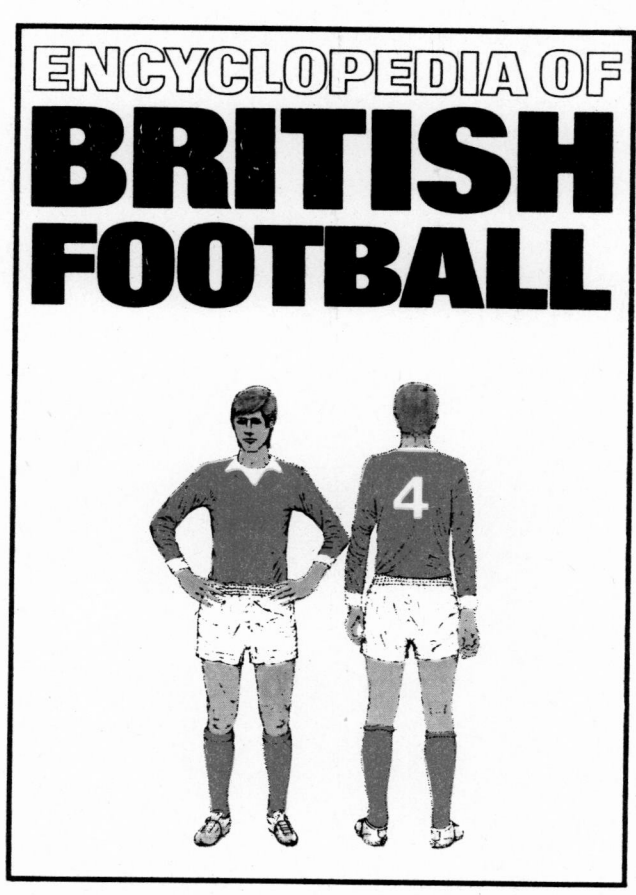

ENCYCLOPEDIA OF
BRITISH FOOTBALL

ENCYCLOPEDIA OF BRITISH FOOTBALL

Marshall Cavendish London & New York

Endpapers: Spurs' new signing Ardiles showed the sort of skill in this League game against Aston Villa that made him a key figure in Argentina's 1978 World Cup winning side.
Title page: Ray Wilkins of Chelsea and Derek Parkin of Wolves clash for the ball in a vital League game. In December 1978, Chelsea were bottom of the League and Danny Blanchflower was invited to take over as manager. The first match under his control, however, against Middlesbrough, resulted in a 7-2 defeat.
Right: Manchester City's Brian Kidd.
Page 6: Brian Clough, voted 1978 Manager of the Year.
Page 8: Kevin Keegan during what many consider to be his greatest individual performance. The match was the 1977 European Cup final, against Borussia Monchengladbach. Liverpool won 3-1.

Written and edited by Phil Soar and Martin Tyler

Artwork by Paul Buckle/Diagram

Published by Marshall Cavendish Books Limited
58 Old Compton Street
London W1V 5PA

© Marshall Cavendish Limited, 1971, 1972, 1973, 1974, 1977, 1979

Most of this material was first published in the partwork *Book of Football*

First printing, William Collins 1974
Updated and revised 1977
Second updating 1979

Printed in Great Britain

ISBN 0 85685 594 4

Introduction

As Bill Shankly said when told that football wasn't really a matter of life-and-death: 'I agree, it's much more serious than that.' For so many people football is not just a game, more a preoccupation, and for everyone who feels that way, young or old, the *Encyclopedia of British Football* is an invaluable companion. Here, in a unique pictorial history, are all the facts and figures that even the most fanatic follower could ever need.

Encyclopedia of British Football was the first publication ever to reproduce *all* of the English and Scottish tables since the Leagues began. Add to that each and every club's complete Cup and League history, a unique record of every single international ever played by *all* of the Home Countries, a history of all the major competitions, and you have an unequalled storehouse of football fact and minutae.

Now easily Britain's biggest selling illustrated football record book, *Encyclopedia of British Football* has yet again been carefully updated with further meticulous research to eradicate the smallest of errors. All of the League tables, English and Scottish, from the nineteenth century onwards are now complete. Each of the League's new clubs is included — as are all the national sides' recent games.

Here you'll find a mine of information, and the answer to virtually any question on Britain's favourite game that you're ever likely to ask. We certainly hope you enjoy reading it as much as we enjoyed putting it together.

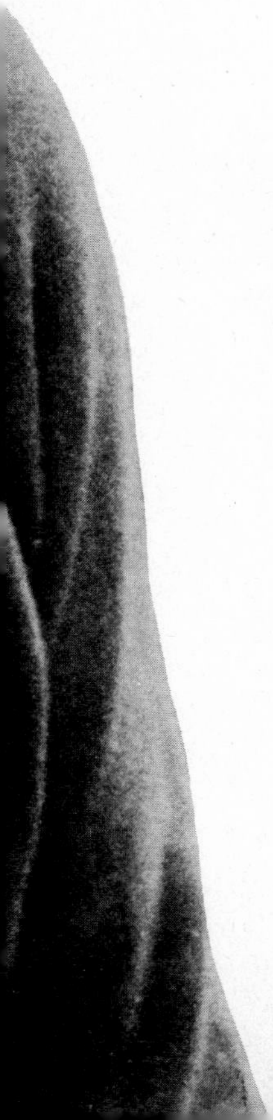

Contents

THE STORY OF FOOTBALL

The game that nobody invented 9
The birth of the FA Cup 12
The founding of the League 15
Scotland before the old firm 19
And the rest came nowhere 22
The Chapman era 28
The golden years 32
1966 and all that 35
The seventies 38

THE MAJOR COMPETITIONS

The story of the FA Cup 44
The League Championship 54
The League Cup 58

THE HOME COUNTRIES

Does charity begin at home? 64
Perfidious Albion 66
A hard road for Scotland 70
A funny thing happened on the way
   to Windsor Park 74
Jonahs in Wales? 78

THE CLUBS

Each club's history and important moments in detailed statistics — including their performance in League and Cup year by year since foundation.

Football League clubs 82
Scottish League clubs 122

THE RECORDS

Year by year complete records of the FA Cup, Scottish FA Cup, Football League and Scottish League. From 1871 to 1978 139
European club competitions 228

![Illustration of a 17th-century football scene in Italy]

The game that nobody invented

Above *A familiar scene, dating back to seventeenth-century Italy.*

Nobody invented football. As soon as an Egyptian, or Assyrian, or Chinese had first kicked or bounced or rolled an object to a companion the seeds of football had been sown. Once the war-games of Greek youths had been adapted to include a ball, all the principles of the modern game had been established—a conflict in which one crowd of combatants tries to force the ball through the territory and into the base guarded by an opposing crowd of combatants. It really is as simple as that, and always has been, whether Association or Rugby, American or Gaelic, Australian Rules or the Eton Wall Game.

Football is, at its simplest, so instinctive and attractive a pastime that it is not surprising to find it growing at numerous points quite independently. Both in China and in ancient Mexico they played a sort of target football, kicking or heading a ball with immense skill through holes in silk screens or through rings set high in a wall. These were games played at royal command, for military training, or at religious festivals. To win a

casket of gold and jewellery was not unknown, though the equivalent of the loser's medal was often even more striking—occasionally the losing team was executed on the spot.

Acrobatic artistry and delicate skills still survive in a charming game played in Burma, where groups of men kick a wicker-work ball between them, the ball never stopping, never touching the ground: there are no goals, no winners or losers—just applause and appreciation of the grace and ball control involved.

Did football arrive with the kicking of a severed head?

The war-games of the Greeks were very different in spirit; they were adapted, as so many things Greek, by the empire-building Romans and were eventually spread throughout the Empire under the name of *harpastum*: two teams on a rectangle of land trying to kick or carry a ball over their rivals' base line.

Inevitably, the game came to Britain. The Britons and Celts adapted it in their own way—there is the legend that the first game played among the Anglo-Saxons was a victory celebration, using the severed head of a defeated Dane as a ball. And so British football evolved in a form that was barely to change for 1,500 years. Every Shrove Tuesday at Ashbourne, in Derbyshire, they still play the ferocious cross-country village game that some historians have traced back as far as the year AD 217. Conflicts of this sort, between hordes of players representing two neighbouring villages or, as in the case of Ashbourne, two halves of the same town, were the norm until the call for stricter and more uniform rules came towards the end of the 18th century.

The Normans, too, had a tradition of football, also adapted from the time of the Roman occupation, which they brought over with them. And within 100 years of William the Conqueror's arrival football had taken root both as a pastime among the Norman ruling elite and as a rampage among their subjects.

In medieval times the game developed very slowly, if at all. Skills took second place to vigour, and no one seems to have been anxious to establish real rules. Twice, between 1280 and 1325, it is recorded that footballers died through falling on their daggers; it is not recorded whether this was done on purpose after conceding a goal, nor whether the daggers were worn as part of the conventional football kit of the day, for discreet use in the thick of the scrimmage.

The only rules the game attracted simply banned it!

Indeed, the only rules that the game did attract at this time were those expressly forbidding it. Edward III, Richard II and Henry IV, all of them concerned with maintaining a strong army against the French, each decreed that football was bad training for battle and that, in any case, its popularity was getting in the way of regular archery practice. The game was banned time and again, both in England and Scotland, without any lasting effect. Then, as the years passed, the game became a natural target for the killjoys; the Puritans furiously condemned the 'bloody and murthering practice'; one Philip Stubbs, in proclaiming that the end of the world was just round the corner, put a fair measure of the blame on 'football playing and other

'develishe pastimes' on the Sabbath.

But the game survived—as 'football' in the English towns and villages, as 'hurling' in Cornwall, and 'knappan' in parts of Wales. It became accepted as part of the English scene on holidays and at festival time. And, by about 1800, football can be said to have reached the threshold of the modern game— the rules still non-existent, the game itself still rough and punishing, but a game that would be understood and appreciated (though probably not enjoyed) by a present-day crowd at Wembley or Twickenham.

It was the public schools that gave the world football

The game, too, had acquired a respectability—not yet the aristocratic backing that cricket was already enjoying, but the respectability that always follows a good spectator sport. The gentry did not yet play the game, but they came along to watch, to lay an occasional bet, and even to raise a subdued cheer.

It was about now that football received the shot in the arm that was eventually to make it the most popular game in the world. The early 19th century saw a tremendous upsurge in education for the privileged; it was the era of the public schools, whose teaching methods impressed the aristocracy and the new industrialists alike. The boys at these schools had little time and even fewer facilities for the more extravagant pastimes of country-house living—no riding, no fishing,

no hunting, no horse-racing. But they quickly adapted the principles of the town and village games —all they needed were two teams and a ball—to the fields or the yards round their school buildings; and they played these games at every opportunity.

And, conveniently for the game, this passion among the boys for the rough, invigorating games of the 'lower classes' coincided with the triumphant peak in the career of that great educationalist, Dr Thomas Arnold of Rugby School. Arnold himself was not a great supporter of the games cult but, seeing that the boys were determined to organize and play games, he brought discipline and a sense of purpose into their pursuit, just as he had done into every other facet of school life. Arnold's followers, and there were many of them, accepted the idea of organized games with enthusiasm. So suddenly, after centuries of official censure and puritan disapproval, people were actually *encouraging* boys to play football!

There was no stopping the game now. In every great public school football of one kind or another became part of the tradition. The rules, as yet, varied drastically from school to school. There was no such thing as the inter-school match, so there was absolutely no need for any one school to play the game to anything like the same rules as the school in the next county. Some of the games that evolved were bizarre in the extreme. At Charterhouse, 20-a-side matches were played in the only space available—a long brick cloister, open at one end, blocked in by a wall at the other:

no long kicks were allowed, no handling the ball, no passing forward—dribbling was the order of the day. At Harrow, where the game had to be adapted to the veritable bog that the winter rains formed in the fields below the hill on which the school stands, a big heavy ball was needed, and rules that encouraged movement. The ground was comparatively big—some 150 yards by 100 yards, and high kicking and catching the ball (though not carrying) were permitted.

Eton's Wall Game —only two goals in seventy years

At Eton, of course, the Wall Game flourished—on an extraordinary pitch 120 yards long and just six yards wide, with, in the early days, 18 or 20 on each side; the goals were a tree at one end and a garden door at the other; progress upfield was painfully slow and very muddy, tries (or 'shies' as Etonians called them) were rare, and converted goals much rarer. The Wall Game still appears to give a lot of Etonians and a lot of newspaper photographers pleasure at the annual St Andrew's Day match; but only two goals have been scored this century!

And at Rugby, too, football was steeped in tradition even before Dr Arnold—a wide-running game with plenty of space, long scrimmages, 'offside' given against a player getting in front of the ball, handling allowed only for a fair catch . . .

Until, that is, the afternoon in

1823 when a Manchester-born boy called William Webb Ellis, later a clergyman and later still to die in obscurity in the South of France, broke all the conventions by catching the ball, tucking it under his arm, and running with it to the opponents' goal line.

This little act of defiance, which might very easily have been shrugged off and forgotten, caused a lot of hard thinking at Rugby School. Eventually, 'running in', as it was called, was accepted into their rules and, in time, led to the basic distinction between the two codes of football.

While boys were still at school, the fact that they played to a strange set of rules hardly mattered. When, however, they left for the universities or for business in the provinces, it became clear that if they were to continue playing football they were going to need a universal set of rules, acceptable to all teams. Up until the 1850s, two teams at, say, Oxford, would only be playing on familiar ground if every player had been to the same school; as things turned out, a major game was often preceded by a long correspondence and lengthy argument about the conventions. Was handling to be allowed? How many players on each side? How long should the pitch be? How wide the goals? Would carrying the ball be permitted? ('Yes', would say all the Old Rugbeians; 'No', would say almost everyone else). And even when the game got under way, confusion and protests would necessitate long midfield conferences between the two captains.

In time it became usual for the Rugby men, and their small but

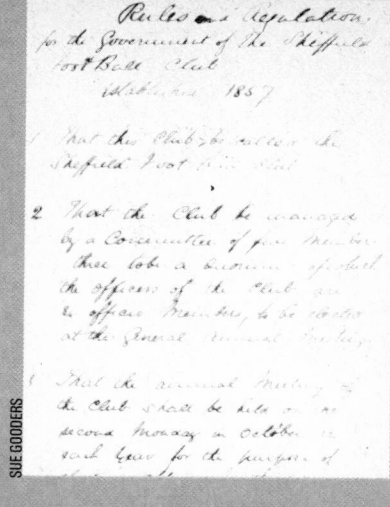

Far left *The early forerunners of modern day matches were generally timeless brawls between two neighbouring villages or parts of the same town. This London street game of around 1300 looks gentler than most.*
Above left *500 years on and the game has hardly changed. This print of a soldiers' friendly is dated 1827.*
Left *The first vestiges of organization; this school game of around 1850 at least has goalposts and approximately the same number on either side. The rules, however, obviously still allow handling and hacking.*
Above *The first minutes of the world's very first 'football club', Sheffield FC. Although the date is given as 1857, it is likely that the club's first members formed a team as early as 1854.*

posts), another great Victorian educationalist, J. C. Thring, issued the rules for what he called *The Simplest Game*. They were indeed very simple, and provided a very straightforward game—no violence, no kicking at the ball in the air, nobody allowed in front of the ball, etc. They were unadventurous, but they provoked great interest, and a number of schools agreed to adopt them.

And at Cambridge, things were moving again. The rules for a match between Cambridge Old Etonians and Cambridge Old Harrovians, in November 1862, specified 11-a-side, an umpire from each side plus a neutral referee, goals 12ft across and up to 20ft high, an hour and a quarter's play only, and the three-man offside rule. These rules were said to have worked well; in the following year they formed a vital part of the revised Cambridge Rules and, in the following months, those of the newly formed Football Association.

Rugby breaks away —over hacking, not handling

In the month of October 1863 football, in the South at least, came of age. The eager young gentlemen of Cambridge University issued their definitive set of rules, but almost at once the control of the game passed from the scholars to the clubs, where it has remained ever since.

The formation of the Football Association was bitter and often ill-tempered, and a certain stubbornness on both sides ensured that the split between the Rugby code and the dribbling code became too wide ever to be mended. The real divergence was not over running with the ball, but over 'hacking'. Rugby men felt it was manly and courageous to tackle an opponent by kicking him on the shin; the dribbling men did not, and voted it out. The Rugby men called the dribbling men cowards, and walked out of the Football Association for ever.

In 1863, football was still far from the game we know today. Every player was still allowed to handle the ball, and when he caught it he could 'make a mark' and so win a free kick; there was, in the first FA laws, a 'touch-down' rule, allowing a free kick at goal after a ball had been kicked over the opposing goal line and touched down (the Rugby 'try', in fact); there was still considerable disagreement over offside, and the FA started off with the Rugby-style 'no one interfering with play in front of the ball' rule.

But within a few years soccer rejected all the distinctive Rugby conventions. Soon only the goalkeeper could handle the ball, the touchdown was abolished, forward passing became the essence of good attacking play and of good entertainment for the spectators. By the early 1870s, England and Scotland were playing internationals and the FA Cup had begun its distinguished and glamorous career. It was only a matter of time before football was to become the most popular pursuit that Britain—and the world—had ever known.

growing company of followers from other schools, to play on their own, and for the others, from Westminster, Charterhouse, Shrewsbury, Harrow and so on, to come to some compromise over the rules of the 'dribbling' game.

Few of these early codes of rules have come down to us intact, but snatches from them give a clear idea of the patterns of the early game, and in particular how boring it must have been to stand in the cold and watch.

In almost every case the game was won or lost (if indeed any goals at all were scored in the one, or two, or three afternoons laid aside for it) in the interminable, seething scrimmage. The aim of the game was, by dint of skilful footwork, to dribble the ball solo through the opposing team, who would all gang up in a scrum to defend. If one man was tackled (and tackling was usually unceremonious and often brutal), another would gather the ball and perform his own solo run until possession was lost and the opposition forwards started the same process in reverse. There may have been the odd instance of inspired, high-speed wing play in the Matthews-Finney tradition, but it is obvious, especially as there was virtually no forward passing, that the games were liable to bog down in the mud. Individual ball-players made as much progress with their lone dribbling as a man trying to push a loaded wheelbarrow into Anfield just as the Kop are on their way out.

The Rugby code may have had too much handling for the purists, but the long kicks and daring runs with the ball might have made it, in those days at any rate, a far more enjoyable afternoon's sport.

The first serious attempts at laying down the rules of football went some way to improving it as a spectacle. In 1848, at Cambridge, 14 men representing Eton, Harrow, Winchester, Rugby and various other public schools, after a seven-hour session, produced the so-called 'Cambridge Rules'—rules that were adapted and tightened up twice in the 1850s.

Under 1848 rules catching the ball was still allowed

Goals were awarded for balls kicked between the flag posts and under the string; goal kicks and throw-ins were given much as today (though throw-ins, taken with one hand only, might travel as far as a kick); catching the ball direct from the foot was allowed, provided the catcher kicked it immediately (no running with the ball, despite that delegate from Rugby); and there was a much more workable offside law—a man could play a ball passed to him from behind, so long as there were *three* opponents between him and the goal.

The game was now established on a common foundation. Competition was possible, and winning became important. By 1855 rules like these were the basis of inter-university matches, and the legendary inter-school matches of public school fiction had begun to blossom.

Amid all this activity in the leisurely atmosphere of the universities and the public schools there

emerged, almost out of the blue, the first recognizable 'football club'.

The old, hard, ruthless town football had been played in Sheffield for many years, but sometime in 1854 or 1855 (though the oldest existing rulebook is dated 1857), after Sheffield Cricket Club had inaugurated a new ground at Bramall Lane, one of the cricketers—William Prest—and some friends from the Collegiate School in Sheffield formed the Sheffield Football Club.

They wrote a constitution and a set of rules (not unlike the Cambridge Rules, though a bit rougher—pushing with the hands was allowed) and specified that every member should have two caps—one red, one dark blue—to distinguish the teams in games played among themselves.

This small band of old school acquaintances, with no apparent encouragement from the gentlemanly scholars from 'down South', had laid the foundations of football in the North of England. Within five years there were 15 different clubs in the Sheffield area, and an 1861 match between the two great local rivals, Sheffield and Hallam, drew a gate of 600 spectators. (Seventy-five years later, at that same Bramall Lane, Sheffield United crammed in 68,000-plus for a Cup-tie.)

Meanwhile, back among the lawmakers, rules and regulations were being hammered out, published, revised, re-negotiated and re-published in a thoroughly confusing burst of activity. At Uppingham School in Rutland, where football was distinguished by an enormously wide goal (with, incidentally, a crossbar rather than tapes between the

The birth of the FA Cup

THE STORY OF FOOTBALL

The most important date in the history of football is 26 October 1863. That was the day on which the Football Association came into being and the point at which 'modern' football can be said to have begun.

In a sense, the most interesting thing about that meeting in the Freemason's Tavern, Great Queen Street, Holborn, was not the teams that were represented but those that were not. There was, for instance, no one from the main provincial centres of the game—Sheffield and Nottingham—nor, more surprisingly, from Cambridge, where the first formal laws had been drawn up in 1848. As a result it was 14 years before the whole country accepted uniform procedures.

The thirteen laws that were eventually approved are indicative of the origins of the men who drew them up. They were, basically, the laws of the game as played at Harrow and by the teams of Harrovian Old Boys—particularly No Names (of Kilburn) and Forest School, who became the famous Wanderers in 1864.

The Blackheath Club, which played to the rules of the game at Rugby, had broken away by the end of 1863, though that alternative game did leave behind it one significant innovation—the more precise name for its competitor. The story may not be true, but one Charles Wreford-Brown, who later became a notable official of the FA, was asked by some friends at Oxford whether he would join them for a game of 'rugger'. He refused, claiming that he was going to play 'soccer'—evidently a play on the word associa-

FOOTBALL.—Last evening a meeting of the captains or other representatives of the football clubs of the metropolis was held at the Freemasons' Tavern, Great Queen-street, Lincoln's Inn-fields. Mr. Pember, N. N. Kilburn Club, having been voted to the chair, observed that the adoption of a certain set of rules by all football players was greatly to be desired, and said that the meeting had been called to carry that object into effect as far as practicable. Mr. E. C. Morley (Barnes) moved, and Mr. Mackenzie (Forest Club, Leytonstone) seconded, the following resolution :—"That it is advisable that a football association should be formed for the purpose of settling a code of rules for the regulation of the game of football." Mr. B. F. Hartshorne said that though he felt it was most desirable that a definite set of rules for football should be generally adopted, yet, as the representative of the Charterhouse School, he could not pledge himself to any course of action without seeing more clearly what other schools would do in the matter. On the part of the Charterhouse he would willingly coalesce if other public schools would do the same. Probably, at a more advanced stage of the association, the opinion of the generality of the great schools would be obtained. The chairman said every association must have a beginning, and they would be very happy to have the co-operation of the last speaker at a future meeting. The resolution for the formation of the association was then put and carried. The officers were elected as follows :—Mr. A. Pember, President ; Mr. E. C. Morley (Barnes), Hon. Secretary; Mr. F. M. Campbell (Blackheath), Treasurer. The annual subscription was fixed at one guinea, all clubs being eligible if of one year's standing, and to be entitled to send two representatives to the yearly meeting, to be held in the last week in September, when the rules would be revised, and the general business arrangements carried out.

ST. GEORGE'S-IN-THE-EAST.—The arrangement which has been for some time past in progress for an ex-

tion. The name caught on.

There was no immediate attempt by the new Football Association to integrate all the various other codes around the country. Not until Charles Alcock, who had been at Harrow from 1855 to 1859, joined the committee did some sort of impetus build up. The rigorous offside law, basically that still employed in rugby, was revised when Westminster and Charterhouse schools joined, but the most important step was the arrival of Yorkshire representatives in 1867.

Yorkshire is the home of the oldest of all football clubs—Sheffield FC. The first written evidence of the club's existence dates from 1857—though it may have been founded by Old Boys of the Collegiate School in Sheffield as early as 1854. By the later date, however, it had its own rules and its secretary approached the newly formed FA in 1863 with a view to integration. The FA did not even bother to reply.

The north Midlands generally was to the provinces what Harrow was to the Home Counties. It was here that the first of the present League clubs originated—Notts County (often referred to as Nottingham before 1882) in 1862, Nottingham Forest in 1865 and Chesterfield in 1866. There have been suggestions that a Stoke club was established by a group of Old Carthusians in 1863—but nineteenth century records give the date as no earlier than 1867.

The first hint of a game that the modern supporter might be able to identify with was the Notts County–Nottingham Forest clash of 1866. The only score of the day came at the end of a 'negative scoreless afternoon' (shades of the present day) when 'there was a sort of steeplechase across the goal-line and over the grandstand railings . . . where W H Revis, of the Forest, touched down. The place-kick, 15 yards at right angles from the goal-line was taken by the same player.' The ball had merely to go between the posts as there was no cross-bar.

As can be deduced, the Nottingham game was a hybrid, relying on a mixture of Rugby, Sheffield and London rules, but with the expansion of the FA to accommodate Sheffield uniformity was not far away. As Alcock himself wrote, '. . . the objects of the Association are to still further remove the barriers which prevent the accomplishment of one universal game'.

By 1870 Alcock, now secretary of the FA, had established unofficial internationals between England and Scotland (or rather a team of Scots resident in London) and a regular London-Sheffield encounter. The growing competitiveness of the game encouraged him to add another suggestion in 1871—a challenge cup 'for which all clubs belonging to the Football Association should be invited to compete'. The idea was unashamedly based on the interhouse knock-out competition at Harrow—the winners being refered to as the 'Cock House'.

The Cup holders chose where the Final was played

The holders of the new trophy, known as the FA Challenge Cup, were to enjoy two invaluable advantages—they were exempt until the Final and they could choose where it was played. Fifteen clubs entered in the first year, though only twelve competed. Of these, two, Maidenhead and Marlow, have entered in each and every subsequent year. The real attraction was the appearance of Queen's Park, the Glasgow side that had been formed in 1867 and had still not had a single goal scored against them. Because of the distance they had to travel they were exempt until the semi-final, when they drew with the Wanderers at the Oval. Unfortunately they could not afford to return for a replay and the Wanderers went on to beat Royal Engineers in the Final at the same venue. The only goal of the match was scored by M P Betts, playing under the assumed name of A H Chequer—meaning that he was a member of the Old Harrovian side Harrow Chequers—and 2,000 people paid the not insubstantial sum of one shilling to watch. Captain of the Wanderers was one Charles W Alcock.

The Wanderers won again the following year, beating Oxford University at the early hour of 11 am so that the event would not clash with the Boat Race. The days of football pre-eminence were still far in the future! Queen's Park again had to withdraw at the semi-final stage. The Cup was dominated for a dozen years by a handful of southern clubs —Wanderers, Royal Engineers, Oxford University, Old Etonians and Clapham Rovers—but the writing was on the wall for these gentlemen amateurs as early as 1877.

In that year, as a result of correspondence between Manchester FC and Marlborough College, the authority of the FA rules was generally accepted throughout the country. Thus the Sheffield version passed into oblivion, but not before it had had a significant effect on the game. The throw-in was used in Yorkshire some five years before the FA accepted it and the free-kick was an innovation from Sheffield; so was the cross-bar. Before 1866 there had been no height

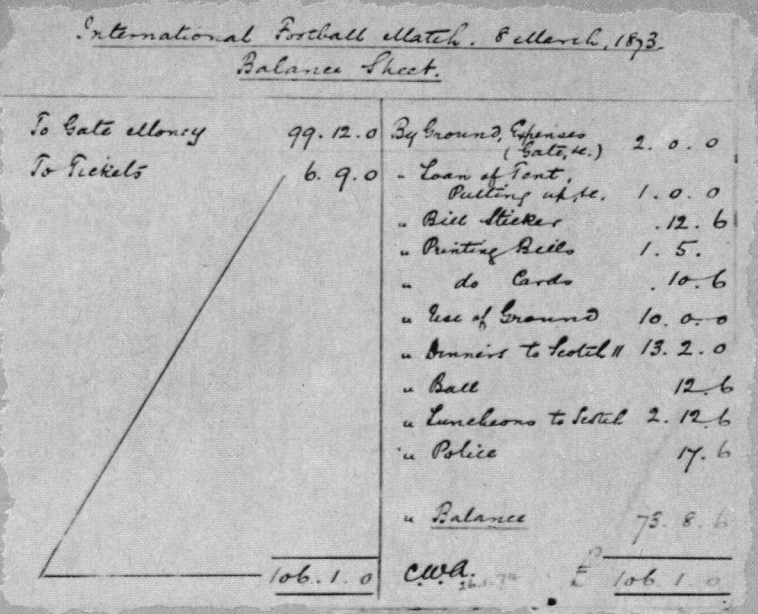

COURTESY OF FOOTBALL ASSOCIATION

Opposite page top The major problem facing the embryonic Football Association was the vast divergence of rules in operation all over the country. At Uppingham in 1862 teams numbered 15-a-side and attacked a goal stretched right across the pitch. Uppingham was one of the first codes to employ a crossbar but, at this time, still penalized kicking at the ball in the air.
Opposite page bottom Organized football arrives. Yet the foundation of the FA warranted just three column inches in The Times of 27 October 1863.
Above The balance sheet from England's very first 'home' international—against Scotland in 1873. The initials CWA are those of Charles Alcock, then secretary of the FA and the man who created the FA Cup competition.
Below Local rivalry in the Midlands. Stoke did not add 'City' until 1925.

STAFFORDSHIRE FOOTBALL ASSOCIATION.

Grand Football Match.

FINAL TIE for COUNTY CHALLENGE CUP,
VALUE 50 GUINEAS.

Winners to receive GOLD MEDALS : Losers, Silver Medals.

STOKE
v.
WEST BROMWICH ALBION.

Stoke Team.		West Bromwich Albion.	
H. WILDIN (Goal).		R. ROBERTS (Goal).	
T. STANFORD,	Backs.	H. BELL,	Backs.
M. MELLOR,		J. STANTON,	
H. R. BROWN,	Half Backs.	E. HORTON,	
F. BETTANY,		F. BUNN,	Half Backs.
E. JOHNSON,		J. WHITE,	
F. POWELL,		H. ASTON,	
G. SHUTT,	Forwards.	J. WHITEHOUSE,	
P. FENNELL,		G. TIMMINS,	
W. MYATT,		G. BELL,	Forwards.
F. BENNETT,		W. BISSEKER,	

Stoke have scored 42 goals to 3; West Bromwich Albion, as above competition. Special Trains from all parts. Kick-off at 4 o'clock.

ADMISSION, 6d. and 1s.
AT STOKE, SATURDAY NEXT, APRIL 21st.
Tickets to be obtained on the way to the ground.

West Bromwich Albion have only been beaten once this season, and are in for the Final of the Wednesbury Charity Cup.

Stoke have played 30 matches—won 19, lost 7, drawn 4, and have scored 111 goals and lost 40. They hold the North Stafford Charity Cup for last Season.

ABBEY AND DANIEL, PERCY STREET PRINTING WORKS, HANLEY.

JACKDAW PUBLICATIONS

restriction on the goal at all—as was seen in that first Nottingham match.

The duration of the game had finally been determined at 90 minutes by 1877, and handling the ball had been restricted to the goalkeeper. In addition neutral referees and umpires (later linesmen) were now an established part of the game and even more so a year later when the familiar blast of the referee's whistle was heard for the first time during a match between Nottingham Forest and Sheffield Norfolk. Before 1878 officials had been forced to attract attention in any way they could—usually by waving a handkerchief.

It is never easy defining the exact moment when a new trend affected any discipline. Yet a casual observer could not fail to have been struck by unusual qualities of the 1878-79 FA Cup competition. It was won by Old Etonians, who beat Clapham Rovers 1-0, but there was nothing remarkable in that fact. A glance at the earlier rounds, however, reveals one very significant feature—the success of two provincial clubs. Nottingham Forest reached the semi-finals and beat Old Harrovians, the real successors to the previous year's Cup winners Wanderers, who had lost most of their players to the Old Boy's clubs on the way.

But the real interest was reserved for Old Etonians' fourth-round tie with Darwen. The Lancashire side were trailing 5-1 with only 15 minutes left, suddenly came to life with a four-goal burst, and were robbed of their likely reward when the Etonians refused to play extra-time. £175 was raised to dispatch Darwen back to London—the result being a 2-2 draw and a second replay which the southerners won 6-2. Darwen had in their ranks two Scots—James Love and Fergus Suter—who were reputedly two of the first players to 'find money in their boots'. They had first appeared in Darwen as members of a Partick team playing a friendly match, and had been persuaded to stay. Lancashire had made its mark and the tide was on the turn.

Football finally takes hold in the industrial North

Football came late to the major industrial conurbations. Aston Villa came into being in 1874 with neighbours Small Heath (to be renamed Birmingham) following a year later. In Lancashire Blackburn and Bolton both saw the light of day in 1874 and the great Newton Heath side (later Manchester United) was founded at the Lancashire and Yorkshire Railway Company's engine depot of that name in 1878.

It was a time of hope for Lancashire. After the near starvation of the 1860s—when cotton supplies were cut off during the American Civil War—and the economic depression of the early 1870s, an industrial boom was absorbing all who needed work. Immigrants flocked in from the agricultural areas and the Celtic fringes and football turned this to its advantage. Advertisements in the Glasgow papers attracted the Scottish 'professors' who taught the English the 'passing' as opposed to 'dribbling' game. Some teams took on so many

Scots that English players felt positively lonely and it is to this era and not the reign of Shankly at Liverpool that we owe the oft-repeated cry of the overlooked, 'you need to wear a kilt to get into that team.'

There were, of course, inducements. A Scot named J J Lang claimed he was the first ever professional when Sheffield Wednesday paid him to move from Glasgow in 1876. By 1880, while most of the players had other jobs, they received substantial remuneration from playing the game—not unlike the 'shamateurs' of the 1960s and, in consequence, football was taken much more seriously than in the south. The days of the gentlemen amateur were almost over.

The 1881 Cup Final—between Old Etonians and Old Carthusians—was the last of the all-amateur finals and, indeed, the last all-southern Final until Spurs met Chelsea in 1967. Old Carthusians later went on to become the first club to win both the FA Cup (1881) and the Amateur Cup (1894 and 1897).

While Etonians managed to defeat Blackburn Rovers the following year, the inevitable happened in 1883 when Blackburn Olympic became the first club to take the trophy out of the Home Counties. It would have been difficult to devise a better pair of teams to illustrate the differences between the game, and the life, in the South and the North. The Old Etonians speak for themselves—representatives of all that was privileged in the South of England; gentlemen amateurs with the time and income to allow their devotion to the game when they thought fit. Blackburn Olympic came from one of the most industrialized areas in the world at that time —the dingy terraces that crawl like centipedes up and down the valleys of the mid-Lancashire weaving towns breeding many of the players that were not imported from Scotland.

Olympic even had a manager, once a travelling organizer of exhibition matches, one Jack Hunter. Like many managers after him, he took his team away to Blackpool to prepare for the Final. Of the players, two were weavers, one a spinner, one a plumber, one a metal-worker and two had no apparent means of support— apart from football.

The Cup retired to Blackburn for all of four years

'The blossom might be in the South, but the roots are in the North' goes the old economic adage, but in football the reverse was nearer the truth. Had the FA not wisely decided to accept professionalism the game must have developed very differently and might even have fallen into the sad split that has contributed to rugby's never having become a world-wide game. The North could never have competed with the South had it accepted the amateur strictures. A working man at the top of his craft might earn £2 for a six-day week; a farm labourer no more than 15/- (75p) at the time. Without some sort of financial inducement no working man could devote the requisite time and energy to the game. The vital decision was approaching; either the

ham St George's in the Midlands and Hearts in Scotland.

William Sudell, the founder of Preston North End, proposed the formation of a British Football Association as a result of these suspensions. In October 1884 he received the support of 26 Lancashire clubs plus Aston Villa and Sunderland.

It was a strange forerunner of the similar situation which was to confront the Rugby Union in Huddersfield a decade later, only on the latter occasion the parent body decided that amateurism was more important than unity and the Northern Football Union (Rugby League) was the result.

The Manchester Guardian read the crisis of 1884 thus: 'The first effect of any change (the legalization of professionalism) will be to make the Rugby game the aristocratic one, and the Association game will probably almost die out in the south of England, where it is already declining in favour.'

Unity was more important than staying amateur

By the start of the 1885-86 season a special general meeting of the FA had legalized the payment of players, basically on the same lines of those employed in cricket (Alcock was also secretary of Surrey CCC).

But it was not harmony everywhere. The Scots banned all professionals from ever playing north of the border and eventually took things further when, in 1887, they decreed that 'clubs belonging to this (the Scottish) Association shall not be members of any other National Association.'

It was something of a blow for the better Glasgow sides—Queen's Park had reached the Cup Final in 1884 and 1885 and the emerging Rangers had been beaten by Aston Villa in an 1887 semi-final at, of all places, Crewe. It was sad in another way for had the Scots maintained contact for just another year that utopia of so many administrators— a British League—might have come into being.

The Scots, nevertheless, had done a great deal for the English game. Before 1872 it was a 'dribbling' game. The public school boy had been taught to exhibit his individual excellence by simply running at the opposition until he lost the ball. As a result most English sides played with a goalkeeper, two backs and eight 'dribbling' forwards. The early contacts with the Scots showed just how inefficient the English system was. Though Royal Engineers and Sheffield had both been noted for a 'combination' style of operation, it was the Scots who had elevated the 'passing' game to a fine and impressive art, depending more on skill and perception than mere force and speed.

The south quickly adopted the 'passing' game and the first twenty years of organized football thus showed tremendous developments in every direction. The amateur dribblers of the 1860s could no more have lived with the professionals of the 1880s than the average League player in 1950 could have found a place in Arsenal's double winning side of 1971.

Top The North's first FA Cup success—Blackburn Olympic's victory in 1883. *Above* The Graphic's impression of the first soccer international in 1872.

South accepted professionalism and kept the game under a single authority or insisted on the amateur ethic and caused the inevitable split.

As it happened the South had very little say on the field for a long time. The Cup stayed in Blackburn for four years—Blackburn Rovers following up the short-lived Olympic's success and equalling Wanderers' three successive wins. The Old Etonian success in 1882 was the last by a southern club until Spurs dramatic intervention in 1901. In fact, between Etonians' last win and Spurs 'double' in 1961, the Cup returned south on only seven occasions. Oddly enough the next eleven seasons saw six London successes.

But to return North. The problem of 'professionalism' so worried the Lancashire FA that they forbade the signing-on of Scots in 1881 and in 1883 Accrington were expelled from the FA for giving an inducement to a particular player. Matters came to a head after a drawn Cup game between Preston North End and Upton Park on 19 January 1884. The London club protested that Preston had paid and played professionals and the Lilywhites were thrown out of the competition. Suspensions on members of the playing staffs followed for Great Lever and Burnley in Lancashire, Walsall and Birming-

It is somehow appropriate that William McGregor, founder and first president of the Football League, should have come from Aston Villa, appropriate because this fine Midland club dominated the early years of the League as no club except the Arsenal of the 30's has done since.

Secure in their vast redbrick mausoleum north of Birmingham—'worth a goal start every home game' one manager said of it—Villa won the Championship six times before the First World War and the FA Cup five times in the same period.

Control of that era fell to very few clubs; primarily Aston Villa and Sunderland, with Manchester United, Newcastle United and the two club sides in both Sheffield and Liverpool providing the main opposition. The first 27 Championships were shared by only ten clubs—those eight plus Preston and Blackburn Rovers. It was to be some years before there was a significant shift of power towards the South. By the end of the First World War, London's trio of Arsenal, Chelsea and Spurs had at last all made their mark and the Southern League was absorbed as the Third Division in 1920.

William McGregor writes his now famous letter

But all this was in the future when Vil' director William McGregor sent his famous letter to Blackburn, Bolton, Preston, West Bromwich and the secretary of his own club, Villa, on 2 March 1888. It had become increasingly difficult for the major clubs to guarantee fixtures; opponents either failed to turn up or were forced to complete postponed or replayed cup ties on dates which were already booked. The real concern, of course, was that gates were dropping off as a result. McGregor saw the great need for a definite list of fixtures

THE STORY OF FOOTBALL

The founding of the League

£10 REWARD.

STOLEN!

From the Shop Window of W. Shillcock, Football Outfitter, Newtown Row, Birmingham, between the hour of 9-30 p.m. on Wednesday, the 11th September, and 7-30 a.m., on Thursday, the 12th inst., the

ENGLISH CUP,

the property of Aston Villa F.C. The premises were broken into between the hours named, and the Cup, together with cash in drawer, stolen.

The above Reward will be paid for the recovery of the Cup, or for information as may lead to the conviction of the thieves.

Information to be given to the Chief of Police, or to Mr. W. Shillcock, 73, Newtown Row.

—as well as the added attraction of competitive football—which would guarantee spectators the game they expected to see.

The initial meeting was held on the eve of the Cup Final, Friday 23 March 1888, at Anderton's Hotel, in London. McGregor's suggestion for a name, the Association Football Union, was rejected because of a possible confusion with the rugby code while McGregor's own objections to the name Football League (because he thought it would be confused with the unpopular and politically extreme Irish National and Land Leagues) were felt to be irrelevant.

No southern club took any part in the foundation

The business was not concluded until 17 April at the Royal Hotel in Manchester, a far more appropriate setting as no southern club had taken any part in the discussions. There it was found that no more than 22 dates could be set aside for fixtures and the League would therefore have to be confined to 12 members. Thus Nottingham Forest, the Wednesday from Sheffield (who did not adopt the present title until 1929) and a long since defunct Lancashire League club called Halliwell went away empty handed while the remaining 12 became the founder members of the oldest League in the world.

Six were from Lancashire, Accring-

Left In 1895 Aston Villa won the FA Cup—and lost it. It was stolen from a shop window and never recovered. Villa were fined £25, and the money was used to purchase the new trophy.
Below The Aston Villa team that did the Double by winning the FA Cup and First Division Championship in 1897. It was 64 years before the feat was repeated—by Tottenham Hotspur.

15

ton, Blackburn Rovers, Bolton Wanderers, Burnley, Everton and Preston North End, five from the loosely-defined Midlands, Aston Villa, Derby County, Notts County, West Bromwich Albion and Wolverhampton Wanderers and one, Stoke, came from the no-man's-land between the two. The twelve have been remarkably durable—only Accrington and Notts County spending the greater part of the first 80 years outside the First Division.

'Proud Preston' get through a season without defeat

McGregor explained: 'It appeared to me that a fixed programme of home-and-away matches between the leading clubs in the country, such fixtures to be kept inviolate, would produce football of a far more interesting nature than we then saw.' It was a fitting prologue.

The first season was dominated by Preston North End; 'Proud Preston', the 'Old Invincibles' that had emerged from the North End Cricket Club in 1881 and whose president was the William Sudell who had forced the professionalism issue with his openly illegal payments.

Sudell's team consisted largely of talented Scots, but in John Goodall he had the finest English centre-forward of his day. Preston's inaugural double was completed without losing a game in the League or conceding a goal in the Cup. They thus became the first—and most likely the last—League side to go through a season without losing a game. But it was a brief flowering. Though they won the Championship the following season, Preston have not won it since, and have only one other Cup success to their credit, in 1938, and then it took a last minute penalty which went in off the bar to take a trophy back to Deepdale.

The Aston Villa story has its similarities, but they were always a far grander club than Preston. Between 1892 and 1905 Villa won five Championships and reached four Cup Finals, winning three of them. That included a double—in 1896-97—which, for 64 years, seemed destined to be the last of all time. Despite all the trophies they won in this period Villa are probably better remembered for one they lost—the FA Cup. After beating neighbours West Bromwich in the 1895 Final, Villa allowed a local boot and shoe manufacturer, William Shillcock, to display it in his shop window. It disappeared on the night of 11 September, and never reappeared in any recognizable form. The FA fined Villa £25, and used the money to buy a new trophy.

The midlanders' great rivals in this period were Sunderland. The north-easterners' rise to fame was astonishingly fast. They relied on Scottish players who cost them no more than a signing-on fee, but the most famous Scotsman to join their ranks proved more expensive. Ned Doig—Arbroath's goalkeeper—was deemed ineligible after his first match, and Sunderland forfeited £50 and two points. The problem was resolved, and Doig proved his worth —between the start of the 1890-91 and 1896-97 seasons they lost only one home game. The results of such defensive excellence were the League Championships of 1892, 1893 and 1895, followed by further successes in 1902 and 1913.

Villa were beaten by a dream that came true

On the last of those five occasions Sunderland finally managed to reach their first Cup Final—only to see their double hopes disappear with a Tom Barber header that gave the trophy to rivals Villa. Early on in the game Clem Stephenson—the Villa forward who was later to captain the great Huddersfield side of the 1920s —told Sunderland's Charlie Buchan that he had dreamed Barber would head the only goal. As well as being accurate it was appropriate—neither club had much more than dreams to live on for the next 60 years.

The Cup had been growing in importance since the founding of the League. By 1893 Surrey County Cricket Club, worried about the size of the crowds, had to withdraw the Oval as the venue and that year the Final was played at Fallowfield, Manchester. The official attendance was 45,000, though at least twice that number managed to get in. Wolves won for the first time, defeating Everton, despite having lost a League game 4-2 to a team of Everton reserves the previous week. The 1894 Final was played at Goodison, Notts County becoming the first Second Division side to take the trophy, but the season after that the wide open spaces of Crystal Palace staged the game for the first time.

Londoners still tended to be a little scathing about the whole event. This was partially because of the sudden invasion from the alien North ('a northern horde of uncouth garb and strange oaths' as the Pall Mall Gazette described Blackburn Rovers' supporters in 1885), but largely because southern clubs had little say in affairs.

But in 1901 Tottenham Hotspur, of the Southern League, became the first and only non-Football League team to win a post-1888 Cup Final— and an amazing affair it turned out to be. The 114,815 crowd still stands as the third largest attendance (after

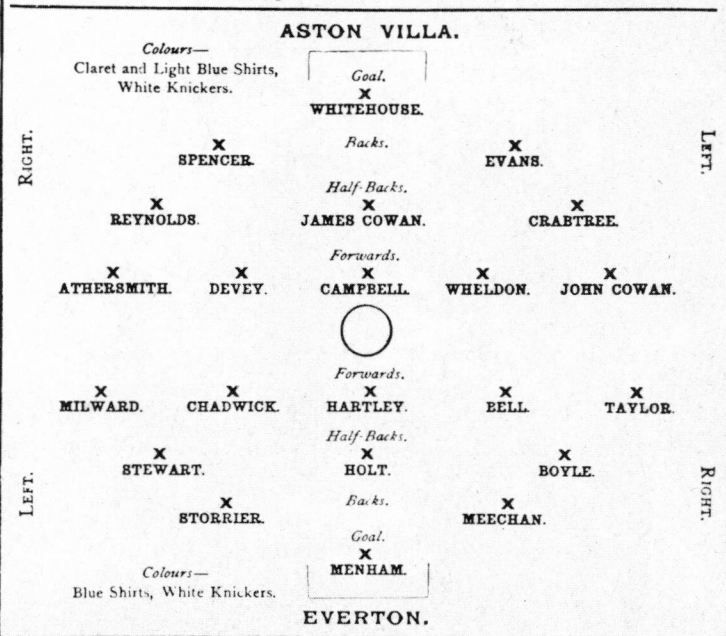
the 1913 and 1923 Finals) at a football match under any code in England and they were treated to one of football's most celebrated disputed goals.

Spurs of the Southern League win the FA Cup

As *The Times*, in typically subdued fashion, said, '. . . the result was not a true reflection of the run of the game. The second goal by Sheffield was the chief incident of the match. Clawley (the Spurs goalkeeper) fumbled a shot slightly but got it away. The referee decided that the ball was over the line and therefore a goal. Clawley says that this was impossible as he must have been behind his line for a goal to have been scored . . .' Most of the crowd it seemed, agreed with Clawley. The game ended at 2-2, but justice was seen to be done at Bolton when Spurs won the replay 3-1. To be fair, the Spurs team consisted of one Irishman, two Welshmen, three northern-Englishmen and five Scots and can hardly be credited with reviving football south of the Trent.

That distinction belongs more fairly to Arsenal. Founded in 1886 by a Scotsman called David Danskin and a group of workmates at the Woolwich Arsenal, the club was originally called Dial Square. The name was changed to Royal Arsenal, then Woolwich Arsenal, The Arsenal and, finally, plain Arsenal. Adopting professionalism in 1891, they found that the southern opposition was simply not strong enough and began to organize fixtures against teams from further north. In 1893 Arsenal became the first southern club to be elected to the Football League.

In 1892 the League had absorbed the rival Football Alliance and now had two divisions and 28 clubs, none south of Birmingham. Until 1898 there was no automatic system of promotion and relegation—the bottom clubs in the First Division and the top clubs in the Second playing 'test' matches to decide which were worthy of the premier places. In that year Stoke and Burnley reasoned that a draw in the last of these test matches would give them both First Division places. The resulting goalless game aroused more than a few suspicions and the system was abolished.

Arsenal's election to the Second Division in 1893 was followed by promotion to the First eleven years later. The subsequent relegation in 1913 proved a blessing in disguise for it led to Henry Norris, then chairman of Fulham, taking an interest in the club. He persuaded them to move right across London, from south of the river Plumstead to Highbury. Their arrival incurred the wrath not only of the local residents, who thought Arsenal an utterly undesirable neighbour, but of nearby Tottenham, to whom the Gunners were not only undesirable but a positive threat.

Norris's machinations gained Arsenal admittance to the First Division after the First World War and joining them were the third of London's great trio, Chelsea. Created out of nothing by the son of a builder —H. A. Mears—Chelsea FC started with a ground in 1905, bought a team and then began looking for someone to play.

The League took in Chelsea—as a brand new club

The Football League were somehow persuaded that it was in their best interests to take in a club that had yet to play a game—and in two years Chelsea had been promoted. 'Chelsea will stagger humanity!' wrote one journalist—though he was referring to the ground. Built in the style of the great Glasgow stadia, with hopes that it would hold 100,000, Stamford Bridge was privileged to hold the first three post-war Cup Finals but has rarely staggered anyone. In fact it had few rivals as the least appealing of the First Division grounds over 60 years later.

The same could never be said about

Left A cavalcade of fans leaving Kingsway, London, bound for the Cup Final of 1906, between Everton and Newcastle United, staged at Crystal Palace. Everton won the game 1-0.
Above The programme of the historic 1897 Cup Final which gave Aston Villa the Double. They beat Everton 3-2. Campbell, Devey and Crabtree scored for Villa, Bell and Hartley for Everton.

Manchester United's new stadium. In 1910 they finally moved across Manchester from Clayton—where the grandstand expressed its dismay and collapsed soon afterwards—to Old Trafford where, bettering Chelsea, it was hoped to seat 100,000. United had finally emerged as the major force they were to remain, winning the League in 1908 and 1911 and the Cup in 1909. The quality of Old Trafford was also soon realized. It staged the 'Khaki' Final (so called because of all the soldiers in the crowd) in 1915, the only time in the twentieth century that the Final has been initially fought for outside London.

The last few years before the First World War have aptly been called 'those strange years of hysteria'. Though Victoria was dead, the era contained the dying vestiges of Victoriana. All in all, it was a very bizarre period. These were the years of the suffragettes, the first great nationwide strikes, a state of open warfare between the political parties over Ireland, the first feeble attempts to create a welfare state and, of course, the inexorable approach of the corporate madness that was the First World War. In its small, strange way football somehow managed to reflect the atmosphere of that era.

When Oldham almost won the Championship

If Oldham Athletic, of all clubs, had won their last game of the 1914–15 season they would have become League Champions. In the Cup Bristol City were finalists in 1909, Barnsley in 1910 and then Bradford City and Barnsley both won the trophy, in 1911 and 1912. None of those four clubs had done anything of note before and none has done anything since. It was a strange time, but it was also a tribute to the strength in depth of the football of the times and a comment on the inability of the bigger clubs—like Villa—to automatically buy success.

There were replays in 1910, 1911 and 1912 and extra time was therefore instituted in 1913. It was fifty-eight years before another replay was needed. Another reflection of the mood of the times was the re-establishment of the Football Players and Trainers' Union. Though the players joined the Federation of Trades Unions in 1909 the Football Association remained violently opposed to any form of organized labour within football. This was a fair indication of the politics of that august body, but, to be fair, there were grounds for fears that football might unwittingly be involved in a

THE GROWTH OF THE FOOTBALL LEAGUE

Period	Seasons	I	II	III	IIIN	IIIS	IV	Total
				Clubs per division				
1888-91	3	12						12
1891-92	1	14						14
1892-93	1	16	12					28
1893-94	1	16	15					31
1894-98	4	16	16					32
1898-05	7	18	18					36
1905-15	10	20	20					40
1919-20	1	22	22					44
1920-21	1	22	22	22				66
1921-23	2	22	22		20	22		86
1923-39	16	22	22		22	22		88
1946-50	4	22	22		22	22		88
1950-58	8	22	22		24	24		92
1958-78	20	22	22	24			24	92
	79							

Centre A Sunderland team line-up reproduced on a lapel badge for the Supporters Club. This was one of the earliest occurrences of what was to become a popular feature 60 years later. The north-easterners were second only to Aston Villa in the pre-First World War era. Depending largely on Scots who cost no more than a signing-on fee they won the League for the fourth time in 1902.

Below The legendary Billy Meredith (centre) in action for Manchester United against Queen's Park Rangers in September 1908.

SUNDERLAND F.C. 1901-2

BY COURTESY OF WILLIAM HEINEMANN LIMITED

general strike. Several players, notably Charlie Roberts of Manchester United, felt that their international careers suffered because of support for the FPTU for the Football Association did not look lightly on the strike that was threatened for the beginning of the 1909-10 season. Most League clubs signed enough amateurs to be sure of fulfilling their fixtures, but nothing came of the threat and the union's real strength can be gauged from the maximum wage legislation, introduced in 1901, which remained in existence until the Eastham case a full six decades later.

A basic structure that has lasted for over 50 years

After the war, in 1920, the Southern League, founded by the professional club at Millwall, became the new Third Division. A year later a northern section was added, initially of 20 clubs but increased to 22 in 1923 and the League structure still in existence half a century later had been established.

RADIO TIMES HULTON PICTURE LIBRARY

The history of Scottish football, to be brutal, is the history of three very great clubs, of an epic series of internationals against the old enemy England, of a constant stream of talent leaving the country for richer rewards south of the border, and of very little else.

Despite occasional flashes from lesser clubs, Celtic and Rangers have dominated the field since the 1890s. And before the turn of the century, Queen's Park, perhaps the greatest amateur football club of all time, *was* Scottish football. They organized football north of the border from the first; excelled at it; beat the English, virtually on their own, time and again, and stamped their high-principled personality on the Scottish game.

Football had flourished in Scotland, of course, long before Queen's Park Football Club was founded. The Scottish game had grown in concert with that of Wales and Ireland and the English countryside, a game of violent celtic fervour characterized by uncompromising battles between neighbouring villages—clan against clan, as often as not, and with plenty of heads broken in the process.

As in England, the game provoked its share of royal disfavour. James I, James II, James III and James IV liberally scattered statutes banning football across the 15th century, and James VI, on ascending the English throne, expressly forbade his son Henry from 'rough and violent exercises at the foot-ball'. (James V was a notable absentee from this bunch of anti-football monarchs, but then he was only one year old when he succeeded to the throne.) Yet football never lost its popularity. By the beginning of the 19th century, while the schools were beginning to take up the game in England, Scottish football found a working champion in the novelist Sir Walter Scott, a fervent supporter of the traditional inter-village game.

'The old clannish spirit is too apt to break out'

Indeed, Scott was himself much in evidence at the most famous of all the matches to be held in football's Dark Ages north of the border. Sir Walter not only backed (financially) the Men of Selkirk against the Men of Yarrow (themselves backed, incidentally, by the Earl of Home)—he also wrote a ballad specially for the day. The game (in two legs, rather like the European Cup) ended even—one leg each; and the food and drink lying ready for the teams dissuaded them from playing a decider. At this date (1815), though, football in Scotland was generally recognized to be in decline, and even Scott himself was declaring that 'it was not always safe to have even the game of football between villages; the old clannish spirit is too apt to break out.'

Nevertheless, football survived in Scotland not through the influence of the public schools as it did in the south of England, but through the young artisans and professional men who recognized the game for the simple, energetic and enjoyable pastime that it was. The game had its greatest following in the industrial areas of Scotland's central lowlands, and in Glasgow the keenest players eventually gravitated, in the mid 1860s, to one of the city's three public parks—Queen's Park.

On 9 July 1867, together with YMCA members and caber-tossing Highlanders who also used the park for recreation, they met to form the 'Queen's Park Football Club', thus

Scotland before the old firm

officially establishing the game in Scotland and founding a tradition in Glasgow which, for single-minded fanaticism, would be difficult to parallel anywhere but in Rio de Janeiro.

The early history of Queen's Park is one of virtually undiluted success. Between their formation in 1867 and 1872 not a single goal was scored against them; they did not lose a single match until February 1876, when they were beaten by London's Wanderers, and only in December of the same year, by which time Scottish competition had become extremely fierce, did they go down at home.

Queen's Park lay down their own rules

In the very early years, Queen's Park were so dominant that not only did they attract the best players and consequently the best results—they also laid down the rules, which were obediently followed by early local opponents such as Thistle, Hamilton Gymnasium and Airdrie (all of whom, incidentally, played their football in the summer months).

In 1870, however, Queen's Park's reputation ensured the acceptance of Scottish football on the national map. Charles Alcock, the recently elected Secretary of the FA wrote a letter to the *Glasgow Herald* announcing that teams of English and Scottish players were to meet at Kennington Oval (the headquarters of Surrey County Cricket Club, but then also the premier football ground in London). He invited nominations from Scotland with a stirring call to arms: 'In Scotland, once essentially the land of football, there should still be a spark left of the old fire, and I confidently appeal to Scotsmen.... etc. etc.'

It was a stroke of genius on Alcock's part. No one, least of all a gentleman footballer, could resist a provocative challenge like that. Queen's Park nominated one Robert Smith, a member of a famous Queen's Park family now based in London, as their player, and the teams met on 19 November 1870, England winning 1-0.

This was not, as yet, international football, or anything like it. The Scottish team was in reality composed of a lot of well-heeled young men who owed family name and background to Scotland, but who were all living in or near, London, and had time on their hands. One of their number was an Old Rugbeian, who had presumably learnt his football in the handling tradition; another was the son of the Prime Minister W E Gladstone, and was himself an MP at the time of the match; yet another was Quintin Hogg, the grandfather of a later Lord Chancellor.

And, most illustrious of all, the Old Etonian A F Kinnaird, aristocrat, football patriarch, successful banker, later Lord High Commissioner of the Church of Scotland—and a football fanatic, who played whenever he possibly could, and whose personality swayed the Football Association for five decades. His influence on the game is

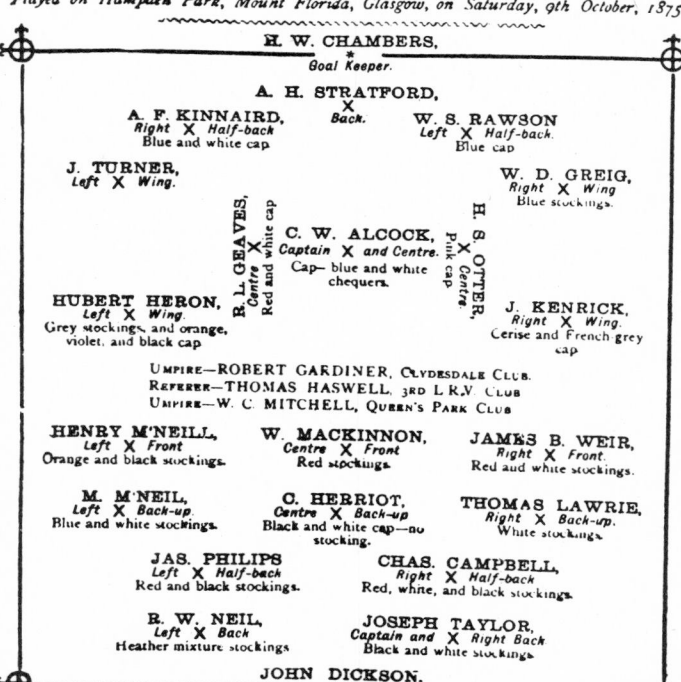

Top A ticket for the first international football match, at Partick in 1872.
Above The programme for an 1875 friendly between Queen's Park and the Wanderers. As players did not wear numbers, they were identified by the colour of their caps or stockings. Queen's Park, despite their strange 2-2-3-3 formation had still not lost a game since their formation 8 years earlier.

19

incalculable; that it came unscathed through the early troubled years of professionalism into the heyday of popularity in the years before World War I is in considerable part due to this remarkable Scot and his 33 years as President of the Football Association.

This first encounter between 'England' and 'London Scottish', was followed by repeat performances on roughly the same lines, twice in 1871 (a 1-1 draw and 2-1 win to 'England') and once in February 1872 (1-0 to 'England').

It was the Queen's Park visit to London for the semi-final of the first FA Cup competition that really formalized inter-national football. Donating a guinea (one sixth of that year's income) toward the purchase of the Cup, Queen's Park drew with Wanderers but could not afford to return for a replay. Nevertheless their style impressed everyone present and also made them aware that the 400 mile journey was not only feasible but might even be worthwhile. The result was the very first football international, played in 1872.

Alcock and Kinnaird probably had most to do with arranging the trip north—Alcock was originally chosen to play for England and Kinnaird for Scotland though neither actually performed—but, looking back, the most interesting feature was the patronizing attitude of the Londoners—that England were going north to show the Scots how to play the game.

Nothing could have been further from reality. Sadly lacking is a photograph of the teams—the players would not promise to buy prints so the official photographer refused to take any frames. At Kennington the following year there was more trouble over photographs—on that occasion they never materialized because the England players insisted on pulling faces.

The match was played at the West of Scotland Cricket Club's ground in Partick. The Scots included nine Queen's Park men (and two more, the brothers Smith, who had played for the club before moving to London a couple of seasons earlier). This provided an understanding between players that the scratch English team could not match, but skilfully though the Scotsmen played, neither side could score—and so the first England-Scotland match ended in a goalless draw. (It happened only twice more in the next century—in 1942 and in 1970).

A shilling entrance but 4,000 still came to watch

The success of the encounter—4,000 spectators turned up, 'including many ladies'—led Queen's Park to search for a suitable ground to play further fixtures. The following season Glasgow Town Council agreed to let 'Hampden Park, Mount Florida' to the club. Ten years later railway construction forced them to move to another site in Hampden Park. The present stadium was completed on yet another site in 1903.

In the spring of 1873, Scotland travelled south to take on the English

giants at Kennington. Again the majority of their side was composed of Queen's Park men and again the crowd was enormous by contemporary standards, 3,000 of them at a shilling a head. They saw a splendidly contested match, with England's powerful dribbling earning them a 2-0 lead, which Scotland equalized only to allow England to score twice more in the closing stages.

The following year, 1874, was a great one for Scottish football. In the first place, Scotland now had its own Football Association, formed in 1873 not specifically to run football north of the border (Queen's Park were doing that very effectively at that time without help from outside), but to institute their own cup competition for the 1873-4 season. Of the original eight SFA members, only Queen's Park now survives (the others were Clydesdale, Dumbreck, Easter, Granville, Rovers, Vale of Leven, and Third Lanark, the last to fade away as late as 1967). There were 16 entrants for the first Scottish Cup, which in 1874 was duly won by Queen's Park, as it was in the two following seasons as well.

And, on 7 March 1874, the Scots defeated England. There were 7000 spectators to watch the 2-1 triumph, and a game which, by all accounts, was notable for its 'beautiful and scientific play'. The English, as usual, excelled in individual brilliance. The Scots, also as usual, knew each other's play (seven men from Queen's Park), and bewildered their opponents with their accurate, defence-splitting passes. The home side's winning goal was described as '. . . a scene which can never be forgotten as long as internationals are played'; Harry McNeil, the midfield wizard, was carried shoulderhigh to the pavilion; and the first of Scottish football's 'finest hours' was complete.

The pattern was to be repeated in the coming few years, all too often for the self respect of the English

clubs. The two countries drew in 1875, Scotland won 3-0 in 1876, beat England in England for the first time in 1877, and thrashed them 7-2 at Hampden in 1878. Of the first eleven matches, from 1872 to 1882, England won two and Scotland seven; on four occasions Scotland scored five or more goals. There was no doubt about it, the Scots had taken on England at their own game and made them look silly.

Both sides were still, of course, amateur but Scotland were playing like professionals. There will always be a dispute about who first developed the passing game—the great Royal Engineers club, which had many successful seasons in London football in the 70s and 80s, claim some credit for 'the combination game', and Sheffield were also early to discover the weaknesses of the individualistic dribbling method, with eight forwards, one half-back, one back and one goalkeeper.

The passing game— not only effective but attractive too

But it is traditionally held that Queen's Park were the first club to perfect football as a *team* game, rather than a game played by a group of individuals. And while the English gentlemen footballers of the 70s and 80s were still vainly dribbling solo at the opposing defenders—just as they had done at school—their undoubted skills were quite impotent when faced with the understanding and team work built up by the Glaswegians.

And this skilled passing game was not only effective, it was attractive too for it increased the scope of the game and the speed of the attacks, and it led to more goals. No wonder they were packing 12,000 into Hampden Park for the internationals as early as 1880.

The popularity of football in Scotland at the start of the 1880s,

Above *The Queen's Park side that won the first Scottish Cup in 1874.*
Opposite top *The Oval was the venue of the England-Scotland match for some years. Here England attack during the 1877 match—the first one they lost at home, Scotland winning 3-1.*
Opposite bottom *Dumbarton challenge Queen's Park in 1883. The Dunbartonshire side were one of the strongest in Scotland before 1900, winning two League Championships.*

and the skill of the young footballers who flocked to the new clubs—long-forgotten names like Renton and Oxford Glasgow, stillfamiliar ones like Kilmarnock and Dumbarton—transformed the game. The non-London clubs were demanding universal laws. Rules for goalkicks and corners were regularized into the form they have today; handling the ball was reserved for the goalkeeper alone; free kicks for infringements were accepted. After a series of squabbles between English and Scottish clubs, the Scottish throw-in was adopted all over the country.

Whereas before the English rule had allowed a one-armed hurl when the ball went out of play, the Scottish had favoured a two-armed throw from behind the head. Before the 1880 match the English refused to take the field unless the referee, a Mr Hamilton, agreed to let them take throws as they liked. He agreed, but as soon as the whistle had blown obviously suffered a kind of selective amnesia which led to him allowing only the 'Scottish' throw—basically that which we know today.

The rules were settled more or less amicably. The dispute over professionalism was not. The rumblings began at the end of the 1870s: rumours started over the alleged payment of players by some of the northern English clubs, and by the early 1880s a full-scale row was brewing. Teams with unashamed working-class origins were making themselves felt, especially as in many

tackling and foul temper. The next year (after a club called Rangers had reached the semi-finals of the FA Cup before going down to Aston Villa), the Scottish Association decreed that '. . . clubs belonging to this association shall not be members of any other national association.' Scotland had broken away, just as it seemed that the still-amateur South of England might be proposing to form a British League.

When the Scots decreed that they should separate

The decision of the Scottish clubs to form a Scottish League in 1891 (and so grant two seasons of glory to Dumbarton, who won the first two Championships) heralded the end of the first chapter in Scottish football. Although professionalism was still banned (until 1893, when the SFA bowed to the inevitable), payments to League players were made quite openly; Queen's Park, still fiercely amateur, refused to join the league until 1900, and the relentless advance of the hard, working-class clubs finally overshadowed these Scottish aristocrats. In 1896, the first year in which the 'Anglos' (the Scottish professionals playing in the English League) were allowed to be selected for Scotland, Queen's Park, for the first time, provided only one member of Scotland's team. But the balance was restored, Scotland's sorry run ended, and they started winning again. And there were 50,000 supporters there to see it.

For Queen's Park it had been a glorious run. In the years between their formation in 1867 and the coming of professionalism, they had, virtually alone, run Scottish football. Losing in two consecutive Finals, they had come closer than any Scottish team to taking the coveted FA Cup out of England; they had, again virtually alone, provided international teams to humble England; they had won the Scottish Cup nine times.

They had provided Scottish crowds with an attractive and fast-moving game which was supported with all the fervour of a new religion. What is more, it grew unopposed. Cricket had never really thrived in Scotland, and rugby was even more haughtily upper-class in Edinburgh and the Borders than it was in southern England. And against all odds and all predictions Queen's Park have remained both amateur and, relatively, talented. In the 1890s, with the advent of professionalism, Celtic and Rangers took over the commanding heights of Scottish football and, sadly perhaps, have shared the battle for supremacy ever since.

The Glaswegian duo owe a lot to Queen's Park—not least for the ground where they regularly contest cup finals and play their more attractive European club matches. And it is a profound commentary on the changing fortunes of a football club that Queen's Park, with a ground that has held 150,000, consider themselves to have a good attendance if they play before one-hundredth of that number.

parts of the country factories and offices were beginning to close after noon on Saturday, allowing the working man a full half-day's leisure every week. And the teams emerging in the North of England—Darwen and Preston, Blackburn and Accrington—often fielded more Scots than Englishmen.

At first, perhaps, the chance of a job in the prosperous factories of Lancashire was as much a lure as the prospect of a weekly shilling or two for playing football, but soon the northern clubs were competing for the services of the Scottish football names and talent scouts were scouring the parks of Glasgow for a likely catch.

The prevailing attitude towards both professionalism and Scots is best illustrated by the infamous story about Major Marindin, referee of the 1887 semi-final between West Brom and Preston. The midlanders won 3-1 and after the game Marindin asked whether they were all English. On being told the team had no Scots Marindin said 'Well then, I am pleased to present you with the ball . . . . I hope you win the Cup.' They didn't, losing to an Aston Villa led by a Scotsman, 2-0.

In 1885 England accepted professionalism, under strict supervision. Scotland held out against it for another eight years. It was a bad time for Scottish football. On the one hand their strong ideological principles forced them to reject the idea of paying sportsmen money; on the other, they saw quite clearly that

the English clubs were ready to snap up those footballers whose principles were less rigid, and Scottish football could only suffer in consequence.

The return of the Anglos—and the return of success

It is surprising, in fact, and a tribute to the deep wells of talent to be tapped in the Scottish Lowlands in those days, that the effect was not worse. The professionalism crisis soured the FA Cup, and the Scottish clubs who still competed. In 1886, the professionals of the fast-rising Preston North End thrashed the amateur Queen's Park 3-0 in Glasgow, and in a game of brutal

![Football match photograph]

And the rest came nowhere

Above The 1978 League Cup final was yet another all-Glasgow Celtic v Rangers affair. Rangers won 2-1 and went on to win both the League Championship and Scottish FA Cup — having been denied completing a hat-trick of Championship wins by Celtic in 1977.
Above right Andy Georgehan, the Don's keeper, loses the ball to Colin Stein at Ibrox.
Right Aberdeen captain Martin Buchan is effectively dispossessed by Celtic's Billy McNeill.

'You might as well attempt to stop the flow of Niagara with a kitchen chair as to endeavour to stem the tide of professionalism,' said the leading voice of one of the factions at the 1893 AGM of the Scottish Football Association. The speaker was J H McLaughlin of Celtic, a prime advocate of the issue at question, the legalization of professionalism in Scotland.

At that meeting – the third inside a year when the question of allowing professionalism was the main item on the agenda – the motion was finally carried. And from that day in May, the story of Scottish football has virtually become the story of Rangers and Celtic. Indeed, of the next 75 Scottish First Division championships contested, only seven different clubs on only 13 occasions took the title away from Glasgow's 'Old Firm.'

Looking back on the first day of 1977, a casual observer would have seen that from 1893 Rangers and Celtic had been champions 63 times —Rangers 35, Celtic 28; their records in the Scottish Cup would be hardly less impressive—44 times they had lifted the trophy out of a possible 71 since the birth of professionalism, Celtic with 23 wins and Rangers 21.

Those figures reflect a situation that was prophesied as far back as 1890 by the almost clairvoyant members of the club which is now the last bastion of amateurism in the senior British game, Queen's Park.

In an aptly titled book, 'The Game for the Game's Sake' (the history of Queen's Park), Glasgow author Robert Crampsey depicts clearly and concisely the attitude of the Hampden club to professionalism at the time: 'Queen's also saw, and warned, that the certain effect of a moneyed game within Scotland would be to tip the scales far too heavily in favour of the big city clubs. As long as those intangible things called honour and prestige were all that were at stake then a local lad might just as well play for his village or small town with which he at least had an affinity. Pay him, and he would sell his sword to the highest bidder.'

Queen's Park, of course, had a lot to lose. Up to the inception of legalized payments, they had been top dogs in Scotland, if not Britain. But it wasn't a mercenary urge to maintain their status that motivated a fierce opposition to professionalism. They were sincerely worried about the effect of financial incentives on the game in Scotland in general. Apart from their prediction about the 'big city clubs' (which they, to an extent, certainly were) they also foresaw the exodus to England, and the reaping of higher rewards available in a far more heavily-populated country, by the cream of Scotland's talent.

The principles which moved the members of Queen's at the time bear the closest scrutiny. Even before payments were legalized, many clubs were obviously practising a form of professionalism. Players would be paid for time off work and for travelling expenses, with sums that clearly exceeded what they were actually due. Queen's Park never did—and indeed still do not—hold with that sort of thing.

And while Queen's Park remained a drawing power right up till the Second World War—and old-time Hampdenites still talk nostalgically of the 'great' Queen's team of the late twenties—it is a fact that since 1893, when they held the Scottish Cup, they have not won a single major trophy.

So the signs of what was to come were manifestly clear to some way back at the very birth of professionalism. Fortunately Queen's Park were only partially right, for Aberdeen, the two Dundee clubs,

Hearts and Hibs are also 'big city clubs'. So why have they never enjoyed a protracted run of success? And since there were six First Division teams in Glasgow—none of them, theoretically at least, enjoying a proportionate population advantage over the other cities—why have Partick Thistle, Clyde, Queen's Park and Third Lanark (sadly now defunct) not even taken a minor share of the 'Old Firm's' success?

The answer—in a word—must be religion. Rangers and Celtic very quickly became more than just football clubs. They were causes—to be fought for, defended, devoted to and, if the need arose, died for. And, but for the dedicated medical staff who man the casualty departments of Glasgow's infirmaries, the supreme sacrifice—martyrdom—would, over the years, have taken its toll of the city's population on many a drunken Saturday night.

Exactly when the religious rift between the two clubs occurred is strangely obscure. Certainly Celtic, founded in 1887 by Brother Walfrid, of the Catholic teaching order of Marist Brothers, had religious influences from the very first. Celtic Football and Athletic Club was formed principally to raise money for food for needy children in the missions of St Mary's, Sacred Heart and St Michael's in the impoverished east end of the city.

Rangers have no such deep-rooted affinity with Protestantism, although Ibrox Park, their wide-open stadium just south of the Clyde, has come to mean to Glasgow's Protestants almost what the Vatican means to the world's Catholics.

Rangers were founded by a group of enthusiastic rowers who used to 'kick the ball' after their strenuous work-outs on the Clyde. In fact, Rangers' first ground was at Glasgow Green, to this day the centre for rowing enthusiasts in the city. A Catholic is known to have played for Rangers in the twenties, and although they had since made 'mistakes' and signed one or two others (who were quickly released) it was only in 1976 that the religious discrimination—against 'left-footers' to use the Glasgow vernacular—was actually formally admitted and abolished.

Celtic, for their part, judge a man solely by his ability. Many of the greatest players in the club's history —John Thomson, Bobby Evans, Bobby Collins, Willie Fernie, and as many as four of the European Cup winning team of 1967 were Protestants. In fact Ronnie Simpson, the goalkeeper in the 1967 side, is the son of an ex-Rangers centre-half, Jimmy Simpson. And in 1965 Celtic appointed a Protestant team manager when they brought Jock Stein in.

But for all that, Celtic's supporters are 99 percent Catholic. Much more to the point, they are Irish Catholic —or of Irish extraction. Those 'needy children' for whom the club was founded were largely the offspring of the droves of Irish workers who came to Glasgow at the end of the last century looking for work and enough to live on.

Their descendants form the basis of Celtic's support nowadays, and on match days at Parkhead many of the songs to be heard are the Irish rebel songs, more suited, perhaps, to a Belfast rally than a Scottish football match.

Rangers' fans counter by pledging their allegiance in song to the cause of Protestantism, or more correctly Irish Protestantism, and epitomized by their parody of the hit song 'Wand'rin Star'.

'I was born under a Union Jack, I was born under a Union Jack, Do I know where hell is? Hell is up the Falls, Heaven is the Shankhill Road, we'll guard old Derry's Walls.'

How many of those Ibrox vocalists, one is tempted to ask, have ever seen Belfast's Shankhill Road or Londonderry's famous town walls?

The Pope, inevitably, comes in for his share of slandering, while William of Orange, England's William III, is the object of much derision from the terracing of Parkhead. Celtic fans insisted 'There's only one King Billy—that's McNeill', surprising no one by feeling more for the Celtic captain of the 1960s, than for an English monarch of the seventeenth century.

With a background like that, of course, Rangers and Celtic are guaranteed the undying allegiance of tens of thousands. So has any provincial outfit a hope of competing with these two over the long term?

Nowadays, it seems extremely unlikely. Outside the 'Old Firm', with the occasional temporary exception, every club in Scotland faces an uphill struggle in the battle for economic survival. The money necessary to build, and maintain, a winning side just does not come in through the turnstiles any more.

So every player in the country outside Ibrox and Parkhead is available for transfer. Players don't have to ask away. If somebody comes along to buy a provincial player, he'll be allowed to go if the price is right; those clubs just can't afford to turn down big money.

Nor can they afford to offer a youngster with potential star quality the same kind of money as Rangers or Celtic. So, as a direct result of the bitter rivalry between two clubs and their fans, Glasgow is generally able to skim the cream of the country's talent, either because of the financial aspect or because many a young fellow would gladly take a cut in wages (though that is not necessary) to play for the club he has been brought up to idolize.

In 1975 the Scottish League split into three divisions in an attempt to bring more competitiveness into the competition. The Premier League was restricted to the top ten clubs who played each other four times during the season. The First and Second Divisions each contained 14 clubs (with Meadowbank Thistle making up the even numbers). After an attempt to increase fixtures for the First and Second Division clubs by the introduction of a Spring Cup

23

had failed, the clubs met each other three times in the 1976-77 season. This new structure, very much on trial, was not helped by the results of its first season. Rangers became the first Premier Division winners—six clear points ahead of who else but Celtic, themselves five points above Hibernian. Even under a new system the old order prevailed with Rangers going on to complete the treble.

It wasn't always like that—until about 1960 the game was thriving in Scotland. It wasn't uncommon for crowds of 30,000 to turn up for a Third Lanark versus Hibs match at Cathkin Park. And, of course, in the years following the last War, the problem for most clubs was simply how quickly they could get people through the turnstiles. Yet Rangers and Celtic still managed to monopolize the top of the heap. The challenge presented by the provincials was often successful, but never lasted long enough to break the overall dominance enjoyed by the Firm.

Joint runners-up in the League Championship stakes to the big two are Hearts and Hibs, with four wins apiece. But two of Hearts' victories were gained in the 1890s, and the other two in 1958 and 1960. Hibs won the League in 1902-3, and then three times in their halcyon days between 1948 and 1952. By 1977 Hibs were still the only club outside Rangers and Celtic to win the title in successive years. Those great Edinburgh teams of the early and late fifties were the nearest anybody ever came to sustaining a serious threat to the Glasgow stranglehold. But even they didn't last long.

Hearts, for instance, with the near-legendary Dave Mackay at wing-half and the formidable inside trio of Conn, Bauld and Wardhaugh up front, looked invincible in their heyday. But sandwiched between their two League titles was one by Rangers, who were only mediocre by comparison. The Old Firm refused to surrender.

Hearts did win a Scottish Cup and two League Cups as well as their League Championships, but never completed the big double in one season. So it was with Hibs. They won three League Championships in five years, with what many Scots still regard as the finest forward line in history (Smith, Johnston, Reilly, Turnbull and Ormond), but never won a cup. Indeed, in the 30 years since the Scottish League Cup became a major competition, only two seasons have gone by when the Old Firm failed to land one of the major trophies. They were 1951-52, when Hibs won the League, Motherwell the Scottish Cup, and Dundee the League Cup, and 1954-55 when Aberdeen won the League, Clyde the Scottish Cup and Hearts the League Cup. Fifteen years later no one expected to see such a season again.

The hopelessness of the provincials was put in a nutshell by the late Tom Preston, chairman of Airdrie. Tom, a great talker who played in Airdrie's Scottish Cup winning team of 1924, rarely thought, never mind spoke, about anything but football. A distinguished Scottish journalist recalls a walk through Airdrie with Parker: 'Two little boys about ten years old skipped past us. They were wearing

Above *The game goes on but the real Rangers-Celtic struggle is off the field.*

Celtic scarves and woollen ski hats. Tom spread his hands and said, "See that? That's what we've got to compete with." He was, of course, referring to the fact that here were two local boys who, even at their age, were leaving the town to follow Celtic.' In the 1960s it was the same all over the country.

Every week managers and directors in Dundee, Edinburgh, Ayr, Kilmarnock, Fife and Aberdeen looked from their windows and saw busloads of Rangers and Celtic supporters departing—and had to watch their own fans trickle through the turnstiles in pitifully small numbers.

But the outlying districts of Scotland are relatively close examples of places where Rangers and Celtic enjoy huge support. There are registered supporters' clubs for this pair all over the world. Rangers have clubs in Mauritius, New Zealand and Australia, to say nothing of their innumerable devotees exiled in North America.

Ironically, Rangers' biggest supporters club is in England. In Corby, the steel town of Northamptonshire, the Rangers Supporters' Association claims that the Corby branch is not only the biggest soccer supporters' club (in the genuine sense) in the country, but in the world.

Considered from a detached viewpoint, Scottish football often adopts the features of a farce. For instance, between the years 1905 and 1947, only once (1931-32) did a team outside the duo manage to win the Scottish First Division. The Motherwell of the thirties were generally regarded as the finest team in the country. Yet at the end of their purple patch that solitary League Championship was all they had to show. Rangers saw to that with an incredible eight wins in nine years. Motherwell were runners-up four times. It is almost as if the Scottish League had a rule prohibiting provincial clubs from even challenging Glasgow.

Unlike English football, where the 'greatest ever team' provokes a fertile discussion never likely to be concluded, Scotland has far fewer choices at its command. One possibility is the Celtic team of just after the First World War, which won three League titles and four Scottish Cups and which included Patsy Gallagher—dubbed by Celtic's late president, Sir Robert Kelly, 'pound for pound the greatest footballer I ever saw'—Tommy McInally, Jimmy 'Napoleon' McMenemy and Jimmy McGrory, whose goal-scoring

feats are unlikely ever to be equalled.

A Protestant alternative is the magnificent Rangers team of the twenties and thirties which included, inevitably, the legendary Alan Morton. Even in the light of the achievements of the Celtic team of more recent years, old-timers still claim nobody before or since could hold a candle to Gallagher and Morton.

But no chronicle of the great teams could be complete without a look at the eleven moulded into the first British outfit to win the European Cup by Jock Stein in 1967. That Celtic side had everything, but Bertie Auld deserves special mention because the Scots believe he was probably the first British player to match the continentals at their own game—or beat them. Slowing it down to his own pace, cockily arrogant in everything he did, Auld had the opposition beaten in the dressing-room before every match with his unshakeable confidence.

Perhaps it was a confidence that should have surprised no one. With Birmingham City, Auld was, on his own admission, a failure. On going to Celtic he joined a team that were on their way to a string of victories that would leave most fans hazy about the last time Celtic had *not* been League Champions. When you play for a team that is *that* successful, you would have to be a very odd character indeed to be anything but confident.

At the other end of the scale, for most First and Second Division sides surviving economically is the name of their game. Kilmarnock, who became one of the privileged ten clubs in the Premier Division in 1976, were committed to a policy of part-time football that no amount of success would change. The majority of clubs gain satisfaction by getting by and taking a pride in hearing their names mentioned on Sports Report every Saturday.

Stranraer are your Mr Average. Their's is an isolated town of only 10,000 inhabitants. They are pleased with an attendance of four figures, but they pride themselves in being better off than they have been for a long time.

'We operate on a shoe-string budget—and we cut our cloth accordingly', says their committee. 'Our gates average about 1,000 and each week we are handed around £100 by our Club Pool. This does us nicely. We have no worries.

'We operate with about 15 players whose wages are average for the

Second Division.' Like several other clubs, they do not even have to worry about a manager's wage. Stranraer are run by a 12-man committee who work entirely for the love of it. In January 1977 this committee even won Scotland's 'Manager of the Month' award!

The fact that Stranraer is rather remote—away in the south-west of Scotland and over 100 miles from the Central Lowland belt of the country where the main action takes place—is not as much of a problem as might be expected. Most of their players are based in Glasgow and this centre is really the starting point for the coach to 'away' matches.

So cleverly do they cut their cloth, in fact, that they are not even forced to sell players regularly. 'We got £10,000 from Dundee United for Jackie Copland a couple of years ago, but he was our first sale in a long time.' The sale of a player, therefore, is a bonus rather than an essential part of the club's income. In fact, discovering good players is probably the only real contribution the average Second Division side makes to Scottish football.

But how do they manage to sign players who later achieve greatness, and who, one would expect, should be holding out for a more glamorous offer? The answer is simple. Great footballers, like any other talent, can come from the unlikeliest corners. Second Division sides are able to sign them before the scouts from the big clubs even hear about them.

The secret of keeping heads above water, as practised so successfully by the Stranraers, the Brechins, the Stenhousemuirs, lies in these clubs' realistic attitude to life. They realize only too well that a town of 10,000 inhabitants—which is about average among the 'rabbits'—just could not support an ambitious football club.

Others, with even bigger populations, have tried to live with the Celtics and in the end all have failed spectacularly. Dunfermline Athletic are the latest and perhaps greatest example.

In the middle of the 1950s, the Fife club were determined to put themselves on the soccer map. By the end of the first decade they had made it to the First Division.

In 1961, under the management of Jock Stein, they won the Scottish Cup, beating Celtic in the final. There was no turning back now. By 1968, when they again won the Scottish Cup, they had proved themselves one of the most progressive—and one of the most feared—provincial clubs in the country.

But the strain of having to maintain their status inevitably proved too much. By season 1971-72 they were reduced to calling for public aid, saying they needed an immediate £50,000 to save the club from extinction. At the end of the same season they were relegated to the Second Division from whence they had come.

Most of the others have learned from these fatal errors over the years, and it would not be unfair to say that every season, from the dozen and a half clubs which form the division, only a handful are seriously looking for, or are capable of, promotion. Of course it was not always so. In fact, the Second Division was formalized at the end of season

SCOTTISH FA CUP FINALS

Year	Venue	Winners		Runners-up	
1874	Hampden Park	Queen's Park	2	Clydesdale	0
1875	Hampden Park	Queen's Park	3	Renton	0
1876	Hampden Park	Queen's Park	1:2	Third Lanark	1:0
1877	Hampden Park	Vale of Leven	0:1:3	Rangers	0:1:2
1878	Hampden Park	Vale of Leven	1	Third Lanark	0
1879¹	Hampden Park	Vale of Leven	1	Rangers	1
1880	Cathkin Park	Queen's Park	3	Thornlibank	0
1881	Kinning Park	Queen's Park	3	Dumbarton	1
1882	Cathkin Park	Queen's Park	2:4	Dumbarton	2:1
1883	Hampden Park	Dumbarton	2:2	Vale of Leven	2:1
1884²	Hampden Park	Queen's Park		Vale of Leven	
1885	Hampden Park	Renton	0:3	Vale of Leven	0:1
1886	Cathkin Park	Queen's Park	3	Renton	1
1887	Hampden Park	Hibernian	2	Dumbarton	1
1888	Hampden Park	Renton	6	Cambuslang	1
1889	Hampden Park	Third Lanark	2	Celtic	1
1890	Ibrox Park	Queen's Park	1:2	Vale of Leven	1:1
1891	Hampden Park	Hearts	1	Dumbarton	0
1893	Ibrox Park	Celtic	5	Queen's Park	1
1893	Ibrox Park	Queen's Park	2	Celtic	1
1894	Hampden Park	Rangers	3	Celtic	1
1895	Ibrox Park	St Bernard's	2	Renton	1
1896	Logie Green	Hearts	3	Hibernian	1
1897	Hampden Park	Rangers	5	Dumbarton	1
1898	Hampden Park	Rangers	2	Kilmarnock	0
1899	Hampden Park	Celtic	2	Rangers	0
1900	Ibrox Park	Celtic	4	Queen's Park	3
1901	Ibrox Park	Hearts	4	Celtic	3
1902	Celtic Park	Hibernian	1	Celtic	0
1903	Celtic Park	Rangers	1:0:2	Hearts	1:0:0
1904	Hampden Park	Celtic	3	Rangers	2
1905	Hampden Park	Third Lanark	0:3	Rangers	0:1
1906	Ibrox Park	Hearts	1	Third Lanark	0
1907	Hampden Park	Celtic	3	Hearts	0
1908	Hampden Park	Celtic	5	St Mirren	1
1909⁴					
1910	Ibrox Park	Dundee	2:0:2	Clyde	2:0:1
1911	Ibrox Park	Celtic	0:2	Hamilton Acad	0:0
1912	Ibrox Park	Celtic	2	Clyde	0
1913	Celtic Park	Falkirk	2	Raith Rovers	0
1914	Ibrox Park	Celtic	0:4	Hibernian	0:1
1919	No competition				
1920	Hampden Park	Kilmarnock	3	Albion Rovers	2
1921	Celtic Park	Partick Thistle	1	Rangers	0
1922	Hampden Park	Morton	1	Rangers	0
1923	Hampden Park	Celtic	1	Hibernian	0
1924	Ibrox Park	Airdrieonians	2	Hibernian	0
1925	Hampden Park	Celtic	2	Dundee	1
1926	Hampden Park	St Mirren	2	Celtic	0
1927	Hampden Park	Celtic	3	East Fife	1
1928	Hampden Park	Rangers	4	Celtic	0
1929	Hampden Park	Kilmarnock	2	Rangers	0
1930	Hampden Park	Rangers	0:2	Partick Thistle	0:1
1931	Hampden Park	Celtic	2:4	Motherwell	2:2
1932	Hampden Park	Rangers	1:3	Kilmarnock	1:0
1933	Hampden Park	Celtic	1	Motherwell	0
1934	Hampden Park	Rangers	5	St Mirren	0
1935	Hampden Park	Rangers	2	Hamilton Acad	1
1936	Hampden Park	Rangers	1	Third Lanark	0
1937	Hampden Park	Celtic	2	Aberdeen	1
1938	Hampden Park	East Fife	1:4	Kilmarnock	1:2
1939	Hampden Park	Clyde	4	Motherwell	0
1946	No competition				
1947	Hampden Park	Aberdeen	2	Hibernian	1
1948	Hampden Park	Rangers	1:1	Morton	1:0
1949	Hampden Park	Rangers	4	Clyde	1
1950	Hampden Park	Rangers	3	East Fife	0
1951	Hampden Park	Celtic	1	Motherwell	0
1952	Hampden Park	Motherwell	4	Dundee	0
1953	Hampden Park	Rangers	1:1	Aberdeen	1:0
1954	Hampden Park	Celtic	2	Aberdeen	1
1955	Hampden Park	Clyde	1:1	Celtic	1:0
1956	Hampden Park	Hearts	3	Celtic	1
1957*	Hampden Park	Falkirk	1:2	Kilmarnock	1:1
1958	Hampden Park	Clyde	1	Hibernian	0
1959	Hampden Park	St Mirren	3	Aberdeen	1
1960	Hampden Park	Rangers	2	Kilmarnock	0
1961	Hampden Park	Dunfermline Ath	0:2	Celtic	0:0
1962	Hampden Park	Rangers	2	St Mirren	0
1963	Hampden Park	Rangers	1:3	Celtic	1:0
1964	Hampden Park	Rangers	3	Dundee	1
1965	Hampden Park	Celtic	3	Dunfermline Ath	2
1966	Hampden Park	Rangers	0:1	Celtic	0:0
1967	Hampden Park	Celtic	2	Aberdeen	0
1968	Hampden Park	Dunfermline Ath	3	Hearts	1
1969	Hampden Park	Celtic	4	Rangers	0
1970	Hampden Park	Aberdeen	3	Celtic	1
1971	Hampden Park	Celtic	1:2	Rangers	1:1
1972	Hampden Park	Celtic	6	Hibernian	1
1973	Hampden Park	Rangers	3	Celtic	2
1974	Hampden Park	Celtic	3	Dundee Utd	0
1975	Hampden Park	Celtic	3	Airdrieonians	1
1976	Hampden Park	Rangers	3	Hearts	1
1977	Hampden Park	Celtic	1	Rangers	0
1978	Hampden Park	Rangers	2	Aberdeen	1

¹Vale of Leven awarded the Cup after Rangers failed to attend the replay.
²Queen's Park awarded the Cup after Vale of Leven failed to attend the final.
³After Queen's Park protested at the first game, which Celtic won 1-0.
⁴Owing to riots the Cup was withheld after two drawn games (2-2, 1-1) at Hampden.

SCOTTISH LEAGUE CHAMPIONSHIP

Season	First	Pts	Second	Pts
1890-91	†Dumbarton	29	†Rangers	29
1891-92	Dumbarton	37	Celtic	35
1892-93	Celtic	29	Rangers	27
1893-94	Celtic	29	Hearts	26
1894-95	Hearts	31	Celtic	26
1895-96	Celtic	30	Rangers	26
1896-97	Hearts	28	Hibernian	26
1897-98	Celtic	33	Rangers	29
1898-99	Rangers	36	Hearts	26
1899-1900	Rangers	32	Celtic	25
1900-01	Rangers	35	Celtic	29
1901-02	Rangers	28	Celtic	26
1902-03	Hibernian	37	Dundee	31
1903-04	Third Lanark	43	Hearts	39
1904-05	‡Celtic	41	Rangers	41
1905-06	Celtic	49	Hearts	43
1906-07	Celtic	55	Dundee	48
1907-08	Celtic	55	Falkirk	51
1908-09	Celtic	51	Dundee	50
1909-10	Celtic	54	Falkirk	52
1910-11	Rangers	52	Aberdeen	48
1911-12	Rangers	51	Celtic	45
1912-13	Rangers	53	Celtic	49
1913-14	Celtic	65	Rangers	59
1914-15	Celtic	65	Hearts	61
1915-16	Celtic	67	Rangers	56
1916-17	Celtic	64	Morton	54
1917-18	Rangers	56	Celtic	55
1918-19	Celtic	58	Rangers	57
1919-20	Rangers	71	Celtic	68
1920-21	Rangers	76	Celtic	66
1921-22	Celtic	67	Rangers	66
1922-23	Rangers	55	Airdrieonians	50
1923-24	Rangers	59	Airdrieonians	50
1924-25	Rangers	60	Airdrieonians	57
1925-26	Celtic	58	Airdrieonians	50
1926-27	Rangers	56	Motherwell	51
1927-28	Rangers	60	*Celtic	55
1928-29	Rangers	67	Celtic	51
1929-30	Rangers	60	Motherwell	55
1930-31	Rangers	60	Celtic	58
1931-32	Motherwell	66	Rangers	61
1932-33	Rangers	62	Motherwell	59
1933-34	Rangers	66	Motherwell	62
1934-35	Rangers	55	Celtic	52
1935-36	Celtic	66	*Rangers	61
1936-37	Rangers	61	Aberdeen	54
1937-38	Celtic	61	Hearts	58
1938-39	Rangers	59	Celtic	48
1939-46	No competition			
1946-47	Rangers	46	Hibernian	44
1947-48	Hibernian	48	Rangers	46
1948-49	Rangers	46	Dundee	45
1949-50	Rangers	50	Hibernian	49
1950-51	Hibernian	48	Rangers	38
1951-52	Hibernian	45	Rangers	41
1952-53	*Rangers	43	Hibernian	43
1953-54	Celtic	43	Hearts	38
1954-55	Aberdeen	49	Celtic	46
1955-56	Rangers	52	Aberdeen	46
1956-57	Rangers	55	Hearts	53
1957-58	Hearts	62	Rangers	49
1958-59	Rangers	50	Hearts	48
1959-60	Hearts	54	Kilmarnock	50
1960-61	Rangers	51	Kilmarnock	50
1961-62	Dundee	54	Rangers	51
1962-63	Rangers	57	Kilmarnock	48
1963-64	Rangers	55	Kilmarnock	49
1964-65	*Kilmarnock	50	Hearts	50
1965-66	Celtic	57	Rangers	55
1966-67	Celtic	58	Rangers	55
1967-68	Celtic	63	Rangers	61
1968-69	Celtic	54	Rangers	49
1969-70	Celtic	57	Rangers	45
1970-71	Celtic	56	Aberdeen	54
1971-72	Celtic	60	Aberdeen	50
1972-73	Celtic	57	Rangers	56
1973-74	Celtic	53	Hibernian	49
1974-75	Rangers	56	Hibernian	49
1975-76	Rangers	54	Celtic	48
1976-77	Celtic	55	Rangers	46
1977-78	Rangers	55	Aberdeen	53

÷ Shared after indecisive play-off (2-2). ‡ Celtic won play-off. *Goal average.

SCOTTISH LEAGUE CUP FINALS

Season	Venue	Winners		Runners-up	
1945-46	Hampden Park	Aberdeen	3	Rangers	2
1946-47	Hampden Park	Rangers	4	Aberdeen	0
1947-48	Hampden Park	East Fife	1:4	Falkirk	1:1
1948-49	Hampden Park	Rangers	2	Raith Rovers	0
1949-50	Hampden Park	East Fife	3	Dunfermline Ath	0
1950-51	Hampden Park	Motherwell	3	Hibernian	0
1951-52	Hampden Park	Dundee	3	Rangers	2
1952-53	Hampden Park	Dundee	2	Kilmarnock	0
1953-54	Hampden Park	East Fife	3	Partick Thistle	2
1954-55	Hampden Park	Hearts	4	Motherwell	2
1955-56	Hampden Park	Aberdeen	2	St Mirren	1
1956-57	Hampden Park	Celtic	0:3	Partick Thistle	0:0
1957-58	Hampden Park	Celtic	7	Rangers	1
1958-59	Hampden Park	Hearts	5	Partick Thistle	1
1959-60	Hampden Park	Hearts	2	Third Lanark	1
1960-61	Hampden Park	Rangers	2	Kilmarnock	0
1961-62	Hampden Park	Rangers	1:3	Hearts	1:1
1962-63	Hampden Park	Hearts	1	Kilmarnock	0
1963-64	Hampden Park	Rangers	5	Morton	0
1964-65	Hampden Park	Rangers	2	Celtic	1
1965-66	Hampden Park	Celtic	2	Rangers	1
1966-67	Hampden Park	Celtic	1	Rangers	0
1967-68	Hampden Park	Celtic	5	Dundee	3
1968-69	Hampden Park	Celtic	6	Hibernian	2
1969-70	Hampden Park	Celtic	1	St Johnstone	0
1970-71	Hampden Park	Rangers	1	Celtic	0
1971-72	Hampden Park	Partick Thistle	4	Celtic	1
1972-73	Hampden Park	Hibernian	2	Celtic	1
1973-74	Hampden Park	Dundee	1	Celtic	0
1974-75	Hampden Park	Celtic	6	Hibernian	3
1975-76	Hampden Park	Rangers	1	Celtic	0
1976-77	Hampden Park	Aberdeen	2	Celtic	1
1977-78	Hampden Park	Rangers	2	Celtic	1

Scotland's traditional 'Second Division' clubs

1 Albion Rovers (Coatbridge)
2 Alloa Athletic
3 Berwick Rangers
4 Brechin City
5 Clydebank
6 East Stirlingshire (Falkirk)
7 Forfar Athletic
8 Hamilton Academicals
9 Montrose
10 Queen's Park (Glasgow)
11 Stenhousemuir
12 Stranraer
13 Arbroath
14 Ayr United
15 Clyde (Glasgow)
16 Cowdenbeath
17 Dumbarton
18 Dunfermline Athletic
19 East Fife (Methil)
20 Morton (Greenock)
21 Queen of the South
22 Raith Rovers (Kirkcaldy)
23 St. Mirren (Paisley)
24 Stirling Albion

Highland League clubs

25 Brora Rangers
26 Buckie Thistle
27 Caledonian (Inverness)
28 Clachnacuddin (Inverness)
29 Deveronvale (Banff)
30 Elgin City
31 Forres Mechanics
32 Fraserburgh
33 Huntly
34 Inverness Thistle
35 Keith
36 Lossiemouth
37 Nairn County
38 Peterhead
39 Ross County (Dingwall)
40 Rothes

1921-22 through the desire of lesser clubs to enjoy the pickings of the First Division.

From the introduction of professionalism in 1893 until the beginning of the First World War the Second Division was only semi-recognized by the Scottish League and promotion to the First Division was by election only.

An aspiring Second Division club had to have plenty of friends to be elected. On the other hand, a club like Queen's Park, whose fortunes faded around 1910, were saved several times from dropping to the Second Division because they had plenty of friends who voted that they stayed where they were.

The system sowed the seeds of discontent. There grew a feeling that, as there were rewards for success, there should be a penalty for failure. That, in fact, there should be a promotion-relegation system between First and Second Division. But all was forgotten when the War began in 1914.

When hostilities ended four years later and football in Scotland began again the Second Division had vanished. In its place was the Central League, a rebel division comprised of clubs who had been in the pre-War lower grade and a few newcomers.

Left *The forty clubs that "make up the numbers" in Scottish soccer. The only major names missing are those of the 13 'traditional' First Division sides in the larger population centres viz: Aberdeen, Airdrie, Celtic, Dundee, Dundee United, Falkirk, Hearts, Hibs, Kilmarnock, Motherwell, Partick, Rangers and St Johnstone (Perth).*
The map shows clearly that the lower division teams cluster round the Central Lowland belt—the only exceptions being the southern isolates, Stranraer, Queen of the South and Berwick, and the group of four to the north of the Firth of Tay. This is relevant in that it shows just how artificial any attempt to divide the Second Division into East/West or North/South sections would be. Only with the addition of the Highland League would regionalization be a meaningful proposition.
The greatest distance between any two present League clubs is the 195 miles from Stranraer to Montrose—about the same distance as London to Leeds or Liverpool. But even this is less of a handicap than it appears as, in Stranraer's case, most of their players live in Glasgow and away journeys start from there.
For most clubs travel is no great problem. The clustering of clubs in the central belt certainly helps in saving travelling expenses—though it is also a problem in that people from all over the area can travel to watch Rangers or Celtic almost as easily as their local club. Nevertheless teams like Falkirk and East Stirlingshire are within 60 miles of 28 of the Scottish League's other 36 teams.
The Highland League operates completely independently and has long resisted attempts to integrate it into a national network. The only League club which comes within 70 miles of its territory is Aberdeen, and attendances at Highland League games are often higher than those in the Second Division and, occasionally, those in the First.

The breakaway League was an immediate success, a real money-spinner in Fife particularly, and clubs like Dunfermline and Cowdenbeath were able to tempt players away from Celtic and Rangers.

Very quickly the Scottish League realized their First Division was threatened, so the idea was hatched that the 'rebels' should be recognized as a Second Division.

'On our terms, though', said the Central League, who of course had been angling after a fair deal all along, anyway. And their terms were that there should be automatic promotion and relegation rather than the vagaries of election.

The Scottish League agreed and in season 1921-22 the official Second Division came into being. The first movement came at the end of that term—Alloa were promoted and three clubs, including Queen's Park, were relegated in order to even the numbers of teams in both Divisions. At the end of the following season began the two-up — two-down system. From then until the Second World War, the only changes in the Second Division were those prompted by clubs dropping out. The number of clubs fluctuated but the overall set-up remained the same.

The entire League programme was suspended, of course, between 1939 and 1945. When normality was restored in season 1946-47 several changes had taken place.

For a start, the separate Leagues were called Division A and Division B as opposed to I and II. And eight teams had dropped from the 1939 Second Division into the newly-formed Division C, which was composed of 'non-League' clubs and reserve teams of the established clubs in the top two divisions.

Stirling Albion, formed only in 1945, were the first champions of 'C' Division and they were promoted to Division B. During the next few years they proceeded to yo-yo their way up and down from 'B' to 'A' and back to 'B'.

In the late forties, with the inevitable 'boom' which followed the War allowing more clubs to run reserve teams, Division C was split into two regionalized groups—South-West and North-East. With the bisection of 'C' Division, it meant the end of promotion to 'B' from that table, as had happened to Stirling previously. It was not until 1955 that the two division system was re-established.

The 'C' divisions were scrapped, and the Reserve League was formed. Five 'non-League' clubs from 'C' were elected to Division II.

And the top two teams in Division II were promoted to the First Division. To even up the teams in each Division, the bottom two in the First Division in 1955 were not relegated.

That is the way it stayed until 1975 when a major reorganisation took place. The top ten clubs of Division One in 1974-75 formed a new Premier Division while the bottom eight along with the top six of Division Two formed the new Division One. The rest of the clubs remained in Division Two. Yet at the top, whatever the structure, the race was never difficult to predict — Rangers or Celtic first, the rest nowhere.

SCOTTISH FIRST DIVISION 1975-78

Season	First	Second
1975-76	Partick Thistle	Kilmarnock
1976-77	St Mirren	Clydebank
1977-78	Morton	Hearts

SCOTTISH SECOND DIVISION 1975-78

Season	First	Second
1975-76	Clydebank	Raith
1976-77	Stirling	Alloa
1977-78	Clyde	Raith

SCOTTISH SECOND DIVISION 1893-1975

Season	First	Second
1893-94[1]	Hibernian	Cowlairs
1894-95[2]	Hibernian	Motherwell
1895-96[3]	Abercorn	Leith Athletic
1896-97[4]	Partick Thistle	Leith Athletic
1897-98	Kilmarnock	Port Glasgow Athletic
1898-99[5]	Kilmarnock	Leith Athletic
1899-1900[6]	Partick Thistle	Morton
1900-01	St Bernard's	Airdrieonians
1901-02[7]	Port Glasgow Athletic	Partick Thistle
1902-03[8]	Airdrieonians	Motherwell
1903-04	Hamilton Academicals	Clyde
1904-05[9]	Clyde	Falkirk
1905-06[10]	Leith Athletic	Clyde
1906-07	St Bernard's	Vale of Leven
1907-08	Raith Rovers	Dumbarton
1908-09	Abercorn	Raith Rovers
1909-10[11]	Leith Athletic	Raith Rovers
1910-11	Dumbarton	Ayr United
1911-12	Ayr United	Abercorn
1912-13[12]	Ayr United	Dunfermline Athletic
1913-14	Cowdenbeath	Albion Rovers
1914-15	Cowdenbeath	St Bernard's
1915-1921	*Competition suspended*	
1921-22[13]	Alloa Athletic	Cowdenbeath
1922-23[14]	Queen's Park	Clydebank
1923-24	St Johnstone	Cowdenbeath
1924-25	Dundee United	Clydebank
1925-26	Dunfermline Athletic	Clyde
1926-27	Bo'ness	Raith Rovers
1927-28	Ayr United	Third Lanark
1928-29	Dundee United	Morton
1929-30	Leith Athletic	East Fife
1930-31	Third Lanark	Dundee United
1931-32	East Stirlingshire	St Johnstone
1932-33	Hibernian	Queen of the South
1933-34	Albion Rovers	Dunfermline Athletic
1934-35	Third Lanark	Arbroath
1935-36	Falkirk	St Mirren
1936-37	Ayr United	Morton
1937-38	Raith Rovers	Albion Rovers
1938-39[15]	Cowdenbeath	Alloa Athletic
1939-1946	*Competition suspended*	
1946-47	Dundee	Airdrieonians
1947-48	East Fife	Albion Rovers
1948-49	Raith Rovers	Stirling Albion
1949-50	Morton	Airdrieonians
1950-51	Queen of the South	Stirling Albion
1951-52	Clyde	Falkirk
1952-53	Stirling Albion	Hamilton Academicals
1953-54	Motherwell	Kilmarnock
1954-55	Airdrieonians	Dunfermline Athletic
1955-56	Queen's Park	Ayr United
1956-57	Clyde	Third Lanark
1957-58	Stirling Albion	Dunfermline Athletic
1958-59	Ayr United	Arbroath
1959-60	St Johnstone	Dundee United
1960-61	Stirling Albion	Falkirk
1961-62	Clyde	Queen of the South
1962-63	St Johnstone	East Stirlingshire
1963-64	Morton	Clyde
1964-65	Stirling Albion	Hamilton Academicals
1965-66	Ayr United	Airdrieonians
1966-67	Morton	Raith Rovers
1967-68	St Mirren	Arbroath
1968-69	Motherwell	Ayr United
1969-70	Falkirk	Cowdenbeath
1970-71	Partick Thistle	East Fife
1971-72	Dumbarton	Arbroath
1972-73	Clyde	Dunfermline Athletic
1973-74	Airdrieonians	Kilmarnock
1974-75	Falkirk	Queen of the South

[1] Clyde (who finished third) elected to First Division
[2] Hibernian elected to First Division
[3] Abercorn elected to First Division
[4] Partick Thistle elected to First Division
[5] Kilmarnock elected to First Division
[6] Partick Thistle and Morton were elected to First Division. So were Queen's Park, but they had not been members of the Second Division
[7] Port Glasgow Athletic and Partick Thistle were elected to the First Division
[8] Airdrieonians and Motherwell elected to First Division
[9] Aberdeen (who finished seventh) and Falkirk elected to First Division
[10] Clyde and Hamilton Academicals (who finished fourth) elected to First Division
[11] Raith Rovers were elected to First Division
[12] Ayr United and Dumbarton (who finished sixth) elected to First Division
[13] Alloa Athletic elected to First Division. Three clubs were relegated to the Second
[14] From season 1922-23 onwards the first two clubs in the Second Division were automatically elected to First Division
[15] No clubs were promoted at the end of 1938-39 because of the Second World War

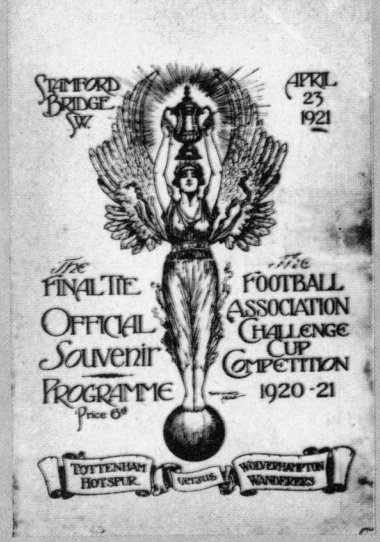

TOPIX

THE STORY OF FOOTBALL

The Chapman era

Above *Bowlers, boaters, trilbies and cloth caps mingle in a section of the crowd for the 1921 Cup Final at Stamford Bridge.*
Right *The cover of the programme for the same match. Spurs won 1-0.*
Top right *Complete with spectacles and plus-fours, Arsenal manager Herbert Chapman poses with his team at Hendon before the trip to Paris and the annual friendly with Racing Club.*
Inset *The bust of Herbert Chapman at Highbury—a memorial to the man who revolutionized football thinking.*

Stamford Bridge SW. April 23 1921
The Final Tie Official Souvenir Programme Price 6d
The Football Association Challenge Cup Competition 1920-21
Tottenham Hotspur versus Wolverhampton Wanderers

COURTESY OF M. KESTON

The twenty years between the First and Second World Wars has been called the era of the manager. That is not quite accurate. In truth it was the era of one manager; just one man, whose achievements found an appropriate setting halfway through two turbulent decades in the 1930 FA Cup Final. Those ninety minutes were, quite simply, a microcosm of the whole period.

The combatants were Huddersfield Town and Arsenal. Just eleven years earlier the Yorkshire club's directors had recommended that the organization move, lock, stock and barrel, to Leeds, support and success being sadly elusive in a Huddersfield obsessed with rugby league. The same year Arsenal crept into the First Division by means which could only be described as devious, being elected after finishing only sixth in the immediate pre-War Second Division.

Four years before the 1930 Final Huddersfield had become the first club ever to win three consecutive League Championships and, five years after it, Arsenal did precisely the same thing. During their great years both were managed by the same man, Herbert Chapman and, appropriately enough, the game in question was won by the club he then managed, Arsenal, over the club he had left, Huddersfield.

Herbert Chapman was born in the very far south of Yorkshire, at Kiveton Park, in 1873. His professional career as a reserve with Spurs was distinguished only by the lemon coloured boots he wore. In 1907 he became manager of the Southern League side Northampton Town and later moved to Second Division Leeds City, who were ignominiously thrown out of the League in 1919 for making illegal payments to players. Their place was taken by Port Vale—who were to suffer exactly the same fate half a century later. Vale, however, were re-elected. Leeds were not and Chapman—suspended though his only involvement was an alleged timely incineration of the club's books—took a partnership in an engineering firm.

Not for long though. Huddersfield, rather than move to Leeds as their directors were then threatening, managed to raise some cash and sign a number of players. When his suspension was lifted, Chapman joined Huddersfield as manager in September 1920. Here the story really begins. Chapman's first success was the FA Cup of 1922, albeit with a disputed Billy Smith penalty, and two years later Huddersfield won the League Championship on goal average from Cardiff. The next season they retained the title with a new defensive record—only 28 goals conceded—and went on to make it a hat-trick in 1926.

By that time, however, Chapman had gone. His success at Huddersfield was remarkable, for he had no great financial resources and the Yorkshiremen, facing the fierce competition of rugby league, had never drawn large crowds. His team had few outstanding players—most notable was Alex Jackson, one of the Scottish 'Wembley Wizards' that crushed England 5-1 in 1928. Jackson was technically a right-winger, though he actually wandered all over the park more in the manner of an Alan Ball. England captains Clem Stephenson and Sam Wadsworth were valuable signings, while Sam Barkas was an excellent full-back partner for Wadsworth. Barkas, in fact, was one of Alf Ramsey's first boyhood idols.

Above *Chapman (far left) with the Cup winning Huddersfield side of 1922. By 1925 he had set them on the way to a League hat-trick and left for Arsenal.*

Chapman's ability lay in choosing and moulding his players as parts of a whole—not just allowing them to function as individuals in the well-defined grooves laid down when 'positional' play was strict. He chose well at Huddersfield, but he was perhaps lucky in that his formation came right immediately. When he moved to Arsenal in 1925 it took rather longer to build a Championship side.

In a sense it was an appropriate time to move, for 1925 was also the year of the most significant tactical development since the 'passing' game had superseded the 'dribbling' game in the 1870s.

The immediate cause was the change in the offside law on 12 June 1925, when the '. . . fewer than three players between the attacker and the goal' clause was changed to '. . . fewer than two . . .' The change had become desirable because so many teams were employing a very simple offside trap, bringing their defenders upfield to render lethargic forwards offside and sometimes confining play to a strip covering no more than 40 yards of the middle of the field.

The Notts County full-backs Morley and Montgomery had been guilty of this before the First World War, but it took their Newcastle counterparts McCracken and Hudspeth to elevate the 'offside game' to a fine art in the early 1920s. The pair became so identified with the ploy that when one side arrived at Newcastle Central station and a guard blew his whistle the centre-forward was heard to remark 'Blimey, offside already!'

When the trend became unacceptable the International Board—the law making body—finally acted; and the results were startling. In the 1924-25 season 1192 goals were scored in the First Division. In the next season that figure read 1703—an increase of almost 50 per cent, or, more graphically, an extra goal for every match played.

But while the immediate result was to move the advantage from defence to attack, the long term effect was probably negative, for the tactical result was, at its simplest, that one attacker became a defender.

Credit for devising the 'third-back game', as it became known, has never been adequately apportioned. Bob Gillespie of Queen's Park quickly made it his job to blot out the opposing centre-forward but folk-lore has it—with some concrete support—that the man behind the innovation was Herbert Chapman.

Chapman's first action on joining Arsenal had been to acquire a scheming inside-forward. His choice was Charlie Buchan from Sunderland, the man selectors said was 'too clever to play for England'. The fee was an imaginative £2,000 down and £100 for every goal he scored in the subsequent season. Buchan scored 19. But it was a transfer significant beyond its immediate impact and strange terms.

In 1929 Henry Norris, Arsenal's chairman, sued the FA for libel after he had been suspended for making illegal payments. The Buchan case was particularly mentioned and it was shown that Buchan had been offered other inducements to join the club. Norris lost his case and far more for, when he died in 1934, he was an exile from football and the club that he had dragged from obscurity.

Charlie Buchan's return to Arsenal, the club he had actually walked out on before the War over eleven shillings expenses, was not a very happy one. One of his, and Chapman's, earliest matches for the club was a humiliating 7-0 defeat at Newcastle on 6 October 1925. Buchan was so upset at such a return to his old home that he and Chapman organized an immediate tactical discussion. One or the other (accounts vary as to who it was) proposed that Arsenal's centre-half, Jack Butler, should adopt a purely defensive role and that one of the inside-forwards should drop back to supply the creative link between defence and attack that the centre-half could no longer provide.

Oddly enough Newcastle's centre-half, Charlie Spencer, claimed he had played just such a defensive role in that vital match, and the Arsenal plan may have come from observing Newcastle's success. Before 1925 the centre-half performed exactly the functions his title implied—he had played in the middle of the field helping in defence and instigating attacks.

Buchan expected to be given the creative inside-forward's job himself, but Chapman valued his goalscoring abilities too highly and detailed a reserve inside-forward, Andy Neil, to perform the midfield role at Upton Park the following week on Monday 8 October 1925. Arsenal won 4-0, with Buchan scoring twice.

Chapman gradually revised his team by pushing the full-backs out to mark the wingers, and using both his wing-halves (now free of their close-marking duties) to perform the midfield duties along with the withdrawn inside-forward. The scheme worked well enough, but was not perfected until Chapman purchased the vital creative link, Alex James, from Preston in 1929. Thus the team played in a formation which could loosely be described as 3-4-3 or 3-3-4, rather than the 2-3-5 of the pre-First World War era. Though most teams quickly copied Chapman's system, club programmes 45 years later were still putting down teams in the outdated 2-3-5 pattern.

One of the secrets of good management is, of course, fitting systems of play to the men available. Some successful managers, like Stan Cullis at Wolves, manage to find just the players to operate a stereotyped formation. Some, like Ramsey at Ipswich, devise a system which suits the limited skills of the players available. Chapman's way was a combination of both, and his spectacular dips into the transfer market were basically a means of filling very specific gaps in both team and system.

For over a decade Arsenal somehow <u>were</u> football

Between 1925 and 1930 Chapman's team and tactics developed in step. Butler's successor as the 'policeman' centre-half was Herbie Roberts, acquired from Oswestry in 1926. His two full-backs were George Male and Eddie Hapgood, often partners for England. David Jack came from Bolton to replace Buchan for the first ever five figure fee (£10,370) in 1928 and, a year later, the key to the whole side arrived from Preston. Alex James was finally persuaded to adopt the midfield general role—spraying out long passes to the flying wingers Hulme and Bastin and to the unrefined but effective Jack Lambert at centre-forward.

That was essentially Chapman's great side of the early 1930s. Having lost the Cup Final of 1927, when Dan Lewis let the ball slide underneath his shiny new jumper and allowed Cardiff to take the Cup out of England for the first time, Arsenal returned to defeat Huddersfield 2-0 three years later.

The League was won for the first time in 1931 with 66 points (which remained a record until Leeds bettered it by one in 1969) and the following year Arsenal were at

Above Fanatical and colourful support in football is nothing new. West Ham followers are optimistic on their way to the 1923 Cup Final.
Right They would have been lucky to find a space. Some estimates say that 200,000 people got into Wembley for the first Final there.
Top right Germany's Graf Zeppelin has a view of Wembley and the 1930 Cup Final. It was the game of the inter-War period, between the only two clubs ever to win a hat-trick of Championships. Arsenal finally beat Huddersfield 2-0.
Far right Chapman's new approach to the whole field of club football prompted Daily Mail cartoonist Tom Webster to produce this strip in 1930.

Wembley to lose by the famous 'over the line' goal to Newcastle: Allen's equalizing goal came from a cross which seemed well over the goal-line when Richardson made it. Between 1933 and 1935 Arsenal completed a hat-trick of League Championships, then beat Sheffield United in the Cup Final of 1936 and were champions again in 1938.

As Chapman died in 1934 he was neither with Huddersfield nor Arsenal when they completed their hat-tricks of Championships. He was succeeded at Highbury by George Allison, a radio commentator.

A simple recitation of Arsenal's successes in the 1930s, impressive though it is, tells only a part of the story. In a way that no other team, before or since, has ever approached, Arsenal somehow *were* football for a decade. In almost every way the Gunners' influence on the game was all-pervasive and Chapman's remarkable success on the field should

never be allowed to conceal some remarkable achievements off it.

His skill as a public relations officer was certainly equal to his skill as a tactician. He claimed that as much energy had been expended getting the name of Gillespie Road tube station changed to Arsenal as had been exerted winning the Cup in 1930. He changed the name of the club from 'The Arsenal' to plain 'Arsenal' because, he explained, 'it will always be first in a list of clubs as well as on the field.' Appreciating the publicity value of the titled, he persuaded the board to accept Lord Lonsdale as one of their number and persuaded the Prince of Wales to open a new stand in 1932. He changed from the original Nottingham Forest colours to a red shirt with white sleeves because it was more distinctive, and later the red socks became blue and white hooped. This was so that the players could recognize each other without looking

up in a melee and not, as Chapman had kidded, because 'red runs in the wash.'

Arsenal: envied, disliked and misunderstood

Chapman was one of the first to experiment with numbering players —the FA finally accepted the idea for the 1933 Cup Final, five years after Chapman—and was in the forefront of schoolboy and youth training schemes.

In his trainer, Tom Whittaker, he appointed the first of the modern day physiotherapist coaches. Modern medical equipment, training routines and individual treatment all arrived at Highbury long before they had been considered anywhere else.

All in all, Arsenal were the very first of the wholly professional football clubs in the British Isles.

CENTRAL PRESS

mitment—one way or the other. Walsall's defeat of Arsenal in the third round of the Cup in 1933 was a cause of widespread celebration all over the country, and the economic conditions of the times go no small way to explaining the peculiar position that one match still holds in the game's folk-lore—it was the perfect example of the poor, underfed weakling rising to humiliate a Goliath which had all the advantages.

On reflection Arsenal gained their reputation not by winning everything going—though they won a lot —but by always being the team to beat. They were really the first professionals to invade a world of semi-amateurs. They disturbed the cosy unthinking mood of the time where even the leading clubs were happy to meander along, appointing an old player as manager, reaching the odd semi-final here, the top five of the League there. This was success, this was football. Arsenal were simply of another generation. Instead of putting down men in chess-board formation—centre forwards with iron foreheads and no feet, wingers on the touchline where they belonged —Arsenal experimented.

But Chapman's two great teams— Huddersfield and Arsenal—should not be allowed to disguise the fact that there were other sides of note in the inter-War period. Bolton, for instance, won the Cup in 1923, 1926 and again in 1929, the first being the occasion of the inaugural Wembley Final and the highest attendance ever at a British football match. West Bromwich won promotion from the Second Division and the FA Cup in 1931—a unique double—and the next year their promotion partners, Everton, went on to become only the second club to win the Second and First Division in consecutive seasons. With a Cup win in 1933, Everton were probably the closest rivals to Arsenal in the period. Dixie Dean had completed his remarkable 60-goal feat with a hat-trick in the last game of the 1927-28 season— against Arsenal—and went on to become a major attraction of the following decade.

The land that gave football to the world stood aloof

On a wider front Britain was barely aware. While Cuba and the Dutch East Indies battled for the World Cup the Home Countries stood aloof from FIFA. England did not enter until 1950, when a traumatic game against the United States showed how 20 years of isolation could take their toll. Chapman may have built the strongest club side in the world, but that was far removed from the true international success that was so long coming.

For the English, then, the era meant Arsenal and in the end that must be Chapman's epitaph. Mention the club in any soccer conscious country in the world and it will produce instant recognition. The word no longer means a place where arms are kept, but rather the club that Herbert Chapman built. The name is a permanent memorial to the achievements of one man—and the club that had the good sense to appoint him.

DAILY MAIL

Herein, perhaps, lies the key to the antipathy that followed, and still follows, the Gunners around the country. No story of the 1930s can be complete without considering this remarkable antagonism.

'Lucky Arsenal' was the cry that flitted across a decade. Time after time, Arsenal seemed happy to absorb the pressure of less talented attacks and win games by the simple expedient of the breakaway goal. It was difficult to convince the unsophisticated terraces or the ageing boardrooms of the 1930s that 80 minutes of unrewarded pressure was less valuable than one goal from a few sudden breaks by Hulme and Bastin. Indeed, it was to be another 30 years before British fans fully appreciated that the best of two teams is, by definition, the one that scores more goals.

It is, of course, impossible to view Arsenal out of historical perspective. The thirties were, for most of provincial Britain, arguably the worst decade for almost a century. In many of the textile towns unemployment reached a third of the workforce; in some places, like Jarrow, literally the whole town was on the dole for years on end. To these towns Arsenal came to represent the wealth, the affluence, and the unfair advantage that London seemed to have stolen from the rest of the country. It was not too unrealistic to see Arsenal as a symbol of the wealth earned in the north but spent and enjoyed in the south.

With the football ground being almost the only entertainment outlet available to the working-classes, it is not surprising that Arsenal became a subject of fierce emotional com-

31

Above The first day of League football for seven long years; spectators cheerfully queue in the rain outside Stamford Bridge on 31 August 1946.
Below But enthusiasm for the game in the late 1940s was not all for the good. A sixth round FA Cup tie at Burnden Park between Bolton and Stoke on 9 March 1946 attracted so many fans that closing the gates had no effect at all. They were broken down by the thousands outside with the result that 33 people were killed and hundreds injured when a wall collapsed.

The golden years

THE STORY OF FOOTBALL

It was an air of tremendous excitement which greeted the men who took the field for the first round of the FA Cup in 1945. It had been six long years since first-class football had been played in the British Isles, and many of the teams that appeared bore little resemblence to those that had played out the first three games of the 1939-40 season, a quickly aborted affair indeed.

Many great players would appear no more, overtaken by age and tiring muscles. Others had been killed during the war, men like Tommy Cooper the great Liverpool full-back who met his end as a despatch rider, Albert Clarke, Blackburn Rovers' gifted inside-forward killed in Normandy on D-Day, Harry Goslin, pre-War captain of Bolton Wanderers, killed in action in Italy, Coen, that fine Luton goalkeeper shot down in a raid over the Ruhr Valley on a RAF bombing raid, or youngsters just making their way in the game in 1939 like Reynolds, transferred from

Charlton to Torquay United a few days before war began, called up and killed in action before he had ever kicked a ball for his new club.

Others again were scattered all over the country, indeed all over the world, retained in the Forces and in essential industries. Consequently clubs gave League chances to men who before the war and again to-day would not have been allowed to lace a boot in a League dressing room.

In 1946-47 in the frantic bid to find and mould a decent combination clubs called on more men than ever before or since. Arsenal had 31 men on first team duty during the season, Huddersfield Town 32. In the Second Division Newport County's League roll call reached the astonishing figure of 41 and Bury, Leicester City, Manchester City, Millwall, Nottingham Forest and Sheffield Wednesday, all topped the 30 mark. Beating them all were Hull City, in the Third North. They fielded 42 men.

Right Bert Turner (third from left) deflects Dally Duncan's shot into his own net to give Derby the lead in the 1946 Cup Final. Less than a minute later Turner made amends by scoring at the other end for Charlton. The game had another memorable incident. In a radio interview before the match a prominent referee had been asked 'What are the chances of the ball bursting?' He gave the odds as a million to one. Strangely enough the ball burst early on and the same thing happened in the 1947 Final. Inferior wartime materials were blamed.

Yet Saturday 31 August 1946 was a symbol to the British people that life was nearly back to normal. On that day a full programme of first class League fixtures was played in the British Isles for the first time since 2 September 1939. In fact the 1945-46 FA Cup competition had been completed under unique rules which required the games to be contested on a home-and-away basis. One resulting oddity was that Charlton became only the second side to reach the Final after undisputably *losing* an earlier game. Fulham beat them 2-1 in one of the Third Round matches but Charlton won on aggregate by taking the other match 3-1.

At the time hundreds of thousands of men were already demobbed with their gratuities burning a hole in their pockets and five or six years of their young lives to make up. Millions in factories and industry had been earning more money than ever before but as the war dragged on found less and less to spend it on. Now, with football back, there would be something exciting to help use up some of that cash, trips to be made by train and coach with meals to buy in towns not visited for many years, and wayside inns to dally at.

Years of austerity turn football into a rare luxury

Rationing still blanketed all the civilizing amenities of life, cars and television sets for all were still a dream, you could not have a house built because of a word called licence. Another period as long as the war they had come through lay ahead before austerity began to fade from people's lives. But in the meantime, there was sport. The fact that once the light evenings had gone the government banned midweek matches in the drive to put the national economy back into a peace time footing made the Saturday afternoon date all the more desirable.

Small wonder then that on 31 August 1946, when clubs opened their grounds to the public shortly after noon, there were long queues outside practically all of them. Small gates were the exceptions, not the rule. In the Third Division South, for example, only two clubs reported attendances of under 10,000. Crowds of 20,000 and 25,000 at this level were commonplace.

This was to be a unique season in many ways. The fixtures were a complete replica of those which had been made for the 1939-40 campaign—a season which died after just seven days. This heightened the illusion that life had been taken up where it had left off. Ahead lay the terrible winter of 1947, by far the worst of the century and at a time when food and fuel were still heavily restricted. The winter struck late, and with floodlighting still another future dream clubs could not get the alarming backlog of fixtures cleared. The season became the longest in history, lasting from 31 August to the following 14 June. The 1947-48 season began only 70 days later.

Both sides of the freeze-up, however, the crowds poured in. This was the time when a Jimmy Hill should have risen and forced through the no-maximum wage for footballers still 15 years or more in the future. Instead, after arbitration, the wage for the best First Division players was increased for the 1947-48 season to £12 a week maximum and £10 a week during the close season.

When the balance sheets for 1946-47 were presented all but half a dozen clubs reported profits, many of them substantial. Stoke City led the way with £32,207, Burnley made £18,000, Liverpool over £17,000, Middlesbrough £15,000 and Wolves nearly £11,000. In Scotland, Rangers made £12,500; Queen of the South, whose home town Dumfries has a population of only 26,000, topped £11,000.

But it was not these figures which created a sensation in the soccer world, rather the £15,000 paid by Derby County to Morton, the Scottish club, for inside forward Billy Steel to succeed Peter Doherty.

On the field the defensive techniques of future years had not even begun to put in an appearance. Clarrie Jordan scored 41 goals for Doncaster Rovers, Wally Ardron of Rotherham United 38; Don Clark (Bristol City) and Dick Yates (Chester) 36 each; four of the Wolves' forwards reached double figures—Dennis Westcott 37, Jesse Pye 20, Jimmy Mullen 12 and Johnny Hancocks 10. Charlie Wayman netted 30 times for Newcastle United. Freddie Steele got 29 for Stoke City, Stan Mortensen 28 for Blackpool with Reg Lewis and Ronnie Rooke getting 49 between them for Arsenal. Jack 'Gunner' Rowley thumped 26 for Manchester United.

There were great names abroad in the land but at the end of an historic and colourful first post-War season such an authority as the late Ivan Sharpe was moved to write: 'More and more players—that's the need to-day.'

The 1946-47 season attracted some 35,000,000 spectators but this record was left far behind in the second post-War campaign. When all the figures were in, the attendance total in first-class football alone topped 40,000,000. This was five million more than ever before and it represented the taking of £4,000,000 at the turnstiles. England won the Home International Championship and against foreign opposition were invincible. This made it possible for Lord Athlone, President of the Football Association to deliver a speech at the annual meeting which smacked faintly of 'showing the flag'.

'At a time when exports are of paramount importance', he said, 'football is far from being insignificant. A successful English referee in the Argentine or our international team in Italy is a way of speaking to other nations in a language ordinary people can understand.' For the first time the magic word 'television' came upon the scene. The FA was all for it, the Football League dead against it.

Two clubs dominated the English scene—Arsenal and Manchester United. United, for the first occasion in modern times, rose to a national eminence which has surrounded Old Trafford ever since. Colchester United, then members of the Southern League, had their first glorious hour when they knocked First Division Huddersfield Town out of the FA Cup. In Scotland Hibernian took the Championship to Edinburgh for the first time since 1903. The team included Gordon Smith, Alec Linwood, Willie Ormond, Eddie Turnbull and an Englishman, Bobby Combe. The most sensational transfer of the season came when Tommy Lawton, England's centre-forward, moved down to the Third Division, joining Notts County for a record £20,000 fee.

Surely 1948-49 could not see a new attendance record? In the event it did—easily. Leaving aside FA Cup games, internationals and the 30 major professional and amateur competitions outside the first class aegis the number of people who attended League matches reached the never surpassed total of 41,271,424.

At the end of it a move was made on the proposal of Plymouth Argyle to increase the minimum admission charge from 1/3d to 1/6d (6p to 7½p). It failed by two votes to go through. The League had just launched its new provident fund for players, railway fares were already 55 per cent up on the 1939 levels and hotel bills had increased by 75 per cent, but this was not passed on to the pub-

Left Tommy Lawton breaks away from Millwall's McMillen during a 1948 Third Division South match. Lawton, then still England's centre-forward, had caused a sensation by moving to Third Division Notts County for the first £20,000 fee a year before. Inspired by his leadership, County were the only club to score more than 100 League goals in 1948-49.

Left below The rise and fall of attendances in the 25 years after the Second World War. British football has never seen a period to compare with the immediate post-War seasons.

and drabness was disappearing. People could now think in terms of cars, clothes, furniture, new fabrics, new colours, television sets, holidays abroad. No longer did sport, and soccer in particular, represent one of the few worthwhile things on which to spend spare money and time. Perhaps some anglicized form of Dolce Vita was in the air.

The season's return for Football League attendances was still extremely good, topping 39,500,000 and it meant that in five campaigns the first class game in England and Wales alone had attracted some 197,000,000. But impressive as the figures for 1950-51 were they represented the first small hole in the dyke. Not only were they one million down on the previous season and nearly two million down on 1948-49, but the League was now bigger by four clubs.

Jackie Sewell— literally worth his weight in gold

In other respects the sky was still the limit. A few days before the transfer deadline in March 1951, Sheffield Wednesday persuaded Notts County to accept £34,000 for Jackie Sewell which made the player the first worth his weight in gold— literally. It caused a furore at the time yet exactly 19 years to the day Martin Peters moved across London from West Ham to Spurs for £200,000.

Talking of Tottenham, they were perhaps the first club to perceive the need to meet the new challenge from outside Britain which was about to engulf the national elevens of the four home countries. Arthur Rowe, Spurs manager, a silver haired Cockney had instituted a style called 'push and run'. Briefly it meant doing the simple things quickly and accurately and it showed the benefits of a higher work rate than previously thought necessary from all eleven members of a side. Newly promoted from Division Two they cast a shadow of the world wide greatness they were to earn a decade later by storming straight on to take the First Division title.

From that season the honeymoon between football and the fans was over. The game is still a crowd puller without parallel in any other form of activity known to twentieth-century man but it is unlikely ever to know again such a golden age at the turn-stiles when in six years it was patronised by 236 million fans, a figure equivalent to the entire population of the United States or Russia. They were, indeed, the Golden Years.

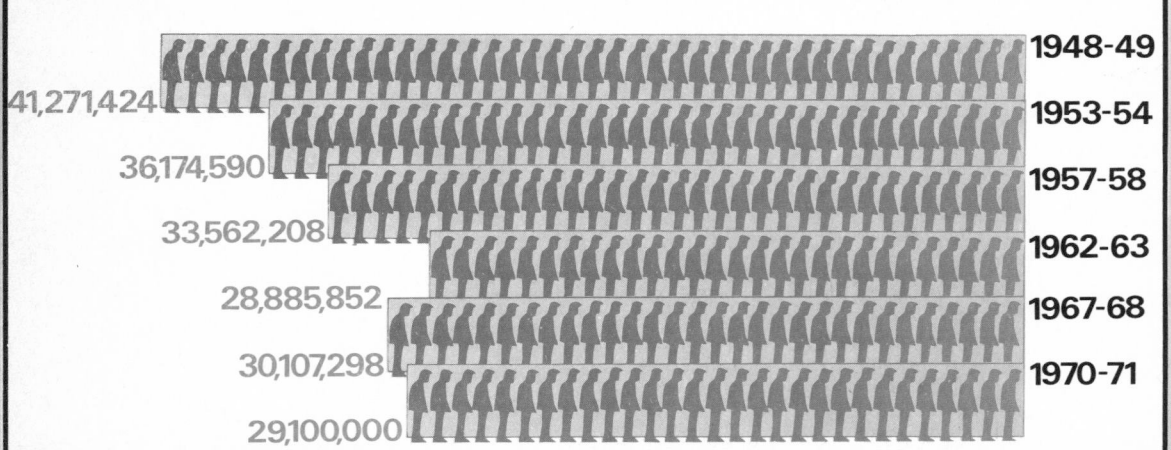

41,271,424	1948-49
36,174,590	1953-54
33,562,208	1957-58
28,885,852	1962-63
30,107,298	1967-68
29,100,000	1970-71

lic. In what was the diamond jubilee season of the League the Victorian illusion of endless security and stability died hard. Goal scoring took a sharp downward trend, the figures dropping to 2.84 goals per match, almost as low as in the 1920s under the old offside law.

The defeat in the Cup of then mighty Sunderland by Yeovil Town of the Southern League on a sloping pitch down in Somerset was the most talked of event in the season. For the first time the Amateur Cup Final was staged at Wembley and a crowd of 95,000 payed over £20,000 to see Bromley beat Romford 1-0. Transfer fees continued to spiral upwards, Derby County paying Manchester United £25,000 for inside-forward Johnny Morris in March 1949.

As the twentieth century came up to its half way mark football reached a watershed. The boom was a long

way from over but 1949-50 was to be the last season in which total League attendances for a season topped 40,000,000. This, too, was the last season of the League in the form of 88 clubs equally divided into four sections, for at the annual meeting four new clubs—Colchester United, Gillingham, Scunthorpe and Lindsey United and Shrewsbury Town—were admitted, two each to both sections of Division Three. The election of Scunthorpe to the Northern group was one of the strangest quirks of post-War football. On the first ballot Shrewsbury were elected easily but Workington and Wigan Athletic tied for second place. Rather than just a straightforward vote between the two tied clubs, the League took it into its head to organize another open ballot—the result being that Scunthorpe defeated both of their seemingly stronger opponents. Workington replaced

New Brighton the following year but, twenty years later, Wigan were still trying to gain entry to the League.

Before this happened there was another very fine act to come. Portsmouth, who the season before had won the First Division Championship for the first time (conveniently in their jubilee year), successfully defended their title, but Wolves gave them a terrific fight which lasted until the final afternoon of the season, 6 May. Rangers were back in the box seat in Scotland taking both League and Cup. Arsenal won the FA Cup—without ever having to leave London! The cry 'Lucky Arsenal' was heard again in the land and perhaps not without justification.

The fifth post-War season, although it was not realised at the time, marked the real beginning in a change in public tastes and habits. At long last the all round austerity

DAILY EXPRESS

No. 17,949   FRIDAY FEBRUARY 7 1958   3 a.m. forecast: Cold; snow or sleet likely   Price 2½

ALIVE   Blanchflower, Edwards, Berry, Scanlon, Morgans, Gregg, Wood, Charlton, Viollet, Foulkes; Busby

DEAD   Byrne, Bent, Jones, Whelan, Colman, Pegg, and Tommy Taylor

SURVIVORS SPEAK

THREE TAKE-OFF ATTEMPTS—AND THEN DISASTER

Matt Busby called out: It's my legs, my legs...

Express Staff Reporters

MANCHESTER United footballers told last night the stark, dramatic story of how the airliner bringing them home from Yugoslavia had .... Munich.

EXPRESS Photo News

SEE PAGES 2, 5, 6, 7 AND 16

LONDON EXPRESS NEWS AND FEATURE SERVICES

THE STORY OF FOOTBALL

1966 and all that

February 1958; the story that stunned a soccer generation. Though the Daily Express *correctly reports Duncan Edwards as being alive he was to die a few days later.*

An Englishman looking at football since the Second World War will inevitably focus on one of two moments in time. One is the evening of 6 February 1958 when the plane carrying Manchester United, undisputably Britain's best club side, crashed on take-off from Munich airport. The other comes eight years later, the afternoon of 30 July 1966, when the country that gave the world the game finally took its place as more than an also-ran. After two decades of international mediocrity, a reputation had been re-established.

The World Cup win came at the midpoint of a decade which saw a complete change in the British game. The vital point was the abolition of the maximum wage in 1961. George Eastham had brought the whole question of players' conditions and contracts into the open and into the courts when Newcastle refused to give him a transfer. Victory for Eastham meant that men who had been restricted to a niggardly maximum wage of £20 a week could command three or four times that amount. Within a year Johnny Haynes, then captain of England, had become the first home footballer earning £100 a week.

It was perhaps unfortunate that this players' revolution should have occurred just as two other forces were changing the fabric of the game, a little more slowly to be sure, but just as vitally. One was the growth of private transport and an effective road system, allowing anyone within forty miles of Manchester, say, to regard United as their local club.

The other factor was the introduction of regular televised games. This affected the game more subtly than the administrators had originally feared. Rather than simply staying at home to watch Spurs rather than going out to see Brentford—a matter of laziness—the really vital change was one of attitude. For spectators were persuaded that the football they wanted to see was that played by the major clubs and, in many cases, that alone.

Television has hardly affected the leading dozen or so clubs at all; it has provided problems for many of the other 80. Youngsters reared on television have begun to think of Bobby Moore or George Best as the archetypal footballer—not the stunning exception. The local Third Division team—though they may be only 400 yards away—have become as remote from their conception of 'today's' football as Alex James or Dixie Dean.

And so the eventual effect of all these changes was to strengthen those already strong and to weaken those already weak. Great old clubs like Bolton and Blackburn found that their reputations meant nothing beside the pull of George Best at Old Trafford; and it is at that vast stadium that we find the greatest of all the great post-War clubs.

In 1971 Manchester United took a quite unprecedented step by making several of their League matches all-ticket. That was the result of 25 consecutive years as the greatest draw in Britain. Three times Sir Matt Busby built great sides—the 1948 combination that won the Cup, the 1958 'Babes' who died at Munich and the 1968 European Cup winning side. But it was not so much the success and hours of incomparable entertainment that has tied United to the hearts of the British people, rather it was a single incident at a German airfield when the team that has been called the greatest English club side ever was destroyed.

Over a decade later people who do not see a football match from one year to the next, religiously go along to their local ground when United play—simply because of the legend of Munich. It made United more than a football team—it made them an article of football faith.

There have been other good club sides—the orthodox fast-running Wolves of the 1950s who first introduced the British to European competition; the two North London 'double' sides of 1961 and 1971, so close geographically yet so far apart in style; Ipswich Town, the most unexpected winners in the history of the League and perfect proof that the age of method had arrived; Leeds United, 'the professionals', never giving anything away, never letting opponents relax, the worshippers of workrate yet destined to become seemingly eternal runners-up; Celtic, so utterly dominant under Stein's command in the 1960s that Scottish football became as predictable as the rising of the sun. And yet, for all this talent, British teams never made the impact they might have done in Europe.

In the first 18 years of the European Cup competition the trophy came to Britain only twice—with Celtic in 1967 and Manchester United in 1968. There was a little more success in the other competitions. Spurs won the Cup Winners Cup in 1963, West Ham in 1965, Manchester City in 1970 and Chelsea in 1971. Leeds won the Fairs Cup in 1968 and 1971, Newcastle United in 1969 and Arsenal in 1970. But all that cannot conceal that Britain could find no competitor for Real Madrid in the late 1950s, nor for Barcelona, Benfica and the two Milan clubs before 1965.

The first steps into Europe had been as painful as the Common Market negotiations. Though Hibernian entered the European Cup in its inaugural season (1955-56), reached the semi-finals and made £25,000 from the venture (a large sum for a Scottish club at the time), the Football League, in traditionally shortsighted fashion, had 'advised' Chelsea not to enter. It is worth remembering that the League had only just begun to allow floodlit fixtures at this time, and they 'advised' Manchester United the same way the following year. But Matt Busby was more farsighted than his superiors and took no notice.

Shortsighted and shabby—the FA's treatment of United

Revenge was swift. After the Munich crash in 1958 the organizing committee invited United to enter the European Cup the following year along with the League Champions, Wolves. A joint committee of the League and FA finally refused permission on the grounds that it was against the competition's rules (rules already waived by the organizers). It was the shabbiest paragraph in a truly parochial chapter.

Europe was a tremendous catalyst for the British. Not only did Football and Scottish League clubs come to adopt entry into European competition as a major goal, but it changed the face of the game in these somewhat isolated Isles. It was not long before club sides realized that the good old-fashioned tackle from behind and charge on the goalkeeper were not going to be tolerated by crowds, opponents or referees in European matches. The less physical game gradually crossed the Channel and its advantages led to a growing rejection of the intimidating behaviour so characteristic of the 1950s. By 1971 the charge on the goalkeeper was no more than a memory and the Football Association felt strongly enough to try and cut out the equally contentious tackle from behind.

So Britain finally came to accept the discipline of Europe, just as she came to accept a new concept in tactics and coaching and the widespread influx of supposedly 'continental' systems. The combination of an emphasis on sheer physical fitness, leading to the 'perpetual motion' players of whom Alan Ball was probably the best example, and the rejec-

Top Part of the West Ham soccer school that was so prominent in the game at the beginning of 1972: From left to right: Jimmy Andrews (coach at Luton), Dave Sexton (Chelsea manager), Noel Cantwell (Coventry manager), Malcolm Allison (team manager at Manchester City), John Bond (Bournemouth manager) and Frank O'Farrell and Malcolm Musgrove (manager and coach at Manchester United) in an East End cafe.
Centre Geoff Hurst scores England's fourth goal in the 1966 World Cup final and the bench leaps up. The man still seated? Alf Ramsey.
Bottom An England squad train at Lilleshall under the eye of Harold Shepherdson.

tion of the more strictly positional 'stopper' or '3-2-5' formation, with its familiar full-backs, inside-forwards and wingers, led to considerable confusion on the terraces in the 1960s.

That a man could wear a number 7 shirt and *not* patrol the right touchline seemed quite revolutionary to many used to watching Matthews and Finney. Dick Graham achieved some early success with an all-purpose Crystal Palace side—once threatening to number his players in alphabetical order as he claimed numbers did not count any more (which assumes that they once did of course)—and Matt Gillies and Bert Johnson took Leicester to the Cup Finals of 1961 and 1963 with similarly revolutionary concepts on how the game should be played.

But while Alf Ramsey achieved the most obvious success with methodical rather than inspired football—neither his Ipswich side of 1962 nor the England of 1966 will ever be categorized among the world's great entertainers—a more appealingly influential figure in the English game of the period was Ron Greenwood, manager of West Ham from 1961. This, in part, was a result of his willingness to allow journalists a view of the inner workings of the football world and his propensity to sit and discuss the game for hours with those who could take his views outside the dressing-room.

But more concrete evidence comes from a look at some of the 'graduates' from his Upton Park college. In 1971 Frank O'Farrell and Malcolm Musgrove, manager and coach at Manchester United, Malcolm Allison, team manager of Manchester City, Noel Cantwell of Coventry, Dave Sexton of Chelsea, Jimmy Bloomfield of Leicester and John Bond, young and startlingly successful manager of Bournemouth, all came into this 'graduate' category and there were several others. Greenwood's West Ham of the mid-sixties are still regarded in some quarters as the most entertaining team of the decade and it was that side that provided Alf Ramsey with the core of his World Cup winning team in Peters, Moore and Hurst.

Greenwood himself has often suggested that the real credit for the new ideas that gained so much currency in the 1960s should go to Walter Winterbottom. The Football Association's Chief Coach from 1946 to 1963, Winterbottom spent most of that period doubling-up as manager of England's various teams, roles whose compatability was not always obvious. While he is widely remembered for a relatively unspectacular spell as team manager, his work on the coaching side at Lilleshall is known only to those inside the game. His tactical appreciation, his encouragement of personal skills and his insistence on a team's corporate knowledge of its objectives are factors that no one who has taken an FA course could ignore. It was at Lilleshall, not Wembley, that the foundations of the 1966 World Cup win and the prospects for home football in the 1970s were laid.

For British football the two decades after 1950 were rather like a child's first few days at school. Suddenly it dawns that there is a lot

more to life than his immediate family group, that there are other children from other families who are not only his equal but sometimes his superior.

So it was with football. It was not that whether Wolves or Manchester United won the League became less significant, more that the most important consequence was that success gained entrance to the European Cup. Whereas a climax used to occur every season—around the time of the Cup Final—it now seemed to occur only once every four years, at the time of the World Cup.

Before 1950 the British regarded the World Cup as an event competed for by foreigners. But the dispute with FIFA having been healed, the four home countries finally agreed to enter and FIFA accepted the Home International Championship as a qualifying competition. The first and second countries were to go through to the final rounds—virtually carte blanche for England and Scotland.

England 0 USA 1 The greatest shock of all time?

In the event, it provided the Scots with a fine opportunity to display that shortsighted foolishness which has often made the English FA appear prophetic visionaries by comparison. England beat Scotland 1-0 at Hampden in the deciding match and the losers, coming only second in the Championship, refused to go to Brazil for the World Cup.

So England went alone and came back even lonelier. At Belo Horizonte they suffered a footballing humiliation not surpassed before or since. The game against the USA was expected to be a canter. That vast country had never adopted the world's most popular version of football, preferring instead its own brutal perversion. The American coach—irony of ironies—was a Scotsman, Bill Jeffrey, and the night before the game his team were up until the early hours at a party; the only unanswered question was the size of the defeat.

Instead they won 1-0; one British press agency assumed the score was a mistake and printed the result as 10-1. To be fair to England, it was one of those days that every team sometimes has—nothing would go right. Looking back, paradoxically, the outcome was more of a disappointment to the Americans than the English. The latter lost 1-0 to Spain in the next game and went home having not even reached the quarter-finals. But the Americans sincerely believed that their victory was going to be the spark that ignited the game across the Atlantic. They could not have been more wrong.

In England the result was not treated seriously—in fact it was dismissed as the fluke it undoubtedly was and the tower of English self-confidence survived, if only for another three years. The main reason for that pride was 80 years of internationals in which England had never lost at home to foreign opposition.

True, Eire had won a poor game 2-0 at Everton in 1949, but as nine

of their side were regular Football League players they can hardly be regarded as aliens. That record was threatened in November 1951 when England drew 2-2 with Austria thanks to an Alf Ramsey penalty. In October 1953 they were 4-3 down to a FIFA side in a full international with only one minute left. Mortensen collided with an opponent and England were awarded a penalty ('although it was still two months to Christmas' as a reporter put it). Ramsey scored again and England's record was safe—but for just four weeks.

The moment of truth arrived on the afternoon of 25 November 1953. Ramsey later said that the game against Hungary had a profound effect on him; it could hardly have had any other. While the game against the USA could be dismissed as a freak the defeat by Hungary was without excuse. A far better team had shown England that reputation was no longer enough.

Eighteen years later that same England side were gathered at a function also attended by Ferenc Puskas. Ramsey greeted his full-back partner that day, Bill Eckersley, rather quizically; 'Hello, it is Bill isn't it?' and Puskas was heard to remark: 'It was like that when they played us—the team hardly seemed to know each other's names.'

England lost 6-3. Far worse, they had made no plans when, six months later, they played a return in Budapest. That one was lost 7-1. England were totally exposed by a side that shamed them in ability, fitness and, above all, in tactical awareness.

English football had entered a period in the doldrums from which it was not to emerge for a dozen years. In the 1954 World Cup the Uruguayan side that had defeated Scotland 7-0 also put out England 4-2. In 1958 England failed even to reach the quarter-finals, losing to the USSR in a group play-off. England's style was summed up by Vittorio Pozzo when he described a goal by Kevan as being scored with the 'outside of his head', implying that England were still not one of the world's more thoughtful soccer nations. That year, at least, Northern Ireland and Wales reached the quarter-finals.

In 1962 England went out 3-1 to Brazil, again in the quarter-finals; Scotland, Wales and Ireland failed to qualify. That was the end of Walter Winterbottom's reign as team manager. Alf Ramsey took over what ought to have been one of the best teams in the world. The first game after his appointment was against France, who declined in the 1960s to the Third Division of European football. England lost that game 5-2, Ramsey declared that they would win the World Cup anyway and the rest is history.

The World Cup victory is not to be denigrated—but what really stands out from 1966 is how sceptical about England's abilities (after previous World Cups) supporters had become and how little chance England were given of winning. Look at the facts. England played six games, all of them at Wembley. In nearly 60 years of internationals against foreign opposition, England had lost only four times at home—to

Eire in 1949, to Hungary in 1953, to Sweden in 1959 and to Austria in 1965. Not even Brazil had managed to win at Wembley. Of the 40 full international games England had played against her six opponents, Uruguay, Mexico, France, Argentina, Portugal and West Germany, she had lost only 8. Not a single one of those had been at home and none of those six countries had managed even a draw at Wembley.

In fact the Germans, the other finalists, had never beaten England anywhere, managing just one draw back in Berlin in 1930. Quite simply each of those six matches should have been won and had they been ordinary mid-week 'friendlies' no one would have expected anything but the eventual results. But it is easy to be wise after the event. At the time there was always Brazil, seeking a hat-trick of victories, a rampant Hungarian attack, Eusebio in startling form and the ever-present threat of West Germany, Russia and Italy.

Ramsey's strength was in his free hand. At long last the FA had realized that the system devised by Stanley Rous during the Second World War—whereby he did everything—was the most effective available. Thus, although there was still an international committee technically in existence, Ramsey was the only man who did any selecting. When asked by one of this committee at a cocktail party exactly what its official duties were, Ramsey is reputed to have replied: 'To come to cocktail parties.'

How could England have failed to win the World Cup?

Being a defender himself, it is not surprising that Ramsey, like a successful First World War general, believed that defence was the key to victory. For the 1966 World Cup final England ended up with just two fulltime forwards, Hurst and Hunt, five defenders (Stiles playing an auxiliary defensive role wherever he was needed) and three providers.

The formation was substantially the same for the traumatic game in Leon four years later—except that now both Peters and Ball were required to be preoccupied in midfield—when it was proved beyond dispute that the best laid schemes of mien, mice and Alf Ramsey can be thwarted by individual error.

Peter Bonetti, deputizing in goal for Banks, was adjudged to have been at fault for the first German goal and was possibly not blameless for the other two. It is sad that one display—albeit the most important of his career—will always be remembered before so many excellent ones elsewhere.

The years 1953 and 1966 must be considered the landmarks of the post-War era for English soccer. The former had the effect of an earthquake—it overthrew all the misconceptions English football had about itself, though it took ten years for all the lessons to filter through. The second date was notable for an atmosphere more akin to VE-day. That was not necessarily inappropriate for it was, after all, the day the national game came in from the cold.

The seventies

The first half of the new decade was a depressing time for England and the rest of the home countries, though Scotland were to enjoy a pocket of consolation in qualifying for, and doing themselves some justice at last, in the finals of the 1974 World Cup. For England, however, there was no consolation — failing in the latter stages of the 1970 World Cup, eliminated in the quarter-finals of the 1972 European Championship and failing to qualify for the 1974 World Cup finals — and, on 1 May 1974, Sir Alf Ramsey paid the traditional price for failure when he was sacked by the Football Association.

Joe Mercer became England's caretaker manager through the 1974 home internationals and a summer tour during which England provided opposition for more fortunate nations warming up to contest the 1974 World Cup finals.

The Football Association then announced that Don Revie, fresh from Leeds' magnificent twenty-nine game unbeaten run at the beginning of the 1973-74 season, would be the new England team manager.

Yet Revie was to experience much the same difficulties as his predecessor. England failed to qualify for the quarter-finals of the 1976 European Championship and in the following post mortem there were some familiar points made: the length and toughness of the English season led to injuries and exhausted players, there was too much football, not enough co-operation between the League and the FA, and not enough time for preparation. Yet, with the wisdom of hindsight, Revie's policy also carried one major flaw. He continually altered his line-up and team work suffered badly. The only unchanged side he ever fielded was his last, against Uruguay in Montevideo. In July 1977, shortly after that match, Revie gave an exclusive interview to the *Daily Mail* in which he announced that he had resigned as England's manager. This was the first the FA knew about it. It provided an unsavoury end to his three-year term in succession to Ramsey, and with England on the brink of failing to qualify for the second successive World Cup, he had been less than successful.

Yet, with English football at its lowest ever for years, with Don Revie's resignation and England's sorry goal-scoring attempts against Finland and Luxembourg, there was Liverpool. Marching magnificently through Europe and England, they were to become only the third English team to reach a European Cup final. The most remarkable moment of their run came in the second leg of the quarter-final against St. Etienne. The French Champions, a goal clear from the home leg, made it 1-1 at Anfield. Liverpool needed three to get through as a result. There seemed to be no chance, but they went on to win 3-1, (a victory reminiscent of Manchester United's 3-3 draw in Madrid in their 1968 semi-final). Their opposition in the semis — Zurich — proved little more than a formality for a team still attempting the treble.

So, Liverpool went to Rome to meet Borussia Monchengladbach having won the League Championship again, but having been surprisingly defeated by Manchester United in the FA Cup final five days earlier. It didn't affect them at all. Playing glorious football, McDermott, Tommy Smith and Phil Neal all scored to demolish the Germans 3-1. Keegan's display against the West German captain Berti Vogts was the outstanding feature — though for Keegan it was to be his last game for Liverpool before moving to SV Hamberg.

Four months later, Ron Greenwood, the new England team manager, included seven Liverpool players in the side to play Switzerland — yet England could manage no more than a goalless draw. More significantly his side, still based on Liverpool, failed to reduce the World Cup deficit with a meagre 2-0 victory in Luxembourg. England then had to achieve an expansive win over Italy to qualify, but they could do no more than reverse the Rome scoreline — Scotland were once again to be Britain's only representatives in the World Cup finals.

Liverpool, however, went on to confirm their status as the best side in Europe — retaining their title as European Champions. The highlight was their semi-final defeat of Borussia Monchengladbach, at Anfield, with Ray Kennedy performing quite brilliantly. The final itself was far less memorable — with Bruges playing defensively and Liverpool below their best. One goal from Keegan's replacement, Kenny Dalglish, however, proved enough in the end.

Certainly in the first half of the decade, the minor European trophies

A sign of the times: in 1974 Manchester United had to erect barriers at Old Trafford to keep their notorious fans off the pitch.

became almost resident in the boardrooms of the League clubs. Manchester City brought home the Cup Winners Cup in 1970, handing it over to Chelsea the following year.

From 1970, the EUFA Cup (once the Fairs Cup) was succesively won by Arsenal, Leeds, Spurs, Liverpool, and Spurs again. In 1976, Liverpool repeated their double of 1973, winning both the EUFA Cup and League Championship. Both EUFA finals provided thrilling finishes. In 1973 Liverpool carried a three-goal lead to Germany for the second leg against Monchengladbach. Two superb goals by Jupp Heynckes before half-time seemed to have broken Liverpool's resistance, but no further cracks appeared and amidst electrifying tension they clung on to their aggregate win.

In 1976 two brilliant counter-attacks from Bruges saw Liverpool two goals down at Anfield before a second half flourish produced a three-goal comeback. It seemed hardly enough for the second leg but Liverpool's consistency had produced just the sort of resilience that earned a winning draw in Belgium and a second EUFA trophy.

In domestic football, Arsenal became the fourth side in the history of the game to complete the League and Cup double. Their triumph in 1971 perhaps has more merit than the previous doubles of Preston, Aston Villa and Tottenham Hotspur. Their unceasing hounding of Leeds United in the League race and the character they showed in coming from behind to win the FA Cup in extra time (after even more of a tightrope performance against Stoke in the semi-final) somehow compensated for the steamrollering style which was often more effective than pretty.

Stoke City added a little glitter to the League Cup when they beat Chelsea in the 1972 final. Appropriately enough for a team which has always recognised the value of age and experience, 35-year-old George Eastham shot the winning goal (his first for three years) and another veteran, Gordon Banks, won his first club medal.

But even Stoke's feat was eclipsed fourteen months later by Stokoe's. As Manager of Second Division Sunderland, Bob Stokoe was the key figure in the most dramatic of FA Cup finals. A solidly struck goal by midfield player Ian Porterfield created the biggest upset of the century, by beating Leeds United, the odds-on favourites.

For Leeds, it was another of the bewildering occasions when they failed at the last hurdle. In four FA Cup finals under Don Revie, they had only once won. Five times they had been runners-up in the First Division; winners again only once.

Above Muller beats Bonetti in extra-time of the 1970 World Cup quarter-final between West Germany and England — completing a remarkable come back. Goals by Beckenbauer and Seeler had pegged back the scores by Mullery and Peters. 
Right Although having left Liverpool for Hamburg, Keegan included a clause in his contract which would guarantee his release for international matches.

In many ways Leeds United are the microcosm of the problems of the early seventies. Their gradual evolution into a strong team has been based on physical play with an emphasis on defence. They had been roundly accused of overstepping the mark in terms of what is called professionalism, of setting a bad example from the top. Their disciplinary record was appalling, and at the start of the 1972-73 season their ground was closed because of the behaviour of the crowd.

Yet there was a significant change at the start of the following campaign. The players, under the threat of the FA, behaved; not only did they win but they became a free scoring side. They extended a League record by going through their first 29 League games of the season unbeaten. Then their character was put to a considerable test when they lost four matches in quick succession and a nine-point advantage over Liverpool had been whittled away. Yet, faced by the threat (and their supporters' expectation) of once again coming second, Revie's squad mustered a final effort and deservedly won their second Championship. It was to be the last success of an ageing side which had still to face the mortification of losing the 1975 European Cup final to Bayern Munich after dominating the game's opening half and having a goal disallowed.

While Leeds were rebuilding under Jimmy Armfield in 1976, many of the side must have felt slightly better about their defeat by Sunderland when Second Division Southampton put paid to Manchester United in the 1976 Cup final.

It was United's first season back in the First Division after being relegated in 1974 — ravaged by the retirements and declines of Charlton, Law, Best, Crerand and company. Tommy Docherty fielded a team of talented but very young players who for most of the season had chased the elusive League and Cup double — the League title going to Liverpool.

Queen's Park Rangers and Derby County had also challenged for the 1976 Championship, but Liverpool's swarming, supremely efficient team work proved too much. Their style and success has characterised both the 1960s and 1970s, but Bob Paisley's success in taking them to that record ninth Championship was generally regretted outside Merseyside. The other three contenders — QPR, Manchester United and Derby — had all contributed rather more originality to a season which, at long last, saw a perceptible upswing in interest and spectator appeal.

A quite remarkable cog in the Liverpool machine was Ian Callaghan, winger in the 1965 Cup winning side and the 1966 World Cup finals, whose ageless midfield prompting earned him the Footballer of the Year award for 1974.

Liverpool also lifted the FA Cup that year — a convincing win over a Newcastle United side who mustered little challenge on the day — but they lost their Championship to Leeds and were runners up the following year to Derby.

Above Bettega, with a flying header, scores Italy's winning goal against England in their World Cup qualifying game — although England managed to reverse the Rome score-line in the return at Wembley.
Right The first leg of an unexpected and little-hailed 'double'. Frank McLintock holds Arsenal's Cup in 1971.
Opposite Les Tibbot of Ipswich (1978 FA Cup winners) and Stuart Pearson of Man Utd (1977 FA Cup winners).

County under Brian Clough had discarded the garb of Second Division also-rans for the cloak of League Champions in 1972. But in 1973 it was Clough himself who was discarded after an undignified boardroom feud.

Clough by this time had established a national reputation as a controversially outspoken pundit. When he and Derby County parted company the story led the front pages as well as the back. Derby's players, bemused and hurt by the incident, threatened a strike, which thankfully did not materialise. Dave Mackay, a former player, was brought back from Nottingham Forest in a successful attempt to quell the storm.

Ironically, both Clough and his assistant Peter Taylor were in charge of Nottingham Forest when Mackay himself was dismissed from County eighteen months after his Derby side had achieved a second Championship of the decade. By that time the tide in the East Midlands seemed to be flowing rapidly back to Nottingham and Clough.

Manchester City moved towards the seventies with their 1969 Cup win when Neil Young's shot made Leicester runners-up for the fourth time in 20 years. City subsequently declined, gradually losing first Mercer, then Allison, then Johnny Hart through nervous exhaustion. Before he left in 1972, Allison

made one of the most questionable decisions of the decade buying the enigmatic Rodney Marsh when City seemed to have the Championship tied up. But the side fell apart, Derby crept through to the title, and Allison's reputation was scarred. As Joe Mercer commented: '£200,000 is a lot of money to spend just to lose the Championship'.

Under the brief reign of Ron Saunders, City lost the 1974 League Cup final, but under Tony Book they were successful in the same competition in 1976. Too often their fluid style could only be produced at Maine Road, and it was not until Bill Taylor, Fulham's coach in the 1975 Cup final, joined the staff that application allied to artistry began to produce away results.

North of the border, Celtic reached a second European Cup final in 1970, but contributed to the game's lack of appeal in Scotland by refusing to give up the League Championship. In 1974, they won their record ninth consecutive title — a whole generation of spectators had grown up without realising that Celtic at the top of the League was not an immutable law. More interesting, perhaps, was their series of consecutive defeats in the first four League Cup finals of the decade. In 1975, Rangers finally broke Celtic's hold on the Championship and went on to retain the title in 1976. They won it again in 1978, after Celtic had denied them a hat-trick in 1977.

In both England and Scotland, two of the reasons most often mentioned for the decline in attendances at first class football matches over recent years have been televised games and hooliganism.

Television is both good and bad for the game. As an advertisement for the best (particularly the leading Premier and First Division clubs) it is a most powerful medium. It also brings in millions of pounds in annual fees to the League and FA. But the tele-presenters are so skilled in their art that their edited weekend package can easily pass for the real thing — or, worse, become a more than satisfactory substitute for it. Young fans in particular, weaned on many hours of televised football, can be disappointed by the real thing — no goals every three or four minutes, no commentary and no action replays. Some critics therefore argue that live games, which the television companies would prefer, must be less damaging to weekly attendances than the more subtle dangers of recorded highlights.

In 1976, even mighty Leeds were only covering three-quarters of their £800,000 outgoings from gate receipts. In fact, only a handful of League clubs were actually operating in the black, something which once again reinforced doubts that the accepted League structure could survive — though legislation the following year allowed the use of lucrative lotteries to boost the ailing coffers. A more serious threat to football as a whole, however, came from violence on the terraces and around League grounds. Whilst accepting that a mindless minority were culprits, the spread of hooliganism — given impetus by its coverage in the media — grew in its intensity and regularity. Fences around grounds, strict segregation of fans and the actual banning of visiting supporters from Manchester United and Chelsea (two notable clubs whose reputations had been particularly scarred by the violent conduct of their so-called followers) helped a little to curb the disturbances within the stadia.

Just how much damage hooliganism has done to football is difficult to assess; the true picture may not emerge for some time because it is the new generations of potential spectators who have been discouraged from falling in love with the game by the real danger of standing amidst brawling mobs; not so much the committed fan who has grown up with an increase in violence.

The loan of Birmingham and England forward Trevor Francis to Philadelphia of the North American Soccer League for the summer of 1978 highlighted a more direct threat to the quality of the game. Coinciding with the passing of the retain-and-transfer system (after years of negotiation, the clubs finally forfeited their rights to keep players once the period of an individual contract had elapsed), the lure of Europe and the United States took on an added glow. With the British tax system vastly penalising stars in all areas, who could blame the country's best footballers from following in the steps of businessmen, golfers and pop-stars?

Ten years earlier the NASL had been a rest-home for ageing professionals, a chance for one final pay-day. All that changed when Pele joined New York Cosmos; no longer could players scoff at the standards. Pele became the catalyst who injected the League with excitement as well as credibility; the big-business that was attracted to invest ensured that the North American clubs could and would bid for the likes of Trevor Francis, at the height of their careers, and no longer for those who were fading into oblivion. With a supply of coaches like Gordon Jago, Freddie Goodwin, Eddie McCreadie, and Ken Furphy they were certainly not short of contacts through whom to make the deals.

Clubs like Luton, whose creditors gave them just one month to live in 1975, were more than happy to off-load players to the States for the summer in order to ease inflated wage bills, even though these players would always miss preseason preparation and often the opening League games.

If the NASL continued its boom at the rate it showed in 1977 the possibility of a large defection was very real. The loaners of today could become the borrowers-back of tomorrow.

Domestically clubs responded to all the threats to their survival with a little more enterprise, though Liverpool's Championship season of 1977 brought them only 15 goals from their 21 away games. A record number of sending-offs in the 1977-78 season told rather more about less tolerant refereeing than any sinister cynicism on the field. And in that season one club — or perhaps one man — gave the First Division a tremendous impetus.

By August 1977 Brian Clough had been out of the First Division for nearly three years, (following his sacking by Leeds United after a tempestuous reign of 42 days as their manager). Now his Nottingham Forest side had just sneaked into the third promotion spot of the Second Division, a point ahead of Bolton Wanderers and Blackpool.

Although Clough had been reunited with his assistant Peter Taylor, who had not been at Leeds with him, Forest were generally tipped for a rapid return from whence they came rather than honours. But Forest became a revelation. Clough strengthened the side for the new season by paying £270,000 for goalkeeper Peter Shilton, by bringing his former Derby midfield lynch-pin Archie Gemmill into the camp and by signing centre half Dave Needham from Queen's Park Rangers. All three transfers took place after the opening jousts in the League Cup competition. This cup-tied the new signings, but did not prevent Forest from winning the trophy — beating Liverpool, the European Champions, with a disputed John Robertson penalty after a draw at Wembley in one of the most one-sided games ever seen there.

After each League Cup-tie men like Frank Clark, John O'Hare, Ian Bowyer and 18-year-old Chris Woods, Shilton's stand-in, would lose their places, but the result was a competition to be in the team that made Forest almost invincible in the League.

They won their first ever Championship by seven points from Liverpool. It was only the fifth time in history that a team had won the Championship first time up, and all of the other four — Liverpool, Everton, Tottenham and Ipswich — had done so from the position of Second Division Champions.

Forest's remarkable triumphs were good for the democracy in the game as was Ipswich reaching their first ever FA Cup final; there they beat Arsenal 1-0, a more attractive if less disciplined side than that

which won the double. The League was not over blessed with the creative skills of a Liam Brady, the all-round talents of a David O'Leary or the sheer presence of a Malcolm MacDonald. But where they did exist, the main problems of the future would be how to keep them from joining a gravy train abroad and how to ensure that those who wished to be thrilled by them could watch them in safety.

Above Viv Anderson of Nottingham Forest loses a boot in a race for the ball with Liverpool's Kenny Dalglish. It was the first round of the 1978/79 European Cup – Forest competing as League Champions and Liverpool as European Champions. Forest won the day, so completing a remarkable hat-trick of major victories over Liverpool – having relegated them to runners-up in both the 1978 League Championship and League Cup final.

Third time lucky for Leeds and Norman Hunter (number 6) as Allan Clarke heads home Mick Jones's cross for the only goal of the Centenary Final.

Kinnaird, of the red beard and long white trousers, stood on his head in front of the pavilion. It was appropriate that his should be the final gesture of an age ready to be confined to the history books; he appeared in 9 of the first 12 Finals, five times on the winning side. Only James Forrest of Blackburn Rovers and C H R Wollaston of the Wanderers received so many winner's medals.

The Wanderers played one game —and won the Cup

Kinnaird's winning appearances were with Old Etonians in 1879 and 1882, and Wanderers, in 1873, 1877 and 1878. His first for the Wanderers was the only occasion on which the Final was contested on the challenge basis that was written into both the competition's title and its original rules. The Wanderers, being the holders, not only had the solitary game to play—the Challenge Final in which they beat Oxford University 2-0—but they were also allowed to choose the venue of that match, which is the reason for Lillie Bridge's one moment of sporting significance.

The Wanderers also entered the records in a unique way in 1878— they won the Cup for the third consecutive time and thus, according to the rules, outright. It was, however, returned with the proviso that it should never again be handed to one team in perpetuity. In fact the scene was a little more comical than that. Charles Alcock, as secretary of the Wanderers, handed back the Cup and asked that it should never be won outright. Charles Alcock, now in his role as secretary of the FA, was only too happy to agree.

In the years that followed only one club—Blackburn Rovers between 1884 and 1886—has repeated the feat, and they were presented with a special shield which still hangs in their boardroom.

It was to Blackburn, in fact, that the Cup fled when it left the gentlemen amateurs of the South. That Lancastrian cotton-weaving town had two fine clubs in the 1880s— Olympic, who became the first side from outside the home counties to win the trophy, in 1883, and Rovers, who won it in the subsequent three seasons.

But the Blackburn clubs were not the first 'outsiders' to make their mark on the competition. In 1879 Nottingham Forest became the first of England's northern sides to reach the semi-finals—and at their first attempt—but more significant was the performance of Darwen, a neighbour of Blackburn, the same year. In the previous round they had held Old Etonians to two draws, the first by scoring four times in the last 15 minutes, but had gone down 6-2 on their third visit to the capital.

Darwen were unlucky that the rule under which all ties after the second round had to be played at the Oval was still in force. No semi final was contested outside London

The story of the FA Cup

'I've got a League Championship medal, a Fairs Cup medal, a League Cup medal and dozens of caps—but sometimes I think I'd swap the lot for a place in a Cup winning side.' The words were those of Billy Bremner before Leeds United's long-awaited success at Wembley in 1972, but they could have come from any of a large number of professionals, that enormous group who have never been lucky enough to carry the Cup around the arena after the highlight of the English season.

The FA Cup has an undeniable aura about it. Not only is it the oldest football competition in the world, not only is its Final watched by hundreds of millions of people *outside* Britain, not only is it the annual showpiece for Britain's national sport, but it has been elevated far beyond that. It is now a ritual, different from a royal wedding or a moon-landing only in that it occurs at more predictable intervals.

In 1971 the BBC published a list of the biggest audiences for single programmes in the history of British television. Four of the top ten were Cup Finals. And despite all the protestations about the League Championship being the ultimate test of professional ability, there is the sneaking suspicion that no-one would sacrifice an FA Cup winners medal for a League Championship equivalent.

For, in the last resort, football must be a game about eleven men against eleven, about one team leaving the field victorious and the other vanquished, about a packed stadium saluting just one team—

just one winner.

In its ultimate simplicity the FA Cup is the forerunner of competitions all over the world. But in a sense it is a lot more than that, for the hundred-year history of the FA Cup is also the history of English football.

It was in the offices of *The Sportsman*, a London newspaper, on 20 July 1871, that seven men took a hesitant step and made football history. The central figure was 29-year-old Charles Alcock, secretary of the FA and the man who suggested that: '. . . it is desirable that a Challenge Cup shall be established in connection with the Association . . .' Among the other six present were M P Betts, who scored the first ever Cup Final goal, and Captain Francis Marindin, later president of the FA, who appeared in two Finals and refereed another eight.

The Harrow School competition that inspired the FA Cup

Alcock had pinched the idea for his competition from his old school, Harrow, where there was a simple knock-out tournament among the houses, the winner being known as the 'Cock House'. The FA ordered a Cup from Martin, Hall and Company; it cost a mere £20 and stood just 18 inches high.

Fifteen clubs entered the first year—all but Donington School, Spalding, and the great Queen's Park of Glasgow coming from the

home counties. In fact Donington scratched without playing a game and never entered again—thus establishing some kind of record— while Queen's Park, thanks to the kindness of the organizing committee, managed to reach the semi-final without kicking a ball.

The strict knock-out principle was not yet in operation; four clubs played in the third round and four in the next, in part through byes and in part through a rule which allowed teams which drew to both go through to the next round.

The Cup's beginnings were undoubtedly humble. Just 2,000 people turned out for the Final to see men dressed in trousers and caps (Royal Engineers wore 'dark blue serge knickerbockers'), who changed ends every time a goal was scored and who won throw-ins by touching the ball down in rugby fashion if it went out of play. The Kennington Oval pitch would have hardly been recognizable to present-day supporters— there was no centre-circle, no half-way line, no penalty area and a tape instead of a cross-bar. Alcock's team, the Wanderers, beat the Engineers 1-0.

The century that followed can be roughly divided into four phases— largely determined by the geographical location of the Final. Firstly there was the amateur era, then the Northern takeover, the Crystal Palace period and, finally, the post-1923 Wembley era.

Ten years after that first Final the Old Etonians beat Blackburn Rovers at the Oval. When the final whistle blew, the victorious captain, A F

until 1882, when Blackburn Rovers drew with Sheffield's The Wednesday at Huddersfield and beat them in Manchester, but for the next few years—before the Irish and Scottish FAs banned their clubs from entering—ties were played all over the United Kingdom. As a result Linfield captured the unique record of never having lost a Cup tie. They drew 2-2 with Nottingham Forest in 1889, and then withdrew before the replay, never to enter again.

Forest had actually arrived in Ireland and played a friendly instead, but it helped create an odd record for them as well, for they are the only club to have been drawn to play FA Cup ties in all four home countries. In 1885, after a drawn game at Derby, Forest had replayed a semi-final with Glasgow's Queen's Park at Merchiston Castle School, Edinburgh, the only semi-final ever contested outside England.

But to return to Darwen, whose performance was in no small way due to the presence of two Scots, Fergus Suter and James Love, both of whom had been 'mislaid' by Partick Thistle on a tour of England. They were, of course, among the first of the professionals that were soon to take over the competition and football south of the border.

The issue of payment did not actually come to a head until January 1884, when Preston North End drew with mighty Upton Park, one of the original entrants in 1872 and still staunch supporters of the lily-white amateur game. The Londoners protested that Preston had included professionals in their team, North End admitted as much, and were disqualified.

Just over a year later the FA sensibly bowed to the inevitable and professionals were allowed provided, among other clauses, they were: '. . . annually registered in a book to be kept by the committee of the FA . . .'

'The Cup'll never go back to London' —and it never did

At least Preston had the satisfaction of seeing Upton Park humbled in the next round by neighbours Blackburn Rovers, on their triumphant march to the first of a hat-trick of wins. At the time Blackburn were also midway through a record of 24 Cup games without defeat, which lasted from a 1-0 setback at the hands of Darwen in the second round of the 1882-83 competition to the December of 1886.

But it was not Rovers who first brought the Cup to Lancashire, rather a long since defunct outfit called Blackburn Olympic. When

Top *100,000 people watch, one cannot as Ronnie Allen tries to put West Bromwich back into the 1954 Cup Final from a penalty. Goalkeeper Sanders missed the moment that brought his club level with Preston North End.*
Centre *The incident from a camera at the other end. Sanders is ringed.*
Bottom *Forty years before and a dozen miles away, Liverpool attack the Burnley goal during the last Final to be played at the Crystal Palace.*

their captain, Warburton, got back to a deserved civic reception in 1883, he declared to the crowd: 'The Cup is very welcome to Lancashire. It'll have a good home and it'll never go back to London.' He was quite right. In the next twelve years it went no further south than Birmingham where, in 1895, it was stolen from the window of a football-boot manufacturer William Shillcock and was never seen again.

In an edition of the *Sunday Pictorial* in February 1958 one Harry Burge, at the age of 83, admitted to having stolen the Cup and melted it down for counterfeit half-crowns. If that is true it is a sad commentary on the economics of the times—the Cup contained less than £20 worth of silver and could hardly have justified the effort.

When Villa won it for a year—and lost it forever

Fortunately for the FA the chairman of Wolverhampton Wanderers had presented his players with scaled-down replicas when they won the trophy in 1893, and it was therefore possible to create an exact reproduction of the original.

That same Wolves victory was on the occasion of the first Final to be contested outside the capital. Surrey CCC, alarmed at the size of the crowd for the 1892 Final, withdrew the Oval as a venue and, in recognition of Lancashire's supremacy, the game's premier event switched to the country's second city, Manchester. There the Fallowfield ground was besieged by a crowd which broke down the barriers and fell through the wooden terracing in a remarkable harbinger of both the first Wembley Final, 30 years later, and the Ibrox disaster, then less than ten years away.

A week earlier Everton's reserve team had thrashed Wolves 4-2 in a First Division game but this time it was a different story with the Midlanders' captain Allen scoring the only goal of the match. The next season saw an equally surprising result. Second Division Notts County beat Bolton, 4-1 at Goodison Park, after reasonably protesting that it was virtually a home game for Bolton, and their centre-forward Jimmy Logan scored a hat-trick to equal William Townley's 1890 feat for Blackburn Rovers.

After the 1894 Final the FA must have concluded that London was the only rightful place for the show-piece of the season, and it has been played there with only one exception (1915) ever since. The obvious choice was Crystal Palace—though the FA's decision to move the game to London can be viewed a little cynically in the light of the fact that only one of the finalists who ever played at the Palace was a London club—Spurs, in 1901—and only two others, Southampton and Bristol City, came from south of Birmingham.

Crystal Palace in 1895 was already a Victorian weekend playground—something like a cross between Battersea Fun Fair and Brighton beach—and it had a huge natural bowl which was used for

sporting events. Terracing as it is known today was never built there; most of the eighty or so thousand who attended Finals stood on the steep grassy slopes of the east side.

The first Final at the Palace (not, incidentally, the present home of Crystal Palace) was the third clash between Birmingham rivals West Bromwich and Aston Villa—they are still the only clubs to have met each other three times in a Final. At kick-off both had won once each, but Villa went on to take the Cup this time, promptly lost it to Mr Burge, but were back again two years later to carry off the new trophy after a Final which must rank along with 1948 and 1953 as one of the greatest ever.

It was also a particularly significant game for it gave Villa a League-Cup double which looked, for 64 years, like being the last of all time. Villa had won the League by the massive margin of 11 points (there were only 16 clubs in the division) and at the Palace defeated Everton 3-2, all the goals coming in the 25 minutes before half-time.

The club that took Villa's mantle of 'the team of all the talents' was Newcastle United—possessors of what is surely the oddest of all Cup Final records. In five Finals at the Crystal Palace they did not win one game, yet they did not lose at Wembley until their sixth match there!

The Geordies' record between 1905 and 1911 is startling in its consistency. They reached the Final in 1905, 1906, 1908, 1910 and 1911. In 1910 they admittedly managed to draw with Second Division Barnsley, and beat them in the replay at Goodison to record their only pre-First World War win. In 1909 they lost a semi-final by the game's only goal to Manchester United, so the only year in the seven between 1905 and 1911 that they did not reach the last four was 1907.

Newcastle's strange relationship with the name Crystal Palace

That season—one in which they won the League—Newcastle suffered a first round knock-out at St James' Park to a club then languishing at the bottom of the Southern League. And the name of that club whose feat must rank alongside the giant-killing exploits of Walsall and Colchester? Irony of ironies . . . Crystal Palace. It was almost as if the very name made the Northumbrians go weak at the knees.

When the two great sides of the era—Villa and Newcastle—met in 1905 they drew a crowd of 101,117 to a game that seemed to have little appeal for the Londoner—but even this figure had been surpassed four years earlier for a game that will surely remain unique for all time.

Since the Final returned in 1895 Londoners had regarded it, more than a little disdainfully, as an affair for provincials—rather like the Agricultural Exhibition at Earls Court is regarded today. In fact London had only one League club—Arsenal—at the turn of the century and had never had a professional interest in the Final.

Then, in the first year of the new century, came a record-breaking Final. 1901 saw Tottenham become the only non-League club to win the Cup since the Football League was founded, though they needed a replay against Sheffield United—winners two years before—to do it. The attendance printed in the following day's papers—114,815—was the largest ever at a football match and has been surpassed in England only twice since—at the 1913 and 1923 Finals.

Sandy Brown, who scored twice at Crystal Palace and once in the replay at Bolton, became the first man to score in every round of the Cup (a feat not equalled until 1935) and his total of 15 Cup goals has yet to be surpassed.

And on top of all this was a violently disputed goal which only the referee and the Sheffield United team of the hundred thousand present thought was justified. The incident was no doubt quite comical to non-partisan spectators. Clawley, the Spurs goalkeeper, clashed with Bennett, a Sheffield forward, and the ball ran behind. Clawley appealed for a goal-kick, Bennett for a corner and the referee silenced them both by awarding a goal. He apparently judged Clawley to have been *behind* his own goal-line before carrying the ball out and being challenged by Bennett.

London's star fell as quickly as it had risen and the capital did not have another representative in the Final until 1915, when Chelsea lost in the muted atmosphere of a wartime Old Trafford, to the side their fellow Londoners had defeated—Sheffield United.

The Yorkshiremen, however, did not carry off the same trophy Spurs

had deprived them of. The design of the latter had been pirated for another competition in Manchester and so the second of the three FA Cups was presented to Lord Kinnaird—whose nine Final appearances is still a record—to mark his 21 years as President of the Football Association.

The present trophy, weighing 175 oz and nineteen inches high, was ordered from Fattorini and Sons of Bradford and, appropriately if strangely, Bradford City were its first holders. Strangely, because neither Bradford club had been near a Final before and neither has been near one since.

As remarkable as the ability of some clubs to keep coming back and taking the Cup is the inability of others to get near it. Take Sunderland for instance. By the time they finally took the trophy back to

Opposite top *The programme for the second of the meetings between West Bromwich and Aston Villa, the last Final to be played at Kennington Oval. No other clubs have ever met in three Cup Finals as Villa and Albion did in 1887, 1892 and 1897.*
Opposite centre *Villa are back, this time at Crystal Palace where Hampton scored the two goals that beat unfortunate Newcastle in 1905.*
Opposite bottom *Villa again but yet another venue for the Final of 1920. The dreary Stamford Bridge produced equally dreary games; in 1920 Villa won with a centre which went in off the back of Kirton's neck.*
Above top *What fans were doing to get into a brand new Wembley in 1923.*
Above *Ricky George scores and Hereford become the first non-League club to defeat First Division opposition (the Newcastle United of 1972) since Yeovil beat Sunderland in 1949.*

Wearside in 1937, they had won the League Championship six times. But near neighbours and rivals Newcastle already had seven Final appearances to their credit—and another three soon to follow. Sunderland's only previous Final was another of the classics—the 1913 game that attracted a crowd even bigger than at the 1901 Final. It assembled for a decisive game, for it was the only Final in the first hundred years of the Cup to be contested by the clubs that finished first and second in the League. In the end honours were shared, Sunderland winning the League and Villa the Cup.

Villa went into the Final, just as they did in 1957, intent on defending their title as the last winners of the double. The Midlanders came very near to making a mess of it though. First their right-winger Charlie Wallace missed a penalty kick—the only time this has happened in a Final—then their England goal-keeper Sam Hardy left the field injured for ten minutes. In the end Barber fulfilled a remarkable prophecy of Clem Stephenson—who had turned to Sunderland's Charlie Buchan early in the match and recounted a dream he had had the night before. 'We won 1-0,' Stephenson is reputed to have said, 'with a goal headed by Barber.' And so it was.

Seven years later Stephenson, Wallace and Hardy provided an illusion of continuity when they again collected winners medals. In the interim Europe had been at war for four years and the Crystal Palace had been requisitioned as a service depot. There was no prospect of it being available before 1923 and the FA had to look elsewhere for a venue for the highlight of the season.

The year Chelsea nearly played the Final at home

Having decided that London was still the only possible home for the Cup Final—a contentious conclusion that was not particularly well received in Manchester, Birmingham or Liverpool—the FA were left with only one choice. The White Hart Lane and Highbury of 1919 were far from the imposing stadiums they are today, and the dreary Stamford Bridge was alone in being large enough.

So Chelsea's impersonal arena it was—a decision that nearly caused the FA a lot more criticism. By the semi-final stage the arrangements for the Final itself were far too advanced for the venue to be changed—but the Chelsea side that had reached the last pre-War Final were alive and well, third in the League, and favourites to reach the first post-War Final as well. The Pensioners went to Bramall Lane for their semi-final against Aston Villa with the prospect of a home tie in the Final—though it was technically against the rules of the competition.

It was Billy Walker who saved the FA's face. He scored two goals, Villa won 3-1 and went on to beat Huddersfield at Stamford Bridge.

The three Stamford Bridge Finals were among the most anonymous

ever. All three were won by the only goal of the match, and the attendances in 1920 and 1922 were among the lowest of the century, coming nowhere near to filling the ground.

The 1922 game was called the most forgettable of all time, but suddenly acquired a new significance after a sequel of 16 years later. The earlier game was a lamentable affair—even the FA minutes commented on the conduct of the players. It was appropriate that it should be decided by a disputed penalty when Preston's right-back Hamilton brought down Huddersfield's winger Billy Smith on the edge of the area, though many said outside it. After a lengthy and heated discussion between the Preston players and the referee, Smith himself took it and scored.

The 1938 game was equally drab, and the contestants were—Huddersfield and Preston. At least it was better tempered and had reached the last minute of extra-time without a goal when Huddersfield's centre-half Young tripped George Mutch and Mutch himself converted the penalty. The story goes that Bill Shankly—then playing for Preston—told Mutch to 'shut your eyes and hit it'. He had obviously been coached in something like that vein, for the ball hit the bar on its way in.

How a white horse disturbed the dreams of West Ham United

But back in 1923 no doubt everyone was glad to get away from Stamford Bridge to Wembley, where the FA had co-operated in a scheme to incorporate a vast new stadium in the British Empire Exhibition, scheduled to open in 1924. The Empire Stadium was ready a year earlier and public enthusiasm was enormous. Unfortunately the FA were lulled by the below capacity crowds at Stamford Bridge and thought that Wembley—capable of holding 127,000 according to the Exhibition authorities—would be more than big enough.

They were perhaps unlucky in that one of the contestants was West Ham, then leading the Second Division and the darlings of East London. In the end the FA publicly thanked a policeman called George Scorey and his white horse Billy that the game took place at all. West Ham were less pleased with the behaviour of the FA's equine saviour. Their game relied on the use of fast-running wingers Richards and Ruffell and, as trainer Charlie Paynter said afterwards: 'It was that white horse thumping its big feet into the pitch that made it hopeless. Our wingers were tumbling all over the place, tripping up in great ruts and holes.' Maybe, but it did not stop Ted Vizard having an excellent game on the left-wing for Bolton. The FA were more generous to PC Scorey, regularly sending him tickets for later Finals—but he was not much interested in football and, in fact, never went to another match. There must have been many who would have given much for a place at the Wembley Finals which followed.

RAY GREEN

Grief and glory on the way to Wembley

When Arsenal returned to Wembley for the centenary Cup Final in 1972 they at least had statistics on their side. Newcastle had won in 1951 and 1952, Spurs in 1961 and 1962 and Arsenal had taken the trophy in 1971. But the portents were to be overcome by Leeds in their third FA Cup Final, for Allan Clarke scored the only goal of the match and Arsenal became the first holders to return to Wembley and lose.

It was a defeat which reminded their followers of the inter-War period. Mighty Arsenal were the giants who strode across the thirties, winning the League five times but having a strangely chequered history in the Cup. True, they did win it twice, but far better remembered are the two occasions when they lost. The first of these was in 1927, when a Cardiff with eight internationals and only one Englishman in their side took the Cup out of England for the first and only time. The solitary goal of the game came from a speculative shot by Cardiff's centre-forward Ferguson. The ball seemed to be easily gathered by Arsenal's Welsh international goalkeeper Dan Lewis, but he seemed to indulge in a grotesque parody of his trade, the ball slipping away from his fumblings and rolling slowly over the line.

Lewis blamed the incident on his new jersey, and to this day Arsenal always wash goalkeepers' jerseys before they are used, to get rid of

any surplus grease. It was a pity that they could not wash away their Cup luck as easily.

Still, there was nothing contentious about Arsenal's 2-0 win over Huddersfield in the 1930 Final, a game remembered for the moment when the *Graf Zeppelin* appeared over the Stadium. The airship—pride of a re-emergent Germany—dipped in salute and passed on sedately.

Two years later Arsenal were back to suffer the greatest of all Cup Final controversies. Their opponents were eternal Cup runners-up Newcastle, and the losers medals seemed destined to make their familiar trek to the North East as early as the fifteenth minute when John put Arsenal ahead. But it was not to be.

Davidson, the Newcastle centre-half, sent a long ball along the right, Richardson went for it but it appeared to be hit too hard for him and looked to have bounced out of play before he hooked it back across the goal. The Arsenal defence stopped and Allen was left free to flick the ball into the net.

The referee, a Mr Harper, carved himself an everlasting niche in soccer history by allowing the goal and Newcastle went on to win via another by Allen. That particular incident—and the photographs of the day tended to support the view of the Arsenal defence rather than that of the referee—probably ranks as the

most arguable Cup Final goal ever.

For a time it was quite impossible to keep Arsenal out of the Cup head-lines. In the third round the following season they went to Walsall, a club of no great pretensions, and lost 2-0 in a game that still ranks above Yeovil-Sunderland and Colchester-Leeds as the greatest of all the giant-killing acts. The reasons are emotional rather than analytical. What more needs to be said than that Arsenal spent more on their boots in 1933 than Walsall had paid in transfer fees for their whole team?

The little clubs can indeed add drama, and one of the most appealing things about the Cup is the periodic appearance of the giantkillers. On occasions it has even gained a club admission to the League—Peterborough after their successes in the 1950s and Hereford and Wimbledon after their exploits in the 70s are perhaps the best examples. Often enough it has cost managers of League clubs their positions. When amateur Blyth Spartans defeated both Crewe and Stockport in successive rounds of the 1971-72 competition, the managers of both the Fourth Division clubs lost their jobs the following week.

Victories by non-League clubs over their League brothers are common enough of course—in 1956-57 it happened as many as eleven times. But since the League added a Third Division in 1920 there have been

The blood runs from Emlyn Hughes' face during his side's vain attempt to prevent Arsenal's double in 1971.

only five instances of a non-League club beating a First Division side, only one away from home. Hereford did well in the third round of 1972, drawing at Newcastle and winning the replay. *Old Moore's Almanac* for the year had predicted that a non-League side would win the Cup and Hereford certainly did their best to oblige—drawing with West Ham in the next round before going down 3-1.

Superstition seems to play a big part in the Cup, where Portsmouth were the arch-adherents. In 1934 they employed manager Jack Tinn's lucky spats to bring them fortune and comedian Bud Flanagan to tell them jokes in the dressing room before the game with Manchester City. It did no good, City coming back to win 2-1 after losing the 1933 Final. City did the same thing in 1956, beating Birmingham with the 'Revie plan' after losing to Newcastle in 1955.

The 1934 Final was the occasion on which Frank Swift fainted. He said that the tension of the last few minutes, when he spent his time between the posts musing on how difficult it would be to clean the Cup and listening to the photographers counting down the seconds, was simply too much and he collapsed as

FOOTBALL ASSOCIATION CHALLENGE CUP FINALS 1872 — 1978

Year	Venue	Winners		Scorers	Runners-up		Scorers	Attendance
1872	Kennington Oval	Wanderers	1	Betts	Royal Engineers	0		2,000
1873[1]	Lillie Bridge	Wanderers	2	Kinnaird, Wollaston	Oxford University	0		3,000
1874	Kennington Oval	Oxford University	2	Mackarness, Patton	Royal Engineers	0		2,000
1875*	Kennington Oval	Royal Engineers	1	Scorer not known	Old Etonians	1	Bonsor	3,000
Replay	Kennington Oval	Royal Engineers	2	Renny-Tailyour, A N Other	Old Etonians	0		3,000
1876	Kennington Oval	Wanderers	0		Old Etonians	0		3,000
Replay	Kennington Oval	Wanderers	3	Hughes (2), Wollaston	Old Etonians	0		3,500
1877*	Kennington Oval	Wanderers	2	Scorers not known	Oxford University	0		3,000
1878[2]	Kennington Oval	Wanderers	3	Scorers not known	Royal Engineers	1	Scorer not known	4,500
1879	Kennington Oval	Old Etonians	1	Scorer not known	Clapham Rovers	0		5,000
1880	Kennington Oval	Clapham Rovers	1	Lloyd-Jones	Oxford University	0		6,000
1881	Kennington Oval	Old Carthusians	3	Scorers not known	Old Etonians	0		4,500
1882	Kennington Oval	Old Etonians	1	Anderson	Blackburn Rovers	0		6,500
1883*	Kennington Oval	Blackburn Olympic	2	Matthews, Costley	Old Etonians	1	Goodhart	8,000
1884	Kennington Oval	Blackburn Rovers	2	Brown, Forrest	Queen's Park (Glasgow)	1	Christie	4,000
1885	Kennington Oval	Blackburn Rovers	2	Brown, Forrest	Queen's Park (Glasgow)	0		12,500
1886	Kennington Oval	Blackburn Rovers	0		West Bromwich Albion	0		15,000
Replay[3]	The Racecourse, Derby	Blackburn Rovers	2	Brown, Sowerbutts	West Bromwich Albion	0		12,000
1887	Kennington Oval	Aston Villa	2	Hunter, Hodgetts	West Bromwich Albion	0		15,500
1888	Kennington Oval	West Bromwich Albion	2	Woodhall, Bayliss	Preston North End	1	Dewhurst	19,000
1889	Kennington Oval	Preston North End	3	Gordon, Goodall, Thompson	Wolverhampton Wanderers	0		22,000
1890	Kennington Oval	Blackburn Rovers	6	Townley (3), Lofthouse, Southworth, Walton	The Wednesday	1	Bennett	20,000
1891	Kennington Oval	Blackburn Rovers	3	Southworth, Townley, Dewar	Notts County	1	Oswald	23,000
1892	Kennington Oval	West Bromwich Albion	3	Nicholls, Geddes, Reynolds	Aston Villa	0		25,000
1893	Fallowfield, Manchester	Wolverhampton Wanderers	1	Allen	Everton	0		45,000
1894	Goodison Park	Notts County	4	Logan (3), Watson	Bolton Wanderers	1	Cassidy	37,000
1895	Crystal Palace	Aston Villa	1	Devey	West Bromwich Albion	0		42,560
1896[4]	Crystal Palace	The Wednesday	2	Spiksley (2)	Wolverhampton Wanderers	1	Black	48,836
1897	Crystal Palace	Aston Villa	3	Campbell, Devey, Crabtree	Everton	2	Bell, Hartley	65,891
1898	Crystal Palace	Nottingham Forest	3	Capes (2), McPherson	Derby County	1	Bloomer	62,017
1899	Crystal Palace	Sheffield United	4	Bennett, Beers, Priest, Almond	Derby County	1	Boag	78,833
1900	Crystal Palace	Bury	4	McLuckie (2), Wood, Plant	Southampton	0		68,945
1901	Crystal Palace	Tottenham Hotspur	2	Brown (2)	Sheffield United	2	Bennett, Priest	114,815
Replay	Burnden Park, Bolton	Tottenham Hotspur	3	Cameron, Smith, Brown	Sheffield United	1	Priest	20,740
1902	Crystal Palace	Sheffield United	1	Common	Southampton	1	Wood	76,914
Replay	Crystal Palace	Sheffield United	2	Hedley, Barnes	Southampton	1	Brown	33,068
1903	Crystal Palace	Bury	6	Leeming (2), Ross, Sagar, Plant, Wood	Derby County	0		63,102
1904	Crystal Palace	Manchester City	1	Meredith	Bolton Wanderers	0		61,374
1905	Crystal Palace	Aston Villa	2	Hampton (2)	Newcastle United	0		101,117
1906	Crystal Palace	Everton	1	Young	Newcastle United	0		75,609
1907	Crystal Palace	The Wednesday	2	Stewart, Simpson	Everton	1	Sharp	84,584
1908	Crystal Palace	Wolverhampton Wanderers	3	Hunt, Hedley, Harrison	Newcastle United	1	Howie	74,967
1909	Crystal Palace	Manchester United	1	Turnbull A	Bristol City	0		71,401
1910	Crystal Palace	Newcastle United	1	Rutherford	Barnsley	1	Tufnell	77,747
Replay	Goodison Park	Newcastle United	2	Shepherd (2 inc a penalty)	Barnsley	0		69,000
1911[5]	Crystal Palace	Bradford City	0		Newcastle United	0		69,098
Replay	Old Trafford	Bradford City	1	Spiers	Newcastle United	0		58,000
1912	Crystal Palace	Barnsley	0		West Bromwich Albion	0		54,556
Replay*	Bramall Lane	Barnsley	1	Tufnell	West Bromwich Albion	0		38,555
1913	Crystal Palace	Aston Villa	1	Barber	Sunderland	0		120,081
1914	Crystal Palace	Burnley	1	Freeman	Liverpool	0		72,778
1915	Old Trafford	Sheffield United	3	Simmons, Kitchen, Fazackerley	Chelsea	0		49,557
1916-1919		Competition suspended						
1920*	Stamford Bridge	Aston Villa	1	Kirton	Huddersfield Town	0		50,018
1921	Stamford Bridge	Tottenham Hotspur	1	Dimmock	Wolverhampton Wanderers	0		72,805
1922	Stamford Bridge	Huddersfield Town	1	Smith (penalty)	Preston North End	0		53,000
1923[6]	Wembley	Bolton Wanderers	2	Jack, Smith J R	West Ham United	0		126,047
1924	Wembley	Newcastle United	2	Harris, Seymour	Aston Villa	0		91,695
1925	Wembley	Sheffield United	1	Tunstall	Cardiff City	0		91,763
1926	Wembley	Bolton Wanderers	1	Jack	Manchester City	0		91,447
1927	Wembley	Cardiff City	1	Ferguson	Arsenal	0		91,206
1928	Wembley	Blackburn Rovers	3	Roscamp (2), McLean	Huddersfield Town	1	Jackson	92,041
1929	Wembley	Bolton Wanderers	2	Butler, Blackmore	Portsmouth	0		92,576
1930	Wembley	Arsenal	2	James, Lambert	Huddersfield Town	0		92,448
1931	Wembley	West Bromwich Albion	2	Richardson W G (2)	Birmingham	1	Bradford	92,406
1932	Wembley	Newcastle United	2	Allen (2)	Arsenal	1	John	92,298
1933	Wembley	Everton	3	Stein, Dean, Dunn	Manchester City	0		92,950
1934	Wembley	Manchester City	2	Tilson (2)	Portsmouth	1	Rutherford	93,258
1935	Wembley	Sheffield Wednesday	4	Rimmer (2), Palethorpe, Hooper	West Bromwich Albion	2	Boyes, Sandford	93,204
1936	Wembley	Arsenal	1	Drake	Sheffield United	0		93,384
1937	Wembley	Sunderland	3	Gurney, Carter, Burbanks	Preston North End	1	O'Donnell	93,495
1938*	Wembley	Preston North End	1	Mutch (penalty)	Huddersfield Town	0		93,497
1939	Wembley	Portsmouth	4	Parker (2), Barlow, Anderson	Wolverhampton Wanderers	1	Dorsett	99,370
1940-1945		Competition suspended						
1946*	Wembley	Derby County	4	Turner H (og), Doherty, Stamps (2)	Charlton Athletic	1	Turner H	98,000
1947*	Wembley	Charlton Athletic	1	Duffy	Burnley	0		99,000
1948	Wembley	Manchester United	4	Rowley (2), Pearson, Anderson	Blackpool	2	Shimwell (penalty), Mortensen	99,000
1949	Wembley	Wolverhampton Wanderers	3	Pye (2), Smyth	Leicester City	1	Griffiths	99,500
1950	Wembley	Arsenal	2	Lewis (2)	Liverpool	0		100,000
1951	Wembley	Newcastle United	2	Milburn (2)	Blackpool	0		100,000
1952	Wembley	Newcastle United	1	Robledo G	Arsenal	0		100,000
1953	Wembley	Blackpool	4	Mortensen (3), Perry	Bolton Wanderers	3	Lofthouse, Moir, Bell	100,000
1954	Wembley	West Bromwich Albion	3	Allen (2 inc a penalty), Griffin	Preston North End	2	Morrison, Wayman	100,000
1955	Wembley	Newcastle United	3	Milburn, Mitchell, Hannah	Manchester City	1	Johnstone	100,000
1956	Wembley	Manchester City	3	Hayes, Dyson, Johnstone	Birmingham City	1	Kinsey	100,000
1957	Wembley	Aston Villa	2	McParland (2)	Manchester United	1	Taylor	100,000
1958	Wembley	Bolton Wanderers	2	Lofthouse (2)	Manchester United	0		100,000
1959	Wembley	Nottingham Forest	2	Dwight, Wilson	Luton Town	1	Pacey	100,000
1960	Wembley	Wolverhampton Wanderers	3	McGrath (og), Deeley (2)	Blackburn Rovers	0		100,000
1961	Wembley	Tottenham Hotspur	2	Smith, Dyson	Leicester City	0		100,000
1962	Wembley	Tottenham Hotspur	3	Greaves, Smith, Blanchflower (penalty)	Burnley	1	Robson	100,000
1963	Wembley	Manchester United	3	Law, Herd (2)	Leicester City	1	Keyworth	100,000
1964	Wembley	West Ham United	3	Sissons, Hurst, Boyce	Preston North End	2	Holden, Dawson	100,000
1965*	Wembley	Liverpool	2	Hunt, St John	Leeds United	1	Bremner	100,000
1966	Wembley	Everton	3	Trebilcock (2), Temple	Sheffield Wednesday	2	McCalliog, Ford	100,000
1967[7]	Wembley	Tottenham Hotspur	2	Robertson, Saul	Chelsea	1	Tambling	100,000
1968*	Wembley	West Bromwich Albion	1	Astle	Everton	0		100,000
1969	Wembley	Manchester City	1	Young	Leicester City	0		100,000
1970*	Wembley	Chelsea	2	Houseman, Hutchinson	Leeds United	2	Charlton, Jones	100,000
Replay*	Old Trafford	Chelsea	2	Osgood, Webb	Leeds United	1	Jones	62,000
1971*	Wembley	Arsenal	2	Kelly, George	Liverpool	1	Heighway	100,000
1972	Wembley	Leeds United	1	Clarke	Arsenal	0		100,000
1973	Wembley	Sunderland	1	Porterfield	Leeds United	0		100,000
1974	Wembley	Liverpool	3	Keegan (2), Heighway	Newcastle United	0		100,000
1975	Wembley	West Ham United	2	Taylor A (2)	Fulham	0		100,000
1976	Wembley	Southampton	1	Stokes	Manchester United	0		100,000
1977	Wembley	Manchester United	2	Pearson, Greenhoff J	Liverpool	1	Case	100,000
1978	Wembley	Ipswich	1	Osborne	Arsenal	0		100,000

*After half-an-hour's extra time. Extra time became compulsory in 1913. [1]Challenge system. The holders, Wanderers, were exempt until the Final.
[2]Wanderers won the trophy outright but restored it to the Association. [3]Blackburn Rovers were also awarded a special shield to mark their third consecutive win.
[4]After the Cup had been stolen in 1895, the FA ordered a replica. The 1896 Final was the first time it was awarded.
[5]After the Cup's design had been duplicated for another competition, it was withdrawn and presented to Lord Kinnaird on his completing 21 years as President of the Football
Association. The present trophy was first awarded in 1911. [6]Official attendance figure. Actual attendance was probably in excess of 200,000. [7]Substitutes allowed for the first time.

the final whistle went.

Portsmouth's rituals proved luckier five years later. Their opponents Wolves arrived at Wembley as the hottest favourites of the century and full of a publicity seeking course of 'monkey glands'. Portsmouth preferred to rely on the spats again and, when the signature book came round, were heartened to see that the Wolves players were so nervous that their signatures were barely legible.

Portsmouth won the Cup easily and proceeded to hold it for the longest period ever—seven years. This, however, was less due to their prowess than the outbreak of the Second World War.

After that lengthy intermission the Cup re-appeared in unfamiliar form. Because of the lack of a League programme, the FA decided to hold the Cup on a home-and-away basis—for the first and only time. It was not really a success, but it created its talking points.

Bradford PA lost 3-1 at home to Manchester City in the fourth round and then went on to win 8-2 at Maine Road, while Charlton became only the third team to *lose* a Cup game and still reach the Final. Fulham beat them 2-1 in the third round at Craven Cottage but Charlton had already won the first leg 3-1 and went through. One previous occasion when this had happened was the second part of a three-match quarter-final fiasco in 1890. Wednesday beat Notts County 5-0 in the first part. County protested to the FA, the game was replayed and County won 3-2. This time it was Sheffield's turn to protest and the eventual result was a 2-1 win for Wednesday —who went on to lose the Final rather ingnominiously 6-1 to Blackburn Rovers.

The 1946 Final was almost as high scoring a game—Derby winning 4-1. That surprised no one for it took

Derby's tally for the competition to 37, the highest aggregate since 1887-88 when Preston beat Hyde 26-0. Charlton's Bert Turner was the central figure of the game, scoring an own goal for Derby and within a minute equalizing with a free-kick which went in off Doherty's legs. He remains the only man to have scored for both sides in a Cup Final.

There followed two years later one of a pair of great Finals that have to be regarded in tandem. In the first the League runners-up, Manchester United, beat Blackpool 4-2 in what has always been regarded as the 'purest' of the Wembley games. Blackpool reached Wembley twice more in the next five years, losing to Newcastle in 1951 and facing Bolton

in 1953, a game consigned to legend as 'the Matthews Final'. Blackpool came back from 3-1 down 20 minutes from time and 3-2 down with just three minutes of normal time left to win 4-3 in the game which will probably always rank—whatever its merits—as *the* Cup Final.

It was a game in keeping with the heady atmosphere of 1953, of the Coronation, of Everest, of Gordon Richards' Derby win, of the Hungarians visit to Wembley. Yet tacticians point to Bolton's strange response to left-half Eric Bell's injury in the first half. Bell moved to the left-wing. Inside-left Harry Hassall, no great tackler, moved to left-half and, when left-back Ralph Banks went down with cramp twenty

Above 'The FA Cup is for the fans,' says Danny Blanchflower. Mansfield Town, average attendance around 5,000, found difficulty accommodating everyone who wanted to watch their sixth round tie with Leicester in 1969. *Left* An over-enthusiastic Evertonian at Wembley in 1966 annoys Brian Labone but gives Brian Harris (far left) the chance to see if the cap fits.

minutes from the end, he was left marking Matthews. As a result, Matthews' right-wing was left as open as the proverbial barn door and Bolton paid the price.

Bell's injury was a portent for the next decade. Between 1952 and 1961 only two Finals—1954 and 1958—were not marred by some vital injury. And, significantly, only two of the teams that suffered —Manchester City in 1956 and Nottingham Forest in 1959— eventually won the Cup. The phenomenon, dubbed 'the Wembley hoodoo', was generally attributed to the turf.

Danny Blanchflower explained after the 1961 Final: 'It was a lush trap; the ideal pitch should have a little give in it. But Wembley is too soft. It pulls at the lower muscles of the leg, braking some efforts and ruining the natural timing.' After that particular game—in which Len Chalmers of Leicester suffered torn ligaments—the hoodoo seemed to die away. Substitutes were first introduced in 1967 and it was never an issue again. Perhaps cutting the grass a little shorter made the difference.

Wolverhampton were the great team of the fifties, winning three Championships, yet their two Cup wins were in the last year of the previous decade and the first of the next. And they were against, perhaps, the two worst post-War finalists. In 1949 Leicester arrived at Wembley with the sole distinction of being the worst placed League club (they finished nineteenth in the Second Division) ever to reach the Final. In fact with one point less they would have been playing Third Division football in the August of the same year. Leicester's 3-1 defeat was the prelude to three more in the next 20 years—leaving them with the undisputed position of chief brides-maid.

Wolves' 1960 opponents were in some ways even more ragged. Black-burn Rovers received a transfer request from centre-forward Derek Dougan on the morning of the match, left-back Dave Whelan broke a leg and right-half McGrath scored an own goal. It was the most one-sided of all the Wembley Finals and, while promising to herald in an even more successful decade than the one before for the Midlanders, it was in fact manager Cullis's swansong. Five years later Wolves were playing Second Division football.

Manchester United's post-war record is far sadder. Despite their wins in 1948, 1963 and 1977, it is the games of 1957 and 1958 that they must be remembered by. Not only did United become the first club to lose successive finals at Wembley, but they did so in tragic circumstances.

United approached Wembley in 1957 as League Champions, having reached the semi-final of the European Cup, and on the verge of becoming perhaps the best British club side ever. Real Madrid had beaten them in the European Cup, but it had disheartened nobody, and Busby had said: '. . . the only difference between the teams was in their experience, and we shall soon acquire that . . .' To add spice to the Cup Final their opponents were Aston Villa, the last club to do the double that United seemed to have so firmly in their grasp.

But within minutes Villa's outside-left McParland had crashed into the United keeper Ray Wood and fractured his cheekbone. Wood went off, Jackie Blanchflower had to take over, and the machine was disturbed. McParland scored two goals to give Villa a record seventh win. As one journalist put it the next day: 'McParland was the man of the match—bagging two goals and one goalkeeper.'

But if 1957 could be called tragic for United, then 1958 was cataclysmic. That was, of course, the year of Munich. Six of the 1957 Wembley side—Byrne, Colman, Edwards, Whelan, Taylor and Pegg—were dead. Two—Johnny Berry and Jackie Blanchflower—survived but never kicked a ball again. And what happened next has become a legend.

POPPERFOTO

RADIO TIMES HULTON PICTURE LIBRARY

FA CUP 1872-1978

The Cup and League Double

1888-89	Preston North End
1896-97	Aston Villa
1960-61	Tottenham Hotspur
1970-71	Arsenal

Cup winners and League runners-up

1903-04	Manchester City
1912-13	Aston Villa
1947-48	Manchester United
1953-54	West Bromwich Albion
1959-60	Wolverhampton Wanderers
1971-72	Leeds United

League Champions and Cup runners-up

1904-05	Newcastle United
1912-13	Sunderland
1956-57	Manchester United
1976-77	Liverpool

Runners-up in Cup and League

1927-28	Huddersfield Town
1931-32	Arsenal
1938-39	Wolverhampton Wanderers
1961-62	Burnley
1964-65	Leeds United
1969-70	Leeds United

Second Division Cup winners

1893-94	Notts County
1907-08	Wolverhampton Wanderers
1911-12	Barnsley
1930-31	West Bromwich Albion
1972-73	Sunderland
1975-76	Southampton

Second Division Cup runners-up

1903-04	Bolton Wanderers
1909-10	Barnsley
1919-20	Huddersfield Town (promoted)
1920-21	Wolverhampton Wanderers
1922-23	West Ham United (promoted)
1935-36	Sheffield United
1946-47	Burnley (promoted)
1948-49	Leicester City
1963-64	Preston North End
1974-75	Fulham

Non-League Cup winners since 1888

1900-01	Tottenham Hotspur

Non-League Cup runners-up since 1888

1889-90	The Wednesday
1899-00	Southampton
1901-02	Southampton

Relegated Cup Winners

None

Relegated Cup runners-up

1914-15	Chelsea*
1925-26	Manchester City
1968-69	Leicester City

*Chelsea finished next to bottom but were elected straight back to the extended First Division after the War.

Hat-trick of Cup wins

1876, 1877, 1878	Wanderers
1884, 1885, 1886	Blackburn Rovers

Consecutive Cup wins

1872, 1873	Wanderers
1890, 1891	Blackburn Rovers
1951, 1952	Newcastle United
1961, 1962	Tottenham Hotspur

Goalscorers in every round

1900-01	A Brown (Tottenham Hotspur)
1934-35	E Rimmer (The Wednesday)
1936-37	F O'Donnell (Preston)
1947-48	S Mortensen (Blackpool)
1950-51	J Milburn (Newcastle)
1952-53	N Lofthouse (Bolton)
1953-54	C Wayman (Preston North End)
1967-68	J Astle (West Bromwich)
1969-70	P Osgood (Chelsea)

The FA waived its rules to allow Stan Crowther, a member of the Villa side that had beaten United in 1957, to play for United after having turned out for Villa already in the competition. Ernie Taylor, already a successful Cup Finalist with Blackpool and Newcastle, was brought to hold the team together. And as if partaking in some medieval ritual, the crowd support bordered on religious fanaticism. Wherever the new United appeared gates were closed. In the Cup Sheffield Wednesday were the first to fall before this uncanny force, then the favourites West Bromwich, then Second Division Fulham after two semi-final games which ended at 2-2 and 5-3.

And so they arrived at the gates of Wembley, where their opponents were to be Bolton. Poor Bolton. Five years earlier every uncommitted observer had wanted them to lose so that Stanley Matthews could get his winner's medal. This time they must have had a sneaking suspicion that even their own fans would not have minded too much if the Cup had ended up just five miles down the road at Old Trafford.

But the fates had let things go far enough. Within three minutes a very unghostly Nat Lofthouse put Bolton one up and, early in the second half, made it two with a charge that bundled both the ball and goalkeeper Gregg into the back of the net.

The myth has grown up that it was Lofthouse's charge that lost United the game. That is unlikely. In many ways they had looked what they were —a team carried along on a wave of fanaticism that could not, in the end, disguise the makeshift nature of the effort. After all, only Foulkes and Charlton had played in both Finals. In the space of six years and three Finals in the 1920s Bolton had used just 17 players. United had been forced to use 20 in successive appearances.

Leeds—the better team that lost a unique replay

Manchester's Yorkshire counterpart—Leeds—have a record almost as sad. The team that Don Revie brought from the shadows became the first to take second place in both major competitions on two separate occasions, 1965 and 1970. What was sadder was the universal opinion that, in the latter Final, Leeds were the better of the two sides. But then the best side is surely the one that scores most goals and Chelsea did precisely that in the first replay since the Final moved to Wembley.

The Cup had long been something of a problem for this team that so much wanted to be loved as well as respected. Between the fifth round in 1952 and the third round in 1963 Leeds had established something of a record, going through 16 Cup games without a win. This included a remarkable spell (1956, 1957 and 1958) when they lost 2-1 at home to Cardiff City in three consecutive third rounds. No doubt they were delighted to get away to a 5-1 defeat at Luton in 1959.

In actual fact Rochdale's record is even worse—they reached the

second round in the 1927-28 season but did not appear there again until 1945-46. For eleven consecutive seasons this unfortunate club was knocked out in the first round.

One club with a very satisfactory post-War Cup record is Tottenham. They have won three Finals, to bring their total to five appearances and five wins. The third, fourth and fifth of these came within the space of six years—1961, 1962 and 1967—and the first of those, a 2-0 win against Leicester, earned Spurs the first double for 64 years.

The first season of the decade seems to have a fascination for White Hart Lane. Spurs won the Cup first in 1901, next in 1921, the League for the first time in 1951, the double in 1961 and the League Cup in 1971.

Newcastle have been even more successful than Tottenham at Wembley. In seven appearances they have won five times and they share with the North Londoners the distinction of being the only club to win in consecutive seasons there. The Magpies were successful in 1924, 1932, 1951, 1952 and 1955, and were not beaten until Liverpool and Manchester City overcame them in the 1974 FA Cup and 1976 League Cup. The fact that they beat Arsenal twice—1932 and 1952—only serves to stress how poor London's record has been in an event that the FA have always insisted should be held there.

A rare spell of success for the capital's supporters

But Spurs' double in 1961 was the precursor of a remarkable run of success for the capital—the more so in comparison with what had gone before—culminating in the Arsenal double of 1971. In the decade 1961-1971 London clubs took six of the eleven Finals; in the previous 60 years of the century they had won precisely the same number.

Arsenal's double was the more remarkable of the two if only for its unpredictability. With Spurs in 1961 the possibility had been discussed from very early on in the season, though that might have reflected the paucity of the opposition as much as anything else. Arsenal came through at the last moment in both competitions—overhauling Leeds after being six points behind with just six weeks to go, and taking 27 points from their last 16 matches, and scoring a last-minute penalty to draw with Stoke in the semi-final.

On the Monday of Cup Final week they beat Spurs—appropriately as their North London neighbours were then the only twentieth-century double winners—to take the League, and five days later squeezed past Liverpool at Wembley to deprive Spurs of their uniqueness.. It was Arsenal's 64th game of the season.

Strangely it was left to Arsenal to try and prevent yet another double the following season. They failed, after a dour game which, if nothing else, epitomized the football of the early seventies and ended in its most familiar score—1-0. Leeds were in no way dispirited by the manner of their victory—it was third time lucky both for the club and for Allan Clarke, the man who scored

GIANT-KILLING BY NON-LEAGUE CLUBS 1919-1978

Victories over First Division sides

*Cardiff City	2	Oldham Athletic	0	1919-20
*Sheffield Wednesday	0	Darlington	2 (after 0-0 draw)	1919-20
†Corinthians	1	Blackburn Rovers	0	1923-24
Colchester United	1	Huddersfield Town	0	1947-48
Yeovil Town	2	Sunderland	1	1948-49
Hereford United	2	Newcastle United	1 (after 2-2 draw)	1971-72
Burnley	0	Wimbledon	1	1974-75

Victories over Second Division sides

*Coventry City	0	Luton Town	1 (after 2-2 draw)	1919-20
*Fulham	1	Swindon Town	2	1919-20
*Plymouth Argyle	4	Barnsley	1	1919-20
*Wolverhampton W	1	Cardiff City	2	1919-20
Wolverhampton W	0	Mansfield Town	1	1928-29
Chelmsford City	4	Southampton	1	1938-39
Colchester United	3	Bradford PA	2	1947-48
Yeovil Town	3	Bury	1	1948-49
†Bishop Auckland	3	Ipswich Town	1 (after 2-2 draw)	1954-55
Lincoln City	4	Peterborough United	5 (after 2-2 draw)	1956-57
Notts County	1	Rhyl	3	1956-57
Worcester City	2	Liverpool	1	1958-59
Ipswich Town	2	Peterborough United	3	1959-60
Newcastle United	1	Bedford Town	2	1963-64
Blyth Spartans	3	Stoke City	2	1977-78

Biggest victories over League sides

Carlisle United	1	Wigan Athletic	6	1934-35
†Walthamstow Avenue	6	Northampton Town	1	1936-37
Derby County	1	Boston United	6	1955-56
Hereford United	6	Queen's Park Rangers	1	1957-58
Barnet	6	Newport County	1	1970-71

Progress to last sixteen (present fifth round)

*1919-20 Cardiff City
*1919-20 Plymouth Argyle
1947-48 Colchester United
1948-49 Yeovil Town
1977-78 Blyth Spartans

*The Third Division did not come into being until 1920. In the 1919-20 season the best Southern League clubs were of a comparable standard with Second Division sides. †Amateur club.

CENTRAL PRESS

the only goal of the Final.

Having won the one that had eluded them for so long however, Leeds went to Wolverhampton just two days later needing a single point for the elusive double. But they lost 2-1.

That Centenary Final at Wembley was the end of a story which had started over seven months earlier. For it was way back in the autumn of 1971 that teams like Guinness Exports and Rawmarsh Welfare had started on the long trek to Wembley. Nowadays, there are initially 36 groups comprised of eight, nine or ten local teams which set the competition rolling.

A club like Boden Colliery Welfare, playing in the North-Eastern Geographical Division in September 1974, was faced with 15 rounds before reaching Wembley. Of course, hardly any of the clubs which start at this early stage even reach the First Round proper. Twenty-four of the best non-League sides are exempt until the Fourth (the last) Qualifying

Round, and the winners from that round go on to the First Round proper where they are joined by the Third and Fourth Division clubs and the previous season's Amateur Cup finalists.

After two rounds this number has been cut to twenty, who are joined by the 44 big boys—the First and Second Division clubs.

It is a system which obviously favours the bigger clubs. The success of Third Division clubs in the League Cup has been attributed, in part, to the fact that bigger clubs have to compete at an earlier stage than they do in the FA Cup.

Yet the thrilling Second Division successes of Sunderland in 1973 and Southampton in 1976 emphasised the democracy of the FA Cup — as did the surprise win of First Division Ipswich in 1978.

The FA Cup, however, has a place for the likes of Abergavenny Thursdays and Irthlingborough Diamonds. It started, and remains, a competition for all the clubs affiliated to

RADIO TIMES HULTON PICTURE LIBRARY

SUNDAY TELEGRAPH

FA CUP SUCCESS 1872 — 1978

	Cup Final wins	Cup Final appearances	Semi-final appearances
Aston Villa	7	9	17
Newcastle United	6	11	13
Blackburn Rovers	6	8	16
West Bromwich Albion	5	10	17
*Tottenham Hotspur	5	5	9
*Wanderers	5	5	4
Arsenal	4	9	13
Wolverhampton Wanderers	4	8	11
Manchester United	4	7	14
Bolton Wanderers	4	7	12
Manchester City	4	7	9
Sheffield United	4	6	10
Everton	3	7	16
Sheffield Wednesday	3	5	13
Preston North End	2	7	10
Old Etonians	2	6	6
Liverpool	2	5	11
West Ham United	2	2	4
Sunderland	2	3	10
*Nottingham Forest	2	2	9
*Bury	2	2	7
Huddersfield Town	1	5	2
Derby County	1	4	13
Leeds United	1	4	6
Oxford University	1	4	6
Royal Engineers	1	4	4
Chelsea	1	3	10
Burnley	1	3	8
Portsmouth	1	3	4
Blackpool	1	3	3
Southampton	1	2	8
Notts County	1	2	4
Cardiff City	1	2	3
Clapham Rovers	1	2	3
Barnsley	1	2	3
Charlton Athletic	1	2	2
*Old Carthusians	1	1	3
*Blackburn Olympic	1	1	2
*Ipswich Town	1	1	2
*Bradford City	1	1	1
Leicester City	–	4	6
Birmingham City	–	2	9
Queen's Park (Glasgow)	–	2	4
Fulham	–	1	5
Bristol City	–	1	2
Luton Town	–	1	1
Millwall	–	–	3
Stoke City	–	–	3
Swifts	–	–	3
Crystal Palace	–	–	2
Darwen	–	–	2
Grimsby Town	–	–	2
Swansea City	–	–	2
Swindon Town	–	–	2
Cambridge University	–	–	1
Crewe Alexandra	–	–	1
Derby Junction	–	–	1
Glasgow Rangers	–	–	1
Hull City	–	–	1
Marlow	–	–	1
Norwich City	–	–	1
Old Harrovians	–	–	1
Oldham Athletic	–	–	1
Port Vale	–	–	1
Reading	–	–	1
Shropshire Wanderers	–	–	1
Watford	–	–	1
York City	–	–	1

*Undefeated in Finals

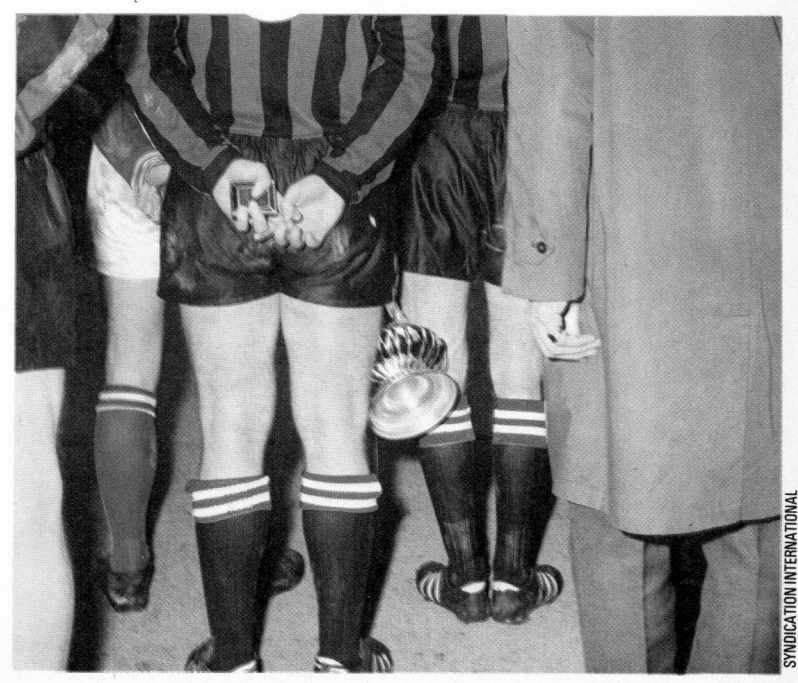

SYNDICATION INTERNATIONAL

Opposite page Geoff Barnett clears from Allan Clarke in 1972. After appearing on the losing side with Leicester in 1969 and with Leeds in 1970, it was third time lucky for Clarke in 1972 when he scored the only goal of the game and was voted 'Man of the Match', just as he was in 1969.
Above Two Welsh international goalkeepers, two sadly similar mistakes; *top* Dan Lewis fumbles Ferguson's shot in the 1927 Final and Arsenal have lost to Cardiff while *bottom* 43 years later Gary Sprake dives over the top of Houseman's speculative effort and allows Chelsea to draw level.
Right 1969, Tony Book holds the trophy, Glyn Pardoe his hard-earned medal.

the Football Association—and it is a place they guard manfully.

Really it is a competition—and most certainly a Final—for the fan. It is the fan who pays £30 for black market tickets, who turns mortals into immortals simply because they scored a goal, who talks about it, dreams about it and relives it for months, who would not give away a Final ticket for a fortune, because the most valuable thing a fortune can buy is a Cup Final ticket.

Danny Blanchflower puts it the players' way: 'In truth we are brainwashed about the Cup Final. A player hears so much about it before

he gets there ... the "majestic" twin towers ... the "hallowed" green turf ... the "royal" greeting ... the crowd singing "Abide With Me" ... It all sounds like some distant religious ceremony that takes place at the end of the season in the promised land. The reality of it can never live up to the dream. The dream is not for the player, it is for the fan ... the lover of the game who doesn't really know what it is like out there and never *will* know. It is the fan's day, which is why some 400 million of them all over the world tune in on Cup Final day. But long may it prosper.'

The League Championship

Below left Peter Shilton of Nottingham Forest making a vital save in the match against Coventry City that decided the 1977/78 League Championship. Although Nottingham has the two oldest clubs in the League this was the first time the Championship had been won by either. By 11 November 1978, Forest had also established four new records — 38 first class games without defeat, 40 League games without defeat, 21 away League games without defeat and 19 consecutive first-class away matches without defeat. Their incredible run finally came to an end at Liverpool on 9 December 1978 with a 2-0 League defeat. **Opposite** Archie Gemmill fending off Coventry's Mick Coop.

On 7 October 1978 Nottingham Forest established a new record of 35 League games without defeat by beating Wolves 3-1. Their last League defeat had been on 19 November 1977 at Leeds, the supplanted record holders. A month later, on 4 November 1978, their goalless draw with Everton established another record – that of 36 consecutive first-class competitive games without defeat. The beaten record, held by Blackburn Rovers, had been established all of 96 years previously, in 1881-82. Since that defeat by Leeds, Forest had played 59 first class games (6 FA Cup, 9 League Cup, 4 European Cup, the FA Charity Shield and 39 First Division) and had been beaten just once (on 11 March 1978) by West Bromwich Albion in an FA Cup quarter-final. Their next game, a 3-2 victory at Everton in the League Cup on 7 November 1978, was also their 18th consecutive *away* first-class game (excluding matches on neutral grounds such as Wembley) without defeat – also a record. The following Saturday, their 3-1 win at Tottenham was their 21st consecutive away League game without defeat – and another record.

Yet, it is not what you do, but what your contemporaries do that brings the difference between success and failure. Hence Leeds could win the 1969 League Championship by scoring 66 times, while forty or so years before, Manchester City mustered 23 goals more and were relegated!

The Yorkshiremen's 66 goal tally—one less than the record 67 points they amassed—was perfectly respectable in a climate of defensive football. City's 1926 total of 89, however, was not—unfortunately for them—as extraordinary then as it would have been forty years on.

For those years saw a decline and fall of positive attacking football. Preventing goals is easier than scoring them, and the 'smash-and-grab' type of football, with goals on the quick break out of defence as introduced by Herbert Chapman during his reign at Arsenal, rapidly became the favoured tactic.

That style of play was perhaps best seen at its peak when the Gunners themselves played against Aston Villa in 1935. Territorially outplayed, Arsenal were restricted to just nine shots at goal, eight of them from their England centre-forward, Ted Drake. The score? Aston Villa 1 Arsenal 7. Drake scored all seven Arsenal goals and struck the crossbar with his eighth shot.

In the early days of the League, Sunderland, for example, won the 1893 title with 100 goals—and 48 points—from just 30 matches. But defences quickly became more sophisticated and the offside trap, brought to a fine art by Bill McCracken of Newcastle in the middle twenties, showed itself as early as 1909. In that year, Newcastle won the title with only 65 goals.

It is interesting to speculate what might have happened if the Football League's original intention to award points only for wins had been carried through. The mind boggles at the goals there might have been had a drawn game remained valueless in terms of points! However, it was not to be, for after 10 weeks of the first season it was decided that drawn games should be worth a point to each side.

At the end of the first season, Preston North End were champions. That inaugural season,

1888-89, when Preston also won the FA Cup without conceding a goal, their League record was so outstanding that it remains an imperishable landmark in soccer history.

In their 22 League matches, they won 18 times and drew four, scoring 74 goals against 15. They are the only British club ever to have gone through a season without a defeat in either League or Cup.

Preston were champions again in the League's second season, though they were beaten four times. In 1890-91, however, they finished second. It was Everton who took the title away from them, and who were to become the most consistent League club, spending all but five of the next 74 seasons in the top division. The record for unbroken membership belongs to Sunderland who, up to their relegation in 1958, had been 57 consecutive seasons in the top bracket.

The League Championship —the preserve of the North and the Midlands

Considering that the North East has produced only three major clubs, Sunderland, Newcastle and Middlesbrough, the area has done well in terms of First Division membership—at least one of the three was there until 1962—especially as none of those was an original League member.

There were twelve of those: Wolves, Everton, Preston, Burnley, Derby, Notts County, Blackburn Rovers, Bolton, Stoke, Accrington, Aston Villa and West Bromwich Albion. The North East was not the only region with no representative in the first League. Not one of that dozen came from London or the South.

By 1976-77 the story was a different one. London had four clubs in the First Division, the Midlands was seven-strong, while Lancashire, a comparative shadow of its former greatness, had only four—two Manchester clubs and the Merseyside pair. Leeds represented Yorkshire and Newcastle, Middlesbrough and Sunderland the North East.

The three remaining clubs—Ipswich, Norwich and Bristol City—came, needless to say, from elsewhere. But that fact is important. Very few First Division teams have come from elsewhere. In the League's first 74 seasons, just nine clubs

have been situated outside the traditional areas of football power—London, the Midlands, Lancashire, Yorkshire and the North East—areas which contain some 80% of the country's population.

They are Grimsby (who joined Division One in 1901), Bristol City (1906), Cardiff (1921), Portsmouth (1927), Luton (1955), Ipswich (1961), Southampton (1966), Norwich (1972) and Carlisle (1974). No more than three have ever been in the First Division at the same time.

But if that signifies any shift in the balance of power, it has been so slight as to be negligible. After all, apart from Portsmouth in 1949 and 1950, and Alf Ramsey's Ipswich in 1962, the Championship has never left the pockets of soccer strength.

This is not because the industrial areas produce the best players, but because they provide more spectators. Crowds paying money at the gate means money to spend on new players. It is a harsh fact of football life that the clubs with the best support tend to get the best players. There are exceptions—of which Aston Villa must be the prime example.

It was different in 1888 when the League started. Professionalism had been legal for only three years; money was not yet all important. Then, the best players came from those parts of the country where there were most young men. And with Lancashire and the Midlands centres of heavy industry, they were able to attract young men from Scotland, Ireland and Wales, where jobs were few. Many a skilful footballer emerged from kickabouts with his workmates.

But as industry began to spread, so did the quality and scope of the game. It is no coincidence that the first team from the South to join the League was a works team—Woolwich Arsenal. The Boer War had made a munitions factory on the banks of the Thames important to the country's war effort. More was to come from that factory than shells.

Not that Arsenal were the first 'outside' club to penetrate the monopoly of the Midlands and Lancashire. Arsenal did not really emerge until 1904, when the League was 16 years old.

The first 'newcomers' were Sunderland, in 1890, who won the Championship in 1891 and 1892, when Sheffield's Wednesday joined the First Division, a year ahead of the other Sheffield club, United.

The arrival of these three was no surprise. Sunderland had a fine team drawn from a mixture of local Northerners and Scotsmen who had been tempted over the border, while Sheffield was one of the first towns in which organized football was played. Indeed, the Sheffield amateur club, formed in 1857, is the oldest in the world.

Sunderland had been champions six times when they were relegated in 1958, which, when added to Newcastle's four, gives the North East an impressive record considering its population. Lancashire, of course, boasting the Liverpool and Manchester clubs in addition to earlier giants of the League such as Blackburn, Preston and Burnley, have easily the best record with 30 of the first 75 Championships.

There have been few discernable patterns with regard to the winning of the League, except perhaps for the years 1963-1970. Then the title seemed to be the preserve of the North. Champions in those years were Everton, Liverpool, Manchester United, Liverpool, United again, Manchester City, Leeds and Everton. Eight Cham-

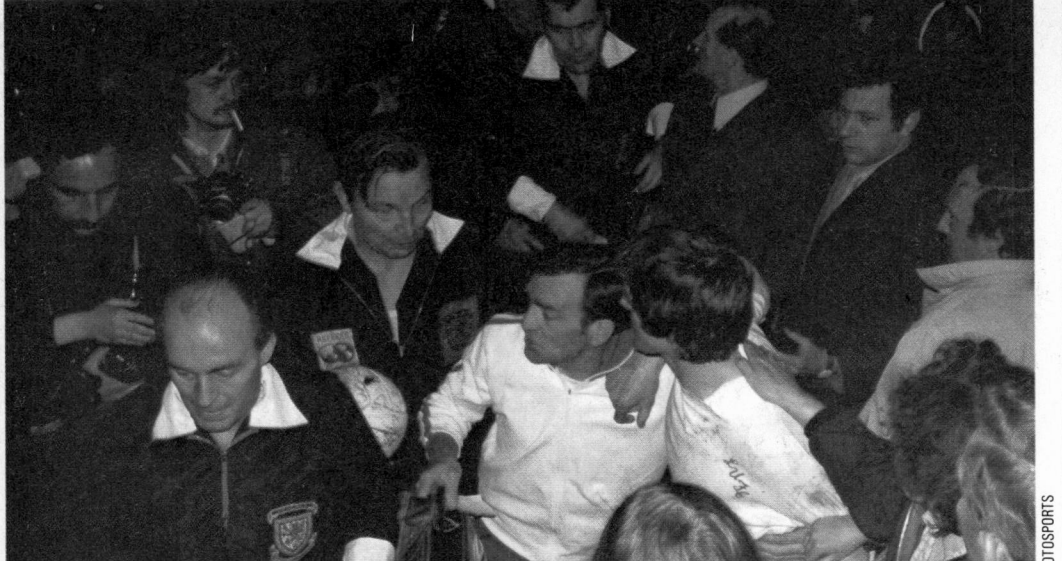

FOTOSPORTS

Above *Despair after Leeds had failed to beat Wolves in their last game of the 1971-72 season and had thus been relegated to the runners-up spot for the third consecutive year and the fifth time in eight seasons. The frustration of having failed to gain the single point necessary to become only the fifth ever double-winners is clear in **bottom** the faces of Billy Bremner and Terry Yorath and **top** in Les Cocker's need to restrain Allan Clarke from discussions with referee Bill Gow. **Opposite** Ex-Liverpool star, Kevin Keegan.*

LEAGUE CHAMPIONSHIP

	Winners	Runners-up
1888-89	Preston North End	Aston Villa
1889-90	Preston North End	Everton
1890-91	Everton	Preston North End
1891-92	Sunderland	Preston North End
1892-93	Sunderland	Preston North End
1893-94	Aston Villa	Sunderland
1894-95	Sunderland	Everton
1895-96	Aston Villa	Derby County
1896-97	Aston Villa	Sheffield United
1897-98	Sheffield United	Sunderland
1898-99	Aston Villa	Liverpool
1899-1900	Aston Villa	Sheffield United
1900-01	Liverpool	Sunderland
1901-02	Sunderland	Everton
1902-03	The Wednesday	Aston Villa
1903-04	The Wednesday	Manchester City
1904-05	Newcastle United	Everton
1905-06	Liverpool	Preston North End
1906-07	Newcastle United	Bristol City
1907-08	Manchester United	Aston Villa
1908-09	Newcastle United	Everton
1909-10	Aston Villa	Liverpool
1910-11	Manchester United	Aston Villa
1911-12	Blackburn Rovers	Everton
1912-13	Sunderland	Aston Villa
1913-14	Blackburn Rovers	Aston Villa
1914-15	Everton	Oldham Athletic
1915-19	No competition	
1919-20	West Bromwich Albion	Burnley
1920-21	Burnley	Manchester City
1921-22	Liverpool	Tottenham Hotspur
1922-23	Liverpool	Sunderland
1923-24	**Huddersfield Town	Cardiff City
1924-25	Huddersfield Town	West Bromwich Albion
1925-26	Huddersfield Town	Arsenal
1926-27	Newcastle United	Huddersfield Town
1927-28	Everton	Huddersfield Town
1928-29	Sheffield Wednesday	Leicester City
1829-30	Sheffield Wednesday	Derby County
1930-31	Arsenal	Aston Villa
1931-32	Everton	Arsenal
1932-33	Arsenal	Aston Villa
1933-34	Arsenal	Huddersfield Town
1934-35	Arsenal	Sunderland
1935-36	Sunderland	Derby County
1936-37	Manchester City	Charlton Athletic
1937-38	Arsenal	Wolverhampton Wanderers
1938-39	Everton	Wolverhampton Wanderers
1939-46	No competition	
1946-47	Liverpool	Manchester United
1947-48	Arsenal	Manchester United
1948-49	Portsmouth	Manchester United
1949-50	**Portsmouth	Wolverhampton Wanderers
1950-51	Tottenham Hotspur	Manchester United
1951-52	Manchester United	Tottenham Hotspur
1952-53	**Arsenal	Preston North End
1953-54	Wolverhampton Wanderers	West Bromwich Albion
1954-55	Chelsea	Wolverhampton Wanderers
1955-56	Manchester United	Blackpool
1956-57	Manchester United	Tottenham Hotspur
1957-58	Wolverhampton Wanderers	Preston North End
1958-59	Wolverhampton Wanderers	Manchester United
1959-60	Burnley	Wolverhampton Wanderers
1960-61	Tottenham Hotspur	Sheffield Wednesday
1961-62	Ipswich Town	Burnley
1962-63	Everton	Tottenham Hotspur
1963-64	Liverpool	Manchester United
1964-65	**Manchester United	Leeds United
1965-66	Liverpool	Leeds United
1966-67	Manchester United	Nottingham Forest
1967-68	Manchester City	Manchester United
1968-69	Leeds United	Liverpool
1969-70	Everton	Leeds United
1970-71	Arsenal	Leeds United
1971-72	Derby County	Leeds United
1972-73	Liverpool	Arsenal
1973-74	Leeds United	Liverpool
1974-75	Derby County	Liverpool
1975-76	Liverpool	Queen's Park Rangers
1976-77	Liverpool	Manchester City
1977-78	Nottingham Forest	Liverpool

**League title won on goal average

FOTOSPORTS

pionships, and seven of them won by Lancashire's two major cities.

Leeds' 1968-69 success was their first. Yorkshire neighbours Huddersfield, however, collected three in consecutive seasons during the twenties, under the guidance of the famous Herbert Chapman, later to build the Arsenal team that became the only club to emulate Huddersfield's feat.

Huddersfield's first Championship they won dramatically. For at the end of the 1923-24 season Cardiff City also had 57 points, and the two clubs' goal averages were remarkably similar. Huddersfield had scored 60 goals against 33, Cardiff 61 against 34. That in fact gave Huddersfield a microscopic advantage.

Cardiff—a penalty away from the title in 1924, re-election in 1934

And that was tragic for Cardiff. For in their last game of the season, the Welshmen had been awarded a penalty in the last minute at Birmingham. No one wanted to take it, but eventually Len Davies stepped up. He missed it, the game ended in a goalless draw and Huddersfield were champions.

If Huddersfield's climb to the top had been dramatic, Cardiff's rise—and their subsequent decline—was even more spectacular. Admitted to the Second Division in 1920, they won promotion

in their first season. Curiously, they were then only a 200th part of a goal behind Birmingham in first place.

Within seven years, Cardiff had been Championship runners-up, beaten FA Cup Finalists, and Cup winners in 1927. Within another seven, they were seeking re-election after finishing bottom of the Third Division South.

That same season, 1933-34, Huddersfield scored more goals than any of their First Division rivals. Perhaps that was some atonement for their poor tally that had deprived Cardiff of what would have been their first and only Championship success. For those 60 goals Huddersfield scored in 1923-24 comprised the lowest aggregate since the War.

The War seemed momentarily to have arrested the trend of fewer and fewer goals, and even the advent of the 'policeman' centre-half, the result of the offside law change in 1925 and exemplified by Arsenal's Herbie Roberts, could do little to stop the surge in goalscoring. In 1931, when the Championship was Arsenal's, they scored 127 goals, while Aston Villa, runners-up that season, themselves scored a record 128.

After the Second World War, football boomed but goals like everything else were in short supply. That was until the great young Manchester United side of the mid-fifties. In 1957, just before the Munich disaster, they scored 103 goals, as did Wolves the next year. In 1959, Wolves surpassed

themselves with 110.

But with the Spurs team that won the double in 1960-61 came one of the last centuries before the massed defences took over. Though Tottenham scored a conspicuous 111 goals in 1962-63, Everton's 84 gave them six more points and thus the title. No club has scored 100 First Division goals since that year.

The fall-off in goalscoring can be clearly seen at the other end of the table. While Spurs won the double, Newcastle went down with 86 goals to their credit. Compared with the miserable 27 Huddersfield scraped together when they were relegated just over a decade later, Newcastle might well curse their misfortune.

Relegated—with a better defensive record than the champions . . .

So too might Cardiff have done in the middle of that chequered spell which took them zooming up and down the League like a car on the big dipper. For back in 1928-29, Wednesday, the champions, conceded 62 goals, Cardiff let in a mere 59, the lowest in the division, and were sent down to Division Two. A little harsh, maybe, but Cardiff's fate bears witness to the fact that no matter how a team's statistics stand in isolation, that is not how the final placings are decided.

The League Cup

'It's a joke. It can never get off the ground. Within three years it'll be scrapped.' That was the reaction of one First Division manager to the news that the move for a Football League Cup had been given official approval.

The millions who saw the passion, excitement and urgency generated by Stoke and West Ham in the four-match semi-final of 1972, or saw the expressions on the faces of the Stoke and Chelsea players as they climbed the Wembley steps a few weeks later, would find it difficult to believe that remark had been made only 12 years before.

'The League Cup has become one of the highlights of the domestic soccer calendar,' asserts Football League secretary Alan Hardaker, who initiated the idea. And the statistics back him up.

Yet for some time it appeared that the pessimists were the realists. The Cup, voted in at the annual meeting of the League in 1960 by a majority of only 15, was a very sickly infant, and the reception it received in some quarters was, to put it kindly, luke-warm. British managers, players and crowds were just beginning to adjust to the thought of European competition and here was another tournament, created to help the smaller sides and not particularly lucrative, to clog up the fixture list still further. It was not right to expect footballers to play 60 times a season.

Five clubs, including those who had finished second, third, fourth and fifth in the First Division the previous season, refused to enter, thus devaluing the competition before it had even started. The following year the number of absentees swelled to 10, including seven of the top ten.

The early, two-legged finals were hardly affairs to shake the football world and in 1962, when it was played out between a Second and a Fourth Division side, the two games pulled in barely 30,000 spectators. So, as the big clubs continued to view it with contempt and the smaller ones entered almost as a matter of form, as the press and the public looked on with detachment, the League Cup went stuttering on.

Hardaker remained the most ardent of its few committed supporters. He had always been obsessed with what was essentially his idea though, as he points out, he could not and did not implement it. 'It's been called Hardaker's baby and even Hardaker's folly,' he explains, 'but I did not take the decision to introduce it. Like everything else done by the League it was a matter for the clubs to vote on.'

Hardaker's early optimism was based on comparisons with the com-petition's much older sister, the FA Cup. 'Every worthwhile development in football has faced initial prob-lems and criticism, and the League Cup was no exception. The early history of the FA Cup shows that it too had to face a variety of problems for several years, not least lack of interest. It was strongly criticised on its inception because it introduced a competitive element into amateur football, namely the winning of a trophy. There were 15 entries. After ten seasons there were 73.'

But the FA Cup was the first national competition. It was the natural result of the enthusiasm and aspirations of an emerging sport. The League Cup, by contrast, was any-thing but; money was its motivating force. It had to be created, and then it took several severe changes—with more commercial carrots being dangled—to drag it from a strug-gling child into a promising adoles-cent. They came in 1966.

The previous season the eight absent clubs had included seven from the top eight in the First Divi-sion—among them League Cham-pions Manchester United, FA Cup holders Liverpool and, most indica-tive of all, Chelsea, the holders of the League Cup itself. Tommy Docherty apparently thought the Fairs Cup a good deal more important. Attend-ances, though slightly improved, remained mediocre.

A new League Cup —with Wembley and European entry

There were two major changes. First, the awkward home and away final was abolished in favour of a more romantic (and lucrative) Satur-day climax at Wembley. Second, the Fairs Cup committee decided to accept the winners as entrants for its competition the following year—provided they were a First Division side. (Though an obvious incentive this move never actually promoted an entrant: in 1967 and 1969 the winners, Queen's Park Rangers and Swindon, were both Third Division sides, in 1968 Leeds—who were to win the Fairs Cup later that season —qualified by coming fourth in the League, and in 1970 Manchester City went on to win the Cup Winners' Cup, thus defending that trophy the following year. Spurs, in 1971, were the first club able to take up the offer, and by then the actual Fairs Cup was no more.)

The changes completely revital-ized a flagging League Cup. All but League Champions Liverpool and Cup winners Everton now entered, and the converts included four sides who had remained aloof from the start—Arsenal, Sheffield Wednes-day, Spurs and Wolves. Perhaps there was a certain justice in the fact that all four of them went out to sides of lesser standing in the League, and not one of them reached the last 16—that is, won more than one game.

In fact West Ham, who had seen something in the League Cup from the start, were responsible for the elimination of the two North London sides who had just joined the fold. They then beat Leeds (7-0) and Blackpool but were stopped short of Wembley by WBA—in a repeat of the previous year's two-legged final —after crashing 4-0 at The Haw-thorns.

Albion's opponents were QPR, then running away with the Third

Top Ron Harris, David Webb, Alan Hudson, John Dempsey and Paddy Mulligan can only stand and watch as Terry Conroy heads Stoke in front in the 1972 League Cup final.
Above Jimmy Greenhoff and friends after Conroy's goal. It was Stoke's twelfth game of the competition and their very first success in a major com-petition—after a 109 year history.
Top right Arsenal's Bobby Gould (10) equalizes in 1969 against Swin-don. But Don Rogers scored twice in extra-time and Third Division Swin-don, like QPR in 1967, had beaten First Division opposition in the final.
Right Football League secretary Alan Hardaker, the most ardent advocate of the competition. But it took six years, a Wembley final and a place in Europe before it succeeded.

Division championship. Rangers had started as they meant to go on with a 5-0 win over Colchester, but they had only one game against a First Division club on the way, beating Leicester 4-2. The match at Wembley, in danger of being a one-sided anti-climax, proved to be the opposite. Lowly QPR, down two goals by an ex-player of their's, Clive Clark, were faced with an apparently impossible task against a club separated from them by about 30 places in the League. But they did do it, with goals from Roger Morgan, Rodney Marsh (a splendid effort that, with the help of television, made him a household name by the Monday morning) and Mark Lazarus.

Had the League Cup come of age? From some quarters came an honest conversion, from others came grudging acknowledgement. Cynics pointed out the fact that no Third Division club had reached the FA Cup Final in the 47 years that section had been in existence, let alone won it, and said that the big sides were still loath to take it at all seriously. But 98,000 at Wembley and millions more in their armchairs thought differently.

The moves had apparently done the trick. Though some clubs committed in Europe continued to opt out—notably Manchester United—the competition grew in stature over the next few years and the average attendance (all for midweek games except the final) soared from just over 11,000 in 1965-66 to over 19,000 in 1971-72.

In 1968 Leeds at last won a domestic honour, with a laboured 1-0 victory over a re-emerging Arsenal on a dreadful Wembley pitch. The following year Arsenal were back (this time on an even worse Wembley surface, thanks to the Horse of the Year Show) to face Swindon, who had played 11 matches to reach the final.

Swindon were trying to repeat Queen's Park Rangers' double of

League Cup and promotion to the Second Division, and they succeeded. Brilliant goalkeeping from Peter Downsborough and two goals from Don Rogers helped them to a 3-1 win, though the effects of a recent 'flu epidemic at Highbury took its toll of the Arsenal players during extra time. Nine of the Arsenal squad appeared in both 1968 and 1969, among them Frank McLintock, who thus finished on the losing side at Wembley for the fourth time.

Extra time was again required in 1970, this time for Manchester City's 2-1 win over West Bromwich Albion. The tie of the competition, however, was the semi-final between the Manchester giants. City—promoted in 1966, League Champions in 1968, FA Cup winners in 1969, and now on their way to a European triumph—had been severely challenging the supremacy of a Manchester United side desperately trying to maintain the status achieved by the European Cup win over Benfica at Wembley in 1968, and a side competing in the League Cup for the first time since 1960-61.

For the first time, perhaps, a League Cup match apart from the final took on a significance outside the competition. The edited versions of both games were televised, and millions saw City confirm their suspicions with a 2-1 win at Maine Road and a 2-2 draw at Old Trafford, the second leg being played in front of 63,418—a record for the League Cup away from Wembley. 'Perhaps now they'll bloody well believe us,' said City wing-half Mick Doyle after the tie. The final, a dull, grinding affair, was a disappointment.

For those who thought the age of the lower clubs was over in the League Cup the 1970-71 competition was something of a revelation. Aston Villa, like QPR and Swindon chasing escape from the Third Division, reached Wembley. They were fortunate in meeting only one

First Division side in their first five ties—a struggling Burnley in the second round—but when they did meet opponents of renown and calibre in Manchester United they proved nothing was missing. First they secured a 1-1 draw at Old Trafford and then, in front of 62,500, beat United 2-1 at Villa Park. But Wembley, Tottenham and Martin Chivers proved to be more difficult. Villa held Spurs for 80 minutes, but then two goals from the England man kept the League Cup firmly in the First Division.

There it was to stay in 1972, when Stoke beat Chelsea at Wembley in the final of what had been the first competition it had been compulsory for all 92 clubs to enter—a rather late and empty gesture at the 1971 annual general meeting. But, like the previous two seasons, it was the semi-final stage that stole the headlines.

The semi-final story dominated by penalty kicks

While Chelsea and Spurs were battling out their tie, West Ham were trying to make the final an all-London affair by beating Stoke. They got off to a good start with a 2-1 win at the Victoria Ground, but John Ritchie pulled a goal back at Upton Park in the return and, in the dying minutes of extra time Gordon Banks (who had been beaten by a Geoff Hurst penalty in the first leg) made a brilliant save to stop his England colleague repeating the feat. A fine replay at Hillsborough produced no goals, and then in the second replay at Old Trafford there was the strange sight of Bobby Moore donning the goalkeeper's jersey while the injured Ferguson was off the field.

Stoke beat him once, with Bernard following up a penalty kick Moore had managed to save first time; then, with Ferguson restored,

Above *West Brom's Jeff Astle after scoring against Manchester City in the 1970 final. His joy was short-lived: City won 2-1 in extra-time*

Top right *Tempers fray during the 1969 final, won by Leeds United (in white), lost by Arsenal.*

Bottom right *Leeds' Gary Sprake and goalscorer Terry Cooper with the Cup after their defeat of Arsenal.*

West Ham took the lead through Bonds and Brooking; Dobing pulled Stoke level before half-time and, as the two sides approached seven hours of battle, Conroy scored the winner.

The final didn't stand a chance. Three of the Stoke-West Ham clashes and both Chelsea-Spurs games had been covered by television and, though the pre-match publicity was as great as for any FA Cup Final, the match was almost inevitably a come-down. Stoke, by no means standing on ceremony or overawed by Wembley, absorbed all Chelsea's subtle pressure and took their chances well to win 2-1. After 12 matches in the tournament that year they deserved some reward.

Following on the heels of Stoke's belated success, Norwich City reached the 1973 final (their first Wembley appearance) despite not having won any of their previous 12 League matches. After the final it was to be another 8 before they recorded a success. Just ten days before Wembley they had sold their star forward Jim Bone, and their resulting contest with Spurs produced a dreadful match.

The only romance came from Ralph Coates who scored the game's only goal after coming on a substitute.

That final began a remarkable hat-trick for Ron Saunders, then the manager of Norwich. Twelve months later he led out Manchester City, his new club, to meet Wolverhampton Wanderers in the 1974 Final. Again he was loser. Yet remarkably 1975 saw Saunders in charge of a third League Cup finalist, Second Division Aston Villa—and this time he was a winner, ironically over Norwich City.

When even Second Division Liverpool stayed out

It was ironic that the League Cup should gain in popularity just as the fixture list was becoming congested, with an increasing number of clubs entering Europe and the emergence of peripheral competitions: the Watney Cup, the Texaco Cup and the Anglo-Italian Tournament.

It may be that the League Cup provided the incentive; that officials and administrators saw the financial rewards to be reaped from competitive matches outside the two established folds. Certainly for a club stuck in the middle of the Third or Fourth Division and eliminated from the first round of the FA Cup in November, a run to the last eight or four can provide the only financial and psychological release during a mundane season.

No exercise can have started so

badly as the League Cup. As Walter Pilkington, one of its most ardent advocates, was to put it later: 'It arrived as an apparent weakling, unwanted and shunned by the rich relations, regarded as an unnecessary affliction, derided by critics who gave it little or no chance of survival.'

It had not even been really intended. The idea was gently mooted in the 'Pattern of Football', published in 1957 by the Football League, with the main proposal being five divisions of 20 clubs. That, pointed out the smaller 'big' clubs who could not afford to lose a single fixture—Preston, Bolton, and the rest—would mean losing four valuable matches. The League Cup then gained favour as a compensation but, somewhere along the line, while that idea was accepted, the restructuring of the League went by the board.

The early tournaments did little or nothing to undermine the conviction that it would die an early death. The first season, for instance, the figures were arranged by mutual agreement of the clubs concerned— an arrangement that proved so cumbersome that the competition dragged on, in front of meagre crowds, for 11 long months, with the final being resolved in the September of 1961. The lowest attendance was 1,737 for a first round tie between Lincoln City and Bradford Park Avenue—a dismal record that stood until 1974. The 20% pool produced £29,982, or £354 for each competing club.

There were, however, more

memorable events: such as Bradford City's 2-1 defeat of Manchester United, Chelsea's 18 goals in three games (including seven against both Millwall and Doncaster), and Gerry Hitchens' 11 goals for Villa before he joined Inter-Milan.

The second season, with the number of absentees doubling—Bill Shankly even kept his Second Division Liverpool out, and they won the title—the result was almost total apathy. The final was an irrelevant affair between Second Division Norwich and Fourth Division Rochdale. This was the only season when all the competing First Division clubs (bar Leicester, who won a bye) competed from the first round.

The fixture pile-up —is it the League Cup's fault?

In the third season the First Division, though still represented by only twelve clubs, at last asserted its authority, Birmingham City beating Villa in the final. The top section retained their monopoly on finalists until 1967, despite the fact that their maximum presence in any year was only 14. Ironically in 1966-67, when all but Liverpool and Everton entered, the League Cup went to a Third Division side.

The competitions up till then were unlikely to have provided standard items for the serious reminiscences of football journalists. Goalscoring, perhaps, was the one thing that caught the eye: Tony

Hateley's 10 in six games for Villa in 1964-65; West Ham's 25 in eight games on the way to the 1966 final, including two fives against Cardiff in the semi-final and 11 of them to Hurst; WBA's 28 in nine games the same season, with 11 to Tony Brown; Orient's 9-2 win over Chester in 1962-63; Workington's 9-1 victory over neighbours Barrow in 1964-65; and Leicester's 8-1 triumph against Coventry the same year.

The rise in popularity of the League Cup after 1966 cannot be put down solely to the introduction of a Wembley final and a promise of a place in Europe. For one thing there was a general stimulation of interest in the game after the World Cup; television coverage was becoming more and more frequent and the League Cup, with its important rounds being played between October and March, plugged the midweek gaps left by a lack of FA Cup replays and European games; and the League Cup proved it produced goals, averaging 3.49 a game up to 1967 and keeping above three for the rest of the decade—well over the figures for the League and the FA Cup. As it rose in popularity the little clubs benefited: the share-out from the 20% pool was £327 for every participating club in 1963-64, but by 1972 it was over £2,000.

The League Cup was bound to cause controversy. It upset a domestic balance that had been carefully evolved and constructed over 72 years. But the eventual success paved the way for other tournaments—though none of them had its logic of

a cup for the League clubs.

The first was the Watney Cup, the first sponsored competition in the British game. Introduced in 1970 and played out in the ten days before the start of the League programme, it received a warm welcome—if only because the invited clubs were the two highest-scoring sides from each division the previous season. Derby won the first, Colchester the second, beating WBA at The Hawthorns in the final.

Though only 19,000 saw that game and the average attendance was 12,000 the competing clubs did well financially: Third Division Halifax, who beat Manchester United before losing to Albion, pulled £7,700 and substantial television fees for their two games, including £4,000 from the sponsors. While they didn't exactly get drunk for weeks, it was a more than fair return after 25% of the net receipts had gone to the county associations of the competing clubs and 10% to the FA fund for the development of youth football.

Following a few weeks behind beer came petrol—in the form of the Texaco Cup. A much bigger and bolder concept—involving the six English First Division sides, six Scottish First Division sides, and two top sides from both Northern Ireland and Eire—its most common criticism was that it was the sides not quite qualifying for Europe, the also-rans, who were the 'attractions'. There was no logic in having second-best clubs playing out a British club championship.

As the economic climate discouraged sponsors from emptying their coffers into peripheral football competitions, the Football League added another tournament in 1975—the Anglo-Scottish competition between selected League clubs from north and south of the border. It was a move greeted with disparaging sounds very similar to those which had met the outset of the League Cup fifteen years earlier.

Yet all the while 'Hardaker's baby' continued to progress, even though the finals rarely produced matches where skill overcame the electric atmosphere of a Wembley occasion. Perhaps the football public were conditioned by similar failings in most FA Cup Finals.

In 1974 Third Division Plymouth Argyle provided the spice by reaching the semi-finals of a competition that kept its interest even though the energy crisis restricted many kick-offs to midweek afternoons. Argyle finally fell to Manchester City after they had achieved sensational wins on the grounds of Burnley, QPR and Birmingham.

City's opponents were Wolverhampton Wanderers in their first Wembley appearance for 14 years. It proved a happy return for the Black Country club largely thanks to an afternoon of inspired goalkeeping by reserve Gary Pierce, on his 23rd birthday. City's flair from Summerbee, Bell, Lee, Law and Marsh wore a transparent look.

Though Bell equalised Wolves' first half goal from a mis-cued shot by Hibbitt, Wolves became League

Main picture Ian Bowyer scores for City in the second leg of the 1970 all-Manchester semi-final.
Inset left The days when the final was not held at Wembley: Bobby Tambling puts Chelsea in front in 1965.
Inset right The Stoke-West Ham semi-final in 1972 had everything, including Mick Bernard's goal after Bobby Moore had saved his penalty.

Cup winners when Richards scored nine minutes from time.

The competition emphasised its democracy in 1975, even if it produced another tedious final. Not one of the semi-finalists came from the First Division—the main giant-toppers being Chester of the Fourth. Manchester United, Aston Villa and Norwich City—the three clubs to be promoted from Division Two—were the other clubs in the last four with Villa and Norwich reaching Wembley. The game seemed destined for a goalless draw until Graydon missed a penalty in the 80th minute but scored from the rebound.

In 1977 and 1978 both Wembley finals produced goalless draws which were eventually resolved at Old Trafford. Aston Villa beat Everton in the second replay of the 1977 final to win the Cup for a record third time and in 1978 Nottingham Forest achieved a remarkable win over Liverpool — who they were to depose in the first round of the 1978/79 European Cup. With teams such as these involved, no one could doubt that the League Cup had come of age.

FOOTBALL LEAGUE CUP FINALS

1960-61 ASTON VILLA
First leg: *Rotherham 22 August 1961 Attendance 12,226*
Rotherham United 2 **Aston Villa** 0
Webster, Kirkman
Second leg: *Villa Park 5 September 1961 Attendance 27,000*
Aston Villa 3 **Rotherham United** 0
O'Neill, Burrows, McParland

1961-62 NORWICH CITY
First leg: *Rochdale 26 April 1962 Attendance 11,123*
Rochdale 0 **Norwich City** 3
Lythgoe 2, Punton
Second leg: *Norwich 1 May 1962 Attendance 19,708*
Norwich City 1 **Rochdale** 0
Hill

1962-63 BIRMINGHAM CITY
First leg: *St Andrew's 23 May 1963 Attendance 31,850*
Birmingham City 3 **Aston Villa** 1
Leek 2, Bloomfield Thomson
Second leg: *Villa Park 27 May 1963 Attendance 37,921*
Aston Villa 0 **Birmingham City** 0

1963-64 LEICESTER CITY
First leg: *Stoke 15 April 1964 Attendance 22,309*
Stoke City 1 **Leicester City** 1
Bebbington Gibson
Second leg: *Leicester 22 April 1964 Attendance 25,372*
Leicester City 3 **Stoke City** 2
Stringfellow, Gibson, Riley Viollet, Kinnell

1964-65 CHELSEA
First leg: *Stamford Bridge 15 March 1965 Attendance 20,690*
Chelsea 3 **Leicester City** 2
Tambling, Venables (pen), Appleton, Goodfellow
McCreadie
Second leg: *Leicester 5 April 1965 Attendance 26,957*
Leicester City 0 **Chelsea** 0

1965-66 WEST BROMWICH ALBION
First leg: *Upton Park 9 March 1966 Attendance 28,341*
West Ham United 2 **West Bromwich Albion** 1
Moore, Byrne Astle
Second leg: *The Hawthorns 23 March 1966 Attendance 31,925*
West Bromwich Albion 4 **West Ham United** 1
Kaye, Brown, Clark, Williams Peters

1966-67 QUEEN'S PARK RANGERS
Final: *Wembley 4 March 1967 Attendance 97,952*
Queen's Park Rangers 3 **West Bromwich Albion** 2
Morgan (R), Marsh, Lazarus Clark 2

1967-68 LEEDS UNITED
Final: *Wembley 2 March 1968 Attendance 97,887*
Leeds United 1 **Arsenal** 0
Cooper

1968-69 SWINDON TOWN
Final: *Wembley 15 March 1969 Attendance 98,189*
Swindon Town 3 **Arsenal** 1
Smart, Rogers 2 Gould

1969-70 MANCHESTER CITY
Final: *Wembley 7 March 1970 Attendance 97,963*
Manchester City 2 **West Bromwich Albion** 1
Doyle, Pardoe Astle

1970-71 TOTTENHAM HOTSPUR
Final: *Wembley 27 February 1971 Attendance 98,096*
Tottenham Hotspur 2 **Aston Villa** 0
Chivers 2

1971-72 STOKE CITY
Final: *Wembley 4 March 1972 Attendance 99,998*
Stoke City 2 **Chelsea** 1
Conroy, Eastham Osgood

1972-73 TOTTENHAM HOTSPUR
Final: *Wembley 3 March 1973 Attendance 100,000*
Tottenham Hotspur 1 **Norwich City** 0
Coates

1973-74 WOLVERHAMPTON WANDERERS
Final: *Wembley 2 March 1974 Attendance 100,000*
Wolverhampton W. 2 **Manchester City** 1
Hibbitt, Richards Bell

1974-75 ASTON VILLA
Final: *Wembley 1 March 1975 Attendance 100,000*
Aston Villa 1 **Norwich City** 0
Graydon

1975-76 MANCHESTER CITY
Final: *Wembley 28 February 1976 Attendance 100,000*
Manchester City 2 **Newcastle United** 1
Barnes, Tueart Gowling

1976-77 ASTON VILLA
Final: *Wembley 12 March 1977 Attendance 100,000*
Aston Villa 0 **Everton** 0
Hillsborough 16 March 1977 Attendance 55,000
Aston Villa 1 **Everton** 1
Kenyon (og) Latchford
Old Trafford 13 April 1977 Attendance 54,749
Aston Villa 3 **Everton** 2
Nicholl, Little 2 Latchford, Lyons

1977-78 NOTTINGHAM FOREST
Final: *Wembley 18 March 1978 Attendance 100,000*
Nottingham Forest 0 **Liverpool** 0
Old Trafford 22 March 1978 Attendance 54,350
Nottingham Forest 1 **Liverpool** 0
Robertson (pen)

This page The 1976 League Cup final was unusually entertaining for an event which, in the 1970s, has built a reputation for somewhat tedious games between teams not particularly well-placed in the other major competitions. Manchester City defeated Newcastle 2-1, the winner being a remarkable bicycle kick from Dennis Tueart.

Above England colleagues Dave Watson and Malcolm Macdonald.

Above right The aftermath and subsequent indignity for Macdonald.

Right Further despair for Macdonald as he fails again at Wembley. It was his second Cup final defeat there with Newcastle – in 1974 Liverpool had taken the FA Cup 3-0.

Opposite page Nottingham Forest manager Brian Clough with Kenny Burns and the spoils of Forest's 1978 League Cup final victory over Liverpool. The European Champions had been beaten by a disputed John Robertson penalty after a draw at Wembley in one of the most one-sided games ever seen there. It concluded a marvellous season for Forest. Not only did they win the League Championship and League Cup, they also established a unique record in carrying off all that seasons individual awards. Kenny Burns was Footballer of the Year, Peter Shilton was Professional Footballer of the Year, Archie Gemmill was runner-up in both those competitions, Tony Woodcock was voted Player of the Year by the First Division managers and also Young Professional of the Year, and Brian Clough was, of course, Manager of the Year. All in all, it was a memorable year for Forest.

Does charity begin at home?

Below This goal by player-manager Terry Neill in 1972 gave Ireland only their second win over England since the War. But perhaps more important to Irish football than the prestige of victory was the Irish FA's cut of television rights and the large Wembley gate.

Right Midfield rivals Billy Bremner and Peter Storey in a tense moment in England's 1-0 win over Scotland in 1972. For Scotsmen, the annual encounter with England was still the highlight of the season.

'It's got to the stage where apart from the England-Scotland game nobody wants to know. The whole thing is a relic from the past. It's out of date, and let's face it, it ought to be scrapped.'

The view of that former First Division manager on the Home International Championship was one which was becoming more and more widespread even before the tournament was moved into eight days at the end of the season in 1968-69. There was a strong feeling among Englishmen and some Scots that it was obsolete and, far worse, irrelevant.

The recent developments in football had meant that the disparity between England and Scotland and the other two associations had grown even wider; and, though the brave fights put up by the Welsh—particularly in the 1976 European Championship—and the Irish have had their moments in the wider spheres of international football, they have been less successful at home.

Northern Ireland's victory at Wembley in 1972 was only her second over England since the War—and in that time Wales had beaten England just once, in 1955.

FIFA threaten to end the Home Championship

The disparity had, of course, always been there—England beat Ireland 13-0 when the countries first met, in 1882—and Ireland's only outright success in the Championship was in 1913-14, and then without gaining the full six points. Wales last won it outright in 1937 and England and Scotland had a share in all but eight of the first 77 contests.

In any reassessment of the Championship, it has to be remembered that, for many years, it provided the only means of international expression for Scotland, Wales and Ireland. England had been playing foreign opposition in full internationals for 22 years when Scotland first ventured outside the fold to play France in 1930. Wales followed suit three years later, but they managed only two games before the War, and in Belfast the decision was not taken until 1951. So, for a very long time, the Home Championship *was* international football in these quarters.

In the mid-seventies political manoeuvres within FIFA showed a lobby for a drastic restriction of the Home Countries international activities. Sections of both the South American and the Afro-Asian blocks campaigned strongly for the representation of the United

Kingdom to be cut from four to one—thus virtually eliminating each of the Home Countries as an individual international force.

The relative performance of a unified United Kingdom squad became a relevant area for debate as each individual country struggled to make a significant impact in the European Championships and World Cups of the decade.

The Home International Championship started in 1884, when the Ireland-Scotland fixture, arranged two years earlier, completed the six-match circle. England and Scotland had already been playing for 14 years, officially for 12, and the Scots continued the dominance they had established in that period. Between 1874 and 1883 England

managed only one win over Scotland, and suffered three crushing defeats. The Scots, ahead in the development of tactics and the passing game, won four outright titles in the first seven years.

England, reaping the rewards from the legalising of professionalism, then took over, with seven clear wins in 11 years. Ireland, with their first win over Scotland, shared the honours in 1903, but it was Wales in 1906-07, who first really broke the duopoly.

A win over Scotland at Wrexham, a draw at Fulham and a 3-2 victory over Ireland in Belfast gave them the five points, and their outright title was assured when Scotland held England 1-1 at Newcastle.

Ireland's turn came in 1914. The

pinnacle of their season came on 14 February at Middlesbrough, when they proved the previous season's shock 2-1 win over England in Belfast was no fluke by winning 3-0 with Billy Gillespie of Sheffield United scoring a magnificent second goal. The Irish had never beaten Wales or England away and now, while still not able to call on all their best players, they accomplished both feats in one season.

The tournament still provides some classic games

It was a remarkable swansong for Ireland. By the time football began again after the First World War the civil war that had been brewing had boiled over and there was never to be a genuinely united Irish team again. It was not, however, until after the next War that the practice of the North choosing players from the Irish Free State for Championship matches finally ceased.

England had made a relatively small impact between the Wars—winning outright only in 1930, 1932 and 1938—but when the Championship restarted in 1946 they and then Scotland started to pull away. Wales, who had won six clear titles between 1920 and 1937, were now struggling to hold their own, despite discovering a mine of talent down at Swansea. In the next quarter-century

SUMMARY OF HOME INTERNATIONALS		
	†First match	Matches played
England v Scotland	1872	96
Scotland v Wales	1876	92
England v Wales	1879	91
England v Ireland	1882	85
Wales v Ireland	1882	85
Scotland v Ireland	1884	83

Wins	Goals
England 36, Scotland 38, drawn 22	England 174, Scotland 163
Scotland 52, Wales 15, drawn 22	Scotland 230, Wales 103
England 60, Wales 12, drawn 19	England 235, Wales 84
England 66, Ireland 6, drawn 13	England 296, Ireland 78
Wales 40, Ireland 26, drawn 19	Wales 175, Ireland 123
Scotland 58, Ireland 13, drawn 12	Scotland 248, Ireland 76

Correct to the end of the 1977-78 season
†The championship itself did not start until 1883-84

neither they nor the Irish ever looked likely champions.

The outright titles all went to England (12) and Scotland (5). The great games between them were all at Wembley: 7-2 to England in 1955, the 9-3 thrashing of 1961, and Scotland's 3-2 win over the world champions in 1967—a match of much drama, but little genuine importance.

The 1955 game is best remembered for the four goals scored by Dennis Wilshaw. This was not, however, a record for the Championship: Joe Bambrick had managed six in Northern Ireland's 7-0 win over Wales in February 1930. Bambrick's feat was all the odder for the fact that Ireland scored only one more goal and obtained not a single point in their other two games that season.

By the late sixties the only fixture that commanded real interest was England versus Scotland. But the Championship as a whole—despite its use as a qualifying group for the European Championship in 1966-68 (it had been used for the World Cup in 1950 and 1954)—was fast becoming an anachronism.

With an increasing number of sides involved in Europe, the League clubs (after EUFA had discarded the use of the Home Championship as a qualifying tournament) protested at the swelling number of internationals England played during the season. In 1968 the League's agreement with the FA stated that this figure should not exceed four and this left Alf Ramsey on a very tight rein indeed.

An unwanted chore or a financial necessity?

The reaction of Ramsey and the FA was understandable if drastic—they suggested the abolition of the Home Internationals, rather than allow England to be left out of European competition. The other three associations predictably fought that idea, and the compromise suggestion was to play the tournament in eight days *after* the end of the season. The Irish and Welsh were not keen, but assurances that all their players would be released by the clubs helped to persuade them—assurances which, with English clubs involved in vital European games, eventually proved to be somewhat shallow. The continuation of the Championship was vital to the Irish and Welsh FAs simply on financial terms. They survive on the money they make from these games—which in a good season will come to nearly three-quarters of their total income. To abolish the Home Internationals would be virtually to abolish the Welsh and Irish Associations.

Even with blanket television coverage offering Ireland and Wales considerable compensation, the experiment was not a success. Attendances at Wembley were healthy, but on a rain-soaked evening only 8,000 paid at Hampden to see Scotland and Northern Ireland draw 1-1; and the millions who watched on television saw a game totally devoid of international flavour, atmosphere—or class.

The system was retained, though it was rather an embarrassment. In the next few years the closing stages of European competitions and the postponement of vital League games meant that players who had already played 50 or more matches still had pressing engagements—or so their clubs would reasonably claim. For some English players and managers, the Home Internationals, squeezed into eight days around the time of the Cup Final and European semi-finals, was little more than a nuisance. The television companies and most of the press battled hopefully to inject enthusiasm, to make out it was one of the great annual events in football, but for all that it was increasingly a tired anti-climax.

Would it keep going on in its solid tradition? There was not much else to help it. It was pointless pretending, certainly for England and possibly for Scotland, that playing Wales and Ireland was complete preparation for the rigours of world-class competition. It had become a duty, like spending Christmas with relations. But then if charity begins at home . . .

HOME CHAMPIONSHIP		
Season	Winners	Pts
1883-84	Scotland	6
1884-85	Scotland	6
1885-86	England	5
	Scotland	5
1886-87	Scotland	5
1887-88	England	6
1888-89	Scotland	5
1889-90	England	5
	Scotland	5
1890-91	England	6
1891-92	England	6
1892-93	England	6
1893-94	Scotland	5
1894-95	England	5
1895-96	Scotland	5
1896-97	Scotland	5
1897-98	England	6
1898-99	England	6
1899-1900	Scotland	6
1900-01	England	5
1901-02	Scotland	5
1902-03	England	4
	Scotland	4
	Ireland	4
1903-04	England	5
1904-05	England	5
1905-06	England	4
	Scotland	4
1906-07	Wales	5
1907-08	England	5
	Scotland	5
1908-09	England	6
1909-10	Scotland	5
1910-11	England	5
1911-12	England	5
	Scotland	5
1912-13	England	4
1913-14	Ireland	5
1919-20	Wales	4
1920-21	Scotland	6
1921-22	Scotland	4
1922-23	Scotland	5
1923-24	Wales	6
1924-25	Scotland	6
1925-26	Scotland	6
1926-27	England	4
	Scotland	4
1927-28	Wales	5
1928-29	Scotland	6
1929-30	England	6
1930-31	England	4
	Scotland	4
1931-32	England	6
1932-33	Wales	5
1933-34	Wales	5
1934-35	England	4
	Scotland	4
1935-36	Scotland	4
1936-37	Wales	6
1937-38	England	4
1938-39	England	4
	Scotland	4
	Wales	4
1946-47	England	5
1947-48	England	5
1948-49	Scotland	6
1949-50	England	6
1950-51	Scotland	6
1951-52	England	5
	Wales	5
1952-53	England	4
	Scotland	4
1953-54	England	6
1954-55	England	6
1955-56	England	3
	Scotland	3
	Wales	3
	N. Ireland	3
1956-57	England	5
1957-58	England	4
	N. Ireland	4
1958-59	England	4
	N. Ireland	4
1959-60	England	4
	Scotland	4
	Wales	4
1960-61	England	6
1961-62	Scotland	6
1962-63	Scotland	6
1963-64	England	4
	Scotland	4
	N. Ireland	4
1964-65	England	5
1965-66	England	5
1966-67	Scotland	5
1967-68	England	5
1968-69	England	6
1969-70	England	4
	Scotland	4
	Wales	4
1970-71	England	5
1971-72	England	4
	Scotland	4
1972-73	England	6
1973-74	England	4
	Scotland	4
1974-75	England	4
1975-76	Scotland	6
1976-77	Scotland	5
1977-78	England	6

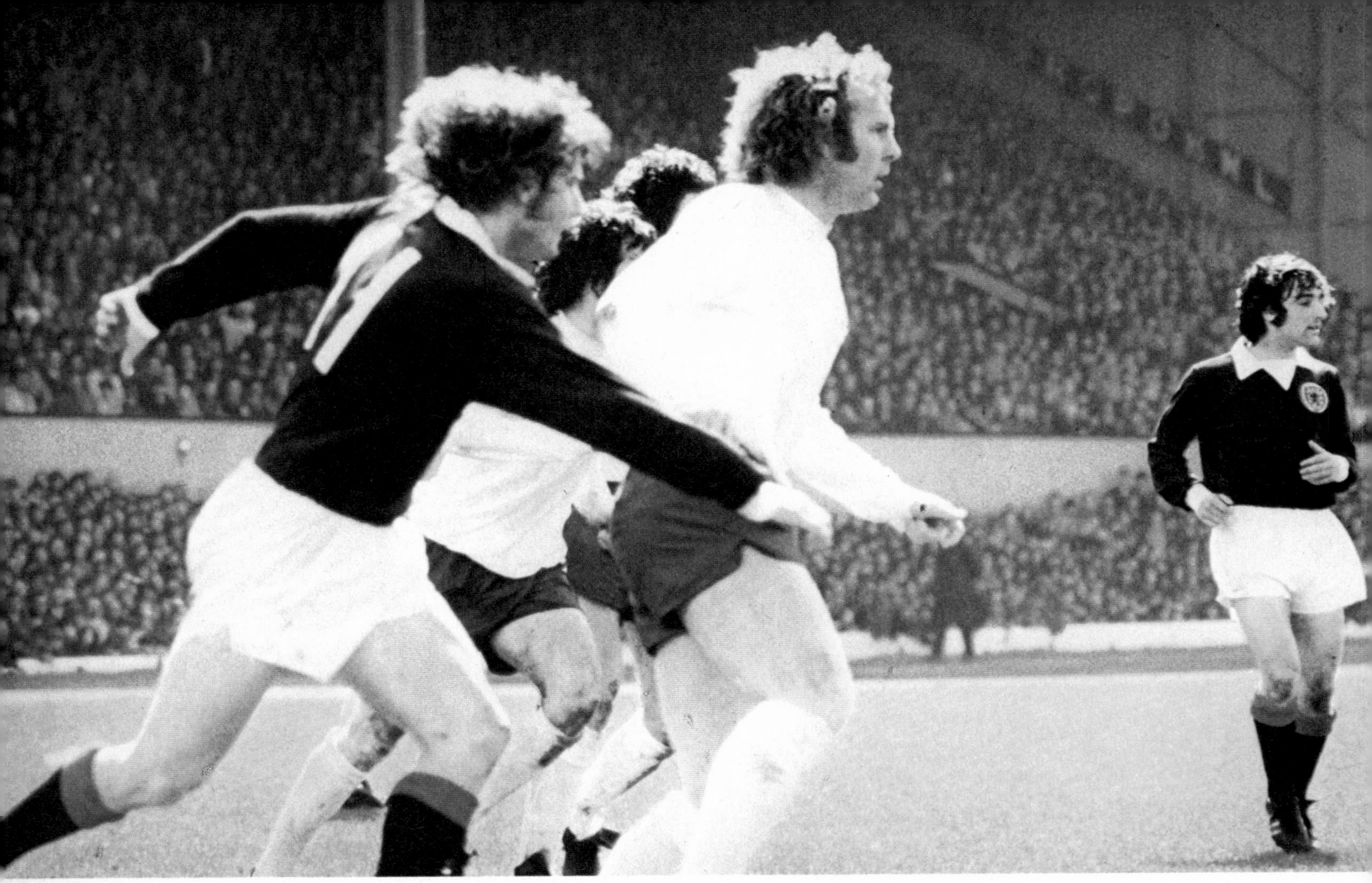

Perfidious Albion

THE HOME COUNTRIES

'The Football Association requires applications from young men who would be prepared to play in an international match against Scotland in Glasgow on November 23.' Imagine the effect of that in the small ad column of a daily paper!

The applications would begin pouring in at once—not only from Kevin Keegan, Ray Clemence and Mick Channon, but from every Fourth Division reserve and public parks amateur—and then the task of choosing the final team would begin.

This massive labour would be accomplished single-handed by the FA Secretary. He would consult nobody and select himself as captain of the side. And, because FA funds would be low, he would suddenly find himself wondering how the visit to Scotland would be financed.

So there would be another newspaper advertisement, and a circular letter to every club in membership of the FA: 'Contributions are required from interested parties to pay the railway and hotel expenses of the England team to play Scotland.' Fantastic as it may seem, that

was exactly what happened when Charles Alcock, the FA Secretary, first put forward the idea of an England v Scotland match in 1872.

Today, over a century later, an international is planned more like a military operation. The players will meet at least four days in advance at a luxury hotel. When Don Revie is satisfied that all his party has arrived, they will dine with the FA Councillors appointed to accompany the team. Then they will retire early in preparation for training the following morning.

For the privilege of playing for England, the players will have all expenses paid, receive £100 for playing, and be entitled to a share of the revenue from the television companies. All they need to bring are their boots, a personal towel, and, of course, themselves. As one FA official put it: 'All we really need is a body. We provide the rest.'

How different it all was in the far-off days of the first international when, on a cold, wet, windy night in 1872, a group of officers and gentlemen gathered in the Royal Garrick

Hotel in Glasgow. Instead of the frugal glasses of orangeade or coca-cola, and the starchless main meals, they tucked into a gargantuan feast with all the gusto of men who had endured the rigours of a train journey from London.

It had been a journey with nothing of the cushioned plushness of a modern Inter-City line. Limbs ached from the buffeting on the wooden austerity of the seats, and the acrid smell of smoke had the travellers still heavy with catarrh.

The game itself ended in a scoreless draw, a surprising result for the Englishmen, who had arranged the fixture, in the words of the FA minutes, 'In order to further the interests of the Association in Scotland'. There was to be ample opportunity to regret the condescending tone of that statement.

In the next 19 years England were to beat Scotland only twice but at least the significance of those defeats was not lost on 'Pa' Jackson, assistant secretary of the FA, who determined that England should create a team on the Queen's Park pattern.

So, in 1882, Jackson formed his Corinthians from former public schools and university men and, in the next seven years, of the 88 players capped by England, '52 were Corinthians. On three occasions when the FA agreed to play Ireland and Wales on the same day, the entire Corinthians side was sent to represent England.

Yet the death of the Corinthians and the true-blue amateur tradition they represented was assured almost from birth. Professionalism was already taking root in the North, and by the end of the century it had completely changed the complexion of international football.

The FA, mainly through the influence of the perceptive Charles Alcock, bowed to the inevitable and, in 1885, James Forrest of Blackburn Rovers became the first acknowledged professional to play for England. Forrest's fee was 10 shillings per match—£99.50 less than the FA offered their players in 1974.

At the start of professionalism, the paid players were treated with suspicion, and the amateur captain would always dine alone to avoid being tainted. At one Birmingham hotel, the manager even asked for guarantees from the FA ensuring that they would pay for any damage caused by professional members of the England team.

But from the day of Forrest's arrival in 1885, the eventual disappearance of the amateur player from the international scene was inevitable. The odd exception, such as Bernard Joy of Casuals and later Arsenal, served only to prove the point.

The amateur player might have had his day, but the amateur administrator most certainly had not. The first England team manager, Walter Winterbottom, did not emerge until after the Second World War and, even then, he was never accorded the right of selection. Perhaps that was not surprising, for the whole process had been haphazard from the beginning.

After the strange 'volunteering' process which selected the team for the original match, clubs were asked by the FA to nominate men for the second. A series of trial matches was held, during which a small army of 71 players was whittled down to the final eleven. As a result, only three men survived from the first international to the second.

The International Selection Committee, later to hold so much sway, was not formed until 1888. Originally it was composed of seven men. This was increased to nine (six from the northern and midland clubs and three from the south) in 1897. The Committee expanded as the years went by. By the fifties there were over 30 members, who were split into sections, one responsible for full internationals, one for amateur internationals and one for youth internationals etc. It was not until Alf Ramsey took over in 1963 that the team selection for full and Under-23 internationals was taken out of the hands of a committee, but certain members still remained responsible for amateur internationals until they were abolished.

Players were not so much selected as voted for. A committee enthusiast from, for example, south-east London would report that he had seen a promising player with Millwall, then a Third Division club. If he could lobby enough support, his discovery would go in to the exclusion of an established star. If the system were still in operation today, it would be technically possible for Kevin Keegan's place in the England team to go to the Workington striker who had impressed in a Fourth Division match!

Caps were won with all the unpredictability of pools dividends. In 1923, Bromley, the London amateur club, had a promising centre-forward called Frank Osborne, a clerk at Thomas Cooks, the travel agents. Fulham persuaded the youngster to join them as an amateur and, within a month, he was playing for England against France in Paris.

'Of course I was proud,' recalled Osborne, years later when he was manager of Fulham, 'but the whole thing was crazy. I was not nearly ready. Today I would have had to wait six years for a cap.'

The statistics tell the whole story. In eleven seasons before the Second

War, England used 99 players; in the following eleven they used 145, 66 of whom never gained a second cap.

Ironically enough, there was much more continuity during the War itself when, with so many leading players serving abroad, the pool of stars available for internationals was restricted.

That meant that the same players —Swift, Scott, Hardwick, Denis and Leslie Compton, Soo, Franklin, Mercer, Matthews, Carter, Lawton, Finney—came up for selection time

after time. In a sense they were the harbingers of the squad system of the 1960s. This historic departure did not, however, set a formal pattern for the future. Sir Alf Ramsey later recalled that when he began playing for England in the 1950s he was barely introduced to his colleagues.

But at least there had been some measure of progress, and a further important step came later in the War when Sir Stanley Rous, later to become President of FIFA, proposed to the FA, of which he was then secretary, that England should have a team manager.

The choice fell upon Walter Winterbottom, a schoolteacher who had been centre-half for Manchester United. A man of charm and insight, Winterbottom was well qualified, but he was to learn unhappily that he had been given responsibility without power. Winterbottom was asked merely to coach and prepare players, while the actual selection remained firmly in the hands of the selection committee. To have a team manager was one thing, but to allow him the license to decide who should play for England was quite different.

It was in this pantomime atmosphere that England, grievously under-prepared, embarked on her first World Cup sortie to Brazil in 1950. The inglorious defeat at the hands of the USA was just one in a whole catalogue of disasters. Things had gone wrong from the very start when two of the England players—Matthews and Taylor—both missed the first game because they had been touring with an FA team in Canada when the England party arrived in Brazil.

That, however, was but one of Walter Winterbottom's problems. When the party took a dislike to the Brazilian food, he even found himself entrusted with the task of cooking. That defeat by the USA and Hungary's historic 6-3 win at Wembley three years later taught the FA what the world has long suspected—that the British were no longer the masters of football.

Something drastic should have been done, but the only significant change came during the 1954 World Cup when some of the senior players were invited to advise on team selection.

Preparations were still as chaotic as ever. The England party arrived in Sweden for the 1958 World Cup finals to find that no training camp had been laid on. The harassed Winterbottom, whose experience of World Cups seemed never less than horrific, was left to chase around for accommodation only days before the first game.

Chile was hardly any better. Incredibly, the England party travelled to the tournament without a team doctor, and the result was that Peter Swan fell ill and, after receiving the wrong treatment, almost died.

The man who achieved more than anyone to create a professional and realistic environment within England's international soccer was, of course, Sir Alf Ramsey. As the successful and unequivocal manager of Ipswich, he did not need to seek the England job when Winterbottom lost, as he was bound to do, his vain battle against administrative incompetence and selectorial vanity in 1962.

Although he was said to have been only third choice for the job, Ramsey could take the post on his own terms. He would not countenance the intolerable pressure which had been laid upon his hamstrung predecessor. He would pick the players and, if the selectors *had* to remain in existence, they would do so only as a rubber stamp.

Ramsey decided that, if a man was selected to play for England, the player had to be first to be told. The Committee, the press and the world could wait. How different from the days when the most frequent morning paper story was how Stanley Accrington came out of the cinema and read in the evening paper that he had been chosen for England!

It was a sign of the times when, in 1964, Bobby Moore complained of the strain of England's pre-match training. Ten years earlier they would hardly have tired a nicotine besotten parks player, but, come Ramsey, those days were clearly over. Stalag Lilleshall was the players' description of their training camp for the 1966 World Cup.

Ten to four thirty, Monday to Thursday, Ramsey would be in his Lancaster Gate office, and he expected the same discipline and punctuality from everyone else. The awesome combination of Harold Shepherdson and Les Cocker—'as cuddly as a sack of cobblestones' said Max Marquis—were brought in as trainers and strict rules of conduct were laid down.

What Ramsey accomplished for England needs little reiteration. He promised that England would win the World Cup in 1966 and they did. Consciously or otherwise, he succeeded by going back to 'Pa' Jackson's concept of running an international side on the same lines as a club.

His stubborn, unsmiling defence of his players did little in the field of public relations; yet on the field of play those players responded to his fierce loyalty. But for England's amazing quarter-final in Leon—quite out of character for a Ramsey side—the World Cup might have been retained.

Finally Ramsey paid the usual managerial price for failure—in his case England's failure to qualify for the 1974 World Cup. His successor, Don Revie, steeped in success at Leeds United, faced similar difficulties and England did not reach the last eight of the 1976 European Championship.

Eventually as Revie's squad set out along the qualification route for the World Cup of 1978, the Football League grudgingly agreed to postpone League matches to increase preparation time.

Temporarily, at least, the massive withdrawals because of club injuries and commitments were ended.

However it made little difference to the team's results and in July 1977 Revie resigned. Ron Greenwood was appointed manager with the then impossible task of getting England to the World Cup finals. England duly failed — eliminated on goal difference — and Scotland were once again to be Britain's only representatives.

FULL INTERNATIONALS PLAYED BY ENGLAND 1870–OCTOBER 1978

Date		*Venue*	*Opponents*	*Score*
*19 November	1870	Kennington Oval	Scotland	1-0
*28 February	1871	Kennington Oval	Scotland	1-1
*18 November	1871	Kennington Oval	Scotland	2-1
*24 February	1872	Kennington Oval	Scotland	1-0
30 November	1872	Glasgow	Scotland	0-0
8 March	1873	Kennington Oval	Scotland	4-2
7 March	1874	Glasgow	Scotland	1-2
6 March	1875	Kennington Oval	Scotland	2-2
4 March	1876	Glasgow	Scotland	0-3
3 March	1877	Kennington Oval	Scotland	1-3
2 March	1878	Glasgow	Scotland	2-7
18 January	1879	Kennington Oval	Wales	2-1
5 April	1879	Kennington Oval	Scotland	5-4
13 March	1880	Glasgow	Scotland	4-5
15 March	1880	Wrexham	Wales	3-2
26 February	1881	Blackburn	Wales	0-1
12 March	1881	Kennington Oval	Scotland	1-6
18 February	1882	Belfast	Ireland	13-0
11 March	1882	Glasgow	Scotland	1-5
13 March	1882	Wrexham	Wales	3-5
3 February	1883	Kennington Oval	Wales	5-0
24 February	1883	Liverpool	Ireland	7-0
10 March	1883	Sheffield	Scotland	2-3
23 February	1884	Belfast	Ireland	8-1
15 March	1884	Glasgow	Scotland	0-1
17 March	1884	Wrexham	Wales	4-0
28 February	1885	Manchester	Ireland	4-0
14 March	1885	Blackburn	Wales	1-1
21 March	1885	Kennington Oval	Scotland	1-1
13 March	1886	Belfast	Ireland	6-1
29 March	1886	Wrexham	Wales	3-1
31 March	1886	Glasgow	Scotland	1-1
5 February	1887	Sheffield	Ireland	7-0
26 February	1887	Kennington Oval	Wales	4-0
19 March	1887	Blackburn	Scotland	2-3
4 February	1888	Crewe	Wales	5-1
17 March	1888	Glasgow	Scotland	5-0
31 March	1888	Belfast	Ireland	5-1
23 February	1889	Stoke-on-Trent	Wales	4-1
2 March	1889	Everton	Ireland	6-1
13 April	1889	Kennington Oval	Scotland	2-3
†15 March	1890	Belfast	Ireland	9-1
†15 March	1890	Wrexham	Wales	3-1
5 April	1890	Glasgow	Scotland	1-1
† 7 March	1891	Sunderland	Wales	4-1
† 7 March	1891	Wolverhampton	Ireland	6-1
6 April	1891	Blackburn	Scotland	2-1
† 5 March	1892	Wrexham	Wales	2-0
† 5 March	1892	Belfast	Ireland	2-0
2 April	1892	Glasgow	Scotland	4-1
25 February	1893	Birmingham	Ireland	6-1
13 March	1893	Stoke-on-Trent	Wales	6-0
1 April	1893	Richmond	Scotland	5-2
3 March	1894	Belfast	Ireland	2-2
12 March	1894	Wrexham	Wales	5-1
7 April	1894	Glasgow	Scotland	2-2
9 March	1895	Derby	Ireland	9-0
18 March	1895	Queen's Club, Kensington	Wales	1-1
6 April	1895	Everton	Scotland	3-0
7 March	1896	Belfast	Ireland	2-0
16 March	1896	Cardiff	Wales	9-1
4 April	1896	Glasgow	Scotland	1-2
20 February	1897	Nottingham	Ireland	6-0
29 March	1897	Sheffield	Wales	4-0
3 April	1897	Crystal Palace	Scotland	1-2
5 March	1898	Belfast	Ireland	3-2
28 March	1898	Wrexham	Wales	3-0
2 April	1898	Glasgow	Scotland	3-1
18 February	1899	Sunderland	Ireland	13-2
20 March	1899	Bristol	Wales	4-1
8 April	1899	Birmingham	Scotland	2-1
17 March	1900	Dublin	Ireland	2-0
26 March	1900	Cardiff	Wales	1-1
7 April	1900	Glasgow	Scotland	1-4
9 March	1901	Southampton	Ireland	3-0
18 March	1901	Newcastle	Wales	6-0
30 March	1901	Crystal Palace	Scotland	2-2
3 March	1902	Wrexham	Wales	0-0
22 March	1902	Belfast	Ireland	1-0
‡ 5 April	1902	Glasgow	Scotland	1-1
3 May	1902	Birmingham	Scotland	2-2
14 February	1903	Wolverhampton	Ireland	4-0
2 March	1903	Portsmouth	Wales	2-1
4 April	1903	Sheffield	Scotland	1-2
29 February	1904	Wrexham	Wales	2-2
12 March	1904	Belfast	Ireland	3-1
9 April	1904	Glasgow	Scotland	1-0
25 February	1905	Middlesbrough	Ireland	1-1
27 March	1905	Liverpool	Wales	3-1
1 April	1905	Crystal Palace	Scotland	1-0
17 February	1906	Belfast	Ireland	5-0
19 March	1906	Cardiff	Wales	1-0
7 April	1906	Glasgow	Scotland	1-2
16 February	1907	Everton	Ireland	1-0
18 March	1907	Fulham	Wales	1-1
6 April	1907	Newcastle	Scotland	1-1
15 February	1908	Belfast	Ireland	3-1
16 March	1908	Wrexham	Wales	7-1
4 April	1908	Glasgow	Scotland	1-1
6 June	1908	Vienna	Austria	6-1
8 June	1908	Vienna	Austria	11-1
10 June	1908	Budapest	Hungary	7-0
13 June	1908	Prague	Bohemia	4-0
13 February	1909	Bradford	Ireland	4-0
15 March	1909	Nottingham	Wales	2-0
3 April	1909	Crystal Palace	Scotland	2-0
29 May	1909	Budapest	Hungary	4-2
31 May	1909	Budapest	Hungary	8-2
1 June	1909	Vienna	Austria	8-1
12 February	1910	Belfast	Ireland	1-1
14 March	1910	Cardiff	Wales	1-0
2 April	1910	Glasgow	Scotland	0-2
C29 June	1910	Durban	South Africa	3-0
C23 July	1910	Johannesburg	South Africa	6-2
C30 July	1910	Capetown	South Africa	6-3
11 February	1911	Derby	Ireland	2-1
13 March	1911	Millwall	Wales	3-0
1 April	1911	Everton	Scotland	1-1
10 February	1912	Dublin	Ireland	6-1
11 March	1912	Wrexham	Wales	2-0
23 March	1912	Glasgow	Scotland	1-1
15 February	1913	Belfast	Ireland	1-2
17 March	1913	Bristol	Wales	4-3
5 April	1913	Stamford Bridge	Scotland	1-0
14 February	1914	Middlesbrough	Ireland	0-3
16 March	1914	Cardiff	Wales	2-0
4 April	1914	Glasgow	Scotland	1-3
V26 April	1919	Everton	Scotland	2-2
V 3 May	1919	Glasgow	Scotland	4-3
V11 October	1919	Cardiff	Wales	1-2
V18 October	1919	Stoke-on-Trent	Wales	2-0
25 October	1919	Belfast	Ireland	1-1
15 March	1920	Highbury	Wales	1-2
10 April	1920	Sheffield	Scotland	5-4
23 October	1920	Sunderland	Ireland	2-0
C26 June	1920	Durban	South Africa	3-1
C17 July	1920	Johannesburg	South Africa	3-1
C19 July	1920	Capetown	South Africa	9-1
14 March	1921	Cardiff	Wales	0-0
9 April	1921	Glasgow	Scotland	0-3
21 May	1921	Brussels	Belgium	2-0
22 October	1921	Belfast	N Ireland	1-1
13 March	1922	Liverpool	Wales	1-0
8 April	1922	Villa Park	Scotland	0-1
21 October	1922	West Bromwich	N Ireland	2-0
5 March	1923	Cardiff	Wales	2-2
19 March	1923	Highbury	Belgium	6-1
14 April	1923	Glasgow	Scotland	2-2
10 May	1923	Paris	France	4-1
21 May	1923	Stockholm	Sweden	4-2
24 May	1923	Stockholm	Sweden	3-1
20 October	1923	Belfast	N Ireland	1-2
1 November	1923	Antwerp	Belgium	2-2
3 March	1924	Blackburn	Wales	1-2
12 April	1924	Wembley	Scotland	1-1
17 May	1924	Paris	France	3-1
22 October	1924	Everton	N Ireland	3-1
8 December	1924	West Bromwich	Belgium	4-0
28 February	1925	Swansea	Wales	2-1
4 April	1925	Glasgow	Scotland	0-2
21 May	1925	Paris	France	3-2
C27 June	1925	Brisbane	Australia	5-1
C 4 July	1925	Sydney	Australia	2-1
C11 July	1925	Maitland	Australia	8-2
C18 July	1925	Sydney	Australia	5-0
C25 July	1925	Melbourne	Australia	2-0
24 October	1925	Belfast	N Ireland	0-0
1 March	1926	Crystal Palace	Wales	1-3
17 April	1926	Manchester	Scotland	1-0
24 May	1926	Antwerp	Belgium	5-3
20 October	1926	Liverpool	N Ireland	3-3
12 February	1927	Wrexham	Wales	3-3
2 April	1927	Glasgow	Scotland	2-1
11 May	1927	Brussels	Belgium	9-1
21 May	1927	Luxembourg	Luxembourg	5-2
26 May	1927	Paris	France	6-0
22 October	1927	Belfast	N Ireland	0-2
28 November	1927	Burnley	Wales	1-2
31 March	1928	Wembley	Scotland	1-5
17 May	1928	Paris	France	5-1
19 May	1928	Antwerp	Belgium	3-1
22 October	1928	Everton	N Ireland	2-1
17 November	1928	Swansea	Wales	3-2
13 April	1929	Glasgow	Scotland	0-1
9 May	1929	Paris	France	4-1
11 May	1929	Brussels	Belgium	5-1
15 May	1929	Madrid	Spain	3-4
C15 June	1929	Durban	South Africa	3-2
C13 July	1929	Johannesburg	South Africa	2-1
C17 July	1929	Capetown	South Africa	3-1
19 October	1929	Belfast	N Ireland	3-0
20 November	1929	Stamford Bridge	Wales	6-0
5 April	1930	Wembley	Scotland	5-2
10 May	1930	Berlin	Germany	3-3
14 May	1930	Vienna	Austria	0-0
20 October	1930	Sheffield	N Ireland	5-1
22 November	1930	Wrexham	Wales	4-0
28 March	1931	Glasgow	Scotland	0-2
14 May	1931	Paris	France	2-5
16 May	1931	Brussels	Belgium	4-1
17 October	1931	Belfast	Ireland	6-2
18 November	1931	Liverpool	Wales	3-1
9 December	1931	Highbury	Spain	7-1
9 April	1932	Wembley	Scotland	3-0
17 October	1932	Blackpool	N Ireland	1-0
16 November	1932	Wrexham	Wales	0-0
7 December	1932	Stamford Bridge	Austria	4-3
1 April	1933	Glasgow	Scotland	1-2
13 May	1933	Rome	Italy	1-1
20 May	1933	Berne	Switzerland	4-0
14 October	1933	Belfast	N Ireland	3-0
15 November	1933	Newcastle	Wales	1-2
6 December	1933	Tottenham	France	4-1
14 April	1934	Wembley	Scotland	3-0
10 May	1934	Budapest	Hungary	1-2
16 May	1934	Prague	Czechoslovakia	1-2
29 September	1934	Cardiff	Wales	4-0
14 November	1934	Highbury	Italy	3-2
6 February	1935	Everton	N Ireland	2-1
6 April	1935	Glasgow	Scotland	0-2
18 May	1935	Amsterdam	Netherlands	1-0
J21 August	1935	Glasgow	Scotland	2-4
19 October	1935	Belfast	N Ireland	3-1
4 December	1935	Tottenham	Germany	3-0
5 February	1936	Wolverhampton	Wales	1-2
4 April	1936	Wembley	Scotland	1-1
6 May	1936	Vienna	Austria	1-2
9 May	1936	Brussels	Belgium	2-3
17 October	1936	Cardiff	Wales	1-2
18 November	1936	Stoke-on-Trent	N Ireland	3-1
2 December	1936	Highbury	Hungary	6-2
17 April	1937	Glasgow	Scotland	1-3
14 May	1937	Oslo	Norway	6-0
17 May	1937	Stockholm	Sweden	4-0
20 May	1937	Helsinki	Finland	8-0
23 October	1937	Belfast	N Ireland	5-1
17 November	1937	Middlesbrough	Wales	2-1
1 December	1937	Tottenham	Czechoslovakia	5-4
9 April	1938	Wembley	Scotland	0-1
14 May	1938	Berlin	Germany	6-3
21 May	1938	Zurich	Switzerland	1-2
26 May	1938	Paris	France	4-2
22 October	1938	Cardiff	Wales	2-4
26 October	1938	Highbury	FIFA	3-0
9 November	1938	Newcastle	Norway	4-0
16 November	1938	Manchester	N Ireland	7-0
15 April	1939	Glasgow	Scotland	2-1

Date		Venue	Opponents	Score
13 May	1939	Milan	Italy	2-2
18 May	1939	Belgrade	Yugoslavia	1-2
24 May	1939	Bucharest	Rumania	2-0
17 June	1939	Johannesburg	South Africa	3-0
24 June	1939	Durban	South Africa	8-2
1 July	1939	Johannesburg	South Africa	2-1
11 November	1939	Cardiff	Wales	1-1
18 November	1939	Wrexham	Wales	3-2
2 December	1939	Newcastle	Scotland	2-1
13 April	1940	Wembley	Wales	0-1
11 May	1940	Glasgow	Scotland	1-1
8 February	1941	Newcastle	Scotland	2-3
26 April	1941	Nottingham	Wales	4-1
3 May	1941	Glasgow	Scotland	3-1
7 June	1941	Cardiff	Wales	3-2
4 October	1941	Wembley	Scotland	2-0
25 October	1941	Birmingham	Wales	2-1
17 January	1942	Wembley	Scotland	3-0
18 April	1942	Glasgow	Scotland	4-5
9 May	1942	Cardiff	Wales	0-1
10 October	1942	Wembley	Scotland	0-0
24 October	1942	Wolverhampton	Wales	1-2
27 February	1943	Wembley	Wales	5-3
17 April	1943	Glasgow	Scotland	4-0
8 May	1943	Cardiff	Wales	1-1
29 May	1943	Wembley	Wales	8-3
16 October	1943	Manchester	Scotland	8-0
19 February	1944	Wembley	Scotland	6-2
22 April	1944	Glasgow	Scotland	3-2
6 May	1944	Cardiff	Wales	2-0
16 September	1944	Liverpool	Wales	2-2
14 October	1944	Wembley	Scotland	6-2
13 February	1945	Birmingham	Scotland	3-2
14 April	1945	Glasgow	Scotland	6-1
5 May	1945	Cardiff	Wales	3-2
26 May	1945	Wembley	France	2-2
15 September	1945	Belfast	N Ireland	1-0
20 October	1945	West Bromwich	Wales	0-1
19 January	1946	Wembley	Belgium	2-0
13 April	1946	Glasgow	Scotland	0-1
11 May	1946	Stamford Bridge	Switzerland	4-1
28 September	1946	Belfast	N Ireland	7-2
30 September	1946	Dublin	Eire	1-0
13 November	1946	Manchester	Wales	3-0
27 November	1946	Huddersfield	Netherlands	8-2
12 April	1947	Wembley	Scotland	1-1
3 May	1947	Highbury	France	3-0
18 May	1947	Zurich	Switzerland	0-1
25 May	1947	Lisbon	Portugal	10-0
21 September	1947	Brussels	Belgium	5-2
18 October	1947	Cardiff	Wales	3-0
5 November	1947	Everton	N Ireland	2-2
19 October	1947	Highbury	Sweden	4-2
10 April	1948	Glasgow	Scotland	2-0
16 May	1948	Turin	Italy	4-0
26 September	1948	Copenhagen	Denmark	0-0
9 October	1948	Belfast	N Ireland	6-2
10 November	1948	Birmingham	Wales	1-0
2 December	1948	Highbury	Switzerland	6-0
9 April	1949	Wembley	Scotland	1-3
13 May	1949	Stockholm	Sweden	1-3
18 May	1949	Oslo	Norway	4-1
22 May	1949	Paris	France	3-1
21 September	1949	Everton	Eire	0-2
15 October	1949	Cardiff	Wales	4-1
16 November	1949	Manchester	N Ireland	9-2
30 November	1949	Tottenham	Italy	2-0
15 April	1950	Glasgow	Scotland	1-0
14 May	1950	Lisbon	Portugal	5-3
18 May	1950	Brussels	Belgium	4-1
25 June	1950	Rio de Janeiro	Chile	2-0
29 June	1950	Belo Horizonte	USA	0-1
2 July	1950	Rio de Janeiro	Spain	0-1
7 October	1950	Belfast	N Ireland	4-1
15 November	1950	Sunderland	Wales	4-2
22 November	1950	Highbury	Yugoslavia	2-2
14 April	1951	Wembley	Scotland	2-3
9 May	1951	Wembley	Argentina	2-1
19 May	1951	Everton	Portugal	5-2
26 May	1951	Sydney	Australia	4-1
30 June	1951	Sydney	Australia	17-0
7 July	1951	Brisbane	Australia	4-1
14 July	1951	Sydney	Australia	6-1
21 July	1951	Newcastle NSW	Australia	5-0
3 October	1951	Highbury	France	2-2
20 October	1951	Cardiff	Wales	1-1
14 November	1951	Birmingham	N Ireland	2-0
28 November	1951	Wembley	Austria	2-2
5 April	1952	Glasgow	Scotland	2-1
18 May	1952	Florence	Italy	1-1
25 May	1952	Vienna	Austria	3-2
28 May	1952	Zurich	Switzerland	3-0
4 October	1952	Belfast	N Ireland	2-2
12 November	1952	Wembley	Wales	5-2
26 November	1952	Wembley	Belgium	5-0
18 April	1953	Wembley	Scotland	2-2
17 May	1953	Buenos Aires	Argentina	0-0
24 May	1953	Santiago	Chile	2-1
31 May	1953	Montevideo	Uruguay	1-2
8 June	1953	New York	USA	6-3
10 October	1953	Cardiff	Wales	4-1
21 October	1953	Wembley	FIFA	4-4
11 November	1953	Liverpool	N Ireland	3-1
25 November	1953	Wembley	Hungary	3-6
3 April	1954	Glasgow	Scotland	4-2
16 May	1954	Belgrade	Yugoslavia	0-1
23 May	1954	Budapest	Hungary	1-7
17 June	1954	Basle	Belgium	4-4
20 June	1954	Berne	Switzerland	2-0
26 June	1954	Basle	Uruguay	2-4
2 October	1954	Belfast	N Ireland	2-0
10 November	1954	Wembley	Wales	3-2
1 December	1954	Wembley	West Germany	3-1
2 April	1955	Wembley	Scotland	7-2
15 May	1955	Paris	France	0-1
18 May	1955	Madrid	Spain	1-1
22 May	1955	Oporto	Portugal	1-3
2 October	1955	Copenhagen	Denmark	5-1
22 October	1955	Cardiff	Wales	1-2
2 November	1955	Wembley	N Ireland	3-0
30 November	1955	Wembley	Spain	4-1
14 April	1956	Glasgow	Scotland	1-1
9 May	1956	Wembley	Brazil	4-2

Date		Venue	Opponents	Score
16 May	1956	Stockholm	Sweden	0-0
20 May	1956	Helsinki	Finland	5-1
26 May	1956	Berlin	West Germany	3-1
6 October	1956	Belfast	N Ireland	1-1
14 November	1956	Wembley	Wales	3-1
28 November	1956	Wembley	Yugoslavia	3-0
WC 5 December	1956	Wolverhampton	Denmark	5-2
6 April	1957	Wembley	Scotland	2-1
WC 8 May	1957	Wembley	Eire	5-1
WC15 May	1957	Copenhagen	Denmark	4-1
WC19 May	1957	Dublin	Eire	1-1
19 October	1957	Cardiff	Wales	4-0
6 November	1957	Wembley	N Ireland	2-3
27 November	1957	Wembley	France	4-0
19 April	1958	Glasgow	Scotland	4-0
7 May	1958	Wembley	Portugal	2-1
11 May	1958	Belgrade	Yugoslavia	0-5
18 May	1958	Moscow	USSR	1-1
WC 8 June	1958	Gothenburg	USSR	2-2
WC11 June	1958	Gothenburg	Brazil	0-0
WC15 June	1958	Boras	Austria	2-2
WC17 June	1958	Gothenburg	USSR	0-1
4 October	1958	Belfast	N Ireland	3-3
22 October	1958	Wembley	USSR	5-0
26 November	1958	Birmingham	Wales	2-2
11 April	1959	Wembley	Scotland	1-0
6 May	1959	Wembley	Italy	2-2
13 May	1959	Rio de Janeiro	Brazil	0-2
17 May	1959	Lima	Peru	1-4
24 May	1959	Mexico City	Mexico	1-2
28 May	1959	Los Angeles	USA	8-1
17 October	1959	Cardiff	Wales	1-1
28 October	1959	Wembley	Sweden	2-3
18 November	1959	Wembley	N Ireland	2-1
9 April	1960	Glasgow	Scotland	1-1
11 May	1960	Wembley	Yugoslavia	3-3
15 May	1960	Madrid	Spain	0-3
22 May	1960	Budapest	Hungary	0-2
8 October	1960	Belfast	N Ireland	5-2
WC19 October	1960	Luxembourg	Luxembourg	9-0
26 October	1960	Wembley	Spain	4-2
23 November	1960	Wembley	Wales	5-1
15 April	1961	Wembley	Scotland	9-3
10 May	1961	Wembley	Mexico	8-0
WC21 May	1961	Lisbon	Portugal	1-1
24 May	1961	Rome	Italy	3-2
27 May	1961	Vienna	Austria	1-3
WC28 September	1961	Highbury	Luxembourg	4-1
14 October	1961	Cardiff	Wales	1-1
WC25 October	1961	Wembley	Portugal	2-0
22 November	1961	Wembley	N Ireland	1-1
4 April	1962	Wembley	Austria	3-1
14 April	1962	Glasgow	Scotland	0-2
9 May	1962	Wembley	Switzerland	3-1
20 May	1962	Lima	Peru	4-0
WC31 May	1962	Rancagua	Hungary	1-2
WC 2 June	1962	Rancagua	Argentina	3-1
WC 7 June	1962	Rancagua	Bulgaria	0-0
WC10 June	1962	Vina del Mar	Brazil	1-3
ENC 3 October	1962	Sheffield	France	1-1
20 October	1962	Belfast	N Ireland	3-1
21 November	1962	Wembley	Wales	4-0
ENC27 February	1963	Paris	France	2-5
6 April	1963	Wembley	Scotland	1-2
8 May	1963	Wembley	Brazil	1-1
29 May	1963	Bratislava	Czechoslovakia	4-2
2 June	1963	Leipzig	East Germany	2-1
5 June	1963	Basle	Switzerland	8-1
12 October	1963	Cardiff	Wales	4-0
23 October	1963	Wembley	FIFA	2-1
20 November	1963	Wembley	N Ireland	8-3
11 April	1964	Glasgow	Scotland	0-1
6 May	1964	Wembley	Uruguay	2-1
17 May	1964	Lisbon	Portugal	4-3
24 May	1964	Dublin	Eire	3-1
27 May	1964	New York	USA	10-0
30 May	1964	Rio de Janeiro	Brazil	1-5
4 June	1964	Sao Paulo	Portugal	1-1
6 June	1964	Rio de Janeiro	Argentina	0-1
3 October	1964	Belfast	N Ireland	4-3
21 October	1964	Wembley	Belgium	2-2
18 November	1964	Wembley	Wales	2-1
9 December	1964	Amsterdam	Netherlands	1-1
10 April	1965	Wembley	Scotland	2-2
5 May	1965	Wembley	Hungary	1-0
9 May	1965	Belgrade	Yugoslavia	1-1
12 May	1965	Nurnberg	West Germany	1-0
16 May	1965	Gothenburg	Sweden	2-1
2 October	1965	Cardiff	Wales	0-0
20 October	1965	Wembley	Austria	2-3
10 November	1965	Wembley	N Ireland	2-1
8 December	1965	Madrid	Spain	2-0
5 January	1966	Everton	Poland	1-1
23 February	1966	Wembley	West Germany	1-0
2 April	1966	Glasgow	Scotland	4-3
4 May	1966	Wembley	Yugoslavia	2-0
26 June	1966	Helsinki	Finland	3-0
29 June	1966	Oslo	Norway	6-1
3 July	1966	Copenhagen	Denmark	2-0
5 July	1966	Chorzow	Poland	1-0
WC11 July	1966	Wembley	Uruguay	0-0
WC16 July	1966	Wembley	Mexico	2-0
WC20 July	1966	Wembley	France	2-0
WC23 July	1966	Wembley	Argentina	1-0
WC26 July	1966	Wembley	Portugal	2-1
WC30 July	1966	Wembley	West Germany	4-2
EC22 October	1966	Belfast	N Ireland	2-0
2 November	1966	Wembley	Czechoslovakia	0-0
EC16 November	1966	Wembley	Wales	5-1
EC15 April	1967	Wembley	Scotland	2-3
24 May	1967	Wembley	Spain	2-0
27 May	1967	Vienna	Austria	1-0
EC21 October	1967	Cardiff	Wales	3-0
EC22 November	1967	Wembley	N Ireland	2-0
6 December	1967	Wembley	USSR	2-2
EC24 February	1968	Glasgow	Scotland	1-1
3 April	1968	Wembley	Spain	1-0
8 May	1968	Madrid	Spain	2-1
22 May	1968	Wembley	Sweden	3-1
1 June	1968	Hanover	West Germany	0-1
EC 5 June	1968	Florence	Yugoslavia	0-1
EC 8 June	1968	Rome	USSR	2-0
6 November	1968	Bucharest	Rumania	0-0
11 December	1968	Wembley	Bulgaria	1-1

Date		Venue	Opponents	Score
15 January	1969	Wembley	Rumania	1-1
12 March	1969	Wembley	France	5-0
3 May	1969	Belfast	N Ireland	3-1
7 May	1969	Wembley	Wales	2-1
10 May	1969	Wembley	Scotland	4-1
1 June	1969	Mexico City	Mexico	0-0
8 June	1969	Montevideo	Uruguay	2-1
12 June	1969	Rio de Janeiro	Brazil	1-2
5 November	1969	Amsterdam	Netherlands	1-0
10 December	1969	Wembley	Portugal	1-0
14 January	1970	Wembley	Netherlands	0-0
25 February	1970	Brussels	Belgium	3-1
18 April	1970	Cardiff	Wales	1-1
21 April	1970	Wembley	N Ireland	3-1
25 April	1970	Glasgow	Scotland	0-0
24 May	1970	Quito	Equador	2-0
WC 2 June	1970	Guadalajara	Rumania	1-0
WC 7 June	1970	Guadalajara	Brazil	0-1
WC11 June	1970	Guadalajara	Czechoslovakia	1-0
WC14 June	1970	Leon	West Germany	2-3
25 November	1970	Wembley	East Germany	3-1
EC 3 February	1971	Valetta	Malta	1-0
EC21 April	1971	Wembley	Greece	3-0
EC12 May	1971	Wembley	Malta	5-0
15 May	1971	Belfast	N Ireland	1-0
19 May	1971	Wembley	Wales	0-0
22 May	1971	Wembley	Scotland	3-1
EC13 October	1971	Basle	Switzerland	3-2
EC10 November	1971	Wembley	Switzerland	1-1
EC 1 December	1971	Athens	Greece	2-0
EC29 April	1972	Wembley	West Germany	1-3
EC13 May	1972	Berlin	West Germany	0-0
20 May	1972	Cardiff	Wales	3-0
23 May	1972	Wembley	N Ireland	0-1
27 May	1972	Glasgow	Scotland	1-0
11 October	1972	Wembley	Yugoslavia	1-1
WC15 November	1972	Cardiff	Wales	1-0
WC24 January	1973	Wembley	Wales	1-1
14 February	1973	Glasgow	Scotland	5-0
12 May	1973	Everton	N Ireland	2-1
15 May	1973	Wembley	Wales	3-0
19 May	1973	Wembley	Scotland	1-0
27 May	1973	Prague	Czechoslovakia	1-1
WC 6 June	1973	Katowice	Poland	0-2
10 June	1973	Moscow	USSR	2-1
14 June	1973	Turin	Italy	0-2
26 September	1973	Wembley	Austria	7-0
WC17 October	1973	Wembley	Poland	1-1
14 November	1973	Wembley	Italy	0-1
3 April	1974	Lisbon	Portugal	0-0
11 May	1974	Cardiff	Wales	2-0
15 May	1974	Wembley	N Ireland	1-0
18 May	1974	Glasgow	Scotland	0-2
22 May	1974	Wembley	Argentina	2-2
29 May	1974	Leipzig	East Germany	1-1
1 June	1974	Sofia	Bulgaria	1-0
5 June	1974	Belgrade	Yugoslavia	2-2
EC30 October	1974	Wembley	Czechoslovakia	3-0
EC20 November	1974	Wembley	Portugal	0-0
12 March	1975	Wembley	West Germany	2-0
EC16 April	1975	Wembley	Cyprus	5-0
EC11 May	1975	Limassol	Cyprus	1-0
17 May	1975	Belfast	N Ireland	0-0
21 May	1975	Wembley	Wales	2-2
24 May	1975	Wembley	Scotland	5-1
3 September	1975	Basle	Switzerland	2-1
EC30 October	1975	Bratislava	Czechoslovakia	1-2
EC19 November	1975	Lisbon	Portugal	1-1
24 March	1976	Wrexham	Wales	2-1
8 May	1976	Cardiff	Wales	1-0
11 May	1976	Wembley	N Ireland	4-0
14 May	1976	Glasgow	Scotland	1-2
23 May	1976	Los Angeles	Brazil	0-1
28 May	1976	New York	Italy	3-2
WC13 June	1976	Helsinki	Finland	4-1
8 September	1976	Wembley	Eire	1-1
WC13 October	1976	Wembley	Finland	2-1
WC17 November	1976	Rome	Italy	0-2
9 February	1977	Wembley	Holland	0-2
WC30 March	1977	Wembley	Luxembourg	5-0
28 May	1977	Belfast	N Ireland	2-1
31 May	1977	Wembley	Wales	0-1
4 June	1977	Wembley	Scotland	1-2
8 June	1977	Rio de Janeiro	Brazil	0-0
12 June	1977	Buenos Aires	Argentina	1-1
15 June	1977	Montevideo	Uruguay	0-0
7 September	1977	Wembley	Switzerland	0-0
WC12 October	1977	Luxembourg	Luxembourg	2-0
WC16 November	1977	Wembley	Italy	2-0
22 February	1978	Munich	West Germany	1-2
19 April	1978	Wembley	Brazil	1-1
13 May	1978	Cardiff	Wales	3-1
16 May	1978	Wembley	N Ireland	1-0
20 May	1978	Glasgow	Scotland	1-0
24 May	1978	Wembley	Hungary	4-1
EC20 September	1978	Copenhagen	Denmark	4-3
EC25 October	1978	Dublin	Eire	1-1

*These four games were all between an England XI and a team of Scots resident in England. The FA does not regard them as official matches

†On each of these days England played two internationals. The FA asked the Corinthian Casuals to provide the teams against Wales, while they themselves selected the sides to play Ireland. Corinthians are the only club side to have represented England in toto

‡This match was abandoned owing to a disaster at the ground. The FA does not regard it as an official match

V – Victory internationals (not regarded as official)

J – Jubilee game (not regarded as official)

WT – War-time internationals (not regarded as official)

WC – World Cup games

ENC – European Nations Cup games

EC – European Championship games

C – Commonwealth tour games. Though billed as 'England' these teams were usually FA Touring XIs. One cap was awarded to each of the players who went on the tour but individual games are not regarded as official internationals

A – Abandoned after 20 minutes owing to torrential rain

A hard road for Scotland

The advertisement appeared in all the Scottish national newspapers. It was, in fact, in the 'Situations Vacant' column. And the vacant situation was that of Scottish international team manager. There is, of course, nothing particularly wrong about advertising for a team manager. It may not be the accepted custom, for the usual practice is to work very much behind the scenes in such circumstances. Even so, the Scottish Football Association's idea was sound enough, for who could be sure what unexpected names might apply?

Sound enough, that is, in all respects but one. Journalists and fans stared disbelievingly at the advert. For the wording made it very clear indeed that the SFA would be willing to hire a team manager on a *part-time basis*.

The storm duly broke. What on earth was happening at Park Gardens, home of the SFA? Did they really think Scotland could compete with the world's greatest football nations without the guidance of a full-time professional manager? How far could the amateur outlook go?

As it happened, wiser minds prevailed and the job did become full-time again. But that advertisement, appearing as it did between the managerships of Jock Stein and John Prentice, is something the SFA will take years to live down.

The incident typified the kind of thinking which has been mainly responsible for Scotland's comparatively poor international record since the War. It is true that, considering the size of her population, Scotland should not be allowed on the same field as nations like England, West Germany, Italy and Russia, countries with a vastly greater number of registered players.

But over the years Scotland has still proved that quality matters far more than quantity. She has produced dozens of players of world class, players whose hallmark has always been pure, natural ability, and the source shows no sign of drying up.

It is this natural feeling of the Scots for football, both in playing the game and watching it, which forced the SFA to bow to the demands of the present, in spite of a strong desire in some quarters to stay safely, comfortably and non-competitively in pre-War days. For while some countries might have grown apathetic about continual failure, the Scots instead became angry.

After the failure to qualify in the summer of 1971 for the European Championship, the uproar reached frightening proportions. Bobby Brown, a man probably far too gentle and likeable for a job which demanded toughness to the point of inflexibility, was sacked. Soon after, the SFA let it be known that they were willing to take on the best man available at a suitable salary —popularly quoted at £10,000.

That autumn, the task was offered to Willie Cunningham, manager of Falkirk, who turned it down. There was a brief period of worry in case the SFA should think that they could do no more and return to their old ways. But then, happily, Tommy Docherty appeared on the scene. He took the job on a trial basis, but there was never any real doubt that he would stay on. His impact on public and players alike was immediate and impressive and the side played confident, thoughtful football in the remaining European Championship qualifying games against Portugal and Belgium.

At last it seemed Scotland had a fighting chance. The conditions and salary of the managership guaranteed some much needed permanency where it mattered. The manager himself was a man of wide experience and proven ability. But perhaps most significant of all were the signs, of which Docherty's appointment was but one, that the progressive voices at the SFA were at last making themselves heard.

Change was certainly long overdue. Before Docherty's appointment few people doubted that the SFA Selection Committee—later called the International Committee— wielded far more power than was good for the game in Scotland. Jock Stein's decision to turn down the full-time job and the £10,000 that was said to go with it, made it quite clear that the conditions of the job were very, very wrong.

Thus, the arrival of Tommy Docherty was generally interpreted as the start of a revolution in Park Gardens. Only a few years previously the appointment of so uncompromising, so determined a man would have been unthinkable.

Even Scottish clubs refuse to release their players

But, of course, only the most naive could have sat back to await with confidence a sudden, irresistible upsurge of Scottish football into the topmost strata of the game. The presence of Tommy Docherty solved one problem. Another remained—one which has bedevilled Scotland's ambitions at least as persist-

ently as the eccentricities of the SFA. For if it is one thing to pick eleven players, it can be quite another thing to get these eleven on the field in the dark blue jerseys of Scotland. Players are not employed by international associations but by clubs. No country, with the possible exception of Northern Ireland, has been worse hit than Scotland by this simple fact of football life.

For Jock Stein was referring not only to any SFA shortcomings when he expressed his dissatisfaction with the conditions of the Scotland job. Crippling as that was, it seemed at times to be only a slight handicap compared to the difficulties in securing the release of players from their clubs. For example, the team Stein eventually fielded in Naples in 1965, for a game in which Scotland had to avoid defeat to stand a chance of qualifying for the World Cup finals, contained barely half of the players he had originally selected. Mackay, Stevenson, Crerand, Baxter, Law and Gilzean were all unavailable. Injuries and the dictates of Football League clubs gave Stein— and Scotland—no chance.

But the root of the problem lies in the economics of Scottish domestic football which have made regular selling of star players a pre-requisite of solvency. Admittedly, lack of imagination and vision at board level in these clubs has contributed to this unenviable situation, but that is another, larger question. The fact remains that English football is liberally sprinkled with high-calibre Scots who until 1976 were only freed to play for Scotland by the grace

and favour of their employers. On a great many occasions, neither the grace nor the favour were particularly forthcoming.

The reasons seemed to vary from diplomatic injuries to more open selfishness. And there was nothing, absolutely nothing, that Scotland was ever able to do about it. The SFA did not even guarantee the release of players with Scottish clubs. Bobby Brown had more than his share of troubles in the release of Scottish-based players, for selfishness knows no natural boundaries, and excuses are easy to invent, almost impossible to disprove. At last in 1976, the Football League agreed to postpone matches to release players in certain weeks for competitive internationals.

It is cruelly ironic that Docherty probably had more trouble with the release of players from the Scottish League than from the Football League. Apart from the Derby County players, the most conspicuous absentees from the squad for the Brazil Independence Tournament were from Scottish League clubs. Hay, Johnstone and Dalglish of Celtic, Jardine of Rangers, Stanton of Hibs all dropped out at one stage or another. It was left largely to the Anglos to earn Scotland their success.

*Below A dispirited Ally MacLeod—the subject of most of the press criticism which followed Scotland's disastrous results in the 1978 World Cup finals. **Opposite** Kenny Dalglish and Gordon McQueen spring an attack on the Welsh goal at Anfield.*

Tommy Docherty could usually be relied upon to figure in controversy but by the seventies his forthright approach was also tempered by a measure of flexibility. Nevertheless his drive lifted the head of Scottish football until, in the eyes of the SFA, he could not combine his national team duties with those of managing Manchester United. He gave way to Willie Ormond, who overcame the depression of a 5-0 thrashing by England in his first match to lead Scotland into the finals of the 1974 World Cup. It was a feat which softened some of Scotland's tragedies of the past.

56 years pass before Scotland play abroad

It is a past in which the lessons are quite as outstanding as the memories. We have already noted that amateurism—and amateurishness—was long a characteristic of the SFA. At one time, this was not only understandable but quite forgivable. The Association was formed, after all, in 1873, the year after what was nearly a complete Queen's Park side had represented Scotland in the first-ever international game against England and had achieved a creditable goal-less draw. Apart from 'missionary' tours to such underdeveloped football areas as North America, the SFA were happy enough to keep the international side within these islands for the next 56 years. There was not, true, an extensive choice of opposition in the first two decades of this century—international associations being relatively scarce—but England were always rather more adventurous. In 1928, just as Scotland were at long last paying more attention to European competition, they joined the other home countries in withdrawing from FIFA over a dispute as to how an amateur should be defined. And so it was that the World Cup started in 1930 without any representatives from the UK.

Immediately after the War, however, the British countries rejoined FIFA and were invited to send the top two in the Home International Championship to compete in Rio for the 1950 World Cup. Scotland finished second, but refused to go. They had already decided they would take part only as outright winners; it was a silly decision.

Even so, the challenge of the ever-growing world of football could not be ignored forever. In February of 1954, the SFA did appoint a team manager of a kind. They chose Andy Beattie, a man of stature and experience who soon found the job, with all its limitations, far too small for him. The SFA still persisted with their time-worn system of selection by committee. At the time Beattie claimed he had no real backing from the authorities and, in retrospect, that can hardly be questioned.

Just before the World Cup finals of 1954, held in Switzerland, Beattie resigned. He was bitter about being allowed only the bare minimum of players—one of whom was Tommy Docherty—and there was

also trouble over expenses. Beattie did fulfil a moral obligation by going with his men to Switzerland, but that campaign was lost before it started. Scotland lost 1-0 to Austria and took a terrible thrashing, 7-0, from Uruguay. One of the players recalled that on his return a selector greeted him with the words: 'Forget about what happened in Switzerland, just so long as we beat England in April.'

Incredibly, the next three years passed in argument... not over what sort of team manager was needed but whether any manager was needed at all. At length, in January 1958, Sir Matt Busby was appointed—still, of course, on a part-time basis, but that plan was soon destroyed by the Munich disaster. The team's trainer, Dawson Walker, took charge during the 1958 World Cup in Sweden—where Scotland finished bottom of their section with one point from a possible six. Sir Matt Busby's return that September was short-lived. He simply was not fit enough, and he resigned three months later.

Then back came Andy Beattie in the spring of the following year. Bygones, hopefully, would be bygones. Yet the selectors and the permanent administration remained all-powerful, and their attitude to the manager was unchanged. The selectors, themselves club directors, had never permitted their own managers too much control, and they could see no reason why the national side should be any different, especially since the English, even then, were little further advanced. Thus Beattie's second chance was no chance at all. He was sacked in the autumn of 1960 on the eve of a match in Cardiff, when he had asked to be excused so he might watch his new club, Nottingham Forest. But who could blame Beattie for putting his bread and butter before the jam?

Beattie's successor, Ian McColl, a former Rangers player of distinction, was still on the Ibrox staff when, in November 1960, he moved in to one of the most dubious jobs in football. Control stayed where it always had been—with the amateurs.

McColl was given neither the power nor the time. He stuck to his task for five years before he was fired in 1965 while training with his players at Largs. Then came Jock Stein, attempting vainly to pick up the pieces for the 1966 World Cup. And, on his exit, that infamous advertisement . . . 'might suit a man with other business interests'. No wonder Willie Waddell and Eddie Turnbull, two of Scotland's most successful club managers, turned down approaches from the SFA.

Those bad days for Scottish international football lasted until the 1974 World Cup when Ormond's squad were unluckily eliminated after two draws and a win. But in 1975 five players, including Bremner the captain, were banned after a night club incident following an international in Denmark. The self-destructive element which has always plagued Scottish football was back and, in fact, followed the team to South America and the 1978 World Cup finals.

In Argentina, they won the game they were expected to lose, drew the one they should have won and lost the one they might have drawn. It was off the field, however, that the most damage was done to their reputation: the conduct of the players was heavily criticised and certain of them hawked their stories round the press — variously blaming the disastrous results against Peru and Iran on each other, the manager and, amazingly, lack of financial incentives. In addition, Willie Johnston was sent home following a positive dope test after the game against Iran and was later banned from international competition for life by the Scottish FA.

The match against Holland, eventual finalists in the competition, had been a totally unexpected, excellent game which the Scots had won 3-2 but which only served to highlight what had gone wrong before. Scotland's international lot rarely seems to be a happy one.

***Right** A typical newpaper headline the morning after Scotland's dismal 1-1 draw with Iran in the 1978 World Cup finals.*

FULL INTERNATIONALS PLAYED BY SCOTLAND 1870–OCTOBER 1978

Date		*Venue*	*Opponents*	*Score*
*19 November	1870	Kennington Oval	England	0-1
*28 February	1871	Kennington Oval	England	1-1
*18 November	1871	Kennington Oval	England	1-2
*24 February	1872	Kennington Oval	England	0-1
30 November	1872	Glasgow	England	0-0
8 March	1873	London	England	2-4
7 March	1874	Glasgow	England	2-1
6 March	1875	London	England	2-2
4 March	1876	Glasgow	England	3-0
25 March	1876	Glasgow	Wales	4-0
3 March	1877	London	England	3-1
15 March	1877	Wrexham	Wales	2-0
2 March	1878	Glasgow	England	7-2
23 March	1878	Glasgow	Wales	9-0
5 April	1879	London	England	4-5
7 April	1879	Wrexham	Wales	3-0
13 March	1880	Glasgow	England	5-4
27 March	1880	Glasgow	Wales	5-1
12 March	1881	London	England	6-1
14 March	1881	Wrexham	Wales	5-1
11 March	1882	Glasgow	England	5-1
25 March	1882	Glasgow	Wales	5-0
10 March	1883	Sheffield	England	3-2
12 March	1883	Wrexham	Wales	3-0
15 March	1884	Glasgow	England	1-0
26 March	1884	Belfast	Ireland	5-0
29 March	1884	Glasgow	Wales	4-1
14 March	1885	Glasgow	Ireland	8-2
21 March	1885	London	England	1-1
23 March	1885	Wrexham	Wales	8-1
20 March	1886	Belfast	Ireland	7-2
27 March	1886	Glasgow	England	1-1
10 April	1886	Glasgow	Wales	4-1
19 February	1887	Glasgow	Ireland	4-1
19 March	1887	Blackburn	England	3-2
21 March	1887	Wrexham	Wales	2-0
10 March	1888	Edinburgh	Wales	5-1
17 March	1888	Glasgow	England	0-5
24 March	1888	Belfast	Ireland	10-2
9 March	1889	Glasgow	Ireland	7-0
13 April	1889	London	England	3-2
15 April	1889	Wrexham	Wales	0-0
22 March	1890	Paisley	Wales	5-0
29 March	1890	Belfast	Ireland	4-1
5 April	1890	Glasgow	England	1-1
21 March	1891	Wrexham	Wales	4-3
28 March	1891	Glasgow	Ireland	2-1
4 April	1891	Blackburn	England	1-2
19 March	1892	Belfast	Ireland	3-2
26 March	1892	Edinburgh	Wales	6-1
2 April	1892	Glasgow	England	1-4
18 March	1893	Wrexham	Wales	8-0
25 March	1893	Glasgow	Ireland	6-1
1 April	1893	London	England	2-5
24 March	1894	Kilmarnock	Wales	5-2
31 March	1894	Belfast	Ireland	2-1
7 April	1894	Glasgow	England	2-2
23 March	1895	Wrexham	Wales	2-2
30 March	1895	Glasgow	Ireland	3-1
6 April	1895	Liverpool	England	0-3
21 March	1896	Dundee	Wales	4-0
28 March	1896	Belfast	Ireland	3-3
4 April	1896	Glasgow	England	2-1
20 March	1897	Wrexham	Wales	2-2
27 March	1897	Glasgow	Ireland	5-1
3 April	1897	London	England	2-1
19 March	1898	Motherwell	Wales	5-2
26 March	1898	Belfast	Ireland	3-0
2 April	1898	Glasgow	England	1-3
18 March	1899	Wrexham	Wales	6-0
25 March	1899	Glasgow	Ireland	9-1
8 April	1899	Birmingham	England	1-2
3 February	1900	Aberdeen	Wales	5-2
3 March	1900	Belfast	Ireland	3-0
7 April	1900	Glasgow	England	4-1
23 February	1901	Glasgow	Ireland	11-0
2 March	1901	Wrexham	Wales	1-1
30 March	1901	London	England	2-2
1 March	1902	Belfast	Ireland	5-1
15 March	1902	Greenock	Wales	5-1
†5 April	1902	Glasgow	England	1-1
3 May	1902	Birmingham	England	2-2
9 March	1903	Cardiff	Wales	1-0
21 March	1903	Glasgow	Ireland	0-2
4 April	1903	Sheffield	England	2-1
12 March	1904	Dundee	Wales	1-1
26 March	1904	Dublin	Ireland	1-1
9 April	1904	Glasgow	England	0-1
6 March	1905	Wrexham	Wales	1-3
18 March	1905	Glasgow	Ireland	4-0
1 April	1905	London	England	0-1
3 March	1906	Edinburgh	Wales	0-2
17 March	1906	Dublin	Ireland	1-0
7 April	1906	Glasgow	England	2-1
4 March	1907	Wrexham	Wales	0-1
16 March	1907	Glasgow	Ireland	3-0
6 April	1907	Newcastle	England	1-1
7 March	1908	Dundee	Wales	2-1
14 March	1908	Dublin	Ireland	5-0
4 April	1908	Glasgow	England	1-1
1 March	1909	Wrexham	Wales	2-3
27 March	1909	Glasgow	Ireland	5-0
3 April	1909	London	England	0-2
5 March	1910	Kilmarnock	Wales	1-0
19 March	1910	Belfast	Ireland	0-1
2 April	1910	Glasgow	England	2-0
6 March	1911	Cardiff	Wales	2-2
18 March	1911	Glasgow	Ireland	2-0
1 April	1911	Liverpool	England	1-1
2 March	1912	Edinburgh	Wales	1-0
16 March	1912	Belfast	Ireland	4-1
23 March	1912	Glasgow	England	1-1
3 March	1913	Wrexham	Wales	0-0
15 March	1913	Dublin	Ireland	2-1
5 April	1913	London	England	0-1
28 February	1914	Glasgow	Wales	0-0
14 March	1914	Belfast	Ireland	1-1
4 April	1914	Glasgow	England	3-1
V26 April	1919	Everton	England	2-2
V 3 May	1919	Glasgow	England	3-4
26 February	1920	Cardiff	Wales	1-1
13 March	1920	Glasgow	Ireland	3-0
10 April	1920	Sheffield	England	4-5
12 February	1921	Aberdeen	Wales	2-1
26 February	1921	Belfast	Ireland	2-0
9 April	1921	Glasgow	England	3-0
4 February	1922	Wrexham	Wales	1-2
4 March	1922	Glasgow	Ireland	2-1
8 April	1922	Birmingham	England	1-0
3 March	1923	Belfast	Ireland	1-0
17 March	1923	Paisley	Wales	2-0
14 April	1923	Glasgow	England	2-2
16 February	1924	Cardiff	Wales	0-2
1 March	1924	Glasgow	N Ireland	2-0
12 April	1924	Wembley	England	1-1
14 February	1925	Edinburgh	Wales	3-1
28 February	1925	Belfast	N Ireland	3-0
4 April	1925	Glasgow	England	2-0
31 October	1925	Cardiff	Wales	3-0
27 February	1926	Glasgow	N Ireland	4-0
17 April	1926	Manchester	England	1-0
30 October	1926	Glasgow	Wales	3-0
26 February	1927	Belfast	N Ireland	2-0
2 April	1927	Glasgow	England	1-2
29 October	1927	Wrexham	Wales	2-2
25 February	1928	Glasgow	N Ireland	0-1
31 March	1928	Wembley	England	5-1
27 October	1928	Glasgow	Wales	4-2
23 February	1929	Belfast	N Ireland	7-3
13 April	1929	Glasgow	England	1-0
1 June	1929	Berlin	Germany	1-1
4 June	1929	Amsterdam	Netherlands	2-0
26 October	1929	Cardiff	Wales	4-2
22 February	1930	Glasgow	N Ireland	3-1
5 April	1930	Wembley	England	2-5
18 May	1930	Paris	France	2-0
25 October	1930	Glasgow	Wales	1-1
21 February	1931	Belfast	N Ireland	0-0
28 March	1931	Glasgow	England	2-0
16 May	1931	Vienna	Austria	0-5
20 May	1931	Rome	Italy	0-3
24 May	1931	Geneva	Switzerland	3-2
19 September	1931	Glasgow	N Ireland	3-1
31 October	1931	Wrexham	Wales	3-2
9 April	1932	Wembley	England	0-3
8 May	1932	Paris	France	3-1
17 September	1932	Belfast	N Ireland	4-0
26 October	1932	Edinburgh	Wales	2-5
1 April	1933	Glasgow	England	2-1
16 September	1933	Glasgow	N Ireland	1-2
4 October	1933	Cardiff	Wales	2-3
29 November	1933	Glasgow	Austria	2-2
14 April	1934	Wembley	England	0-3
20 October	1934	Belfast	N Ireland	1-2
21 November	1934	Aberdeen	Wales	3-2
6 April	1935	Glasgow	England	2-0
J21 August	1935	Glasgow	England	4-2
5 October	1935	Cardiff	Wales	1-1
13 November	1935	Edinburgh	N Ireland	2-1
4 April	1936	Wembley	England	1-1
14 October	1936	Glasgow	Germany	2-0
31 October	1936	Belfast	N Ireland	3-1
2 December	1936	Dundee	Wales	1-2
17 April	1937	Glasgow	England	3-1
9 May	1937	Vienna	Austria	1-1
15 May	1937	Prague	Czechoslovakia	3-1
30 October	1937	Cardiff	Wales	1-2
10 November	1937	Aberdeen	N Ireland	1-1
8 December	1937	Glasgow	Czechoslovakia	5-0
9 April	1938	Wembley	England	1-0
21 May	1938	Amsterdam	Netherlands	3-1
8 October	1938	Belfast	N Ireland	2-0
9 November	1938	Edinburgh	Wales	3-2
7 December	1938	Glasgow	Hungary	3-1
15 April	1939	Glasgow	England	1-2
WT 2 December	1939	Newcastle	England	1-2
WT11 May	1940	Glasgow	England	1-1
WT 8 February	1941	Newcastle	England	3-2
WT 3 May	1941	Glasgow	England	1-3
WT 4 October	1941	Wembley	England	0-2
WT17 January	1942	Wembley	England	0-3
WT18 April	1942	Glasgow	England	5-4
WT10 October	1942	Wembley	England	0-0
WT17 April	1943	Glasgow	England	0-4
WT16 October	1943	Manchester	England	0-8
WT19 February	1944	Wembley	England	2-6
WT22 April	1944	Glasgow	England	2-3
WT14 October	1944	Wembley	England	2-6
WT 3 February	1945	Villa Park	England	3-2
WT14 April	1945	Glasgow	England	1-6
V13 April	1946	Glasgow	England	1-0
23 January	1946	Glasgow	Belgium	2-2
15 May	1946	Glasgow	Switzerland	3-1
19 October	1946	Wrexham	Wales	1-3
27 November	1946	Glasgow	N Ireland	0-0
12 April	1947	Wembley	England	1-1
18 May	1947	Brussels	Belgium	1-2
24 May	1947	Luxembourg	Luxembourg	6-0
4 October	1947	Belfast	N Ireland	0-2
12 November	1947	Glasgow	Wales	1-2
10 April	1948	Glasgow	England	0-2
28 April	1948	Glasgow	Belgium	2-0
17 May	1948	Berne	Switzerland	1-2
23 May	1948	Paris	France	0-3
23 October	1948	Cardiff	Wales	3-1

Jeers for Ally after World Cup disgrace

THE SHAME  OF SCOTLAND

Date		Venue	Opponents	Score
17 November	1948	Glasgow	N Ireland	3-2
9 April	1949	Wembley	England	3-1
27 April	1949	Glasgow	France	2-0
WC 1 October	1949	Belfast	N Ireland	8-2
WC 9 November	1949	Glasgow	Wales	2-0
WC15 April	1950	Glasgow	England	0-1
26 April	1950	Glasgow	Switzerland	3-1
21 May	1950	Lisbon	Portugal	2-2
27 May	1950	Paris	France	1-0
21 October	1950	Cardiff	Wales	3-1
1 November	1950	Glasgow	N Ireland	6-1
13 December	1950	Glasgow	Austria	0-1
14 April	1951	Wembley	England	3-2
12 May	1951	Glasgow	Denmark	3-1
16 May	1951	Glasgow	France	1-0
20 May	1951	Brussels	Belgium	5-0
27 May	1951	Vienna	Austria	0-4
6 October	1951	Belfast	N Ireland	3-0
14 November	1951	Glasgow	Wales	0-1
5 April	1952	Glasgow	England	1-2
30 April	1952	Glasgow	USA	6-0
25 May	1952	Copenhagen	Denmark	2-1
30 May	1952	Stockholm	Sweden	1-3
18 October	1952	Cardiff	Wales	2-1
5 November	1952	Glasgow	N Ireland	1-1
18 April	1953	Wembley	England	2-2
6 May	1953	Glasgow	Sweden	1-2
WC 3 October	1953	Belfast	N Ireland	3-1
WC 4 November	1953	Glasgow	Wales	3-3
WC 3 April	1954	Glasgow	England	2-4
5 May	1954	Glasgow	Norway	1-0
19 May	1954	Oslo	Norway	1-1
25 May	1954	Helsinki	Finland	2-1
WC16 June	1954	Zurich	Austria	0-1
WC19 June	1954	Basle	Uruguay	0-7
16 October	1954	Cardiff	Wales	1-0
3 November	1954	Glasgow	N Ireland	2-2
8 December	1954	Glasgow	Hungary	2-4
2 April	1955	Wembley	England	2-7
4 May	1955	Glasgow	Portugal	3-0
15 May	1955	Belgrade	Yugoslavia	2-2
19 May	1955	Vienna	Austria	4-1
29 May	1955	Budapest	Hungary	1-3
8 October	1955	Belfast	N Ireland	1-2
9 November	1955	Glasgow	Wales	2-0
14 April	1956	Glasgow	England	1-1
2 May	1956	Glasgow	Austria	1-1
20 October	1956	Cardiff	Wales	2-2
7 November	1956	Glasgow	N Ireland	1-0
21 November	1956	Glasgow	Yugoslavia	2-0
6 April	1957	Wembley	England	1-2
WC 8 May	1957	Glasgow	Spain	4-2
WC19 May	1957	Basle	Switzerland	2-1
22 May	1957	Stuttgart	West Germany	3-1
WC26 May	1957	Madrid	Spain	1-4
5 October	1957	Belfast	N Ireland	1-1
WC 6 November	1957	Glasgow	Switzerland	3-2
13 November	1957	Glasgow	Wales	1-1
19 April	1958	Glasgow	England	0-4
7 May	1958	Glasgow	Hungary	1-1
1 June	1958	Warsaw	Poland	2-1
WC 8 June	1958	Vasteras	Yugoslavia	1-1
WC11 June	1958	Norrkoping	Paraguay	2-3
WC15 June	1958	Orebro	France	1-2
18 October	1958	Cardiff	Wales	3-0
5 November	1958	Glasgow	N Ireland	2-2
11 April	1959	Wembley	England	0-1
6 May	1959	Glasgow	West Germany	3-2
27 May	1959	Amsterdam	Netherlands	2-1
3 June	1959	Lisbon	Portugal	0-1
3 October	1959	Belfast	N Ireland	4-0
4 November	1959	Glasgow	Wales	1-1
9 April	1960	Glasgow	England	1-1
4 May	1960	Glasgow	Poland	2-3
29 May	1960	Vienna	Austria	1-4
5 June	1960	Budapest	Hungary	3-3
8 June	1960	Ankara	Turkey	2-4
22 October	1960	Cardiff	Wales	0-2
9 November	1960	Glasgow	N Ireland	5-2
15 April	1961	Wembley	England	3-9
WC 3 May	1961	Glasgow	Eire	4-1
WC 7 May	1961	Dublin	Eire	3-0
WC14 May	1961	Bratislava	Czechoslovakia	0-4
WC26 September	1961	Glasgow	Czechoslovakia	3-2
7 October	1961	Belfast	N Ireland	6-1
8 November	1961	Glasgow	Wales	2-0
WC29 November	1961	Brussels	Czechoslovakia	2-4
14 April	1962	Glasgow	England	2-0
2 May	1962	Glasgow	Uruguay	2-3
20 October	1962	Cardiff	Wales	3-2
7 November	1962	Glasgow	N Ireland	5-1
6 April	1963	Wembley	England	2-1
‡8 May	1963	Glasgow	Austria	4-1
4 June	1963	Bergen	Norway	3-4
9 June	1963	Dublin	Eire	0-1
13 June	1963	Madrid	Spain	6-2
12 October	1963	Belfast	N Ireland	1-2
7 November	1963	Glasgow	Norway	6-1
20 November	1963	Glasgow	Wales	2-1
11 April	1964	Glasgow	England	1-0
12 May	1964	Hanover	West Germany	2-2
3 October	1964	Cardiff	Wales	2-3
WC21 October	1964	Glasgow	Finland	3-1
25 November	1964	Glasgow	N Ireland	3-2
10 April	1965	Wembley	England	2-2
8 May	1965	Glasgow	Spain	0-0
WC23 May	1965	Chorzow	Poland	1-1
WC27 May	1965	Helsinki	Finland	2-1
2 October	1965	Belfast	N Ireland	2-3
WC13 October	1965	Glasgow	Poland	1-2
WC 9 November	1965	Glasgow	Italy	1-0
24 November	1965	Glasgow	Wales	4-1
WC 7 December	1965	Naples	Italy	0-3
2 April	1966	Glasgow	England	3-4
11 May	1966	Glasgow	Holland	0-3
18 June	1966	Glasgow	Portugal	0-1
25 June	1966	Glasgow	Brazil	1-1
22 October	1966	Cardiff	Wales	1-1
16 November	1966	Glasgow	N Ireland	2-1
15 April	1967	Wembley	England	3-2
10 May	1967	Glasgow	Russia	0-2
21 October	1967	Belfast	N Ireland	0-1
22 November	1967	Glasgow	Wales	3-2
24 February	1968	Glasgow	England	1-1
30 May	1968	Amsterdam	Holland	0-0
16 October	1968	Copenhagen	Denmark	1-0
WC 6 November	1968	Glasgow	Austria	2-1
WC11 December	1968	Nicosia	Cyprus	5-0
WC16 April	1969	Glasgow	West Germany	1-1
3 May	1969	Wrexham	Wales	5-3
6 May	1969	Glasgow	N Ireland	1-1
10 May	1969	Wembley	England	1-4
WC12 May	1969	Glasgow	Cyprus	8-0
21 September	1969	Dublin	Eire	1-1
WC22 October	1969	Hamburg	West Germany	2-3
WC 5 November	1969	Vienna	Austria	0-2
18 April	1970	Belfast	N Ireland	1-0
22 April	1970	Glasgow	Wales	0-0
25 April	1970	Glasgow	England	0-0
EC11 November	1970	Glasgow	Denmark	1-0
EC 3 February	1971	Liege	Belgium	0-3
EC21 April	1971	Lisbon	Portugal	0-2
15 May	1971	Cardiff	Wales	0-0
18 May	1971	Glasgow	N Ireland	0-1
22 May	1971	Wembley	England	1-3
EC 9 June	1971	Copenhagen	Denmark	0-1
14 June	1971	Moscow	Russia	0-1
EC13 October	1971	Glasgow	Portugal	2-1
EC10 November	1971	Glasgow	Belgium	1-0
1 December	1971	Rotterdam	Holland	1-2
26 April	1972	Glasgow	Peru	2-0
20 May	1972	Glasgow	N Ireland	2-0
24 May	1972	Glasgow	Wales	1-0
28 May	1972	Glasgow	England	0-1
28 June	1972	Belo Horizonte	Yugoslavia	2-2
2 July	1972	Porto Alegre	Czechoslovakia	0-0
5 July	1972	Rio de Janeiro	Brazil	0-1
WC18 October	1972	Copenhagen	Denmark	4-1
WC15 November	1973	Glasgow	Denmark	2-0
14 February	1973	Glasgow	England	0-5
12 May	1973	Wrexham	Wales	2-0
16 May	1973	Glasgow	N Ireland	1-2
19 May	1973	Wembley	England	0-1
22 June	1973	Berne	Switzerland	0-1
30 June	1973	Glasgow	Brazil	0-1
WC26 September	1973	Glasgow	Czechoslovakia	2-1
WC17 October	1973	Bratislava	Czechoslovakia	0-1
14 November	1973	Glasgow	West Germany	1-1
27 March	1974	Frankfurt	West Germany	1-2
27 May	1974	Glasgow	N Ireland	0-1
14 May	1974	Glasgow	Wales	2-0
18 May	1974	Glasgow	England	2-0
1 June	1974	Bruges	Belgium	1-2
6 June	1974	Oslo	Norway	2-1
WC14 June	1974	Dortmund	Zaire	2-0
WC18 June	1974	Frankfurt	Brazil	0-0
WC22 June	1974	Frankfurt	Yugoslavia	1-1
30 October	1974	Glasgow	East Germany	3-0
EC20 November	1974	Glasgow	Spain	1-2
EC 5 February	1975	Valencia	Spain	1-1
16 April	1975	Gothenburg	Sweden	1-1
13 May	1975	Glasgow	Portugal	1-0
17 May	1975	Cardiff	Wales	2-2
20 May	1975	Glasgow	N Ireland	3-0
24 May	1975	Wembley	England	1-5
EC 1 June	1975	Bucharest	Rumania	1-1
EC 3 September	1975	Copenhagen	Denmark	1-0
EC29 October	1975	Glasgow	Denmark	3-1
EC17 December	1975	Glasgow	Rumania	1-1
7 April	1976	Glasgow	Switzerland	1-0
6 May	1976	Glasgow	Wales	3-1
8 May	1976	Glasgow	N Ireland	3-0
15 May	1976	Glasgow	England	2-1
8 September	1976	Glasgow	Finland	6-0
WC13 October	1976	Prague	Czechoslovakia	0-2
WC17 November	1976	Glasgow	Wales	1-0
27 April	1977	Glasgow	Sweden	3-1
28 May	1977	Wrexham	Wales	0-0
1 June	1977	Glasgow	N Ireland	3-0
4 June	1977	Wembley	England	2-1
15 June	1977	Santiago	Chile	4-2
18 June	1977	Buenos Aires	Argentina	1-1
23 June	1977	Rio de Janeiro	Brazil	0-2
7 September	1977	East Berlin	East Germany	0-1
WC21 September	1977	Glasgow	Czechoslovakia	3-1
WC12 October	1977	Liverpool	Wales	2-0
22 February	1978	Glasgow	Bulgaria	2-1
13 May	1978	Glasgow	N Ireland	1-1
17 May	1978	Glasgow	Wales	1-1
20 May	1978	Glasgow	England	0-1
WC 3 June	1978	Cordoba	Peru	1-3
WC 7 June	1978	Cordoba	Iran	1-1
WC11 June	1978	Mendoza	Holland	3-2
EC20 September	1978	Vienna	Austria	2-3
25 October	1978	Glasgow	Norway	3-2

* These matches were played by a team of Scots resident in London. They are not regarded as official.
†This match was abandoned after a disaster at the ground. It is not regarded as official.
‡Abandoned after 79 minutes. V – Victory games. J – Jubilee game. WT – War-time game. WC – World Cup. EC – European Championship.

A funny thing happened on the way to Windsor Park

Vanishing Best keeps Ireland waiting again

'The whole thing,' Peter Doherty once said of Irish international football, 'is a complete joke.' There 'was no trace of vindictiveness in that comment. There was nothing the manager liked better than a laugh, and if Irish football has been a joke, it certainly has never been a bad one.

Besides, Doherty's contribution to the comic side of Irish football has been as rich as anyone's. There was the time when he was up until the late hours playing cards with his players before a match with Scotland. A worried supporter pointed out the time, mentioning that the Scots, like all good footballers, were safely tucked up in bed. 'Ah yes,' came the reply, 'but are they sleeping?'

Doherty talks with fond nostalgia about his eleven years spell as Ireland's manager, but he is not without his regrets. 'At times when I look back, I feel ashamed of what went on. I am convinced that if we had been organized we would have done much much better.'

Haphazard administration as well as circumstances outside any Irishman's control have long blighted Ireland's record. For years there was not even the chance for players to meet each other before the day of the match. Tom Priestley, the Chelsea and Coleraine winger of the 1930s recalled his introduction to the national team.

What would the FA have done to George Best?

'Elisha Scott, one of the world's greatest ever goalkeepers was then captain. To me and most fans of Irish football Scott had seemed like a God. I was really looking forward to meeting him, but it wasn't until we were in the dressing room before the kick-off that I actually spoke to him. Although he was my captain, I barely talked to him for five minutes. There was nothing unusual about that in those days. That was the way things were.'

Things had clearly changed for the better by the time Terry Neill took over the managership in 1971. But the cavalier approach to international football still remained. No one actually missed the boat for the Home Championship in 1972, but there was still one conspicuous absentée from the Irish party. For the third time in a year George Best failed to report on time for the Irish team. In England, where the punishments for Alan Hudson and Colin Todd showed how harsh the disciplinary machine could be, Best's international career would surely

have been finished. Yet so far from being censorious, Terry Neill generously kept Best's place in the team open until the last possible minute and even after the magnificent victory over England at Wembley, he was prepared to say how much he wished Best had been there to share his pleasure.

But then anyone whose task it is to get eleven Irish footballers to appear together at any one place has to be unusually tolerant. The history of Irish international football, if not quite a comedy of errors, is certainly littered with episodes which could only have happened to Irishmen.

Even in 1913-14, the season of Ireland's outright win in the Home Championship, there was the usual last minute chase for that elusive eleventh man. Ireland's right-winger at the time was a Manchester United player by the name of Hamill, whose reputation was for whole hearted effort at all times. Well . . . not quite at all times for on the Saturday before the crucial match against England, United officials noted an unusual lethargy about Hamill's play. Asked for an explanation, the unfortunate winger admitted that he had been conserving his energy in anticipation of the international. His patriotism cost him dear for he was promptly forbidden to play for his country. But, as so often, Ireland triumphed in adversity, winning against England and Wales and drawing with Scotland for the fifth point that gave them the Championship outright.

That success was to be an isolated one. Ireland did not win another international until 1923 and only won another eleven in the years before the Second World War. The poor record is largely attributable to the partition in 1921 and the formation of the breakaway Football Association of Ireland in the same year.

The years between the partition and the appointment of Doherty in 1951 are not recalled by Ulstermen with relish. It was left to Eire to provide the two highlights of the era. Against Belgium in a 1934 World Cup qualifying game, the Aberdeen centre-forward, Paddy Moore, scored all four goals in a remarkable comeback with which Eire pulled back a four goal deficit to draw 4-4. As the FAI Annual put it: 'This was Paddy Moore's finest hour, despite the honours he won afterwards. We were behind. Paddy brought his total of goals to four, to earn a draw, when we seemed to be licked.' That game may well have been Moore's finest hour, but Eire's was definitely on 21 September 1949 when, with a team that

MANCHESTER UNITED'S vanishing super-star George Best scored an international hat-trick when he failed to report on schedule for Northern Ireland in Glasgow yesterday.

It is the third time in 12 months that he has broken the rules of the game for his country.

He was a late-comer exactly a year ago when he missed the first training session for the England game in Belfast.

By ALEX TOMER

disappointed but guarded a hint of No te

included a carpenter and a printer of a Dublin newspaper, they became the first ever 'foreign' side to beat England at home. Eire's 2-0 win was a personal triumph for captain Johnny Carey, who in the absence of any team manager, worked out the tactics and took care of the pre-match training session.

Carey's contribution to Irish football was as great as anyone's. Before the Second World War the northern Irish Football Association regularly selected players from the Free State for its international sides,

and Carey was one of several to play for both Northern Ireland and Eire. In one week he actually managed to play for both sides —on September 26 and 28 1946— against the full England side.

The fault of Northern Ireland's poor record between the Wars did not lie with the players so much as the system under which they played. One anecdote, told by Hugh Davey, throws some light on what was wrong. Davey and his Reading colleague, Billy McConnell, had travelled up to Belfast via London.

SYNDICATION INTERNATIONAL

OWEN BARNES

Top left In May 1972, for the third time in twelve months, George Best failed to report on time for an Irish international. This time he had taken to the Spanish beaches, threatening to give up the game.
Top Without Best and forced to play away from home, the Irish defence conceded two goals to the Scots, but a 1-0 win against England in the next game was ample consolation for that. It was only Ireland's third ever win in England.
Above Port Vale's Sammy Morgan scores Northern Ireland's equalizing goal against Spain at Hull City's Boothferry Park. Unable to play in Ireland, the Irish settled instead for the club ground of manager Terry Neill.
Left Manchester United's Johnny Carey, winner of 28 caps for Eire and seven for Northern Ireland.

Irish international in 1882, were happily things of the past. There were meritorious draws, occasional victories against Scotland and above all the 3-2 win of 1957 on Ireland's second visit to Wembley.

That match was a tribute to Blanchflower's captaincy. Twice he ordered new tactical dispositions on the field in response to the changing phases of the game. Ireland took the lead with a Jimmy McIlroy penalty which went into the net via a post and the back of the diving England goalkeeper. 'Brother, when we do it, we do it clever,' Blanchflower commented after the game. The second goal was scored by Sammy McCrory, the Southend United inside-forward. In the morning papers Duncan Edwards had asked: 'What is an old man like McCrory doing in a game like this.' 'Not bad for an old man, eh!' McCrory said as he passed Edwards on his way back to the centre after the goal.

That match was the prelude to what was Ireland's golden era—the 1958 World Cup finals in Sweden. For the Irish it was a carnival as well as the most important competition in the world. They became the heroes of Sweden and the darlings of the world's press. While the Germans, Brazilians, Argentinians, Czechs and even the English had strict security and 'no interview' rules, the Irish camp, in a dreamy little seaside haunt at Tylosand, was open to all.

'We like to train on whiskey and potato bread'

The lovable Gerry Morgan, with his Jimmy Durante profile, and rakishly worn head gear, was the most photographed and most quoted character in Sweden. He had an unlimited supply of stories, most of them unadulterated blarney. He told one credulous scribe that the Irish trained on whisky and potato bread. Another went away with the story that the players would each receive a £1,000 bonus for each victory, and to cap that he said Jimmy McIlroy would be knighted if Northern Ireland won the cup.

It was all good, clean fun and valuable publicity for the 'mad Irish' who won thousands of supporters and were 'adopted' by the residents of Halmstad, where they played their first two matches. A goal from Wilbur Cush gave the team an encouraging 1-0 win against Czechoslovakia but that was soon followed by a 3-1 defeat by Argentina.

Even in defeat the Irish won friends. After the game the Irish party made their way, as usual, to 'The Black Kat', Halmstad's one night club. As one player put it: 'Well, you can never miss a chance to drown your sorrows can you.' For once the Argentinians were there, but they were closeted in an upstairs reception room. The revelry, meanwhile, was all downstairs, where the defeated Irish team were drinking to finer prospects in the next game.

A stirring 2-2 draw against West Germany meant a sectional play-off with Czechoslovakia, which the

As usual they put in for their expenses: 'Three bob for a taxi and half a crown for a meal. As soon as we sent in the bill the officials were on to us, saying that that was far too much and that we'd have to cut down for the next game or we wouldn't be sure of our places in the team. We just laughed.'

The renaissance began in August 1951, when the international selectors wisely, if rather belatedly, decided that it was time to introduce professionalism at the top and appointed Peter Doherty as manager.

Why Doherty? There could have been no other choice. The man who had decorated the game with his magical artistry and was rated by Sepp Herberger, the wily West German team manager, as 'one of the greatest all-round players' was steeped in football.

He had all the qualities, but his main assets were his fierce dedication, honesty, sense of humour, hypnotic homespun eloquence and stern, sensibly imposed, discipline. He was the saviour of Irish football. But the revival was not instant. It took years of hard work, patience and the enthusiasm of the players to change Northern Ireland's image from that of 'Aunt Sallies' to a team that was to prove itself of true international stature.

Doherty was a players' man. He shared their jokes, their triumphs, their disasters and he never lost his sense of humour. Only once did he lose his temper. That was in Bologna in 1961, when Northern Ireland were playing Italy in a tour friendly. Peter had persuaded Wilbur Cush, than a Portadown player, to abandon his idea of retiring and had earmarked him for the job of marking Omar Sivori, the great inside-

forward. The selectors, who still selfishly clung to the job of picking the team, omitted Cush from the side.

'I don't think I have ever been so mad in my life,' said Doherty. 'I went to my hotel to pack my bags, I inquired about planes back home and I would have left on the spot. I stayed on only because it would have broken my heart to leave the players.'

Under the guidance of Doherty and his chief lieutenant, Danny Blanchflower, and with the infectious good humour of the late Gerry Morgan, a former international centre-half and one of the last of the traditional cloth cap trainers, results began to improve. Victories were still hard to come by, but the horrible hidings from England, which had been all too regular since the 13-0 catastrophe in the first ever

FULL INTERNATIONALS PLAYED BY IRELAND AND NORTHERN IRELAND FEBRUARY 1882 – OCTOBER 1978

Date		Venue	Opponents	Score
18 February	1882	Belfast	England	0-13
25 February	1882	Wrexham	Wales	1-7
24 February	1883	Liverpool	England	0-7
17 March	1883	Belfast	Wales	1-1
9 February	1884	Wrexham	Wales	0-6
23 February	1884	Belfast	England	1-8
26 March	1884	Belfast	Scotland	0-5
28 February	1885	Manchester	England	0-4
14 March	1885	Glasgow	Scotland	2-8
11 April	1885	Belfast	Wales	2-8
27 February	1886	Wrexham	Wales	0-5
13 March	1886	Belfast	England	1-6
20 March	1886	Belfast	Scotland	2-7
5 February	1887	Sheffield	England	0-7
19 February	1887	Glasgow	Scotland	1-4
12 March	1887	Belfast	Wales	4-1
3 March	1888	Wrexham	Wales	0-11
24 March	1888	Belfast	Scotland	2-10
31 March	1888	Belfast	England	1-5
2 March	1889	Liverpool	England	1-6
9 March	1889	Glasgow	Scotland	0-7
27 April	1889	Belfast	Wales	1-3
8 February	1890	Shrewsbury	Wales	2-5
15 March	1890	Belfast	England	1-9
29 March	1890	Belfast	Scotland	1-4
7 February	1891	Belfast	Wales	7-2
7 March	1891	Wolverhampton	England	1-6
28 March	1891	Glasgow	Scotland	1-2
27 February	1892	Bangor (Wales)	Wales	1-1
5 March	1892	Belfast	England	0-2
19 March	1892	Belfast	Scotland	2-3
25 February	1893	Birmingham	England	1-6
25 March	1893	Glasgow	Scotland	1-6
8 April	1893	Belfast	Wales	4-3
24 February	1894	Swansea	Wales	1-4
3 March	1894	Belfast	England	2-2
31 March	1894	Belfast	Scotland	1-2
9 March	1895	Derby	England	0-9
16 March	1895	Belfast	Wales	2-2
30 March	1895	Glasgow	Scotland	1-3
29 February	1896	Wrexham	Wales	1-6
7 March	1896	Belfast	England	0-2
28 March	1896	Belfast	Scotland	3-3
20 February	1897	Nottingham	England	0-6
•6 March	1897	Belfast	Wales	4-3
27 March	1897	Glasgow	Scotland	1-5
19 February	1898	Llandudno	Wales	1-0
5 March	1898	Belfast	England	2-3
26 March	1898	Belfast	Scotland	0-3
18 February	1899	Sunderland	England	2-13
4 March	1899	Belfast	Wales	1-0
25 March	1899	Glasgow	Scotland	1-9
24 February	1900	Llandudno	Wales	0-2
3 March	1900	Belfast	Scotland	0-3
17 March	1900	Dublin	England	0-2
23 February	1901	Glasgow	Scotland	0-11
9 March	1901	Southampton	England	0-3
23 March	1901	Llandudno	Wales	0-1
1 March	1902	Belfast	Scotland	1-5
22 March	1902	Belfast	England	0-1
22 March	1902	Cardiff	Wales	3-0
14 February	1903	Wolverhampton	England	0-4
21 March	1903	Glasgow	Scotland	2-0
28 March	1903	Belfast	Wales	2-0
12 March	1904	Belfast	England	1-3
21 March	1904	Bangor (Wales)	Wales	1-0
26 March	1904	Dublin	Scotland	1-1
25 February	1905	Middlesbrough	England	1-1
18 March	1905	Glasgow	Scotland	0-4
8 April	1905	Belfast	Wales	2-2
17 February	1906	Belfast	England	0-5
17 March	1906	Dublin	Scotland	0-1
2 April	1907	Wrexham	Wales	4-4
16 February	1907	Liverpool	England	0-1
23 February	1908	Belfast	Wales	2-3
16 March	1908	Glasgow	Scotland	0-3
15 February	1908	Belfast	England	1-3
14 March	1908	Dublin	Scotland	0-5
11 April	1908	Aberdare	Wales	1-0
13 February	1909	Bradford	England	0-4
20 March	1909	Belfast	Wales	2-3
27 March	1909	Glasgow	Scotland	0-5
12 February	1910	Belfast	England	1-1
11 March	1910	Wrexham	Wales	1-4
19 March	1910	Belfast	Scotland	1-0
11 February	1911	Derby	England	1-2
18 March	1911	Glasgow	Scotland	0-2
28 March	1911	Belfast	Wales	1-2
10 February	1912	Dublin	England	1-6
16 March	1912	Belfast	Scotland	1-4
13 April	1912	Cardiff	Wales	3-2
18 January	1913	Belfast	Wales	0-1
15 February	1913	Belfast	England	2-1
15 March	1913	Dublin	Scotland	1-2
19 January	1914	Wrexham	Wales	2-1
14 February	1914	Middlesbrough	England	3-0
14 March	1914	Belfast	Scotland	1-1
25 October	1919	Belfast	England	1-1
14 February	1920	Belfast	Wales	2-2
13 March	1920	Glasgow	Scotland	0-3
23 October	1920	Sunderland	England	0-2
26 February	1921	Belfast	Scotland	0-2
9 April	1921	Swansea	Wales	1-2
22 October	1921	Belfast	England	1-1
4 March	1922	Glasgow	Scotland	1-2
1 April	1922	Belfast	Wales	1-1
21 October	1922	West Bromwich	England	0-2
3 March	1923	Belfast	Scotland	0-1

Date		Venue	Opponents	Score
14 April	1923	Wrexham	Wales	3-0
20 October	1923	Belfast	England	2-1
1 March	1924	Glasgow	Scotland	0-2
15 March	1924	Belfast	Wales	0-1
22 October	1924	Liverpool	England	1-3
28 February	1925	Belfast	Scotland	0-3
18 April	1925	Wrexham	Wales	0-0
24 October	1925	Belfast	England	0-0
13 January	1926	Belfast	Wales	3-0
27 February	1926	Glasgow	Scotland	0-4
20 October	1926	Liverpool	England	3-3
26 February	1927	Belfast	Scotland	0-2
9 April	1927	Cardiff	Wales	2-2
22 October	1927	Belfast	England	2-0
4 February	1928	Belfast	Wales	1-2
25 February	1928	Glasgow	Scotland	1-0
22 October	1928	Liverpool	England	1-2
2 February	1929	Wrexham	Wales	2-2
23 February	1929	Belfast	Scotland	3-7
19 October	1929	Belfast	England	0-3
1 February	1930	Belfast	Wales	7-0
22 February	1930	Glasgow	Scotland	1-3
20 October	1930	Sheffield	England	1-5
21 February	1931	Belfast	Scotland	0-0
22 April	1931	Wrexham	Wales	2-3
19 September	1931	Glasgow	Scotland	1-3
17 October	1931	Belfast	England	2-6
5 December	1931	Belfast	Wales	4-0
17 September	1932	Belfast	Scotland	0-4
17 October	1932	Blackpool	England	0-1
7 December	1932	Wrexham	Wales	1-4
16 September	1933	Glasgow	Scotland	2-1
14 October	1933	Belfast	England	0-3
4 November	1933	Belfast	Wales	1-1
20 October	1934	Belfast	Scotland	2-1
6 February	1935	Liverpool	England	1-2
27 March	1935	Wrexham	Wales	1-3
19 October	1935	Belfast	England	1-3
13 November	1935	Edinburgh	Scotland	1-2
11 March	1936	Belfast	Wales	3-2
31 October	1936	Belfast	Scotland	1-3
18 November	1936	Stoke	England	1-3
17 March	1937	Wrexham	Wales	1-4
23 October	1937	Belfast	England	1-5
10 November	1937	Aberdeen	Scotland	1-1
16 March	1938	Belfast	Wales	1-0
8 October	1938	Belfast	Scotland	0-2
16 November	1938	Manchester	England	0-7
15 March	1939	Wrexham	Wales	1-3
V15 September	1945	Belfast	England	0-1
28 September	1946	Belfast	England	2-7
27 November	1946	Glasgow	Scotland	0-0
16 April	1947	Belfast	Wales	2-1
4 October	1947	Belfast	Scotland	2-0
5 November	1947	Liverpool	England	2-2
10 March	1948	Wrexham	Wales	0-2
9 October	1948	Belfast	England	2-6
17 November	1948	Glasgow	Scotland	2-3
9 March	1949	Belfast	Wales	0-2
WC 1 October	1949	Belfast	Scotland	2-8
WC16 November	1949	Manchester	England	2-9
WC 8 March	1950	Wrexham	Wales	0-0
7 October	1950	Belfast	England	1-4
1 November	1950	Glasgow	Scotland	1-6
7 March	1951	Belfast	Wales	1-2
12 May	1951	Belfast	France	2-2
6 October	1951	Belfast	Scotland	0-3
14 November	1951	Birmingham	England	0-2
19 March	1952	Swansea	Wales	0-3
4 October	1952	Belfast	England	2-2
5 November	1952	Glasgow	Scotland	1-1
11 November	1952	Paris	France	1-3
15 April	1953	Belfast	Wales	2-3
WC 3 October	1953	Belfast	Scotland	1-3
WC11 November	1953	Liverpool	England	1-3
WC31 March	1954	Wrexham	Wales	2-1
2 October	1954	Belfast	England	0-2
3 November	1954	Glasgow	Scotland	2-2
20 April	1955	Belfast	Wales	2-3
8 October	1955	Belfast	Scotland	2-1
2 November	1955	Wembley	England	0-3
11 April	1956	Cardiff	Wales	1-1
6 October	1956	Belfast	England	1-1
7 November	1956	Glasgow	Scotland	0-1
WC16 January	1957	Lisbon	Portugal	1-1
10 April	1957	Belfast	Wales	0-0
WC25 April	1957	Rome	Italy	0-1
WC 1 May	1957	Belfast	Portugal	3-0
5 October	1957	Belfast	Scotland	1-1
6 November	1957	Wembley	England	3-2
4 December	1957	Belfast	Italy	2-2
WC15 January	1958	Belfast	Italy	2-1
16 April	1958	Cardiff	Wales	1-1
WC 8 June	1958	Halmstad	Czechoslovakia	1-0
WC11 June	1958	Halmstad	Argentina	1-3
WC15 June	1958	Malmo	West Germany	2-2
WC17 June	1958	Malmo	Czechoslovakia	2-1
WC19 June	1958	Norrkoping	France	0-4
4 October	1958	Belfast	England	3-3
15 October	1958	Madrid	Spain	2-6
5 November	1958	Glasgow	Scotland	2-2
22 April	1959	Belfast	Wales	4-1
3 October	1959	Belfast	Scotland	0-4
18 November	1959	Wembley	England	1-2
6 April	1960	Wrexham	Wales	2-3
8 October	1960	Belfast	England	2-5
WC26 October	1960	Belfast	West Germany	3-4
9 November	1960	Glasgow	Scotland	2-5

Date		Venue	Opponents	Score
12 April	1961	Belfast	Wales	1-5
25 April	1961	Bologna	Italy	2-3
WC 3 May	1961	Athens	Greece	1-2
WC10 May	1961	West Berlin	West Germany	1-2
7 October	1961	Belfast	Scotland	1-6
WC17 October	1961	Belfast	Greece	2-0
22 November	1961	Wembley	England	1-1
11 April	1962	Cardiff	Wales	0-4
9 May	1962	Rotterdam	Netherlands	0-4
ENC10 October	1962	Katowice	Poland	2-0
20 October	1962	Belfast	England	1-3
7 November	1962	Glasgow	Scotland	1-5
ENC28 November	1962	Belfast	Poland	2-0
3 April	1963	Belfast	Wales	1-4
30 May	1963	Bilbao	Spain	1-1
12 October	1963	Belfast	Scotland	2-1
30 October	1963	Belfast	Spain	0-1
20 November	1963	Wembley	England	3-8
15 April	1964	Swansea	Wales	3-2
29 April	1964	Belfast	Uruguay	3-0
3 October	1964	Belfast	England	3-4
WC14 October	1964	Belfast	Switzerland	1-0
WC14 November	1964	Lausanne	Switzerland	1-2
25 November	1964	Glasgow	Scotland	2-3
WC17 March	1965	Belfast	Holland	2-1
31 March	1965	Belfast	Wales	0-5
WC 7 April	1965	Rotterdam	Holland	0-0
WC 7 May	1965	Belfast	Albania	4-1
2 October	1965	Belfast	Scotland	3-2
10 November	1965	Wembley	England	1-2
WC24 November	1965	Tirana	Albania	1-1
30 March	1966	Cardiff	Wales	4-1
7 May	1966	Belfast	West Germany	0-2
22 June	1966	Belfast	Mexico	4-1
22 October	1966	Belfast	England	0-2
16 November	1966	Glasgow	Scotland	1-2
12 April	1967	Belfast	Wales	0-0
21 October	1967	Belfast	Scotland	1-0
22 November	1967	Wembley	England	0-2
28 February	1968	Wrexham	Wales	0-2
10 September	1968	Jaffa	Israel	3-2
WC23 October	1968	Belfast	Turkey	4-1
WC11 December	1968	Istanbul	Turkey	3-0
3 May	1969	Belfast	England	1-3
6 May	1969	Glasgow	Scotland	1-1
10 May	1969	Belfast	Wales	0-0
WC10 September	1969	Belfast	Russia	0-0
WC22 October	1969	Moscow	Russia	0-2
18 April	1970	Belfast	Scotland	0-1
21 April	1970	Wembley	England	1-3
25 April	1970	Swansea	Wales	0-1
EC11 November	1970	Seville	Spain	0-3
EC 3 February	1971	Nicosia	Cyprus	3-0
EC21 April	1971	Belfast	Cyprus	5-0
15 May	1971	Belfast	England	0-1
18 May	1971	Glasgow	Scotland	1-0
22 May	1971	Belfast	Wales	1-0
EC22 September	1971	Moscow	Russia	0-1
EC13 October	1971	Belfast	Russia	1-1
EC16 February	1972	Hull	Spain	1-1
20 May	1972	Glasgow	Scotland	0-2
24 May	1972	Wembley	England	1-0
27 May	1972	Wrexham	Wales	0-0
WC18 October	1972	Sofia	Bulgaria	0-3
WC14 February	1973	Nicosia	Cyprus	0-1
WC28 March	1973	Coventry	Portugal	1-1
WC 8 May	1973	Fulham	Cyprus	3-0
12 May	1973	Everton	England	1-2
16 May	1973	Glasgow	Scotland	2-1
19 May	1973	Everton	Wales	1-0
WC26 September	1973	Sheffield	Bulgaria	0-0
WC14 November	1973	Lisbon	Portugal	1-1
11 May	1974	Glasgow	Scotland	1-0
15 May	1974	Wembley	England	0-1
18 May	1974	Wrexham	Wales	0-1
EC 4 September	1974	Oslo	Norway	1-2
EC30 October	1974	Solna	Sweden	2-0
EC16 March	1975	Belfast	Yugoslavia	1-0
17 May	1975	Belfast	England	0-0
20 May	1975	Glasgow	Scotland	0-3
23 May	1975	Belfast	Wales	1-0
EC 3 September	1975	Belfast	Sweden	1-2
EC29 October	1975	Belfast	Norway	3-0
EC19 November	1975	Belgrade	Yugoslavia	0-1
3 March	1976	Tel Aviv	Israel	1-1
8 May	1976	Glasgow	Scotland	0-3
11 May	1976	Wembley	England	0-4
14 May	1976	Swansea	Wales	0-1
WC13 October	1976	Rotterdam	Holland	2-2
WC10 November	1976	Liege	Belgium	0-2
27 April	1977	Cologne	West Germany	0-5
28 May	1977	Belfast	England	1-2
1 June	1977	Glasgow	Scotland	0-3
3 June	1977	Belfast	Wales	1-1
WC11 June	1977	Reykjavik	Iceland	0-1
WC29 September	1977	Belfast	Iceland	2-0
WC12 October	1977	Belfast	Holland	0-1
WC16 November	1977	Belfast	Belgium	3-0
13 May	1978	Glasgow	Scotland	1-1
16 May	1978	Wembley	England	0-1
19 May	1978	Wrexham	Wales	0-1
EC20 September	1978	Dublin	Eire	0-0
EC25 October	1978	Belfast	Denmark	2-1

ENC – European Nations Cup games
EC – European Championship games
WC – World Cup games
V – Victory International

Irish won 2-1 despite playing with a goalkeeper with a broken hand and an injured ankle. Unbelievably they had reached the quarter finals, but their tired, injury-ridden side had to surrender to the French, who sauntered to a 4-0 win at Norkopping.

When the Doherty regime ended with his retirement in 1961, Bertie Peacock, left-half in the Irish team in Sweden, and then player manager of Coleraine, took over after Danny Blanchflower had turned down the job he later accepted in 1976.

Peacock it was who introduced George Best to international football. 'Harry Gregg was really responsible, for he kept telling me what a wonderful player Best was. After his first game against Wales at Swansea it was easy to see that he was going to be one of the world's great players,' he said.

Peacock's resignation was followed in 1967 by the appointment of Billy Bingham, another Doherty old boy, who was later to manage the Greek national team. After resounding victories against Turkey and Cyprus and a draw against Russia in Belfast hopes of a World Cup trip to Mexico were shattered when George Best was injured and could not play against the Russians, who won 2-0 in Moscow.

And so on to the appointment of Terry Neill, who played for and managed Hull City besides taking care of the Irish team. The humour was there as ever—after he had scored the goal that gave Ireland their second ever win over England at Wembley Neill was quick to remark that it doubled his tally.

The omens in 1976 were promising. Football had returned to Belfast, and George Best, revived at Fulham, wore the green shirt again. Johnny Giles had led Eire to an excellent draw at Wembley. Blanchflower's side had held Holland in Rotterdam in the World Cup.

1977 and 1978 saw both Northern Ireland and Eire continue to do reasonably well internationally. In the World Cup, Eire managed a win and a draw from their three matches and Northern Ireland two wins from four games. It was obviously not enough for either team to get to the finals but it did confirm that their football was no longer just another Irish joke.

Right Peter Storey robs George Best at Belfast's Windsor Park during what was to be the last international the two countries played there for six years. England won on both occasions – 1-0 in May 1971 and 2-1 in May 1977.

FULL INTERNATIONALS PLAYED BY EIRE
1924–OCTOBER 1978

Date		Venue	Opponents	Score
28 May	1924	Paris	Bulgaria	1-0
2 June	1924	Paris	Netherlands	1-2
3 June	1924	Paris	Estonia	3-1
16 June	1925	Dublin	USA	3-1
21 March	1926	Turin	Italy	0-3
23 April	1927	Dublin	Italy	1-2
12 February	1928	Liege	Belgium	4-2
20 April	1929	Dublin	Belgium	4-0
11 May	1930	Brussels	Belgium	3-1
26 April	1931	Barcelona	Spain	1-1
13 December	1931	Dublin	Spain	0-5
8 May	1932	Amsterdam	Netherlands	2-0
WC25 February	1934	Dublin	Belgium	4-4
WC 8 April	1934	Amsterdam	Netherlands	2-5
15 December	1934	Dublin	Hungary	2-4
5 May	1935	Basle	Switzerland	0-1
8 May	1935	Dortmund	Germany	1-3
8 December	1935	Dublin	Netherlands	3-5
17 March	1936	Dublin	Switzerland	1-0
3 May	1936	Budapest	Hungary	3-3
9 May	1936	Luxembourg	Luxembourg	5-1
17 October	1936	Dublin	Germany	5-2
6 December	1936	Dublin	Hungary	2-3
17 May	1937	Berne	Switzerland	1-0
23 May	1937	Paris	France	2-0
WC10 October	1937	Oslo	Norway	2-3
WC 7 November	1937	Dublin	Norway	3-3
18 May	1938	Prague	Czechoslovakia	2-2
22 May	1938	Warsaw	Poland	0-6
18 September	1938	Dublin	Switzerland	4-0
13 November	1938	Dublin	Poland	3-2
19 March	1939	Cork	Hungary	2-2
18 May	1939	Budapest	Hungary	2-2
23 May	1939	Bremen	Germany	1-1
16 June	1946	Lisbon	Portugal	1-3
23 June	1946	Madrid	Spain	1-0
30 September	1946	Dublin	England	0-1
2 March	1947	Dublin	Spain	3-2
4 May	1947	Dublin	Portugal	0-2
23 May	1948	Lisbon	Portugal	0-2
30 May	1948	Barcelona	Spain	1-2
5 December	1948	Dublin	Switzerland	0-1
24 April	1949	Dublin	Belgium	0-2
22 May	1949	Dublin	Portugal	1-0
WC 2 June	1949	Stockholm	Sweden	1-3
12 June	1949	Dublin	Spain	1-4
WC 8 September	1949	Dublin	Finland	3-0
21 September	1949	Everton	England	2-0
WC 9 October	1949	Helsinki	Finland	1-1
WC13 November	1949	Dublin	Sweden	1-3
10 May	1950	Brussels	Belgium	1-5
26 November	1950	Dublin	Norway	2-2
13 May	1951	Dublin	Argentina	0-1
30 May	1951	Oslo	Norway	3-1
17 October	1951	Dublin	West Germany	3-2
4 May	1952	Cologne	West Germany	0-3
7 May	1952	Vienna	Austria	0-6
1 June	1952	Madrid	Spain	0-6
16 November	1952	Dublin	France	1-1
25 March	1953	Dublin	Austria	4-0
WC 4 October	1953	Dublin	France	3-5
WC28 October	1953	Dublin	Luxembourg	4-0
WC25 November	1953	Paris	France	0-1
WC 7 March	1954	Luxembourg	Luxembourg	1-0
8 November	1954	Dublin	Norway	2-1
1 May	1955	Dublin	Netherlands	1-0
25 May	1955	Oslo	Norway	3-1
28 May	1955	Hamburg	West Germany	1-2
19 September	1955	Dublin	Yugoslavia	1-4
27 November	1955	Dublin	Spain	2-2
10 May	1956	Rotterdam	Netherlands	4-1
WC 3 October	1956	Dublin	Denmark	2-1
25 November	1956	Dublin	West Germany	3-0
WC 8 May	1957	Wembley	England	1-5
WC19 May	1957	Dublin	England	1-1
WC 2 October	1957	Copenhagen	Denmark	2-0
11 May	1958	Katowice	Poland	2-2
14 May	1958	Vienna	Austria	1-3
5 October	1958	Dublin	Poland	2-2
ENC 5 May	1959	Dublin	Czechoslovakia	2-0
ENC10 May	1959	Bratislava	Czechoslovakia	0-4
1 November	1959	Dublin	Sweden	3-2
30 March	1960	Dublin	Chile	2-0
11 May	1960	Dusseldorf	West Germany	1-0
18 May	1960	Malmo	Sweden	1-4
28 September	1960	Dublin	Wales	2-3
6 November	1960	Dublin	Norway	3-2
WC 3 May	1961	Glasgow	Scotland	1-4
WC 7 May	1961	Dublin	Scotland	0-3
WC 8 October	1961	Dublin	Czechoslovakia	1-3
WC29 October	1961	Prague	Czechoslovakia	1-7
8 April	1962	Dublin	Austria	2-3
ENC12 August	1962	Dublin	Iceland	4-2
ENC 2 September	1962	Reykjavik	Iceland	1-1
9 June	1963	Dublin	Scotland	1-0
25 September	1963	Vienna	Austria	0-0
13 October	1963	Dublin	Austria	3-2
11 March	1964	Seville	Spain	1-5
8 April	1964	Dublin	Spain	0-2
10 May	1964	Oslo	Norway	4-1
13 May	1964	Dublin	Poland	3-2
24 May	1964	Dublin	England	1-3
25 October	1964	Dublin	Poland	3-2
24 March	1965	Dublin	Belgium	0-2
WC 5 May	1965	Dublin	Spain	1-0
WC21 October	1965	Seville	Spain	1-4
WC10 November	1965	Paris	Spain	0-1
4 May	1966	Dublin	West Germany	0-4
22 May	1966	Vienna	Austria	2-3
25 May	1966	Liege	Belgium	3-2
ENC23 October	1966	Dublin	Spain	0-0
16 November	1966	Dublin	Turkey	2-1
ENC 7 December	1966	Valencia	Spain	0-2
22 February	1967	Ankara	Turkey	1-2
21 May	1967	Dublin	Czechoslovakia	0-2
22 November	1967	Prague	Czechoslovakia	2-1
30 October	1968	Katowice	Poland	0-1
10 November	1968	Dublin	Austria	2-2
4 December	1968	Dublin	Denmark	1-1
WC 4 May	1969	Dublin	Czechoslovakia	1-2
WC27 May	1969	Copenhagen	Denmark	2-0
21 September	1969	Dublin	Scotland	1-1
WC 7 October	1969	Prague	Czechoslovakia	0-3
6 May	1970	Dublin	Poland	1-2
9 May	1970	Berlin	West Germany	1-2
23 September	1970	Dublin	Poland	0-2
EC14 October	1970	Dublin	Sweden	1-1
EC28 October	1970	Malmo	Sweden	0-1
EC 8 December	1970	Rome	Italy	0-3
EC10 May	1971	Dublin	Italy	1-2
EC30 May	1971	Dublin	Austria	1-4
EC10 October	1971	Linz	Austria	0-6
11 June	1972	Recife	Iran	2-1
18 June	1972	Natal (Brazil)	Equador	3-2
21 June	1972	Recife	Chile	1-2
25 June	1972	Recife	Portugal	1-2
WC18 October	1972	Dublin	Russia	1-2
WC15 November	1972	Dublin	France	2-1
WC13 May	1973	Moscow	USSR	0-1
16 May	1973	Wroclaw	Poland	0-2
WC19 May	1973	Paris	France	1-1
6 June	1973	Oslo	Norway	1-1
21 October	1973	Dublin	Poland	1-0
5 May	1974	Rio de Janeiro	Brazil	1-2
8 May	1974	Montevideo	Uruguay	0-2
12 May	1974	Santiago	Chile	2-1
EC30 October	1974	Dublin	USSR	3-0
EC20 November	1974	Izmin	Turkey	1-1
EC10 May	1975	Dublin	Switzerland	2-1
EC18 May	1975	Kiev	USSR	1-2
EC21 May	1975	Berne	Switzerland	0-1
EC29 October	1975	Dublin	Turkey	4-0
24 March	1976	Dublin	Norway	3-0
26 May	1976	Poznan	Poland	2-0
8 September	1976	Wembley	England	1-1
13 October	1976	Ankara	Turkey	3-3
WC17 November	1976	Paris	France	0-2
9 February	1977	Dublin	Spain	0-1
WC30 March	1977	Dublin	France	1-0
24 April	1977	Dublin	Poland	0-0
WC 1 June	1977	Sofia	Bulgaria	1-2
WC12 October	1977	Dublin	Bulgaria	0-0
5 April	1978	Dublin	Turkey	4-2
12 April	1978	Lodz	Poland	0-3
21 May	1978	Oslo	Norway	0-0
EC24 May	1978	Copenhagen	Denmark	3-3
EC20 September	1978	Dublin	N Ireland	0-0
EC25 September	1978	Dublin	England	1-1

ENC — European Nations Cup games   WC — World Cup games
EC — European Championship games

Jonahs in Wales?

A penalty decision by an East German referee and a lack of temperament at a vital time was all that came between Wales and the semi-finals of the 1976 European Championship.

Under the studious managership of Mike Smith, an Englishman whose playing days were confined to Corinthian Casuals, Wales reached the quarter finals with splendid performances against Austria, Hungary and Luxembourg.

The signs were still good when they returned from Yugoslavia only two goals down. But that contentious penalty in the early minutes of the second leg only provoked a physical, over-emotional response from Wales —and from the Cardiff crowd, whose aggrieved ferocity spoiled one of the principality's finest hours and earned a ban on internationals at Ninian Park after an original ruling against all home grounds.

From the very earliest days Wales have been confined to an inferior status. On three occasions in the 1890s England even sent a second team to play Wales on the *same day* as the fixture with Ireland.

This derisory treatment, which continued for some years, was not immediately justified by results. In the first three matches against England, played between 1879 and 1881, Wales lost two by the odd goal and won the third.

Wales' first international matches were against Scotland and, from the start in 1876, they represented a devastating run of failure. In the first 11 years, Scotland scored 54 goals against five.

International football became a little like the law of the ocean where the big fish eat the smaller fish and the smaller ones eat the tiny ones. Wales turned to Ireland for her whipping boys, winning 7-1, 6-0, 8-2, 5-0 and 11-0 during the first six years and losing only once—1-4 in Belfast in 1887.

With the creation of the FA in 1863 and the commencement of the England v Scotland series, it became inevitable that organized football would spread to the hills of Wales and across the sea to Ireland.

In 1873 the Wrexham club was formed and they have the reputation of being the first organized club to emerge in the Principality. There is, however, considerable evidence that the Druids, who played at Plasmadoc Park, Ruabon, were formed even earlier.

Soon Chirk, Aberystwyth, Newton, Corwen, Bala, Bangor and Caernarvon had clubs. So did Oswestry who, although just across the border in England, played their part in the development of Welsh football.

The earliest clubs were exclusively in the North of Wales where the gentlemen farmers and university graduates had the leisure to take up sport.

The original idea of an international match came from G A Clay-Thomas, a London Welshman, who made the proposal to the *Field* magazine. In February 1876, a meeting was arranged and the 'Cambrian FA', which was the Welsh body's first title, advertised for players in the *Field*.

The inaugural match, played on 25 March 1876, resulted in a 4-0 defeat. This first team contained two Daviesas, a Jones, an Evans and a Williams. For nearly 100 years, scarcely a Welsh team would take the field without the possessor of at least one of these names in the side.

The earliest Welsh team did not contain any representatives from the South. Welsh football was North Wales football, and they were to guard that tradition into the 20th century, when the professionals of the industrial south had left the northern amateurs far behind.

'The parish pump politics of Welsh football'

But the first professional clubs were from the South: Merthyr, Aberdare, later followed by Cardiff in 1910 and Newport and Swansea in 1911. All of them later gained election to the Football League.

Despite this, the Northerners regarded these clubs as upstarts, and the international team had a preponderance of northerners until the 1920s. Whatever the current form of individuals, there was an insistence that there should be at least a 6-5 bias in favour of northern-born players. This idiotic system, perpetuated by generations of unwieldy selection committees—who far outnumbered the players—persisted even until after the First World War.

Not only soccer suffered from this stubborn parochialism. In rugby union selection committees the same divisions arose. The representatives of the east always demanded their quota of players from Cardiff and Newport, while the men from the west insisted that Swansea and Llanelli should provide the bulk of the team.

Incredibly, the soccer selectors persisted with their parish pump politics even when all the player-candidates were members of English football league clubs. 'You can't have Dai Astley of Aston Villa *and* Leslie Jones of Arsenal in the forward line', someone would say. 'They're

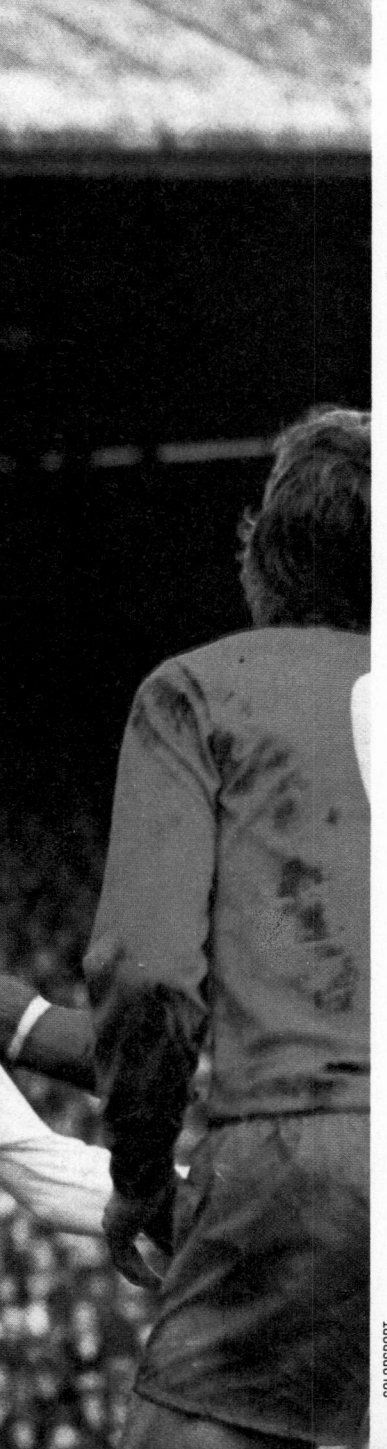

Top left *Terry Medwin, the Spurs reserve winger, scores the first of the two goals that beat Hungary in the play-off for a place in the quarter-final of the 1958 World Cup. Drawn against Brazil, Wales were only beaten by a last minute goal from Pele.*

Bottom left *Mike England (left) in his usual commanding form in the middle of the Welsh defence. It was the attack that gave manager Dave Bowen his main problems. Between 1970 and 1972 Wales could only muster seven goals in fifteen internationals.*

both South Walians and you've already got four from there.'

Apart from this internal warfare, Welsh international football had another cross to bear. While the English selectors could demand the release of any player in the Football League, the Welsh, like the Irish and Scots, had to rely on the generosity of the English.

Some, like Arsenal, believed that any man had the right to play for the country of his birth and put few difficulties in the way. But others were totally unco-operative, and the burden has been carried right up to modern times.

Dave Bowen, the former Welsh team manager, had claimed that only twice in his long period in control was he able to field his chosen side. Small wonder that Wales, despite producing some of the most outstanding players in the world, has never been able to produce results commensurate with her potential.

The selfishness of the English clubs did, however, produce one memorable moment of glory. It came in 1930 when the Football League banned the release of all League players for Saturday afternoon internationals played by Wales, Ireland and Scotland.

The situation provided few problems for the Scots. At the time their domestic football had never been of a higher standard and they could call upon a powerful team of home-based players. But Wales, who had to play them at Hampden, could demand players only from the four clubs affiliated to the Welsh FA.

These were Cardiff, already sliding from the greatness which had won them the FA Cup in 1927 and in the Second Division, Swansea, also in the Second Division, Wrexham (Third Division North) and Newport (Third Division South).

The harrassed Welsh selectors realized that even these clubs did not have sufficient players of quality. So they were forced to delve deeply into the amateur ranks. So emerged, under the captaincy of Fred Keenor, 'the Welsh unknowns'.

By any standards the team looked a strange one with Dewey of Cardiff Corinthians, Ellis of Oswestry and Collins of Llanelli all amateurs. Rightly, the team was dubbed Fred Keenor and 10 others.

Incredibly, Wrexham's Bamford shot Wales into the lead in five minutes but, when Battles put Scotland level in the 50th minute, everyone expected an avalanche of goals. But Wales, gallant little Wales, defending majestically, hung on to achieve one of the most remarkable results in soccer history.

How did it happen? Apart from the inspiring Keenor, one man

deserves the credit: Ted Robbins, the doyen of football secretaries, who, from 1910, had guided the fortunes of what had often been a motley collection of players.

Robbins, with his white hair, astrakhan coat and Edwardian wing collar, did not appear, on the face of it, the man to establish a rapport with professional footballers. Yet, somehow, he injected fire and brimstone into the most ordinary players. A Third Division nonentity would go out like the traditional Welsh dragon.

Robbins and the red shirt of Wales worked a strange alchemy which turned pigmies into giants. But perhaps it was that Welsh dragon too. One of the oldest Welsh proverbs is 'Y draig goch d dyry gychwen' (The Red Dragon gives impetus).

Robbins, the human dynamo, devoted his life to the cause of Wales. He travelled everywhere pleading in his soft North Walian voice for a more open handed attitude from the English clubs. Ivan Sharpe, that great journalist, once recalled how Robbins would ring up on a Friday and say 'I'm still two short for tomorrow's international. But I'm not worried. Wales are never whacked.'

Nor were they. The inspiration of that Hampden triumph—for, in the context, triumph it was—set the pattern for the arrival of the great Welsh side of the thirties which won the Home Championship three times (1933, 1934 and 1937) and was undefeated from 1932 to 1934.

Ted Robbins and his men brought back a little of the pride to these men. The Welsh football team, triumphing over the English, was something in which they could believe.

It used to be said that Robbins only had to shout down a pitshaft and up would come a ready-made international. There was almost a grain of truth in it. For men with no money to spare, football and rugby were the only recreations.

Dai Astley, whose football weight became well over 12 stone—he was over 6 feet tall—was nine stone when he left the mines. In the mid-thirties, Cardiff signed two forwards who had been unemployed since they left school. Both had suffered so long from an inadequate diet that they had to be 'enormously fattened-up' before they could be tried in the reserve team.

It says much for the tenacity of the Welsh, and the insight of the talent scouts, that these boys were able to show they had something even when they were on the edge of malnutrition.

In 1934 came a grim reminder of what life was like when the Gresford colliery disaster in North Wales took the lives of hundreds of Welshmen. England agreed to play Wales at Ninian Park for the disaster fund. It was one of Stanley Matthews' earliest internationals and Wales were beaten 4-0.

Before the Second World War began in 1939, Wales had one more moment of glory when England sent their star-studded team to Ninian Park with a new name in the ranks—Tommy Lawton, the 19-year-old Everton centre-forward. Wales con-

founded everyone by winning 4-2.

Ted Robbins remained at the helm during the War when the authorities recognized that international football was essential for morale. Wales, barely able to raise a team, suffered a number of humiliating defeats and once, if you please, had to field an Englishman at Wembley.

When Ivor Powell, the Villa half-back, was injured early in the game, Wales were down to ten men. In the interests of making it a fair contest, Wales were invited to send on one of their reserves. But, from the Welsh bench, came an embarrassing shaking of heads. They had only brought the bare eleven players!

So, Stanley Mortensen of Blackpool, the England reserve, was asked to make up the number. In the most curious circumstances, he made his first international appearance.

The post-War years brought an upsurge in the talent available to Wales. Cardiff City won promotion to the Second Division in 1947 and Swansea did likewise.

So did Trevor Ford, a former Swansea reserve, who became a highly priced firebrand centre-forward with Aston Villa, Sunderland and Cardiff. Later there were the brilliant Allchurch brothers, Ivor and Len, and, of course, Cliff Jones, all of whom were the product of a brilliant Swansea schools' side.

But the greatest of them all was another Swansea boy, John Charles, who, having moved to Leeds as a youngster, became, simultaneously, a profoundly gifted centre-half and centre-forward.

With his £65,000 transfer to Juventus in 1957, Charles became the forerunner of the British born players who succumbed to the blandishments of Gigi Peronace, that irrepressible agent, and moved to Italy before the removal of the maximum wage.

Although in Italy, Charles came back to join the Welsh party for the 1958 World Cup in Sweden. They qualified in their group with draws against Hungary, Sweden, the eventual finalists, and Mexico. And then, their finest hour, Wales beat Hungary, finalists in 1954, in the group play-off.

In the quarter-final, they came up against the powerful Brazil side. John Charles had been injured and Wales would have gained another draw but for the late arrival of a Brazilian substitute of 17, who scored the only goal with only minutes to go. His name? Pele.

The 1958 World Cup remained the last real impact Wales made on the international arena until Mike Smith took charge. His achievement lay in welding together a team based on the midfield strength of Terry Yorath, John Mahoney and Brian Flynn, with the extra ingredient of a fairy story return to international football from Arfon Griffiths, the 35-year old Wrexham player-coach.

If Liverpool's John Toshack had received greater support in attack, Wales might have carried that European Championship foray even further.

1977 and 1978 saw Wales make an equally spirited attempt to reach the finals of the 1978 World Cup — unlucky to win only one of the three matches.

FULL INTERNATIONALS PLAYED BY WALES 1876–OCTOBER 1978

Date		Venue	Opponents	Score
25 March	1876	Glasgow	Scotland	0-4
15 March	1877	Wrexham	Scotland	0-2
23 March	1878	Glasgow	Scotland	0-9
18 January	1879	London	England	1-2
7 April	1879	Wrexham	Scotland	0-3
15 March	1880	Wrexham	England	2-3
27 March	1880	Glasgow	Scotland	1-5
26 February	1881	Blackburn	England	1-0
14 March	1881	Wrexham	Scotland	1-5
25 February	1882	Wrexham	Ireland	7-1
13 March	1882	Wrexham	England	5-3
25 March	1882	Glasgow	Scotland	0-5
3 February	1883	London	England	0-5
12 March	1883	Wrexham	Scotland	0-3
17 March	1883	Belfast	Ireland	1-1
9 February	1884	Wrexham	Ireland	6-0
17 March	1884	Wrexham	England	0-4
29 March	1884	Glasgow	Scotland	1-4
14 March	1885	Blackburn	England	1-1
23 March	1885	Wrexham	Scotland	1-8
11 April	1885	Belfast	Ireland	8-2
27 February	1886	Wrexham	Ireland	5-0
29 March	1886	Wrexham	England	1-3
10 April	1886	Glasgow	Scotland	1-4
26 February	1887	London	England	0-4
12 March	1887	Belfast	Ireland	1-4
21 March	1887	Wrexham	Scotland	0-2
4 February	1888	Crewe	England	1-5
3 March	1888	Wrexham	Ireland	11-0
10 March	1888	Edinburgh	Scotland	1-5
23 February	1889	Stoke	England	1-4
15 April	1889	Wrexham	Scotland	0-0
27 April	1889	Belfast	Ireland	3-1
8 February	1890	Shrewsbury	Ireland	5-2
15 March	1890	Wrexham	England	1-3
22 March	1890	Paisley	Scotland	0-5
7 February	1891	Belfast	Ireland	2-7
7 March	1891	Sunderland	England	1-4
21 March	1891	Wrexham	Scotland	3-4
27 February	1892	Bangor (Wales)	Ireland	1-1
5 March	1892	Wrexham	England	0-2
26 March	1892	Edinburgh	Scotland	1-6
13 March	1893	Stoke	England	0-6
18 March	1893	Wrexham	Scotland	0-8
8 April	1893	Belfast	Ireland	3-4
24 February	1894	Swansea	Ireland	4-1
12 March	1894	Wrexham	England	1-5
24 March	1894	Kilmarnock	Scotland	2-5
16 March	1895	Belfast	Ireland	2-2
18 March	1895	London	England	1-1
23 March	1895	Wrexham	Scotland	2-2
29 February	1896	Wrexham	Ireland	6-1
16 March	1896	Cardiff	England	1-9
21 March	1896	Dundee	Scotland	0-4
6 March	1897	Belfast	Ireland	3-4
20 March	1897	Wrexham	Scotland	2-2
29 March	1897	Sheffield	England	0-4
19 February	1898	Llandudno	Ireland	0-1
19 March	1898	Motherwell	Scotland	2-5
28 March	1898	Wrexham	England	0-3
4 March	1899	Belfast	Ireland	0-1
18 March	1899	Wrexham	Scotland	0-6
20 March	1899	Bristol	England	1-4
3 February	1900	Aberdeen	Scotland	2-5
24 February	1900	Llandudno	Ireland	2-0
26 March	1900	Cardiff	England	1-1
2 March	1901	Wrexham	Scotland	1-1
18 March	1901	Newcastle	England	0-6
23 March	1901	Llandudno	Ireland	1-0
3 March	1902	Wrexham	England	0-0
15 March	1902	Greenock	Scotland	1-5
22 March	1902	Cardiff	Ireland	0-3
2 March	1903	Portsmouth	England	1-2
9 March	1903	Cardiff	Scotland	0-1
28 March	1903	Belfast	Ireland	0-2
29 February	1904	Wrexham	England	2-2
12 March	1904	Dundee	Scotland	1-1
21 March	1904	Bangor (Wales)	Ireland	0-1
6 March	1905	Wrexham	Scotland	3-1
27 March	1905	Liverpool	England	1-3
8 April	1905	Belfast	Ireland	2-2
3 March	1906	Edinburgh	Scotland	2-0
19 March	1906	Cardiff	England	0-1
2 April	1906	Wrexham	Ireland	4-4
23 February	1907	Belfast	Ireland	3-2
4 March	1907	Wrexham	Scotland	1-0
18 March	1907	London	England	1-1
7 March	1908	Dundee	Scotland	1-2
16 March	1908	Wrexham	England	1-7
11 April	1908	Aberdare	Ireland	0-1
1 March	1909	Wrexham	Scotland	3-2
15 March	1909	Nottingham	England	0-2
20 March	1909	Belfast	Ireland	3-2
5 March	1910	Kilmarnock	Scotland	0-1
11 March	1910	Wrexham	Ireland	4-1
14 March	1910	Cardiff	England	0-1
6 March	1911	Cardiff	Scotland	2-2
13 March	1911	London	England	0-3
28 March	1911	Belfast	Ireland	2-1
2 March	1912	Edinburgh	Scotland	0-1
11 March	1912	Wrexham	England	0-2
13 April	1912	Cardiff	Ireland	2-3
18 January	1913	Belfast	Ireland	1-0
3 March	1913	Wrexham	Scotland	0-0
17 March	1913	Bristol	England	3-4
19 January	1914	Wrexham	Ireland	1-2
28 February	1914	Glasgow	Scotland	0-0
16 March	1914	Cardiff	England	0-2
V11 October	1919	Cardiff	England	2-1
V18 October	1919	Stoke	England	0-2
14 February	1920	Belfast	Ireland	2-2
26 February	1920	Cardiff	Scotland	1-1
15 March	1920	London	England	2-1
12 February	1921	Aberdeen	Scotland	1-2
14 March	1921	Cardiff	England	0-0
9 April	1921	Swansea	Ireland	2-1
4 February	1922	Wrexham	Scotland	2-1
13 March	1922	Liverpool	England	0-1
1 April	1922	Belfast	Ireland	1-1
5 March	1923	Cardiff	England	2-2
17 March	1923	Paisley	Scotland	0-2
14 April	1923	Wrexham	Ireland	0-3

Date		Venue	Opponents	Score
16 February	1924	Cardiff	Scotland	2-0
3 March	1924	Blackburn	England	2-1
15 March	1924	Belfast	N Ireland	1-0
14 February	1925	Edinburgh	Scotland	1-3
28 February	1925	Swansea	England	1-2
18 April	1925	Wrexham	N Ireland	0-0
31 October	1925	Cardiff	Scotland	0-3
13 January	1926	Belfast	N Ireland	0-3
1 March	1926	London	England	3-1
30 October	1926	Glasgow	Scotland	0-3
12 February	1927	Wrexham	England	3-3
9 April	1927	Cardiff	N Ireland	2-2
29 October	1927	Wrexham	Scotland	2-2
28 November	1927	Burnley	England	2-1
4 February	1928	Belfast	N Ireland	2-1
27 October	1928	Glasgow	Scotland	2-4
17 November	1928	Swansea	England	2-3
2 February	1929	Wrexham	N Ireland	2-2
26 October	1929	Cardiff	Scotland	2-4
20 November	1929	London	England	0-6
1 February	1930	Belfast	N Ireland	0-7
25 October	1930	Glasgow	Scotland	1-1
22 November	1930	Wrexham	England	0-4
22 April	1931	Wrexham	N Ireland	3-2
31 October	1931	Wrexham	Scotland	2-3
18 November	1931	Liverpool	England	1-3
5 December	1931	Belfast	N Ireland	0-4
26 October	1932	Edinburgh	Scotland	5-2
16 November	1932	Wrexham	England	0-0
7 December	1932	Wrexham	N Ireland	4-1
25 May	1933	Paris	France	1-1
4 October	1933	Cardiff	Scotland	3-2
4 November	1933	Belfast	N Ireland	1-1
15 November	1933	Newcastle	England	2-1
29 September	1934	Cardiff	England	0-4
21 November	1934	Aberdeen	Scotland	2-3
27 March	1935	Wrexham	N Ireland	3-1
5 October	1935	Cardiff	Scotland	1-1
5 February	1936	Wolverhampton	England	2-1
11 March	1936	Belfast	N Ireland	2-3
17 October	1936	Cardiff	England	2-1
2 December	1936	Dundee	Scotland	2-1
17 March	1937	Wrexham	N Ireland	4-1
30 October	1937	Cardiff	Scotland	2-1
17 November	1937	Middlesbrough	England	1-2
16 March	1938	Belfast	N Ireland	0-1
22 October	1938	Cardiff	England	4-2
9 November	1938	Edinburgh	Scotland	2-3
15 March	1939	Wrexham	N Ireland	3-1
20 May	1939	Paris	France	1-2
WT11 November	1939	Cardiff	England	1-1
WT18 November	1939	Wrexham	England	2-3
WT13 April	1940	Wembley	England	1-0
WT26 April	1941	Nottingham	England	1-4
WT 7 June	1941	Cardiff	England	2-3
WT25 October	1941	Birmingham	England	1-2
WT 9 May	1942	Cardiff	England	1-0
WT24 October	1942	Wolverhampton	England	2-1
WT27 February	1943	Wembley	England	3-5
WT 8 May	1943	Cardiff	England	1-1
WT25 September	1943	Wembley	England	3-8
WT 6 May	1944	Cardiff	England	0-2
WT16 September	1944	Liverpool	England	2-2
WT 5 May	1945	Cardiff	England	2-3
V20 October	1945	West Bromwich	England	1-0
19 October	1946	Wrexham	Scotland	3-1
13 November	1946	Manchester	England	0-3
16 April	1947	Belfast	N Ireland	1-2
18 October	1947	Cardiff	England	0-3
12 November	1947	Glasgow	Scotland	2-1
10 March	1948	Wrexham	N Ireland	2-0
23 October	1948	Cardiff	Scotland	1-3
10 November	1948	Birmingham	England	0-1
9 March	1949	Belfast	N Ireland	2-0
15 May	1949	Lisbon	Portugal	2-3
22 May	1949	Liege	Belgium	1-3
26 May	1949	Berne	Switzerland	0-4
WC15 October	1949	Cardiff	England	1-4
WC 9 November	1949	Glasgow	Scotland	0-2
23 November	1949	Cardiff	Belgium	5-1
WC 8 March	1950	Wrexham	N Ireland	0-0
21 October	1950	Cardiff	Scotland	1-3
15 November	1950	Sunderland	England	2-4
7 March	1951	Belfast	N Ireland	2-1
12 May	1951	Cardiff	Portugal	2-1
16 May	1951	Wrexham	Switzerland	3-2
20 October	1951	Cardiff	England	1-1
14 November	1951	Glasgow	Scotland	1-0
19 March	1952	Swansea	N Ireland	3-0
18 October	1952	Cardiff	Scotland	1-2
12 November	1952	Wembley	England	2-5
15 April	1953	Belfast	N Ireland	3-2
14 May	1953	Paris	France	1-6
21 May	1953	Belgrade	Yugoslavia	2-5
WC10 October	1953	Cardiff	England	1-4
WC 4 November	1953	Glasgow	Scotland	3-3
WC31 March	1954	Wrexham	N Ireland	1-2
9 May	1954	Vienna	Austria	0-2
22 September	1954	Cardiff	Yugoslavia	1-3
16 October	1954	Cardiff	Scotland	0-1
10 November	1954	Wembley	England	2-3
20 April	1955	Belfast	N Ireland	3-2
22 October	1955	Cardiff	England	2-1
9 November	1955	Glasgow	Scotland	0-2
23 November	1955	Wrexham	Austria	1-2
11 April	1956	Cardiff	N Ireland	1-1
20 October	1956	Cardiff	Scotland	2-2
14 November	1956	Wembley	England	1-3
10 April	1957	Belfast	N Ireland	0-0
WC 1 May	1957	Cardiff	Czechoslovakia	1-0
WC19 May	1957	Leipzig	East Germany	1-2
WC26 May	1957	Prague	Czechoslovakia	0-2
WC25 September	1957	Cardiff	East Germany	4-1
19 October	1957	Cardiff	England	0-4
13 November	1957	Glasgow	Scotland	1-1
WC15 January	1958	Tel-Aviv	Israel	2-0
WC 5 February	1958	Cardiff	Israel	2-0
16 April	1958	Cardiff	N Ireland	1-1
WC 8 June	1958	Sandviken	Hungary	1-1
WC11 June	1958	Stockholm	Mexico	1-1
WC15 June	1958	Stockholm	Sweden	0-0
WC17 June	1958	Stockholm	Hungary	2-1

Date		Venue	Opponents	Score
WC19 June	1958	Gothenburg	Brazil	0-1
18 October	1958	Cardiff	Scotland	0-3
26 November	1958	Birmingham	England	2-2
22 April	1959	Belfast	N Ireland	1-4
17 October	1959	Cardiff	England	1-1
4 November	1959	Glasgow	Scotland	1-1
6 April	1960	Wrexham	N Ireland	3-2
28 September	1960	Dublin	Eire	3-2
22 October	1960	Cardiff	Scotland	2-0
23 November	1960	Wembley	England	1-5
12 April	1961	Belfast	N Ireland	5-1
WC19 April	1961	Cardiff	Spain	1-2
WC18 May	1961	Madrid	Spain	1-1
28 May	1961	Budapest	Hungary	2-3
14 October	1961	Cardiff	England	1-1
8 November	1961	Glasgow	Scotland	0-2
11 April	1962	Cardiff	N Ireland	4-0
12 May	1962	Rio de Janiero	Brazil	1-3
16 May	1962	Sao Paulo	Brazil	1-3
22 May	1962	Mexico City	Mexico	1-2
20 October	1962	Cardiff	Scotland	2-3
ENC 7 November	1962	Budapest	Hungary	1-3
21 November	1962	Wembley	England	0-4
ENC20 March	1963	Cardiff	Hungary	1-1
3 April	1963	Belfast	N Ireland	4-1
12 October	1963	Cardiff	England	0-4
20 November	1963	Glasgow	Scotland	1-2
15 April	1964	Swansea	N Ireland	3-2
3 October	1964	Cardiff	Scotland	3-2
WC21 October	1964	Copenhagen	Denmark	0-1
18 November	1964	Wembley	England	1-2
WC 9 December	1964	Athens	Greece	0-2
WC17 March	1965	Cardiff	Greece	4-1
31 March	1965	Belfast	N Ireland	5-0
1 May	1965	Florence	Italy	1-4
WC30 May	1965	Moscow	Russia	1-2
2 October	1965	Cardiff	England	0-0
WC27 October	1965	Cardiff	Russia	2-1
24 November	1965	Glasgow	Scotland	1-4
WC 1 December	1965	Wrexham	Denmark	4-2
30 March	1966	Cardiff	N Ireland	1-4
14 May	1966	Rio de Janeiro	Brazil	1-3
18 May	1966	Belo Horizonte	Brazil	0-1
22 May	1966	Santiago	Chile	0-2
22 October	1966	Glasgow	Scotland	1-1
16 November	1966	Wembley	England	1-5
12 April	1967	Belfast	N Ireland	0-0
21 October	1967	Cardiff	England	0-3
22 November	1967	Glasgow	Scotland	2-3
28 February	1968	Wrexham	N Ireland	2-0
8 May	1968	Cardiff	West Germany	1-1
WC23 October	1968	Cardiff	Italy	0-1
26 March	1969	Frankfurt	West Germany	1-1
WC16 April	1969	Dresden	East Germany	1-2
3 May	1969	Wrexham	Scotland	3-5
7 May	1969	Wembley	England	1-2
10 May	1969	Belfast	N Ireland	0-0
28 July	1969	Cardiff	Rest of Britain	0-1
WC22 October	1969	Cardiff	East Germany	1-3
WC 4 November	1969	Rome	Italy	1-4
18 April	1970	Cardiff	England	1-1
22 April	1970	Glasgow	Scotland	0-0
25 April	1970	Swansea	N Ireland	1-0
EC11 November	1970	Cardiff	Rumania	0-0
EC21 April	1971	Swansea	Czechoslovakia	1-3
15 May	1971	Cardiff	Scotland	0-0
18 May	1971	Wembley	England	0-0
22 May	1971	Belfast	N Ireland	0-1
EC26 May	1971	Helsinki	Finland	1-0
EC13 October	1971	Swansea	Finland	3-0
EC27 October	1971	Prague	Czechoslovakia	0-1
EC24 November	1971	Bucharest	Rumania	0-2
20 May	1972	Cardiff	England	0-3
24 May	1972	Glasgow	Scotland	0-1
28 May	1972	Wrexham	N Ireland	0-0
WC15 November	1972	Cardiff	England	0-1
WC24 January	1973	Wembley	England	1-1
WC28 March	1973	Cardiff	Poland	2-0
12 May	1973	Wrexham	Scotland	0-2
15 May	1973	Wembley	England	0-3
19 May	1973	Everton	N Ireland	0-1
WC26 September	1973	Katowice	Poland	0-3
11 May	1974	Cardiff	England	0-2
14 May	1974	Glasgow	Scotland	0-2
18 May	1974	Wrexham	N Ireland	1-0
EC 4 September	1974	Vienna	Austria	1-2
EC30 October	1974	Cardiff	Hungary	2-0
EC20 November	1974	Swansea	Luxembourg	5-0
EC16 April	1975	Budapest	Hungary	2-1
EC 1 May	1975	Luxembourg	Luxembourg	3-1
17 May	1975	Cardiff	Scotland	2-2
21 May	1975	Wembley	England	2-2
23 May	1975	Belfast	N Ireland	0-1
EC19 November	1975	Wrexham	Austria	1-0
24 March	1976	Wrexham	England	1-2
EC24 April	1976	Zagreb	Yugoslavia	0-2
6 May	1976	Glasgow	Scotland	1-3
8 May	1976	Cardiff	England	0-1
14 May	1976	Swansea	N Ireland	1-0
EC22 May	1976	Cardiff	Yugoslavia	1-1
6 October	1976	Cardiff	West Germany	0-2
WC17 November	1976	Glasgow	Scotland	0-1
WC30 March	1977	Wrexham	Czechoslovakia	3-0
28 May	1977	Wrexham	Scotland	0-0
31 May	1977	Wembley	England	1-0
3 June	1977	Belfast	N Ireland	1-1
6 September	1977	Wrexham	Kuwait	0-0
20 September	1977	Kuwait	Kuwait	0-0
WC12 October	1977	Liverpool	Scotland	0-2
WC17 November	1977	Prague	Czechoslovakia	0-1
14 December	1977	Dortmund	West Germany	1-1
18 April	1978	Teheran	Iran	1-0
13 May	1978	Cardiff	England	1-3
17 May	1978	Glasgow	Scotland	1-1
19 May	1978	Wrexham	N Ireland	1-0
EC25 October	1978	Wrexham	Malta	7-0

WC – World Cup games
EC – European Championship games
V – Victory International WT – War-time International
ENC – European Nations Cup games

The Clubs

Club colours as worn in the 1977/78 season.

Club information is correct up to the close of the 1977/78 season.

Key

q – qualifying rounds/competition
P – promoted
R – relegated
IIIS – Third Division South
IIIN – Third Division North
C – Football/Scottish League champions
p – preliminary round
L – failed to gain re-election

ALDERSHOT

Founded: 1926
Address: Recreation Ground, High Street, Aldershot
Telephone: Aldershot 20211
Ground capacity: 20,000 (2,000 seated)
Playing area: 117 by 76 yards
Record attendance: 19,138 v Carlisle United, FA Cup 4th round replay, 28.1.70
Record victory: 8-1 v Gateshead, Division IV, 1958-59
Record defeat: 0-9 v Bristol City, Division III(S), 28.12.46
Most League points: 56, Division IV, 1972-73
Most League goals: 83, Division IV, 1963-64
League scoring record: 25, Jack Howarth, Division III, 1973-74
Record League aggregate: 172, Jack Howarth, 1965-77
Most League appearances: 450, Len Walker, 1964-76
Most capped player: None

THE ALDERSHOT RECORD

	Division & place	Cup round reached				
1933	SIII 17	5	1959	IV 22		1
1934	SIII 14	3	1960	IV 13		1
1935	SIII 18	3	1961	IV 10		4
1936	SIII 11	1	1962	IV 7		2
1937	SIII 22	1	1963	IV 11		2
1938	SIII 18	3	1964	IV 9		4
1939	SIII 10	2	1965	IV 18		2
1946		4	1966	IV 17		2
1947	SIII 20	2	1967	IV 10		3
1948	SIII 19	2	1968	IV 9		1
1949	SIII 21	3	1969	IV 15		1
1950	SIII 20	1	1970	IV 6		4
1951	SIII 18	3	1971	IV 13		3
1952	SIII 12	2	1972	IV 17		2
1953	SIII 19	1	1973	IV 4P		2
1954	SIII 17	2	1974	111 8		2
1955	SIII 14	2	1975	111 20		1
1956	SIII 15	3	1976	111 21R		3
1957	SIII 19	1	1977	IV 17		1
1958	SIII 18	3	1978	IV 5		1

ARSENAL

Founded: 1886
Address: Arsenal Stadium, Highbury, London N.5
Telephone: (01) 226 0304
Ground capacity: 60,000
Playing area: 110 by 71 yards
Record attendance: 73,295 v Sunderland, Division 1, 9.3.35
Record victory: 12-0 v Loughborough Town, Division II, 12.3.1900
Record defeat: 0-8 v Loughborough Town, Division II, 12.12.96
Most League points: 66, Division I, 1930-31
Most League goals: 127, Division I, 1930-31
League scoring record: 42, Ted Drake, Division I, 1934-35
Record League aggregate: 150, Cliff Bastin, 1930-1947
Most League appearances: 500, George Armstrong, 1960-1977
Most capped player: 44 (59 in all), Terry Neill, Northern Ireland

FA Cup	Year	Opponents	Score	Scorers
Winners	1930	Huddersfield Town	2-0	James, Lambert
	1936	Sheffield United	1-0	Drake
	1950	Liverpool	2-0	Lewis 2
	1971	Liverpool	*2-1	Kelly, George
Runners-up	1927	Cardiff City	0-1	
	1932	Newcastle United	1-2	John
	1952	Newcastle United	0-1	
	1972	Leeds United	0-1	
	1978	Ipswich Town	0-1	

League Cup				
Runners-up	1968	Leeds United	0-1	
	1969	Swindon Town	*1-3	Gould

* — after extra time

THE ARSENAL RECORD

	Division & place	Cup round reached		Division & place	Cup round reached
1890		q	1934	I 1C	q-f
1891		1	1935	I 1C	q-f
1892		1	1936	I 6	Winners
1893		1	1937	I 3	q-f
1894	II 9	1	1938	I 1C	5
1895	II 8	1	1939	I 5	3
1896	II 7	1	1946		3
1897	II 10	q	1947	I 13	3
1898	II 5	1	1948	I 1C	3
1899	II 7	1	1949	I 5	4
1900	II 8	q	1950	I 6	Winners
1901	II 7	2	1951	I 5	5
1902	II 4	1	1952	I 3	Final
1903	II 3	1	1953	I 1C	q-f
1904	II 2P	2	1954	I 12	4
1905	I 10	1	1955	I 9	4
1906	I 12	s-f	1956	I 5	q-f
1907	I 7	s-f	1957	I 5	q-f
1908	I 14	1	1958	I 12	3
1909	I 6	2	1959	I 3	5
1910	I 18	2	1960	I 13	3
1911	I 10	2	1961	I 11	3
1912	I 10	1	1962	I 10	4
1913	I 20R	2	1963	I 7	5
1914	II 3	1	1964	I 8	5
1915	II 6P	2	1965	I 13	4
1920	I 11	2	1966	I 14	3
1921	I 9	1	1967	I 7	5
1922	I 17	q-f	1968	I 9	5
1923	I 11	1	1969	I 4	5
1924	I 19	2	1970	I 12	3
1925	I 20	1	1971	I 1C	Winners
1926	I 2	q-f	1972	I 5	Final
1927	I 11	Final	1973	I 2	s-f
1928	I 10	s-f	1974	I 10	4
1929	I 9	q-f	1975	I 16	q-f
1930	I 14	Winners	1976	I 17	3
1931	I 1C	4	1977	I 8	5
1932	I 2	Final	1978	I 5	Final
1933	I 1C	3			

ASTON VILLA

Founded: 1874
Address: Villa Park, Trinity Road, Birmingham 6
Telephone: (021) 327 6604
Ground capacity: 53,000
Playing area: 115 by 75 yards
Record attendance: 76,588 v Derby County, FA Cup quarter-final, 2.3.46
Record victory: 13-0 v Wednesday Old Alliance, FA Cup 1st round, 30.10.86
Record defeat: 1-8 v Blackburn Rovers, FA Cup 3rd round, 1888-89
Most League points: 70, Division III, 1971-72
Most League goals: 128, Division I, 1930-31
League scoring record: 49, Pongo Waring, Division I, 1930-31
Record League aggregate: 213, Harry Hampton, 1904-1920
and Billy Walker, 1919-1934
Most League appearances: 560, Charlie Aitken, 1961-76
Most capped player: 33 (34 in all), Peter McParland, Northern Ireland

FA Cup	Year	Opponents	Score	Scorers
Winners	1887	West Bromwich Albion	2-0	Hodgetts, Hunter
	1895	West Bromwich Albion	1-0	Chatt
	1897	Everton	3-2	Campbell, Wheldon, Crabtree
	1905	Newcastle United	2-0	Hampton 2
	1913	Sunderland	1-0	Barber
	1920	Huddersfield Town	1-0	Kirton
	1957	Manchester United	2-1	McParland 2
Runners-up	1892	West Bromwich Albion	0-3	
	1924	Newcastle United	0-2	
League Cup	1961	Rotherham United	A0-2	
Winners			H3-0	O'Neill, Burrows, McParland
	1975	Norwich City	1-0	Graydon
	1977	Everton	0-0	
		Replay	* 1-1	Kenyon og
		Replay	* 3-2	Nicholl, Little 2
Runners-up	1963	Birmingham City	A1-3	Thomson
			H0-0	
	1971	Tottenham Hotspur	0-2	

*after extra time

THE VILLA RECORD

	Division & place	Cup round reached		Division & place	Cup round reached
1880		3	1927	I 10	3
1881		4	1928	I 8	5
1882		4	1929	I 3	s-f
1883		q-f	1930	I 4	q-f
1884		4	1931	I 2	3
1885		3	1932	I 5	4
1886		2	1933	I 2	4
1887		Winners	1934	I 13	s-f
1888		1	1935	I 13	3
1889	I 2	q-f	1936	I 21R	3
1890	I 8	2	1937	II 9	3
1891	I 9	2	1938	II 1P	s-f
1892	I 4	Final	1939	I 12	4
1893	I 4	1	1946		q-f
1894	I 1C	q-f	1947	I 8	3
1895	I 3	Winners	1948	I 6	3
1896	I 1C	1	1949	I 10	4
1897	I 1C	Winners	1950	I 12	3
1898	I 6	1	1951	I 15	4
1899	I 1C	1	1952	I 6	3
1900	I 1C	q-f	1953	I 11	q-f
1901	I 15	s-f	1954	I 13	3
1902	I 8	1	1955	I 6	4
1903	I 2	s-f	1956	I 20	4
1904	I 5	2	1957	I 10	Winners
1905	I 4	Winners	1958	I 14	3
1906	I 8	3	1959	I 21R	s-f
1907	I 5	2	1960	II 1P	s-f
1908	I 2	3	1961	I 9	5
1909	I 7	1	1962	I 7	q-f
1910	I 1C	3	1963	I 15	4
1911	I 2	2	1964	I 19	3
1912	I 6	2	1965	I 16	5
1913	I 2	Winners	1966	I 16	3
1914	I 2	s-f	1967	I 21R	4
1915	I 13	2	1968	II 16	4
1920	I 9	Winners	1969	II 18	5
1921	I 10	q-f	1970	II 21R	3
1922	I 5	q-f	1971	III 4	1
1923	I 6	1	1972	III 1P	1
1924	I 6	Final	1973	II 3	3
1925	I 15	3	1974	II 14	5
1926	I 6	5	1975	II 2P	5
			1976	I 16	3
			1977	I 4	q-f
			1978	I 8	3

BARNSLEY

Formed: 1887 (as Barnsley St Peter's)
Address: Oakwell Ground, Grove Street, Barnsley, Yorkshire
Telephone: 0226 84113
Ground capacity: 38,500
Playing area: 111 by 75 yards
Record attendance: 40,255 v Stoke City, FA Cup 5th round, 15.2.36
Record victory: 9-0 v Loughborough Town, Division II, 28.1.1899
9-0 v Accrington Stanley, Division III(N), 3.2.34
Record defeat: 0-9 v Notts County, Division II, 19.11.27
Most League points: 67, Division III(N), 1938-39
Most League goals: 118, Division III(N), 1933-34
League scoring record: 33, Cecil McCormack, Division II, 1950-51
Record League aggregate: 123, Ernest Hine, 1921-1926 and 1934-1938
Most League appearances: 514, Barry Murphy, 1962-1978
Most capped player: 9 (15 in all), Eddie McMorran, Ireland

FA Cup	Year	Opponents	Score	Scorers
Winners	1912	West Bromwich Albion	0-0	
		Replay	1-0	Tufnell
Runners-up	1910	Newcastle United	1-1	Tufnell
		Replay	0-2	

THE BARNSLEY RECORD

	Division & place	Cup round reached		Division & place	Cup round reached
1895		1	1936	II 20	q-f
1896		p	1937	II 14	3
1897		1	1938	II 21R	4
1898		p	1939	NIII 1P	3
1899	II 11	1	1946		5
1900	II 16	p	1947	II 10	4
1901	II 15	p	1948	II 12	3
1902	II 11	p	1949	II 9	3
1903	II 8	2	1950	II 13	3
1904	II 8	1	1951	II 15	3
1905	II 7	1	1952	II 20	4
1906	II 12	2	1953	II 22R	4
1907	II 8	q-f	1954	NIII 2	2
1908	II 16	1	1955	NIII 1P	2
1909	II 17	1	1956	II 18	4
1910	II 9	Final	1957	II 19	5
1911	II 19	2	1958	II 14	3
1912	II 6	Winners	1959	II 22R	3
1913	II 4	2	1960	III 17	1
1914	II 5	1	1961	III 8	q-f
1915	II 3	1	1962	III 20	2
1920	II 12	2	1963	III 18	3
1921	II 16	1	1964	III 20	2
1922	II 3	3	1965	III 24R	2
1923	II 9	2	1966	IV 16	2
1924	II 11	1	1967	IV 16	3
1925	II 15	2	1968	IV 2P	1
1926	II 18	1	1969	III 10	3
1927	II 11	4	1970	III 7	3
1928	II 14	3	1971	III 12	2
1929	II 16	3	1972	III 22R	2
1930	II 17	3	1973	IV 14	1
1931	II 19	5	1974	IV 13	2
1932	II 21R	3	1975	IV 15	1
1933	NIII 8	3	1976	IV 12	1
1934	NIII 1P	1	1977	IV 6	2
1935	II 16	3	1978	IV 7	2

BIRMINGHAM CITY

Founded: 1875
Address: St. Andrew's, Birmingham 9
Telephone: (021) 772 0101
Ground capacity: 51,000
Playing area: 115 by 75 yards
Record attendance: 66,844 v Everton, FA Cup 5th round, 11.2.39
Record victory: 12-0 v Walsall Town Swifts, Division II, 17.12.1892
12-0 v Doncaster Rovers, Division II, 11.4.03
Record defeat: 1-9 v Sheffield Wednesday, 13.12.30
Most League points: 59, Division II, 1947-48
Most League goals: 103, Division II, 1893-94
League scoring record: 29, Joe Bradford, Division I, 1927-28
Record League aggregate: 249, Joe Bradford, Division I, 1920-35
Most capped player: 25, Harry Hibbs, England
Most League appearances: 486, Gil Merrick, 1946-60

FA Cup	Year	Opponents	Score	Scorers
Runners-up	1931	West Bromwich Albion	1-2	Bradford
	1956	Manchester City	1-3	Kinsey
League Cup				
Winners	1963	Aston Villa	h3-1 a0-0	Leek 2, Bloomfield

THE BIRMINGHAM RECORD

Year	Division & place	Cup round reached		Year	Division & place	Cup round reached
1889*		1		1936	I 12	3
1890		2		1937	I 11	3
1891		d		1938	I 18	3
1892		2		1939	I 21R	5
1893	II 1	1		1946††		s-f
1894	II 2P	1		1947	II 3	q-f
1895	II 12	1		1948	II 1P	3
1896	I 15R	1		1949	I 17	3
1897	II 4	1		1950	I 22R	3
1898	II 6	q		1951	II 4	s-f
1899	II 8	2		1952	II 3	4
1900	II 3	q		1953	II 6	q-f
1901	II 2P	3		1954	II 7	4
1902	I 17R	p		1955	II 1P	q-f
1903	II 2P	1		1956	I 6	Final
1904	I 11	p		1957	I 12	s-f
1905	I 7	1		1958	I 13	3
1906†	I 7	4		1959	I 9	5
1907	I 9	1		1960	I 19	3
1908	I 20R	1		1961	I 19	5
1909	II 11	1		1962	I 17	3
1910	II 20	1		1963	I 20	3
1911	II 16	1		1964	I 20	3
1912	II 12	1		1965	I 22R	3
1913	II 3	3		1966	II 10	4
1914	II 14	3		1967	II 10	q-f
1915	II 5	3		1968	II 4	s-f
1920	II 5	3		1969	II 7	5
1921	II 1P	1		1970	II 18	3
1922	II 18	§		1971	II 9	3
1923	I 17	1		1972	II 2P	s-f
1924	I 14	2		1973	I 10	3
1925	I 8	3		1974	I 19	4
1926	I 14	4		1975	I 17	s-f
1927	I 17	4		1976	I 19	3
1928	I 11	5		1977	I 13	4
1929	I 15	4		1978	I 11	3
1930	I 11	4				
1931	I 19	Final				
1932	I 9	4				
1933	I 13	6				
1934	I 20	5				
1935	I 19	6				

* – as Small Heath until 1905
† – as Birmingham until 1945
†† – as Birmingham City
§ – did not enter
d – disqualified for fielding an ineligible player

BLACKBURN ROVERS

Founded: 1875
Address: Ewood Park, Blackburn
Telephone: Blackburn 55432
Ground capacity: 47,500 (7,000 seated)
Playing area: 116 by 72 yards
Record attendance: 61,783 v Bolton Wanderers, FA Cup quarter-final, 2.3.29
Record victory: 11-0 v Rossendale United, FA Cup, 1884-85
Record defeat: 0-8 v Arsenal, Division I, 25.2.33
Most League points: 60, Division III, 1974-75
Most League goals: 114, Division II, 1954-55
League scoring record: 43, Ted Harper, Division I, 1925-26
Record League aggregate: 140, Tom Briggs, 1952-1958
Most League appearances: 580, Ronnie Clayton, 1950-1969
Most capped player: 41, Bob Crompton, England

FA Cup	Year	Opponents	Score	Scorers
Winners	1884	Queen's Park	2-1	Brown, Forrest
	1885	Queen's Park	2-0	Forrest, Brown
	1886	West Bromwich Albion	0-0	
			2-0	Sowerbutts, Brown
	1890	Sheffield Wednesday	6-1	Dewar, Southworth, Lofthouse, Townley 3
	1891	Notts County	3-1	Dewar, Southworth, Townley
	1928	Huddersfield Town	3-1	Roscamp 2, McLean
Runners-up	1882	Old Etonians	0-1	
	1960	Wolverhampton Wanderers	0-3	

THE BLACKBURN RECORD

Year	Division & place	Cup round reached		Year	Division & place	Cup round reached
1880		3		1929	I 7	q-f
1881		2		1930	I 6	5
1882		Final		1931	I 10	5
1883		2		1932	I 16	4
1884		Winners		1933	I 15	4
1885		Winners		1934	I 8	3
1886		Winners		1935	I 15	5
1887		2		1936	I 15	5
1888		2		1936	I 22R	4
1889	I 4	s-f		1937	II 12	3
1890	I 3	Winners		1938	II 16	3
1891	I 6	Winners		1939	II 1P	q-f
1892	I 9	2		1946		3
1893	I 9	s-f		1947	I 17	5
1894	I 4	s-f		1948	I 22R	4
1895	I 5	2		1949	II 14	3
1896	I 8	1		1950	II 16	3
1897	I 14	3		1951	II 6	3
1898	I 15	1		1952	II 14	s-f
1899	I 6	1		1953	II 9	3
1900	I 4	2		1954	II 3	4
1901	I 9	1		1955	II 6	3
1902	I 4	1		1956	II 4	5
1903	I 16	2		1957	II 4	3
1904	I 15	3		1958	II 2P	s-f
1905	I 13	1		1959	I 10	4
1906	I 9	1		1960	I 17	Final
1907	I 12	2		1961	I 18	5
1908	I 14	1		1962	I 16	q-f
1909	I 4	3		1963	I 11	3
1910	I 3	3		1964	I 7	5
1911	I 12	s-f		1965	I 10	3
1912	I 1C	s-f		1966	I 22R	q-f
1913	I 5	q-f		1967	II 4	3
1914	I 1C	3		1968	II 9	3
1915	I 3	1		1969	II 19	5
1920	I 20	1		1970	II 8	3
1921	I 11	1		1971	II 21R	3
1922	I 15	3		1972	III 10	1
1923	I 14	2		1973	III 3	2
1924	I 8	1		1974	III 13	4
1925	I 16	s-f		1975	III 1P	3
1926	I 12	4		1976	II 15	3
1927	I 18	3		1977	II 12	5
1928	I 12	Winners		1978	II 5	4

BLACKPOOL

Founded: 1887
Address: Bloomfield Road, Blackpool
Telephone: Blackpool 46118
Ground capacity: 38,000 (6,500 seated)
Playing area: 111 by 73 yards
Record attendance: 39,118 v Manchester United, Division I, 19.4.32
Record victory: 10-0 v Lanerossi Vincenza, Anglo-Italian tournament, 10.6.72
Record defeat: 1-10 v Huddersfield Town, Division I, 13.12.30
Most League points: 58, Division II, 1929-30 & 1967-68
Most League goals: 98, Division II, 1929-30
League scoring record: 45, Jimmy Hampson, Division II, 1929-30
Record League aggregate: 247, Jimmy Hampson, 1927-1938
Most League appearances: 568, Jimmy Armfield, 1952-1971
Most capped player: 43, Jimmy Armfield, England

FA Cup	Year	Opponents	Score	Scorers
Winners	1953	Bolton Wanderers	4-3	Mortensen 3, Perry
Runners-up	1948	Manchester United	2-4	Shimwell (pen), Mortensen
	1951	Newcastle United	0-2	

THE BLACKPOOL RECORD

Year	Division & place	Cup round reached	Year	Division & place	Cup round reached
1892		1	1935	II 4	3
1893		1	1936	II 3	4
1894		p	1937	II 2P	3
1895		p	1938	I 12	4
1896		1	1939	I 15	3
1897	II 8	1	1946		4
1898	II 11	p	1947	I 5	3
1899	II 16	2	1948	I 9	Final
1900*			1949	I 16	4
1901	II 12	p	1950	I 7	q-f
1902	II 12	p	1951	I 3	Final
1903	II 14	q	1952	I 9	3
1904	II 15		1953	I 7	Winners
1905	II 15	1	1954	I 6	5
1906	II 14	3	1955	I 19	3
1907	II 13	1	1956	I 2	3
1908	II 15	1	1957	I 4	5
1909	II 20	2	1958	I 7	3
1910	II 12	1	1959	I 8	q-f
1911	II 9	1	1960	I 11	4
1912	II 14	2	1961	I 20	3
1913	II 20	1	1962	I 13	3
1914	II 16	1	1963	I 13	3
1915	II 10	1	1964	I 18	3
1920	II 4	2	1965	I 17	3
1921	II 4	2	1966	I 13	3
1922	II 19	1	1967	I 22R	3
1923	II 5	1	1968	II 3	4
1924	II 4	2	1969	II 8	3
1925	II 17	q-f	1970	II 2P	4
1926	II 6	3	1971	I 22R	4
1927	II 9	3	1972	II 6	3
1928	II 19	3	1973	II 7	3
1929	II 8	3	1974	II 5	3
1930	II 1P	4	1975	II 7	3
1931	I 20	4	1976	II 10	4
1932	I 20	3	1977	II 5	3
1933	I 22R	5	1978	II 20R	3
1934	II 11	4			

* — failed to obtain re-election in 1899

BOLTON WANDERERS

Founded: 1874
Address: Burnden Park, Bolton, BL3 2QR
Telephone: Bolton 21101
Ground capacity: 51,000
Playing area: 113 by 76 yards
Record attendance: 69,912 v Manchester City, FA Cup 5th round, 18.2.33
Record victory: 13-0 v Sheffield United, FA Cup 2nd round, 1.2.1890
Record defeat: 0-7 v Manchester City, Division I, 21.3.36
Most League points: 61, Division III, 1972-73
Most League goals: 96, Division II, 1934-35
League scoring record: 38, Joe Smith, Division I, 1920-21
Record League aggregate: 255, Nat Lofthouse, 1946-1961
Most League appearances: 519, Eddie Hopkinson, 1956-1970
Most capped player: 33, Nat Lofthouse, England

FA Cup	Year	Opponents	Score	Scorers
Winners	1923	West Ham United	2-0	Jack, J R Smith
	1926	Manchester City	1-0	Jack
	1929	Portsmouth	2-0	Butler, Blackmore
	1958	Manchester United	2-0	Lofthouse (2)
Runners-up	1894	Notts County	1-4	Cassidy
	1904	Manchester City	0-1	
	1953	Blackpool	3-4	Lofthouse, Moir, Bell

THE BOLTON WANDERERS RECORD

Year	Division & place	Cup round reached	Year	Division & place	Cup round reached
1882		2	1930	I 15	3
1883		3	1931	I 14	4
1884		4	1932	I 17	3
1885		q	1933	I 21R	5
1886		3	1934	II 3	q-f
1887		q	1935	II 2P	s-f
1888		q	1936	I 13	3
1889	I 5	q	1937	I 20	5
1890	I 9	s-f	1938	I 7	3
1891	I 5	1	1939	I 8	3
1892	I 3	1	1946		s-f
1893	I 5	1	1947	I 18	4
1894	I 13	Final	1948	I 17	3
1895	I 10	q-f	1949	I 14	3
1896	I 4	s-f	1950	I 16	4
1897	I 8	2	1951	I 8	4
1898	I 11	q-f	1952	I 5	3
1899	I 17R	1	1953	I 14	Final
1900	II 2P	1	1954	I 5	q-f
1901	I 10	2	1955	I 18	4
1902	I 12	2	1956	I 8	4
1903	I 18R	1	1957	I 9	3
1904	II 7	Final	1958	I 15	Winners
1905	II 2P	q-f	1959	I 4	q-f
1906	I 6	1	1960	I 6	4
1907	I 6	3	1961	I 18	4
1908	I 19R	3	1962	I 11	3
1909	II 1P	1	1963	I 18	3
1910	I 20R	1	1964	I 21R	4
1911	II 2P	1	1965	II 3	5
1912	I 4	3	1966	II 9	4
1913	I 8	1	1967	II 9	4
1914	I 6	3	1968	II 12	3
1915	I 17	s-f	1969	II 17	4
1920	I 6	1	1970	II 16	3
1921	I 3	1	1971	II 22R	3
1922	I 6	2	1972	III 8	4
1923	I 13	Winners	1973	III 1P	5
1924	I 4	2	1974	II 11	4
1925	I 3	2	1975	II 10	3
1926	I 8	Winners	1976	II 4	5
1927	I 4	5	1977	II 4	3
1928	I 7	4	1978	II 1P	5
1929	I 14	Winners			

AFC BOURNEMOUTH

Founded: 1899 (as Boscombe)
Address: Dean Court, Bournemouth, Hampshire
Telephone: Bournemouth 35381
Ground capacity: 22,000
Playing area: 115 by 75 yards
Record attendance: 28,799 v Manchester United, FA Cup quarter-final, 2.3.57
Record victory: 11-0 v Margate, FA Cup 1st round, 20.11.71
Record defeat: 1-8 v Bradford City, Division III, 24.1.70
Most League points: 62, Division III, 1971-72
Most League goals: 88, Division III(S), 1956-57
League scoring record: 42, Ted Macdougall, 1970-71
Record League aggregate: 202, Ron Eyre, 1924-1933
Most League appearances: 412, Ray Bumstead, 1958-1970
Most capped player: 4 (13 in all), Tommy Godwin, Eire

THE BOURNEMOUTH RECORD

	Division & place	Cup round reached		Division & place	Cup round reached
1924	SIII 21		1955	SIII 17	3
1925	SIII 20	q	1956	SIII 9	1
1926	SIII 8	4	1957	SIII 5	q-f
1927	SIII 7	3	1958	SIII 9	2
1928	SIII 14	3	1959	III 12	1
1929	SIII 9	5	1960	III 10	4
1930	SIII 10	3	1961	III 19	3
1931	SIII 10	1	1962	III 3	1
1932	SIII 15	4	1963	III 5	1
1933	SIII 18	1	1964	III 4	1
1934	SIII 21	2	1965	III 11	2
1935	SIII 17	1	1966	III 18	3
1936	SIII 8	3	1967	III 20	2
1937	SIII 6	3	1968	III 12	3
1938	SIII 13	2	1969	III 4	2
1939	SIII 15	3	1970	III 21R	1
1946		1	1971	IV 2P	3
1947	SIII 7	3	1972	III 3	2
1948	SIII 2	3	1973	III 7	3
1949	SIII 3	3	1974	III 11	3
1950	SIII 12	4	1975	III 21R	2
1951	SIII 9	2	1976	IV 6	2
1952	SIII 14	1	1977	IV 13	1
1953	SIII 9	1	1978	IV 17	1
1954	SIII 19	2		∗ – did not enter	

BRADFORD CITY

Founded: 1903
Address: Valley Parade Ground, Bradford BD8 7DY
Telephone: Bradford 26565
Ground capacity: 23,469
Playing area: 110 by 70 yards
Record attendance: 39,146 v Burnley, FA Cup 4th round, 11.3.11
Record victory: 11-1 v Rotherham United, Division III(N), 25.8.28
Record defeat: 1-9 v Colchester United, Division IV, 30.12.61
Most League points: 63, Division III(N), 1928-29
Most League goals: 128, Division III(N), 1928-29
League scoring record: 34, David Layne, Division IV, 1961-62
Record League aggregate: 88, Frank O'Rourke, 1906-13
Most League appearances: 443, Ian Cooper, 1965-1977
Most capped player: 9, H. Hampton, Ireland

FA Cup	Year	Opponents	Score	Scorers
Winners	1911	Newcastle United	0-0	
	Replay		1-0	Spiers

THE BRADFORD CITY RECORD

	Division & place	Cup round reached		Division & place	Cup round reached
1904	II 10	p	1947	NIII 5	1
1905	II 8	p	1948	NIII 14	2
1906	II 11	3	1949	NIII 22	2
1907	II 5	3	1950	NIII 19	2
1908	II 1P	1	1951	NIII 7	1
1909	I 18	3	1952	NIII 15	2
1910	I 7	2	1953	NIII 16	2
1911	I 5	Winners	1954	NIII 5	1
1912	I 11	q-f	1955	NIII 21	3
1913	I 13	1	1956	NIII 8	2
1914	I 9	2	1957	NIII 9	1
1915	I 10	q-f	1958	NIII 3	3
1920	I 15	q-f	1959	III 11	4
1921	I 15	2	1960	III 19	5
1922	I 21R	2	1961	III 22R	2
1923	II 15	1	1962	IV 5	3
1924	II 18	1	1963	IV 23	3
1925	II 16	3	1964	IV 5	1
1926	II 16	3	1965	IV 19	3
1927	II 22R	3	1966	IV 23	1
1928	NIII 6	2	1967	IV 11	1
1929	NIII 1P	4	1968	IV 5	2
1930	II 18	5	1969	IV 4P	1
1931	II 10	4	1970	III 10	3
1932	II 7	3	1971	III 19	2
1933	II 11	3	1972	III 24R	1
1934	II 6	3	1973	IV 16	4
1935	II 20	4	1974	IV 8	4
1936	II 12	5	1975	IV 10	1
1937	II 21R	3	1976	IV 17	q-f
1938	NIII 14	3	1977	IV 4P	1
1939	NIII 3	1	1978	III 22R	1
1946		1			

BRENTFORD

Founded: 1889
Address: Griffin Park, Braemar Road, Brentford, Middlesex TW8 0NT
Telephone: (01) 560 2021
Ground capacity: 37,000
Playing area: 114 by 75 yards
Record attendance: 39,626 v Preston North End, FA Cup quarter-final, 5.3.38
Record victory: 9-0 v Wrexham, Division III, 15.10.63
Record defeat: 0-7 v Swansea Town, Division III(S), 8.11.24
0-7 v Walsall, Division III(S), 19.1.57
Most League points: 62, Division III(S), 1932-33; Division IV, 1962-63
Most League goals: 98, Division IV, 1962-63
League scoring record: 36, John Holliday, Division III(S), 1932-33
Record League aggregate: 153, Jim Towers, 1954-1961
Most League appearances: 514, Ken Coote, 1949-1964
Most capped player: 12, Idris Hopkins, Wales

THE BRENTFORD RECORD

Year	Division & place	Cup round reached	Year	Division & place	Cup round reached
1920		1	1953	II 17	4
1921	III 21	1	1954	II 21R	3
1922	SIII 9	1	1955	SIII 11	4
1923	SIII 14	p	1956	SIII 6	2
1924	SIII 17	p	1957	SIII 8	2
1925	SIII 21	p	1958	SIII 2	1
1926	SIII 18	2	1959	III 3	4
1927	SIII 11	5	1960	III 6	2
1928	SIII 12	3	1961	III 17	1
1929	SIII 13	2	1962	III 23R	3
1930	SIII 2	1	1963	IV 1P	1
1931	SIII 3	4	1964	III 16	4
1932	SIII 5	4	1965	III 5	3
1933	SIII 1P	1	1966	III 23R	3
1934	II 4	3	1967	IV 9	3
1935	II 1P	3	1968	IV 14	1
1936	I 5	3	1969	IV 11	2
1937	I 6	4	1970	IV 5	1
1938	I 6	q-f	1971	IV 14	5
1939	I 18	3	1972	IV 3P	1
1946		q-f	1973	III 22R	1
1947	I 21R	4	1974	IV 19	1
1948	II 15	4	1975	IV 8	2
1949	II 18	q-f	1976	IV 18	3
1950	II 9	3	1977	IV 15	2
1951	II 9	3	1978	IV 4P	2
1952	II 10	4			

Year	Division & place	Cup round reached	Year	Division & place	Cup round reached
1936	SIII 7	3	1961	II 16	4
1937	SIII 3	1	1962	II 22R	3
1938	SIII 5	3	1963	III 22R	1
1939	SIII 3	1	1964	IV 8	1
1946		5	1965	IV 1P	1
1947	SIII 17	1	1966	III 15	2
1948	SIII 22	3	1967	III 19	4
1949	SIII 6	1	1968	III 10	2
1950	SIII 8	1	1969	III 12	2
1951	SIII 13	4	1970	III 5	2
1952	SIII 5	1	1971	III 14	3
1953	SIII 7	3	1972	III 2P	2
1954	SII 2	2	1973	II 22R	3
1955	SIII 6	3	1974	III 19	1
1956	SIII 2	2	1975	III 19	3
1957	SIII 6	1	1976	III 4	3
1958	SIII 1P	2	1977	III 2P	1
1959	II 12	3	1978	II 4	4
1960	II 14	5			

BRIGHTON AND HOVE ALBION

Founded: 1900
Address: Goldstone Ground, Old Shoreham Road, Hove, Sussex
Telephone: Brighton 739535
Ground capacity: 36,000
Playing area: 112 by 75 yards
Record attendance: 36,747 v Fulham, Division II. 27.12.58
Record victory: 10-1 v Wisbech, FA Cup 1st round, 13.11.65
Record defeat: 0-9 v Middlesbrough, Division II, 23.8.58
Most League points: 65, Division III(S), 1955-56, Division III, 1971-72
Most League goals: 112, Division III(S), 1955-56
League scoring record: 32, Peter Ward, Division III, 1976-77
Record League aggregate: 113, Tommy Cook, 1922-29
Most League appearances: 509, Tug Wilson, 1922-36
Most capped player: 8, Jack Jenkins, Wales

THE BRIGHTON RECORD

Year	Division & place	Cup round reached	Year	Division & place	Cup round reached
1906		2	1923	SIII 4	2
1907		1	1924	SIII 5	3
1908		2	1925	SIII 8	2
1909		1	1926	SIII 5	1
1910		1	1927	SIII 4	3
1911		2	1928	SIII 4	2
1912		1	1929	SIII 15	1
1913		2	1930	SIII 5	5
1914		3	1931	SIII 4	4
1915		2	1932	SIII 8	3
1920		p	1933	SIII 12	5
1921	III 18	2	1934	SIII 10	4
1922	SIII 19	2	1935	SIII 9	3

BRISTOL CITY

Founded: 1894
Address: Ashton Gate, Bristol BS3 2EJ
Telephone: Bristol 664093
Ground capacity: 37,000
Playing area: 115 by 75 yards
Record attendance: 43,335 v Preston North End, FA Cup 5th round, 16.2.35
Record victory: 11-0 v Chichester, FA Cup 1st round, 5.11.60
Record defeat: 0-9 v Coventry City, Division III(S), 28.4.34
Most League points: 70, Division III(S), 1954-55
Most League goals: 104, Division III(S), 1926-27
League scoring record: 36, Don Clark, Division III(S), 1946-47
Record League aggregate: 315, John Atyeo, 1951-1966
Most League appearances: 597, John Atyeo, 1951-1966
Most capped player: 26, Billy Wedlock, England

FA Cup	Year	Opponents	Score
Runners-up	1909	Manchester United	0-1

THE CITY RECORD

Year	Division & place	Cup round reached	Year	Division & place	Cup round reached
1899		1	1938	SIII 2	2
1900		2	1939	SIII 8	1
1901		q	1946		4
1902	II 6	4q	1947	SIII 3	2
1903	II 4	2	1948	SIII 7	2
1904	II 4	1	1949	SIII 16	3
1905	II 4	2	1950	SIII 15	1
1906	II 1P	1	1951	SIII 10	5
1907	I 2	2	1952	SIII 15	2
1908	I 10	1	1953	SIII 5	1
1909	I 8	Final	1954	SIII 3	3
1910	I 16	2	1955	SIII 1P	1
1911	I 19R	1	1956	II 11	3
1912	II 13	1	1957	II 13	5
1913	II 16	1	1958	II 17	5
1914	II 8	1	1959	II 10	4
1915	II 13	2	1960	II 22R	3
1920	II 8	s-f	1961	III 14	4
1921	II 3	1	1962	III 6	3
1922	II 22R	1	1963	III 14	3
1923	SIII 1P	2	1964	III 5	4
1924	II 22R	3	1965	III 2P	3
1925	SIII 3	2	1966	II 5	3
1926	SIII 4	3	1967	II 15	5
1927	SIII 1P	2	1968	II 19	3
1928	II 12	3	1969	II 16	3
1929	II 20	3	1970	II 14	3
1930	II 20	3	1971	II 19	3
1931	II 16	3	1972	II 8	3
1932	II 22R	4	1973	II 5	4
1933	SIII 15	2	1974	II 16	q-f
1934	SIII 19	3	1975	II 5	3
1935	SIII 15	5	1976	II 2P	3
1936	SIII 13	1	1977	I 18	3
1937	SIII 16	1	1978	I 17	3

BRISTOL ROVERS

Founded: 1883
Address: Bristol Stadium, Eastville, Bristol BS5 6NN
Telephone: Bristol 558620/551905
Ground capacity: 39,333
Playing area: 110 by 70 yards
Record attendance: 38,472 v Preston North End, FA Cup 4th round, 30.1.60
Record victory: 15-1 v Weymouth, FA Cup preliminary round, 17.11.1900
Record defeat: 0-12 v Luton Town, Division III(S), 13.4.36
Most League points: 64, Division III(S), 1952-53
Most League goals: 92, Division III(S), 1952-53
League scoring record: 33, Geoff Bradford, Division III(S), 1952-53
Record League aggregate: 245, Geoff Bradford, 1949-1964
Most League appearances: 487, Harry Bamford, 1946-1958
Most capped player: 7, Matt O'Mahoney, 6 Eire, 1 Northern Ireland

THE BRISTOL ROVERS RECORD

Year	Division & place	Cup round reached		Year	Division & place	Cup round reached	
1921	III 10	1		1953	SIII 1P		3
1922	SIII 14	q		1954	II 9		3
1923	SIII 13	q		1955	II 9		4
1924	SIII 9	q		1956	II 6		4
1925	SIII 17	1		1957	II 9		4
1926	SIII 19	1		1958	II 10		6
1927	SIII 10	3		1959	II 6		3
1928	SIII 19	2		1960	II 9		4
1929	SIII 19	2		1961	II 17		3
1930	SIII 20	3		1962	II 21R		3
1931	SIII 15	4		1963	III 19		1
1932	SIII 18	2		1964	III 12		4
1933	SIII 9	3		1965	III 6		3
1934	SIII 7	2		1966	III 16		1
1935	SIII 8	3		1967	III 5		3
1936	SIII 17	3		1968	III 15		3
1937	SIII 15	3		1969	III 16		5
1938	SIII 15	1		1970	III 3		2
1939	SIII 22	2		1971	III 6		2
1946		2		1972	III 6		3
1947	SIII 14	1		1973	III 5		1
1948	SIII 20	4		1974	II 2P		3
1949	SIII 5	1		1975	II 19		4
1950	SIII 9	1		1976	II 18		3
1951	SIII 6	6		1977	II 15		3
1952	SIII 7	4		1978	II 18		5

BURNLEY

Founded: 1882
Address: Turf Moor, Burnley, Lancashire
Telephone: Burnley 27777
Ground capacity: 38,000
Playing area: 115 by 73 yards
Record attendance: 54,755 v Huddersfield Town, FA Cup 3rd round, 23.2.24
Record victory: 9-0 v Darwen, Division I, 9.1.1892
9-0 v Crystal Palace, FA Cup 2nd round replay, 1908-09
9-0 v New Brighton, FA Cup 4th round, 26.1.57
Record defeat: 0-10 v Aston Villa, Division I, 29.8.25
0-10 v Sheffield United, Division I, 19.1.29
Most League points: 62, Division II, 1972-73
Most League goals: 102, Division I, 1960-61
League scoring record: 35, George Beel, Division I, 1927-28
Record League aggregate: 178, George Beel, 1923-1932
Most League appearances: 530, Jerry Dawson, 1906-1929
Most capped player: 51 (55 in all), Jimmy McIlroy, Northern Ireland

FA Cup	Year	Opponents	Score	Scorers
Winners	1914	Liverpool	1-0	Freeman
Runners-up	1947	Charlton Athletic	0-1	
	1962	Tottenham Hotspur	1-3	Robson

THE BURNLEY RECORD

Year	Division & place	Cup round reached		Year	Division & place	Cup round reached
1889	I 9	2		1933	II 19	q-f
1890	I 11	1		1934	II 13	3
1891	I 8	2		1935	II 12	s-f
1892	I 7	2		1936	II 15	3
1893	I 6	2		1937	II 13	5
1894	I 5	1		1938	II 6	4
1895	I 9	1		1939	II 14	3
1896	I 10	2		1946		3
1897	I 16R	1		1947	II 2P	Final
1898	II 1P	3		1948	I 3	3
1899	I 3	1		1949	I 15	5
1900	I 17R	1		1950	I 10	5
1901	II 3	2		1951	I 10	3
1902	II 9	1		1952	I 14	q-f
1903	II 18	q		1953	I 6	5
1904	II 5	q		1954	I 7	4
1905	II 11	q		1955	I 10	3
1906	II 9	1		1956	I 7	4
1907	II 7	1		1957	I 7	q-f
1908	II 7	1		1958	I 6	4
1909	II 14	q-f		1959	I 7	q-f
1910	II 14	2		1960	I 1C	q-f
1911	II 8	q-f		1961	I 4	s-f
1912	II 3	1		1962	I 2	Final
1913	II 2P	s-f		1963	I 3	4
1914	I 12	Winners		1964	I 9	q-f
1915	I 4	3		1965	I 12	5
1920	I 2	2		1966	I 3	4
1921	I 1C	3		1967	I 14	3
1922	I 3	1		1968	I 13	3
1923	I 15	1		1969	I 14	4
1924	I 17	s-f		1970	I 14	4
1925	I 19	1		1971	I 21R	3
1926	I 20	3		1972	II 7	3
1927	I 5	5		1973	II 1P	3
1928	I 18	3		1974	I 6	s-f
1929	I 19	4		1975	I 10	3
1930	I 21R	3		1976	I 21R	3
1931	II 8	4		1977	II 16	4
1932	II 19	3		1978	II 11	4

BURY

Founded: 1885
Address: Gigg Lane, Bury, Lancs
Telephone: (061) 764 4881/2
Ground capacity: 35,000
Playing area: 112 by 72 yards
Record attendance: 35,000 v Bolton, FA Cup 3rd round, 9.1.60
Record victory: 12-1 v Stockton, FA Cup 1st round replay, 1896-97
Record defeat: 0-10 v Blackburn Rovers, FA Cup preliminary round, 1887-88
Most League points: 68, Division III, 1960-61
Most League goals: 108, Division III, 1960-61
League scoring record: 31, Norman Bullock, Division I, 1925-26
Record League aggregate: 124, Norman Bullock, 1920-1935
Most League appearances: 506, Norman Bullock, 1920-1935
Most capped player: 11 (14 in all), W Gorman, Republic of Ireland and 4, Northern Ireland

FA Cup	Year	Opponents	Score	Scorers
Winners	1900	Southampton	4-0	McLuckie 2, Wood, Plant
	1903	Derby County	6-0	Ross, Sagar, Leeming 2, Wood, Plant

THE BURY RECORD

Year	Division & place	Cup round reached	Year	Division & place	Cup round reached
1895	II 1P	2	1936	II 14	4
1896	I 11	q-f	1937	II 3	4
1897	I 9	2	1938	II 10	4
1898	I 14	1	1939	II 16	3
1899	I 10	2	1946		4
1900	I 12	Winners	1947	II 17	3
1901	I 5	2	1948	II 20	3
1902	I 7	q-f	1949	II 12	3
1903	I 8	Winners	1950	II 18	4
1904	I 12	2	1951	II 20	3
1905	I 17	2	1952	II 17	3
1906	I 17	1	1953	II 20	4
1907	I 16	3	1954	II 17	3
1908	I 7	2	1955	II 13	3
1909	I 17	2	1956	II 16	3
1910	I 13	2	1957	II 21R	3
1911	I 18	1	1958	NIII 4	2
1912	I 20R	2	1959	III 10	3
1913	II 11	2	1960	III 7	3
1914	II 10	2	1961	III 1P	3
1915	II 11	2	1962	II 18	3
1920	II 5	2	1963	II 8	4
1921	II 11	1	1964	II 18	4
1922	II 11	1	1965	II 16	3
1923	II 6	3	1966	II 19	3
1924	II 2P	1	1967	II 22R	4
1925	I 5	1	1968	III 2P	3
1926	I 4	4	1969	II 21R	3
1927	I 19	3	1970	III 19	1
1928	I 5	4	1971	III 22R	2
1929	I 21R	5	1972	IV 8	3
1930	II 5	3	1973	IV 13	3
1931	II 13	4	1974	IV 4P	1
1932	II 5	q-f	1975	III 14	4
1933	II 4	4	1976	III 13	4
1934	II 12	4	1977	III 7	2
1935	II 10	3	1978	III 15	1

THE CAMBRIDGE RECORD

Year	Division & place	Cup round reached	Year	Division & place	Cup round reached
1971	IV 20	2	1975	IV 6	3
1972	IV 10	2	1976	IV 13	1
1973	IV 3P	1	1977	IV 1P	1 1
1974	III 21R	3	1978	III 2P	2

CARDIFF CITY

Founded: 1899
Address: Ninian Park, Cardiff, CF1 8SX
Telephone: 0222 28501
Ground capacity: 46,000
Playing area: 112 by 76 yards
Record attendance: *57,800 v Arsenal, Division I, 22.4.53
(*Ground record: 61,566, Wales v England, 14.10.61)
Record victory: 9-2 v Thames, Division III(S), 6.2.32
Record defeat: 2-11 v Sheffield United, Division I, 1.1.26
Most League points: 66, Division III(S), 1946-47
Most League goals: 93, Division III(S), 1946-47
League scoring record: 31, Stan Richards, Division III(S), 1946-47
Record League aggregate: 127, Len Davies, 1923-1929
Most League appearances: 445, Tom Farquharson, 1922-1935
Most capped player: 39 (41 in all), Alf Sherwood, Wales

FA Cup	Year	Opponents	Score	Scorer
Winners	1927	Arsenal	1-0	Ferguson
Runners-up	1925	Sheffield United	0-1	

CAMBRIDGE UNITED

Founded: 1919*
Address: Abbey Stadium, Newmarket Road, Cambridge
Telephone: Teversham 2170/2488
Ground capacity: 12,000 (1,200 seated)
Playing area: 115 by 75 yards
Record attendance: †8,691 v Grimsby Town, Division IV, 27.12.71
Record victory: 6-0 v Darlington, Division IV, 18.9.71
Record defeat: 0-6 v Aldershot, Division III, 13.4.74
0-6 v Darlington, Division IV, 28.9.74
Most League points: 65, Division IV, 1976-77
Most League goals: 87, Division IV, 1976-77
League scoring record: 21, Alan Biley, 1977-78
Record League aggregate: 47, Brian Greenhalgh, 1971-74
Most League appearances: 248, Terry Eades, 1970-77
Most capped player: None
* as Abbey United. Changed name to Cambridge United in 1949
† ground record: 14,000 v Chelsea, Friendly, 1.5.70

THE CARDIFF RECORD

Year	Division & place	Cup round reached	Year	Division & place	Cup round reached
1920		3	1953	I 12	3
1921	II 2P	s-f	1954	I 10	4
1922	I 4	q-f	1955	I 20	3
1923	I 9	3	1956	I 17	4
1924	I 2	q-f	1957	I 21R	3
1925	I 11	Final	1958	II 15	5
1926	I 16	4	1959	II 9	4
1927	I 14	Winners	1960	II 2P	3
1928	I 6	5	1961	I 15	3
1929	I 22R	3	1962	I 21R	3
1930	II 8	4	1963	II 10	3
1931	II 22R	3	1964	II 15	3
1932	SIII 9	3	1965	II 13	3
1933	SIII 19	1	1966	II 20	4
1934	SIII 22	2	1967	II 20	4
1935	SIII 19	1	1968	II 13	3
1936	SIII 20	1	1969	II 5	3
1937	SIII 18	3	1970	II 7	3
1938	SIII 10	3	1971	II 3	4
1939	SIII 13	4	1972	II 19	5
1946		3	1973	II 20	4
1947	SIII 1P	3	1974	II 17	3
1948	II 5	3	1975	II 21R	3
1949	II 4	5	1976	III 2P	4
1950	II 10	3	1977	II 18	5
1951	II 3	3	1978	II 19	3
1952	II 2P	3			

CARLISLE UNITED

Founded: 1904
Address: Brunton Park, Carlisle
Telephone: Carlisle 26237
Ground capacity: 28,000
Playing area: 117 by 78 yards
Record attendance: 27,500 v Birmingham City, FA Cup 3rd round, 5.1.57
Record victory: 8-0 v Hartlepools United, Division III(N), 1.9.28
v Scunthorpe United, Division III(N), 25.12.52
Record defeat: 1-11 v Hull City, Division III(N), 14.1.39
Most League points: 62, Division III(N), 1950-51
Most League goals: 113, Division IV, 1963-64
League scoring record: 42, Jimmy McConnell, Division III(N), 1928-29
Record League aggregate: 126, Jimmy McConnell, 1928-1932
Most League appearances: 465, Alan Ross, 1963-1978
Most capped player: 4, Eric Welsh, Northern Ireland

THE CARLISLE RECORD

	Division & place	Cup round reached			Division & place	Cup round reached
1929	NIII 8	2		1957	NIII 15	3
1930	NIII 15	3		1958	NIII 16	2
1931	NIII 8	3		1959	IV 10	2
1932	NIII 18	2		1960	IV 19	1
1933	NIII 19	2		1961	IV 19	2
1934	NIII 13	2		1962	IV 4P	3
1935	NIII 22	1		1963	III 23R	3
1936	NIII 13	1		1964	IV 2P	5
1937	NIII 10	3		1965	III 1P	1
1938	NIII 12	1		1966	II 14	4
1939	NIII 19	1		1967	II 3	4
1946		2		1968	II 10	4
1947	NIII 16	3		1969	II 12	3
1948	NIII 9	1		1970	II 12	5
1949	NIII 15	1		1971	II 4	4
1950	NIII 9	3		1972	II 10	3
1951	NIII 3	3		1973	II 18	5
1952	NIII 7	1		1974	II 3P	4
1953	NIII 9	1		1975	I 22R	q-f
1954	NIII 13	1		1976	II 19	3
1955	NIII 20	2		1977	II 20R	4
1956	NIII 21	1		1978	III 13	3

CHARLTON ATHLETIC

Founded: 1905
Address: The Valley, Floyd Road, Charlton, London SE7 8AW
Telephone: (01) 858 3711/3712
Ground capacity: 66,000 (2,900 seated)
Playing area: 114 by 78 yards
Record attendance: 75,031 v Aston Villa, FA Cup 5th round, 12.2.38
Record victory: 8-1 v Middlesbrough, Division I, 12.9.53
Record defeat: 1-11 v Aston Villa, Division II, 14.11.59
Most League points: 61, Division III(S), 1934-35
Most League goals: 107, Division II, 1957-58
League scoring record: 32, Ralph Allen, Division III(S), 1934-35
Record League aggregate: 153, Stuart Leary, 1953-62
Most League appearances: 583, Sam Bartram, 1934-56
Most capped player: 19, John Hewie, Scotland

FA Cup	Year	Opponents	Score	Scorers
Winners	1947	Burnley	1-0	Duffy
Runners-up	1946	Derby County	1-4	Turner H

THE CHARLTON RECORD

	Division & place	Cup round reached			Division & place	Cup round reached
1922	SIII 16	q		1954	I 9	3
1923	SIII 12	4		1955	I 15	3
1924	SIII 14	2		1956	I 14	5
1925	SIII 15	p		1957	I 22R	3
1926	SIII 21	3		1958	II 3	4
1927	SIII 13	2		1959	II 8	4
1928	SIII 11	3		1960	II 7	4
1929	SIII 1P	3		1961	II 10	3
1930	II 13	4		1962	II 15	4
1931	II 15	3		1963	II 20	3
1932	II 10	3		1964	II 4	3
1933	II 22R	3		1965	II 18	4
1934	SIII 5	4		1966	II 16	3
1935	SIII 1P	1		1967	II 19	3
1936	II 2P	3		1968	II 15	3
1937	I 2	3		1969	II 3	4
1938	I 4	5		1970	II 20	4
1939	I 3	3		1971	II 20	3
1946		Final		1972	II 21R	3
1947	I 19	Winners		1973	III 11	3
1948	I 13	5		1974	III 14	1
1949	I 9	3		1975	III 3P	2
1950	I 20	4		1976	II 9	5
1951	I 17	3		1977	II 7	3
1952	I 10	3		1978	II 17	3
1953	I 5	3				

CHELSEA

Founded: 1905
Address: Stamford Bridge, London SW6
Telephone: (01) 385 5545
Ground capacity: 60,000
Playing area: 114 by 71 yards
Record attendance: 82,905 v Arsenal, Division I, 12.10.35
Record victory: 13-0 v Jeunesse Hautcharage, 1st Rd European Cup Winners Cup 29.9.71
Record defeat: 1-8 v Wolverhampton Wanderers, Division I, 26.9.53
Most League points: 57, Division II, 1906-07
Most League goals: 98, Division I, 1960-61
League scoring record: 41, Jimmy Greaves, 1960-61
Record League aggregate: 164, Bobby Tambling, 1958-1970
Most League appearances: 584, Peter Bonetti, 1960-1978
Most capped player: 23, Eddie McCreadie, Scotland

FA Cup	Year	Opponents	Score	Scorers
Winners	1970	Leeds United	*2-2	Houseman, Hutchinson
			*2-1	Osgood, Webb
Runners-up	1915	Sheffield United	0-3	
	1967	Tottenham Hotspur	1-2	Tambling
League Cup				
Winners	1965	Leicester City	H3-2	Tambling, Venables (pen)
				McCreadie
			A0 0	
Runners up	1972	Stoke City	1 2	Osgood

THE CHELSEA RECORD

Year	Division & place	FA Cup round reached	Year	Division & place	FA Cup round reached
1906	II 3	3q	1948	I 18	4
1907	II 2P	1	1949	I 13	5
1908	I 13	2	1950	I 13	s-f
1909	I 11	2	1951	I 20	5
1910	I 19R	2	1952	I 19	s-f
1911	II 3	s-f	1953	I 19	5
1912	II 2P	2	1954	I 8	3
1913	I 18	2	1955	I 1C	5
1914	I 8	1	1956	I 16	5
1915	I 19	Final	1957	I 12	4
1920	I 3	s-f	1958	I 11	4
1921	I 18	q-f	1959	I 14	4
1922	I 9	1	1960	I 18	4
1923	I 19	2	1961	I 12	3
1924	I 21R	1	1962	I 22R	3
1925	II 5	1	1963	II 2P	5
1926	II 3	4	1964	I 5	4
1927	II 4	q-f	1965	I 3	s-f
1928	II 3	3	1966	I 5	s-f
1929	II 9	5	1967	I 9	Final
1930	II 2P	3	1968	I 6	q-f
1931	I 12	q-f	1969	I 5	q-f
1932	I 12	s-f	1970	I 3	Winners
1933	I 18	3	1971	I 6	4
1934	I 19	5	1972	I 7	5
1935	I 12	3	1973	I 12	6
1936	I 8	5	1974	I 17	3
1937	I 13	4	1975	I 21R	4
1938	I 10	3	1976	II 11	5
1939	I 20	q-f	1977	II 2P	3
1946		5	1978	I 16	5
1947	I 15	4			

THE CHESTER RECORD

CHESTER

Founded: 1884
Address: Sealand Road, Chester, CH1 4LW
Telephone: Chester 21048
Ground capacity: 20,500 (2,100 seated)
Playing area: 114 by 76 yards
Record attendance: 20,500 v Chelsea, FA Cup 3rd round replay, 16.1.52
Record victory: 12-0 v York City, Division III(N), 1.2.36
Record defeat: 2-11 v Oldham Athletic, Division III(N), 19.1.52
Most League points: 56, Division III(N), 1946-47; Division IV, 1964-65
Most League goals: 119, Division IV, 1964-65
League scoring record: 36, Dick Yates, Division III(N), 1946-47
Record League aggregate: 83, Gary Talbot, 1963-1967 and 1968-1970
Most League appearances: 408, Ray Gill, 1951-1962
Most capped player: 9 (30 in all), W Lewis, Wales

Year	Division & place	Cup round reached	Year	Division & place	
1932	NIII 3	2	1957	NIII 21	1
1933	NIII 4	4	1958	NIII 21	2
1934	NIII 10	2	1959	IV 13	2
1935	NIII 3	3	1960	IV 20	2
1936	NIII 2	2	1961	IV 24	1
1937	NIII 3	4	1962	IV 23	2
1938	NIII 9	3	1963	IV 21	1
1939	NIII 6	4	1964	IV 12	2
1946		3	1965	IV 8	3
1947	NIII 3	4	1966	IV 7	3
1948	NIII 20	4	1967	IV 19	1
1949	NIII 18	2	1968	IV 22	2
1950	NIII 12	2	1969	IV 14	2
1951	NIII 13	1	1970	IV 11	4
1952	NIII 19	3	1971	IV 5	3
1953	NIII 20	1	1972	IV 20	1
1954	NIII 24	1	1973	IV 15	1
1955	NIII 24	1	1974	IV 7	3
1956	NIII 17	1	1975	IV 4P	1
			1976	III 17	2
			1977	III 13	5
			1978	III 5	2

CHESTERFIELD

Founded: 1866
Address: Recreation Ground, Saltergate, Chesterfield, Derbyshire
Telephone: Chesterfield 32318
Ground capacity: 28,500 (3,000 seated)
Playing area: 114 by 72 yards
Record attendance: 30,968 v Newcastle United, Division II, 7.4.39
Record victory: 10-0 v Glossop North End, Division II, 17.1.03
Record defeat: 1-9 v Port Vale, Division II, 24.9.32
Most League points: 64, Division IV, 1969-70
Most League goals: 102, Division III(N), 1930-31
League scoring record: 44, Jimmy Cookson, Division III(N), 1925-26
Record League aggregate: 112, Herbert Munday, 1899-1909
Most League appearances: 613, Dave Blakey, 1948-1967
Most capped player: 4 (7 in all), Walter McMillen, Northern Ireland

THE CHESTERFIELD RECORD

Year	Division & place	Cup round reached	Year	Division & place	
1900	II 7	p	1939	II 6	3
1901	II 14	1	1946		3
1902	II 16	p	1947	II 4	4
1903	II 6	p	1948	II 16	3
1904	II 11	p	1949	II 6	3
1905*	II 5	p	1950	II 14	5
1906*	II 18	2	1951	II 21R	3
1907*	II 18	1	1952	NIII 13	2
1908*	II 19	2	1953	NIII 12	2
1909*	II 19L	1	1954	NIII 6	4
1910		1	1955	NIII 6	1
1911		p	1956	NIII 6	2
1912		p	1957	NIII 6	3
1913		1	1958	NIII 8	1
1914		1	1959	III 16	3
1915		p	1960	III 18	1
1920		p	1961	III 24R	3
1921		p	1962	IV 19	2
1922	NIII 13	p	1963	IV 15	2
1923	NIII 4	p	1964	IV 16	3
1924	NIII 3	p	1965	IV 12	3
1925	NIII 7	p	1966	IV 20	1
1926	NIII 4	3	1967	IV 15	1
1927	NIII 7	3	1968	IV 7	3
1928	NIII 16	1	1969	IV 20	3
1929	NIII 11	3	1970	IV 1P	1
1930	NIII 4	3	1971	III 5	2
1931	NIII 1P	1	1972	III 13	3
1932	II 17	4	1973	III 16	2
1933	II 21R	5	1974	III 5	1
1934	NIII 2	3	1975	III 15	3
1935	NIII 10	3	1976	III 15	1
1936	NIII 1P	2	1977	III 18	2
1937	II 15	3	1978	III 9	2
1938	II 11	5			

* – as Chesterfield Town

COLCHESTER UNITED

Founded: 1937
Address: Layer Road, Colchester, Essex
Telephone: Colchester 74042
Ground capacity: 16,150 (1,205 seated)
Playing area: 110 by 71 yards
Record attendance: 19,072 v Reading, FA Cup 1st round, 27.11.48
Record victory: 9-1 v Bradford City, Division IV, 30.9.61
Record defeat: 0-7 v Leyton Orient, Division III(S), 5.1.52
0-7 v Reading, Division III(S), 18.9.57
Most League points: 60, Division IV, 1973-74
Most League goals: 104, Division IV, 1961-62
League scoring record: 37, Bobby Hunt, Division IV, 1961-62
Record League aggregate: 131, Martyn King, 1959-65
Most League appearances: 421, Peter Wright, 1952-64
Most capped player: None

THE COLCHESTER RECORD

	Division & place	Cup round reached		Division & place	Cup round reached
1946		p	1963	III 12	1
1947		1	1964	III 17	2
1948		5	1965	III 23R	2
1949		1	1966	IV 4P	1
1950		p	1967	III 13	2
1951	SIII 16	1	1968	III 22R	3
1952	SIII 10	3	1969	IV 6	2
1953	SIII 22	3	1970	IV 10	1
1954	SIII 23	1	1971	IV 6	q-f
1955	SIII 24	1	1972	IV 11	1
1956	SIII 12	1	1973	IV 22	2
1957	SIII 3	1	1974	IV 3P	1
1958	SIII 12	1	1975	III 11	2
1959	III 5	4	1976	III 22R	1
1960	III 9	1	1977	IV 3P	4
1961	III 23R	2	1978	III 8	2
1962	IV 2P	1			

Founded: 1883
Address: Highfield Road, Coventry
Telephone: Coventry 57171
Ground capacity: 48,000
Playing area: 110 by 75 yards
Record attendance: 51,457 v Wolverhampton Wanderers, Division II, 29.4.67
Record victory: 9-0 v Bristol City, Division III(S), 28.4.34
Record defeat: 2-10 v Norwich City, Division III(S), 15.3.30
Most League points: 60, Division IV, 1958-59 & Division III, 1963-64
Most League goals: 108, Division III(S), 1931-32
League scoring record: 49, Clarrie Bourton, Division III(S), 1931-32
Record League aggregate: 171, Clarrie Bourton, 1931-37
Most League appearances: 486, George Curtis, 1956-1970
Most capped player: 21 (48 in all), Dave Clements, Northern Ireland

THE COVENTRY RECORD

	Division & place	Cup round reached				
1908		1	1949	II	16	3
1909		q	1950	II	12	3
1910		q-f	1951	II	7	3
1911		3	1952	II	21R	4
1912		2	1953	SIII	6	3
1913		1	1954	SIII	14	1
1914		4q	1955	SIII	9	3
1915		6q	1956	SIII	8	1
1920	II 20	1	1957	SIII	16	1
1921	II 21	6q	1958	SIII	19	2
1922	II 20	2	1959	IV	2P	2
1923	II 18	5q	1960	III	5	1
1924	II 19	1	1961	III	15	3
1925	II 22R	1	1962	III	14	2
1926	NIII 16	1	1963	III	4	q-f
1927	SIII 15	2	1964	III	1P	2
1928	SIII 20	1	1965	II	10	3
1929	SIII 11	1	1966	II	3	5
1930	SIII 6	3	1967	II	1P	3
1931	SIII 14	2	1968	I	20	4
1932	SIII 12	1	1969	I	20	4
1933	SIII 6	2	1970	I	6	3
1934	SIII 2	2	1971	I	10	3
1935	SIII 3	1	1972	I	18	4
1936	SIII 1P	1	1973	I	18	6
1937	II 8	5	1974	I	16	5
1938	II 4	3	1975	I	14	4
1939	II 4	3	1976	I	14	4
1946		3	1977	I	19	4
1947	II 8	4	1978	I	7	3
1948	II 10	4				

COVENTRY CITY

CREWE ALEXANDRA

Founded: 1877
Address: Gresty Road, Crewe, Cheshire
Telephone: Crewe 3014
Ground capacity: 17,000
Playing area: 113 by 75 yards
Record attendance: 20,000 v Tottenham Hotspur, FA Cup 4th round, 30.1.60
Record victory: 8-0 v Rotherham United, Division III(N), 1.10.32
Record defeat: 2-13 v Tottenham Hotspur, FA Cup 4th round replay, 3.2.60
Most League points: 59, Division IV, 1962-63
Most League goals: 95, Division III(N), 1931-32
League scoring record: 34, Terry Harkin, Division IV, 1964-65
Record League aggregate: 126, Bert Swindells, 1928-1937
Most League appearances: 436, Tommy Lowry, 1966-1977
Most capped player: 12 (30 in all), William Lewis, Wales

THE CREWE RECORD

Year	Division & place	Cup round reached	Year	Division & place	Cup round reached
1886		3	1932	NIII 6	1
1887		p	1933	NIII 10	2
1888		s-f	1934	NIII 14	1
1889		1	1935	NIII 13	1
1890		p	1936	NIII 6	3
1891		1	1937	NIII 20	3
1892		1	1938	NIII 8	2
1893	II 10	p	1939	NIII 8	2
1894	II 12	p	1946		1
1895	II 16	p	1947	NIII 8	1
1896	II 16L	1	1948	NIII 10	4
1897		p	1949	NIII 12	3
1898		p	1950	NIII 7	2
1899		p	1951	NIII 9	2
1900		p	1952	NIII 16	1
1901		p	1953	NIII 10	1
1902		p	1954	NIII 16	2
1903		p	1955	NIII 22	1
1904		p	1956	NIII 24	1
1905		p	1957	NIII 24	1
1906		1	1958	NIII 24	1
1907		1	1959	IV 18	1
1908		p	1960	IV 14	4
1909		p	1961	IV 9	4
1910		p	1962	IV 10	2
1911		2	1963	IV 3P	2
1912		1	1964	III 22R	2
1913		p	1965	IV 10	1
1914		p	1966	IV 14	4
1915		p	1967	IV 5	3
1920		p	1968	IV 4P	1
1921		p	1969	III 23R	1
1922	NIII 6	p	1970	IV 15	1
1923	NIII 6	p	1971	IV 15	2
1924	NIII 20	p	1972	IV 24	1
1925	NIII 15	p	1973	IV 21	3
1926	NIII 11	2	1974	IV 21	1
1927	NIII 15	3	1975	IV 18	1
1928	NIII 17	4	1976	IV 16	1
1929	NIII 9	1	1977	IV 12	1
1930	NIII 11	2	1978	IV 15	2
1931	NIII 18	2			

CRYSTAL PALACE

Founded: 1905
Address: Selhurst Park, SE25 6PU
Telephone: 01-653 2223/4
Ground capacity: 51,000 (9,000 seated)
Playing area: 110 by 75 yards
Record attendance: 49,498 v Chelsea, Division I, 27.12.69
Record victory: 9-0 v Barrow, Division IV, 10.10.59
Record defeat: 4-11 v Manchester City, FA Cup 5th round, 20.2.26
Most League points: 64, Division IV, 1960-61
Most League goals: 110, Division IV, 1960-61
League scoring record: 46, Peter Simpson, Division III(S), 1930-31
Record League aggregate: 154, Peter Simpson, 1930-1936
Most League appearances: 432, Terry Long, 1956-1969
Most capped player: 13, Ian Evans, Wales

THE PALACE RECORD

Year	Division & place	Cup round reached	Year	Division & place	Cup round reached
1921	III 1P	2	1953	SIII 13	2
1922	II 14	2	1954	SIII 22	1
1923	II 16	1	1955	SIII 20	2
1924	II 15	3	1956	SIII 23	1
1925	II 21R	2	1957	SIII 20	3
1926	SIII 13	5	1958	SIII 14	3
1927	SIII 6	1	1959	IV 7	3
1928	SIII 5	2	1960	IV 8	3
1929	SIII 2	5	1961	IV 2P	2
1930	SIII 9	3	1962	III 15	3
1931	SIII 2	4	1963	III 11	2
1932	SIII 4	2	1964	III 2P	2
1933	SIII 5	1	1965	II 7	q-f
1934	SIII 12	4	1966	II 11	3
1935	SIII 5	1	1967	II 7	3
1936	SIII 6	2	1968	II 11	3
1937	SIII 14	1	1969	II 2P	3
1938	SIII 7	3	1970	I 20	5
1939	SIII 2	1	1971	I 18	3
1946		3	1972	I 20	3
1947	SIII 18	3	1973	I 21R	4
1948	SIII 13	3	1974	II 20R	3
1949	SIII 22	1	1975	III 5	3
1950	SIII 7	1	1976	III 5	s-f
1951	SIII 24	1	1977	III 3P	3
1952	SIII 19	1	1978	II 9	3

DARLINGTON

Founded: 1883
Address: Feethams Ground, Darlington, County Durham
Telephone: Darlington 65097
Ground capacity: 20,000
Playing area: 110 by 74 yards
Record attendance: 21,023 v Bolton Wanderers, League cup 3rd round, 14.11.60
Record victory: 9-2 v Lincoln City, Division III(N), 7.1.28
Record defeat: 0-10 v Doncaster Rovers, Division IV, 25.1.64
Most League points: 59, Division IV, 1965-66
Most League goals: 108, Division III(N), 1929-30
League scoring record: 39, David Brown, Division III(N), 1924-5
Record League aggregate: 74, David Brown, 1923-1926
Most League appearances: 442, Ron Greener, 1955-1967
Most capped player: None

THE DARLINGTON RECORD

Year	Division & place	Cup round reached	Year	Division & place	Cup round reached
1911		3	1950	NIII 17	1
1912		2	1951	NIII 18	1
1913		p	1952	NIII 23	1
1914		p	1953	NIII 21	1
1915		1	1954	NIII 21	1
1920		2	1955	NIII 15	3
1921		1	1956	NIII 15	2
1922	NIII 2	1	1957	NIII 18	2
1923	NIII 9	p	1958	NIII 20	5
1924	NIII 6	1	1959	IV 16	3
1925	NIII 1P	1	1960	IV 15	2
1926	II 15	2	1961	IV 7	2
1927	II 21R	4	1962	IV 13	1
1928	NIII 7	3	1963	IV 12	1
1929	NIII 19	3	1964	IV 19	1
1930	NIII 3	1	1965	IV 17	3
1931	NIII 11	1	1966	IV 2P	2
1932	NIII 11	3	1967	III 22R	2
1933	NIII 22	4	1968	IV 16	1
1934	NIII 16	1	1969	IV 5	2
1935	NIII 5	2	1970	IV 22	1
1936	NIII 12	3	1971	IV 12	2
1937	NIII 22	4	1972	IV 19	2
1938	NIII 19	1	1973	IV 24	1
1939	NIII 18	2	1974	IV 20	1
1946		2	1975	IV 21	2
1947	NIII 17	2	1976	IV 20	1
1948	NIII 16	1	1977	IV 11	3
1949	NIII 4	3	1978	IV 19	1

DERBY COUNTY

Founded: 1884
Address: Baseball Ground, Shaftesbury Crescent, Derby DE3 8NB
Telephone: 0332 40105
Ground capacity: 38,500 (15,250 seated)
Playing area: 110 by 71 yards
Record attendance: 41,826 v Tottenham Hotspur, Division I, 20.9.69
Record victory: 12-0 v Finn Harps, UEFA Cup 3rd round, 15.9.76
Record defeat: 2 ,11 v Everton, FA Cup 1st round, 18.1.90
Most League points: 63, Division II, 1968-69, Division III(N), 1955-56, 1956-57
Most League goals: 111, Division III(N), 1956-57
League scoring record: 37, Jack Bowers, Division I, 1930-31 and Ray Straw, Division III(N) .1956-57
Record League aggregate: 291, Steve Bloomer, 1892-1906 and 1910-1914
Most League appearances: 478, Jack Parry, 1949-1966
Most capped player: 28, Roy McFarland, England (as at 1.1.77)

FA Cup	Year	Opponents	Score	Scorers
Winners	1946	Charlton Athletic	*4-1	Stamps 2, Doherty, og
Runners-up	1898	Nottingham Forest	1-3	Bloomer
	1899	Sheffield United	1-4	Boag
	1903	Bury	0-6	

*—after extra time

THE DERBY RECORD

	Division & place	Cup round reached		Division & place	Cup round reached
1885		1	1932	I 15	5
1886		3	1933	I 7	s-f
1887		2	1934	I 4	5
1888		2	1935	I 6	5
1889	I 10	2	1936	I 2	q-f
1890	I 7	1	1937	I 4	5
1891	I 11	2	1938	I 13	3
1892	I 10	1	1939	I 6	3
1893	I 13	1	1946		Winners
1894	I 3	q-f	1947	I 14	5
1895	I 15	1	1948	I 4	s-f
1896	I 2	s-f	1949	I 3	q-f
1897	I 3	s-f	1950	I 11	q-f
1898	I 10	Final	1951	I 11	4
1899	I 9	Final	1952	I 17	3
1900	I 6	1	1953	I 22R	3
1901	I 12	1	1954	II 18	3
1902	I 6	s-f	1955	II 22R	3
1903	I 9	Final	1956	NIII 2	2
1904	I 14	s-f	1957	NIII 1P	2
1905	I 11	1	1958	II 16	3
1906	I 15	2	1959	II 7	3
1907	I 19R	3	1960	II 18	3
1908	II 6	1	1961	II 12	3
1909	II 5	s-f	1962	II 16	4
1910	II 4	2	1963	II 18	4
1911	II 6	q-f	1964	II 13	3
1912	II 1P	2	1965	II 9	3
1913	I 7	1	1966	II 8	3
1914	I 20R	2	1967	II 17	3
1915	II 1P	1	1968	II 18	3
1920	I 18	1	1969	II 1P	3
1921	I 21R	2	1970	I 4	5
1922	II 12	1	1971	I 9	5
1923	II 14	s-f	1972	I 1C	5
1924	II 3	2	1973	I 7	6
1925	II 3	1	1974	I 3	4
1926	II 2P	4	1975	I 1C	5
1927	I 12	4	1976	I 4	s-f
1928	I 4	4	1977	I 15	q-f
1929	I 6	4	1978	I 12	5
1930	I 2	4			
1931	I 6	3			

DONCASTER ROVERS

Founded: 1879
Address: Belle Vue Ground, Doncaster
Telephone: Doncaster 55281
Ground capacity: 30,000
Playing area: 118 by 79 yards
Record attendance: 37,149 v Hull City, Division III(N), 2.10.48
Record victory: 10-0 v Darlington, Division IV, 25.1.64
Record defeat: 0-12 v Small Heath, Division II, 11.4.03
Most League points: 72, Division III(N), 1946-47
Most League goals: 123, Division III(N), 1946-47
League scoring record: 42, Clarrie Jordan, Division III(N), 1946-47
Record League aggregate: 180, Tom Kettley, 1923-29
Most League appearances: 406, Fred Emery, 1925-1936
Most capped player: 14, Len Graham, Northern Ireland

THE DONCASTER ROVERS RECORD

	Division & place	Cup round reached		Division & place	Cup round reached
1902	II 7	p	1954	II 12	5
1903*	II 16	q	1955	II 18	5
1905*	II 18	q	1956	II 17	5
1924	NIII 9	q	1957	II 14	3
1925	NIII 18	1	1958	II 22R	3
1926	NIII 10	2	1959	III 22R	3
1927	NIII 8	2	1960	IV 17	3
1928	NIII 4	1	1961	IV 11	1
1929	NIII 5	1	1962	IV 21	1
1930	NIII 14	4	1963	IV 16	2
1931	NIII 15	2	1964	IV 14	3
1932	NIII 15	2	1965	IV 9	3
1933	NIII 6	3	1966	IV 1P	1
1934	NIII 5	1	1967	III 23R	1
1935	NIII 1P	1	1968	IV 10	3
1936	II 18	3	1969	IV 1P	3
1937	II 22R	3	1970	III 11	2
1938	NIII 2	3	1971	III 23R	1
1939	NIII 2	4	1972	IV 12	1
1946		1	1973	IV 17	3
1947	NIII 1P	3	1974	IV 22	3
1948	II 21R	3	1975	IV 17	2
1949	NIII 3	1	1976	IV 10	1
1950	NIII 1P	4	1977	IV 8	1
1951	II 11	3	1978	IV 12	1
1952	II 16	5			
1953	II 13	3			

*Doncaster failed to gain re-election. Elected in 1904 and 1923.

EVERTON

Founded: 1878
Address: Goodison Park, Liverpool L4 4EL
Telephone: (051) 525 5283/4
Ground capacity: 58,000 (25,000 seated)
Playing area: 112 by 78 yards
Record attendance: 78,299 v Liverpool, Division I, 18.8.48
Record victory: 11-2 v Derby County, FA Cup 1st round, 18.1.1890
Record defeat: 4-10 v Tottenham Hotspur, Division I, 11.10.58
Most League points: 66, Division I, 1969-70
Most League goals: 121, Division II, 1930-31
League scoring record: 60, Dixie Dean, Division I, 1927-28
Record League aggregate: 349, Dixie Dean, 1925-1937
Most League appearances: 465, Ted Sagar, 1929-1953
Most capped player: 37 (72 in all), Alan Ball, England

FA Cup	Year	Opponents	Score	Scorers
Winners	1906	Newcastle United	1-0	Young
	1933	Manchester City	3-0	Stein, Dean, Dunn
	1966	Sheffield Wednesday	3-2	Trebilcock 2, Temple
Runners-up	1893	Wolverhampton Wanderers	0-1	
	1897	Aston Villa	2-3	Bell, Boyle
	1907	Sheffield Wednesday	1-2	Sharp
	1968	West Bromwich Albion	*0-1	
League Cup				
Runners up	1977	Aston Villa	0-0	
	Replay		*1-1	Latchford
*after extra time	Replay		*2-3	Latchford, Lyons

THE EVERTON RECORD

	Division & place	Cup round reached				
1887		1	1932	I	1C	3
1888		2	1933	I	11	Winners
1889	I 8	q	1934	I	14	3
1890	I 2	2	1935	I	8	q-f
1891	I 1C	1	1936	I	16	3
1892	I 5	1	1937	I	17	5
1893	I 3	Final	1938	I	14	4
1894	I 6	1	1939	I	1C	q-f
1895	I 2	q-f	1946			3
1896	I 3	q-f	1947	I	10	4
1897	I 7	Final	1948	I	14	5
1898	I 4	s-f	1949	I	18	4
1899	I 4	2	1950	I	18	s-f
1900	I 11	1	1951	I	22R	3
1901	I 7	2	1952	II	7	3
1902	I 2	1	1953	II	16	s-f
1903	I 12	q-f	1954	II	2P	5
1904	I 3	1	1955	I	11	4
1905	I 2	s-f	1956	I	15	q-f
1906	I 11	Winners	1957	I	15	5
1907	I 3	Final	1958	I	16	4
1908	I 11	q-f	1959	I	16	5
1909	I 2	2	1960	I	15	3
1910	I 10	s-f	1961	I	5	3
1911	I 4	3	1962	I	4	5
1912	I 2	q-f	1963	I	1C	5
1913	I 11	q-f	1964	I	3	5
1914	I 15	1	1965	I	4	4
1915	I 1C	s-f	1966	I	11	Winners
1920	I 16	1	1967	I	6	q-f
1921	I 7	q-f	1968	I	5	Final
1922	I 20	1	1969	I	3	s-f
1923	I 5	1	1970	I	1C	3
1924	I 7	2	1971	I	14	s-f
1925	I 17	3	1972	I	15	5
1926	I 11	3	1973	I	17	4
1927	I 20	4	1974	I	7	4
1928	I 1C	4	1975	I	4	5
1929	I 18	3	1976	I	11	3
1930	I 22R	4	1977	I	9	s-f
1931	II 1P	s-f	1978	I	3	4

Founded: 1904
Address: St. James' Park, Exeter
Telephone: Exeter 54073
Ground capacity: 18,500 (1,940 seated)
Playing area: 114 by 73 yards
Record attendance: 20,984 v Sunderland, FA Cup 6th Rd. replay, 4.3.31
Record victory: 8-1 v Coventry City, Division III(S), 4.12.26
8-1 v Aldershot, Division III(S), 4.5.35
Record defeat: 0-9 v Notts County, Division III(S), 16.10.48, and
0-9 v Northampton Town, Division III(S), 12.4.58
Most League points: 62, Division IV, 1976-77
Most League goals: 88, Division III(S), 1932-33
League scoring record: 34, Fred Whitlow, Division III(S), 1932-33
Record League aggregate: 105, Alan Banks, 1963-66, 1967-1973
Most League appearances: 495, Arnold Mitchell, 1952-66
Most capped player: 1 (17 in all), Dermot Curtis, Eire

THE EXETER CITY RECORD

	Division & place	Cup round reached				
1909		2	1949	SIII	12	3
1910		5q	1950	SIII	16	4
1911		1	1951	SIII	14	4
1912		4q	1952	SIII	23	2
1913		4q	1953	SIII	17	1
1914		2	1954	SIII	9	1
1915		1	1955	SIII	22	1
1920		6q	1956	SIII	16	3
1921	SIII 19	1	1957	SIII	21	1
1922	SIII 21	5q	1958	SIII	24	1
1923	SIII 20	5q	1959	IV	5	1
1924	SIII 16	2	1960	IV	9	3
1925	SIII 7	1	1961	IV	21	1
1926	SIII 20	1	1962	IV	18	1
1927	SIII 12	3	1963	IV	17	1
1928	SIII 8	4	1964	IV	4P	2
1929	SIII 21	3	1965	III	17	2
1930	SIII 16	1	1966	III	22R	1
1931	SIII 13	6	1967	IV	14	1
1932	SIII 7	3	1968	IV	20	2
1933	SIII 2	1	1969	IV	17	3
1934	SIII 9	1	1970	IV	18	2
1935	SIII 11	2	1971	IV	15	1
1936	SIII 22	1	1972	IV	15	2
1937	SIII 21	5	1973	IV	8	1
1938	SIII 17	2	1974	IV	10	1
1939	SIII 14	1	1975	IV	9	1
1946		2	1976	IV	7	1
1947	SIII 15	1	1977	IV	2P	1
1948	SIII 11	1	1978	III	17	3

EXETER CITY

FULHAM

Founded: 1880
Address: Craven Cottage, Stevenage Road, London SW6
Telephone: (01) 736 5621/7035/0511
Ground capacity: 42,000
Playing area: 110 by 75 yards
Record attendance: 49,335 v Millwall, Division II, 8.10.38
Record victory: 10-1 v Ipswich Town, Division I, 26.12.63
Record defeat: 0-9 v Wolverhampton Wanderers, Division I, 16.9.59
Most League points: 60, Division II, 1958-59 & Division III, 1970-71
Most League goals: 111, Division III(S), 1931-32
League scoring record: 41, Frank Newton, Division III(S), 1931-32
Record League aggregate: 159, Johnny Haynes, 1952-70
Most League appearances: 598, Johnny Haynes, 1952-70
Most capped player: 56, Johnny Haynes, England

FA Cup	Year	Opponents	Score
Runners-up	1975	West Ham United	0-2

THE FULHAM RECORD

Year	Division & place	Cup round reached	Year	Division & place	Cup round reached
1904		1	1947	II 15	3
1905		q-f	1948	II 11	q-f
1906		2	1949	II 1P	3
1907		2	1950	I 17	3
1908	II 4	s-f	1951	I 18	q-f
1909	II 10	2	1952	I 22R	3
1910	II 7	2	1953	II 8	3
1911	II 10	1	1954	II 8	4
1912	II 8	q-f	1955	II 14	3
1913	II 9	1	1956	II 9	4
1914	II 11	1	1957	II 11	4
1915	II 12	2	1958	II 5	s-f
1920	II 6	1	1959	II 2P	4
1921	II 9	3	1960	I 10	4
1922	II 7	2	1961	I 17	3
1923	II 10	1	1962	I 20	s-f
1924	II 20	2	1963	I 16	3
1925	II 12	2	1964	I 15	4
1926	II 19	q-f	1965	I 20	3
1927	II 18	4	1966	I 20	3
1928	II 21R	3	1967	I 19	4
1929	SIII 5	2	1968	I 22R	4
1930	SIII 7	4	1969	II 22R	4
1931	SIII 9	3	1970	III 4	1
1932	SIII 1P	3	1971	III 2P	1
1933	II 3	3	1972	II 20	4
1934	II 16	3	1973	II 9	3
1935	II 7	3	1974	II 13	4
1936	II 9	s-f	1975	II 9	Final
1937	II 11	3	1976	II 12	3
1938	II 8	3	1977	II 17	3
1939	II 12	4	1978	II 10	3
1946		3			

Year	Division & place	Cup round reached	Year	Division & place	Cup round reached
1951	SIII 22	2	1968	III 11	1
1952	SIII 22	2	1969	III 20	2
1953	SIII 20	2	1970	III 20	5
1954	SIII 10	1	1971	III 24R	1
1955	SIII 4	2	1972	IV 13	3
1956	SIII 10	1	1973	IV 9	1
1957	SIII 22	2	1974	IV 2P	1
1958	SIII 22	3	1975	III 10	1
1959	IV 11	1	1976	III 14	2
1960	IV 7	3	1977	III 12	1
1961	IV 15	3	1978	III 7	2
1962	IV 20	1			
1963	IV 5	3			
1964	IV 1P	1			
1965	III 7	2			
1966	III 6	1			
1967	III 11	2			

*New Brompton Excelsior until 1913
†Not re-elected   Re-elected 1950

GILLINGHAM

Founded: 1893
Address: Priestfield Stadium, Gillingham, Kent
Telephone: Medway 51854
Ground capacity: 22,000
Playing area: 114 by 75 yards
Record attendance: 23,002 v Queen's Park Rangers, FA Cup 3rd round, 10.1.48
Record victory: 10-1 v Gorleston, FA Cup 1st round, 16.11.57
Record defeat: 2-9 v Nottingham Forest, Division III(S), 18.11.50
Most League points: 62, Division IV, 1973-4
Most League goals: 90, Division IV, 1973-4
League scoring record: 31, Ernie Morgan, Division III(S), 1954-55, Brian Yeo, Division IV, 1973-74
Record League aggregate: 135, Brian Yeo, 1963-75
Most League appearances: 571, John Simpson, 1957-72
Most capped player: 1, Frank Fox, England; 1 (2), Damien Richardson, Eire

THE GILLINGHAM RECORD

Year	Division & place	Cup round reached	Year	Division & place	Cup round reached
1899*		1	1924	SIII 15	1
1900		p	1925	SIII 13	p
1901		p	1926	SIII 10	2
1902		p	1927	SIII 20	2
1903		p	1928	SIII 16	3
1904		p	1929	SIII 22	1
1905		p	1930	SIII 21	1
1906		1	1931	SIII 16	2
1907		2	1932	SIII 21	1
1908		2	1933	SIII 7	2
1909		p	1934	SIII 17	2
1910		p	1935	SIII 20	1
1911		1	1936	SIII 16	2
1912		p	1937	SIII 11	2
1913		1	1938†	SIII 22	1
1914		2	1939		q
1915		1	1946		q
1920		1	1947		3
1921	III 22	p	1948		3
1922	SIII 18	1	1949		q
1923	SIII 16	p	1950		2

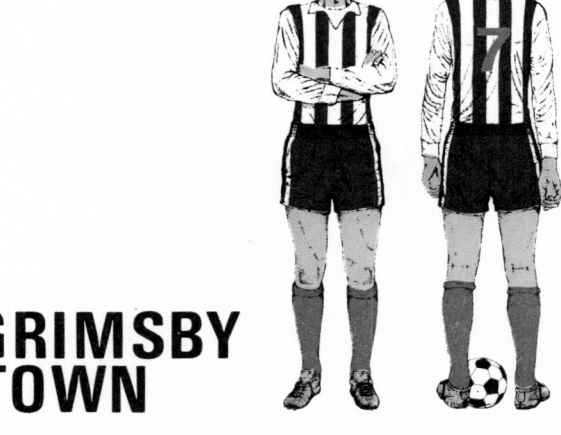

GRIMSBY TOWN

Founded: 1878 (as Grimsby Pelham)
Address: Blundell Park, Cleethorpes, Lincolnshire
Telephone: Cleethorpes 61420/61803
Ground capacity: 28,000
Playing area: 111 by 74 yards
Record attendance: 31,657 v Wolves, FA Cup 5th round, 20.2.37
Record victory: 9-2 v Darwen, Division II, 15.4.1899
Record defeat: 1-9 v Arsenal, Division I, 28.1.31
Most League points: 68, Division III(N), 1955-56
Most League goals: 103, Division II, 1933-34
League scoring record: 42, Pat Glover, Division II, 1933-34
Record League aggregate: 182, Pat Glover, 1930-1939
Most League appearances: 448, Keith Jobling, 1953-1969
Most capped player: 7, Pat Glover, Wales

THE GRIMSBY RECORD

Year	Division & place	Cup round reached	Year	Division & place	Cup round reached
1893	II 4	2	1938	I 20	3
1894	II 5	1	1939	I 10	s-f
1895	II 5	p	1946		3
1896	II 3	2	1947	I 16	4
1897	II 3	1	1948	I 22R	3
1898	II 12	1	1949	II 11	4
1899	II 10	1	1950	II 11	4
1900	II 6	1	1951	II 22R	3
1901	II 1P	p	1952	NIII 2	2
1902	I 15	1	1953	NIII 5	3
1903	I 17R	2	1954	NIII 17	3
1904	II 6	1	1955	NIII 23	3
1905	II 13	1	1956	NIII 1P	3
1906	II 8	1	1957	II 16	3
1907	II 11	1	1958	II 13	3
1908	II 18	q-f	1959	II 21R	4
1909	II 13	1	1960	III 4	2
1910	II 19L	1	1961	III 6	1
1911		3	1962	III 2P	1
1912	II 9	p	1963	II 19	3
1913	II 7	1	1964	II 21R	3
1914	II 15	1	1965	III 10	2
1915	II 17	1	1966	III 11	4
1920	II 22M	1	1967	III 17	1
1921	III 13	2	1968	III 21R	1
1922	NIII 3	1	1969	IV 23	1
1923	NIII 14	p	1970	IV 16	1
1924	NIII 11	1	1971	IV 1P	1
1925	NIII 12	p	1972	IV 9	4
1926	NIII 1P	3	1973	III 9	4
1927	II 17	3	1974	III 6	3
1928	II 11	3	1975	III 16	2
1929	II 2P	3	1976	III 18	1
1930	I 18	3	1977	III 23R	2
1931	I 13	5	1978	IV 6	3
1932	I 21R	5			
1933	II 13	4			
1934	II 1P	4			
1935	I 5	3			
1936	I 17	s-f			
1937	I 11	5			

M—not re-elected to Second Division but invited to join newly formed Third Division.

HALIFAX TOWN

Founded: 1911
Address: Shay Ground, Halifax HX1 2YS
Telephone: Halifax 53423
Ground capacity: 25,000
Playing area: 110 by 70 yards
Record attendance: 36,885 v Tottenham Hotspur, FA Cup 5th round, 14.2.53
Record victory: 7-0 v Bishop Auckland, FA Cup 2nd round replay, 10.1.67
Record defeat: 0,13 v Stockport County, Division III(N), 6.1.34
Most League points: 57, Division IV, 1968-69
Most League goals: 83, Division III(N), 1957-58
League scoring record: 34, Albert Valentine, Division III(N), 1934-35
Record League aggregate: 129, Ernest Dixon .1922-1930
Most League appearances: 367, John Pickering, 1965-74
Most capped player: 1, Mick Meagan, Eire

THE HALIFAX RECORD

Year	Division & place		Cup round reached	Year	Division & place		Cup round reached
1922	NIII	19	p	1954	NIII	23	1
1923	NIII	7	1	1955	NIII	14	1
1924	NIII	14	2	1956	NIII	19	2
1925	NIII	9	p	1957	NIII	11	1
1926	NIII	5	1	1958	NIII	7	1
1927	NIII	4	1	1959	III	9	2
1928	NIII	12	2	1960	III	15	2
1929	NIII	13	1	1961	III	9	2
1930	NIII	21	1	1962	III	18	1
1931	NIII	17	2	1963	III	24R	2
1932	NIII	17	3	1964	IV	10	1
1933	NIII	15	5	1965	IV	23	1
1934	NIII	9	3	1966	IV	15	1
1935	NIII	2	1	1967	IV	12	3
1936	NIII	17	2	1968	IV	11	3
1937	NIII	7	1	1969	IV	2P	4
1938	NIII	18	1	1970	III	18	1
1939	NIII	12	3	1971	III	3	1
1946			1	1972	III	16	1
1947	NIII	22	2	1973	III	20	2
1948	NIII	21	1	1974	III	9	2
1949	NIII	19	1	1975	III	17	2
1950	NIII	21	1	1976	III	24R	3
1951	NIII	22	1	1977	IV	21	3
1952	NIII	20	1	1978	IV	20	1
1953	NIII	14	5				

HARTLEPOOL

Founded: 1908
Address: The Victoria Ground, Clarence Road, Hartlepool
Telephone: Hartlepool 72584
Ground capacity: 16,500
Playing area: 113 by 77 yards
Record attendance: 17,426 v Manchester United, FA Cup 3rd round, 5.1.57
Record victory: 10-1 v Barrow, Division IV, 4.4.59
Record defeat: 1-10 v Wrexham, Division IV, 3.3.62
Most League points: 60, Division IV, 1967-68
Most League goals: 90, Division III(N), 1956-57
League scoring record: 28, Bill Robinson, Division III(N), 1927-28
Record League aggregate: 98, Ken Johnson, 1949-1964
Most League appearances: 448, Watty Moore, 1948-1964
Most capped player: 1 (11 in all), Ambrose Fogarty, Eire

THE HARTLEPOOL RECORD

Year	Division & place		Cup round reached	Year	Division & place		Cup round reached
1922	NIII	4	p	1954	NIII	18	1
1923	NIII	15	p	1955	NIII	5	4
1924	NIII	21	p	1956	NIII	4	3
1925	NIII	20	1	1957	NIII	2	3
1926	NIII	6	p	1958	NIII	17	2
1927	NIII	17	1	1959	IV	19	2
1928	NIII	15	1	1960	IV	24	1
1929	NIII	21	1	1961	IV	23	1
1930	NIII	8	1	1962	IV	22	3
1931	NIII	20	1	1963	IV	24	1
1932	NIII	13	1	1964	IV	23	1
1933	NIII	14	2	1965	IV	15	2
1934	NIII	11	2	1966	IV	18	3
1935	NIII	12	2	1967	IV	8	1
1936	NIII	8	3	1968	IV	3P	1
1937	NIII	6	2	1969	III	22R	1
1938	NIII	20	2	1970	IV	23	2
1939	NIII	21	2	1971	IV	23	1
1946			1	1972	IV	18	2
1947	NIII	13	2	1973	IV	20	1
1948	NIII	19	2	1974	IV	11	1
1949	NIII	16	1	1975	IV	13	3
1950	NIII	18	2	1976	IV	14	3
1951	NIII	16	2	1977	IV	22	1
1952	NIII	9	3	1978	IV	21	4
1953	NIII	17	2				

HEREFORD UNITED

Founded: 1924
Address: Edgar Street, Hereford
Telephone: Hereford 4037
Ground capacity: 17,500
Playing area: 111 by 80 yards
Record attendance: 18,114 v Sheffield Wednesday, FA Cup 3rd round, 4.1.58
Record victory: 11-0 v Thynnes, FA Cup qualifying rounds, September 1947
Record defeat: 2-9 v Yeovil Town, Southern League, April 1957
Most capped player: 1 (7 in all), Brian Evans, Wales
Most League points: 63, Division III, 1975-76
Most League goals: 86, Division III, 1975-76
League scoring record: 35, Dixie McNeil, Division III, 1975-76
Record League aggregate: 85, Dixie McNeil, 1974-77
Most League appearances: 137, Billy Tucker, 1972-77

THE HEREFORD RECORD

Year	Division & place		Cup round reached	Year	Division & place		Cup round reached
1973	IV	2P	1	1976	III	1P	3
1974	III	18	4	1977	II	22R	4
1975	III	12	2	1978	III	23R	1

HUDDERSFIELD TOWN

Founded: 1908
Address: Leeds Road, Huddersfield HD1 6PE
Telephone: Huddersfield 20335/6
Ground capacity: 48,000 (6,200 seated)
Playing area: 115 by 75 yards
Record attendance: 67,037 v Arsenal, FA Cup quarter-final, 27.2.32
Record victory: 10-1 v Blackpool .Division I, 13.12.30
Record defeat: 0-8 v Middlesbrough, Division I, 1950-51
Most League points: 64, Division II, 1919-20
Most League goals: 97, Division II, 1919-20
League scoring record: 35, George Brown, Division I, 1925-26, Sam Taylor, Division II, 1919-20
Record League aggregate: 142, George Brown, Division I, 1921-1929
Most League appearances: 520, Billy Smith, 1914-1934
Most capped player: 31 (41 in all), Jimmy Nicholson, Northern Ireland

FA Cup	Year	Opponents	Score	Scorers
Winners	1922	Preston North End	1-0	Smith (pen)
Runners-up	1920	Aston Villa	*0-1	
	1928	Blackburn Rovers	1-3	Jackson
	1930	Arsenal	0-2	
	1938	Preston North End	*0-1	

*after extra time

THE HUDDERSFIELD RECORD

	Division & place	Cup round reached			Division & place		
1911	II 13			1951	I 19	5	
1912	II 17	1		1952	I 21R	3	
1913	II 5	2		1953	II 2P	4	
1914	II 13	2		1954	I 3	3	
1915	II 8	1		1955	I 12	q-f	
1920	II 2P	Final		1956	I 21R	3	
1921	I 17	3		1957	II 12	5	
1922	I 14	Winners		1958	II 9	3	
1923	I 3	3		1959	II 14	3	
1924	I 1C	3		1960	II 6	4	
1925	I 1C	1		1961	II 20	4	
1926	I 1C	4		1962	II 7	4	
1927	I 2	3		1963	II 6	3	
1928	I 2	Final		1964	II 12	5	
1929	I 16	s-f		1965	II 8	4	
1930	I 10	Final		1966	II 4	5	
1931	I 5	3		1967	II 6	3	
1932	I 4	q-f		1968	II 14	3	
1933	I 6	4		1969	II 6	4	
1934	I 2	4		1970	II 1F	3	
1935	I 16	3		1971	I 15	4	
1936	I 3	4		1972	I 22R	q-f	
1937	I 15	3		1973	II 21R	3	
1938	I 15	Final		1974	III 10	2	
1939	I 19	s-f		1975	III 24R	1	
1946		3		1976	IV 5	4	
1947	I 20	3		1977	IV 9	1	
1948	I 19	3		1978	IV 11	1	
1949	I 20	4					
1950	I 15	3					

HULL CITY

Founded: 1904
Address: Boothferry Park, Hull HU4 6EU
Telephone: 0482 52195/6
Ground capacity: 42,000 (9,000 seated)
Playing area: 112 by 75 yards
Record attendance: 55,019 v Manchester United, FA Cup quarter-final, 26.2.49
Record victory: 11-1 v Carlisle United, Division III (N), 14.1.39
Record defeat: 0-8 v Wolverhampton Wanderers, Division II, 4.11.11
Most League points: 69, Division III, 1965-66
Most League goals: 109, Division III, 1965-66
League scoring record: 39, Bill McNaughton, Division III (N), 1932-33
Record League aggregate: 195, Chris Chilton, 1960-1971
Most League appearances: 511, Andy Davidson, 1947-1967
Most capped player: 15 (59 in all), Terry Neill, Northern Ireland

THE HULL RECORD

	Division & place	Cup round reached			Division & place		
1906	II 5	1		1949	NIII 1P	q-f	
1907	II 9	1		1950	II 7	4	
1908	II 8	2		1951	II 10	5	
1909	II 4	1		1952	II 18	4	
1910	II 3	1		1953	II 18	4	
1911	II 5	1		1954	II 15	5	
1912	II 7	1		1955	II 19	3	
1913	II 12	2		1956	II 22R	3	
1914	II 7	1		1957	NIII 8	3	
1915	II 7	q-f		1958	NIII 5	4	
1920	II 11	1		1959	III 2P	1	
1921	II 13	q-f		1960	II 21R	3	
1922	II 5	2		1961	III 11	3	
1923	II 12	1		1962	III 10	2	
1924	II 17	1		1963	III 10	3	
1925	II 10	3		1964	III 8	3	
1926	II 13	3		1965	III 4	2	
1927	II 7	5		1966	III 1P	q-f	
1928	II 14	3		1967	II 12	3	
1929	II 12	3		1968	II 17	3	
1930	II 21R	s-f		1969	II 11	3	
1931	NIII 6	3		1970	II 13	3	
1932	NIII 8	3		1971	II 5	q-f	
1933	NIII 1P	3		1972	II 12	5	
1934	II 15	4		1973	II 13	5	
1935	II 13	3		1974	II 9	3	
1936	II 22R	3		1975	II 8	3	
1937	NIII 5	1		1976	II 14	4	
1938	NIII 3	3		1977	II 14	3	
1939	NIII 7	2		1978	II 22R	3	
1947	NIII 11	3					
1948	NIII 5	3		Did not compete in 1946 Cup			

IPSWICH TOWN

Founded: 1887
Address: Portman Road, Ipswich, Suffolk IP1 2DA
Telephone: Ipswich 51306/57107
Ground capacity: 38,000
Playing area: 112 by 72 yards
Record attendance: 38,010 v Leeds United, FA Cup 6th round, 8.3.75
Record victory: 10-0 v Floriana, Malta, European Cup, 1962-63
Record defeat: 1-10 v Fulham, Division I, 26.12.63
Most League points: 64, Division III(S), 1953-54 & 1955-56
Most League goals: 106, Division III(S), 1955-56
League scoring record: 41, Ted Phillips, Division III(S), 1956-57
Record League aggregate: 203, Ray Crawford, 1958-1963 & 1966-1969
Most League appearances: 428, Tom Parker, 1946-1957
Most capped player: 40, Allan Hunter, Northern Ireland

FA Cup	Year	Opponents	Score	Scorer
Winners	1978	Arsenal	1-0	Osborne

THE IPSWICH RECORD

	Division & place	Cup round reached			Division & place	Cup round reached
1939	SIII 7	3		1962	I 1C	4
1946		2		1963	I 17	4
1947	SIII 6	2		1964	I 22R	4
1948	SIII 4	1		1965	II 5	4
1949	SIII 7	1		1966	II 15	3
1950	SIII 17	3		1967	II 5	5
1951	SIII 8	2		1968	II 1P	3
1952	SIII 17	3		1969	I 12	3
1953	SIII 16	3		1970	I 18	3
1954	SIII 1P	5		1971	I 19	5
1955	II 21R	3		1972	I 13	4
1956	SIII 3	1		1973	I 4	4
1957	SIII 1P	3		1974	I 4	5
1958	II 8	4		1975	I 3	s-f
1959	II 16	5		1976	I 6	4
1960	II 11	3		1977	I 3	4
1961	II 1P	3		1978	I 18	Winners

THE LEEDS RECORD

	Division & place	FA Cup round reached			Division & place	FA Cup round reached
1906†	II 6			1952	II 6	5
1907†	II 10	1		1953	II 10	3
1908†	II 12	1		1954	II 10	3
1909†	II 12	2		1955	II 4	3
1910†	II 17	1		1956	II 2P	3
1911†	II 11	1		1957	I 8	3
1912†	II 19	2		1958	I 17	3
1913†	II 6	1		1959	I 15	3
1914†	II 4	2		1960	I 21R	3
1915†	II 15	2		1961	II 14	3
1920‡	II			1962	II 19	3
1921	II 14	1q		1963	II 5	5
1922	II 8	1		1964	II 1P	4
1923	II 7	2		1965	I 2	Final
1924	II 1P	3		1966	I 2	4
1925	I 18	1		1967	I 4	s-f
1926	I 19	3		1968	I 4	s-f
1927	I 21R	4		1969	I 1C	3
1928	II 2P	3		1970	I 2	Final
1929	I 13	4		1971	I 2	5
1930	I 5	4		1972	I 2	Winners
1931	I 21R	5		1973	I 3	Final
1932	II 2P	3		1974	I 1C	5
1933	I 8	5		1975	I 9	q-f
1934	I 9	3		1976	I 5	4
1935	I 18	4		1977	I 10	s-f
1936	I 11	5		1978	I 9	3
1937	I 19	3				
1938	I 9	4				
1939	I 13	4				
1946		3				
1947	I 22R	3				
1948	II 18	3				
1949	II 15	3				
1950	II 5	q-f				
1951	II 5	4				

†as Leeds City
‡Leeds expelled from the League after 8 matches. Fixtures transferred to Port Vale, who finished 13th.

LEEDS UNITED

Founded: 1904†
Address: Elland Road, Leeds LS11 0ES **Telephone:** 0532 716037
Ground capacity: 50,000 **Playing area:** 117 by 76 yards
Record attendance: 57,892 v Sunderland, FA Cup 5th round, 15.3.67
Record victory: 10-0 v Lyn Oslo, European Cup, 1st Rd, 17.9.69
Record defeat: 1-8 v Stoke City, Division I, 27.8.34
Most League points: 67, Division I, 1968-69
Most League goals: 98, Division II, 1927-28
League scoring record: 42, John Charles, 1953-54
Record League aggregate: 154, John Charles, 1949-1957 & 1962
Most League appearances: 629, Jack Charlton, 1953-1973
Most capped player: 54, Billy Bremner, Scotland

FA Cup	Year	Opponents	Score	Scorers
Winners	1972	Arsenal	1-0	Clarke
Runners-up	1965	Liverpool	*1-2	Bremner
	1970	Chelsea	*2-2	Charlton, Jones
			*1-2	Jones
	1973	Sunderland	0-1	
League Cup				
Winners	1968	Arsenal	1-0	Cooper

†as Leeds City. Reconstituted as Leeds United 1920   *after extra time

LEICESTER CITY

Founded: 1884
Address: Filbert Street, Leicester
Telephone: Leicester 57111/2
Ground capacity: 34,000
Playing area: 112 by 75 yards
Record attendance: 47,298 v Tottenham Hotspur, FA Cup 5th round, 18.2.28
Record victory: 10-0 v Portsmouth, Division I, 20.10.28
Record defeat: 0-12 v Nottingham Forest, Division I, 21.4.09
Most League points: 61, Division II, 1956-57
Most League goals: 109, Division II, 1956-57
League scoring record: 44, Arthur Rowley, Division II, 1956-57
Record League aggregate: 262, Arthur Chandler, 1923-1935
Most League appearances: 530, Adam Black, 1919-1935
Most capped player: 37 (73 in all), Gordon Banks, England

THE LEICESTER RECORD

Year	Division & place	Cup round reached		Year	Division & place	Cup round reached
1894		2		1936	II 6	5
1895	II 4	1		1937	II 1P	4
1896	II 8	4q		1938	I 16	4
1897	II 9	4q		1939	I 22R	4
1898	II 7	1		1946		3
1899	II 3	4q		1947	II 9	5
1900	II 5	1		1948	II 9	5
1901	II 11	1		1949	II 19	Final
1902	II 14	p		1950	II 15	3
1903	II 15	2q		1951	II 14	3
1904	II 18	4q		1952	II 5	3
1905	II 14	1		1953	II 5	3
1906	II 7	1		1954	II 1P	q-f
1907	II 3	1		1955	I 21R	3
1908	II 2P	2		1956	II 5	4
1909	I 20R	2		1957	II 1P	3
1910	II 5	q-f		1958	I 18	3
1911	II 15	2		1959	I 19	4
1912	II 10	2		1960	I 12	q-f
1913	II 15	1		1961	I 6	Final
1914	II 18	1		1962	I 14	3
1915	II 19	6q		1963	I 4	Final
1920	II 14	3		1964	I 11	3
1921	II 12	1		1965	I 18	q-f
1922	II 9	3		1966	I 7	5
1923	II 3	2		1967	I 8	3
1924	II 12	1		1968	I 13	q-f
1925	II 1P	q-f		1969	I 21R	Final
1926	I 17	3		1970	II 3	5
1927	I 7	1		1971	II 1P	q-f
1928	I 3	5		1972	I 12	4
1929	I 2	5		1973	I 16	3
1930	I 8	3		1974	I 9	s-f
1931	I 16	3		1975	I 18	5
1932	I 19	5		1976	I 7	5
1933	I 19	3		1977	I 11	3
1934	I 17	s-f		1978	I 22R	4
1935	I 21R	4				

THE LINCOLN RECORD

Year	Division & place	Cup round reached		Year	Division & place	Cup round reached
1885		3		1931	NIII 2	2
1886		1		1932	NIII 1P	2
1887		1		1933	II 18	3
1888		p		1934	II 22R	3
1889		p		1935	NIII 4	2
1890		2		1936	NIII 4	1
1891		1		1937	NIII 2	2
1892		p		1938	NIII 7	2
1893	II 9	p		1939	NIII 17	3
1894	II 8	p		1946		2
1895	II 13	q		1947	NIII 12	3
1896	II 13	p		1948	NIII 1P	1
1897	II 16	p		1949	II 22R	3
1898	II 14	p		1950	NIII 4	1
1899	II 12	p		1951	NIII 5	1
1900	II 9	p		1952	NIII 1P	3
1901	II 8	p		1953	II 15	3
1902	II 5	2		1954	II 16	4
1903	II 10	1		1955	II 16	3
1904	II 12	q		1956	II 8	3
1905	II 9	1		1957	II 18	3
1906	II 13	2		1958	II 20	3
1907	II 19	2		1959	II 19	3
1908	II 20L			1960	II 13	3
1909		1		1961	II 22R	4
1910	II 15	p		1962	III 22R	1
1911	II 21L	p		1963	IV 22	3
1912		2		1964	IV 11	3
1913	II 8	p		1965	IV 22	3
1914	II 19	1		1966	IV 22	1
1915	II 16	1		1967	IV 24	1
1920	II 21L	1		1968	IV 13	1
1921		2		1969	IV 8	3
1922	NIII 14	p		1970	IV 8	2
1923	NIII 13	q		1971	IV 21	3
1924	NIII 19	p		1972	IV 5	1
1925	NIII 8	p		1973	IV 10	1
1926	NIII 15	1		1974	IV 12	1
1927	NIII 11	3		1975	IV 5	3
1928	NIII 2	3		1976	IV 1P	4
1929	NIII 6	3		1977	III 9	3
1930	NIII 5	2		1978	III 16	1

LINCOLN CITY

LIVERPOOL

Founded: 1892
Address: Anfield Road, Liverpool 4 **Telephone**: (051) 263 2361
Ground capacity: 56,318
Playing area: 110 by 75 yards
Record attendance: 61,905 v Wolverhampton Wanderers, FA Cup 4th Rd, 2.2.52
Record victory: 11-0 v Strömgodset, European Cup Winners Cup, 17.9.74
Record defeat: 1-9 v Birmingham City, Division II, 11.12.54
Most League points: 62, Division II, 1961-62
Most League goals: 106, Division II, 1895-96
League scoring record: 41, Roger Hunt, Division II, 1961-62
Record League aggregate: 245, Roger Hunt, 1959-1969
Most League appearances: 640, Ian Callaghan, 1960-1978
Most capped player: 54, Emlyn Hughes, England

FA Cup	Year	Opponents	Score	Scorers
Winners	1965	Leeds United	*2-1	Hunt, St John
	1974	Newcastle United	3-0	Keegan 2, Heighway
Runners-up	1914	Burnley	0-1	
	1950	Arsenal	0-2	
	1971	Arsenal	*1-2	Heighway
	1977	Manchester United	1-2	Case
League Cup				
Runners-up	1978	Nottingham Forest	0-0	
		Replay	0-1	

*After extra time

THE LIVERPOOL RECORD

Year	Division & place	F.A. Cup round reached	Year	Division & place	Cup round
1894	II 1P	q-f	1936	I 19	4
1895	I 16R	2	1937	I 18	3
1896	II 1P	2	1938	I 11	5
1897	I 5	s-f	1939	I 11	5
1898	I 9	q-f	1946		4
1899	I 2	s-f	1947	I 1C	s-f
1900	I 10	2	1948	I 11	4
1901	I 1C	1	1949	I 12	5
1902	I 11	2	1950	I 8	Final
1903	I 5	1	1951	I 9	3
1904	I 17R	1	1952	I 11	5
1905	II 1P	1	1953	I 17	3
1906	I 1C	s-f	1954	I 22R	3
1907	I 15	q-f	1955	II 11	5
1908	I 8	3	1956	II 3	5
1909	I 16	2	1957	II 3	3
1910	I 2	1	1958	II 4	q-f
1911	I 13	2	1959	II 4	3
1912	I 17	2	1960	II 3	4
1913	I 12	3	1961	II 3	4
1914	I 16	Final	1962	II 1P	5
1915	I 14	2	1963	I 8	s-f
1920	I 4	q-f	1964	I 1C	q-f
1921	I 4	2	1965	I 7	Winners
1922	I 1C	2	1966	I 1C	3
1923	I 1C	3	1967	I 5	5
1924	I 12	q-f	1968	I 3	q-f
1925	I 4	q-f	1969	I 2	5
1926	I 7	4	1970	I 5	q-f
1927	I 9	5	1971	I 5	Final
1928	I 16	4	1972	I 3	4
1929	I 5	4	1973	I 1C	q-f
1930	I 12	3	1974	I 2	Winners
1931	I 9	3	1975	I 2	4
1932	I 10	q-f	1976	I 1C	4
1933	I 14	3	1977	1 1C	Final
1934	I 18	5	1978	1 2	3
1935	I 7	4			

LUTON
TOWN

Founded: 1885
Address: 70 Kenilworth Road, Luton
Telephone: Luton 411622
Ground capacity: 25,000
Playing area: 112 by 72 yards
Record attendance: 30,069 v Blackpool, FA Cup 6th round replay, 4.3.59
Record victory: 12-0 v Bristol Rovers, Division III(S), 13.4.36
Record defeat: 1-9 v Swindon Town, Division III(S), 28.8.21
Most League points: 66, Division IV, 1967-68
Most League goals: 103, Division III(S), 1936-37
League scoring record: 55, Joe Payne, Division III(S), 1936-37
Record League aggregate: 243, Gordon Turner, 1949-1964
Most League appearances: 494, Bob Morton, 1949-1964
Most capped player: 19, George Cummins, Eire

FA Cup	Year	Opponents	Score	Scorers
Runners-up	1959	Nottingham Forest	1-2	Pacey

THE LUTON TOWN RECORD

Year	Division & place	Cup round reached	Year	Division & place	Cup round
1898	II 8	1	1952	II 8	q-f
1899	II 15	p	1953	II 3	5
1900	II 17L	p	1954	II 6	3
1921	SIII 9	3	1955	II 2P	5
1922	SIII 4	2	1956	I 10	3
1923	SIII 5	1	1957	I 16	3
1924	SIII 7	1	1958	I 8	3
1925	SIII 16	1	1959	I 17	Final
1926	SIII 7	2	1960	I 22R	5
1927	SIII 8	3	1961	II 13	5
1928	SIII 13	3	1962	II 13	3
1929	SIII 7	3	1963	II 22R	3
1930	SIII 13	1	1964	III 18	3
1931	SIII 7	2	1965	III 21R	3
1932	SIII 6	3	1966	IV 6	2
1933	SIII 14	q-f	1967	IV 17	2
1934	SIII 6	3	1968	IV 1P	2
1935	SIII 4	4	1969	III 3	3
1936	SIII 2	4	1970	III 2P	2
1937	SIII 1P	4	1971	II 6	3
1938	II 12	5	1972	II 13	3
1939	II 7	3	1973	II 12	q-f
1946		3	1974	II 2P	5
1947	II 13	5	1975	I 20R	3
1948	II 13	5	1976	II 7	4
1949	II 10	5	1977	II 6	4
1950	II 17	3	1978	II 13	4
1951	II 19	4			

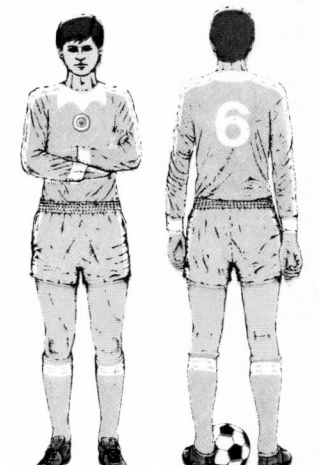

MANCHESTER
CITY

Founded: 1887
Address: Maine Road, Moss Side, Manchester M14 7WN
Telephone: (061) 226 1191/2
Ground capacity: 52,500
Playing area: 117 by 79 yards
Record attendance: 84,569 v Stoke City, FA Cup quarter-final, 3.3.34
Record victory: 11-3 v Lincoln City, Division II, 23.3.95
Record defeat: 1-9 v Everton, Division I, 3.9.06
Most League points: 62, Division II, 1946-47
Most League goals: 108, Division II, 1926-27
League scoring record: 38, Tom Johnson, Division I, 1928-29
Record League aggregate: 158, Tom Johnson, 1919-1930
Most League appearances: 565, Alan Oakes, 1959-76
Most capped player: 48, Colin Bell, England

FA Cup	Year	Opponents	Score	Scorers
Winners	1904	Bolton Wanderers	1-0	Meredith
	1934	Portsmouth	2-1	Tilson, 2
	1956	Birmingham City	3-1	Hayes, Dyson, Johnstone
	1969	Leicester City	1-0	Young
Runners-up	1926	Bolton Wanderers	0-1	
	1933	Everton	0-3	
	1955	Newcastle United	1-3	Johnstone
League Cup				
Winners	1970	West Bromwich Albion	2-1	Doyle, Pardoe
	1976	Newcastle United	2-1	Barnes, Tueart
Runners-up	1974	Wolverhampton		
		Wanderers	1-2	Bell

THE CITY RECORD

Year	Division & place	Cup round reached	Year	Division & place	Cup round
1893†	II 5		1937	I 1C	q-f
1894†	II 13		1938	I 21R	q-f
1895	II 9		1939	II 5	4
1896	II 2		1946		4
1897	II 6	1	1947	II 1P	5
1898	II 3	2	1948	I 10	5
1899	II 1P	2	1949	I 7	3
1900	I 7	1	1950	I 21R	3
1901	I 11	1	1951	II 2P	3
1902	I 18R	2	1952	I 15	3
1903	II 1P	1	1953	I 20	4
1904	I 2	Winners	1954	I 17	4
1905	I 3	2	1955	I 7	Final
1906	I 5	1	1956	I 4	Winners
1907	I 17	1	1957	I 18	3
1908	I 3	3	1958	I 5	3
1909	I 19R	1	1959	I 20	3
1910	II 1P	q-f	1960	I 16	4
1911	I 17	2	1961	I 13	4
1912	I 15	2	1962	I 12	4
1913	I 6	2	1963	I 21R	5
1914	I 13	q-f	1964	II 6	3
1915	I 5	3	1965	II 11	3
1920	I 7	2	1966	II 1P	q-f
1921	I 2	1	1967	I 15	q-f
1922	I 10	3	1968	I 1C	4
1923	I 8	1	1969	I 13	Winners
1924	I 11	s-f	1970	I 9	4
1925	I 10	1	1971	I 11	5
1926	I 21R	Final	1972	I 4	3
1927	II 3	3	1973	I 11	5
1928	II 1P	5	1974	I 14	4
1929	I 8	3	1975	I 8	3
1930	I 3	5	1976	I 8	4
1931	I 8	3	1977	I 2	5
1932	I 14	s-f	1978	I 4	4
1933	I 16	Final			
1934	I 5	Winners			
1935	I 4	3			
1936	I 9	5			

†as Ardwick

Runners-up	1957	Aston Villa	1-2	Taylor
	1958	Bolton Wanderers	0-2	
	1976	Southampton	0-1	

*Ground record: 76,962 for Wolverhampton Wanderers v Grimsby Town, FA Cup semi-final, 25.3.39

THE UNITED RECORD

Year	Division & place	Cup round reached	Year	Division & place	Cup round
1890+		1	1934	II 20	3
1891+			1935	II 5	4
1892+			1936	II 1P	4
1893+	I 16	1	1937	I 21R	4
1894+	I 16R	2	1938	II 2P	5
1895+	II 3	1	1939	I 14	3
1896+	II 6	2	1946		4
1897+	II 2	q-f	1947	I 2	4
1898+	II 4	2	1948	I 2	Winners
1899+	II 4	1	1949	I 2	s-f
1900+	II 4		1950	I 4	q-f
1901+	II 10	1	1951	I 2	q-f
1902+	II 15		1952	I 1C	3
1903	II 5	2	1953	I 8	5
1904	II 3	2	1954	I 4	3
1905	II 3		1955	I 5	4
1906	II 2P	q-f	1956	I 1C	3
1907	I 8	1	1957	I 1C	Final
1908	I 1C	q-f	1958	I 9	Final
1909	I 13	Winners	1959	I 2	3
1910	I 5	1	1960	I 7	5
1911	I 1C	3	1961	I 7	4
1912	I 13	q-f	1962	I 15	s-f
1913	I 4	3	1963	I 19	Winners
1914	I 14	1	1964	I 2	s-f
1915	I 18	1	1965	I 1C	s-f
1920	I 12	2	1966	I 4	s-f
1921	I 13	1	1967	I 1C	4
1922	I 22R	1	1968	I 2	3
1923	II 4	2	1969	I 11	q-f
1924	II 14	2	1970	I 8	s-f
1925	II 2P	1	1971	I 8	3
1926	I 9	s-f	1972	I 8	4
1927	I 15	3	1973	I 18	3
1928	I 19	q-f	1974	I 21R	4
1929	I 12	4	1975	II 1P	3
1930	I 17	3	1976	I 3	Final
1931	I 22R	4	1977	I 6	Winners
1932	II 12	3	1978	I 10	4
1933	II 6	3			

+ — as Newton Heath

MANCHESTER UNITED

Founded: 1878
Address: Old Trafford, Manchester M16 0RA
Telephone: (061) 872 1661/2
Ground capacity: 60,500
Playing area: 116 by 76 yards
Record attendance: *70,504 v Aston Villa, Division I, 27.12.20
Record victory: 10-0 v Anderlecht, European Cup 1956-57
Record defeat: 0-7 v Aston Villa, Division I, 27.12.30
Most League points: 64, Division I, 1956-57
Most League goals: 103, Division I, 1956-57 & Division I, 1958-59
League scoring record: 32, Dennis Viollet, Division I, 1959-60
Record League aggregate: 198, Bobby Charlton, 1956-1973
Most League appearances: 606, Bobby Charlton, 1956-1973
Most capped player: 106, Bobby Charlton, England

FA Cup	Year	Opponents	Score	Scorers
Winners	1909	Bristol City	1-0	Turnbull (A)
	1948	Blackpool	4-2	Rowley 2, Pearson, Anderson
	1963	Leicester City	3-1	Herd 2, Law
	1977	Liverpool	2-1	Pearson, Greenhoff, J.

MANSFIELD TOWN

Founded: 1905
Address: Field Mill Ground, Quarry Lane, Mansfield, Notts.
Telephone: Mansfield 23567
Ground capacity: 23,500
Playing area: 115 by 72 yards
Record attendance: 24,467 v Nottingham Forest, FA Cup 3rd round, 10.1.53
Record victory: 9-2 v Rotherham United, Division III(N), 27.12.32
9-2 v Hounslow Town, FA Cup 1st round replay, 5.11.62
Record defeat: 1-8 v Walsall, Division III(N), 19.1.33
Most League points: 68, Division IV, 1974-75
Most League goals: 108, Division IV, 1962-63
League scoring record: 55, Ted Harston, Division III(N), 1936-37
Record League aggregate: 104, Harry Johnson, 1931-1936
Most League appearances: 417, Don Bradley, 1949-1962
Most capped player: None

THE MANSFIELD RECORD

Year	Division & place	Cup round reached	Year	Division & place	Cup round reached
1932	SIII 20	1	1957	NIII 16	1
1933	NIII 16	1	1958	NIII 6	3
1934	NIII 17	1	1959	III 20	1
1935	NIII 8	3	1960	III 22R	3
1936	NIII 19	1	1961	IV 20	2
1937	NIII 9	2	1962	IV 14	2
1938	SIII 14	3	1963	IV 4P	3
1939	SIII 16	2	1964	III 7	1
1946		3	1965	III 3	2
1947	SIII 22	1	1966	III 19	1
1948	NIII 8	3	1967	III 9	4
1949	NIII 10	3	1968	III 20	1
1950	NIII 8	2	1969	III 15	q-f
1951	NIII 2	5	1970	III 6	5
1952	NIII 6	1	1971	III 7	2
1953	NIII 18	3	1972	III 21R	1
1954	NIII 7	1	1973	IV 6	1
1955	NIII 13	1	1974	IV 17	2
1956	NIII 18	2	1975	IV 1P	5
			1976	III 11	2
			1977	III 1P	1
			1978	II 21R	3

Year	Division & place	Cup round reached	Year	Division & place	Cup round reached
1936	I 14	q-f	1961	II 5	3
1937	I 7	3	1962	II 12	5
1938	I 5	5	1963	II 4	4
1939	I 4	4	1964	II 10	3
1946		5	1965	II 17	5
1947	I 11	q-f	1966	II 21R	3
1948	I 16	5	1967	III 2P	3
1949	I 19	4	1968	II 6	4
1950	I 9	4	1969	II 4	3
1951	I 6	3	1970	II 4	q-f
1952	I 18	4	1971	II 7	4
1953	I 13	3	1972	II 9	5
1954	I 21R	3	1973	II 4	3
1955	II 12	3	1974	II 1P	4
1956	II 14	4	1975	I 7	q-f
1957	II 6	4	1976	I 13	3
1958	II 7	4	1977	I 12	q-f
1959	II 13	3	1978	I 14	q-f
1960	II 5	3			

MIDDLESBROUGH

Founded: 1876
Address: Ayresome Park, Middlesbrough
Telephone: Middlesbrough 89659
Ground capacity: 42,000 (10,200 seated)
Playing area: 115 by 75 yards
Record attendance: 53,596 v Newcastle United, Division I, 27.12.49
Record victory: 9-0 v Brighton, Division II, 23.8.58
Record defeat: 0-9 v Blackburn Rovers, Division II, 6.11.54
Most League points: 65, Division II, 1973-74
Most League goals: 122, Division II, 1926-27
League scoring record: 59, George Camsell, Division II, 1926-27
Record League aggregate: 326, George Camsell, 1925-1939
Most League appearances: 563, Tim Williamson, 1902-1923
Most capped player: 26, Wilf Mannion, England

FA Amateur Cup	Year	Opponents	Score	Scorers
Winners	1895	Old Carthusians	2-1	Mullen, Nelmes
	1898	Uxbridge	2-1	Bishop, Kempley

THE MIDDLESBROUGH RECORD

Year	Division & place	Cup round reached	Year	Division & place	Cup round reached
1888		q-f	1910	I 17	1
1889		q	1911	I 16	3
1890		q	1912	I 7	2
1891		q	1913	I 16	3
1892		2	1914	I 4	1
1893		2	1915	I 12	2
1894		1	1920	I 13	2
1895		2	1921	I 8	1
1896		2q	1922	I 8	1
1897		1q	1923	I 18	2
1898		5q	1924	I 22R	1
1899		2q	1925	II 13	1
1900	II 14	p	1926	II 10	4
1901	II 6	q-f	1927	II 1P	5
1902	II 2P	1	1928	I 22R	5
1903	I 13	p	1929	II 1P	4
1904	I 10	q-f	1930	I 16	5
1905	I 15	1	1931	I 7	3
1906	I 18	3	1932	I 18	3
1907	I 11	2	1933	I 17	5
1908	I 6	1	1934	I 16	3
1909	I 9	1	1935	I 20	3

MILLWALL

Founded: 1885
Address: The Den, Cold Blow Lane, New Cross, London SE14 5RH
Telephone: (01) 639 3143
Ground capacity: 40,000 (3,500 seated)
Playing area: 112 by 74 yards
Record attendance: 48,672 v Derby County, FA Cup 5th round, 20.2.37
Record victory: 9-1 v Torquay United, Division III(S), 29.8.27
9-1 v Coventry City, Division III(S), 19.11.27
Record defeat: 1-9 v Aston Villa, FA Cup 4th round, 28.1.46
Most League points: 65, Division III(S), 1927-28; Division III, 1965-66
Most League goals: 127, Division III(S), 1927-28
League scoring record: 37, Dick Parker, Division III(S), 1926-27
Record League aggregate: 79, Derek Possee, 1967-1973
Most League appearances: 449, Barry Kitchener, 1967-1978
Most capped player: 26 (27 in all), Eamonn Dunphy, Eire

THE MILLWALL RECORD

Year	Division & place	Cup round reached	Year	Division & place	Cup round reached
1895		1	1936	SIII 12	3
1896		1	1937	SIII 8	s-f
1897		1	1938	SIII 1P	3
1898		q	1939	II 13	4
1899		q	1946		4
1900		s-f	1947	II 18	3
1901		1	1948	II 22R	3
1902		p	1949	SIII 8	2
1903		s-f	1950	SIII 22	1
1904		1	1951	SIII 5	4
1905		1	1952	SIII 4	2
1906		2	1953	SIII 2	3
1907		2	1954	SIII 12	2
1908		1	1955	SIII 5	3
1909		3	1956	SIII 22	1
1910		1	1957	SIII 17	5
1911		1	1958	SIII 23	2
1912		1	1959	IV 9	2
1913		1	1960	IV 6	1
1914		3	1961	IV 6	1
1915		2	1962	IV 1P	1
1920		1	1963	III 16	2
1921	III 7	1	1964	III 21R	1
1922	SIII 12	q-f	1965	IV 2P	4
1923	SIII 6	2	1966	III 2P	2
1924	SIII 3	1	1967	II 8	3
1925	SIII 5	1	1968	II 7	3
1926	SIII 3	5	1969	II 10	4
1927	SIII 3	q-f	1970	II 10	3
1928	SIII 1P	3	1971	II 8	3
1929	II 14	4	1972	II 3	4
1930	II 14	5	1973	II 11	5
1931	II 14	3	1974	II 12	3
1932	II 9	3	1975	II 20R	3
1933	II 7	4	1976	III 3P	2
1934	II 21R	4	1977	II 10	3
1935	SIII 12	4	1978	II 16	q-f

NEWCASTLE UNITED

Founded: 1882
Address: St James' Park, Newcastle-on-Tyne, NE1 4ST
Telephone: (0632) 28361/2
Ground capacity: 54,000
Playing area: 115 by 75 yards
Record attendance: 68,386 v Chelsea, Division I, 3.9.30
Record victory: 13-0 v Newport County, Division II, 5.10.46
Record defeat: 0-9 v Burton Wanderers, Division II, 15.4.95
Most League points: 57, Division II, 1964-65
Most League goals: 98, Division I, 1951-52
League scoring record: 36, Hughie Gallacher, Division I, 1926-27
Record League aggregate: 178, Jackie Milburn, 1946-1957
Most League appearances: 432, Jim Lawrence, 1904-1922
Most capped player: 40, Alf McMichael, Northern Ireland

FA Cup	Year	Opponents	Score	Scorers
Winners	1910	Barnsley	*1-1	Rutherford
			2-0	Shepherd 2 (1 pen)
	1924	Aston Villa	2-0	Harris, Seymour
	1932	Arsenal	2-1	Allen 2
	1951	Blackpool	2-0	Milburn 2
	1952	Arsenal	1-0	Robledo (G)
	1955	Manchester City	3-1	Milburn, Mitchell, Hannah
Runners-up	1905	Aston Villa	0-2	
	1906	Everton	0-1	
	1908	Wolverhampton Wanderers	1-3	Howie
	1911	Bradford City	*0-0	
			0-1	
	1974	Liverpool	0-3	
League Cup				
Runners-up	1976	Manchester City	1-2	Gowling

*After extra time.

THE NEWCASTLE RECORD

	Division & place	Cup round reached		Division & place	Cup round reached
1893		1	1935	II 6	4
1894	II 4	2	1936	II 8	5
1895	II 10	2	1937	II 4	3
1896	II 5	2	1938	II 19	3
1897	II 5	1	1939	II 9	5
1898	II 2P	2	1946		3
1899	I 13	2	1947	II 5	s-f
1900	I 5	2	1948	II 2P	3
1901	I 6	1	1949	I 4	3
1902	I 3	q-f	1950	I 5	4
1903	I 14	1	1951	I 4	Winners
1904	I 4	1	1952	I 8	Winners
1905	I 1C	Final	1953	I 16	4
1906	I 4	Final	1954	I 15	5
1907	I 1C	1	1955	I 8	Winners
1908	I 4	Final	1956	I 11	q-f
1909	I 1C	s-f	1957	I 17	4
1910	I 4	Winners	1958	I 19	4
1911	I 8	Final	1959	I 11	3
1912	I 3	1	1960	I 8	3
1913	I 14	q-f	1961	I 21R	q-f
1914	I 11	1	1962	II 11	3
1915	I 15	q-f	1963	II 7	4
1920	I 8	2	1964	II 8	3
1921	I 5	3	1965	II 1P	3
1922	I 7	2	1966	I 15	4
1923	I 4	1	1967	I 20	4
1924	I 9	Winners	1968	I 10	3
1925	I 6	2	1969	I 9	4
1926	I 10	5	1970	I 7	3
1927	I 1C	5	1971	I 12	3
1928	I 9	3	1972	I 11	3
1929	I 10	3	1973	I 9	4
1930	I 19	q-f	1974	I 15	Final
1931	I 17	4	1975	I 15	4
1932	I 11	Winners	1976	I 15	q-f
1933	I 5	3	1977	I 5	4
1934	I 21R	3	1978	I 21R	4

NEWPORT COUNTY

Founded: 1912
Address: Somerton Park, Newport, Monmouthshire
Telephone: Newport 71543/71271
Ground capacity: 22,060 (672 seated)
Playing area: 112 by 78 yards
Record attendance: 24,268 v Cardiff City, Division III(S), 16.10.37
Record victory: 10-0 v Merthyr Town, Division III(S), 10.4.30
Record defeat: 0-13 v Newcastle United, Division II, 5.10.46
Most League points: 56, Division IV, 1972-73
Most League goals: 85, Division IV, 1964-65
League scoring record: 34, Tudor Martin, Division III(S), 1929-30
Record League aggregate: 99, Reg Parker, 1948-1954
Most League appearances: 530, Ray Wilcox, 1946-1960
Most capped player: 2, Billy Thomas, Wales
2 (4 in all), Jack Nicholls, Wales
2 (9 in all), Freddie Cook, Wales
2 (41 in all), Alf Sherwood, Wales
2, Harold Williams, Wales

THE NEWPORT RECORD

	Division & place	Cup round reached		Division & place	Cup round reached
1920		1	1955	SIII 19	1
1921	III 15	q	1956	SIII 19	1
1922	SIII 20	1	1957	SIII 12	4
1923	SIII 22	p	1958	SIII 11	1
1924	SIII 10	q	1959	III 17	4
1925	SIII 6	p	1960	III 13	3
1926	SIII 17	2	1961	III 13	1
1927	SIII 9	1	1962	III 24R	2
1928	SIII 9	1	1963	IV 20	1
1929	SIII 16	2	1964	IV 15	4
1930	SIII 18	2	1965	IV 16	3
1931	SIII 22	2	1966	IV 9	1
1932	*		1967	IV 18	1
1933	SIII 21	2	1968	IV 12	3
1934	SIII 18	2	1969	IV 22	1
1935	SIII 22	1	1970	IV 21	3
1936	SIII 21	1	1971	IV 22	1
1937	SIII 19	2	1972	IV 14	1
1938	SIII 16	3	1973	IV 5	2
1939	SIII 1P	3	1974	IV 9	1
1946		3	1975	IV 12	2
1947	II 22R	3	1976	IV 22	1
1948	SIII 12	2	1977	IV 19	2
1949	SIII 15	5	1978	IV 16	1
1950	SIII 21	3			
1951	SIII 11	4			
1952	SIII 6	3			
1953	SIII 15	3			
1954	SIII 15	1			

*Newport were not re-elected in 1931, and took Thames' place in 1932.

NORTHAMPTON TOWN

Founded: 1897
Address: County Ground, Abingdon Avenue, Northampton NN1 4PS
Telephone: Northampton 31553
Ground capacity: 20,000 (2,000 seated)
Playing area: 120 by 75 yards
Record attendance: 24,523 v Fulham, Division I, 23.4.66
Record victory: 11-1 v Southend United, Southern League, 30.12.09
10-0 v Walsall, Division III(S), 5.11.27
Record defeat: 0-11 v Southampton, Southern League, 28.12.01
Most League points: 62, Division III(S), 1952-53 & Division III, 1962-63
Most League goals: 109, Division III(S), 1952-53 & Division III, 1962-63
League scoring record: 36, Cliff Holton, Division III, 1961-62
Record League aggregate: 135, Jack English, 1947-1960
Most League appearances: 521, Tommy Fowler, 1946-1961
Most capped player: 12 (16 in all), E Lloyd Davies, Wales

THE NORTHAMPTON RECORD

	Division & place	Cup round reached			Division & place	Cup round reached
1906		1		1948	SIII 14	2
1907		1		1949	SIII 20	2
1908		1		1950	SIII 2	5
1909		1		1951	SIII 21	4
1910		2		1952	SIII 8	1
1911		2		1953	SIII 3	2
1912		3		1954	SIII 5	2
1913		1		1955	SIII 13	1
1914		p		1956	SIII 11	3
1915		2		1957	SIII 14	1
1920		p		1958	SIII 13	4
1921	IIi 14	1		1959	IV 8	2
1922	SIII 17	2		1960	IV 6	1
1923	SIII 8	p		1961	IV 3P	3
1924	SIII 8	1		1962	III 8	3
1925	SIII 9	1		1963	III 1P	1
1926	SIII 12	3		1964	II 11	3
1927	SIII 18	2		1965	II 2P	3
1928	SIII 2	3		1966	I 21R	3
1929	SIII 3	3		1967	II 21R	3
1930	SIII 4	3		1968	III 17	1
1931	SIII 6	1		1969	III 21R	3
1932	SIII 14	4		1970	IV 14	5
1933	SIII 8	2		1971	IV 7	1
1934	SIII 13	5		1972	IV 21	2
1935	SIII 7	3		1973	IV 23	1
1936	SIII 15	1		1974	IV 5	2
1937	SIII 7	1		1975	IV 16	2
1938	SIII 9	1		1976	IV 2P	1
1939	SIII 17	1		1977	III 22R	1
1946		3		1978	IV 10	2
1947	SIII 13	3				

NORWICH CITY

Founded: 1905
Address: Carrow Road, Norwich NOR 22
Telephone: 0603 21514/5
Ground capacity: 32,000
Playing area: 114 by 74 yards
Record attendance: 43,984 v Leicester City, FA Cup quarter-final, 30.3.63
Record victory: 10-2 v Coventry City, Division III(S), 15.3.30
Record defeat: 2-10 v Swindon Town, Southern League, 5.9.08
Most League points: 64, Division III(S), 1950-51
Most League goals: 99, Division III(S), 1952-53
League scoring record: 31, Ralph Hunt, Division III(S), 1955-56
Record League aggregate: 122, Johnny Gavin, 1945-1954 & 1955-1958
Most League appearances: 590, Ron Ashman, 1947-1964
Most capped player: 7, Ted MacDougall, Scotland

League Cup	Year	Opponents	Score	Scorers
Winners	1962	Rochdale	A3-0	Lythgoe 2, Punton
			H1-0	Hill
Runners-up	1973	Tottenham Hotspur	0-1	
	1975	Aston Villa	0-1	

THE NORWICH RECORD

	Division & place	Cup round reached			Division & place	Cup round reached
1906		2		1948	SIII 21	2
1907		2		1949	SIII 9	2
1908		2		1950	SIII 11	3
1909		3		1951	SIII 2	5
1910		1		1952	SIII 3	3
1911		2		1953	SIII 4	2
1912		1		1954	SIII 7	5
1913		2		1955	SIII 11	2
1914		1		1956	SIII 7	3
1915		3		1957	SIII 24	1
1920		q-f		1958	SIII 8	3
1921	III 16	1		1959	III 4	s-f
1922	SIII 15	1		1960	III 2P	1
1923	SIII 18	1		1961	II 4	5
1924	SIII 11	1		1962	II 17	5
1925	SIII 12	2		1963	II 11	q-f
1926	SIII 16	1		1964	II 17	3
1927	SIII 16	3		1965	II 6	3
1928	SIII 17	2		1966	II 13	5
1929	SIII 17	3		1967	II 11	5
1930	SIII 8	1		1968	II 9	4
1931	SIII 21	2		1969	II 13	3
1932	SIII 10	2		1970	II 11	3
1933	SIII 3	1		1971	II 10	3
1934	SIII 1P	1		1972	II 1P	3
1935	II 14	5		1973	I 20	3
1936	II 11	3		1974	I 22R	3
1937	II 17	4		1975	II 3P	3
1938	II 14	3		1976	I 10	5
1939	II 21R	3		1977	I 16	3
1946		3		1978	I 13	3
1947	SIII 21	2				

NOTTINGHAM FOREST

Founded: 1865
Address: City Ground, Nottingham NG2 5FJ
Telephone: Nottingham 868236
Ground capacity: 49,000
Playing area: 115 by 78 yards
Record attendance: 49,946 v Manchester United, Division I, 28.10.67
Record victory: 14-0 v Clapton, FA Cup 1st round, 17.1.1891
Record defeat: 1-9 v Blackburn Rovers, Division II, 10.4.37
Most League points: 70, Division III(S), 1950-51
Most League goals: 110, Division III(S), 1950-51
League scoring record: 36, Wally Ardron, Division III(S), 1950-51
Record League aggregate: 199, Grenville Morris, 1898-1913
Most League appearances: 614, Bob McKinlay, 1951-1970
Most capped player: 20, Liam O'Kane, Northern Ireland

FA Cup	Year	Opponents	Score	Scorers
Winners	1898	Derby County	3-1	Capes 2, McPherson
	1959	Luton Town	2-1	Dwight, Wilson
League Cup				
Winners	1978	Liverpool	0-0	
		Replay	1-0	Robertson (pen)

THE FOREST RECORD

Year	Division & place	Cup round reached	Year	Division & place	Cup round reached
1879		s-f	1928	II 10	q-f
1880		s-f	1929	II 11	3
1881		2	1930	II 10	q-f
1882		1	1931	II 17	3
1883		3	1932	II 11	3
1884		2	1933	II 5	3
1885		s-f	1934	II 17	4
1886		3	1935	II 9	5
1887		3	1936	II 19	4
1888		5	1937	II 19	3
1889		2	1938	II 20	4
1890		1	1939	II 20	3
1891		q-f	1946		3
1892		s-f	1947	II 11	5
1893	I 10	2	1948	II 19	3
1894	I 7	q-f	1949	II 21R	3
1895	I 7	q-f	1950	SIII 4	2
1896	I 13	1	1951	SIII 1P	2
1897	I 11	q-f	1952	II 4	3
1898	I 8	Winners	1953	II 4	4
1899	I 11	q-f	1954	II 4	3
1900	I 8	s-f	1955	II 15	5
1901	I 4	2	1956	II 7	3
1902	I 5	s-f	1957	II 2P	q-f
1903	I 10	2	1958	I 10	4
1904	I 9	2	1959	I 13	Winners
1905	I 16	2	1960	I 20	4
1906	I 19R	3	1961	I 14	3
1907	II 1P	1	1962	I 19	4
1908	I 9	1	1963	I 9	q-f
1909	I 14	q-f	1964	I 13	3
1910	I 14	3	1965	I 5	5
1911	I 20R	1	1966	I 18	4
1912	II 15	1	1967	I 2	s-f
1913	II 17	2	1968	I 11	4
1914	II 20	1	1969	I 18	3
1915	II 18	1	1970	I 15	3
1920	II 18	1	1971	I 16	5
1921	II 18	1	1972	I 21R	3
1922	II 1P	3	1973	II 14	3
1923	I 20	1	1974	II 7	q-f
1924	I 20	1	1975	II 16	4
1925	I 22R	2	1976	II 8	3
1926	II 17	q-f	1977	11 3P	4
1927	II 5	4	1978	I 1C	q-f

FA Cup	Year	Opponents	Score	Scorers
Winners	1894	Bolton Wanderers	4-1	Watson, Logan 3
Runners-up	1891	Blackburn Rovers	1-3	Oswald

THE COUNTY RECORD

Year	Division & place	Cup round reached	Year	Division & place	Cup round reached
1878		1	1928	II 15	3
1879		1	1929	II 5	3
1880		1	1930	II 22R	3
1881		3	1931	SIII 1P	4
1882		3	1932	II 16	3
1883		s-f	1933	II 15	3
1884		s-f	1934	II 18	3
1885		q-f	1935	II 22R	3
1886		5	1936	SIII 9	3
1887		q-f	1937	SIII 2	1
1888		q	1938	SIII 11	4
1889	I 11	2	1939	SIII 11	4
1890	I 10	3	1946		2
1891	I 3	Final	1947	SIII 12	3
1892	I 8	q	1948	SIII 6	2
1893	I 14R	2	1949	SIII 11	4
1894	II 3	Winners	1950	SIII 1P	3
1895	II 2	1	1951	II 17	3
1896	II 10	1	1952	II 15	4
1897	II 1P	2	1953	II 19	4
1898	I 13	1	1954	II 14	3
1899	I 5	2	1955	II 7	q-f
1900	I 15	2	1956	II 20	3
1901	I 3	2	1957	II 20	3
1902	I 13	1	1958	II 21R	4
1903	I 15	3	1959	III 23R	1
1904	I 13	1	1960	IV 2P	2
1905	I 18	1	1961	III 5	1
1906	I 16	1	1962	III 13	2
1907	I 18	q-f	1963	III 7	1
1908	I 18	2	1964	III 24R	2
1909	I 15	1	1965	IV 13	2
1910	I 19	1	1966	IV 8	1
1911	I 11	1	1967	IV 20	1
1912	I 16	2	1968	IV 17	1
1913	I 19R	1	1969	IV 19	1
1914	II 1P	1	1970	IV 7	1
1915	I 16	1	1971	IV 1P	3
1920	I 21R	3	1972	III 4	4
1921	II 6	2	1973	III 2P	3
1922	II 13	s-f	1974	III 10	3
1923	II 1P	1	1975	II 14	4
1924	I 10	2	1976	II 5	3
1925	I 9	3	1977	II 8	3
1926	I 22R	5	1978	II 15	5
1927	II 16	3			

NOTTS COUNTY

Founded: 1862
Address: Meadow Lane, Nottingham NG2 3HS
Telephone: Nottingham 868494
Ground capacity: 40,000 (4,470 seated)
Playing area: 117 by 76 yards
Record attendance: 47,301 v York City, FA Cup quarter-final, 12.3.55
Record victory: 15-0 v Thornhill United, 1st round FA Cup, 1884-85
Record defeat: 1-9 v Aston Villa, Division I, 29.9.1889
1-9 v Bristol Rovers, Division I, 16.11.1889
1-9 v Portsmouth, Division II, 9.4.27
Most League points: 69, Division IV, 1970-71
Most League goals: 107, Division IV, 1959-60
League scoring record: 39, Tom Keetley, Division III(S), 1930-31
Record League aggregate: 125, Les Bradd, 1967-78
Most League appearances: 564, Albert Iremonger, 1904-1926
Most capped player: 7 (10 in all), Bill Fallon, Republic of Ireland

OLDHAM ATHLETIC

Founded: 1894*
Address: Boundary Park, Oldham
Telephone: 061 624 4972
Ground capacity: 30,000
Playing area: 110 by 74 yards
Record attendance: 47,671 v Sheffield Wednesday, FA Cup 4th round, 25.1.30
Record victory: 11-0 v Southport, Division IV, 26.12.62
Record defeat: 4-13 v Tranmere Rovers, Division III(N), 26.12.35
Most League points: 62, Division III, 1973-74
Most League goals: 95, Division IV, 1962-63
League scoring record: 33, Tommy Davis, Division III(N), 1936-37
Record League aggregate: 110, Eric Gemmell, 1947-54
Most League appearances: 452, Ian Wood, 1966-1978
Most capped player: 9 (24 in all), Albert Gray, Wales
*as Pine Villa, name changed to Oldham Athletic in 1899

	Division & place	Cup round reached				
1907		2	1948	NIII 11	2
1908	II 3	2	1949	NIII 6	3
1909	II 6	1	1950	NIII 11	3
1910	II 2P	1	1951	NIII 15	3
1911	I 7	2	1952	NIII 4	2
1912	I 18	3	1953	NIII 1P	3
1913	I 9	s-f	1954	II 22R	3
1914	I 3	1	1955	NIII 10	2
1915	I 2	q-f	1956	NIII 20	1
1920	I 17	1	1957	NIII 19	2
1921	I 19	1	1958	NIII 15	2
1922	I 19	2	1959	IV 21	3
1923	I 22R	1	1960	IV 23	2
1924	II 7	2	1961	IV 12	2
1925	II 18	1	1962	IV 11	4
1926	II 7	3	1963	IV 2P	1
1927	II 10	4	1964	III 9	3
1928	II 7	4	1965	III 20	3
1929	II 18	3	1966	III 20	3
1930	II 3	4	1967	III 10	3
1931	II 12	3	1968	III 16	1
1932	II 18	3	1969	III 24R	1
1933	II 16	3	1970	IV 19	2
1934	II 9	4	1971	IV 3P	1
1935	II 21R	3	1972	III 11	1
1936	NIII 7	2	1973	III 4	1
1937	NIII 4	3	1974	III 1P	4
1938	NIII 4	1	1975	II 18	3
1939	NIII 5	1	1976	II 17	3
1946		2	1977	II 13	5
1947	NIII 19	2	1978	II 8	3

	Division & place	Cup round reached				
1906*	II 20	1	1950	SIII 18	1
1907	II 17	q	1951	SIII 17	1
1908	II 14	p	1952	SIII 16	5
1909	II 15	1	1953	SIII 14	1
1910	II 16	1	1954	SIII 11	q-f
1911	II 4	1	1955	SIII 2	2
1912	II 4	1	1956	SIII 1P	4
1913	II 14	1	1957	II 15	3
1914	II 6	2	1958	II 12	4
1915	II 9	1	1959	II 17	3
1920	II 15	1	1960	II 10	3
1921	II 7	1	1961	II 19	5
1922	II 15	1	1962	II 2P	4
1923	II 19	1	1963	I 22R	5
1924	II 10	1	1964	II 16	4
1925	II 11	1	1965	II 19	3
1926	II 20	q-f	1966	II 22	3
1927	II 20	3	1967	II 14	2
1928	II 20	3	1968‡	III 18	4
1929	II 22R	4	1969	III 18	1
1930	SIII 12	4	1970	III 1P	4
1931	SIII 19	1	1971	II 17	4
1932	SIII 16	2	1972	II 17	q-f
1933	SIII 20	1	1973	II 15	3
1934	SIII 11	3	1974	II 4	4
1935	SIII 14	2	1975	II 12	3
1936	SIII 14	4	1976	II 13	3
1937	SIII 12	2	1977	II 19	4
1938	SIII 19	2	1978	II 14	s-f
1939	SIII 20	2			
1946		1			
1947†	SIII 19	1			
1948	SIII 17	1			
1949	SIII 19	2			

* – as Clapton Orient 1881–1946
† – as Leyton Orient 1946–1968
‡ – as Orient 1968–

ORIENT

Founded: 1881
Address: Leyton Stadium, Brisbane Road, Leyton, London E10 5NE
Telephone: (01) 539 2223/4
Ground capacity: 34,000 (3,600 seated)
Playing area: 110 by 80 yards
Record attendance: 34,345 v West Ham United, FA Cup 4th round, 25.1.64
Record victory: 9-2 v Aldershot, Division III(S), 10.2.34
9-2 v Chester, League Cup 3rd round, 15.10.62
Record defeat: 0-8 v Aston Villa, FA Cup 4th round, 30.1.29
Most League points: 66, Division III(S), 1955-56
Most League goals: 106, Division III(S), 1955-56
League scoring record: 35, Tommy Johnston, Division II, 1957-58
Record League aggregate: 119, Tommy Johnston, 1956-1962
Most League appearances: 430, Peter Allen, 1965-1978
Most capped player: 4, Mal Lucas, Wales

OXFORD UNITED

Founded: 1896*
Address: Manor Ground, Beech Road, Headington, Oxford
Telephone: Oxford 61503
Ground capacity: 18,000
Playing area: 112 by 78 yards
Record attendance: 22,730 v Preston North End, FA Cup quarter-final, 29.2.64
Record victory: 7-1 v Barrow, Division IV, 19.12.64
Record defeat: 0-5 v Cardiff City, Division II, 8.2.69
0-5 v Cardiff City, Division II, 12.9.73
Most League points: 61, Division IV, 1964-65
Most League goals: 87, Division IV, 1964-65
League scoring record: 23, Colin Booth, Division IV, 1964-65
Record League aggregate: 73, Graham Atkinson, 1962-1973
Most League appearances: 480, John Shuker, 1962-1977
Most capped player: 6 (11 in all), Dave Roberts, Wales
*as Headington United. Name changed to Oxford United 25.6.60

	Division & place	Cup round reached				
1961		3	1970	II 15	3
1962		1	1971	II 14	5
1963	IV 18	3	1972	II 15	3
1964	IV 18	q-f	1973	II 8	4
1965	IV 4P	1	1974	II 18	3
1966	III 14	1	1975	II 11	3
1967	III 15	1	1976	II 20R	3
1968	III 1P	3	1977	III 17	1
1969	II 20	3	1978	III 18	1

PETERBOROUGH UNITED

Founded: 1934
Address: London Road, Peterborough, PE2 8AL
Telephone: 0733 69347
Ground capacity: 30,000
Playing area: 112 by 76 yards
Record attendance: 30,096 v Swansea Town, FA Cup 5th round, 20.2.65
Record victory: 8-1 v Oldham Athletic, Division IV, 26.11.69
Record defeat: 1-8 v Northampton Town, FA Cup 2nd round, 1946-47
Most League points: 66, Division IV, 1960-61
Most League goals: 134, Division IV, 1960-61
League scoring record: 52, Terry Bly, Division IV, 1960-61
Record League aggregate: 120, Jim Hall, 1967-75
Most League appearances: 385, Tommy Robson, 1968-1978
Most capped player: 8 (21 in all), Tony Millington, Wales

THE PETERBOROUGH RECORD

	Division & place	Cup round reached			Division & place	Cup round reached
1957		4		1969	IV 18	1
1958		1		1970	IV 9	4
1959		3		1971	IV 16	2
1960		4		1972	IV 8	3
1961	IV 1P	4		1973	IV 19	3
1962	III 5	4		1974	IV 1P	4
1963	III 6	3		1975	III 7	5
1964	III 10	1		1976	III 10	4
1965	III 8	q-f		1977	III 16	2
1966	III 13	2		1978	III 4	3
1967	III 15	4				
1968	III 24R	3		R—relegated (for illegal payments)		
				Actually finished ninth		

PLYMOUTH ARGYLE

Founded: 1886
Address: Home Park, Plymouth, Devon
Telephone: Plymouth 52561
Ground capacity: 40,000
Playing area: 112 by 75 yards
Record attendance: 43,596 v Aston Villa, Division II, 10.10.36
Record victory: 8-1 v Millwall, Division II, 16.1.32
Record defeat: 0-9 v Stoke City, Division II, 17.12.60
Most League points: 68, Division III(S), 1929-30
Most League goals: 107, Division III(S), 1925-26 and 1951-52
League scoring record: 32, Jack Cock, Division III(S), 1925-26
Record League aggregate: 180, Sammy Black, 1924-1938
Most League appearances: 470, Sammy Black, 1924-1938
Most capped player: 20 (23 in all), Moses Russell, Wales

THE PLYMOUTH RECORD

	Division & place	Cup round reached				Division & place	Cup round reached
1904		1		1947	II	19	3
1905		1		1948	II	17	3
1906		2		1949	II	20	3
1907		1		1950	II	21R	3
1908		2		1951	SIII	4	3
1909		3		1952	SIII	1P	1
1910		1		1953	II	4	5
1911		1		1954	II	19	4
1912		1		1955	II	20	3
1913		2		1956	II	21R	3
1914		2		1957	SIII	18	2
1915		1		1958	SIII	3	3
1920		3		1959	III	1P	3
1921	III 11	3		1960	II	19	3
1922	SIII 2	1		1961	II	11	3
1923	SIII 2	3		1962	II	5	4
1924	SIII 2	1		1963	II	12	3
1925	SIII 2	1		1964	II	20	3
1926	SIII 2	3		1965	II	15	4
1927	SIII 2	3		1966	II	18	4
1928	SIII 3	1		1967	II	16	3
1929	SIII 4	4		1968	II	22R	3
1930	SIII 1P	3		1969	III	5	1
1931	II 18	3		1970	III	17	2
1932	II 4	4		1971	III	15	1
1933	II 14	3		1972	III	8	1
1934	II 10	3		1973	III	8	4
1935	II 8	4		1974	III	17	3
1936	II 7	4		1975	III	2P	4
1937	II 5	4		1976	II	16	3
1938	II 13	3		1977	II	21R	3
1939	II 15	3		1978	III	19	3
1946		3					

PORTSMOUTH

Founded: 1898
Address: Fratton Park, Frogmore Road, Portsmouth
Telephone: Portsmouth 31204/5
Ground capacity: 46,000
Playing area: 116 by 73 yards
Record attendance: 51,385 v Derby County, FA Cup quarter-final, 26.2.49
Record victory: 9-1 v Notts County, Division II, 9.4.27
Record defeat: 0-10 v Leicester City, Division I, 20.10.28
Most League points: 65, Division III, 1961-62
Most League goals: 87, Division II, 1923-24, 1926-27; Division III, 1961-62
League scoring record: 40, Billy Haines, Division II, 1926-27
Record League aggregate: 194, Peter Harris, 1946-1960
Most League appearances: 764, Jimmy Dickinson, 1946-1965
Most capped player: 48, Jimmy Dickinson, England

FA Cup	Year	Opponents	Score	Scorers
Winners	1939	Wolverhampton Wanderers	4-1	Parker 2, Barlow, Anderson
Runners-up	1929	Bolton Wanderers	0-2	
	1934	Manchester City	1-2	Rutherford

THE PORTSMOUTH RECORD

	Division & place	Cup round reached				
1900		1	1939	I	17	Winners
1901		q-f	1946			3
1902		q-f	1947	I	12	4
1903		1	1948	I	8	4
1904		1	1949	I	1C	s-f
1905		2	1950	I	1C	5
1906		1	1951	I	7	3
1907		2	1952	I	4	q-f
1908		3	1953	I	15	3
1909		2	1954	I	14	5
1910		2	1955	I	3	3
1911		1	1956	I	12	4
1912		2	1957	I	19	4
1913		1	1958	I	20	4
1914		1	1959	I	22R	5
1915		1	1960	II	20	3
1920		1	1961	II	21R	3
1921	SIII	12	1	1962	III 1P	1
1922	SIII	3	1	1963	II 16	4
1923	SIII	6	1	1964	II 9	3
1924	SIII	1P	1	1965	II 20	3
1925	II	4	2	1966	II 12	3
1926	II	11	3	1967	II 14	4
1927	II	2P	4	1968	II 5	5
1928	I	20	3	1969	II 15	4
1929	I	20	Final	1970	II 17	3
1930	I	13	4	1971	II 16	4
1931	I	4	5	1972	II 16	5
1932	I	8	5	1973	II 17	3
1933	I	9	3	1974	II 15	5
1934	I	10	Final	1975	II 17	3
1935	I	14	4	1976	II 22R	4
1936	I	10	3	1977	III 20	3
1937	I	9	3	1978	III 24R	2
1938	I	19	4			

THE PORT VALE RECORD

	Division & place	Cup round reached				
1893*	II 11	q	1950	SIII	13	4
1894*	II 7	q	1951	SIII	12	3
1895*	II 15	q	1952	SIII	13	1
1896*	II 14L	p	1953	NIII	2	2
1897*		p	1954	NIII	1P	s-f
1898*		2	1955	II	17	4
1899*	II 9	1	1956	II	12	4
1900*	II 11	1	1957	II	22R	3
1901*	II 9	1	1958	SIII	15	2
1902*	II 13	1	1959	IV	1P	1
1903*	II 9	p	1960	III	14	5
1904*	II 13	p	1961	III	7	3
1905*	II 16	2	1962	III	12	5
1906*	II 17	1	1963	III	3	4
1907*	†II 16	2	1964	III	13	4
1908*		p	1965	III	22R	2
1909*		p	1966	IV	19	3
1910*		p	1967	IV	13	2
1911*		p	1968	‡IV	18	1
1912*		p	1969	IV	13	3
1913*		p	1970	IV	4P	2
1914		1	1971	III	17	1
1915		q	1972	III	15	3
1920	§II 13	1	1973	III	6	3
1921	II 17	p	1974	III	20	3
1922	II 18	1	1975	III	6	1
1923	II 17	p	1976	III	12	2
1924	II 16	p	1977	III	19	5
1925	II 8	1	1978	III	21R	2
1926	II 8	3				
1927	II 8	4				
1928	II 9	5				
1929	II 21R	3				
1930	NIII 1P	2				
1931	II 5	4				
1932	II 20	4				
1933	II 17	3				
1934	II 8	3				
1935	II 18	3				
1936	II 21R	4				
1937	NIII 11	3				
1938	NIII 15	1				
1939	SIII 18	2				
1946		3				
1947	SIII 10	4				
1948	SIII 8	1				
1949	SIII 13	1				

*– As Burslem Port Vale.
Name changed in 1913
L – failed to obtain re-election
† – Burslem Port Vale resigned from the League
§ – Port Vale returned to the League, taking over the fixtures and record of Leeds City on 9 October 1919
‡ – Expelled from the League for financial irregularities and therefore technically finished 24th. Obtained re-election immediately.

PORT VALE

Founded: 1876
Address: Vale Park, Hamil Road, Burslem, Stoke-on-Trent
Telephone: Stoke-on-Trent 87626/85524
Ground capacity: 50,000 (7,700 seated)
Playing area: 116 by 76 yards
Record attendance: 50,000 v Aston Villa, FA Cup 5th round, 20.2.60
Record victory: 9-1 v Chesterfield, Division II, 24.9.32
Record defeat: 0-10 v Sheffield United, Division II, 10.12.1892
0-10 v Notts County, Division II, 26.2.1895
Most League points: 69, Division III(N), 1953-54
Most League goals: 110, Division IV, 1958-59
League scoring record: 38, Wilf Kirkham, Division II, 1926-27
Record League aggregate: 154, Wilf Kirkham, 1923-29, 1931-33
Most League appearances: 761, Roy Sproson, 1950-1972
Most capped player: 7 (17 in all), Sammy Morgan, Northern Ireland

PRESTON NORTH END

Founded: 1881
Address: Deepdale, Preston PR1 6RU
Telephone: Preston 795919
Ground capacity: 38,000
Playing area: 112 by 78 yards
Record attendance: 42,684 v Arsenal, Division I, 23.4.38
Record victory: 26-0 v Hyde, FA Cup 1st series 1st round, 15.10.1887
Record defeat: 0-7 v Blackpool, Division I, 1.5.48
Most League points: 61, Division III, 1970-71
Most League goals: 100, Division II, 1927-28 & Division I, 1957-58
League scoring record: 37, Ted Harper, Division II, 1932-33
Record League aggregate: 187, Tom Finney, 1946-1960
Most League appearances: 447, Allan Kelly, 1961-75
Most capped player: 76, Tom Finney, England

FA Cup	Year	Opponents	Score	Scorers
Winners	1889	Wolverhampton Wanderers	3-0	Dewhurst, Ross, Thompson
	1938	Huddersfield Town	*1-0	Mutch (pen)
Runners-up	1888	West Bromwich Albion	1-2	Goodall
	1922	Huddersfield Town	0-1	
	1937	Sunderland	1-3	O'Donnell (F)
	1954	West Bromwich Albion	2-3	Morrison, Wayman
	1964	West Ham United	2-3	Holden, Dawson

*after extra time

THE PRESTON RECORD

Year	Division & place	Cup round reached	Year	Division & place	Cup round reached
1884		4	1932	II 13	5
1885		†	1933	II 9	3
1886		3	1934	II 2P	q-f
1887		s-f	1935	I 11	q-f
1888		Final	1936	I 7	4
1889	I 1C	Winners	1937	I 14	Final
1890	I 1C	q-f	1938	I 3	Winners
1891	I 2	1	1939	I 9	q-f
1892	I 2	q-f	1946		5
1893	I 2	s-f	1947	I 7	q-f
1894	I 14	2	1948	I 7	q-f
1895	I 4	2	1949	I 21R	4
1896	I 9	1	1950	II 6	3
1897	I 4	q-f	1951	II 1P	4
1898	I 12	1	1952	I 7	3
1899	I 15	2	1953	I 2	4
1900	I 16	q-f	1954	I 11	Final
1901	I 17R	1	1955	I 14	4
1902	II 3	1	1956	I 19	3
1903	II 7	2	1957	I 3	5
1904	II 1P	2	1958	I 2	3
1905	I 8	q-f	1959	I 12	5
1906	I 2	1	1960	I 9	q-f
1907	I 14	1	1961	I 22R	4
1908	I 12	1	1962	II 10	q-f
1909	I 10	2	1963	II 17	3
1910	I 12	1	1964	II 3	Final
1911	I 14	2	1965	II 12	4
1912	I 19R	1	1966	II 17	q-f
1913	II 1P	1	1967	II 13	3
1914	I 19R	3	1968	II 20	4
1915	II 2P	1	1969	II 14	4
1920	I 19	3	1970	II 22R	3
1921	⊦ 16	s-f	1971	III 1P	1
1922	I 16	Final	1972	II 18	4
1923	I 16	2	1973	II 19	3
1924	I 18	1	1974	II 21R	3
1925	I 21R	2	1975	III 9	3
1926	II 12	3	1976	III 8	2
1927	I 6	4	1977	III 6	2
1928	II 4	3	1978	III 3P	2
1929	II 13	3			
1930	II 16	3			
1931	II 7	3			

† – Preston expelled by FA

THE QPR RECORD

Year	Division & place	Cup round reached	Year	Division & place	Cup round reached
1900		2	1946		5
1901		q	1947	SIII 2	3
1902		q	1948	SIII 1P	q-f
1903		q	1949	II 13	3
1904		q	1950	II 20	3
1905		q	1951	II 16	3
1906		1	1952	II 22R	3
1907		1	1953	SIII 21	1
1908		2	1954	SIII 18	3
1909		1	1955	SIII 15	1
1910		q-f	1956	SIII 18	1
1911		1	1957	SIII 10	3
1912		1	1958	SIII 10	2
1913		2	1959	III 13	2
1914		q-f	1960	III 8	2
1915		3	1961	III 4	2
1920		1	1962	III 4	3
1921	SIII 3	2	1963	III 13	3
1922	SIII 5	1	1964	III 15	3
1923	SIII 11	q-f	1965	III 14	2
1924	SIII 22	1	1966	III 3	3
1925	SIII 19	1	1967	III 1P	3
1926	SIII 22	2	1968	II 2P	3
1927	SIII 14	*	1969	I 22R	3
1928	SIII 10	1	1970	II 9	q-f
1929	SIII 6	1	1971	II 10	3
1930	SIII 3	3	1972	II 4	3
1931	SIII 8	3	1973	II 2P	5
1932	SIII 13	4	1974	I 8	q-f
1933	SIII 16	3	1975	I 11	5
1934	SIII 4	3	1976	I 2	3
1935	SIII 13	2	1977	I 14	4
1936	SIII 4	1	1978	I 19	5
1937	SIII 9	3			
1938	SIII 3	2			
1939	SIII 6	3			

* – did not enter

QUEEN'S PARK RANGERS

Founded: 1885
Address: South Africa Road, London W12 7PA
Telephone: (01) 743 2618
Ground capacity: 30,000
Playing area: 112 by 72 yards
Record attendance: 35,353 v Leeds United, Division I, 28.4.74
Record victory: 9-2 v Tranmere Rovers, Division III, 3.12.60
Record defeat: 1-8 v Mansfield Town, Division III, 15.3.65
1-8 v Manchester United, Division I, 12.2.69
Most League points: 67, Division III, 1966-67
Most League goals: 111, Division III, 1961-62
League scoring record: 37, George Goddard, Division III(S), 1929-30
Record League aggregate: 172, George Goddard, 1926-1934
Most League appearances: 519, Tony Ingham, 1950-1963
Most capped player: 19 (39 in all), Don Givens, Eire

League Cup	Year	Opponents	Score	Scorers
Winners	1967	West Bromwich Albion	3-2	Morgan (R), Marsh, Lazarus

READING

Founded: 1871
Address: Elm Park, Norfolk Road, Reading
Telephone: Reading 57878 9 0
Ground capacity: 27,000 (3,200 seated)
Playing area: 112 by 77 yards
Record attendance: 33,042 v Brentford, FA Cup 5th round, 19.2.27
Record victory: 10-2 v Crystal Palace, Division III(S), 4.9.46
Record defeat: 0-18 v Preston North End, FA Cup 1st round, 1893-94
Most League points: 61, Division III(S), 1951-52
Most League goals: 112, Division III(S), 1951-52
League scoring record: 39, Ronnie Blackman, Division III(S), 1951-52
Record League aggregate: 156, Ronnie Blackman, 1947-1954
Most League appearances: 453, Dick Spiers, 1955-1970
Most capped player: 8, Pat McConnell, Ireland

THE READING RECORD

Year	Division & place	Cup round reached		Year	Division & place	Cup round reached	
1900		1		1939	SIII 5	1	
1901		3		1946		1	
1902		2		1947	SIII 9	3	
1903		1		1948	SIII 10	3	
1904		1		1949	SIII 2	2	
1905		1		1950	SIII 10	3	
1906		1		1951	SIII 3	3	
1907		1		1952	SIII 2	3	
1908		1		1953	SIII 11	1	
1909		1		1954	SIII 8	1	
1910		1		1955	SIII 18	3	
1911		q		1956	SIII 17	2	
1912		3		1957	SIII 13	3	
1913		3		1958	SIII 5	3	
1914		1		1959	III 6	1	
1915		1		1960	III 11	3	
1920		1		1961	III 18	3	
1921	III 20	1		1962	III 7	1	
1922	SIII 13	1		1963	III 20	3	
1923	SIII 19	1		1964	III 6	2	
1924	SIII 18	1		1965	III 13	4	
1925	SIII 14	2		1966	III 8	3	
1926	SIII 1P	3		1967	III 4	2	
1927	II 14	s-f		1968	III 5	3	
1928	II 18	4		1969	III 14	3	
1929	II 15	5		1970	III 8	1	
1930	II 19	3		1971	III 21R	3	
1931	II 21R	3		1972	IV 16	4	
1932	SIII 2	1		1973	IV 7	4	
1933	SIII 4	3		1974	IV 6	2	
1934	SIII 3	3		1975	IV 7	1	
1935	SIII 2	5		1976	IV 3P	1	
1936	SIII 3	3		1977	III 21R	3	
1937	SIII 5	3		1978	IV 8	2	
1938	SIII 6	1					

(Rochdale record continued:)

Year	Division & place	Cup round reached		Year	Division & place	Cup round reached	
1961	IV 17	1		1970	III 9	1	
1962	IV 12	2		1971	III 16	4	
1963	IV 7	1		1972	III 18	1	
1964	IV 20	2		1973	III 13	1	
1965	IV 6	1		1974	III 24R	2	
1966	IV 21	2		1975	IV 19	2	
1967	IV 21	1		1976	IV 15	3	
1968	IV 19	1		1977	IV 18	1	
1969	IV 3P	1		1978	IV 24	1	

ROTHERHAM UNITED

Founded: 1884
Address: Millmoor Ground, Rotherham, Yorkshire
Telephone: Rotherham 2434
Ground capacity: 24,000 (1,392 seated)
Playing area: 115 by 76 yards
Record attendance: 25,000 v Sheffield Wednesday, Division II, 26.1.52
25,000 v Sheffield United, Division II, 13.12.52
Record victory: 8-0 v Oldham Athletic, Division III(N), 26.5.47
Record defeat: 1-11 v Bradford City, Division III(N), 25.8.28
Most League points: 71, Division III(N), 1950-51
Most League goals: 114, Division III(N), 1946-47
League scoring record: 38, Wally Ardron, Division III(N), 1946-47
Record League aggregate: 130, Gladstone Guest, 1946-1956
Most League appearances: 459, Danny Williams, 1946-1962
Most capped player: 6, Harry Millership, Wales

	Season	Opponents	Score	Scorers
League Cup Runners-up	1960-61	Aston Villa	H2-0 A0-3	Webster, Kirkman

ROCHDALE

Founded: 1907
Address: Spotland, Willbutts Lane, Rochdale, Lancashire
Telephone: 0706 44648
Ground capacity: 28,000 (700 seated)
Playing area: 113 by 75 yards
Record attendance: 24,231 v Notts County, FA Cup 2nd round, 10.12.49
Record victory: 8-1 v Chesterfield, Division III(N), 18.12.26
Record defeat: 0-8 v Wrexham, Division III(N), 28.12.29
Most League points: 62, Division III(N), 1923-24
Most League goals: 105, Division III(N), 1926-27
League scoring record: 44, Albert Whitehurst, Division III(N), 1926-27
Record League aggregate: 117, Albert Whitehurst, 1923-1928
Most League appearances: 317, Graham Smith, 1966-74
Most capped player: None

	Year	Opponents	Score
League Cup Runners-up	1962	Norwich City	h0-3 a0-1

THE ROCHDALE RECORD

Year	Division & place	Cup round reached		Year	Division & place	Cup round reached	
1913		1		1936	NIII 20	1	
1914		p		1937	NIII 18	1	
1915		2		1938	NIII 17	1	
1920		1		1939	NIII 15	1	
1921		1		1946		3	
1922	NIII 20	p		1947	NIII 6	3	
1923	NIII 12	p		1948	NIII 12	2	
1924	NIII 2	p		1949	NIII 7	1	
1925	NIII 6	p		1950	NIII 3	2	
1926	NIII 3	2		1951	NIII 11	3	
1927	NIII 2	1		1952	NIII 21	3	
1928	NIII 13	2		1953	NIII 22	1	
1929	NIII 17	1		1954	NIII 19	1	
1930	NIII 10	1		1955	NIII 12	3	
1931	NIII 21	1		1956	NIII 12	1	
1932	NIII 21	1		1957	NIII 13	1	
1933	NIII 18	1		1958	NIII 11	1	
1934	NIII 22	1		1959	III 24R	1	
1935	NIII 20	1		1960	IV 12	2	

THE ROTHERHAM RECORD

Year	Division & place	Cup round reached		Year	Division & place	Cup round reached	
1894*	II 14	q		1957	II 17	3	
1895*	II 12	q		1958	II 18	3	
1896*	II 15	1		1959	II 20	3	
1920†	II 17	q		1960	II 8	4	
1921†	II 19	q		1961	II 15	4	
1922†	II 16	q		1962	II 9	3	
1923†	II 21R	1		1963	II 14	3	
1924†	NIII 4	q		1964	II 7	3	
1925†	NIII 22	q		1965	II 14	4	
1926‡	NIII 14	3		1966	II 7	4	
1927	NIII 19	1		1967	II 18	4	
1928	NIII 14	3		1968	II 21R	5	
1929	NIII 16	1		1969	III 11	2	
1930	NIII 20	3		1970	III 14	2	
1931	NIII 14	1		1971	III 8	3	
1932	NIII 19	1		1972	III 5	4	
1933	NIII 17	1		1973	III 21R	2	
1934	NIII 21	3		1974	IV 15	2	
1935	NIII 9	2		1975	IV 3P	3	
1936	NIII 11	2		1976	III 16	2	
1937	NIII 17	1		1977	III 4	3	
1938	NIII 6	2		1978	III 20	3	
1939	NIII 11	1					
1946		4					
1947	NIII 2	3					
1948	NIII 2	3					
1949	NIII 2	4					
1950	NIII 6	3					
1951	NIII 1P	4					
1952	II 9	4					
1953	II 12	5					
1954	II 5	4					
1955	II 3	4					
1956	II 19	3					

* — Rotherham Town, who resigned from the League in 1896
† — Rotherham County elected to the League in 1919
‡ — Rotherham County and Rotherham Town amalgamated to form Rotherham United at the start of the 1925-26 season.

SCUNTHORPE UNITED

Founded: 1904
Address: Old Show Ground, Scunthorpe, South Humberside
Telephone: Scunthorpe 2954
Ground capacity: 27,000
Playing area: 112 by 78 yards
Record attendance: 23,935 v Portsmouth, FA Cup 4th round, 30.1.54
Record victory: 9-0 v Boston United, FA Cup 1st round, 21.11.53
Record defeat: 0-8 v Carlisle United, Division III(N), 25.12.52
Most League points: 66, Division III(N), 1957-58
Most League goals: 88, Division III(N), 1957-58
League scoring record: 31, Barry Thomas, Division II, 1961-62
Record League aggregate: 92, Barry Thomas, 1959-1962, 1964-1966
Most League appearances: 600, Jack Brownsword, 1950-1965
Most capped player: None

THE SCUNTHORPE RECORD

	Division & place	Cup round reached				
1951	NIII 12	q	1965	III 18	1
1952	NIII 14	3	1966	III 4	1
1953	NIII 15	3	1967	III 18	2
1954	NIII 3	4	1968	III 23R	2
1955	NIII 3	2	1969	IV 16	1
1956	NIII 9	4	1970	IV 12	5
1957	NIII 14	2	1971	IV 17	3
1958	NIII 1P	5	1972	IV 4P	1
1959	II 18	3	1973	III 24R	3
1960	II 15	4	1974	IV 18	4
1961	II 9	4	1975	IV 24	1
1962	II 4	3	1976	IV 19	1
1963	II 9	3	1977	IV 20	1
1964	II 22R	3	1978	IV 14	1

Founded: 1889
Address: Bramall Lane, Sheffield S2 4SU
Telephone: 0742 25585
Ground capacity: 49,000 (15,300 seated)
Playing area: 117 by 75 yards
Record attendance: 68,287 v Leeds United, FA Cup 5th round, 15.2.36
Record victory: 11-2 v Cardiff City, Division 1, 1.1.26
Record defeat: 0-13 v Bolton Wanderers, FA Cup 2nd round, 1.2.90
Most League points: 60, Division II, 1952–53
Most League goals: 102, Division I, 1925–26
League scoring record: 41, Jimmy Dunne, Division I, 1930-31
Record League aggregate: 205, Harry Johnson, 1919-1930
Most League appearances: 629, Joe Shaw, 1948-1966
Most capped player: 25, Billy Gillespie, Ireland

FA Cup	Year	Opponents	Score	Scorers
Winners	1899	Derby County	4-1	Bennett, Beers, Almond, Priest
	1902	Southampton	1-1	Common
			2-1	Hedley, Barnes
	1915	Chelsea	3-0	Simmons, Fazackerley, Kitchen
	1925	Cardiff City	1-0	Tunstall
Runners-up	1901	Tottenham Hotspur	2-2	Bennett, Priest
			1-3	Priest
	1936	Arsenal	0-1	

THE UNITED RECORD

	Division & place	Cup round reached			Division & place	Cup round reached
1890		2	1934	I 22R	3
1891		1	1935	II 11	4
1892		2	1936	II 3	Final
1893	II 2P	2	1937	II 7	4
1894	I 10	1	1938	II 3	4
1895	I 6	2	1939	II 2P	5
1896	I 12	2	1946		4
1897	I 2	1	1947	I 6	q-f
1898	I 1C	1	1948	I 12	3
1899	I 16	Winners	1949	I 22R	4
1900	I 2	q-f	1950	II 3	4
1901	I 14	Final	1951	II 8	4
1902	I 10	Winners	1952	II 11	q-f
1903	I 4	2	1953	II 1P	4
1904	I 7	q-f	1954	I 20	3
1905	I 6	1	1955	I 13	3
1906	I 13	2	1956	I 22R	5
1907	I 4	1	1957	II 7	3
1908	I 17	1	1958	II 6	5
1909	I 12	1	1959	II 3	q-f
1910	I 6	1	1960	II 4	q-f
1911	I 9	1	1961	II 2P	s-f
1912	I 14	1	1962	I 5	q-f
1913	I 15	1	1963	I 10	5
1914	I 10	s-f	1964	I 12	4
1915	I 6	Winners	1965	I 19	4
1920	I 14	2	1966	I 9	4
1921	I 20	1	1967	I 10	5
1922	I 11	1	1968	I 21R	q-f
1923	I 10	s-f	1969	II 9	3
1924	I 5	1	1970	II 6	4
1925	I 14	Winners	1971	II 2P	3
1926	I 5	4	1972	I 10	3
1927	I 8	3	1973	I 14	4
1928	I 13	s-f	1974	I 13	3
1929	I 11	3	1975	I 6	4
1930	I 20	4	1976	I 22R	3
1931	I 15	5	1977	II 11	3
1932	I 7	4	1978	II 12	3
1933	I 10	4			

SHEFFIELD UNITED

SHEFFIELD WEDNESDAY

Founded: 1867
Address: Hillsborough, Sheffield S6 1SW
Telephone: Sheffield 343123
Ground capacity: 55,000
Playing area: 115 by 75 yards
Record attendance: 72,841 v Manchester City, FA Cup 5th round, 17.2.34
Record victory: 12-0 v Halliwell, FA Cup 1st round, 17.1.1891
Record defeat: 0-10 v Aston Villa, Division I, 5.10.1912
Most League points: 62, Division II, 1958-59
Most League goals: 106, Division II, 1958-59
League scoring record: 46, Derek Dooley, Division II, 1951-52
Record League aggregate: 200, Andy Wilson, 1900-20
Most League appearances: 502, Andy Wilson, 1900-20
Most capped player: 33, Ron Springett, England

FA Cup	Year	Opponents	Score	Scorers
Winners	1896	Wolverhampton Wanderers	2-1	Spiksley 2
	1907	Everton	2-1	Stewart, Simpson
	1935	West Bromwich Albion	4-2	Rimmer 2, Palethorpe, Hooper
Runners-up	1890	Blackburn Rovers	1-6	Bennett
	1966	Everton	2-3	McCalliog, Ford

THE WEDNESDAY RECORD

	Division & place	Cup round reached		Division & place	Cup round reached
1881		4	1930	I 1C	s-f
1882		s-f	1931	I 3	4
1883		4	1932	I 3	5
1884		2	1933	I 3	3
1885		3	1934	I 11	5
1886			1935	I 3	Winners
1887			1936	I 20	4
1888		q-f	1937	I 22R	4
1889		q-f	1938	II 17	3
1890		Final	1939	II 3	5
1891		q-f	1946		5
1892		q-f	1947	II 20	5
1893	I 12	q-f	1948	II 4	4
1894	I 12	s-f	1949	II 8	4
1895	I 8	s-f	1950	II 2P	3
1896	I 7	Winners	1951	I 21R	3
1897	I 6	1	1952	II 1P	3
1898	I 5	2	1953	I 18	3
1899	I 18R	1	1954	I 19	s-f
1900	II 1P	2	1955	I 22R	4
1901	I 8	1	1956	II 1P	3
1902	I 9	1	1957	I 14	3
1903	I 1C	1	1958	I 22R	5
1904	I 1C	s-f	1959	II 1P	3
1905	I 9	s-f	1960	I 5	s-f
1906	I 3	q-f	1961	I 2	q-f
1907	I 13	Winners	1962	I 6	5
1908	I 5	1	1963	I 6	4
1909	I 5	3	1964	I 6	3
1910	I 11	1	1965	I 8	3
1911	I 6	1	1966	I 17	Final
1912	I 5	1	1967	I 11	q-f
1913	I 3	3	1968	I 19	5
1914	I 18	q-f	1969	I 15	4
1915	I 7	3	1970	I 22R	4
1920	I 22R	1	1971	II 15	3
1921	II 10	2	1972	II 14	3
1922	II 10	1	1973	II 10	5
1923	II 8	3	1974	II 19	3
1924	II 8	2	1975	II 22R	3
1925	II 14	2	1976	III 20	3
1926	II 1P	3	1977	III 8	1
1927	I 16	4	1978	III 14	2
1928	I 14	5			
1929*	I 1C	4			

*The club officially changed their name to Sheffield Wednesday in the summer of 1929. Before then they were known as The Wednesday.
†Did not enter

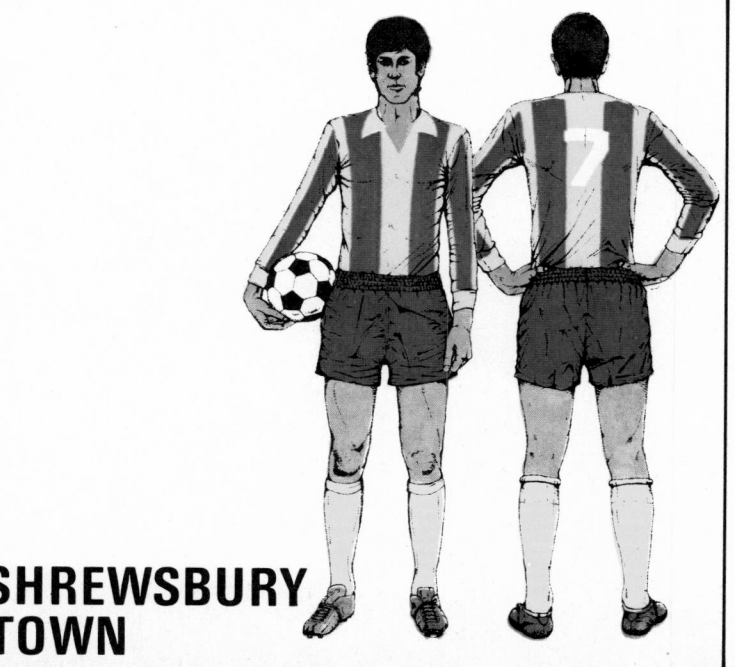

SHREWSBURY TOWN

Founded: 1886
Address: Gay Meadow, Shrewsbury, Shropshire
Telephone: Shrewsbury 56068
Ground capacity: 18,000
Playing area: 116 by 76 yards
Record attendance: 18,917 v Walsall, Division III, 26.4.61
Record victory: 7-0 v Swindon Town, Division III(S), 1954-55
Record defeat: 1-8 v Norwich City, Division III(S), 1952-53
1-8 v Coventry City, Division III, 22.10.63
Most League points: 62, Division IV, 1974-75
Most League goals: 101, Division IV, 1958-59
League scoring record: 38, Arthur Rowley, 1958-59
Record League aggregate: 152, Arthur Rowley, 1958-1965
Most League appearances: 329, Joe Wallace, 1954-1963
Most capped player: 5 (12 in all), Jimmy McLaughlin, Northern Ireland

THE SHREWSBURY RECORD

	Division & place	Cup round reached			Division & place	Cup round reached
1951	NIII 20	*		1968	III 3	3
1952	SIII 20	1		1969	III 17	1
1953	SIII 23	4		1970	III 15	2
1954	SIII 21	1		1971	III 13	2
1955	SIII 16	1		1972	III 12	3
1956	SIII 13	2		1973	III 15	2
1957	SIII 9	1		1974	III 22R	1
1958	SIII 17	1		1975	IV 2P	1
1959	IV 4P	2		1976	III 9	3
1960	III 3	1		1977	III 10	3
1961	III 10	3		1978	III 11	3
1962	III 19	4				
1963	III 15	3				
1964	III 11	1				
1965	III 16	5				
1966	III 10	5				
1967	III 6	3				

*Shrewsbury withdrew, refusing to play in the qualifying rounds after being elected to the Football League

SOUTHAMPTON

Founded: 1885
Address: The Dell, Milton Road, Southampton SO9 4XX
Telephone: Southampton 23408
Ground capacity: 31,000 (6,500 seated)
Playing area: 110 by 72 yards
Record attendance: 31,044 v Manchester United, Division I, 8.10.69
Record victory: 11-0 v Northampton, Southern League, 28.12.01
Record defeat: 0-8 v Tottenham Hotspur, Division II, 28.3.36
0-8 v Everton, Division I, 20.11.71
Most League points: 61, Division III(S), 1921-22 & Division III, 1959-60
Most League goals: 112, Division III(S), 1957-58
League scoring record: 39, Derek Reeves, Division III, 1959-60
Record League aggregate: 160, Terry Paine, 1956-74
Most League appearances: 713, Terry Paine, 1956-74
Most capped player: 45, Mick Channon, England

FA Cup	Year	Opponents	Score	Scorers
Winners	1976	Manchester United	1-0	Stokes
Runners-up	1900	Bury	0-4	
	1902	Sheffield United	1-1	Wood
	Replay		1-2	Brown

THE SOUTHAMPTON RECORD

Year	Division & place		Cup round reached	Year	Division & place		Cup round reached
1895		1		1936	II	17	3
1896		1		1937	II	18	3
1897		2		1938	II	15	3
1898		s-f		1939	II	18	3
1899		q-f		1946			4
1900		Final		1947	II	14	4
1901		1		1948	II	3	q-f
1902		Final		1949	II	3	3
1903		1		1950	II	4	3
1904		2		1951	II	12	4
1905		q-f		1952	II	13	3
1906		q-f		1953	II	21R	5
1907		2		1954	SIII	6	1
1908		s-f		1955	SIII	3	2
1909		1		1956	SIII	14	2
1910		2		1957	SIII	4	3
1911		1		1958	SIII	6	2
1912		1		1959	III	14	3
1913		1		1960	III	1P	4
1914		1		1961	II	8	4
1915		3		1962	II	6	3
1920		1		1963	II	13	s-f
1921	III	2	3	1964	II	5	3
1922	SIII	1P	2	1965	II	4	4
1923	II	11	q-f	1966	II	2P	3
1924	II	5	3	1967	I	19	4
1925	II	7	s-f	1968	I	15	4
1926	II	14	3	1969	I	7	4
1927	II	13	s-f	1970	I	11	4
1928	II	17	3	1971	I	7	5
1929	II	4	3	1972	I	19	3
1930	II	7	3	1973	I	13	5
1931	II	9	3	1974	I	20R	5
1932	II	14	3	1975	II	13	3
1933	II	12	3	1976	II	6	Winners
1934	II	14	3	1977	II	9	5
1935	II	19	4	1978	II	2P	4

THE SOUTHEND RECORD

Year	Division & place		Cup round reached	Year	Division & place		Cup round reached
1910		2		1950	SIII	3	3
1911		1		1951	SIII	7	1
1912		q		1952	SIII	9	5
1913		1		1953	SIII	8	1
1914		1		1954	SIII	16	2
1915		2		1955	SIII	10	3
1920		1		1956	SIII	4	4
1921	III	17	3	1957	SIII	7	4
1922	SIII	22	2	1958	SIII	7	3
1923	SIII	15	q	1959	III	8	1
1924	SIII	19	2	1960	III	12	2
1925	SIII	10	q	1961	III	20	2
1926	SIII	11	5	1962	III	16	1
1927	SIII	19	2	1963	III	8	2
1928	SIII	7	2	1964	III	14	1
1929	SIII	12	1	1965	III	12	1
1930	SIII	11	2	1966	III	21R	3
1931	SIII	5	1	1967	IV	6	1
1932	SIII	3	2	1968	IV	6	1
1933	SIII	13	4	1969	IV	7	4
1934	SIII	16	3	1970	IV	17	1
1935	SIII	21	3	1971	IV	18	3
1936	SIII	18	3	1972	IV	2P	2
1937	SIII	10	2	1973	III	14	1
1938	SIII	12	3	1974	III	12	3
1939	SIII	12	4	1975	III	18	3
1946		1		1976	III	23R	5
1947	SIII	8	3	1977	IV	10	3
1948	SIII	9	1	1978	IV	2P	3
1949	SIII	18	1				

SOUTHEND UNITED

Founded: 1906
Address: Roots Hall Ground, Victoria Avenue, Southend-on-Sea, Essex
Telephone: Southend 40707
Ground capacity: 35,000 (3,000 seated)
Playing area: 110 by 74 yards
Record attendance: 28,059 v Birmingham City, FA Cup 4th round, 26.1.57
Record victory: 10-1 v Golders Green, FA Cup 1st round, 24.11.34
10-1 v Brentwood, FA Cup 2nd round, 2.12.68
Record defeat: 1-11 v Northampton, Southern League, 30.12.09
Most League points: 60, Division IV, 1971-72
60, Division IV, 1977-78
Most League goals: 92, Division III(S), 1950-51
League scoring record: 31, Jim Shankly, Division III(S), 1928-29 &
Sammy McCrory, Division III(S), 1957-58
Record League aggregate: 122, Roy Hollis, 1953-1960
Most League appearances: 451, Sandy Anderson, 1950-1963
Most capped player: 9, George Mackenzie, Republic of Ireland

STOCKPORT COUNTY

Founded: 1883
Address: Edgeley Park, Stockport, Cheshire
Telephone: Stockport 8888/9
Ground capacity: 24,900 (3,000 seated)
Playing area: 110 by 75 yards
Record attendance: 27,833 v Liverpool, FA Cup 5th round, 11.2.50
Record victory: 13-0 v Halifax Town, Division III(N), 6.1.34
Record defeat: 1-8 v Chesterfield, Division II, 19.4.02
Most League points: 64, Division IV, 1966-67
Most League goals: 115, Division III(N), 1933-34
League scoring record: 46, Alf Lythgoe, Division III(N), 1933-34
Record League aggregate: 132, Jack Connor, 1951-1956
Most League appearances: 465, Robert Murray, 1952-1963
Most capped player: 1, Harry Hardy, England

THE STOCKPORT RECORD

Year	Division & place		Cup round reached	Year	Division & place		Cup round reached
1901	II	17	q	1915	II	14	1
1902	II	17	p	1920	II	16	1
1903	II	17	q	1921	II	20R	1
1904	II	16	p	1922	NIII	1P	p
1905*			p	1923	II	20	p
1906	II	10	1	1924	II	13	p
1907	II	12	1	1925	II	19	2
1908	II	13	1	1926	II	22R	3
1909	II	18	2	1927	NIII	6	1
1910	II	13	2	1928	NIII	3	2
1911	II	17	p	1929	NIII	2	3
1912	II	16	1	1930	NIII	2	3
1913	II	19	1	1931	NIII	7	2
1914	II	12	p	1932	NIII	12	1

Year	Division & place		Cup round
1933	NIII	3	2
1934	NIII	3	2
1935	NIII	7	5
1936	NIII	5	1
1937	NIII	1P	1
1938	II	22R	3
1939	NIII	9	4
1946			1
1947	NIII	4	3
1948	NIII	17	4
1949	NIII	8	3
1950	NIII	10	5
1951	NIII	10	4
1952	NIII	3	1
1953	NIII	11	3
1954	NIII	10	3
1955	NIII	9	1
1956	NIII	7	1
1957	NIII	5	1
1958	NIII	9	4
1959	III	21R	3
1960	IV	10	2
1961	IV	13	4
1962	IV	16	1
1963	IV	19	1
1964	IV	17	1
1965	IV	24	4
1966	IV	13	2
1967	IV	1P	1
1968	III	13	1
1969	III	9	3
1970	III	24R	2
1971	IV	11	1
1972	IV	23	2
1973	IV	11	3
1974	IV	24	1
1975	IV	20	1
1976	IV	21	1
1977	IV	14	1
1978	IV	18	2

*Failed to gain re-election in 1904. Returned when Division II increased from 19 to 20 clubs in 1905

Year	Division & place		Cup round
1929	II	6	3
1930	II	11	3
1931	II	11	3
1932	II	3	5
1933	II	1P	4
1934	I	12	q-f
1935	I	10	3
1936	I	4	5
1937	I	10	4
1938	I	17	4
1939	I	7	3
1946			q-f
1947	I	4	5
1948	I	15	4
1949	I	11	5
1950	I	19	3
1951	I	13	5
1952	I	20	4
1953	I	21R	4
1954	II	11	4
1955	II	5	4
1956	II	13	5
1957	II	5	3
1958	II	11	5
1959	II	5	4
1960	II	17	3
1961	II	18	5
1962	II	8	4
1963	II	1P	3
1964	I	17	5
1965	I	11	4
1966	I	10	3
1967	I	12	3
1968	I	18	4
1969	I	19	5
1970	I	9	4
1971	I	13	s-f
1972	I	17	s-f
1973	I	15	3
1974	I	5	3
1975	I	5	3
1976	I	12	5
1977	I	21R	3
1978	II	7	3

resigned from League
†name changed to Stoke City in 1925

STOKE CITY

Founded: 1863 (though no recorded reference before 1867)
Address: Victoria Ground, Stoke-on-Trent, Staffordshire
Telephone: 0782 44660
Ground capacity: 48,000
Playing area: 116 by 75 yards
Record attendance: 51,380 v Arsenal, Division I, 29.3.37
Record victory: 10-3 v West Bromwich Albion, Division I, 4.2.37
Record defeat: 0-10 v Preston North End, Division I, 14.9.1889
Most League points: 63, Division III(N), 1926-27
Most League goals: 92, Division III(N), 1926-27
League scoring record: 33, Freddie Steele, Division I, 1936-37
Record League aggregate: 142, Freddie Steele, 1934-1939
Most League appearances: 506, Eric Skeels, 1958-76
Most capped player: 36 (73 in all), Gordon Banks, England

League Cup	Year	Opponents	Score	Scorers
Winners	1972	Chelsea	2-1	Conroy, Eastham
Runners-up	1964	Leicester City	1-1	Bebbington
		(aggregate)	2-3	Viollet, Kinnell

THE STOKE CITY RECORD

Year	Division & place		Cup round reached
1889	I	12	p
1890	I	12L	q-f
1891			q-f
1892	I	13	q-f
1893	I	7	1
1894	I	11	2
1895	I	14	2
1896	I	6	q-f
1897	I	13	2
1898	I	16	2
1899	I	12	s-f
1900	I	9	1
1901	I	16	1
1902	I	16	q-f
1903	I	6	q-f
1904	I	16	1
1905	I	12	2
1906	I	10	2
1907	I	20R	1
1908	II	10	q-f
1909			1
1910			1
1911			1
1912			p
1913			1
1914			1
1915			p
1920	II	10	1
1921	II	20	1
1922	II	2P	3
1923	I	21R	2
1924	II	6	1
†1925	II	20	1
1926	II	21R	4
1927	NIII	1P	1
1928	II	5	q-f

SUNDERLAND

Founded: 1879
Address: Roker Park Ground, Sunderland, Co. Durham
Telephone: Sunderland 72077/58638
Ground capacity: 53,500
Playing area: 112 by 72 yards
Record attendance: 75,118 v Derby County, FA Cup quarter-final replay, 8.3.33
Record victory: 11-1 v Fairfield, FA Cup 1st round, 2.2.1895
Record defeat: 0-8 v West Ham United, Division 1, 19.10.68
Most League points: 61, Division II, 1963-64
Most League goals: 109, Division I, 1935-36
League scoring record: 43, David Halliday, Division I, 1928-29
Record League aggregate: 209, Charlie Buchan, 1911-1925
Most League appearances: 537, Jim Montgomery, 1962-1977
Most capped player: 33 (56 in all), Billy Bingham & 33, Martin Harvey, N. Ireland

FA Cup	Year	Opponents	Score	Scorers
Winners	1937	Preston North End	3-1	Gurney, Carter, Burbanks
	1973	Leeds United	1-0	Porterfield
Runners-up	1913	Aston Villa	0-1	

THE SUNDERLAND RECORD

Year	Division & place		Cup round reached
1890			1
1891	I	7	q-f
1892	I	1C	s-f
1893	I	1C	q-f
1894	I	2	2
1895	I	1C	s-f
1896	I	5	2
1897	I	15	2
1898	I	2	1
1899	I	7	2
1900	I	3	2
1901	I	2	1
1902	I	1C	2
1903	I	3	1
1904	I	6	1
1905	I	5	1
1906	I	14	3
1907	I	10	3
1908	I	16	1
1909	I	3	q-f
1910	I	8	3
1911	I	3	1
1912	I	8	3
1913	I	1C	Final
1914	I	7	q-f
1915	I	8	1
1920	I	5	3
1921	I	12	1
1922	I	12	1
1923	I	2	2
1924	I	3	1
1925	I	7	2
1926	I	3	5
1927	I	3	3
1928	I	15	4
1929	I	4	3
1930	I	9	5
1931	I	11	s-f
1932	I	13	4
1933	I	12	q-f
1934	I	6	4
1935	I	2	4
1936	I	1C	3
1937	I	8	Winners
1938	I	8	s-f
1939	I	16	5
1946			5
1947	I	9	3
1948	I	20	3
1949	I	8	4

Year	Div	Pl	Cup		Year	Div	Pl	Cup
1950	I	3	4		1965	I	15	4
1951	I	12	q-f		1966	I	19	3
1952	I	12	3		1967	I	17	5
1953	I	9	4		1968	I	16	3
1954	I	18	3		1969	I	17	3
1955	I	4	s-f		1970	I	21R	3
1956	I	9	s-f		1971	II	13	3
1957	I	20	4		1972	II	5	4
1958	I	21R	3		1973	II	6	Winners
1959	II	15	3		1974	II	6	3
1960	II	16	3		1975	II	4	4
1961	II	6	q-f		1976	II	1P	q-f
1962	II	3	4		1977	I	20R	3
1963	II	3	5		1978	II	6	3
1964	II	2P	q-f					

SWANSEA CITY

Founded: 1900 (as Swansea Town)
Address: Vetch Field, Swansea
Telephone: Swansea 42855
Ground capacity: 35,000
Playing area: 110 by 70 yards
Record attendance: 32,796 v Arsenal, FA Cup 4th round, 17.2.68
Record victory: 8-0 v Hartlepool United, Division IV, 1.4.78
Record defeat: 1-8 v Fulham, Division II, 22.1.38
Most League points: 62, Division III(S), 1948-49
Most League goals: 90, Division II, 1956-57
League scoring record: 35, Cyril Pearce, Division II, 1931-32
Record League aggregate: 166, Ivor Allchurch, 1949-1958, 1965-1968
Most League appearances: 585, Wilfred Milne, 1919-1937
Most capped player: 42 (68 in all), Ivor Allchurch, Wales

THE SWANSEA RECORD

Year	Division & place		Cup round reached		Year	Division & place		Cup round reached
1921	III	5	2		1955	II	10	5
1922	SIII	10	3		1956	II	10	3
1923	SIII	3	p		1957	II	10	3
1924	SIII	4	2		1958	II	19	3
1925	SIII	1P	2		1959	II	11	3
1926	II	5	s-f		1960	II	12	4
1927	II	12	q-f		1961	II	7	5
1928	II	6	3		1962	II	20	3
1929	II	19	4		1963	II	15	4
1930	II	15	3		1964	II	19	s-f
1931	II	20	3		1965	II	22R	5
1932	II	15	3		1966	III	17	1
1933	II	10	3		1967	III	21R	2
1934	II	19	5		1968	IV	15	4
1935	II	17	4		1969	IV	10	3
1936	II	13	3		1970*	IV	3P	3
1937	II	16	5		1971	III	11	4
1938	II	18	3		1972	II	13	4
1939	II	19	3		1973	III	23R	1
1946			3		1974	IV	14	1
1947	II	21R	4		1975	IV	22	1
1948	SIII	5	3		1976	IV	11	1
1949	SIII	1P	2		1977	IV	5	1
1950	II	8	4		1978	IV	3P	3
1951	II	18	3					
1952	II	19	5					
1953	II	11	3					
1954	II	20	4					

*Name changed to Swansea City during 1969-70 season

SWINDON TOWN

Founded: 1881
Address: County Ground, Swindon, Wiltshire
Telephone: Swindon 22118
Ground capacity: 28,000 (6,500 seated)
Playing area: 114 by 72 yards
Record attendance: 32,000 v Arsenal, FA Cup 3rd round, 15.1.72
Record victory: 10-1 v Farnham United Brewery, FA Cup 1st round, 28.11.25
Record defeat: 1-10 v Manchester City, FA Cup 4th round replay, 25.1.30
Most League points: 64, Division III, 1968-69
Most League goals: 100, Division III(S), 1926-27
League scoring record: 47, Harry Morris, Division III(S), 1926-27
Record League aggregate: 216, Harry Morris, 1926-1933
Most League appearances: 738, John Trollope, 1960-1978
Most capped player: 30 (43 in all), Rod Thomas, Wales

League Cup	Year	Opponents	Score	Scorers
Winners	1969	Arsenal	3-1	Smart, Rogers 2

after extra time

THE SWINDON RECORD

Year	Division & place		Cup round reached		Year	Division & place		Cup round reached
1906		1			1948	SIII	16	5
1907		q			1949	SIII	4	3
1908		3			1950	SIII	14	2
1909		1			1951	SIII	17	2
1910		s-f			1952	SIII	16	5
1911		q-f			1953	SIII	18	3
1912		s-f			1954	SIII	19	2
1913		3			1955	SIII	21	1
1914		2			1956	SIII	24	4
1915		1			1957	SIII	23	2
1920		2			1958	SIV	4	1
1921	III	4	2		1959	III	15	2
1922	SIII	6	2		1960	III	16	1
1923	SIII	9	1		1961	III	16	2
1924	SIII	6	q-f		1962	III	9	1
1925	SIII	4	1		1963	III	2P	4
1926	SIII	6	4		1964	II	14	5
1927	SIII	5	1		1965	II	21R	3
1928	SIII	6	4		1966	III	7	3
1929	SIII	10	5		1967	III	8	2
1930	SIII	14	4		1968	III	9	4
1931	SIII	12	1		1969	III	2P	q-f
1932	SIII	17	1		1970	II	5	4
1933	SIII	22	3		1971	II	12	4
1934	SIII	8	3		1972	II	11	3
1935	SIII	16	4		1973	II	16	4
1936	SIII	19	1		1974	II	22R	3
1937	SIII	13	2		1975	III	4	4
1938	SIII	8	4		1976	III	19	3
1939	SIII	9	2		1977	III	11	4
1946			1		1978	III	10	3
1947	SIII	4	2					

TORQUAY UNITED

Founded: 1898
Address: Plainmoor, Torquay, Devon
Telephone: Torquay 38666/7
Ground capacity: 22,000
Playing area: 112 by 74 yards
Record attendance: 21,908 v Huddersfield Town, FA Cup 4th round, 29.1.55
Record victory: 9-0 v Swindon Town, Division III(S), 8.3.52
Record defeat: 2-10 v Fulham, Division III(S), 7.9.31
            2-10 v Luton Town, Division III(S), 2.9.33
Most League points: 60, Division IV, 1959-60
Most League goals: 89, Division III(S), 1956-57
League scoring record: 40, 'Sammy' Collins, Division III(S), 1955-56
Record League aggregate: 204, 'Sammy' Collins, 1948-1958
Most League appearances: 443, Dennis Lewis, 1947-1959
Most capped player: None

THE TORQUAY RECORD

	Division & place	Cup round reached		Division & place	Cup round reached
1928	SIII 22	Sc	1955	SIII 8	4
1929	SIII 18	2	1956	SIII 5	3
1930	SIII 19	1	1957	SIII 2	3
1931	SIII 11	3	1958	SIII 21	2
1932	SIII 19	1	1959	IV 12	3
1933	SIII 10	2	1960	IV 3P	2
1934	SIII 20	2	1961	III 12	2
1935	SIII 10	2	1962	III 21R	2
1936	SIII 10	2	1963	IV 6	2
1937	SIII 20	1	1964	IV 6	2
1938	SIII 20	1	1965	IV 11	3
1939	SIII 19	2	1966	IV 3P	1
1946		1	1967	III 7	1
1947	SIII 11	1	1968	III 4	1
1948	SIII 18	3	1969	III 6	2
1949	SIII 9	4	1970	III 13	1
1950	SIII 5	2	1971	III 10	4
1951	SIII 20	1	1972	III 23R	3
1952	SIII 11	2	1973	IV 18	2
1953	SIII 12	1	1974	IV 16	1
1954	SIII 13	1	1975	IV 14	1
			1976	IV 9	1
			1977	IV 16	1
			1978	IV 9	1

Sc—scratched

TOTTENHAM HOTSPUR

Founded: 1882
Address: 748 High Road, Tottenham, London N17
Telephone: (01) 808 2046
Ground capacity: 52,000
Playing area: 110 by 73 yards
Record attendance: 75,038 v Sunderland, FA Cup quarter-final, 5.3.38
Record victory: 13-2 v Crewe Alexandra, FA Cup 4th round, 3.2.60
Record defeat: 2-8 v Derby County, Division I, 16.10.76
Most League points: 70, Division II, 1919-20
Most League goals: 115, Division I, 1960-61
League scoring record: 37, Jimmy Greaves, Division I, 1962-63
Record League aggregate: 220, Jimmy Greaves, 1961-1970
Most League appearances: 472, Pat Jennings, 1964-1977
Most capped player: 66 (68 in all), Pat Jennings, Northern Ireland

FA Cup	Year	Opponents	Score	Scorers
Winners	1901	Sheffield United	2-2	Brown 2
			3-1	Cameron, Smith, Brown
	1921	Wolverhampton W	1-0	Dimmock
	1961	Leicester City	2-0	Smith, Dyson
	1962	Burnley	3-1	Greaves, Smith, Blanchflower (pen)
	1967	Chelsea	2-1	Robertson, Saul
League Cup				
Winners	1971	Aston Villa	2-0	Chivers 2
	1973	Norwich City	1-0	Coates

THE SPURS RECORD

	Division & place	F.A. Cup round reached		Division & place	F.A. Cup round reached
1895		4q	1936	II 5	q-f
1896		1	1937	II 10	q-f
1897		3q	1938	II 5	q-f
1898		2q	1939	II 8	4
1899		q-f	1946		3
1900		1	1947	II 6	3
1901		Winners	1948	II 8	s-f
1902		1	1949	II 5	3
1903		q-f	1950	II 1P	5
1904		q-f	1951	I 1C	3
1905		2	1952	I 2	4
1906		3	1953	I 10	s-f
1907		3	1954	I 16	q-f
1908		1	1955	I 16	5
1909	II 2P	3	1956	I 18	s-f
1910	I 15	3	1957	I 2	5
1911	I 15	2	1958	I 3	4
1912	I 12	1	1959	I 18	5
1913	I 17	2	1960	I 3	5
1914	I 17	2	1961	I 1C	Winners
1915	I 20R	2	1962	I 3	Winners
1920	II 1P	q-f	1963	I 2	3
1921	I 6	Winners	1964	I 4	3
1922	I 2	s-f	1965	I 6	5
1923	I 12	q-f	1966	I 8	5
1924	I 15	1	1967	I 3	Winners
1925	I 12	3	1968	I 7	5
1926	I 15	4	1969	I 6	q-f
1927	I 13	3	1970	I 11	4
1928	I 21R	5	1971	I 3	q-f
1929	II 10	3	1972	I 6	q-f
1930	II 12	3	1973	I 8	4
1931	II 3	4	1974	I 11	3
1932	II 8	3	1975	I 19	3
1933	II 2P	4	1976	I 9	3
1934	I 3	5	1977	I 22R	3
1935	I 22R	5	1978	II 3P	3

TRANMERE ROVERS

Tranmere Rovers

Founded: 1883
Address: Prenton Park, 14 Prenton Road West, Birkenhead
Telephone: 051 608 3677/4194
Ground capacity: 25,000
Playing area: 112 by 74 yards
Record attendance: 24,424 v Stoke City, FA Cup 4th round, 5.2.72
Record victory: 13-4 v Oldham Athletic, Division III(N), 26.12.35
Record defeat: 1-9 v Tottenham Hotspur, FA Cup 3rd round replay, 14.1.53
Most League points: 60, Division IV, 1964-65
Most League goals: 111, Division III(N), 1930-31
League scoring record: 35, Robert 'Bunny' Bell, Division III(N), 1933-34
Record League aggregate: 104, Robert 'Bunny' Bell, 1931-1936
Most League appearances: 595, Harold Bell, 1946-1964
Most capped player: 3 (4 in all), John Brown, Ireland;
3 (23 in all), Bert Gray, Wales

THE TRANMERE RECORD

Year	Division & place	Cup round reached	Year	Division & place	Cup round reached
1922	NIII 18	q	1954	NIII 14	3
1923	NIII 16	q	1955	NIII 19	1
1924	NIII 12	p	1956	NIII 16	2
1925	NIII 21	p	1957	NIII 23	1
1926	NIII 7	p	1958	NIII 11	3
1927	NIII 9	1	1959	III 7	2
1928	NIII 5	3	1960	III 20	1
1929	NIII 7	2	1961	III 21R	2
1930	NIII 12	1	1962	IV 15	1
1931	NIII 3	1	1963	IV 8	3
1932	NIII 4	3	1964	IV 7	1
1933	NIII 11	4	1965	IV 5	1
1934	NIII 7	4	1966	IV 5	1
1935	NIII 6	2	1967	IV 4P	2
1936	NIII 3	4	1968	III 19	5
1937	NIII 19	1	1969	III 7	1
1938	NIII 1P	3	1970	III 16	4
1939	II 22R	3	1971	III 18	1
1946		2	1972	III 19	4
1947	NIII 10	1	1973	III 10	2
1948	NIII 18	2	1974	III 16	2
1949	NIII 11	1	1975	III 22R	3
1950	NIII 5	2	1976	IV 4P	1
1951	NIII 4	2	1977	III 14	1
1952	NIII 11	4	1978	III 12	1
1953	NIII 12	3			

THE WALSALL RECORD

Year	Division & place	Cup round reached	Year	Division & place	Cup round reached
1893*	II 12	p	1950	SIII 19	1
1894*	II 10	p	1951	SIII 15	1
1895*	II 14L	q	1952	SIII 24	1
1896		p	1953	SIII 24	1
1897	II 12	p	1954	SIII 24	3
1898	II 10	1	1955	SIII 23	3
1899	II 6	p	1956	SIII 20	3
1900	II 12	1	1957	SIII 15	1
1901	II 16L	p	1958	SIII 20	1
1922	NIII 8	1	1959	IV 6	1
1923	NIII 3	p	1960	IV 1P	2
1924	NIII 17	p	1961	III 2P	1
1925	NIII 19	p	1962	II 14	4
1926	NIII 21	1	1963	II 21R	3
1927	NIII 14	3	1964	III 19	1
1928	SIII 18	1	1965	III 19	1
1929	SIII 14	3	1966	III 9	4
1930	SIII 17	4	1967	III 12	3
1931	SIII 17	3	1968	III 7	4
1932	NIII 16	1	1969	III 13	3
1933	NIII 5	4	1970	III 12	3
1934	NIII 4	2	1971	III 20	2
1935	NIII 14	3	1972	III 9	4
1936	NIII 10	3	1973	III 17	2
1937	SIII 17	4	1974	III 15	2
1938	SIII 21	2	1975	III 8	5
1939	SIII 21	5	1976	III 7	1
1946		1	1977	III 15	3
1947	SIII 5	3	1978	III 6	5
1948	SIII 3	3			
1949	SIII 14	4			

* – as Walsall Town Swifts

WALSALL

Founded: 1888 (as Walsall Town Swifts)
Address: Fellows Park, Walsall, Staffordshire
Telephone: Walsall 22791
Ground capacity: 24,100
Playing area: 113 by 73 yards
Record attendance: 25,453 v Newcastle United, Division II, 29.8.61
Record victory: 10-0 v Darwen, Division II, 4.3.1899
Record defeat: 0-12 v Small Heath, Division II, 17.12.1892
0-12 v Darwen, Division II, 26.12.1896
Most League points: 65, Division IV, 1959-60
Most League goals: 102, Division IV, 1959-60
League scoring record: 40, Gilbert Alsop, Division III(N), 1933-34 & 1934-35
Record League aggregate: 184, Tony Richards, 1954-1963, Colin Taylor, 1958-73
Most League appearances: 459, Colin Taylor, 1958-1963, 1964-1968
and 1969-1973
Most capped player: 11, Mick Kearns, Eire

WATFORD

Founded: 1891
Address: Vicarage Road, Watford WD1 8ER
Telephone: Watford 21759
Ground capacity: 36,500
Playing area: 113 by 73 yards
Record attendance: 34,099 v Manchester United, FA Cup 4th round, 3.2.69
Record victory: 10-1 v Lowestoft, FA Cup, 1st round, 27.11.26
Record defeat: 0-10 v Wolverhampton Wanderers, FA Cup 1st round replay, 13.1.12
Most League points: 71, Division IV, 1977-78
Most League goals: 92, Division IV, 1959-60
League scoring record: 42, Cliff Holton, Division IV, 1959-60
Record League aggregate: 144, Tommy Barnett, 1928-1939
Most League appearances: 411, Duncan Welbourne, 1963-74
Most capped player: 2, Frank Hoddinott, Wales
2 (68 in all), Pat Jennings, Northern Ireland

THE WATFORD RECORD

Year	Division & place	Cup round reached	Year	Division & place	Cup round reached
1906		2	1933	SIII 11	3
1907		1	1934	SIII 15	1
1908		1	1935	SIII 6	2
1909		1	1936	SIII 5	4
1910		1	1937	SIII 4	1
1911		1	1938	SIII 4	3
1912		1	1939	SIII 4	3
1913		p	1946		4
1914		p	1947	SIII 16	2
1915		p	1948	SIII 15	1
1920		p	1949	SIII 17	1
1921	III 6	2	1950	SIII 6	4
1922	SIII 7	2	1951	SIII 23	1
1923	SIII 10	1	1952	SIII 21	2
1924	SIII 20	3	1953	SIII 10	2
1925	SIII 11	1	1954	SIII 4	1
1926	SIII 15	2	1955	SIII 7	3
1927	SIII 21	2	1956	SIII 20	2
1928	SIII 15	1	1957	SIII 11	2
1929	SIII 8	4	1958	SIII 16	1
1930	SIII 15	2	1959	IV 15	2
1931	SIII 18	5	1960	IV 4P	5
1932	SIII 11	q-f	1961	III 4	3

<table>
<tr><td>1962</td><td>III 17</td><td>3</td><td>1971</td><td>II 18</td><td>4</td></tr>
<tr><td>1963</td><td>III 17</td><td>4</td><td>1972</td><td>II 22R</td><td>3</td></tr>
<tr><td>1964</td><td>III 3</td><td>2</td><td>1973</td><td>III 19</td><td>3</td></tr>
<tr><td>1965</td><td>III 9</td><td>1</td><td>1974</td><td>III 7</td><td>2</td></tr>
<tr><td>1966</td><td>III 12</td><td>2</td><td>1975</td><td>III 23R</td><td>1</td></tr>
<tr><td>1967</td><td>III 3</td><td>3</td><td>1976</td><td>IV 8</td><td>1</td></tr>
<tr><td>1968</td><td>III 6</td><td>3</td><td>1977</td><td>IV 7</td><td>3</td></tr>
<tr><td>1969</td><td>III 1P</td><td>4</td><td>1978</td><td>IV 1P</td><td>3</td></tr>
<tr><td>1970</td><td>II 19</td><td>s-f</td><td></td><td></td><td></td></tr>
</table>

<table>
<tr><td>1959</td><td>I 5</td><td>5</td><td>1969</td><td>I 10</td><td>s-f</td></tr>
<tr><td>1960</td><td>I 4</td><td>5</td><td>1970</td><td>I 16</td><td>3</td></tr>
<tr><td>1961</td><td>I 10</td><td>3</td><td>1971</td><td>I 17</td><td>4</td></tr>
<tr><td>1962</td><td>I 9</td><td>5</td><td>1972</td><td>I 16</td><td>3</td></tr>
<tr><td>1963</td><td>I 14</td><td>4</td><td>1973</td><td>I 22R</td><td>5</td></tr>
<tr><td>1964</td><td>I 10</td><td>4</td><td>1974</td><td>II 8</td><td>5</td></tr>
<tr><td>1965</td><td>I 14</td><td>3</td><td>1975</td><td>II 6</td><td>4</td></tr>
<tr><td>1966</td><td>I 6</td><td>3</td><td>1976</td><td>II 3P</td><td>5</td></tr>
<tr><td>1967</td><td>I 13</td><td>4</td><td>1977</td><td>I 7</td><td>3</td></tr>
<tr><td>1968</td><td>I 8</td><td>Winners</td><td>1978</td><td>I 6</td><td>s-f</td></tr>
</table>

WEST BROMWICH ALBION

Founded: 1879
Address: The Hawthorns, West Bromwich, B71 4LF
Telephone: (021) 553 0095
Ground capacity: 44,000
Playing area: 115 by 75 yards
Record attendance: 64,815 v Arsenal, FA Cup quarter-final, 6.3.37
Record victory: 12-0 v Darwen, Division I, 4.4.1892
Record defeat: 3-10 v Stoke City, Division I, 4.2.37
Most League points: 60, Division I, 1919-20
Most League goals: 105, Division II, 1929-30
League scoring record: 39, William G Richardson, Division I, 1935-36
Record League aggregate: 208, Ronnie Allen, 1950-1961
Most League appearances: 527, Tony Brown, 1963-1978
Most capped player: 33 (43 in all), Stuart Williams, Wales

FA Cup

	Year	Opponents	Score	Scorers
Winners	1888	Preston North End	2-1	Bayliss, Woodhall
	1892	Aston Villa	3-0	Geddes, Nicholls, Reynolds
	1931	Birmingham City	2-1	W G Richardson 2
	1954	Preston North End	3-2	Allen 2, Griffin
	1968	Everton	*1-0	Astle
Runners-up	1886	Blackburn	0-0	
replay			0-2	
	1887	Aston Villa	0-2	
	1895	Aston Villa	0-1	
	1912	Barnsley	0-0,	
replay			0-1	
	1935	Sheffield Wednesday	2-4	Boyes, Sandford

*after extra time

League Cup

	Year	Opponents	Score	Scorers
Winners	1966	West Ham United	(a) 1-2	Astle
			(h) 4-1	Kaye, Brown, Clark (C), Williams
Runners-up	1967	Queen's Park Rangers	2-3	Clark (C) 2
	1970	Manchester City	1-2	Astle

THE ALBION RECORD

	Division & place	Cup round reached		Division & place	
1885		q-f	1921	I 14	1
1886		Final	1922	I 13	3
1887		Final	1923	I 17	3
1888		Winners	1924	I 16	q-f
1889	I 6	s-f	1925	I 2	q-f
1890	I 5	1	1926	I 13	4
1891	I 12	s-f	1927	I 22R	3
1892	I 12	Winners	1928	II 8	3
1893	I 8	1	1929	II 7	q-f
1894	I 8	1	1930	II 6	3
1895	I 13	Final	1931	II 2P	Winners
1896	I 16	q-f	1932	I 6	3
1897	I 12	2	1933	I 4	4
1898	I 7	q-f	1934	I 7	3
1899	I 14	q-f	1935	I 9	Final
1900	I 13	q-f	1936	I 18	4
1901	I 18R	s-f	1937	I 16	s-f
1902	II 1P	1	1938	I 22R	4
1903	I 7	1	1939	II 10	4
1904	I 18R	1	1946		4
1905	II 10	p	1947	II 7	4
1906	II 4	1	1948	II 7	4
1907	II 4	s-f	1949	II 2P	q-f
1908	II 5	2	1950	I 14	3
1909	II 3	2	1951	I 16	3
1910	II 11	3	1952	I 13	5
1911	II 1P	2	1953	I 4	4
1912	I 9	Final	1954	I 2	Winners
1913	I 10	1	1955	I 17	4
1914	I 5	3	1956	I 13	5
1915	I 11	1	1957	I 11	s-f
1920	I 1C	1	1958	I 4	q-f

WEST HAM UNITED

Founded: 1900
Address: Boleyn Ground, Green Street, Upton Park, London E13
Telephone: (01) 472 0704
Ground capacity: 41,000
Playing area: 110 by 72 yards
Record attendance: 42,322 v Tottenham Hotspur, Division I, 17.10.70
Record victory: 8-0 v Rotherham United, Division II, 8.3.58
8-0 v Sunderland, Division I, 19.10.68
Record defeat: 2-8 v Blackburn Rovers, Division I, 26.12.63
Most League points: 57, Division II, 1957-58
Most League goals: 101, Division II, 1957-58
League scoring record: 41, Vic Watson, Division I, 1929-30
Record League aggregate: 306, Vic Watson, 1920-1935
Most League appearances: 545, Bobby Moore, 1958-1974
Most capped player: 108, Bobby Moore, England

FA Cup

	Year	Opponents	Score	Scorers
Winners	1964	Preston North End	3-2	Sissons, Hurst, Boyce
	1975	Fulham	2-0	A. Taylor 2
Runners-up	1923	Bolton Wanderers	0-2	

League Cup

	Year	Opponents	Score	Scorers
Runners-up	1966	West Bromwich Albion	h2-1	Moore, Byrne
			a1-4	Peters

THE HAMMERS RECORD

	Division & place	Cup round reached		Division & place	
1913		2	1952	II 12	4
1914		3	1953	II 14	3
1915		1	1954	II 13	4
1920	II 7	3	1955	II 8	3
1921	II 5	1	1956	II 16	q-f
1922	II 4	1	1957	II 8	4
1923	II 2P	Final	1958	II 1P	5
1924	I 13	2	1959	I 6	3
1925	I 13	3	1960	I 14	3
1926	I 18	3	1961	I 16	3
1927	I 6	4	1962	I 8	3
1928	I 17	4	1963	I 12	q-f
1929	I 17	q-f	1964	I 14	Winners
1930	I 7	q-f	1965	I 9	4
1931	I 18	3	1966	I 12	4
1932	I 22R	4	1967	I 16	3
1933	I 20	s-f	1968	I 12	5
1934	II 7	4	1969	I 8	4
1935	II 3	3	1970	I 17	3
1936	II 4	3	1971	I 20	3
1937	II 6	3	1972	I 14	5
1938	II 9	3	1973	I 6	4
1939	II 11	5	1974	I 18	3
1946		4	1975	I 13	Winners
1947	II 11	3	1976	I 18	4
1948	II 6	3	1977	I 17	3
1949	II 7	4	1978	I 20R	4
1950	II 19	4			
1951	II 13	4			

WIGAN ATHLETIC

Founded: 1932*
Address: Springfield Park, Wigan
Telephone: Wigan 44433
Ground capacity: 30,000
Playing area: 117 by 73 yards
Record attendance: 27,500 v Hereford, December 1953
Most capped player: None
*Following the disbanding of Wigan Borough in 1931— the first club to resign from the League mid-season. Wigan Athletic were elected to the League at the end of the 1977-78 season.

WIMBLEDON

Founded: 1889
Address: Plough Lane, Durensford Road, Wimbledon, London SW19
Telephone: 01-946 6311
Ground capacity: 15,000
Record attendance: 18,000 v H.M.S. Victory, FA Amateur Cup, 1930
Record victory: 15-1 v London Polytechnic, FA Amateur Cup, 1929
Most League points: 44, Division IV, 1977-78
Most League goals: 66, Division IV, 1977-78
League scoring record: Roger Connell, Division IV, 1977-78
Most League appearances: 42, Jeff Bryant, 1977-78
Most capped player: None

THE WIMBLEDON RECORD

	Division & place	Cup round reached
1978	IV 13	1

WOLVERHAMPTON WANDERERS

Founded: 1876 (as St Luke's School, Blakenhall)
Address: Molineux, Wolverhampton, WV1 4QR
Telephone: Wolverhampton 24053/4
Ground capacity: 53,000
Playing area: 115 by 72 yards
Record attendance: 61,315 v Liverpool, FA Cup 5th round, 11.2.39
Record victory: 14-0 v Crosswell's Brewery, FA Cup qualifying rounds, 1886-87
Record defeat: 1-10 v Newton Heath, Division I, 15.10.1892
Most League points: 64, Division I, 1957-58
Most League goals: 115, Division II, 1931-32
League scoring record: 37, Dennis Westcott, Division I, 1946-47
Record League aggregate: 164, Billy Hartill, 1928-1935
Most League appearances: 491, Billy Wright, 1946-1959
Most capped player: 105, Billy Wright, England

FA Cup	Year	Opponents	Score	Scorers
Winners	1893	Everton	1-0	Allen
	1908	Newcastle United	3-1	Hunt, Hedley, Harrison on
	1949	Leicester City	3-1	Pye 2, Smyth
	1960	Blackburn Rovers	3-0	McGrath (og), Deeley 2
Runners-up	1889	Preston North End	0-3	
	1896	Sheffield Wednesday	1-2	Black
	1921	Tottenham Hotspur	0-1	
	1939	Portsmouth	1-4	Dorsett
League Cup				
Winners	1974	Manchester City	2-1	Hibbit, Richards

THE WOLVES RECORD

Year	Division & place	Cup round reached	Year	Division & place	Cup round reached
1884	2		1931	II 4	q-f
1885	1		1932	II 1P	4
1886	4		1933	I 20	3
1887	3		1934	I 15	4
1888	3		1935	I 17	4
1889	I 3	Final	1936	I 15	3
1890	I 4	s-f	1937	I 5	q-f
1891	I 4	q-f	1938	I 2	4
1892	I 6	q-f	1939	I 2	Final
1893	I 11	Winners	1946		4
1894	I 9	1	1947	I 3	4
1895	I 11	q-f	1948	I 5	4
1896	I 14	Final	1949	I 6	Winners
1897	I 10	2	1950	I 2	5
1898	I 3	2	1951	I 14	s-f
1899	I 8	2	1952	I 16	4
1900	I 4	1	1953	I 3	3
1901	I 13	q-f	1954	I 1C	3
1902	I 14	1	1955	I 2	q-f
1903	I 11	1	1956	I 3	3
1904	I 8	2	1957	I 6	4
1905	I 14	2	1958	I 1C	q-f
1906	I 20R	2	1959	I 1C	4
1907	II 6	1	1960	I 2	Winners
1908	II 9	Winners	1961	I 3	3
1909	II 7	1	1962	I 18	4
1910	II 8	2	1963	I 5	3
1911	II 9	3	1964	I 16	3
1912	II 5	3	1965	I 21R	q-f
1913	II 10	2	1966	II 6	5
1914	II 9	2	1967	II 2P	4
1915	II 4	2	1968	I 17	3
1920	II 19	2	1969	I 16	4
1921	II 15	Final	1970	I 13	3
1922	II 17	1	1971	I 4	4
1923	II 22R	2	1972	I 9	3
1924	NIII 1P	3	1973	I 5	s-f
1925	II 6	1	1974	I 12	3
1926	II 4	3	1975	I 12	3
1927	II 15	q-f	1976	I 20R	q-f
1928	II 16	4	1977	II 1P	q-f
1929	II 17	3	1978	I 15	4
1930	II 9	3			

WREXHAM

Founded: 1873
Address: Racecourse Ground, Mold Road, Wrexham
Telephone: Wrexham 2414
Ground capacity: 30,000
Playing area: 117 by 75 yards
Record attendance: 34,445 v Manchester United, FA Cup 4th round, 26.1.57
Record victory: 10-1 v Hartlepool, Division IV, 3.3.62
Record defeat: 0-9 v Brentford, Division III, 15.10.63
Most League points: 61, Division IV, 1969-70
61, Division III, 1977-78
Most League goals: 106, Division III(N), 1932-33
League scoring record: 44, Tom Bamford, Division III(N), 1933-34
Record League aggregate: 175, Tom Bamford, 1928-1934
Most League appearances: 588, Arfon Griffiths, 1959-1961, 1962-1978
Most capped player: 22, Horace Blew, Wales

THE WREXHAM RECORD

	Division & place	Cup round reached			Division & place	Cup round reached	
1922	NIII 12	2		1954	NIII 8	3	
1923	NIII 10	3		1955	NIII 18	2	
1924	NIII 16	2		1956	NIII 14	1	
1925	NIII 16	q		1957	NIII 12	4	
1926	NIII 19	1		1958	NIII 12	1	
1927	NIII 13	2		1959	III 18	1	
1928	NIII 11	4		1960	III 23R	3	
1929	NIII 3	1		1961	IV 16	1	
1930	NIII 17	4		1962	IV 3P	3	
1931	NIII 4	3		1963	III 9	3	
1932	NIII 10	1		1964	III 23R	2	
1933	NIII 2	2		1965	IV 14	2	
1934	NIII 6	1		1966	IV 24	2	
1935	NIII 18	2		1967	IV 7	2	
1936	NIII 18	1		1968	IV 8	1	
1937	NIII 8	3		1969	IV 9	2	
1938	NIII 10	2		1970	IV 2P	4	
1939	NIII 14	1		1971	III 9	1	
1946		3		1972	III 16	3	
1947	NIII 7	2		1973	III 12	2	
1948	NIII 3	2		1974	III 4	q-f	
1949	NIII 9	1		1975	III 13	1	
1950	NIII 20	2		1976	III 6	1	
1951	NIII 14	2		1977	III 5	4	
1952	NIII 18	2		1978	III 1P	q-f	
1953	NIII 3	3					

YORK CITY

Founded: 1922
Address: Bootham Crescent, York
Telephone: York 24447
Ground capacity: 17,000
Playing area: 115 by 75 yards
Record attendance: 28,123 v Huddersfield Town, FA Cup 5th round, 5.3.38
Record victory: 9-1 v Southport, Division III(N), 2.2.57
Record defeat: 0-12 v Chester, Division III(N), 1.2.36
Most League points: 62, Division IV, 1964-65
Most League goals: 92, Division III(N), 1954-55
League scoring record: 31, Bill Fenton, Division III(N), 1951-52
31, Alf Bottom, Division III(N), 1955-56
Record League aggregate: 125, Norman Wilkinson, 1954-1966
Most League appearances: 481, Barry Jackson, 1958-1970
Most capped player: 5 (7 in all), Peter Scott, Northern Ireland

THE YORK RECORD

	Division & place	Cup round reached			Division & place	Cup round reached	
1930	NIII 6	3		1958	NIII 13	4	
1931	NIII 12	3		1959	IV 3P	1	
1932	NIII 10	1		1960	III 21R	3	
1933	NIII 20	1		1961	IV 5	3	
1934	NIII 12	1		1962	IV 6	1	
1935	NIII 15	3		1963	IV 14	3	
1936	NIII 16	1		1964	IV 22	1	
1937	NIII 12	4		1965	IV 3P	2	
1938	NIII 11	q-f		1966	III 24R	1	
1939	NIII 20	3		1967	IV 22	2	
1946		4		1968	IV 21	1	
1947	NIII 15	1		1969	IV 21	3	
1948	NIII 13	1		1970	IV 13	4	
1949	NIII 14	2		1971	IV 4P	4	
1950	NIII 22	1		1972	III 19	2	
1951	NIII 17	3		1973	III 18	3	
1952	NIII 10	1		1974	III 3P	1	
1953	NIII 4	1		1975	II 15	3	
1954	NIII 22	1		1976	II 21R	4	
1955	NIII 4	s-f		1977	III 24R	2	
1956	NIII 11	4		1978	IV 22	1	
1957	NIII 7	2					

ABERDEEN

Founded: 1903
Address: Pittodrie Stadium, Aberdeen AB2 1QH
Telephone: 0224 21428
Ground capacity: 30,000 (15,000 seated)
Playing area: 110 by 71 yards
Record attendance: 46,061 v Heart of Midlothian, Scottish Cup 4th round, 13.3.54
Record victory: 13-0 v Peterhead, Scottish Cup 3rd round, 9.2.23
Record defeat: 2-9 v Dundee, Division I, 17.4.09
Most League points: 61, Division I, 1935-36
Most League goals: 96, Division I, 1935-36
League scoring record: 38, Benny Yorston, Division I, 1929-30
Record League aggregate: 160, Harry Yorston, 1950-57
Most League appearances: *Not available*
Most capped player: 17, Bobby Clark, Scotland

Scottish Cup	Year	Opponents	Score	Scorers
Winners	1947	Hibernian	2-1	Hamilton, Williams
	1970	Celtic	3-1	Harper, McKay 2
Runners-up	1937	Celtic	1-2	Armstrong
	1953	Rangers	1-1	Yorston
			0-1	
	1954	Celtic	1-2	Buckley
	1959	St Mirren	1-3	Baird
	1967	Celtic	0-2	
	1978	Rangers	1-2	Ritchie

League Cup				
Winners	1946	Rangers	3-2	Baird, Williams, Taylor
	1956	St Mirren	2-1	og, Leggat
	1977	Celtic	2-1	Jarvie, Robb
Runners-up	1947	Rangers	0-4	

THE ABERDEEN RECORD

Year	Division & place	Cup round reached	Year	Division & place	Cup round reached
1906	I 12	2	1949	I 13	1
1907	I 11	2	1950	I 8	q-f
1908	I 8	s-f	1951	I 5	q-f
1909	I 8	2	1952	I 11	q-f
1910	I 4	3	1953	I 11	Final
1911	I 2	s-f	1954	I 9	Final
1912	I 9	3	1955	I 1C	s-f
1913	I 8	2	1956	I 2	5
1914	I 14	3	1957	I 6	6
1915	I 14		1958	I 12	q-f
1916	I 11		1959	I 13	Final
1917	I 20		1960	I 15	2
1918	†		1961	I 6	3
1919	†		1962	I 12	3
1920	I 17	4	1963	I 6	q-f
1921	I 11	3	1964	I 9	3
1922	I 15	s-f	1965	I 12	1
1923	I 5	4	1966	I 8	s-f
1924	I 13	s-f	1967	I 4	Final
1925	I 15	4	1968	I 5	2
1926	I 11	s-f	1969	I 15	s-f
1927	I 8	2	1970	I 8	Winners
1928	I 7	4	1971	I 2	s-f
1929	I 7	4	1972	I 2	q-f
1930	I 3	3	1973	I 4	q-f
1931	I 6	q-f	1974	I 4	3
1932	I 7	1	1975	I 5	q-f
1933	I 5	2	1976	P 7	4
1934	I 5	q-f	1977	P 3	4
1935	I 6	s-f	1978	P 2	Final
1936	I 3	q-f			
1937	I 2	Final			
1938	I 6	3			
1939	I 3	s-f			
1947	I 3	Winners			
1948	I 10	3			

† Aberdeen did not compete

AIRDRIEONIANS

Founded: 1878
Address: Broomfield Park, Airdrie, Lanarkshire
Telephone: Airdrie 62067
Ground capacity: 26,000 (2,000 seated)
Playing area: 112 by 68 yards
Record attendance: 24,000 v Hearts, Scottish Cup 4th round, 8.3.52
Record victory: 11-1 v Falkirk, Division I, 28.4.51
Record defeat: 1-11 v Hibernian, Division I, 24.10.59
Most League points: 60, Division II, 1973-74
Most League goals: 107, Division II, 1965-66
League scoring record: 45, H G Yarnall, Division I, 1916-17
Most capped player: 9, Jimmy Crapnell, Scotland

Scottish Cup	Year	Opponents	Score	Scorers
Winners	1924	Hibernian	2-0	Russell 2
Runners-up	1975	Celtic	1-3	McCann

THE AIRDRIEONIANS RECORD

Year	Division & place	Cup round reached	Year	Division & place	Cup round reached
1895	II 6	1	1934	I 18	1
1896	II 5	p	1935	I 14	q-f
1897	II 4	p	1936	I 19R	2
1898	II 8	p	1937	II 4	2
1899	II 6	1	1938	II 3	1
1900	II 9	1	1939	II 4	2
1901	II 2	1	1947	II 2P	1
1902	II 4	1	1948	I 15R	q-f
1903	II 1P	1	1949	II 3	1
1904	I 12	1	1950	II 2P	1
1905	I 4	s-f	1951	I 14	q-f
1906	I 3	3	1952	I 13	q-f
1907	I 4	1	1953	I 14	3
1908	I 6	1	1954	I 15R	1
1909	I 5	3	1955	II 1P	s-f
1910	I 9	2	1956	I 7	q-f
1911	I 11	2	1957	I 11	q-f
1912	I 10	2	1958	I 16	1
1913	I 4	3	1959	I 5	2
1914	I 6	3	1960	I 16	3
1915	I 10		1961	I 13	s-f
1916	I 15		1962	I 15	1
1917	I 4		1963	I 11	2
1918	I 15		1964	I 15	3
1919	I 13		1965	I 17R	2
1920	I 7	1	1966	II 2P	1
1921	I 10	1	1967	I 13	2
1922	I 16	3	1968	I 13	q-f
1923	I 2	2	1969	I 7	q-f
1924	I 2	Winners	1970	I 12	2
1925	I 2	3	1971	I 10	s-f
1926	I 2	q-f	1972	I 15	4
1927	I 4	2	1973	I 18R	q-f
1928	I 13	3	1974	II 1P	3
1929	I 15	3	1975	I 11	Final
1930	I 12	3	1976	I 7	3
1931	I 9	2	1977	I 6	3
1932	I 14	s-f	1978	I 10	3
1933	I 18	2			

ALBION ROVERS

Founded: 1881
Address: Cliftonhill Park, Coatbridge, Lanarkshire
Telephone: Coatbridge 21865
Ground capacity: 20,000 (580 seated)
Record attendance: 27,381 v Rangers, Scottish Cup 2nd round, 8.2.36
Record victory: 10-0 v Brechin City, Division II, 1937-38
Record defeat: 1-9 v Motherwell, Division I, 1936-37
Most League points: 54, Division II, 1929-30
Most League goals: 101, Division II, 1929-30
League scoring record: 41, Jim Renwick, Division II, 1932-33
Record League aggregate: *Not available*
Most League appearances: *Not available*
Most capped player: 1, Jock White, Scotland

Scottish Cup

	Year	Opponents	Score	Scorers
Runners-up	1920	Kilmarnock	2-3	Watson, Hillhouse

THE ALBION ROVERS RECORD

	Division & place	Cup round reached		Division & place	Cup round reached
1904	II 9	2	1939	I 16R	1
1905	II 8	p	1947	II 4	3
1906	II 3	p	1948	II 2P	1
1907	II 6	p	1949	I 16R	2
1908	II 9	1	1950	II 11	2
1909	II 10	1	1951	II 8	2
1910	II 9	p	1952	II 14	3
1911	II 3	p	1953	II 16	3
1912	II 11	p	1954	II 7	2
1913	II 9	p	1955	II 11	5
1914	II 2	1	1956	II 17	4
1915	II 9		1957	II 5	4
1916			1958	II 17	2
1917			1959	II 10	1
1918			1960	II 10	2
1919			1961	II 17	1
1920	*I 22	Final	1962	II 18	2
1921	I 17	s-f	1963	II 7	1
1922	I 11	2	1964	II 9	3
1923	I 19R	1	1965	II 11	p
1924	II 5	1	1966	II 7	1
1925	II 15	1	1967	II 8	p
1926	II 9	3	1968	II 8	p
1927	II 16	1	1969	II 7	p
1928	II 8	4	1970	II 11	1
1929	II 4	3	1971	II 7	3
1930	II 3	3	1972	II 18	3
1931	II 9	2	1973	II 18	1
1932	II 16	2	1974	II 17	2
1933	II 5	q-f	1975	II 12	4
1934	II 1P	q-f	1976	II 9	3
1935	I 16	2	1977	II 6	4
1936	I 16	2	1978	II 8	3
1937	I 20R	2			
1938	II 2P	3			

*Elected to First Division in 1919

ALLOA ATHLETIC

Founded: 1878
Address: Recreation Ground, Alloa, Clackmannanshire
Telephone: Alloa 2695
Ground capacity: 9,000
Playing area: 110 by 75 yards
Record attendance: 12,800 v Dunfermline, Scottish Cup 3rd round replay, 22.2.39
Record victory: 9-2 v Forfar Athletic, Division II, 18.3.33
Record defeat: 0-10 v Dundee, Division II, 8.3.47
Most League points: 60, Division II, 1921-22
Most League goals: 92, Division II, 1961-62
League scoring record: 49, Wee Crilley, Division II, 1921-22
Most capped player: 1, Jock Hepburn, Scotland

THE ALLOA RECORD

	Division & place	Cup round reached		Division & place	Cup round reached
1920		2	1953	II 9	2
1921		3	1954	II 11	1
1922	II 1P	3	1955	II 15	5
1923	I 20R	1	1956	II 13	5
1924	II 16	2	1957	II 15	5
1925	II 4	2	1958	II 8	1
1926	II 16	2	1959	II 13	3
1927	II 15	3	1960	II 13	2
1928	II 15	3	1961	II 11	q-f
1929	II 13	1	1962	II 4	2
1930	II 19	1	1963	II 9	2
1931	II 13	2	1964	II 16	2
1932	II 13	1	1965	II 10	p
1933	II 11	1	1966	II 8	1
1934	II 15	2	1967	II 13	1
1935	II 10	1	1968	II 17	1
1936	II 4	1	1969	II 18	p
1937	II 9	1	1970	II 6	p
1938	II 11	1	1971	II 16	3
1939	II 2	q-f	1972	II 16	3
1947	II 5	1	1973	II 12	2
1948	II 12	2	1974	II 12	2
1949	II 14	2	1975	II 15	3
1950	II 16	1	1976	II 3	3
1951	II 16	1	1977	II 2P	4
1952	II 7	2	1978	I 13R	3

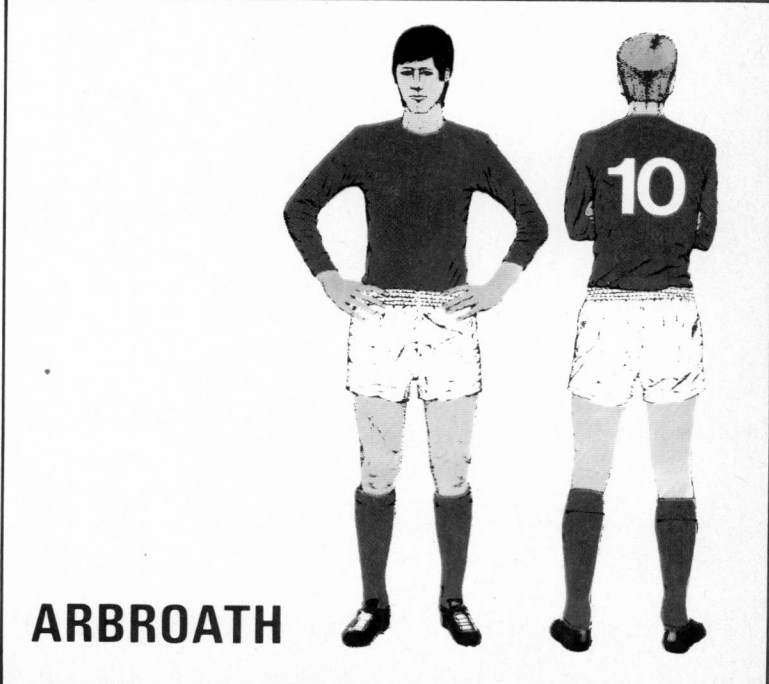

ARBROATH

Founded: 1878
Address: Gayfield Park
Telephone: 02414 2157
Ground capacity: 15,000
Record attendance: 13,510 v Rangers, Scottish Cup 3rd round, 23.2.52
Record victory: 36-0 v Bon Accord, Scottish Cup 1st round, 12.9.85
Record defeat: 0-8 v Kilmarnock, Division II, 1948–49
Most League points: 57, Division II, 1966–67
Most League goals: 87, Division II, 1967–68
League scoring record: 45, Dave Easson, Division II, 1958-59
Record League aggregate: 120, Jimmy Jack, 1966-1971
Most League appearances: 319, Ian Stirling, 1960-1971
Most capped player: 2 (6 in all), Ned Doig, Scotland

THE ARBROATH RECORD

Year	Division & place	Cup round reached	Year	Division & place	Cup round reached
1922	II 16	1	1954	II 14	2
1923	II 20	1	1955	II 12	5
1924	II 17	2	1956	II 18	5
1925	II 5	3	1957	II 10	5
1926	II 10	2	1958	II 3	2
1927	II 19	1	1959	II 2P	2
1928	II 10	1	1960	I 18R	2
1929	II 3	3	1961	II 12	2
1930	II 9	2	1962	II 6	2
1931	II 15	3	1963	II 6	2
1932	II 11	2	1964	II 3	2
1933	II 10	1	1965	II 7	1
1934	II 3	2	1966	II 6	p
1935	II 2P	1	1967	II 3	1
1936	I 12	1	1968	II 2P	2
1937	I 14	2	1969	I 18R	1
1938	I 11	1	1970	II 5	1
1939	I 17R	1	1971	II 3	3
1947	II 12	s-f	1972	II 2P	3
1948	II 13	2	1973	I 15	3
1949	II 7	1	1974	I 13	4
1950	II 14	1	1975	I 18	q-f
1951	II 13	1	1976	I 5	3
1952	II 16	3	1977	I 8	q-f
1953	II 7	1	1978	I 9	3

AYR UNITED

Founded: 1910
Address: Somerset Park, Ayr, Scotland
Telephone: Ayr 63435
Ground capacity: 25,000 (1,500 seated)
Playing area: 111 by 75 yards
Record attendance: 25,225 v Rangers, Division I, 13.9.69
Record victory: 11-1 v Dumbarton, League Cup, 13.8.52
Record defeat: 0-9 v Rangers, Division I, 16.11.29; v Hearts, Division I, 28.2.31
Most League points: 60, Division II, 1958-59
Most League goals: 117, Division II, 1927-28
League scoring record: 66, J Smith, Division II, 1927-28
Most capped player: 1 (2 in all), John Crosbie, Scotland

THE AYR RECORD

Year	Division & place	Cup round reached	Year	Division & place	Cup round reached
1899*	II 8	p	1936	I 20R	1
1900*	II 8	p	1937	II 1P	1
1901*	II 6	2	1938	I 17	q-f
1902*	II 8	1	1939	I 14	1
1903*	II 3	2	1947	II 11	2
1904*	II 3	1	1948	II 10	1
1905*	II 5	1	1949	II 9	2
1906*	II 7	p	1950	II 13	1
1907*	II 8	2	1951	II 3	q-f
1908*	II 3	p	1952	II 3	1
1909*	II 5	1	1953	II 5	3
1910*	II 7	2	1954	II 9	2
1911	II 2	p	1955	II 8	5
1912	II 1	1	1956	II 2P	6
1913	II 1P	2	1957	I 18R	5
1914	I 10	1	1958	II 5	1
1915	I 5		1959	II 1P	3
1916	I 4		1960	I 8	q-f
1917	I 15		1961	I 18R	2
1918	I 18		1962	II 9	1
1919	I 7		1963	II 13	2
1920	I 10	3	1964	II 14	q-f
1921	I 14	3	1965	II 18	1
1922	I 10	2	1966	II 1P	1
1923	I 10	3	1967	I 18R	1
1924	I 14	q-f	1968	II 5	1
1925	I 19R	2	1969	II 2P	2
1926	II 3	1	1970	I 14	1
1927	II 8	1	1971	I 14	3
1928	II 1P	2	1972	I 12	4
1929	I 16	2	1973	I 6	s-f
1930	I 9	2	1974	I 7	q-f
1931	I 18	3	1975	I 7	3
1932	I 17	1	1976	P 6	4
1933	I 16	2	1977	P 8	4
1934	I 8	2	1978	P 9R	3
1935	I 18	2			

*—Ayr FC (combined with Ayr Parkhouse in 1910)
p—preliminary round

BERWICK RANGERS

Founded: 1881
Address: Shielfield Park, Tweedmouth, Berwick-on-Tweed, Northumberland
Telephone: Berwick 7424
Ground capacity: 16,000
Playing area: 112 by 76 yards
Record attendance: 13,365 v Rangers, Scottish Cup 1st round, 28.1.67
Record victory: 8-2 v Dundee United, 1957-58
Record defeat: 0-8 v Morton & 1-9 v Dundee United
Most League points: 45, Division II, 1973-74
Most League goals: 83, Division II, 1961-62
League scoring record: 38, Ken Bowron, Division II, 1963-64
Record League aggregate: 98, Ken Bowron, 1963-1966 & 1968-1969
Most League appearances: 282, Alistair Campbell, 1955-1962

THE BERWICK RECORD

Year	Division & place	Cup round reached	Year	Division & place	Cup round reached
1956	II 14	1	1968	II 14	1
1957	II 18	1	1969	II 16	1
1958	II 19	1	1970	II 9	1
1959	II 10	1	1971	II 13	2
1960	II 9	1	1972	II 13	2
1961	II 11	1	1973	II 9	3
1962	II 8	1	1974	II 6	1
1963	II 17	1	1975	II 10	3
1964	II 12	1	1976	II 11	1
1965	II 8	1	1977	II 8	1
1966	II 11	1	1978	II 4	3
1967	II 10	2			

BRECHIN CITY

Founded: 1906
Address: Glebe Park, Brechin, Angus
Telephone: Brechin 2856
Ground capacity: 10,000
Playing area: 110 by 67 yards
Record attendance: 8,123 v Aberdeen, Scottish Cup 3rd round, 3.2.73
Record victory: 12-1 v Thornhill, Scottish Cup, 1st round, 28.1.26
Record defeat: 0-10 v Albion Rovers, Division II, 1937-38
Most League points: 42, Division II, 1955-56, 1958-59
Most League goals: 80, Division II, 1957-58
Most capped player: None

THE BRECHIN RECORD

Year	Division & place	Cup round reached		Year	Division & place	Cup round reached
1924		1		1956	II 6	6
1925		1		1957	II 6	5
1926		3		1958	II 7	1
1927		2		1959	II 5	2
1928		2		1960	II 12	1
1929		2		1961	II 14	3
1930	II 20	1		1962	II 19	2
1931	II 16	1		1963	II 19	2
1932	II 19	1		1964	II 15	2
1933	II 15	1		1965	II 19	p
1934	II 14	2		1966	II 16	p
1935	II 15	3		1967	II 20	1
1936	II 16	1		1968	II 16	1
1937	II 16	1		1969	II 17	p
1938	II 18	1		1970	II 14	p
1939	II 10	1		1971	II 19	3
1947	*	p		1972	II 15	2
1948	*	p		1973	II 19	3
1949	*	p		1974	II 19	3
1950	*	1		1975	II 17	1
1951	*	2		1976	II 13	2
1952	*	1		1977	II 13	3
1953	*	1		1978	II 14	3
1954	*	2				
1955	II 16	4				

* – Brechin competed in Division 'C'

CELTIC

Founded: 1888
Address: Celtic Park (Parkhead), Glasgow SE
Telephone: (041) 554 2710
Ground capacity: 80,000
Playing area: 115 by 75 yards
Record attendance: 92,000 v Rangers, Division I, 1.1.38
Record victory: 11-0 v Dundee, Division I, 26.10.95
Record defeat: 0-8 v Motherwell, Division I, 1936-37
Most League points: 67, Division I, 1915-16 & 1921-22
Most League goals: 115, Division I, 1935-36
League scoring record: 50, Jimmy McGrory, Division I, 1935-36
Record League aggregate: 397, Jimmy McGrory, 1922-23 & 1924-1938
Most League appearances: 378, Jimmy McGrory, 1922-23 & 1924-1938
Most capped player: 45 (48 in all), Bobby Evans, Scotland

Scottish Cup	Year	Opponents	Score	Scorers
Winners	1892	Queen's Park	†5-1	Campbell 2, McMahon 2, og
	1899	Rangers	2-0	Hodge, McMahon
	1900	Queen's Park	4-3	Divers 3, McMahon
	1904	Rangers	3-2	Quinn 3
	1907	Hearts	3-0	Orr (pen), Somers 2
	1908	St Mirren	5-1	Bennett 2, Quinn, Hamilton, Somers
	1911	Hamilton A.	0-0	
			2-0	Quinn, McAtee
	1912	Clyde	2-0	McMenemy, Gallagher
	1914	Hibernian	0-0	
			4-1	McColl 2, Browning, McAtee
	1923	Hibernian	1-0	Cassidy
	1925	Dundee	2-1	Gallagher, McGrory
	1927	East Fife	3-1	McLean, Connelly, og
	1931	Motherwell	2-2	McGrory, og
			4-2	Thomson 2, McGrory 2
	1933	Motherwell	1-0	McGrory
	1937	Aberdeen	2-1	Crum, Buchan
	1951	Motherwell	1-0	McPhail
	1954	Aberdeen	2-1	Fallon, og
	1965	Dunfermline A.	3-2	Auld 2, McNeill
	1967	Aberdeen	2-0	Wallace 2
	1969	Rangers	4-0	McNeill, Lennox, Connelly, Chalmers
	1971	Rangers	1-1	Lennox
			2-1	Macari, Hood (pen)
	1972	Hibernian	6-1	McNeill, Deans 3, Macari 2
	1974	Dundee United	3-0	Hood, Murray, Deans
	1975	Airdrieonians	3-1	Wilson 2, McCluskey (pen)
	1977	Rangers	1-0	Lynch (pen)
Runners-up	1889	Third Lanark	1-2	McCallum
	1893	Queen's Park	1-2	Blessington
	1894	Rangers	1-3	Maley
	1901	Hearts	3-4	McOustra 2, McMahon
	1902	Hibernian	0-1	
	1909	Rangers	2-2, 1-1	
	1926	St Mirren	0-2	
	1928	Rangers	0-4	
	1955	Clyde	1-1	Walsh
			0-1	
	1956	Hearts	1-3	Haughney
	1961	Dunfermline A.	0-0	
			0-2	
	1963	Rangers	1-1	Murdoch
			0-3	
	1966	Rangers	0-0	
			0-1	
	1970	Aberdeen	1-3	Lennox
	1973	Rangers	2-3	Dalglish, Connelly (pen)

Scottish League Cup

	Year	Opponents	Score	Scorers
Winners	1957	Partick Thistle	0-0	
			3-0	McPhail 2, Collins
	1958	Rangers	7-1	Wilson, Mochan 2, McPhail 3, Fernie
	1966	Rangers	2-1	Hughes (2 pen)
	1967	Rangers	1-0	Lennox
	1968	Dundee	5-3	Chalmers 2, Wallace, Lennox, Hughes
	1969	Hibernian	6-2	Wallace, Auld, Lennox 3, Craig
	1970	St Johnstone	1-0	Auld
	1975	Hibernian	6-3	Deans 3, Johnstone, Wilson, Johnstone
Runners-up	1965	Rangers	1-2	Murray
	1971	Rangers	0-1	
	1972	Partick T.	1-4	Dalglish
	1973	Hibernian	1-2	Dalglish
	1974	Dundee	0-1	
	1976	Rangers	0-1	
	1977	Aberdeen	1-2	Dalglish
	1978	Rangers	1-2	Edvaldsson

THE CELTIC RECORD

Year	Division & place	Cup round reached		Year	Division & place	Cup round reached
1889		Final		1920	I 2	3
1890		1		1921	I 2	3
1891	I 3	s-f		1922	I 1C	3
1892	I 2	Winners		1923	I 3	Winners
1893	I 1C	Final		1924	I 3	1
1894	I 1C	Final		1925	I 4	Winners
1895	I 2	3		1926	I 1C	Final
1896	I 1C	1		1927	I 3	Winners
1897	I 4	1		1928	I 2	Final
1898	I 1C	2		1929	I 2	s-f
1899	I 3	Winners		1930	I 4	3
1900	I 2	Winners		1931	I 2	Winners
1901	I 2	Final		1932	I 3	3
1902	I 2	Final		1933	I 4	Winners
1903	I 5	3		1934	I 3	4
1904	I 3	Winners		1935	I 2	4
1905	I 1C	4		1936	I 1C	2
1906	I 1C	3		1937	I 3	Winners
1907	I 1C	Winners		1938	I 1C	3
1908	I 1C	Winners		1939	I 2	4
1909	I 1C	Final		1947	I 7	1
1910	I 1C	4		1948	I 12	s-f
1911	I 5	Winners		1949	I 6	1
1912	I 2	Winners		1950	I 4	3
1913	I 2	3		1951	I 7	Winners
1914	I 1C	Winners		1952	I 9	1
1915	I 1C			1953	I 8	4
1916	I 1C			1954	I 1C	Winners
1917	I 1C			1955	I 2	Final
1918	I 2			1956	I 5	Final
1919	I 1C			1957	I 5	s-f

Year	Div	Place	Cup		Year	Div	Place	Cup
1958	I	3	3		1969	I	1C	Winners
1959	I	6	s-f		1970	I	1C	Final
1960	I	9	s-f		1971	I	1C	Winners
1961	I	4	Final		1972	I	1C	Winners
1962	I	3	s-f		1973	I	1C	Final
1963	I	4	Final		1974	I	1C	Winners
1964	I	3	4		1975	I	3	Winners
1965	I	8	Winners		1976	P	2	3
1966	I	1C	Final		1977	P	1C	Winners
1967	I	1C	Winners		1978	P	5	4
1968	I	1C	1					

Year	Div	Place	Cup		Year	Div	Place	Cup
1961	I	17R	1		1970	I	16	1
1962	II	1P	2		1971	I	15	4
1963	I	17R	2		1972	I	17R	3
1964	II	2P	2		1973	II	1P	3
1965	I	7	1		1974	I	15	3
1966	I	11	1		1975	I	16	3
1967	I	3	s-f		1976	I	14R	3
1968	I	8	2		1977	II	7	3
1969	I	13	2		1978	II	1P	1

CLYDE

Founded: 1878
Address: Shawfield Park, Glasgow C.5
Telephone: (041) 647 6329
Ground capacity: 25,000 (2,000 seated)
Playing area: 110 by 70 yards
Record attendance: 52,000 v Rangers, Division I, 21.11.08
Record victory: 11-1 v Cowdenbeath, Division II, 6.10.51
Record defeat: 0-11 v Rangers, Scottish Cup 4th round, 1880-81
Most League points: 64, Division II, 1956-57*
Most League goals: 122, Division II, 1956-57
League scoring record: 32, Bill Boyd, Division I, 1932-33
Most capped player: 12, Tommy Ring, Scotland

Scottish Cup	Year	Opponents	Score	Scorers
Winners	1939	Motherwell	4-0	Martin 2, Wallace, Noble
	1955	Celtic	1-1	Robertson
	Replay		1-0	Ring
	1958	Hibernian	1-0	Coyle
Runners-up	1910	Dundee	2-2	Chalmers, Booth
	First replay		0-0	
	Second replay		1-2	Chalmers
	1912	Celtic	0-2	
	1949	Rangers	1-4	Galletly

THE CLYDE RECORD

Year	Division & place		Cup round reached		Year	Division & place		Cup round reached
1892	I	7	p		1923	I	16	1
1893	I	10	1		1924	I	19R	3
1894	II	3P	3		1925	II	3	2
1895	I	7	3		1926	II	2P	3
1896	I	9	2		1927	I	17	3
1897	I	9	1		1928	I	15	1
1898	I	10	1		1929	I	17	3
1899	I	8	3		1930	I	11	2
1900	I	10R	2		1931	I	12	2
1901	II	4	2		1932	I	13	q-f
1902	II	12	p		1933	I	12	s-f
1903	II	12	1		1934	I	14	1
1904	II	2	1		1935	I	10	2
1905	II	1	1		1936	I	18	s-f
1906	II	2P	1		1937	I	10	s-f
1907	I	8	1		1938	I	15	1
1908	I	17	p		1939	I	9	Winners
1909	I	3	s-f		1947	I	10	1
1910	I	5	Final		1948	I	6	3
1911	I	7	q-f		1949	I	14	Final
1912	I	3	Final		1950	I	13	2
1913	I	9	s-f		1951	I	15R	3
1914	I	9	2		1952	II	1P	2
1915	I	17			1953	I	5	q-f
1916	I	16			1954	I	8	2
1917	I	13			1955	I	7	Winners
1918	I	17			1956	I	17R	s-f
1919	I	17			1957	II	1P	q-f
1920	I	16	1		1958	I	4	Winners
1921	I	7	2		1959	I	15	2
1922	I	10	3		1960	I	6	s-f

CLYDEBANK

Founded: 1965 (new club)
Address: New Kilbowie Park, Clydebank
Telephone: (041) 952 2887
Ground capacity: 13,500
Playing area: 110 by 68 yards
Record attendance: 14,900 v Hibernian, Scottish Cup 1st round, 10.2.65
Record victory: 7-1 v Queen's Park, Division II, 1970-71
Record defeat: 0-7 v Falkirk, Division II, 20.9.69
Most League points: 44, Division II, 1974-75
Most League goals: 62, Division II, 1967-68
League scoring record: 27, Joe McCallan, 1976-77

THE CLYDEBANK RECORD

Year	Division & place		Cup round reached		Year	Division & place		Cup round reached
1918	I	9			1968	II	9	p
1919	I	10			1969	II	13	p
1920	I	5			1970	II	13	2
1921	I	20			1971	II	5	3
1922	I	22R			1972	II	9	4
1923	II	2P			1973	II	17	1
1924	I	20R			1974	II	10	3
1925	II	2P			1975	II	7	4
1926	I	20R			1976	II	1P	2
1927	II	3			1977	I	2P	4
1928	II	14			1978	P	10R	3
1929	II	16						
1930	II	18						
1931*	II	19			*Old Clydebank disbanded			
1965†	II	5	1		†East Stirlingshire Clydebank			
1966‡			p		‡Clydebank juniors			
1967§	II	18	p		§Clydebank			

COWDENBEATH

126

Founded: 1881
Address: Central Park, Cowdenbeath, Fife, Scotland
Telephone: Cowdenbeath 511205
Ground capacity: 25,000
Playing area: 110 by 70 yards
Record attendance: 25,586 v Rangers, League Cup quarter-final, 21.9.49
Record victory: 12-0 v Johnstone, Scottish Cup 1st round, 21.1.28
Record defeat: 1-11 v Clyde, Division II, 6.10.51
Most League points: 60, Division II, 1938-39
Most League goals: 120, Division II, 1938-39
League scoring record: 40, Willie Devlin, 1925-26
Most capped player: 1 (3 in all), Alec Venters, Scotland

THE COWDENBEATH RECORD

Year	Division & place	Cup round reached		Year	Division & place	Cup round reached
1906	II 9	p		1937	II 6	3
1907	II 7	1		1938	II 6	2
1908	II 12	p		1939	II 1	2
1909	II 11	p		1947	II 14	3
1910	II 11	p		1948	II 5	2
1911	II 5	p		1949	II 13	2
1912	II 4	p		1950	II 5	2
1913	II 5	p		1951	II 11	1
1914	II 1	p		1952	II 8	2
1915	II 1			1953	II 13	2
1916				1954	II 13	2
1917				1955	II 14	4
1918				1956	II 7	5
1919				1957	II 3	4
1920		1		1958	II 6	1
1921		p		1959	II 14	1
1922	II 2	2		1960	II 19	3
1923	II 11	2		1961	II 8	2
1924	II 2P	2		1962	II 14	1
1925	I 5	1		1963	II 8	2
1926	I 7	1		1964	II 17	1
1927	I 7	2		1965	II 12	1
1928	I 9	2		1966	II 10	2
1929	I 13	2		1967	II 6	1
1930	I 16	2		1968	II 12	1
1931	I 7	q-f		1969	II 12	1
1932	I 12	2		1970	II 2P	p
1933	I 17	1		1971	I 18R	4
1934	I 20R	3		1972	II 5	3
1935	II 12	1		1973	II 7	3
1936	II 10	3		1974	II 13	3
				1975	II 19	2
				1976	II 9	4
				1977	II 12	1
				1978	II 10	3

THE DUMBARTON RECORD

Year	Division & place	Cup round reached		Year	Division & place	Cup round reached
1891	I 1C†	Final		1932	II 12	1
1892	I 1C	3		1933	II 9	2
1893	I 7	2		1934	II 6	1
1894	I 5	2		1935	II 16	2
1895	I 10	2		1936	II 18	3
1896	I 10R	1		1937	II 15	2
1897	II 10	Final		1938	II 7	1
1898	*	1		1939	II 11	1
1899	*	1		1947	II 13	q-f
1900	*	p		1948	II 11	3
1901	*	p		1949	II 15	3
1902	*	p		1950	II 15	2
1903	*	p		1951	II 9	1
1904	*	p		1952	II 10	3
1905	*	p		1953	II 10	1
1906	*	p		1954	II 16L	4
1907	II 4	p		1955	*	4
1908	II 2	p		1956	II 4	4
1909	II 4	p		1957	II 9	q-f
1910	II 4	1		1958	II 4	1
1911	II 1	p		1959	II 4	2
1912	II 3	1		1960	II 6	1
1913	II 6E	q-f		1961	II 10	2
1914	I 19	1		1962	II 17	1
1915	I 13			1963	II 12	1
1916	I 9			1964	II 6	2
1917	I 10			1965	II 14	1
1918	I 8			1966	II 12	q-f
1919	I 15			1967	II 14	1
1920	I 11	1		1968	II 10	p
1921	I 21	4		1969	II 14	1
1922	I 20R	1		1970	II 7	1
1923	II 4	1		1971	II 4	2
1924	II 10	1		1972	II 1P	4
1925	II 8	2		1973	I 16	4
1926	II 11	q-f		1974	I 10	3
1927	II 18	2		1975	I 14	q-f
1928	II 11	1		1976	I 4	s-f
1929	II 14	3		1977	I 7	3
1930	II 16	1		1978	I 4	q-f
1931	II 10	1				

† shared jointly with Rangers
* not members of League
E – elected to First Division

DUMBARTON

Founded: 1872 (as Dumbarton Athletic)
Address: Boghead Park, Dumbarton, Strathclyde
Telephone: Dumbarton 62569
Ground capacity: 18,000
Record attendance: 18,000 v Raith Rovers, Scottish Cup quarter-final, 2.3.57
Record victory: 8-0 v Cowdenbeath, Division II, 28.3.64
Record defeat: 1-11 v Ayr United, League Cup, 13.8.52
Most League points: 52, Division II, 1971-72
Most League goals: 101, Division II, 1956-57
League scoring record: 38, Kenny Wilson, Division II, 1971-72
Most capped player: 18, John Lindsay, Scotland
18, James McAulay, Scotland

Scottish Cup	Year	Opponents	Score
Winners	1883	Vale of Leven	2-2
		Replay	2-1
Runners-up	1881	Queen's Park	1-3
	1882	Queen's Park	2-2
		Replay	1-4
	1887	Hibernian	1-2
	1891	Hearts	0-1
	1897	Rangers	1-5

DUNDEE

Founded: 1893
Address: Dens Park, Dundee, Angus
Telephone: Dundee 86104
Ground capacity: 38,500
Playing area: 110 by 75 yards
Record attendance: 43,024 v Rangers, Scottish Cup 2nd round, 7.2.53
Record victory: 10-0 v Alloa Athletic, Division II, 8.3.47
10-0 v Dunfermline Athletic, Division II, 22.3.47
Record defeat: 0-11 v Celtic, Division I, 26.10.1895
Most League points: 54, Division I, 1961-62
Most League goals: 113, Division II, 1946-47
League scoring record: 38, David Halliday, Division I, 1923-24
Record League aggregate: 111, Alan Gilzean, 1960-1964
Most League appearances: 341, Doug Cowie, 1947-1961
Most capped player: 24, Alex Hamilton, Scotland

Scottish Cup	Year	Opponents	Score	Scorers
Winners	1910	Clyde	2-2	Hunter, Langlands
			0-0	
			2-1	Bellamy, Hunter
Runners-up	1925	Celtic	1-2	McLean (D)
	1952	Motherwell	0-4	
	1964	Rangers	1-3	Cameron
League Cup				
Winners	1952	Rangers	3-2	Flavell, Pattillo, Boyd
	1953	Kilmarnock	2-0	Flavell 2
	1974	Celtic	1-0	Wallace
Runners-up	1968	Celtic	3-5	McLean (G) 2, McLean (J)

THE DUNDEE RECORD

Year	Division & place	Cup round reached		Year	Division & place	Cup round reached
1894	I 8	p		1935	I 8	1
1895	I 8	s-f		1936	I 13	3
1896	I 5	2		1937	I 9	3
1897	I 5	q-f		1938	I 19R	1
1898	I 7	s-f		1939	II 6	2
1899	I 10	1		1947	II 1P	q-f
1900	I 6	q-f		1948	I 4	1
1901	I 7	q-f		1949	I 2	s-f
1902	I 9	2		1950	I 6	1
1903	I 2	s-f		1951	I 3	q-f
1904	I 5	q-f		1952	I 8	Final
1905	I 7	1		1953	I 7	2
1906	I 7	1		1954	I 7	3
1907	I 2	2		1955	I 8	5
1908	I 4	2		1956	I 13	6
1909	I 2	2		1957	I 10	5
1910	I 6	Winners		1958	i 11	3
1911	I 6	s-f		1959	I 4	1
1912	I 8	2		1960	I 4	2
1913	I 14	q-f		1961	I 10	2
1914	I 7	2		1962	I 1C	1
1915	I 15			1963	I 9	q-f
1916	I 8			1964	I 6	Final
1917	I 16R			1965	I 6	1
1918†				1966	I 9	2
1919†				1967	I 6	1
1920	I 4	2		1968	I 9	2
1921	I 4	q-f		1969	I 9	1
1922	I 4	3		1970	I 6	s-t
1923	I 7	1-f		1971	I 5	q-f
1924	I 5	2		1972	I 5	4
1925	I 8	Final		1973	I 5	s-f
1926	I 10	2		1974	I 5	s-f
1927	I 5	3		1975	I 6	s-f
1928	I 14	3		1976	P 9R	3
1929	I 18	3		1977	I 3	s-f
1930	I 14	q-f		1978	I 3	3
1931	I 8	3				
1932	I 11	2				
1933	I 15	3				
1934	I 12	2		† No Second Division		

THE DUNDEE UNITED RECORD

Year	Division & place	Cup round reached		Year	Division & place	Cup round reached
1911*	II 8	p		1954	II 15	1
1912*	II 10	p		1955	II 13	4
1913*	II 10	2		1956	II 8	5
1914*	II 4	1		1957	II 13	6
1915*	II 11			1958	II 9	2
1920*	†	p		1959	II 17	2
1921*	†	p		1960	II 2P	2
1922*	II 19	1		1961	I 9	2
1923‡		2		1962	I 10	2
1924	II 9	1		1963	I 7	s-f
1925	II 1P	2		1964	I 8	1
1926	I 17	1		1965	I 9	2
1927	I 20R	q-f		1966	I 9	2
1928	II 6	2		1967	I 9	s-f
1929	II 1P	q-f		1968	I 11	2
1930	I 19R	2		1969	I 5	q-f
1931	II 2P	2		1970	I 5	2
1932	II 19R	3		1971	I 6	4
1933	II 13	2		1972	I 7	3
1934	II 17	1		1973	I 7	3
1935	II 4	3		1974	I 8	Final
1936	II 7	2		1975	I 4	4
1937	II 14	1		1976	P 8	4
1938	II 14	2		1977	P 4	3
1939	II 9	2		1978	P 3	s-f
1947	II 10	1				
1948	II 15	2				
1949	II 8	2				
1950	II 8	2				
1951	II 4	1				
1952	II 4	3				
1953	II 8	1				

*as Dundee Hibernians
† Scottish Second Division not reformed until 1921
‡ Name changed to Dundee United. Dundee Hibernians did not compete in the League 1922-23.

DUNDEE UNITED

Founded: 1910*
Address: Tannadice Park, Dundee, Angus
Telephone: Dundee 86289
Ground capacity: 28,500 (2,500 seated)
Playing area: 110 by 74 yards
Record attendance: 28,000 v Barcelona, Fairs Cup 2nd round, 16.11.66
Record victory: 14-0 v Nithsdale Wanderers, Scottish Cup 1st round, 17.1.31
Record defeat: 1-12 v Motherwell, Division II, 23.1.54
Most League points: 51, Division II, 1928-29
Most League goals: 99, Division II, 1928-29
League scoring record: 41, John Coyle, Division II, 1955-56
Record League aggregate: 202, Peter McKay, 1947-1954
Most League appearances: Not available
Most capped player: 3 (11 in all) Orjan Persson, Sweden
*As Dundee Hibernians. Name changed to Dundee United in 1923

Scottish Cup	Year	Opponents	Score
Runners-up	1974	Celtic	0-3

DUNFERMLINE ATHLETIC

Founded: 1885
Address: East End Park, Dunfermline
Telephone: Dunfermline 24295
Ground capacity: 27,000 (3,100 seated)
Playing area: 112 by 72 yards
Record attendance: 27,816 v Celtic, Division I, 1968-69
Record victory: 11-2 v Stenhousemuir, Division II, 1930-31
Record defeat: 0-10 v Dundee, Division II, 22.3.47
Most League points: 59, Division II, 1925-26
Most League goals: 120, Division II, 1957-58
League scoring record: 53, Bobby Skinner, Division II, 1925-26
Record League aggregate: 154, Charlie Dickson, 1955-64
Most League appearances: 301, George Peebles, 1956-66
Most capped player: 6 (12 in all), Andy Wilson, Scotland

Scottish Cup	Year	Opponents	Score	Scorers
Winners	1961	Celtic	0-0	
			2-0	Thomson, Dickson
	1968	Hearts	3-1	Gardner 2, Lister (pen)
Runners-up	1965	Celtic	2-3	Melrose, McLaughlin
Scottish League Cup				
Runners-up	1950	East Fife	0-3	

THE DUNFERMLINE RECORD

Year	Division & place	Cup round reached	Year	Division & place	Cup round reached
1922	II 8	2	1955	II 2P	6
1923	II 13	3	1956	I 16	5
1924	II 7	1	1957	I 17R	6
1925	II 13	1	1958	II 2P	3
1926	II 1P	1	1959	I 16	q-f
1927	I 18	3	1960	I 13	2
1928	I 20R	4	1961	I 12	Winners
1929	II 11	1	1962	I 4	q-f
1930	II 10	1	1963	I 8	3
1931	II 3	1	1964	I 5	s-f
1932	II 10	q-f	1965	I 3	Final
1933	II 3	1	1966	I 4	s-f
1934	II 2P	1	1967	I 8	q-f
1935	I 15	q-f	1968	I 4	Winners
1936	I 10	1	1969	I 3	2
1937	I 19R	1	1970	I 9	1
1938	II 9	1	1971	I 16	4
1939	II 5	3	1972	I 18R	3
1947	II 8	1	1973	II 2P	4
1948	II 7	2	1974	I 16	q-f
1949	II 4	1	1975	I 15	3
1950	II 4	3	1976	I 13R	3
1951	II 10	1	1977	II 3	3
1952	II 6	3	1978	II 3	2
1953	II 11	1			
1954	II 8	2			

Year	Div & place	Cup	Year	Div & place	Cup
1964	II 4	2	1972	I 16	3
1965	II 9	2	1973	I 9	3
1966	II 4	1	1974	I 17R	3
1967	II 5	2	1975	II 5	3
1968	II 3	2	1976	I 12	3
1969	II 3	1	1977	I 12	q-f
1970	II 10	q-f	1978	I 14R	3
1971	II 2P	3			

EAST FIFE

Founded: 1903
Address: Bayview Park, Methil, Fife
Telephone: Leven 26323
Ground capacity: 25,000
Record attendance: 22,515 v Raith Rovers, Division I, 2.1.50
Record victory: 13-2 v Edinburgh City, Division II, 11.12.37
Record defeat: 0-9 v Hearts, Division I, 5.10.57
Most League points: 57, Division II, 1929-30
Most League goals: 114, Division II, 1929-30
League scoring record: 33, Alex McGauchie, Division II, 1929-30
Most capped player: 5 (8 in all), George Aitken, Scotland

Scottish Cup	Year	Opponents	Score	Scorers
Winners	1938	Kilmarnock	1-1	McLeod
		Replay	4-2	McKerrell 2, McLeod Miller
Runners-up	1927	Celtic	1-3	Wood
	1950	Rangers	0-3	
Scottish League Cup				
Winners	1948	Falkirk	0-0	
		Replay	4-1	Duncan 3, Adams
	1950	Dunfermline	3-0	Fleming, Duncan, Morris
	1954	Partick Thistle	3-2	Gardiner, Fleming, Christie

THE EAST FIFE RECORD

Year	Division & place	Cup round reached	Year	Division & place	Cup round reached
1921		3	1939	II 3	1
1922	II 12	1	1947	II 3	q-f
1923	II 9	3	1948	II 1P	q-f
1924	II 13	2	1949	I 4	s-f
1925	II 9	1	1950	I 4	Final
1926	II 4	1	1951	I 10	1
1927	II 6	Final	1952	I 3	2
1928	II 4	1	1953	I 3	2
1929	II 8	1	1954	I 6	1
1930	II 2P	1	1955	I 11	5
1931	I 20R	1	1956	I 12	5
1932	II 8	1	1957	I 15	6
1933	II 7	1	1958	I 17R	1
1934	II 13	1	1959	II 8	1
1935	II 9	1	1960	II 18	1
1936	II 6	1	1961	II 13	2
1937	II 5	3	1962	II 10	3
1938	II 5	Winners	1963	II 11	2

EAST STIRLINGSHIRE

Founded: 1881
Address: Firs Park, Falkirk, Stirlingshire
Telephone: Falkirk 23583
Ground capacity: 12,000
Record attendance: 11,500 v Hibernian, Scottish Cup, 10.2.60
Record victory: 8-2 v Brechin City, Division II, 31.3.62
Record defeat: 0-10 v Dundee United, Division II, 25.3.39
Most League points: 55, Division II, 1931-32
Most League goals: 111, Division II, 1931-32
League scoring record: 36, Malcolm Morrison, Division II, 1938-39
Record League aggregate: *Not available*
Most League appearances: *Not available*
Most capped player: 2, David Alexander, Scotland

THE EAST STIRLINGSHIRE RECORD

Year	Division & place	Cup round reached	Year	Division & place	Cup round reached
1902	II 9	p	1949	‡	1
1903	II 8	p	1950	‡	1
1904	II 6	p	1951	‡	2
1905	II 9	p	1952	‡	1
1906	II 12	p	1953	‡	2
1907	II 11	p	1954	‡	1
1908	II 5	p	1955	‡	4
1909	II 9	p	1956	II 16	4
1910	II 8	p	1957	II 19	4
1911	II 7	1	1958	II 15	1
1912	II 9	2	1959	II 15	1
1913	II 3	2	1960	II 15	3
1914	II 8	2	1961	II 16	1
1915	II 4		1962	II 11	2
1920	†	2	1963	II 2P	3
1921	†	3	1964	I 18R	3
1922	II 15	3	1965††	II 5	p
1923	II 19	1	1966	II 17	1
1924	*	3	1967	II 19	p
1925	II 18	2	1968	II 15	1
1926	II 18	1	1969	II 9	2
1927	II 5	1	1970	II 12	p
1928	II 9	1	1971	II 17	2
1929	II 12	2	1972	II 8	1
1930	II 12	1	1973	II 13	2
1931	II 7	1	1974	II 16	1
1932	II 1P	1	1975	II 9	3
1933	I 20R	1	1976	II 8	1
1934	II 9	3	1977	II 10	3
1935	II 14	1	1978	II 9	2
1936	II 8	1			
1937	II 7	1			
1938	II 13	1			
1939	II 17	1			
1947	‡	2			
1948	‡	2			

* – Did not compete
† – No Second Division
‡ – Competed in Division 'C'
†† – as East Stirlingshire Clydebank

FALKIRK

Founded: 1876
Address: Brockville Park, Falkirk, Scotland
Telephone: Falkirk 24121
Ground capacity: 24,000 (2,750 seated)
Playing area: 110 by 70 yards
Record attendance: 23,100 v Celtic, Scottish Cup 3rd round, 21.2.53
Record victory: 10-0 v Breadalbane, Scottish Cup 1st round, 13.1.23 and 23.1.26
Record defeat: 1-11 v Airdrieonians, Division I, 28.4.51
Most League points: 59, Division II, 1935-36
Most League goals: 132, Division II, 1935-36
League scoring record: 43, Evelyn Morrison, Division I, 1928-29
Most capped player: 14 (15 in all), Alec Parker, Scotland

Scottish Cup

	Year	Opponents	Score	Scorers
Winners	1913	Raith Rovers	2-0	Robertson, Logan
	1957	Kilmarnock	1-1	Prentice
	Replay		2-1	Merchant, Moran

Scottish League Cup

	Year	Opponents	Score	Scorers
Runners-up	1948	East Fife	0-0	
	Replay		1-4	Aikman

THE FALKIRK RECORD

Year	Division & place	Cup round reached	Year	Division & place	Cup round reached
1902		q-f	1937	I 7	2
1903	II 7	q	1938	I 4	q-f
1904	II 4	q	1939	I 5	3
1905	II 2P	q	1947	I 11	3
1906	I 13	1	1948	I 7	2
1907	I 5	1	1949	I 5	1
1908	I 2	1	1950	I 14	2
1909	I 9	s-f	1951	I 16R	1
1910	I 2	2	1952	II 2P	q-f
1911	I 3	2	1953	I 13	3
1912	I 7	2	1954	I 13	2
1913	I 5	Winners	1955	I 12	7
1914	I 5	1	1956	I 14	5
1915	I 6		1957	I 14	Winners
1916	I 12		1958	I 10	q-f
1917	I 12		1959	I 17R	2
1918	I 14		1960	II 8	2
1919	I 16		1961	II 2P	1
1920	I 20	2	1962	I 14	1
1921	I 18	1	1963	I 13	1
1922	I 5	2	1964	I 14	q-f
1923	I 4	3	1965	I 16	1
1924	I 15	s-f	1966	I 10	1
1925	I 16	3	1967	I 14	2
1926	I 8	3	1968	I 15	1
1927	I 6	s-f	1969	I 17R	1
1928	I 10	3	1970	II 1P	q-f
1929	I 11	3	1971	I 7	3
1930	I 7	q-f	1972	I 14	3
1931	I 14	3	1973	I 14	4
1932	I 18	1	1974	I 18R	3
1933	I 11	2	1975	II 1	4
1934	I 10	3	1976	I 8	4
1935	I 20R	1	1977	I 14R	3
1936	II 1P	s-f	1978	II 5	1

FORFAR ATHLETIC

Founded: 1884
Address: Station Park, Forfar, Angus
Telephone: Forfar 3576/2817
Ground capacity: 11,800 (850 seated)
Record attendance: 10,800 v Rangers, Scottish Cup 2nd round, 7.2.70
Record victory: 9-1 v Stenhousemuir, Division II, 1968-69
Record defeat: 2-10 v Dundee, Division II, 1938-39
Most League points: 47, Division II, 1968-69
Most League goals: 90, Division II, 1931-32
League scoring record: 45, Davie Kilgour, Division II, 1929-30

THE FORFAR RECORD

Year	Division & place	Cup round reached	Year	Division & place	Cup round reached
1922	II 14	1	1955	II 10	5
1923	II 15	1	1956	II 15	5
1924	II 14	2	1957	II 16	4
1925	II 20	1	1958	II 12	2
1926	*	2	1959	II 12	1
1927	II 9	2	1960	II 16	2
1928	II 5	2	1961	II 18	3
1929	II 7	1	1962	II 16	1
1930	II 8	2	1963	II 18	1
1931	II 12	1	1964	II 18	3
1932	II 6	1	1965	II 17	1
1933	II 14	1	1966	II 19	p
1934	II 11	2	1967	II 16	p
1935	II 11	1	1968	II 7	1
1936	II 13	1	1969	II 6	p
1937	II 12	1	1970	II 18	2
1938	II 15	2	1971	II 15	3
1939	II 15	1	1972	II 17	3
1947	*	1	1973	II 16	2
1948	*	1	1974	II 18	3
1949	*	1	1975	II 20	2
1950	II 10	1	1976	II 12	3
1951	II 14	1	1977	II 14	2
1952	II 12	1	1978	II 6	2
1953	II 15	2			
1954	II 12	2	* – Competed in Division 'C'		

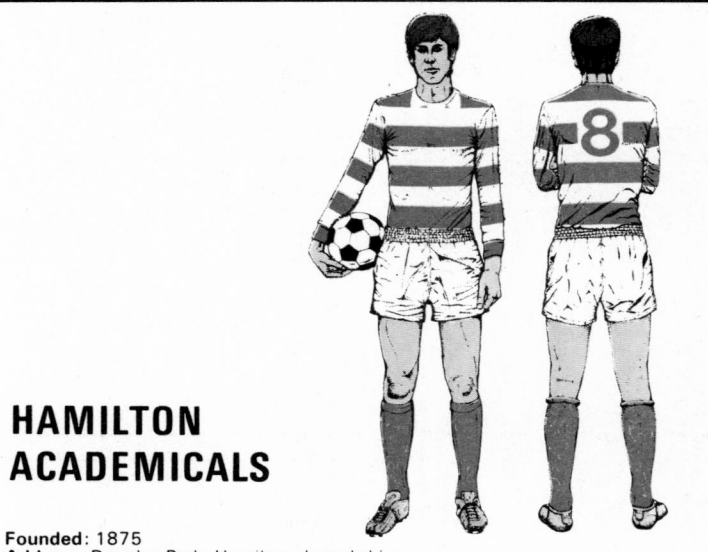

HAMILTON ACADEMICALS

Founded: 1875
Address: Douglas Park, Hamilton, Lanarkshire
Telephone: Hamilton 23108
Ground capacity: 24,000
Playing area: 110 by 72 yards
Record attendance: 28,281 v Heart of Midlothian, Scottish Cup 3rd round, 3.3.37
Record victory: 10-2 v Cowdenbeath, Division I, 1932-33
Record defeat: 1-11 v Hibernian, Division I, 6.11.65
Most League points: 55, Division II, 1973-74
Most League goals: 92, Division I, 1932-33
League scoring record: 34, David Wilson, Division I, 1936-37
Record League aggregate: 246, David Wilson, 1928-1939
Most League appearances: *Not available*
Most capped player: 2, Jimmy King, Scotland

Runners-up	Year	Opponents	Score	Scorer
	1911	Celtic	0-0	
			0-2	
	1935	Rangers	1-2	Harrison

THE HAMILTON RECORD

Year	Division & place	Cup round reached	Year	Division & place	Cup round reached
1899	II 5	p	1934	I 11	2
1900	II 7	1	1935	I 4	Final
1901	II 9	p	1936	I 6	1
1902	II 5	p	1937	I 8	q-f
1903	II 6	2	1938	I 13	3
1904	II 1	p	1939	I 7	2
1905	II 3	p	1947	I 16R	1
1906	II 4P	2	1948	II 3	1
1907	I 16	p	1949	II 10	1
1908	I 11	1	1950	II 6	1
1909	I 16	1	1951	II 7	2
1910	I 15	p	1952	II 9	2
1911	I 16	Final	1953	II 2P	3
1912	I 12	1	1954	I 16R	q-f
1913	I 10	2	1955	II 3	q-f
1914	I 18	2	1956	II 11	5
1915	I 7		1957	II 11	6
1916	I 7		1958	II 10	1
1917	I 11		1959	II 7	3
1918	I 12		1960	II 4	1
1919	I 14		1961	II 6	3
1920	I 21	1	1962	II 13	2
1921	I 15	3	1963	II 4	3
1922	I 18	4	1964	II 13	2
1923	I 18	3	1965	II 2P	1
1924	I 12	3	1966	I 18R	1
1925	I 13	s-f	1967	II 4	q-f
1926	I 12	2	1968	II 11	1
1927	I 15	3	1969	II 15	p
1928	I 18	2	1970	II 19	1
1929	I 12	2	1971	II 18	2
1930	I 13	s-f	1972	II 19	3
1931	I 10	2	1973	II 8	4
1932	I 10	s-f	1974	II 3	1
1933	I 8	1	1975	II 3	4
			1976	I 9	3
			1977	I 10	3
			1978	I 7	3

Year			Year		
1888	4		1930	I 10	s-f
1889	4		1931	I 5	2
1890	5		1932	I 8	3
1891	I 6	Winners	1933	I 3	s-f
1892	I 3	3	1934	I 6	3
1893	I 5	3	1935	I 3	s-f
1894	I 2	1	1936	I 5	1
1895	I 1C	s-f	1937	I 5	3
1896	I 4	Winners	1938	I 2	1
1897	I 1C	2	1939	I 4	3
1898	I 4	3	1947	I 4	q-f
1899	I 2	1	1948	I 9	2
1900	I 4	s-f	1949	I 8	q-f
1901	I 10	Winners	1950	I 4	2
1902	I 3	3	1951	I 4	s-f
1903	I 4	Final	1952	I 4	s-f
1904	I 2	1	1953	I 2	q-f
1905	I 8	2	1954	I 4	q-f
1906	I 2	Winners	1955	I 4	q-f
1907	I 9	Final	1956	I 3	Winners
1908	I 12	3	1957	I 2	5
1909	I 12	2	1958	I 1C	3
1910	I 12	3	1959	I 2	2
1911	I 14	1	1960	I 1C	2
1912	I 4	s-f	1961	I 8	q-f
1913	I 3	s-f	1962	I 6	3
1914	I 3	2	1963	I 5	2
1915	I 2		1964	I 4	3
1916	I 6		1965	I 2	q-f
1917	I 14		1966	I 7	q-f
1918	I 10		1967	I 11	1
1919	I 6		1968	I 12	Final
1920	I 15	3	1969	I 8	2
1921	I 3	s-f	1970	I 4	2
1922	I 19	3	1971	I 11	4
1923	I 12	2	1972	I 6	q-f
1924	I 9	4	1973	I 10	3
1925	I 10	2	1974	I 6	s-f
1926	I 3	3	1975	I 4	q-f
1927	I 13	1	1976	P 5	Final
1928	I 4	3	1977	P 9R	s-f
1929	I 4	1	1978	I 2P	4

HEART OF MIDLOTHIAN

Founded: 1874
Address: Tynecastle Park, Gorgie Road, Edinburgh 11
Telephone: (031) 337 6132
Ground capacity: 49,000 (4,000 seated)
Record attendance: 53,496 v Rangers, Scottish Cup 2nd round, 13.2.32
Record victory: 15-0 v King's Park, Scottish Cup 2nd round, 13.2.37
Record defeat: 0-7 v Hibernian, 1.1.73
Most League points: 62, Division I, 1957-58
Most League goals: 132, Division I, 1957-58
League scoring record: 44, Barney Battles, Division I, 1930-31
Record League aggregate: 206, Jimmy Wardhaugh, 1946-1959
Most capped player: 29, Bobby Walker, Scotland

Scottish Cup

	Year	Opponents	Score	Scorers
Winners	1891	Dumbarton	1-0	Mason
	1896	Hibernian	3-1	Baird (pen), King, Michael
	1901	Celtic	4-3	Walker (R), Bell 2, Thomson
	1906	Third Lanark	1-0	Wilson
	1956	Celtic	3-1	Crawford 2, Conn
Runners-up	1903	Rangers	1-1	Walker (R)
			0-0	
			0-2	
	1907	Celtic	0-3	
	1968	Dunfermline Athletic	1-3	Lunn og
	1976	Rangers	1-3	Shaw

Scottish League Cup

	Year	Opponents	Score	Scorers
Winners	1955	Motherwell	4-2	Bauld 3, Wardhaugh
	1959	Partick Thistle	5-1	Bauld 2, Murray 2, Hamilton
	1960	Third Lanark	2-1	Hamilton, Young
	1963	Kilmarnock	1-0	Davidson
Runners-up	1962	Rangers	1-1	Cumming
			1-3	Davidson

THE HEARTS RECORD

Year	Division & place	Cup round reached	Year		
1876		2	1882		1
1877		1	1883		3
1878		1	1884		3
1879		4	1885		2
1880		3	1886		2
1881		5	1887		3

HIBERNIAN

Founded: 1875
Address: Easter Road, Edinburgh
Telephone: (031) 661 2159
Ground capacity: 50,000
Playing area: 112 by 74 yards
Record attendance: 65,850 v Hearts, Division I, 2.1.1950
Record victory: 15-1 v Peebles Rovers, Scottish Cup 2nd round, 11.2.61
Record defeat: 2-9 v Morton, Division I, 1918-19
Most League points: 54, Division II, 1932-33
Most League goals: 106, Division I, 1959-60
League scoring record: 42, Joe Baker, Division I, 1959-60
Record League aggregate: 185, Lawrie Reilly, 1946-58
Most League appearances: 348, Eddie Turnbull, 1946-59
Most capped player: 39, Lawrie Reilly, Scotland

Scottish Cup

	Year	Opponents	Score	Scorers
Winners	1887	Dumbarton	2-1	Not known
	1902	Celtic	1-0	McGeachan
Runners-up	1896	Hearts	1-3	O'Neill
	1914	Celtic	0-0	
			1-4	Smith
	1923	Celtic	0-1	
	1924	Airdrieonians	0-2	
	1947	Aberdeen	1-2	Cuthbertson
	1958	Clyde	0-1	
	1972	Celtic	1-6	Gordon

Scottish League Cup

	Year	Opponents	Score	Scorers
Winners	1973	Celtic	2-1	Stanton, O'Rourke
Runners-up	1951	Motherwell	0-3	
	1969	Celtic	2-6	O'Rourke, Stevenson
	1975	Celtic	3-6	Harper 3

THE HIBERNIAN RECORD

Year	Division & place	Cup round reached	Year	Division & place	Cup round reached
1894	II 1	p	1933	II 1P	q-f
1895	II 1P	2	1934	I 16	3
1896	I 3	Final	1935	I 11	3
1897	I 2	2	1936	I 17	2
1898	I 3	q-f	1937	I 17	2
1899	I 4	2	1938	I 10	1
1900	I 3	2	1939	I 13	s-f
1901	I 3	s-f	1947	I 2	Final
1902	I 6	Winners	1948	I 1C	s-f
1903	I 1C	q-f	1949	I 3	q-f
1904	I 10	2	1950	I 2	1
1905	I 5	1	1951	I 1C	s-f
1906	I 11	q-f	1952	I 1C	1
1907	I 12	s-f	1953	I 2	q-f
1908	I 5	q-f	1954	I 5	3
1909	I 6	1	1955	I 5	5
1910	I 8	s-1	1956	I 4	5
1911	I 9	1	1957	I 9	5
1912	I 13	1	1958	I 9	Final
1913	I 6	3	1959	I 10	q-f
1914	I 13	Final	1960	I 7	q-f
1915	I 11		1961	I 7	q-f
1916	I 19		1962	I 8	1
1917	I 17		1963	I 16	3
1918	I 16		1964	I 10	1
1919	I 18		1965	I 4	s-f
1920	I 18	2	1966	I 6	2
1921	I 13	1	1967	I 5	q-f
1922	I 7	2	1968	I 3	2
1923	I 8	Final	1969	I 12	1
1924	I 7	Final	1970	I 3	1
1925	I 3	1	1971	I 12	s-f
1926	I 16	2	1972	I 4	Final
1927	I 9	1	1973	I 3	4
1928	I 12	s-f	1974	I 2	q-f
1929	I 14	1	1975	I 2	3
1930	I 17	3	1976	P 3	q-f
1931	I 19R	3	1977	P 6	4
1932	II 7	1	1978	P 4	4

THE KILMARNOCK RECORD

Year	Division & place	Cup round reached	Year	Division & place	Cup round reached
1896	II 4	1	1934	I 7	2
1897	II 3	s-f	1935	I 9	2
1898	II 1	Final	1936	I 8	2
1899	II 1P	q-f	1937	I 11	1
1900	I 5	q-f	1938	I 18	Final
1901	I 5	2	1939	I 10	2
1902	I 7	3	1947	I 15R	1
1903	I 9	2	1948	II 6	1
1904	I 14	q-f	1949	II 11	1
1905	I 9	1	1950	II 7	1
1906	I 14	2	1951	II 12	1
1907	I 17	2	1952	I 5	2
1908	I 14	s-f	1953	II 4	2
1909	I 10	1	1954	II 2P	2
1910	I 11	1	1955	I 10	6
1911	I 10	1	1956	I 8	6
1912	I 16	2	1957	I 3	Final
1913	I 11	3	1958	I 5	3
1914	I 12	3	1959	I 8	q-f
1915	I 12		1960	I 2	Final
1916	I 10		1961	I 2	2
1917	I 6		1962	I 5	q-f
1918	I 3		1963	I 2	2
1919	I 9		1964	I 2	s-f
1920	I 9	Winners	1965	I 1C	q-f
1921	I 12	2	1966	I 3	q-f
1922	I 17	2	1967	I 7	1
1923	I 15	2	1968	I 7	1
1924	I 16	2	1969	I 4	q-f
1925	I 12	q-f	1970	I 7	s-f
1926	I 9	1	1971	I 13	q-f
1927	I 16	2	1972	I 11	s-f
1928	I 8	4	1973	I 17R	4
1929	I 10	Winners	1974	II 2P	3
1930	I 8	2	1975	II 12	3
1931	I 11	s-f	1976	I 2P	q-f
1932	I 9	Final	1977	P 10R	3
1933	I 14	q-f	1978	I 6	q-f

KILMARNOCK

Founded: 1869
Address: Rugby Park, Kilmarnock
Telephone: Kilmarnock 25184
Ground capacity: 34,500 (4,200 seated)
Playing area: 115 by 75 yards
Record attendance: 34,246 v Rangers, League Cup, August 1963
Record victory: 11-1 v Paisley Academicals, Scottish Cup 1st round, 18.1.30
Record defeat: 0-8 v Hibernian, Division I, 1925-26
0-8 v Rangers, Division I, 1936-37
Most League points: 50, Division I, 1959-60, 1960-61 & 1964-65
Most League goals: 92, Division I, 1962-63
League scoring record: 35, Peerie Cunningham, Division I, 1927-28
Record League aggregate: 102, Jimmy Maxwell, 1931-1934
Most League appearances: 424, Frank Beattie, 1954-1971
Most capped player: 9, Joe Nibloe, Scotland

Scottish Cup	Year	Opponents	Score	Scorers
Winners	1920	Albion Rovers	3-2	Culley, J R Smith, Shortt
	1929	Rangers	2-0	Aitken, Williamson
Runners-up	1898	Rangers	0-2	
	1932	Rangers	1-1	Maxwell
			0-3	
	1938	East Fife	1-1	McAvoy
			2-4	Thomson (pen), McGrogan
	1957	Falkirk	1-1	Curlett
			1-2	Curlett
	1960	Rangers	0-2	
Scottish League Cup				
Runners-up	1953	Dundee	0-2	
	1961	Rangers	0-2	
	1963	Hearts	0-1	

MEADOWBANK THISTLE

Founded: 1974 (formerly Ferranti Thistle)
Address: Meadowbank Stadium, Edinburgh
Telephone: 031 337 2442
Ground capacity: 16,000
Playing area: 105 by 75 yards
Record attendance: 4,000 v Albion Rovers, Scottish League Cup, 9.8.74
Record victory: 4-1 v Forfar, Scottish League Cup, 23.8.75
4-1 v Albion Rovers, Division II, 17.1.76
Record defeat: 0-8 v Hamilton Academicals, Division II, 14.12.74
Most League points: 23, Division II, 1974-75
Most League goals: 26, Division II, 1974-75

THE MEADOWBANK RECORD

Year	Division & place	Cup round reached	Year	Division & place	Cup round reached
1975	II 18		1977	II 11	2
1976	II 14	2	1978	II 13	4

MONTROSE

Founded: 1879
Address: Links Park, Montrose
Telephone: Montrose 3200
Ground capacity: 9,000
Playing area: 114 by 66 yards
Record attendance: 8,983 v Dundee, Scottish Cup 3rd round, 17.3.73
Record victory: 12-0 v Vale of Leithen, Scottish Cup 2nd round, 4.1.75
Record defeat: 0-13 v Aberdeen Reserves, Division C, 17.3.51
Most League points: 53, Division II, 1974-75
Most League goals: 78, Division II, 1970-71
Most capped player: 2 (6 in all), A Keillor, Scotland

THE MONTROSE RECORD

	Division & place	Cup round reached				
1930	II 11	q-f	1959	II	19	2
1931	II 8	3	1960	II	7	2
1932	II 17	1	1961	II	7	2
1933	II 17	2	1962	II	5	2
1934	II 16	1	1963	II	15	2
1935	II 17	1	1964	II	5	1
1936	II 12	1	1965	II	16	1
1937	II 13	1	1966	II	9	1
1938	II 16	1	1967	II	12	p
1939	II 14	2	1968	II	13	p
1947	※	p	1969	II	10	2
1948	※	q-f	1970	II	8	1
1949	※	1	1971	II	6	2
1950	※	1	1972	II	10	3
1951	※	1	1973	II	6	q-f
1952	※	1	1974	II	8	3
1953	※	3	1975	II	3	3
1954	※	1	1976	I	3	q-f
1955	※	4	1977	I	5	3
1956	II 19	4	1978	I	11	3
1957	II 17	5				
1958	II 14	2				

※—Montrose compete in C Division

1934	II 5	1	1961	II	19	2
1935	II 6	2	1962	II	3	2
1936	II 3	q-f	1963	II	3	1
1937	II 2P	s-f	1964	II	1P	2
1938	I 20R	3	1965	I	10	2
1939	II 12E	1	1966	I	17R	1
1947	I 6	3	1967	II	1P	1
1948	I 14	Final	1968	I	6	s-f
1949	I 15R	3	1969	I	10	s-f
1950	II 1P	2	1970	I	10	2
1951	I 12	2	1971	I	8	4
1952	I 15R	3	1972	I	13	4
1953	II 6	3	1973	I	12	3
1954	II 5	3	1974	I	14	4
1955	II 9	5	1975	I	17	3
1956	II 9	5	1976	I	11	3
1957	II 4	5	1977	I	4	3
1958	II 13	2	1978	I	1P	q-f
1959	II 11	3				
1960	II 14	1				

E—elected to First Division

MORTON

Founded: 1874
Address: Cappielow Park, Greenock
Telephone: Greenock 23571
Ground capacity: 25,000 (2,900 seated)
Playing area: 110 by 71 yards
Record attendance: 23,500 v Celtic, Division I, 1921
and v Rangers, Scottish Cup 3rd round, 21.2.53
Record victory: 11-0 v Carfin Shamrock, Scottish Cup, 1886
Record defeat: 2-8 v Rangers, Division I, 15.3.27
Most League points: 69, Division II, 1966-67
Most League goals: 135, Division II, 1963-64
League scoring record: 51, Allan McGraw, Division II, 1963-64
Most capped player: 25, Jimmy Cowan, Scotland

Scottish Cup	Year	Opponents	Score	Scorers
Winners	1922	Rangers	1-0	Gourlay
Runners-up	1948	Rangers	1-1	Whyte
		Replay	0-1	
Scottish League Cup				
Runners-up	1964	Rangers	0-5	

THE MORTON RECORD

	Division & place	Cup round reached				
1894	II 8	p	1914	I	4	2
1895	II 5	p	1915	I	4	
1896	II 9	1	1916	I	3	
1897	II 5	s-f	1917	I	2	
1898	II 3	2	1918	I	4	
1899	II 7	2	1919	I	3	
1900	II 2E	1	1920	I	6	s-f
1901	I 4	q-f	1921	I	9	2
1902	I 10	1	1922	I	12	Winners
1903	I 12	1	1923	I	14	1
1904	I 11	s-f	1924	I	11	1
1905	I 13	2	1925	I	14	1
1906	I 10	2	1926	I	15	q-f
1907	I 13	2	1927	I	19R	1
1908	I 13	2	1928	II	18	2
1909	I 17	1	1929	II	2P	1
1910	I 17	2	1930	I	18	1
1911	I 13	2	1931	I	16	3
1912	I 6	q-f	1932	I	15	1
1913	I 13	2	1933	I	19R	1

MOTHERWELL

Founded: 1885*
Address: Fir Park, Motherwell, Lanarkshire
Telephone: Motherwell 63229
Ground capacity: 31,000
Playing area: 110 by 72 yards
Record attendance: 35,632 v Rangers, Scottish Cup 4th round replay, 12.3.52
Record victory: 12-1 v Dundee United, Division II, 1953-54
Record defeat: 0-10 v St Mirren, Scottish Southern League, 1945-46
Most League points: 66, Division I, 1931-32
Most League goals: 119, Division I, 1931-32
League scoring record: 52, Bill McFadyen, Division I, 1931-32
Record League aggregate: 283, Hugh Ferguson, 1916-1925
Most League appearances: 626, Bob Ferrier, 1918-1937
Most capped player: 12, George Stevenson, Scotland
※As Wee Alpha. Changed name to Motherwell in 1886.

Scottish Cup	Year	Opponents	Score	Scorers
Winners	1952	Dundee	4-0	Watson, Redpath, Humphries, Kelly
Runners-up	1931	Celtic	2-2	Stevenson, McMenemy
			2-4	Murdoch, Stevenson
	1933	Celtic	0-1	
	1939	Clyde	0-4	
	1951	Celtic	0-1	
League Cup				
Winners	1951	Hibernian	3-0	Kelly, Forrest, Watters
Runners-up	1955	Hearts	2-4	Redpath (pen), Bain

THE MOTHERWELL RECORD

	Division & place	Cup round reached				
1904	J 13	2	1915	I	18	
1905	I 14	2	1916	II	14	
1906	I 9	1	1917	I	8	
1907	I 10	1	1918	I	5	
1908	I 10	2	1919	I	5	
1909	I 14	2	1920	I	3	1
1910	I 10	3	1921	I	5	q-f
1911	I 17	3	1922	I	13	3
1912	I 14	3	1923	I	13	s-f
1913	I 7	2	1924	I	10	3
1914	I 17	4	1925	I	18	3

133

Year	Div & place		Cup round	Year	Div & place		Cup round
1926	I	5	1	1956	I	10	5
1927	I	2	1	1957	I	7	6
1928	I	3	q-f	1958	I	8	s-f
1929	I	3	q-f	1959	I	3	3
1930	I	2	3	1960	I	5	3
1931	I	3	Final	1961	I	5	q-f
1932	I	1C	q-f	1962	I	9	s-f
1933	I	2	Final	1963	I	10	2
1934	I	2	s-f	1964	I	11	q-f
1935	I	7	q-f	1965	I	14	s-f
1936	I	4	q-f	1966	I	13	2
1937	I	4	q-f	1967	I	10	1
1938	I	5	q-f	1968	I	17R	1
1939	I	12	Final	1969	II	1P	1
1947	I	8	s-f	1970	I	11	q-f
1948	I	8	3	1971	I	9	3
1949	I	12	2	1972	I	10	q-f
1950	I	10	1	1973	I	8	4
1951	I	9	Final	1974	I	9	q-f
1952	I	7	Winners	1975	I	10	s-f
1953	I	15R	3	1976	P	4	s-f
1954	II	1P	s-f	1977	P	7	q-f
1955	I	15	q-f	1978	P	6	4

Year	Div & place		Cup round	Year	Div & place		Cup round
1938	I	7	3	1962	I	7	2
1939	I	11	1	1963	I	3	3
1947	I	5	1	1964	I	7	3
1948	I	3	3	1965	I	11	2
1949	I	11	q-f	1966	I	12	1
1950	I	7	s-f	1967	I	12	2
1951	I	6	1	1968	I	10	q-f
1952	I	6	1	1969	I	14	1
1953	I	9	2	1970	I	18R	1
1954	I	3	q-f	1971	II	1P	3
1955	I	9	5	1972	I	7	3
1956	I	9	q-f	1973	I	13	q-f
1957	I	8	5	1974	I	11	4
1958	I	6	2	1975	I	13	3
1959	I	9	3	1976	I	1P	4
1960	I	10	q-f	1977	P	5	3
1961	I	11	3	1978	P	7	s-f

PARTICK THISTLE

Founded: 1876
Address: Firhill Park, Glasgow
Telephone: 041-946 2673
Ground capacity: 36,000 (3,500 seated)
Playing area: 110 by 71 yards
Record attendance: 49,838 v Rangers, Division I, 18.2.22
Record victory: 16-0 v Royal Albert, Scottish Cup 1st round, 17.1.31
Record defeat: 1-10 v Dunfermline Athletic, Division I, 1958-59
Most League points: 56, Division II, 1970-71
Most League goals: 91, Division I, 1928-29
League scoring record: 41, Alec Hair, Division I, 1926-27
Most capped player: 9, John McKenzie, Scotland

Scottish Cup	Year	Opponents	Score	Scorers
Winners	1921	Rangers	1-0	Blair
Runners-up	1930	Rangers	0-0	
		Replay	1-2	Torbet
Scottish League Cup				
Winners	1972	Celtic	4-1	Rae, Lawrie, McQuade, Bone
Runners-up	1954	East Fife	2-3	Walker, McKenzie
	1957	Celtic	0-0	
		Replay	0-3	
	1959	Hearts	1-5	Smith

THE PARTICK RECORD

Year	Div & place		Cup round reached	Year	Div & place		Cup round reached
1894	II	5	p	1916	I	5	
1895	II	7	p	1917	I	9	
1896	II	6	p	1918	I	6	
1897	II	1P	1	1919	I	4	
1898	I	8	1	1920	I	13	3
1899	I	9R	q-f	1921	I	6	Winners
1900	II	1P	q-f	1922	I	6	s-f
1901	I	11R	1	1923	I	11	1
1902	II	2P	1	1924	I	8	q-f
1903	I	8	q-f	1925	I	7	3
1904	I	7	1	1926	I	14	3
1905	I	6	q-f	1927	I	11	s-f
1906	I	5	2	1928	I	6	q-f
1907	I	14	1	1929	I	6	2
1908	I	15	2	1930	I	6	Final
1909	I	18	2	1931	I	4	2
1910	I	16	1	1932	I	6	q-f
1911	I	4	2	1933	I	10	3
1912	I	5	1	1934	I	13	2
1913	I	17	3	1935	I	13	2
1914	I	15	q-f	1936	I	9	1
1915	I	8		1937	I	13	3

QUEEN OF THE SOUTH

Founded: 1919
Address: Palmerston Park, Dumfries
Telephone: Dumfries 4853
Ground capacity: 20,000
Playing area: 111 by 73 yards
Record attendance: 25,000 v Hearts, Scottish Cup 3rd round, 23.2.52
Record victory: 11-1 v Stranraer, Scottish Cup 1st round, 16.1.32
Record defeat: 2-10 v Dundee, Division I, 1.12.62
Most League points: 53, Division II, 1961-62; Division II, 1974-75
Most League goals: 94, Division II, 1959-60
League scoring record: 33, Jimmy Gray, Division II, 1927-28
Most capped player: 3, Billy Houliston, Scotland

THE QUEEN OF THE SOUTH RECORD

Year	Div & place		Cup round reached	Year	Div & place		Cup round reached
1926	II	17	1	1956	I	6	q-f
1927	II	11	1	1957	I	16	5
1928	II	12	1	1958	I	15	q-f
1929	II	9	2	1959	I	18R	1
1930	II	7	2	1960	II	3	3
1931	II	5	1	1961	II	5	2
1932	II	9	2	1962	II	2P	2
1933	II	2P	1	1963	I	15	q-f
1934	I	4	q-f	1964	I	17R	2
1935	I	17	1	1965	II	3	1
1936	I	15	3	1966	II	3	2
1937	I	18	q-f	1967	II	9	1
1938	I	16	2	1968	II	6	2
1939	I	6	q-f	1969	II	5	1
1947	I	12	1	1970	II	3	1
1948	I	13	3	1971	II	11	3
1949	I	10	2	1972	II	7	3
1950	I	15R	s-f	1973	II	11	3
1951	II	1P	1	1974	II	4	4
1952	I	10	3	1975	II	2	4
1953	I	10	q-f	1976	I	10	q-f
1954	I	10	3	1977	I	9	q-f
1955	I	13	5	1978	I	12	4

1947	I	13	3	1965	II	4	2
1948	I	16R	3	1966	II	13	1
1949	II	5	1	1967	II	7	q-f
1950	II	9	1	1968	II	4	p
1951	II	6	2	1969	II	11	†
1952	II	15	2	1970	II	15	p
1953	II	3	2	1971	II	14	3
1954	II	10	1	1972	II	12	2
1955	II	4	4	1973	II	14	2
1956	II	1P	6	**1974**	II	14	3
1957	I	13	6	**1975**	II	16	4
1958	I	18R	3	**1976**	II	4	1
1959	II	18	2	**1977**	II	5	3
1960	II	11	3	**1978**	II	7	q-f
1961	II	15	1				
1962	II	12	1				
1963	II	14	3				
1964	II	7	2	(†) – progress in the FA Cup			

QUEEN'S PARK

Founded: 1867
Address: Hampden Park, Glasgow
Telephone: 041 632 1275 4090
Ground capacity: 88,000
Record attendance: 97,000 v Rangers, Scottish Cup 2nd round, 18.2.33
(*Ground record:* 149,547, Scotland v England, 17.4.37)
Record victory: 16-0 v St Peter's, Scottish Cup 1st round, 1885-86
Record defeat: 0-9 v Motherwell, Division I, 26.4.30
Most League points: 57, Division II, 1922-23
Most League goals: 100, Division I, 1928-29
League scoring record: 30, Willie Martin, Division I, 1937-38
Most capped player: 14, Watty Arnott, Scotland

Scottish Cup

	Year	Opponents	Score
Winners	1874	Clydesdale	2-0
	1875	Renton	3-0
	1876	Third Lanark	1-1
		Replay	2-0
	1880	Thornlibank	3-0
	1881	Dumbarton	3-1
	1882	Dumbarton	2-2
		Replay	4-1
	†1884	Vale of Leven	
	1886	Renton	3-1
	]1890	Vale of Leven	1-1
		Replay	2-1
	1893	Celtic	2-1
Runners-up	‡1892	Celtic	1-5
	1900	Celtic	3-4

After a protested game which Queen's Park won 2-1
†Queen's Park awarded the cup after Vale of Leven failed to appear
‡After protested game which Celtic won 1-0

FA Cup

	Year	Opponents	Score	Scorer
Runners up	1884	Blackburn Rovers	1-2	Christie
	1885	Blackburn Rovers	0-2	

THE QUEEN'S PARK RECORD

	Division & place	Cup round reached				
1872		(s-f†)	1906	I	16	2
1873		(s-f†)	1907	I	15	s-f
1874		Winners	1908	I	16	q-f
1875		Winners	1909	I	15	q-f
1876		Winners	1910	I	14	q-f
1877		q-f (3†)	1911	I	18	2
1878		3 (1†)	1912	I	17	p
1879		q-f	1913	I	18	3
1880		Winners	1914	I	16	q-f
1881		Winners	1915	I	20	
1882		Winners	1916	I	18	
1883		q-f	1917	I	18	
1884		Winners (Final†)	1918	I	7	
1885		3 (Final†)	1919	I	8	
1886		Winners	1920	I	12	3
1887		s-f	1921	I	19	1
1888		s-f	1922		21R	2
1889		3	1923	II	1P	3
1890		Winners	1924	I	17	3
1891		q-f	1925	I	17	2
1892		Final	1926	I	13	2
1893		Winners	1927	I	12	2
1894		s-f	1928	I	16	s-f
1895		1	1929	I	5	2
1896		q-f	1930	I	15	1
1897		1	1931	I	13	2
1898		q-f	1932	I	16	2
1899		q-f	1933	I	9	2
1900		Final	1934	I	12	2
1901	I 8	2	1935	I	12	2
1902	I 8	q-f	1936	I	14	1
1903	I 10	1	1937	I	15	2
1904	I 8	1	1938	I	12	2
1905	I 12	1	1939	I	19	2

RAITH ROVERS

Founded: 1893
Address: Stark's Park, Pratt Street, Kirkcaldy, Fife
Telephone: Kirkcaldy 3514
Ground capacity: 28,000
Record attendance: 32,000 v Herts, Scottish Cup 2nd round, 7.2.53
Record victory: 10-1 v Coldstream, Scottish Cup 2nd round, 13.2.54
Record defeat: 2-11 v Morton, Division II, 1935-36
Most League points: 59, Division II, 1937-38
Most League goals: 142, Division II, 1937-38
League scoring record: 39, Norman Haywood, Division II, 1937-38
Most capped player: 6, Dave Morris, Scotland

Scottish Cup	Year	Opponents	Score
Runners-up	1913	Falkirk	0-2

Scottish League Cup			
Runners-up	1949	Rangers	0-2

THE RAITH ROVERS RECORD

	Division & place	Cup round reached				
1903	II 11	p	1930	II	5	1
1904	II 5	p	1931	II	4	1
1905	II 10	p	1932	II	3	2
1906	II 8	p	1933	II	6	1
1907	II 10	q-f	1934	II	8	1
1908	II 1	q-f	1935	II	13	2
1909	II 2	p	1936	II	17	1
1910	II 2P	p	1937	II	8	1
1911	I 15	p	1938	II	1P	q-f
1912	I 16	1	1939	I	20R	1
1913	I 16	Final	1947	II	6	3
1914	I 11	3	1948	II	4	3
1915	I 19		1949	II	1P	2
1916	I 20		1950	I	9	q-f
1917	I 19		1951	I	8	s-f
1918	*		1952	I	5	2
1919	*		1953	I	12	2
1920	I 19	3	1954	I	12	3
1921	I 16	1	1955	I	14	6
1922	I 3	1	1956	I	11	s-f
1923	I 9	q-f	1957	I	4	s-f
1924	I 4	3	1958	I	7	2
1925	I 9	3	1959	I	14	1
1926	I 19R	2	1960	I	11	1
1927	II 2P	2	1961	I	16	3
1928	I 17	2	1962	I	13	3
1929	I 20R	q-f	1963	I	18R	s-f

1964	II 10	1	
1965	II 13	p	
1966	II 5	p	
1967	II 2P	1	
1968	I 16	1	
1969	I 16	1	
1970	I 17R	1	
1971	II 8		
1972	II 11	5	
1973	II 3	3	
1974	II 5	3	
1975	II 13	3	
1976	II 2P	4	
1977	I 13R	2	
1978	II 2P	2	

*Raith Rovers did not compete

RANGERS

Founded: 1873
Address: Ibrox Stadium, Glasgow SW1
Telephone: (041) 427 0159
Ground capacity: 71,000
Playing area: 115 by 75 yards
Record attendance: 118,567 v Celtic, Division I, 2.1.39
Record victory: 14-2 v Blairgowrie, Scottish Cup 1st round, 20.1.34
Record defeat: 2-10 v Airdrie, 1886
Most League points: 76, Division I, 1920-21
Most League goals: 118, Division I, 1931-32 & 1933-34
League scoring record: 44, Sam English, Division I, 1931-32
Record League aggregate: 233, Bob McPhail, 1927-1939
Most League appearances: 492, Davie Meiklejohn, 1920-1936
Most capped player: 53, George Young, Scotland

Scottish Cup

	Year	Opponents	Score	Scorers
Winners	1894	Celtic	3-1	McCreadie, Barker, McPherson
	1897	Dumbarton	5-1	Miller, Hyslop, McPherson 2, Smith
	1898	Kilmarnock	2-0	Smith, Hamilton
	1903	Heart of Midlothian	1-1	
			0-0	
			2-0	Mackie, Campbell
	1928	Celtic	4-0	Meiklejohn (pen), McPhail, Archibald 2
	1930	Partick Thistle	0-0	
			2-1	Marshall, Craig
	1932	Kilmarnock	1-1	McPhail
			3-0	Fleming, McPhail, English
	1934	St Mirren	5-0	Nicholson 2, McPhail, Smith, Main
	1935	Hamilton	2-1	Smith 2
	1936	Third Lanark	1-0	McPhail
	1948	Morton	1-1	Gillick
			1-0	Williamson
	1949	Clyde	4-1	Young (2 pens), Williamson, Duncanson
	1950	East Fife	3-0	Findlay, Thornton 2
	1953	Aberdeen	1-1	Prentice
			1-0	Simpson
	1960	Kilmarnock	2-0	Millar 2
	1962	St Mirren	2-0	Brand, Wilson
	1963	Celtic	1-1	Brand
			3-0	Wilson, Brand 2,
	1964	Dundee	3-1	Millar 2, Brand
	1966	Celtic	0-0	
			1-0	Johansen
	1973	Celtic	3-2	Parlane, Conn, Forsyth
	1976	Heart of Midlothian	3-1	Johnstone 2, MacDonald
	1978	Aberdeen	2-1	MacDonald, Johnstone

	Year	Opponents	Score	Scorers
Runners-up	1877	Vale of Leven	0-0	
			1-1	
			2-3	Campbell, McNeil
	1879	Vale of Leven	1-1	Struthers
	1899	Celtic	0-2	
	1904	Celtic	2-3	Speedie 2
	1905	Third Lanark	0-0	
			1-3	
	1909	Celtic	2-2	Gilchrist, Bennett
			1-1	Gordon
	1921	Partick Thistle	0-1	
	1922	Morton	0-1	
	1929	Kilmarnock	0-2	
	1969	Celtic	0-4	
	1971	Celtic	1-1	Johnstone
			1-2	og
	1977	Celtic	0-1	

Scottish League Cup

	Year	Opponents	Score	Scorers
Winners	1947	Aberdeen	4-0	Duncanson 2, Williamson, Gillick
	1949	Raith Rovers	2-0	Gillick, Paton
	1961	Kilmarnock	2-0	Brand, Scott
	1962	Heart of Midlothian	1-1	Millar
			3-1	Millar, Brand, McMillan
	1964	Morton	5-0	Forrest 4, Willoughby
	1965	Celtic	2-1	Forrest 2
	1971	Celtic	1-0	Johnstone
	1976	Celtic	1-0	MacDonald
	1978	Celtic	2-1	Cooper, Smith
Runners-up	1952	Dundee	2-3	Findlay, Thornton
	1958	Celtic	1-7	Simpson
	1966	Celtic	1-2	og
	1967	Celtic	0-1	

THE RANGERS RECORD

	Division & place	Cup round reached		Division & place	Cup round reached
1875	2		1924	I 1C	3
1876	2		1925	I 1C	s-f
1877	Final		1926	I 6	s-f
1878	4		1927	I 1C	q-f
1879	Final		1928	I 1C	Winners
1880	1		1929	I 1C	Final
1881	q-f		1930	I 1C	Winners
1882	q-f		1931	I 1C	2
1883	2		1932	I 2	Winners
1884	s-f		1933	I 1C	3
1885	q-f		1934	I 1C	Winners
1886	1		1935	I 1C	Winners
1887	3		1936	I 2	Winners
1888	2		1937	I 1C	1
1889	2		1938	I 3	s-f
1890	3		1939	I 1C	3
1891	I 1	1	1947	I 1C	3
1892	I 4	4	1948	I 2	Winners
1893	I 2	3	1949	I 1C	Winners
1894	I 4	Winners	1950	I 1C	Winners
1895	I 3	1	1951	I 2	2
1896	I 2	3	1952	I 2	q-f
1897	I 3	Winners	1953	I 1C	Winners
1898	I 2	Winners	1954	I 4	s-f
1899	I 1C	Final	1955	I 3	6
1900	I 1C	s-f	1956	I 1C	q-f
1901	I 1C	1	1957	I 1C	6
1902	I 1C	s-f	1958	I 2	s-f
1903	I 3	Winners	1959	I 1C	3
1904	I 4	Final	1960	I 3	Winners
1905	I 2	Final	1961	I 1C	3
1906	I 4	3	1962	I 2	Winners
1907	I 3	3	1963	I 1C	Winners
1908	I 3	2	1964	I 1C	Winners
1909	I 4	Final	1965	I 5	q-f
1910	I 3	2	1966	I 2	Winners
1911	I 1C	3	1967	I 2	1
1912	I 1C	2	1968	I 2	q-f
1913	I 1C	3	1969	I 2	Final
1914	I 2	3	1970	I 2	q-f
1915	I 3		1971	I 4	Final
1916	I 2		1972	I 3	s-f
1917	I 3		1973	I 2	Winners
1918	I 1C		1974	I 3	4
1919	I 2		1975	I 1C	3
1920	I 1C	s-f	1976	P 1C	Winners
1921	I 1C	Final	1977	P 2	Final
1922	I 2	Final	1978	P 1C	Winners
1923	I 1C	2			

ST JOHNSTONE

Founded: 1884
Address: Muirton Park, Perth
Telephone: Perth 26961
Ground capacity: 28,000 (2,500 seated)
Playing area: 115 by 74 yards
Record attendance: 29,972 v Dundee, Scottish Cup 2nd round, 10.2.52
Record victory: 8-1 v Partick Thistle, Scottish League Cup, 16.8.69
Record defeat: 1-10 v Third Lanark, Scottish Cup 1st round, 24.1.03
Most League points: 56, Division II, 1923-24
Most League goals: 102, Division II, 1931-32
League scoring record: 36, Jimmy Benson, Division II, 1931-32
Most capped player: 2, Alex McLaren, Scotland

Scottish League Cup

	Year	Opponents	Score
Runners up	1970	Celtic	0 1

THE ST JOHNSTONE RECORD

Year	Division & place	Cup round reached	Year	Division & place	Cup round reached
1912	II 5	1	1950	II 3	2
1913	II 11	3	1951	II 5	2
1914	II 5	1	1952	II 11	2
1915	II 8		1953	II 14	2
1916			1954	II 6	1
1917			1955	II 7	6
1918			1956	II 3	5
1919			1957	II 12	5
1920		2	1958	II 11	2
1921		p	1959	II 6	3
1922	II 13	1	1960	II 1P	1
1923	II 3	1	1961	I 15	1
1924	II 1P	2	1962	I 17R	2
1925	I 11	1	1963	II 1P	2
1926	I 18	3	1964	I 13	2
1927	I 14	1	1965	I 13	2
1928	I 11	1	1966	I 14	q·f
1929	I 9	2	1967	I 15	2
1930	I 20R	2	1968	I 14	s·f
1931	II 6	2	1969	I 6	q·f
1932	II 2P	2	1970	I 13	1
1933	I 5	3	1971	I 3	3
1934	I 9	s·f	1972	I 8	3
1935	I 5	q·f	1973	I 11	3
1936	I 7	3	**1974**	**I 12**	**4**
1937	I 12	2	**1975**	**I 9**	**4**
1938	I 8	2	**1976**	**P 10R**	**3**
1939	I 8	1	**1977**	**I 11**	**3**
1947	II 9	1	**1978**	**I 8**	**4**
1948	II 9	2			
1949	II 6	1			

ST MIRREN

Founded: 1876
Address: St Mirren Park, Love Street, Paisley, Renfrewshire
Telephone: 041 840 1337
Ground capacity: 53,000
Playing area: 112 by 75 yards
Record attendance: 47,428 v Celtic, Scottish Cup 4th round, 7.3.25
Record victory: 15-0 v Glasgow University, Scottish Cup 1st round, 30.1.60
Record defeat: 2-9 v Dundee, Division I, 29.2.64
Most League points: 62, Division II, 1967-68
Most League goals: 114, Division II, 1935-36
League scoring record: 45, Dunky Walker, Division I, 1921-22
Most capped player: 6, Tommy Jackson, Scotland

Scottish Cup

	Year	Opponents	Score	Scorers
Winners	1926	Celtic	2-0	McCrae, Harrison
	1959	Aberdeen	3-1	Bryceland, Miller, Baker
Runners-up	1908	Celtic	1-5	Cunningham
	1934	Rangers	0-5	
	1962	Rangers	0-2	

Scottish League Cup

	Year	Opponents	Score	Scorers
Runners-up	1956	Aberdeen	1-2	Holmes

THE ST MIRREN RECORD

Year	Division & place	Cup round reached	Year	Division & place	Cup round reached
1891	I 8	5	1932	I 5	1
1892	I 10	1	1933	I 7	2
1893	I 3	q·f	1934	I 17	Final
1894	I 6	2	1935	I 19R	3
1895	I 5	2	1936	II 2P	3
1896	I 8	2	1937	I 16	q·f
1897	I 6	2	1938	I 14	2
1898	I 6	2	1939	I 18	3
1899	I 5	2	1947	I 14	1
1900	I 8	1	1948	I 5	q·f
1901	I 9	s·f	1949	I 9	2
1902	I 5	s·f	1950	I 11	1
1903	I 6	1	1951	I 11	1
1904	I 6	q·f	1952	I 14	2
1905	I 10	q·f	1953	I, 6	2
1906	I 8	s·f	1954	I 11	1
1907	I 7	q·f	1955	I 6	5
1908	I 7	Final	1956	I 15	6
1909	I 7	q·f	1957	I 12	q·f
1910	I 13	2	1958	I 13	2
1911	I 12	1	1959	I 7	Winners
1912	I 18	1	1960	I 14	2
1913	I 12	q f	1961	I 14	s·f
1914	I 20	s f	1962	I 16	Final
1915	I 9		1963	I 12	q f
1916	I 13		1964	I 12	3
1917	I 7		1965	I 15	1
1918	I 11		1966	I 16	1
1919	I 11		1967	I 17R	2
1920	I 14	2	1968	II 1P	1
1921	I 22	1	1969	I 11	2
1922	I 8	q·f	1970	I 15	2
1923	I 6	2	1971	I 17R	4
1924	I 6	2	1972	II 4	4
1925	I 6	q·f	1973	II 5	
1926	I 4	Winners	**1974**	**II 11**	**3**
1927	I 10	2	**1975**	**II 6**	**2**
1928	I 5	3	**1976**	**I 6**	**3**
1929	I 8	s·f	**1977**	**I 1P**	**4**
1930	I 5	q·f	**1978**	**P 8**	**3**
1931	I 15	s·f			

STENHOUSEMUIR

Founded: 1884
Address: Ochilview Park, Stenhousemuir, Scotland
Telephone: Larbert 2992
Ground capacity: 12,000 (500 seated)
Record attendance: 13,000 v East Fife, Scottish Cup 4th round, 11.3.50
Record victory: 9-2 v Dundee United, Division II, 1936-37
Record defeat: 2-11 v Dunfermline Athletic, Division II, 1930-31
Most League points: 50, Division II, 1960-61
Most League goals: 99, Division II, 1960-61

THE STENHOUSEMUIR RECORD

	Division & place	Cup round reached		Division & place	Cup round reached
1922	II 10	1	1955	II 6	5
1923	II 14	1	1956	II 5	q-f
1924	II 4	2	1957	II 14	5
1925	II 11	1	1958	II 16	2
1926	II 5	2	1959	II 3	2
1927	II 10	1	1960	II 5	3
1928	II 16	2	1961	II 3	1
1929	II 18	2	1962	II 15	3
1930	II 17	1	1963	II 16	1
1931	II 17	1	1964	II 11	1
1932	II 4	1	1965	II 15	1
1933	II 4	q-f	1966	II 18	p
1934	II 4	1	1967	II 17	p
1935	II 5	1	1968	II 18	p
1936	II 11	2	1969	II 19	1
1937	II 10	1	1970	II 16	p
1938	II 8	2	1971	II 10	2
1939	II 8	1	1972	II 14	1
1947	II 7	1	1973	II 10	2
1948	II 14	1	1974	II 15	2
1949	II 12	q-f	1975	II 11	1
1950	II 12	q-f	1976	II 10	3
1951	II 15	1	1977	II 9	1
1952	II 13	1	1978	II 12	1
1953	II 12	1			
1954	II 4	1	p – preliminary round		

STIRLING ALBION

Founded: 1945
Address: Annfield Park, Stirling
Telephone: Stirling 3584
Ground capacity: 25,000 (900 seated)
Record attendance: 26,400 v Celtic, Scottish Cup, 4th round, 14.3.59
Record victory: 7-0 v Albion Rovers, Division II, 1947-48
        7-0 v Montrose, Division II, 1957-58
        7-0 v St Mirren, Division I, 1959-60
        7-0 v Arbroath, Division II, 1960-61
Record defeat: 0-9 v Dundee United, Division I, 30.12.67
Most League points: 59, Division II, 1964-65
Most League goals: 105, Division II, 1957-58
League scoring record: 22, Bobby Gilmour, Division I, 1958-59
Most capped player: None

THE STIRLING ALBION RECORD

	Division & place	Cup round reached		Division & place	Cup round reached
1947		p	1963	II 10	1
1948	II 8	2	1964	II 19	1
1949	II 2P	1	1965	II 1P	q-f
1950	I 16R	q-f	1966	I 15	2
1951	II 2P	1	1967	I 16	1
1952	I 16R	2	1968	I 18R	1
1953	II 1P	2	1969	II 4	1
1954	I 14	3	1970	II 4	1
1955	I 16	5	1971	II 12	4
1956	I 18R	6	1972	II 3	2
1957	II 8	5	1973	II 4	4
1958	II 1P	2	1974	II 7	4
1959	I 12	q-f	1975	II 8	2
1960	I 17R	2	1976	II 6	4
1961	II 1P	1	1977	II 1P	3
1962	I 18R	q-f	1978	I 5	4

STRANRAER

Founded: 1870
Address: Stair Park, Stranraer, Wigtownshire, Scotland
Telephone: Stranraer 3271
Ground capacity: 5,000
Record attendance: 6,500 v Rangers, Scottish Cup 1st round, 24.1.48
Record victory: 7-0 v Brechin City, Division II, 1964-65
Record defeat: 1-11 v Queen of the South, Scottish Cup 1st round, 1931-32
Most League points: 44, Division II, 1960-61 and 1971-72
Most League goals: 83, Division II, 1960-61
League scoring record: 27, Derek Frye, Division II, 1977-78
Most capped player: None

THE STRANRAER RECORD

	Division & place	Cup round reached		Division & place	Cup round reached
1956	II 12	4	1968	II 19	p
1957	II 7	5	1969	II 8	2
1958	II 18	2	1970	II 17	1
1959	II 16	2	1971	II 9	3
1960	II 17	1	1972	II 6	2
1961	II 4	2	1973	II 15	4
1962	II 7	3	1974	II 9	2
1963	II 5	1	1975	II 14	2
1964	II 8	2	1976	II 7	2
1965	II 6	p	1977	II 4	2
1966	II 15	1	1978	II 11	2
1967	II 15	p			

The Records

FA CUP 1871-72

FIRST ROUND
Clapham Rovers v Upton Park	3-0
Crystal Palace v Hitchin	0-0*
Maidenhead v Great Marlow	2-0
Barnes v Civil Service	2-0
Wanderers v Harrow Chequers (scratched)	wo
Royal Engineers v Reigate Priory (scratched)	wo
Queen's Park	bye
Donington School	bye
Hampstead Heathens	bye

SECOND ROUND
Wanderers v Clapham Rovers	3-1
Crystal Palace v Maidenhead	3-0
Royal Engineers v Hitchin	3-1
Hampstead Heathens v Barnes	2-0
Queen's Park v Donington School (scratched)	wo

THIRD ROUND
Wanderers v Crystal Palace	†*
Royal Engineers v Hampstead Heathens	2-0
Queen's Park	‡bye

†Drawn game for which no score is available.
‡Queen's Park were granted a bye from the third round into the semi-final because of travelling.

SEMI-FINAL
Royal Engineers v Crystal Palace	3-0
Wanderers v Queen's Park (scratched)††	0-0, wo

††Queen's Park could not afford to travel to London for the replay.

FINAL AT KENNINGTON OVAL
Wanderers v Royal Engineers	1-0

*The progress of Crystal Palace and Hitchin into the second round and Crystal Palace and Wanderers into the semi-final round was covered by Rule 8 of the competition whereby in the case of a draw both clubs could compete in the next round.

FA CUP 1872-73

FIRST ROUND
Oxford University v Crystal Palace	3-2
Royal Engineers v Civil Service	3-0
1st Surrey Rifles v Upton Park	2-0
Maidenhead v Great Marlow	1-0
South Norwood v Barnes	1-0
Windsor Home Park v Reigate Priory	4-2
Clapham Rovers v Hitchin (scratched)	wo
Queen's Park	*bye
Wanderers	†bye

*Queen's Park, Glasgow, because of the travelling involved, were awarded byes to the semi-final round.
†This was the only occasion when the Cup holders were excused from taking part until the Final.

SECOND ROUND
Clapham Rovers v Oxford University	0-3
1st Surrey Rifles v Maidenhead	1-3
South Norwood v Windsor Home Park	0-3
Royal Engineers	bye
Queen's Park	bye
Wanderers	bye

THIRD ROUND
Oxford University v Royal Engineers	1-0
Maidenhead v Windsor Home Park	1-0
Queen's Park	bye
Wanderers	bye

FOURTH ROUND
Oxford University v Maidenhead	4-0
Queen's Park	bye
Wanderers	bye

SEMI-FINAL
Oxford University v Queen's Park (scratched)	*wo
Wanderers	bye

*Queen's Park apparently beat Oxford but could not afford to travel to London for the Final.

FINAL AT LILLIE BRIDGE*
Wanderers v Oxford University	2-0

*Wanderers, as Cup holders, had choice of ground.

FA CUP 1873-74

FIRST ROUND
Oxford University v Upton Park	4-0
Barnes v 1st Surrey Rifles	1-0
Cambridge University v South Norwood	1-0
Pilgrims v Great Marlow	1-0
Royal Engineers v Brondesbury	5-0
Uxbridge v Gitanos	3-0
Swifts v Crystal Palace	1-0
Woodford Wells v Reigate Priory	3-0
Sheffield v Shropshire Wanderers	††
Wanderers v Southall (scratched)	wo
Trojans v Farningham (scratched)	wo
Clapham Rovers v A A C (scratched)	wo
Maidenhead v Civil Service (scratched)	wo
High Wycombe v Old Etonians (scratched)	wo

††After two drawn games Sheffield won on the toss of a coin

SECOND ROUND
Oxford University v Barnes	2-1
Clapham Rovers v Cambridge University	4-1
Sheffield v Pilgrims	1-0
Royal Engineers v Uxbridge	2-1
Maidenhead v High Wycombe	1-0
Swifts v Woodford Wells	2-1
Wanderers v Trojans (scratched)	wo

THIRD ROUND
Oxford University v Wanderers	1-0
Clapham Rovers v Sheffield	2-1
Royal Engineers v Maidenhead	7-0
Swifts	bye

SEMI-FINAL
Oxford University v Clapham Rovers	1-0
Royal Engineers v Swifts	2-0

FINAL AT KENNINGTON OVAL
Oxford University v Royal Engineers	2-0

Top *Queen's Park in 1874, still undefeated and the first winners of the Scottish Cup.*
Bottom *Royal Engineers in 1872, 7-4 on favourites for the FA Cup, but only runners-up.*

SCOTTISH FA CUP 1873-74

FIRST ROUND
Queen's Park v Dumbreck	7-0
Clydesdale v Granville	6-0
Western v Blythwood	0-1
Alexandria Athletic v Callander	2-0
Eastern v Rovers	4-0
Renton v Kilmarnock	2-0
Dumbarton v Vale of Leven (scratched)	wo
3rd Lanark Rifle Volunteers v Southern (scratched)	wo

SECOND ROUND
Queen's Park v Eastern	1-0
Alexandria Athletic v Blythwood	0-2
Renton v Dumbarton	0-0, 1-0
Clydesdale v 3rd Lanark Rifle Volunteers	1-1, 0-0, 2-0

SEMI-FINAL
Queen's Park v Renton	2-0
Clydesdale v Blythwood	4-0

FINAL AT HAMPDEN PARK
Queen's Park v Clydesdale	2-0

The first FA Cup competitions were far less organised than those a century later. The first winners, Wanderers, won only one game before defeating Royal Engineers in the Final. They received a walk over in the first round, beat Clapham in the second, went through after only drawing in the third and received a walk-over in the semi-final after Queen's Park had been unable to pay for the long journey to London for a replay.

Wanderers' goal in the Final — the first in an FA Cup Final — was scored by M P Betts, who played under the name of A H Chequer, indicating that he had come from Harrow Chequers, who had scratched to Wanderers in the first round. Queen's Park had the same trouble the next year. After defeating Oxford they were unable to travel to the Final and Oxford took their place — thus being one of only three clubs to have reached a Final after losing an earlier match.

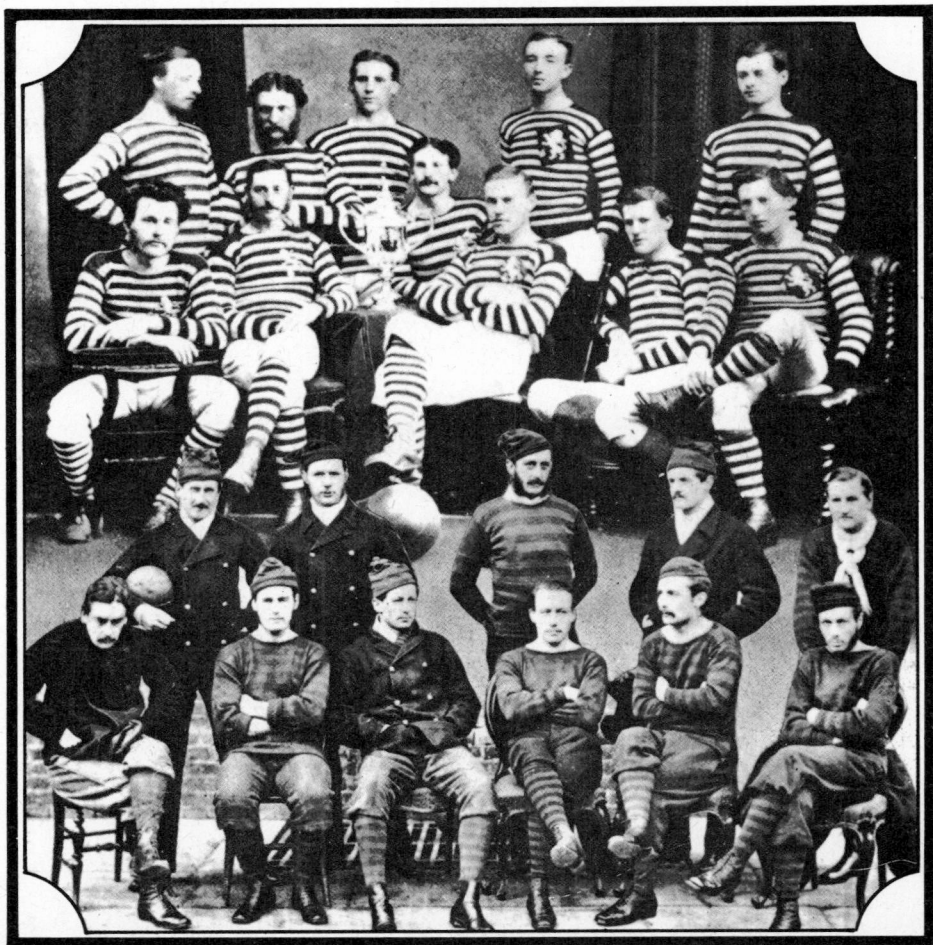

COURTESY OF DR PERCY YOUNG

FA CUP 1874-75

FIRST ROUND
Royal Engineers v Great Marlow	3-0
Cambridge University v Crystal Palace	†2-1
Clapham Rovers v Panthers	3-0
Pilgrims v South Norwood	2-1
Oxford University v Brondesbury	6-0
Wanderers v Farningham	16-0
Barnes v Upton Park	3-0
Old Etonians v Swifts	††3-0
Maidenhead v Hitchin	1-0
Woodford Wells v High Wycombe	1-0
Southall v Leyton	†5-0
Windsor Home Park v Uxbridge (scratched)	wo
Shropshire Wanderers v Sheffield (scratched)	wo
Civil Service v Harrow Chequers (scratched)	wo
Reigate Priory	bye

†Drawn game for which no score is available

SECOND ROUND
Royal Engineers v Cambridge University	5-0
Clapham Rovers v Pilgrims	2-0
Wanderers v Barnes	4-0
Maidenhead v Reigate Priory	2-1
Woodford Wells v Southall	3-0
Oxford University v Windsor Home Park (scratched)	wo
Shropshire Wanderers v Civil Service (scratched)	†two
Old Etonians	bye

†Drawn game for which no score is available

THIRD ROUND
Royal Engineers v Clapham Rovers	3-2
Oxford University v Wanderers	2-1
Old Etonians v Maidenhead	1-0
Shropshire Wanderers v Woodford Wells	†2-0

†Drawn game for which no score is available

SEMI-FINAL
Royal Engineers v Oxford University	†1-0
Old Etonians v Shropshire Wanderers	1-0

†Drawn game for which no score is available

FINAL AT KENNINGTON OVAL
Royal Engineers v Old Etonians	1-1, 2-0

SCOTTISH FA CUP 1874-75

FIRST ROUND
Helensburgh v 3rd Edinburgh Rifle Volunteers	3-0
Rangers v Oxford	2-0
West End v Star of Leven	3-0
Kilmarnock v Vale of Leven Rovers	4-0
Dumbreck v Alexandria Athletic	5-1
3rd Lanark Rifle Volunteers v Barrhead	1-0
Dumbarton v Arthurlie	3-0
Queen's Park v Western	1-0
Eastern v 23rd Renfrew Rifle Volunteers	3-0
Renton v Blythwood (scratched)	wo
Clydesdale v Vale of Leven (scratched)	wo
Rovers v Hamilton Academicals (scratched)	wo
Standard	bye

SECOND ROUND
Eastern v Kilmarnock	3-0
Renton v Helensburgh	2-0
3rd Lanark Rifle Volunteers v Standard	2-0
Queen's Park v West End	7-0
Clydesdale v Dumbreck	2-0
Dumbarton v Rangers	1-0
Rovers	bye

THIRD ROUND
Renton v Eastern	1-0
Dumbarton v 3rd Lanark Rifle Volunteers	1-0
Queen's Park v Rovers (scratched)	wo
Clydesdale	bye

SEMI-FINAL
Renton v Dumbarton	1-0
Queen's Park v Clydesdale	1-0

FINAL AT HAMPDEN PARK
Queen's Park v Renton	3-0

FA CUP 1875-76

FIRST ROUND
Wanderers v 1st Surrey Rifles	5-0
Crystal Palace v 105th Regiment	†3-0
Upton Park v Southall	1-0
Swifts v Great Marlow	2-0
Royal Engineers v High Wycombe	15-0
Panthers v Woodford Wells	1-0
Reigate Priory v Barnes	1-0
Oxford University v Forest School	6-0
Hertfordshire Rangers v Rochester	4-0
Old Etonians v Pilgrims	4-1
Maidenhead v Ramblers	2-0
Sheffield v Shropshire Wanderers (scratched)	wo
South Norwood v Clydesdale (scratched)	wo
Cambridge University v Civil Service (scratched)	wo
Clapham Rovers v Hitchin (scratched)	wo
Leyton v Harrow Chequers (scratched)	wo

†Drawn game for which no score is available

SECOND ROUND
Wanderers v Crystal Palace	3-0
Swifts v South Norwood	5-0
Reigate Priory v Cambridge University	0-8
Oxford University v Hertfordshire Rangers	8-2
Old Etonians v Maidenhead	8-0
Clapham Rovers v Leyton	12-0
Sheffield v Upton Park (scratched)	wo
Royal Engineers v Panthers (scratched)	wo

THIRD ROUND
Wanderers v Sheffield	2-0
Swifts v Royal Engineers	3-1
Cambridge University v Oxford University	0-4
Old Etonians v Clapham Rovers	1-0

SEMI-FINAL
Wanderers v Swifts	2-1
Oxford University v Old Etonians	0-1

FINAL AT KENNINGTON OVAL
Wanderers v Old Etonians	0-0, 3-0

SCOTTISH FA CUP 1875-76

SECOND ROUND
3rd Edinburgh Rifle Volunteers v Edinburgh Thistle	1-0
Levern v Hamilton Academicals	3-0
Drumpellier v Heart of Midlothian	2-0
Vale of Leven v Renton	3-0
Queen's Park v Northern	5-0
3rd Lanark Rifle Volunteers v Rangers	2-1
Helensburgh v 23rd Renfrew Rifle Volunteers	1-0
Clydesdale v Kilmarnock	6-0
Dumbarton v Renton Thistle	2-1
Western v Sandyford	3-0
Dumbreck v St Andrew's	2-0
Rovers v West End	6-0
Partick Thistle v Towerhill	2-0
Mauchline v Kilbirnie (scratched)	wo

THIRD ROUND
Queen's Park v Clydesdale	2-0
Vale of Leven v Mauchline	6-0
3rd Lanark Rifle Volunteers v Levern	3-0
Dumbreck v Partick Thistle	5-0
Rovers v 3rd Edinburgh Rifle Volunteers	4-0
Western v Helensburgh	2-0
Dumbarton v Drumpellier	5-1

FOURTH ROUND
Queen's Park v Dumbreck	2-0
3rd Lanark Rifle Volunteers v Western	5-0
Vale of Leven v Rovers	2-0
Dumbarton	bye

SEMI-FINAL
Queen's Park v Vale of Leven	3-1
3rd Lanark Rifle Volunteers v Dumbarton	3-0

FINAL AT HAMPDEN PARK
Queen's Park v 3rd Lanark Rifle Volunteers	1-1, 2-0

FA CUP 1876-77

FIRST ROUND
Pilgrims v Ramblers	4-1
Panthers v Wood Grange	3-0
Clapham Rovers v Reigate Priory	5-0
Rochester v Union	5-0
Swifts v Reading Hornets	2-0
Royal Engineers v Old Harrovians	2-1
South Norwood v Saxons	4-1
105th Regiment v 1st Surrey Rifles	3-0
Upton Park v Leyton	7-0
Great Marlow v Hertfordshire Rangers	2-1
Forest School v Gresham	4-1
Wanderers v Saffron Walden (scratched)	wo
Southall v Old Wykehamists (scratched)	wo
Cambridge University v High Wycombe (scratched)	wo
Shropshire Wanderers v Druids (scratched)	wo
Sheffield v Trojans (scratched)	wo
Oxford University v Old Salopians (scratched)	wo
Barnes v Old Etonians (scratched)	wo
Queen's Park	bye

SECOND ROUND
Wanderers v Southall	6-1
Pilgrims v Panthers	1-0
Cambridge University v Clapham Rovers	2-1
Rochester v Swifts	1-0
Royal Engineers v Shropshire Wanderers	3-0
Sheffield v South Norwood	7-0
Oxford University v 105th Regiment	6-1
Upton Park v Barnes	1-0
Great Marlow v Forest School	1-0
Queen's Park	bye

THIRD ROUND
Wanderers v Pilgrims	3-0
Cambridge University v Rochester	4-0
Royal Engineers v Sheffield	1-0
Upton Park v Great Marlow	†1-0
Oxford University v Queen's Park (scratched)	wo

†Drawn game for which no score is available.

FOURTH ROUND
Cambridge University v Royal Engineers	1-0
Oxford University v Upton Park	†1-0
Wanderers	bye

†Drawn game for which no score is available

SEMI-FINAL
Wanderers v Cambridge University	1-0
Oxford University	bye

FINAL AT KENNINGTON OVAL
Wanderers v Oxford University	2-0

SCOTTISH FA CUP 1876-77

FOURTH ROUND
Queen's Park v Northern	4-0
Vale of Leven v Busby	4-0
Lennox v Swifts	4-0
Lancefield v Hamilton	2-0
Rangers v Mauchline	3-0
Ayr Thistle v Partick Thistle (disqualified)	wo

FIFTH ROUND
Rangers v Lennox	3-0
Vale of Leven v Queen's Park	2-1
Ayr Thistle v Lancefield	1-0

SEMI-FINAL
Vale of Leven v Ayr Thistle	9-0
Rangers	bye

FINAL AT HAMPDEN PARK
Vale of Leven v Rangers	0-0, 1-1, 3-2

Queen's Park conceded their first ever goal in the Scottish Cup semi-final against Vale of Leven early in 1876. They had been in existence for almost nine years. Their first ever defeat in Scotland was also at the hands of Vale of Leven on 30 December 1876. The latter won a fifth round Scottish Cup tie 2-1.

FA CUP 1877-78

FIRST ROUND

Wanderers v Panthers	9-1
High Wycombe v Wood Grange	4-0
Great Marlow v Hendon	2-0
Sheffield v Notts County	3-0
Darwen v Manchester	3-1
Pilgrims v Ramblers	†1-0
Druids v Shropshire Wanderers	1-0
Oxford University v Hertfordshire Rangers	5-2
Clapham Rovers v Grantham	2-0
Swifts v Leyton	8-2
Old Harrovians v 105th Regiment	2-0
1st Surrey Rifles v Forest School	1-0
Cambridge University v Southill Park	3-1
Maidenhead v Reading Hornets	10-0
Upton Park v Rochester	3-0
Reading v South Norwood	2-0
Remnants v St Stephens	4-1
Hawks v Minerva	5-2
Barnes v St Marks (scratched)	wo
Royal Engineers v Union (scratched)	wo
Old Foresters v Old Wykehamists (scratched)	wo
Queen's Park	*bye

†Drawn game for which no score is available
*Queen's Park later withdrew

SECOND ROUND

Wanderers v High Wycombe	9-0
Barnes v Great Marlow	3-1
Sheffield v Darwen	1-0
Royal Engineers v Pilgrims	6-0
Oxford University v Old Foresters	1-0
Clapham Rovers v Swifts	4-0
Old Harrovians v 1st Surrey Rifles	6-0
Cambridge University v Maidenhead	4-2
Upton Park v Reading	1-0
Remnants v Hawks	2-0
Druids	bye

THIRD ROUND

Wanderers v Barnes	4-1
Royal Engineers v Druids	8-0
Oxford University v Clapham Rovers	3-2
Old Harrovians v Cambridge University	2-0
Upton Park v Remnants	3-0
Sheffield	bye

FOURTH ROUND

Wanderers v Sheffield	3-0
Royal Engineers v Oxford University	4-2
Old Harrovians v Upton Park	3-1

SEMI-FINAL

Royal Engineers v Old Harrovians	2-1
Wanderers	bye

FINAL AT KENNINGTON OVAL

Wanderers v Royal Engineers	3-1

The first ever Welsh Cup tie was played on Saturday 30 October, 1877, between Druids of Ruabon and Newtown at Newtown. The founder of the Welsh FA, Llewelyn Kenrick, captained Druids that day; they won the game and eventually reached the final to meet Wrexham. Wrexham won 1-0, apparently using a 2-3-5 line up. If that is in fact correct, then it is the first recorded instance of what remained the standard formation for half a century. At the time the Welsh FA had not even purchased a trophy, but when they did it was a magnificent affair which dwarfed the FA Cup.

Because of the dearth of clubs in Wales, the Cup has always been open to English sides. This produced an English winner as early as 1884 when Oswestry defeated Druids 3-2. The situation became a little absurd in 1934, however, with a final replay which is surely unparalleled in any cup competition. The game was between two English clubs — Bristol City and Tranmere Rovers — and was played on an English ground, Chester's Sealand Road. City won 3-0 and it was not until 1948 that the Cup actually returned to a Welsh club.

SCOTTISH FA CUP 1877-78

FOURTH ROUND

Renton v Rovers	4-0
South Western v Glengowan	5-0
Mauchline v Kilbirnie	2-1
Parkgrove v Drumpellier	3-1
3rd Lanark Rifle Volunteers v Govan	7-0
Vale of Leven v Rangers	5-0
Thornliebank v Hibernian	**
Beith v Dundas St Clement's (scratched)	wo
Partick Thistle v Barrhead (disqualified)	wo
Jordanhill	bye
Renfrew	†bye

**After two draws, both teams went through to the next round
†Renfrew, who had earlier been beaten by Barrhead, were reinstated on the latter's disqualification

FIFTH ROUND

Vale of Leven v Jordanhill	10-0
Parkgrove v Partick Thistle	2-1
South Western v Hibernian	3-1
Renton v Thornliebank	2-1
3rd Lanark Rifle Volunteers v Beith	4-0
Mauchline v Renfrew (scratched)	wo

SIXTH ROUND

Vale of Leven v Parkgrove	5-0
3rd Lanark Rifle Volunteers v South Western	2-1
Renton v Mauchline	3-1

SEMI-FINAL

3rd Lanark Rifle Volunteers v Renton	1-0
Vale of Leven	bye

FINAL AT HAMPDEN PARK

Vale of Leven v 3rd Lanark Rifle Volunteers	1-0

SCOTTISH FA CUP 1878-79

FOURTH ROUND

Hibernian v Roy Roy	9-0
3rd Lanark Rifle Volunteers v Renfrew	4-0
Vale of Leven v Govan	11-1
Dumbarton v Portland	6-1
Queen's Park v Mauchline	5-0
Rangers v Alexandria Athletic	3-0
Beith v Kilmarnock Athletic	9-1
Helensburgh v Heart of Midlothian (scratched)	wo
Stonelaw v Thistle (disqualified)	wo
Partick Thistle	bye

FIFTH ROUND

Queen's Park v 3rd Lanark Rifle Volunteers	5-0
Rangers v Partick Thistle	4-0
Helensburgh v Hibernian	2-1
Dumbarton v Stonelaw	9-1
Vale of Leven v Beith	6-1

SIXTH ROUND

Rangers v Queen's Park	1-0
Vale of Leven v Dumbarton	3-1
Helensburgh	bye

SEMI-FINAL

Vale of Leven v Helensburgh	3-0
Rangers	bye

FINAL AT HAMPDEN PARK

Vale of Leven v Rangers	1-1*

*Cup awarded to Vale of Leven. Rangers refused to play the replay within the time allotted by the SFA. Rangers refused to turn up after the SFA had turned down a protest that they had scored a perfectly legitimate second goal in the first game.

The Scottish Cup of 1878-79 saw two scenes unfamiliar a century later. Hearts failed to turn up for their tie at Helensburgh and, later, mighty Rangers refused to play a final replay against Vale of Leven in a fit of pique over a disputed goal.

FA CUP 1878-79

FIRST ROUND

Old Etonians v Wanderers	7-2
Reading v Hendon	1-0
Grey Friars v Great Marlow	2-1
Pilgrims v Brentwood	3-1
Nottingham Forest v Notts County	†1-0
Sheffield v Grantham	†3-1
Old Harrovians v Southill Park	8-0
Oxford University v Wednesbury Strollers	7-0
Royal Engineers v Old Foresters	3-0
Barnes v Maidenhead	†4-0
Upton Park v Saffron Walden	5-0
Forest School v Rochester	4-2
Cambridge University v Hertfordshire Rangers	2-0
Swifts v Hawks	2-1
Romford v Ramblers	3-1
Minerva v 105th Regiment (scratched)	wo
Darwen v Birch (scratched)	wo
Remnants v Unity (scratched)	wo
Panthers v Runnymede (scratched)	†two
Clapham Rovers v Finchley (scratched)	wo
South Norwood v Leyton (scratched)	wo
Eagley	bye

†Drawn game for which no score is available

SECOND ROUND

Old Etonians v Reading	1-0
Minerva v Grey Friars	3-0
Darwen v Eagley	4-1
Remnants v Pilgrims	6-2
Nottingham Forest v Sheffield	2-0
Old Harrovians v Panthers	3-0
Oxford University v Royal Engineers	4-0
Barnes v Upton Park	3-2
Clapham Rovers v Forest School	10-1
Cambridge University v South Norwood	3-0
Swifts v Romford	3-1

THIRD ROUND

Old Etonians v Minerva	5-2
Darwen v Remnants	3-2
Nottingham Forest v Old Harrovians	2-0
Oxford University v Barnes	2-1
Clapham Rovers v Cambridge University	1-0
Swifts	bye

FOURTH ROUND

Old Etonians v Darwen	5-5, 2-2, 6-2
Nottingham Forest v Oxford University	2-1
Clapham Rovers v Swifts	8-1

SEMI-FINAL

Old Etonians v Nottingham Forest	2-1
Clapham Rovers	bye

FINAL AT KENNINGTON OVAL

Old Etonians v Clapham Rovers	1-0

The 1878-79 Cup season was notable for the arrival of the northern teams. Nottingham Forest became the first northern side to reach the semi-finals (and the only one of the present League clubs to have got so far at the first attempt) but Darwen's displays were more newsworthy. In their fourth round tie against Old Etonians at the Oval, Darwen scored four times in the last 15 minutes to draw 5-5. Etonians refused to play extra time and it took a public subscription to bring Darwen back for a 2-2 draw. A third game was decisive, Etonians winning 6-2 and eventually taking the Cup.

Darwen had in their ranks two Scots — James Love and Fergus Suter — who were reputedly the first of the 'professionals' to find money in their boots. They had come down to Darwen as part of a touring Partick Thistle side, played a friendly, and been persuaded to stay. The tide was on the turn and the days of the gentlemen amateurs almost at an end. Wanderers, after a hat-trick of successes in 1876-78, were defeated in the very first round of the 1878-79 competition by Old Etonians, who went on to become their successors as Cup holders.

FA CUP 1879-80

SECOND ROUND
Clapham Rovers v South Norwood	4-0
Hendon v Mosquitoes	7-1
Wanderers v Old Carthusians	1-0
West End v Hotspurs	1-0
Oxford University v Birmingham	6-0
Aston Villa v Stafford Road Works	3-1
Maidenhead v Henley	3-1
Royal Engineers v Upton Park	4-1
Grey Friars v Gresham	9-0
Nottingham Forest v Turton	6-0
Blackburn Rovers v Darwen	3-1
Sheffield v Sheffield Providence	3-0
Pilgrims v Hertfordshire Rangers (scratched)	wo
Old Harrovians	bye
Old Etonians	bye

THIRD ROUND
Clapham Rovers v Pilgrims	7-0
Old Etonians v Wanderers	3-1
Royal Engineers v Old Harrovians	2-0
Nottingham Forest v Blackburn Rovers	6-0
Oxford University v Aston Villa (scratched)	wo
Hendon	bye
West End	bye
Maidenhead	bye
Grey Friars	bye
Sheffield	bye

FOURTH ROUND
Clapham Rovers v Hendon	2-0
Old Etonians v West End	5-1
Oxford University v Maidenhead	1-0
Royal Engineers v Grey Friars	1-0
Nottingham Forest v Sheffield	* 2-2

*Sheffield disqualified for refusing to play extra time

FIFTH ROUND
Clapham Rovers v Old Etonians	1-0
Oxford University v Royal Engineers	†1-0
Nottingham Forest	bye

†Drawn game for which no score is available

SEMI-FINAL
Oxford University v Nottingham Forest	1-0
Clapham Rovers	bye

FINAL AT KENNINGTON OVAL
Clapham Rovers v Oxford University	1-0

SCOTTISH FA CUP 1879-80

FOURTH ROUND
South Western v Arbroath	4-0
Pollockshields Athletic v Renfrew	2-1
Dumbarton v Clyde	11-1
Third Lanark v Kirkintilloch	5-1
Rob Roy v Johnstone Athletic	4-2
Thornliebank v Fossilbank	13-0
Mauchline v Hamilton Academicals	2-0
Cambuslang v Plains	3-0
Queen's Park v Strathblane	10-1
Parkgrove v Hibernian	**
Hurlford v Kilbirnie	**

**After two draws both teams went through to the next round

FIFTH ROUND
South Western v Parkgrove	3-2
Dumbarton v Kilbirnie	6-2
Queen's Park v Hurlford	15-1
Thornliebank v Rob Roy	12-0
Pollockshields Athletic v Cambuslang	4-0
Hibernian v Mauchline	2-0
Third Lanark	bye

SIXTH ROUND
Pollockshields Athletic v South Western	6-1
Dumbarton v Hibernian	6-2
Thornliebank v Third Lanark	2-1
Queen's Park	bye

SEMI-FINAL
Queen's Park v Dumbarton	1-0
Thornliebank v Pollockshields Athletic	2-1

FINAL AT CATHKIN PARK
Queen's Park v Thornliebank	3-0

SCOTTISH FA CUP 1880-81

FOURTH ROUND
Heart of Midlothian v Cambridge	3-0
Hurlford v Cartside	3-1
Central v Edinburgh University	1-0
Dumbarton v Glasgow University	9-0
Rangers v Clyde	11-0
Queen's Park v Beith	11-2
St Mirren v Cowlairs	1-0
Arthurlie v South Western (scratched)	wo
Mauchline v Clarkston (scratched)	wo
Vale of Leven v Arbroath (scratched)	wo
Thistle	bye

FIFTH ROUND
Vale of Leven v Thistle	7-1
Dumbarton v St Mirren	5-1
Arthurlie v Heart of Midlothian	4-0
Queen's Park v Mauchline	2-0
Rangers v Hurlford	3-0
Central	bye

SIXTH ROUND
Queen's Park v Central	10-0
Dumbarton v Rangers	3-1
Vale of Leven v Arthurlie	2-0

SEMI-FINAL
Dumbarton v Vale of Leven	2-0
Queen's Park	bye

FINAL AT KINNING PARK
Queen's Park v Dumbarton	2-1*, 3-1

*Dumbarton's protest about spectators on the pitch during the first game was upheld

FA CUP 1880-81

SECOND ROUND
Old Carthusians v Dreadnought	5-1
Royal Engineers v Pilgrims	1-0
Swifts v Reading	1-0
Upton Park v Weybridge	3-0
Darwen v Sheffield	5-1
The Wednesday v Blackburn Rovers	4-0
Turton v Astley Bridge	3-0
Reading Abbey v Acton	2-1
Great Marlow v West End	4-0
Old Etonians v Hendon	2-0
Grey Friars v Maidenhead	1-0
Stafford Road Works v Grantham	†7-1
Aston Villa v Nottingham Forest	2-1
Notts County	bye
Rangers	bye
Clapham Rovers	bye
Romford	bye
Hertfordshire Rangers	bye

†Drawn game for which no score is available

THIRD ROUND
Royal Engineers v Rangers	6-0
Clapham Rovers v Swifts	2-1
The Wednesday v Turton	2-0
Romford v Reading Abbey	2-0
Old Etonians v Hertfordshire Rangers	3-0
Aston Villa v Notts County	3-1
Old Carthusians	bye
Upton Park	bye
Darwen	bye
Great Marlow	bye
Stafford Road Works	bye
Grey Friars	bye

FOURTH ROUND
Old Carthusians v Royal Engineers	2-1
Clapham Rovers v Upton Park	5-4
Darwen v The Wednesday	5-1
Romford v Great Marlow	2-1
Old Etonians v Grey Friars	4-0
Stafford Road Works v Aston Villa	3-2

FIFTH ROUND
Old Carthusians v Clapham Rovers	4-1
Darwen v Romford	15-0
Old Etonians v Stafford Road Works	2-1

SEMI-FINAL
Old Carthusians v Darwen	4-1
Old Etonians	bye

FINAL AT KENNINGTON OVAL
Old Carthusians v Old Etonians	3-0

Above The reason Blackburn Rovers won the Cup so often? F H Ayres and Company ran this advertisement regularly for ten years, but 1879-80 was a little premature for it. In their first expedition into the Cup, which was that season, Rovers were rudely dismissed 6-0 by Nottingham Forest, who were at the time on the way to a second consecutive semi-final.

Old Carthusians' defeat of Old Etonians in the 1881 Cup Final was the first leg of a rare double. In 1894 they also won the first Amateur Cup final by defeating Casuals 2-1. In fact this oft repeated 'unique' record is not so: Royal Engineers, FA Cup winners in 1875, later went on to win the Amateur Cup in 1908 as Depot Battalion, Royal Engineers.

The two Scottish Cup finals of 1881 between Queen's Park and Dumbarton resulted in quite unprecedented scenes. The game was played at Rangers' home, Kinning Park, and the crowds were so great that many spent most of the game on the pitch. Because of this Dumbarton protested that Queen's second and winning goal was invalid, the pitch having virtually been invaded, and the SFA ordered a replay. Queen's threatened to withdraw from the Association, but eventually turned out and won 3-1. At the second game the gates had to be closed, the first time that this had happened in Scottish history. This was not really surprising for Dumbarton and Queen's were the Rangers and Celtic of pre-1900 Scotland.
The next year, 1882, there was even more trouble when the two met in the final. The crowd was bad-tempered and there were protests over yet another disputed goal — this time to level at 2-2. Queen's Park went on to win the replay, 4-1, before a record 15,000 crowd, but the two games left a remarkably bitter taste. Up to that point there had been a well-attended friendly every year between the clubs, but this was abandoned and, indeed, never reinstated. Dumbarton finally won the Cup the following year, beating Vale of Leven, after defeating Queen's Park in the sixth round.

FA CUP 1881-82

SECOND ROUND

Blackburn Rovers v Bolton Wanderers	6-2
Darwen v Accrington	3-1
Turton v Bootle	4-0
Wednesbury Old Alliance v Small Heath Alliance	6-0
Notts County v Wednesbury Strollers	11-1
Staveley v Grantham	3-1
Heeley v Sheffield	4-1
Upton Park v Hanover United	3-1
Hotspur v Reading Abbey	4-1
Reading Minster v Romford	3-1
Swifts v Old Harrovians	7-1
Maidenhead v Acton	2-1
Great Marlow v St Bartholomew's Hospital	2-0
Reading v West End (scratched)	*wo
Old Foresters v Pilgrims	3-1
Old Carthusians v Barnes	7-1
Aston Villa	bye
The Wednesday	bye
Old Etonians	bye
Dreadnought	bye
Royal Engineers	bye

*West End scratched after a drawn game

THIRD ROUND

Darwen v Turton	4-2
Aston Villa v Notts County	**4-1
The Wednesday v Staveley	**5-1
Hotspur v Reading Minster	2-0
Old Etonians v Swifts	3-0
Great Marlow v Dreadnought	2-1
Royal Engineers v Old Carthusians	2-0
Blackburn Rovers	bye
Wednesbury Old Alliance	bye
Heeley	bye
Upton Park	bye
Maidenhead	bye
Reading	bye
Old Foresters	bye

**two drawn games for which no scores are available

FOURTH ROUND

Blackburn Rovers v Darwen	5-1
Wednesbury Old Alliance v Aston Villa	4-2
The Wednesday v Heeley	3-1
Upton Park v Hotspur	5-0
Old Etonians v Maidenhead	6-3
Great Marlow v Reading (scratched)	wo
Old Foresters v Royal Engineers	2-1

FIFTH ROUND

Blackburn Rovers v Wednesbury Old Alliance	3-1
The Wednesday v Upton Park	6-0
Great Marlow v Old Foresters	*1-0
Old Etonians	bye

*drawn game for which no score is available

SEMI-FINAL

Blackburn Rovers v The Wednesday	0-0, 5-1
Old Etonians v Great Marlow	5-0

FINAL AT KENNINGTON OVAL

Old Etonians v Blackburn Rovers	1-0

The 1882 FA Cup Final was the real bridging point between the old 'gentlemen's' football and the new professionalism. It was the first appearance of a northern club – Blackburn Rovers – and the last time a Southern side was to win for 30 years. After the game Lord Kinnaird, the victorious captain, stood on his head in front of the pavillion. He had appeared in 8 Finals and won 5 winners medals, a record that was to be equalled but never surpassed. He also appeared in the following year's Final, when he collected a ninth medal.

Before a first round FA Cup tie against Everton late in 1881, Bootle discovered that they only had eight players. Three spectators were asked to play and Bootle won the tie. In the second round, with a full team, Bootle lost 4-0 to a team called Turton.

SCOTTISH FA CUP 1881-82

FOURTH ROUND

Falkirk v Milton of Campsie	3-1
Rangers v Thornliebank	2-0
Clyde v Edinburgh University	3-2
Kilmarnock v Our Boys	9-2
Queen's Park v Johnstone	3-2
Cartvale v Glasgow University	5-4
Hibernian v West Benhar	*8-0
Kilmarnock Athletic v Mauchline	3-2
Partick Thistle v Glasgow Athletic	1-0
Arthurlie v Helensburgh	*1-0
West Calder v Stranraer (scratched)	wo
South Western	bye
Dumbarton	bye
Beith	bye
Vale of Teith	bye
Shotts	bye

*after a drawn game

FIFTH ROUND

Arthurlie v Kilmarnock	4-1
West Calder v Falkirk	4-2
Queen's Park v Partick Thistle	10-0
Shotts v Vale of Teith	5-0
Kilmarnock Athletic v Beith	2-1
Cartvale v Clyde	5-4
Rangers v South Western	†6-4
Dumbarton v Hibernian	†4-1

†after a protested game

SIXTH ROUND

Queen's Park v Shotts	15-0
Kilmarnock Athletic v Arthurlie	5-2
Dumbarton v Rangers	†5-1
Cartvale v West Calder	5-3

†after a protested game

SEMI-FINAL

Queen's Park v Kilmarnock Athletic	3-2
Dumbarton v Cartvale	11-2

FINAL AT CATHKIN PARK

Queen's Park v Dumbarton	2-2, 4-1

SCOTTISH FA CUP 1882-83

FOURTH ROUND

Hurlford v Vale of Teith	3-2
Hibernian v Thistle	2-2, 4-1
Arthurlie v Queen of the South Wanderers	3-1
Dumbarton v Thornliebank	3-0
Queen's Park v Cambuslang	5-0
Lugar Boswell v Renton	5-3
Third Lanark v Dunblane	7-1
Kilmarnock Athletic v Abercorn	5-2
Pollockshields Athletic v Johnstone	3-1
Vale of Leven v Edinburgh University	2-0
Partick Thistle v Glasgow University (scratched)	wo

FIFTH ROUND

Vale of Leven v Lugar Boswell	5-0
Queen's Park v Hurlford	7-2
Arthurlie v Hibernian	†6-0
Third Lanark	bye
Dumbarton	bye
Kilmarnock Athletic	bye
Partick Thistle	bye
Pollockshields Athletic	bye

†after a protested game

SIXTH ROUND

Vale of Leven v Partick Thistle	4-0
Pollockshields Athletic v Third Lanark	5-2
Dumbarton v Queen's Park	3-1
Kilmarnock Athletic v Arthurlie	***1-0

***after three drawn games

SEMI-FINAL

Vale of Leven v Kilmarnock Athletic	*2-0
Dumbarton v Pollockshields Athletic	*5-0

*after a drawn game

FINAL AT HAMPDEN PARK

Dumbarton v Vale of Leven	2-2, 2-1

FA CUP 1882-83

SECOND ROUND

Blackburn Olympic v Lower Darwen	9-1
Darwen Ramblers v Haslingden	3-2
Darwen v Blackburn Rovers	1-0
Druids v Northwich Victoria	5-0
Bolton Wanderers v Liverpool Ramblers	3-0
Eagley v Halliwell	3-1
Old Carthusians v Etonian Ramblers	7-0
Royal Engineers v Reading	8-0
Clapham Rovers v Hanover United	7-1
Windsor v United Hospitals	3-1
Old Etonians v Brentwood	2-1
Swifts v Upton Park	*3-2
Hendon v Chatham	2-1
Great Marlow v Reading Minster (scratched)	wo
Phoenix Bessemer v Grimsby	8-1
The Wednesday v Lockwood Brothers	6-0
Nottingham Forest v Heeley	7-2
Aston Villa v Wednesbury Old Alliance	4-1
Aston Unity v Mitchell's St George's	3-0
Walsall Town v Stafford Road Works	4-1
Church	bye
Old Westminsters	bye
Rochester	bye
South Reading	bye
Notts County	bye

*drawn game for which no score is available

THIRD ROUND

Blackburn Olympic v Darwen Ramblers	8-0
Church v Darwen	*2-0
Druids v Bolton Wanderers	**1-0
Old Carthusians v Old Westminsters	3-2
Clapham Rovers v Windsor	3-0
Old Etonians v Rochester	7-0
Hendon v South Reading	11-1
Notts County v Phoenix Bessemer	*3-2
The Wednesday v Nottingham Forest	*3-2
Aston Villa v Aston Unity	3-1
Eagley	bye
Royal Engineers	bye
Swifts	bye
Great Marlow	bye
Walsall Town	bye

*drawn game for which no score is available
**two drawn games for which no scores are available

FOURTH ROUND

Blackburn Olympic v Church	2-0
Druids v Eagley	2-1
Old Carthusians v Royal Engineers	6-2
Old Etonians v Swifts	2-0
Hendon v Great Marlow	3-0
Notts County v The Wednesday	4-1
Aston Villa v Walsall Town	2-1
Clapham Rovers	bye

FIFTH ROUND

Blackburn Olympic v Druids	4-0
Old Carthusians v Clapham Rovers	5-3
Old Etonians v Hendon	4-2
Notts County v Aston Villa	4-3

SEMI-FINAL

Blackburn Olympic v Old Carthusians	4-0
Old Etonians v Notts County	2-1

FINAL AT KENNINGTON OVAL

Blackburn Olympic v Old Etonians	2-1

Blackburn Olympic, the first winners of the Cup to come from the North of England, and the first overtly professional winners, are perhaps the least known of all successful Cup Finalists. Their star rose suddenly and declined just as quickly. After reaching the semi-final the following season they were never heard of again. Olympic even had a manager, one Jack Hunter, whose earlier career had been with a travelling circus. He took his team away to Blackpool before the Final. Of his players, two were weavers, one a spinner, one a plumber, one a metal worker and two were unemployed other than football. A far cry from Old Etonians, last of the English amateur finalists.

WEST BROMWICH

Albion Football Club.

SEASON TICKET.

1883-1884.

To Admit to all Matches on the

FOUR ACRES,

SITUATE IN SEAGAR STREET.

PRICE :—THREE SHILLINGS.

Above *A West Bromwich Albion season ticket for 1883-84. For one third of the price of admission to the popular side for a single game in 1974, the Throstles fan could watch a whole season's football in the Midlands.*

Top *The first Blackburn Rovers side to win the FA Cup in 1884. Their opponents were the Scots side Queen's Park. If the latter had won they would have completed a remarkable double, for they had already won the Scottish Cup. In fact they returned to Glasgow extremely bitter at the game's refereeing. Under Scottish rules at the time the offside law only required two defenders between the ball and the goal, but English law required three. Queen's scored two goals that would have been allowed in Scotland and felt thoroughly deprived. They were also upset that Blackburn had four full-time professionals, payment of players still being illegal in Scotland.*

When Blackburn Rovers reached The Oval for the Cup Final in 1882 they had gone 35 consecutive games without defeat, still recognised to be the longest run of first-class fixtures without setback in English football. Since Darwen defeated them in the first round of the 1880-81 competition, Rovers had won 31 games and drawn four. One of those victories was against mighty Preston North End in the latter's first ever professional game. Blackburn won reasonably convincingly, 16-0.

FA CUP 1883-84

THIRD ROUND

Blackburn Rovers v Padiham	3-0
Staveley v Lockwood Brothers	1-0
Upton Park v Reading	6-1
Eagley v Preston North End	1-9
Swifts v Clapham Rovers	2-1
Notts County v Grantham	4-1
Bolton Wanderers v Irwell Springs	8-1
Queen's Park v Oswestry	7-1
Aston Villa v Wednesbury Old Alliance	7-4
Wednesbury Town v Derby Midland	1-0
Romford v Brentwood	1-4
Old Foresters	bye
Old Westminsters	bye
Blackburn Olympic	bye
Old Wykehamists	bye
Northwich Victoria	bye

FOURTH ROUND

Blackburn Rovers v Staveley	5-0
Upton Park v Preston North End	1-1, wo*
Swifts v Old Foresters	2-1
Notts County v Bolton Wanderers	2-2, 2-1
Queen's Park v Aston Villa	6-1
Old Westminsters v Wednesbury Town	5-1
Blackburn Olympic v Old Wykehamists	9-1
Brentwood v Northwich Victoria	1-3

*Upton Park protested that Preston paid their players. The FA upheld the protest and disqualified Preston before the replay.

FIFTH ROUND

Blackburn Rovers v Upton Park	3-0
Swifts v Notts County	1-1, 0-1
Queen's Park v Old Westminsters	1-0
Blackburn Olympic v Northwich Victoria	9-1

SEMI-FINAL

Blackburn Rovers v Notts County	1-0
Queen's Park v Blackburn Olympic	4-1

FINAL AT KENNINGTON OVAL

Blackburn Rovers v Queen's Park	2-1

SCOTTISH FA CUP 1883-84

FOURTH ROUND

Mauchline v Royal Albert	4-0
St Bernard's v Thornliebank	2-0
Vale of Leven v Harp	6-0
Pollockshields Athletic v Our Boys	11-0
Dunblane v Rangers	0-6
Kilmarnock Athletic v Cambuslang	2-3
5th KRV v Hibernian	1-8
Partick Thistle v Queen's Park	0-4
Cartvale v Abercorn	4-2
Battlefield v Edinburgh University (scratched)	wo
Arthurlie	bye

FIFTH ROUND

Arthurlie v Vale of Leven	0-0, 1-3
Mauchline v Pollockshields Athletic	2-3
St Bernard's v Rangers	0-3
Queen's Park	bye
Battlefield	bye
Hibernian	bye
Cambuslang	bye
Cartvale	bye

SIXTH ROUND

Cambuslang v Rangers	2-5
Queen's Park v Cartvale	6-1
Vale of Leven v Pollockshields Athletic	4-2
Hibernian v Battlefield	6-1

SEMI-FINAL

Vale of Leven v Rangers	3-0
Hibernian v Queen's Park	1-5

FINAL

Cup awarded to Queen's Park	†

†Vale of Leven wanted to postpone the final because of the illness of two players and the family bereavement of another. But the FA, although sympathetic, decided that was impossible due to other engagements, such as the international against England. Vale did not turn up for the final and the Cup was awarded to Queen's Park.

FA CUP 1884-85

THIRD ROUND

Blackburn Rovers v Witton	6-1
West Bromwich Albion v Aston Villa	††3-0
Druids v Chirk	4-1
Grimsby Town v Lincoln City	1-0
Chatham v Hanover United	2-0
Lower Darwen v Darwen Old Wanderers	4-2
Church v Southport	10-0
Queen's Park v Leek	3-2
Old Wykehamists v Upton Park	2-1
Notts County v Sheffield	9-0
Walsall Swifts v Mitchell's St George's	3-2
Nottingham Forest v The Wednesday	2-1
Swifts v Old Westminsters	2-1
Romford	bye
Old Carthusians	bye
Darwen	bye
Old Etonians	bye
Middlesbrough	bye

††Two drawn games (scores unavailable)

FOURTH ROUND

Blackburn Rovers v Romford	8-0
West Bromwich Albion v Druids	1-0*
Old Carthusians v Grimsby Town	3-0
Chatham v Lower Darwen	1-0
Church v Darwen	3-0
Queen's Park v Old Wykehamists	7-0
Notts County v Walsall Swifts	4-1
Nottingham Forest v Swifts	1-0
Old Etonians v Middlesbrough	5-2

*Druids arrived with only ten men and refused to take the field. West Bromwich therefore scored within five seconds of the kick-off, whereupon Druids decided to take part. This 'goal' is not normally recorded and West Bromwich scored again to 'officially' win 1-0

FIFTH ROUND

Old Carthusians v Chatham	3-0
Blackburn Rovers	bye
West Bromwich Albion	bye
Church	bye
Queen's Park	bye
Notts County	bye
Nottingham Forest	bye
Old Etonians	bye

SIXTH ROUND

Blackburn Rovers v West Bromwich Albion	2-0
Old Carthusians v Church	1-0
Queen's Park v Notts County	2-2, 2-1
Nottingham Forest v Old Etonians	2-0

SEMI-FINAL

Blackburn Rovers v Old Carthusians	5-0
Queen's Park v Nottingham Forest	1-1, 3-0

FINAL AT KENNINGTON OVAL

Blackburn Rovers v Queen's Park	2-0

SCOTTISH FA CUP 1884-85

FOURTH ROUND

Hibernian v Ayr	5-1
Morton v Wishaw Swifts	2-1
Vale of Leven v Arthurlie	2-1
Annbank v Queen of the South Wanderers	5-2
Battlefield v Pollockshields Athletic	3-0
Our Boys v West Benhar	3-3, 3-8
Renton v St Mirren	2-1
Rangers v Arbroath	3-4†, 8-1
Dumbarton v Partick Thistle	6-3
Cambuslang v Thornliebank	2-2, 0-0*

†Rangers protested the result and the SFA ordered a replay
*Both teams went through to the next round

FIFTH ROUND

Hibernian v Morton	4-0
Cambuslang v Dumbarton	4-1
Annbank v West Benhar	5-1
Rangers	bye
Renton	bye
Battlefield	bye
Vale of Leven	bye
Thornliebank	bye

SIXTH ROUND

Hibernian v Annbank	5-0
Vale of Leven v Thornliebank	4-3
Renton v Rangers	5-3
Cambuslang v Battlefield	3-1

SEMI-FINAL

Renton v Hibernian	3-2
Vale of Leven v Cambuslang	0-0, 3-1

FINAL AT HAMPDEN PARK

Renton v Vale of Leven	0-0, 3-1

SCOTTISH FA CUP 1885-86

FOURTH ROUND

Dumbarton v Partick Thistle	3-0
Queen of the South Wanderers v Arthurlie	†
Cambuslang v Wishaw Swifts	9-0
Hibernian v Arbroath	5-3
Renton v Cowlairs	4-0
Queen's Park v Airdrieonians	1-0
Third Lanark v Ayr	3-2*, 3-3, 5-1
Abercorn v Strathmore	7-2
Vale of Leven v Harp	6-0
Port Glasgow Athletic	bye

* replayed after Ayr protested
† Arthurlie won the tie. There is no record of the score

FIFTH ROUND

Renton v Vale of Leven	2-2, 3-0
Third Lanark v Port Glasgow Athletic	1-1, 1-1, 4-1
Arthurlie v Queen's Park	1-2
Abercorn v Cambuslang	0-1
Dumbarton v Hibernian	2-2, 3-4

SIXTH ROUND

Hibernian v Cambuslang	3-2
Third Lanark	bye
Renton	bye
Queen's Park	bye

SEMI-FINAL

Hibernian v Renton	0-2
Third Lanark v Queen's Park	0-3

FINAL AT CATHKIN PARK

Queen's Park v Renton	3-1

FA CUP 1885-86

THIRD ROUND

Blackburn Rovers v Darwen Old Wanderers	6-1
Staveley v Nottingham Forest	2-1
South Reading v Clapham Rovers*	wo
Burslem Port Vale v Leek (scratched)	wo
Swifts v Old Harrovians*	wo
Church v Rossendale	5-1
South Shore v Halliwell	6-1
Notts County v Notts Rangers	3-0
Wolverhampton Wanderers v Walsall Swifts	2-1
Old Westminsters v Romford	5-1
Preston North End* v Bolton Wanderers	3-2‡
Small Heath Alliance v Derby County	4-2
Davenham v Crewe Alexandra	2-1
Middlesbrough v Grimsby Town	2-1
Brentwood	bye
West Bromwich Albion	bye
Old Carthusians	bye
Redcar	bye

*disqualified
‡Preston disqualified after a protest

FOURTH ROUND

West Bromwich Albion v Wolverhampton Wanderers	3-1
Brentwood v South Reading	3-0
Blackburn Rovers	bye
Staveley	bye
Burslem Port Vale	bye
Swifts	bye
Church	bye
South Shore	bye
Notts County	bye
Old Carthusians	bye
Old Westminsters	bye
Bolton Wanderers	bye
Small Heath Alliance	bye
Davenham	bye
Redcar	bye
Middlesbrough	bye

FIFTH ROUND

Blackburn Rovers v Staveley	7-1
Brentwood v Burslem Port Vale †	wo
Swifts v Church	6-2
South Shore v Notts County	2-1
West Bromwich Albion v Old Carthusians	1-0
Old Westminsters v Bolton Wanderers*	wo
Small Heath Alliance v Davenham	2-1
Redcar v Middlesbrough	2-1

*disqualified
† Burslem Port Vale scratched after one drawn game

SIXTH ROUND

Blackburn Rovers v Brentwood	3-1
Swifts v South Shore	2-1
West Bromwich Albion v Old Westminsters	6-0
Small Heath Alliance v Redcar	2-0

SEMI-FINAL

Blackburn Rovers v Swifts	2-1
West Bromwich Albion v Small Heath Alliance	4-0

FINAL AT KENNINGTON OVAL

Blackburn Rovers v West Bromwich Albion	0-0, 2-0*

*replay at The Racecourse, Derby

Blackburn Rovers defeated Queen's Park in both the 1884 and 1885 FA Cup Finals. These remain the only occasions on which the same clubs have contested consecutive Finals. Queen's Park were also the last amateur club to appear in an English Cup Final.

On the way to the 1885 Cup Final Queen's Park defeated both the Nottingham clubs, then considered second only to Blackburn, after a replay. The second semi-final against Nottingham Forest is the only semi-final ever to be played outside England. It was staged at Merchiston Castle School in Edinburgh and it helped Forest set up their remarkable record of having been drawn to play Cup ties in all four home countries. In the first round of the 1888-89 competition they were drawn to play Linfield in Belfast. In fact by the time they arrived Linfield had withdrawn so the game became a friendly instead. No Scottish club ever reached the final again and three years later, the Scottish Football Association banned its members from entering competitions other than its own.

Rangers were drawn to play Arbroath in the Fourth Round of the 1884-85 Scottish Cup. Having lost 4-3 they sent home a telegram reading 'beaten on a back green'. Having measured the pitch they found it was only 49 yards 2 ft 1 in wide, 11 inches short of the minimum. They protested, the game was replayed, and Rangers won 8-1.

The 1886 Cup Final replay, played at The Racecourse, Derby, was the first Final ever played outside London. In winning the game Blackburn Rovers completed a hat-trick of successes never since repeated and were presented with a special shield – which still hangs in their boardroom – to mark the feat. The match is far more famous however, for the performance of the Blackburn captain Jimmy Brown. In his last ever game for the club, Brown dribbled the length of the pitch to score one of the greatest goals in the history of the Cup. In so doing he became the only man ever to score in three consecutive Cup Finals, and, more surprisingly, was immortalized in Arnold Bennett's 'The Card' for the feat.

FA CUP 1886-87†

THIRD ROUND
Aston Villa v Wolverhampton Wanderers	
	2-2, 3-3, 2-0
Horncastle v Grantham	2-0
Darwen v Bolton Wanderers	4-3
Chirk v Goldenhill (disqualified)	wo
Glasgow Rangers v Cowlairs	3-2
Lincoln City v Gainsborough Trinity	2-2, 1-0
Old Westminsters v Old Etonians	3-0
Partick Thistle v Cliftonville	11-1
Mitchell's St George's v Walsall Town	7-2
Lockwood Brothers v Nottingham Forest	2-1
Notts County v Staveley	3-0
Great Marlow v Dulwich	2-0
Preston North End v Renton	2-0
Old Foresters v Chatham	4-1
Old Carthusians v Caledonians (absent)	wo
Leek v Burslem Port Vale	2-2, 1-1, 3-1
Crewe Alexandra	bye
Swifts	bye
West Bromwich Albion	bye

FOURTH ROUND
Leek v Crewe Alexandra	1-0
Old Foresters v Swifts	2-0
West Bromwich Albion v Mitchell's St George's	1-0
Aston Villa	bye
Horncastle	bye
Darwen	bye
Chirk	bye
Glasgow Rangers	bye
Lincoln City	bye
Old Westminsters	bye
Partick Thistle	bye
Lockwood Brothers	bye
Notts County	bye
Great Marlow	bye
Preston North End	bye
Old Carthusians	bye

FIFTH ROUND
Aston Villa v Horncastle	5-0
Darwen v Chirk	3-1
Glasgow Rangers v Lincoln City	3-0
Old Westminsters v Partick Thistle	1-0
West Bromwich Albion v Lockwood Brothers	2-1*
Notts County v Great Marlow	5-2
Preston North End v Old Foresters	3-0
Old Carthusians v Leek	2-0
*after a disputed game	

SIXTH ROUND
Aston Villa v Darwen	3-2
Glasgow Rangers v Old Westminsters	5-1
West Bromwich Albion v Notts County	4-1
Preston North End v Old Carthusians	2-1

SEMI-FINAL
Aston Villa v Glasgow Rangers	3-1
West Bromwich Albion v Preston North End	3-1

FINAL AT KENNINGTON OVAL
Aston Villa v West Bromwich Albion	2-0

†There is some confusion as to the exact specification of the rounds. The *Football Annual for 1887*, edited by the honorary secretary of the Football Association, Charles Alcock, gives seven rounds and a Final. Later historys, such as the official *History of the Cup* give only three rounds and a Final after qualifying matches.

Hibernian's defeat of Dumbarton in the 1887 Scottish Cup final was the first time that an Edinburgh club had won the Scottish Cup. It was also the first and only time that the final was contested at Crosshills. The same year Hibs played and defeated Preston North End at their new ground, Easter Road, in what was billed as the 'Association Football Championship of the World' More remotely Hibernian's success was one of the main promptings for the founding of Celtic in Glasgow.

SCOTTISH FA CUP 1886-87

FIFTH ROUND
Hibernian v Queen of the South Wanderers	7-3
Vale of Leven v Cambuslang Hibernians	2-0
Clyde v Third Lanark	0-0, 2-4
Queen's Park v Cambuslang	1-1, 5-4
Hurlford v Morton	5-1
Kilmarnock v Dunblane	6-0
Port Glasgow Athletic v St Bernard's	6-2
Dumbarton v Harp (scratched)	wo

SIXTH ROUND
Port Glasgow Athletic v Vale of Leven	1-3
Kilmarnock v Queen's Park	0-5
Third Lanark v Hibernian	1-2
Hurlford v Dumbarton	0-0, 2-1*, 1-3

*Hurlford insisted on playing on a frozen pitch; the result was declared null and void by the Scottish FA

SEMI-FINAL
Hibernian v Vale of Leven	3-1
Queen's Park v Dumbarton	1-2

FINAL AT CROSSHILLS
Hibernian v Dumbarton	2-1

Below *The West Bromwich Albion side that won the FA Cup in 1888. It was their third consecutive Final but their first ever success. Billy Bassett is seated, second from the left. After defeating Preston North End at Trent Bridge in the 1887 semi-final, West Bromwich met them again in the actual Final in 1888. To say that Preston were confident is to put it mildly. One of their modest requests was that they might be photographed with the Cup before the game. They explained that they would be dirty afterwards and that this would spoil the picture. The referee, Major Marindin, who controlled eight Finals in all as well as playing in two, suggested that 'Had you not better win it first?' Apparently they had ten good scoring chances to Albion's two, but Albion converted 100% and Preston only 10%. It was called the greatest upset in the history of the Cup, and perhaps remained so until Sunderland defeated Leeds. West Bromwich's inspiration was 5ft 5in Billy Bassett, who went on to win eight consecutive caps against the Scots. Albion went on to beat Aston Villa in a series of three games to become the 'Champions of the Midlands'. Then then went to Scotland to play Scottish Cup winners Renton for the title of 'Champions of the World'. The game was played in a blinding snowstorm and Renton won.*

FA CUP 1887-88†

FIFTH ROUND
West Bromwich Albion v Stoke	4-1
Old Carthusians v Bootle	2-0
Derby Junction v Chirk	1-0
Darwen v Blackburn Rovers	0-3
Nottingham Forest v The Wednesday	2-4
Aston Villa v Preston North End	1-3
Middlesbrough v Old Foresters (scratched)	4-0*
Crewe Alexandra v Derby County	1-0

*Old Foresters protested at the state of the pitch and the FA ordered a replay. Meanwhile, Old Foresters scratched and Middlesbrough thus went through without a second game

SIXTH ROUND
West Bromwich Albion v Old Carthusians	4-2
Derby Junction v Blackburn Rovers	2-1
The Wednesday v Preston North End	1-3
Middlesbrough v Crewe Alexandra	0-2

SEMI-FINAL
West Bromwich Albion v Derby Junction	3-0
Preston North End v Crewe Alexandra	4-0

FINAL AT KENNINGTON OVAL
West Bromwich Albion v Preston North End	2-1

†There is confusion about the exact specification of the rounds. The *Football Annual for 1888* gives seven rounds and a Final, as do newspapers for that year.

SCOTTISH FA CUP 1887-88

FIFTH ROUND
Arbroath v Cowlairs	5-1
Cambuslang v Ayr	10-0
Thistle v Vale of Leven Wanderers	2-9
Abercorn v St Bernard's	9-0
Queen's Park v Partick Thistle	2-0
St Mirren v Renton	2-3
Our Boys v Albion Rovers	4-1
Dundee Wanderers v Carfin Shamrock	5-2

SIXTH ROUND
Abercorn v Arbroath	3-1
Renton v Dundee Wanderers	5-1
Cambuslang v Our Boys	6-0
Queen's Park v Vale of Leven Wanderers	7-1

SEMI-FINAL
Renton v Queen's Park	3-1
Abercorn v Cambuslang	1-1, 1-10

FINAL AT HAMPDEN PARK
Renton v Cambuslang	6-1

FA CUP 1888-89

FIRST ROUND
Grimsby Town v Sunderland Albion	3-1
Bootle v Preston North End	0-3
Halliwell v Crewe Alexandra	2-2, 5-1
Birmingham St George's v Long Eaton Rangers	3-2
Chatham v South Shore	2-1
Nottingham Forest v Linfield (scratched)	2-2, wo*
Small Heath v West Bromwich Albion	2-3
Burnley v Old Westminsters	4-3
Wolverhampton Wanderers v Old Carthusians	4-3
Walsall Town Swifts v Sheffield Heeley	5-1
The Wednesday v Notts Rangers	1-1, 3-0
Notts County v Old Brightonians	2-0
Blackburn Rovers v Accrington	1-1, 5-0
Swifts v Wrexham	3-1
Aston Villa v Witton	3-2
Derby County v Derby Junction	1-0

*Nottingham Forest travelled to Belfast for the replay but Linfield had scratched in the interim and the clubs played a friendly instead

SECOND ROUND
Grimsby Town v Preston North End	0-2
Halliwell v Birmingham St George's	2-3
Chatham v Nottingham Forest	1-1, 2-2, 3-2
West Bromwich Albion v Burnley	5-1
Wolverhampton Wanderers v Walsall Town Swifts	6-1
The Wednesday v Notts County	3-2
Blackburn Rovers v Swifts (scratched)	wo
Aston Villa v Derby County	5-3

THIRD ROUND
Preston North End v Birmingham St George's	2-0
Chatham v West Bromwich Albion	1-10
Wolverhampton Wanderers v The Wednesday	5-0
Blackburn Rovers v Aston Villa	8-1

SEMI-FINAL
Preston North End v West Bromwich Albion	1-0
Wolverhampton Wanderers v Blackburn Rovers	1-1, 3-1

FINAL AT KENNINGTON OVAL
Preston North End v Wolverhampton Wanderers	3-0

SCOTTISH FA CUP 1888-89

FIFTH ROUND
Third Lanark v Abercorn	5-4*, 2-2, 2-2, 3-1
Renton v Arbroath	3-3, 4-0
Celtic v Clyde	0-1†, 9-2
Dumbarton v Mossend Swifts	3-1
St Mirren v Queen of the South Wanderers	3-1
Campsie	bye
Dumbarton Athletic	bye
East Stirlingshire	bye

*Abercorn protested about bad light
†Celtic protested about bad light and the state of the pitch

SIXTH ROUND
Third Lanark v Campsie	6-0
Dumbarton v St Mirren	1-1, 2-2, 2-2, 3-1
Dumbarton Athletic v Renton	1-2
East Stirlingshire v Celtic	1-2

SEMI-FINAL
Dumbarton v Celtic	1-4
Third Lanark v Renton	2-0

FINAL AT HAMPDEN PARK
Third Lanark v Celtic	3-0‡, 2-1

‡The first game was declared unofficial because of a snowstorm. Third Lanark tried to claim the Cup but the SFA ordered a replay.

William Townley scored the first ever Cup Final hat-trick for Blackburn against The Wednesday in the 1890 Final. Rovers won 6-1 to record the highest score in a Final tie. Wednesday arrived for the Final having lost a disputed earlier tie against Notts County.

FOOTBALL LEAGUE 1888-89

		P	W	D	L	F	A	Pts
1	Preston	22	18	4	0	74	15	40
2	Aston Villa	22	12	5	5	61	43	29
3	Wolves	22	12	4	6	50	37	28
4	Blackburn	22	10	6	6	66	45	26
5	Bolton	22	10	2	10	63	59	22
6	WBA	22	10	2	10	40	46	22
7	Accrington	22	6	8	8	48	48	20
8	Everton	22	9	2	11	35	46	20
9	Burnley	22	7	3	12	42	62	17
10	Derby	22	7	2	13	41	60	16
11	Notts County	22	5	2	15	39	73	12
12	Stoke	22	4	4	14	26	51	12

Top *William McGregor of Aston Villa, whose open letter of 2 March 1888 led to the formation of the Football League. A meeting was held at Anderton's Hotel on the eve of the Cup Final (23 March 1888) and the idea was approved in principle. The details were finalized on 17 April at the Royal Hotel in Manchester by the twelve member clubs. With only 22 fixture dates available, other hopefuls—including Sheffield Wednesday and Nottingham Forest—had to be turned down. The League had grown in simple response to the need to guarantee fixtures. While there were only Cup competitions fixtures would always be called off at short notice for replays, and friendlies could never be guaranteed. Because of the uncertainty, spectators were increasingly reluctant to commit themselves to turning up to a match that might never be played—and so emerged McGregor's inevitable solution. Preston were the first winners of the League. Their performance in 1888-89 was unique for they remain the only side in England and Scotland to have gone a whole season without a League or or Cup defeat.*

FOOTBALL LEAGUE 1889-90

		P	W	D	L	F	A	Pts
1	Preston	22	15	3	4	71	30	33
2	Everton	22	14	3	5	65	40	31
3	Blackburn	22	12	3	7	78	41	27
4	Wolves	22	10	5	7	51	38	25
5	WBA	22	11	3	8	47	50	25
6	Accrington	22	9	6	7	53	56	24
7	Derby	22	9	3	10	43	55	21
8	Aston Villa	22	7	5	10	43	51	19
9	Bolton	22	9	1	12	54	65	19
10	Notts County	22	6	5	11	43	51	17
11	Burnley	22	4	5	13	36	65	13
12	Stoke	22	3	4	15	27	69	10

FA CUP 1889-90

FIRST ROUND
Preston North End v Newton Heath	6-1
Lincoln City v Chester	2-0
Bolton Wanderers v Belfast Distillery	10-1
Sheffield United v Burnley	2-1
The Wednesday v Swifts	6-1
Accrington v West Bromwich Albion	3-1
Notts County v Birmingham St George's	4-4, 6-2
South Shore v Aston Villa	2-4
Bootle v Sunderland Albion*	1-3
Derby Midland v Nottingham Forest	3-0
Blackburn Rovers v Sunderland	4-2
Newcastle West End v Grimsby Town	1-2
Wolverhampton Wanderers v Old Carthusians	2-0
Small Heath v Clapton	3-1
Stoke v Old Westminsters	3-0
Everton v Derby County	11-2

*Sunderland Albion were disqualified

SECOND ROUND
Preston North End v Lincoln City	4-0
Bolton Wanderers v Sheffield United	13-0
The Wednesday v Accrington	2-1
Notts County v Aston Villa	4-1
Bootle v Derby Midland	2-1
Blackburn Rovers v Grimsby Town	3-0
Wolverhampton Wanderers v Small Heath	2-1
Stoke v Everton	4-2

THIRD ROUND
Preston North End v Bolton Wanderers	2-3
The Wednesday v Notts County	5-0*, 2-3*, 2-1
Bootle v Blackburn Rovers	0-7
Wolverhampton Wanderers v Stoke	3-2

*replayed after protest on both occasions

SEMI-FINAL
Bolton Wanderers v The Wednesday	1-2
Blackburn Rovers v Wolverhampton Wanderers	1-0

FINAL AT KENNINGTON OVAL
Blackburn Rovers v The Wednesday	6-1

SCOTTISH FA CUP 1889-90

FOURTH ROUND
Aberdeen v Queen's Park	1-13
Airdrieonians v Abercorn	2-3
Grangemouth v Vale of Leven	1-7
Third Lanark v Linthouse	2-0
Lanemark v St Mirren	2-8
Moffat v Carfin Shamrock	4-2
Ayr v Leith Athletic	1-4
Cowdenbeath v Dunblane	†
Hibernian v Queen of the South Wanderers	†
Kilbirnie v East Stirlingshire	†
Heart of Midlothian v Alloa Athletic	†
East End v Cambuslang	†

†No scores are available. The first named team won in each case.

FIFTH ROUND
Queen's Park v St Mirren	1-0
Cowdenbeath v Abercorn	2-8
Vale of Leven v Heart of Midlothian	3-1
East End v Moffat	2-2*
Third Lanark	bye
Hibernian	bye
Leith Athletic	bye
Kilbirnie	bye

*East End won the replay

SIXTH ROUND
Queen's Park v Leith Athletic	1-0
Abercorn v Hibernian	6-2
Vale of Leven v East End	4-0
Third Lanark v Kilbirnie	4-1

SEMI-FINAL
Vale of Leven v Third Lanark	3-0
Queen's Park v Abercorn	2-0

FINAL AT IBROX PARK
Queen's Park v Vale of Leven	1-1, 2-1

FA CUP 1890-91

FIRST ROUND

Middlesbrough Ironopolis v Blackburn Rovers	1-2*, 0-3
Chester v Lincoln City	1-0
Accrington v Bolton Wanderers	2-2, 5-1
Long Eaton Rangers v Wolverhampton Wanderers	2-3
Royal Arsenal v Derby County	1-2
The Wednesday v Halliwell	12-0
Crusaders v Birmingham St George's	0-2
West Bromwich Albion v Old Westminsters (scratched)	wo
Darwen v Kidderminster	3-1*, 13-0
Sunderland v Everton	1-0
Clapton v Nottingham Forest	0-14
Sunderland Albion v 93rd Highlanders	2-0
Sheffield United v Notts County	1-9
Burnley v Crewe Alexandra	4-2
Stoke v Preston North End	3-0
Aston Villa v Casuals	13-1

*replayed after protest

SECOND ROUND

Blackburn Rovers v Chester	7-0
Accrington v Wolverhampton Wanderers	2-3
Derby County v The Wednesday	2-3
Birmingham St George's v West Bromwich Albion	0-3
Darwen v Sunderland	0-2
Nottingham Forest v Sunderland Albion	1-1, 0-0, 5-0
Notts County v Burnley	2-1
Stoke v Aston Villa	3-0

THIRD ROUND

Blackburn Rovers v Wolverhampton Wanderers	2-0
The Wednesday v West Bromwich Albion	0-2
Sunderland v Nottingham Forest	4-0
Notts County v Stoke	1-0

SEMI-FINAL

Blackburn Rovers v West Bromwich Albion	3-2
Sunderland v Notts County	3-3, 0-2

FINAL AT KENNINGTON OVAL

Blackburn Rovers v Notts County	3-1

SCOTTISH FA CUP 1890-91

FIFTH ROUND

Dumbarton v 5th KRV	8-0
Heart of Midlothian v Morton	5-1
Royal Albert v Celtic	0-4*, 0-2
St Mirren v Queen's Park	2-3
Abercorn	bye
Third Lanark	bye
East Stirlingshire	bye
Leith Athletic	bye

*Crowd invaded the pitch 10 minutes before time and forced a replay, which was played at Ibrox.

SIXTH ROUND

Dumbarton v Celtic	3-0
Heart of Midlothian v East Stirlingshire	3-1
Third Lanark v Queen's Park	1-1, 2-2, 4-1
Leith Athletic v Abercorn	2-3

SEMI-FINAL

Dumbarton v Abercorn	3-1
Heart of Midlothian v Third Lanark	4-1

FINAL AT HAMPDEN PARK

Heart of Midlothian v Dumbarton	1-0

FOOTBALL LEAGUE 1890-91

		P	W	D	L	F	A	Pts
1	Everton	22	14	1	7	63	29	29
2	Preston	22	12	3	7	44	23	27
3	Notts County	22	11	4	7	52	35	26
4	Wolves	22	12	2	8	39	50	26
5	Bolton	22	12	1	9	47	34	25
6	Blackburn	22	11	2	9	52	43	24
7	Sunderland	22	10	5	7	51	31	23*
8	Burnley	22	9	3	10	52	63	21
9	Aston Villa	22	7	4	11	45	58	18
10	Accrington	22	6	4	12	28	50	16
11	Derby	22	7	1	14	47	81	15
12	WBA	22	5	2	15	34	57	12

*Two points deducted for fielding Ned Doig against WBA on 20 September 1890 before the League had approved his registration from Arbroath.

SCOTTISH LEAGUE 1890-91

		P	W	D	L	F	A	Pts
1=	Dumbarton†	18	13	3	2	61	21	29
1=	Rangers†	18	13	3	2	58	25	29
3	Celtic*	18	11	3	4	48	21	21
4	Cambuslang	18	8	4	6	47	42	20
5	Third Lanark*	18	8	3	7	38	39	15
6	Hearts	18	6	2	10	31	37	14
7	Abercorn	18	5	2	11	36	47	12
8	St Mirren	18	5	1	12	39	62	11
9	Vale of Leven	18	5	1	12	27	65	11
10	Cowlairs*	18	4	3	11	24	50	6

†Dumbarton and Rangers drew 2-2 in a play-off and were declared joint Champions.
*Each had four points deducted for infringements.

FOOTBALL LEAGUE 1891-92

		P	W	D	L	F	A	Pts
1	Sunderland	26	21	0	5	93	36	42
2	Preston	26	18	1	7	61	31	37
3	Bolton	26	17	2	7	51	37	36
4	Aston Villa	26	15	0	11	89	56	30
5	Everton	26	12	4	10	49	49	28
6	Wolves	26	11	4	11	59	46	26
7	Burnley	26	11	4	11	49	45	26
8	Notts County	26	11	4	11	55	51	26
9	Blackburn	26	10	6	10	58	65	26
10	Derby	26	10	4	12	46	52	24
11	Accrington	26	8	4	14	40	78	20
12	WBA	26	6	6	14	51	58	18
13	Stoke	26	5	4	17	38	61	14
14	Darwen	26	4	3	19	38	112	11

SCOTTISH LEAGUE 1891-92

		P	W	D	L	F	A	Pts
1	Dumbarton	22	18	1	3	81	26	37
2	Celtic	22	16	3	3	64	19	35
3	Hearts	22	15	4	3	64	36	34
4	Rangers	22	12	2	8	57	49	26
5	Leith	22	12	1	9	52	38	25
6	Third Lanark	22	9	4	9	44	38	22
7	Clyde	22	8	4	10	64	60	20
8	Renton	22	8	4	10	43	41	20
9	Abercorn	22	6	5	11	45	59	17
10	St Mirren	22	4	5	13	43	56	13
11	Cambuslang	22	2	6	14	21	79	10
12	Vale of Leven	22	0	5	17	24	101	5

FA CUP 1891-92

FIRST ROUND

Old Westminsters v West Bromwich Albion	2-3
Blackburn Rovers v Derby County	4-1
The Wednesday v Bolton Wanderers	4-1
Small Heath v Royal Arsenal	5-1
Sunderland Albion v Birmingham St George's	4-0
Nottingham Forest v Newcastle East End	2-1
Luton v Middlesbrough	0-3
Preston North End v Middlesbrough Ironopolis	2-2, 6-0
Crewe Alexandra v Wolverhampton Wanderers	2-2, 1-4
Blackpool v Sheffield United	0-3
Aston Villa v Heanor Town	4-1
Bootle v Darwen	0-2
Crusaders v Accrington	1-4
Sunderland v Notts County	4-0
Everton v Burnley	1-3
Stoke v Casuals	3-0

SECOND ROUND

West Bromwich Albion v Blackburn Rovers	3-1
The Wednesday v Small Heath	2-0
Sunderland Albion v Nottingham Forest	0-1
Middlesbrough v Preston North End	1-2
Wolverhampton Wanderers v Sheffield United	3-1
Aston Villa v Darwen	2-0
Accrington v Sunderland	1-3
Burnley v Stoke	1-3

THIRD ROUND

West Bromwich Albion v The Wednesday	2-1
Nottingham Forest v Preston North End	2-0
Wolverhampton Wanderers v Aston Villa	1-3
Sunderland v Stoke	2-2, 4-0

SEMI-FINAL

West Bromwich Albion v Nottingham Forest	1-1, 1-1, 6-2
Aston Villa v Sunderland	4-1

FINAL AT KENNINGTON OVAL

West Bromwich Albion v Aston Villa	3-0

SCOTTISH FA CUP 1891-92

SECOND ROUND

Rangers v Kilmarnock	0-0, 1-1, 3-1
Third Lanark v Dumbarton	1-3
Broxburn Shamrock v Heart of Midlothian	4-5
Annbank v Leith Athletic	2-1
Queen's Park v Bathgate Rovers	6-0
Arbroath v Renton	0-3
Celtic v Kilmarnock Athletic	3-0
Cowlairs v Mid-Annandale	11-2

THIRD ROUND

Celtic v Cowlairs	4-1
Rangers v Annbank	2-0
Renton v Heart of Midlothian	4-4, 1-1, 3-2
Dumbarton v Queen's Park	2-2, 1-4

SEMI-FINAL

Renton v Queen's Park	1-1, 0-3
Celtic v Rangers	5-3

FINAL AT IBROX PARK

Celtic v Queen's Park	1-0*, 5-1

*The final had to be replayed, the first game having been disrupted by an unexpectedly large crowd.

In the first round of the FA Cup in 1890–91, Nottingham Forest beat Clapton 14-0 at Clapton. This remains the highest away win in any English first-class fixture. In the same round Darwen scored 13 against Kidderminster, Villa 13 against Casuals and Sheffield Wednesday 12 against Halliwell. Forest's performance was part of a good day for Nottingham – County also won 9-1 away from home.

During the 1890–91 FA Cup quarter-final between Notts County and Stoke at Trent Bridge a shot was punched off the line by County's left-back Hendry with his goalkeeper Toone well beaten. As the laws made no mention of penalties at the time, Stoke had to take a free-kick on the goal-line which Toone smothered easily. County won the match 1-0 and went on to the Final. The incident provoked so much comment that, partially as a result, penalties were introduced by the FA from September 1891. This led to another controversial incident in which Stoke were also the sufferers the next season. During a League game at Aston Villa, Stoke were losing 1-0 when a penalty was awarded them just two minutes from time. The Villa keeper picked up the ball and booted it out of the ground. By the time it had been found the referee had blown for full time. The law was soon changed to allow referees to add on time for penalties. The penalty law was changed again as late as 1892 when players were banned from touching the ball twice – and hence dribbling into the net.

FIRST DIVISION

		P	W	D	L	F	A	Pts
1	Sunderland	30	22	4	4	100	36	48
2	Preston	30	17	3	10	57	39	37
3	Everton	30	16	4	10	74	51	36
4	Aston Villa	30	16	3	11	73	62	35
5	Bolton	30	13	6	11	56	55	32
6	Burnley	30	13	4	13	51	44	30
7	Stoke	30	12	5	13	58	48	29
8	WBA	30	12	5	13	58	69	29
9	Blackburn	30	8	13	9	47	56	29
10	Nottm Forest	30	10	8	12	48	52	28
11	Wolves	30	12	4	14	47	68	28
12	Wednesday	30	12	3	15	55	65	27
13	Derby	30	9	9	12	52	64	27
14	Notts County	30	10	4	16	53	61	24
15	Accrington	30	6	11	13	57	81	23
16	Newton Heath	30	6	6	18	50	85	18

SCOTTISH FA CUP 1892-93

FIRST ROUND

Celtic v Linthouse	3-1
Airdrieonians v Third Lanark	3-6
Cowlairs v Queen's Park	1-4
Clyde v Dumbarton	1-6*
Motherwell v Campsie	9-2†, 6-4
St Mirren v Aberdeen	6-4
Dunblane v Broxburn Shamrock	0-3
Stenhousemuir v Heart of Midlothian	1-1, 0-8
Northern v Leith Athletic	1-3
Royal Albert v Cambuslang	6-1
Abercorn v Renton	6-0
St Bernard's v Queen of South Wanderers	5-1
Rangers v Annbank	7-0
King's Park v Monkcastle	6-1
5th KVR v Camelon	5-3
Albion Rovers v Kilmarnock	1-2

*The invasion of the pitch by the crowd caused the game to be abandoned with 25 minutes left to play. The SFA awarded the tie to Dumbarton.
† After a protest about the size of the pitch the tie was replayed.

SECOND ROUND

Celtic v 5th KVR	7-0
Leith Athletic v St Mirren	0-2
Abercorn v Third Lanark	4-5
St Bernard's v Royal Albert	5-2
Broxburn Shamrock v King's Park	3-0
Heart of Midlothian v Motherwell	4-2
Dumbarton v Rangers	0-1
Kilmarnock v Queen's Park	0-8

THIRD ROUND

Heart of Midlothian v Queen's Park	1-1, 2-5
Celtic v Third Lanark	5-1
St Bernard's v Rangers	3-2
Broxburn Shamrock v St Mirren	4-3

SEMI-FINAL

Queen's Park v Broxburn Shamrock	4-2
Celtic v St Bernard's	5-0

FINAL AT IBROX PARK

Queen's Park v Celtic	2-1

Right *Wolverhampton's 1893 team which won the only Final ever to be played at Fallowfield, Manchester, and the first to be initially contested outside London. An Everton reserve side had beaten the Wolves first team 4-2 the week before, but the underdogs won the real thing with a long-range headed goal from captain Harry Allen. The crowd, officially 45,000 but probably twice that number, broke down the gates and invaded the pitch and the match was played in near chaos.*

On 10 December 1892 Sheffield United defeated Burslem Port Vale 10-0 in a League fixture at Burslem. This remains the biggest away win in any Football League match. A contemporary report commented that: 'The Vale keeper lost his spectacles in the mud.'

SECOND DIVISION

		P	W	D	L	F	A	Pts
1	Small Heath	22	17	2	3	90	35	36
2	Sheff United	22	16	3	3	62	19	35
3	Darwen	22	14	2	6	60	36	30
4	Grimsby	22	11	1	10	42	41	23
5	Ardwick	22	9	3	10	45	40	21
6	Burton Swifts	22	9	2	11	47	47	20
7	Northwich Vic	22	9	2	11	42	58	20
8	Bootle	22	8	3	11	49	63	19
9	Lincoln	22	7	3	12	45	51	17
10	Crewe	22	6	3	13	42	69	15
11	Burslem PV	22	6	3	13	30	57	15
12	Walsall TS	22	5	3	14	37	75	13

TEST MATCHES 1892-93

Sheffield United 1 Accrington 0
Darwen 3 Notts County 2
Newton Heath 1 Small Heath 1

Play-off
Newton Heath 5 Small Heath 2

Sheffield United and Darwen promoted
Notts County relegated
Accrington resigned from the League

SCOTTISH LEAGUE

		P	W	D	L	F	A	Pts
1	Celtic	18	14	1	3	54	25	29
2	Rangers	18	12	4	2	41	27	28
3	St Mirren	18	9	2	7	40	39	20
4	Third Lanark	18	9	1	8	53	39	19
5	Hearts	18	8	2	8	39	42	18
6	Leith	18	8	1	9	36	31	17
7	Dumbarton	18	8	1	9	35	35	17
8	Renton	18	5	5	8	31	44	15
9	Abercorn	18	5	1	12	35	52	11
10	Clyde	18	2	2	14	25	55	6

1892-93 Champions Sunderland were the second side to be called 'The Team of all the Talents'. They became the first to score 100 goals or more in a single League season. In fact this total was not surpassed until after the First World War though, by then of course teams were playing far more games. Sunderland's winning margin of 11 points over the second club, Preston North End, has been equalled but never beaten in the division since. Aston Villa equalled it in 1897 as did Manchester United in 1956.

FA CUP 1892-93

FIRST ROUND

Everton v West Bromwich Albion	4-1
Nottingham Forest v Casuals	4-0
The Wednesday v Derby County	3-2*, 0-1†, 4-2
Burnley v Small Heath	2-0
Accrington v Stoke	2-1
Preston North End v Burton Swifts	9-2
Marlow v Middlesbrough Ironopolis	1-3
Notts County v Shankhouse	4-0
Wolverhampton Wanderers v Bolton Wanderers	1-1, 2-1
Newcastle United v Middlesbrough	2-3
Darwen v Aston Villa	5-4
Grimsby Town v Stockton	5-0
Blackburn Rovers v Newton Heath	4-0
Loughborough Town v Northwich Victoria	1-2
Blackpool v Sheffield United	1-3
Sunderland v Woolwich Arsenal	6-0

*Replay after protest
† Replay after second protest

SECOND ROUND

Everton v Nottingham Forest	4-2
The Wednesday v Burnley	1-0
Accrington v Preston North End	1-4
Middlesbrough Ironopolis v Notts County	3-2
Wolverhampton Wanderers v Middlesbrough	2-1
Darwen v Grimsby Town	2-0
Blackburn Rovers v Northwich Victoria	4-1
Sheffield United v Sunderland	1-3

THIRD ROUND

Everton v The Wednesday	3-0
Preston North End v Middlesbrough Ironopolis	2-2, 7-0
Wolverhampton Wanderers v Darwen	5-0
Blackburn Rovers v Sunderland	3-0

SEMI-FINAL

Everton v Preston North End	2-2, 0-0, 2-1
Wolverhampton Wanderers v Blackburn Rovers	2-1

FINAL AT FALLOWFIELD (MANCHESTER)

Wolverhampton Wanderers v Everton	1-0

With the introduction of a Second Division in 1892 – in fact the Football League simply absorbed the Football Alliance – a promotion/relegation system of test matches was instituted. This lasted until 1898 when Stoke and Burnley, realising that if they drew their match they would both be in the First Division, contrived a scoreless draw. Suspicions were aroused and a system of two up/two down was introduced.

COLORSPORT

FIRST DIVISION

		P	W	D	L	F	A	Pts
1	Aston Villa	30	19	6	5	84	42	44
2	Sunderland	30	17	4	9	72	44	38
3	Derby	30	16	4	10	73	62	36
4	Blackburn	30	16	2	12	69	53	34
5	Burnley	30	15	4	11	61	51	34
6	Everton	30	15	3	12	90	57	33
7	Nottm Forest	30	14	4	12	57	48	32
8	WBA	30	14	4	12	66	59	32
9	Wolves	30	14	3	13	52	63	31
10	Sheff United	30	13	5	12	47	61	31
11	Stoke	30	13	3	14	65	79	29
12	Wednesday	30	9	8	13	48	57	26
13	Bolton	30	10	4	16	38	52	24
14	Preston	30	10	3	17	44	56	23
15	Darwen	30	7	5	18	37	83	19
16	Newton Heath	30	6	2	22	36	72	14

SECOND DIVISION

		P	W	D	L	F	A	Pts
1	Liverpool	28	22	6	0	77	18	50
2	Small Heath	28	21	0	7	103	44	42
3	Notts County	28	18	3	7	70	31	39
4	Newcastle	28	15	6	7	66	39	36
5	Grimsby	28	15	2	11	71	58	32
6	Burton Swifts	28	14	3	11	79	61	31
7	Burslem PV	28	13	4	11	66	64	30
8	Lincoln	28	11	6	11	59	58	28
9	Woolwich A	28	12	4	12	52	55	28
10	Walsall TS	28	10	3	15	51	61	23
11	Md Ironopolis	28	8	4	16	37	72	20
12	Crewe	28	6	7	15	42	73	19
13	Ardwick	28	8	2	18	47	71	18
14	Rotherham Twn	28	6	3	19	44	91	15
15	Northwich Vic	28	3	3	22	30	98	9

TEST MATCHES 1893-94

Preston North End 4 Notts County 0
Small Heath 3 Darwen 1
Liverpool 2 Newton Heath 0

Liverpool and Small Heath promoted
Darwen and Newton Heath relegated

At the beginning of the 1894-95 season Liverpool completed what remained the longest League run without defeat until Leeds broke it in 1969. They had joined the Second Division in 1893 and remained undefeated in the 28-game season. They then won their Test Match to gain promotion to the First, where they drew the first two games before suffering their first ever League defeat by Aston Villa. This was after a run of 31 games.

Aston Villa turned the tables on Sunderland in Season 1893-94 by taking the League Championship with a margin of 6 points. It was the start of an era in which they became the leading club in the land. Over a period of seven years Villa won five Championships and two FA Cup Finals. They also become only the second club to win the double (after Preston North End) in 1897. Yet as recently as 1891 they had finished fourth from bottom and had had to seek re-election to the League.

When the FA made Goodison the venue for the 1894 Cup Final Notts County protested that it was virtually a home tie for Bolton. They won anyway, with Jimmy Logan (seated centre) scoring a hat-trick to equal William Townley's feat of 1890. Only one man, Stan Mortensen in 1953, has done it since.

During the 1893-94 season Everton scored 22 goals in the space of four matches. Jack Southworth claimed 15 of these, including six on the trot against West Bromwich on 30 December 1893. Everton won 7-1.

FA CUP 1893-94

FIRST ROUND

Middlesbrough Ironopolis v Luton Town	2-1
Nottingham Forest v Heanor Town	1-0
Notts County v Burnley	1-0
Stockport County v Burton Wanderers	0-1
Leicester Fosse v South Shore	2-1
Derby County v Darwen	2-0
Newton Heath v Middlesbrough	4-0
West Bromwich Albion v Blackburn Rovers	2-3
Newcastle United v Sheffield United	2-0
Small Heath v Bolton Wanderers	3-4
Liverpool v Grimsby Town	3-0
Preston North End v Reading	18-0
Woolwich Arsenal v The Wednesday	1-2
Stoke v Everton	1-0
Sunderland v Accrington	3-0
Aston Villa v Wolverhampton Wanderers	4-2

SECOND ROUND

Middlesbrough Ironopolis v Nottingham Forest	0-2
Notts County v Burton Wanderers	2-1
Leicester Fosse v Derby County	0-0, 0-3
Newton Heath v Blackburn Rovers	0-0, 1-5
Newcastle United v Bolton Wanderers	1-2
Liverpool v Preston North End	3-2
The Wednesday v Stoke	1-0
Sunderland v Aston Villa	2-2, 1-3

THIRD ROUND

Nottingham Forest v Notts County	1-1, 1-4
Derby County v Blackburn Rovers	1-4
Bolton Wanderers v Liverpool	3-0
The Wednesday v Aston Villa	3-2

SEMI-FINAL

Notts County v Blackburn Rovers	1-0
Bolton Wanderers v The Wednesday	2-1

FINAL AT GOODISON PARK

Notts County v Bolton Wanderers	4-1

SCOTTISH FIRST DIVISION

		P	W	D	L	F	A	Pts
1	Celtic	18	14	1	3	53	32	29
2	Hearts	18	11	4	3	46	32	26
3	St Bernard's	18	11	1	6	53	41	23
4	Rangers	18	8	4	6	44	30	20
5	Dumbarton	18	7	5	6	32	35	19
6	St Mirren	18	7	3	8	50	46	17
7	Third Lanark	18	7	3	8	37	45	17
8	Dundee	18	6	3	9	43	58	15
9	Leith	18	4	2	12	36	46	10
10	Renton	18	1	2	15	23	52	4

Below *Notts County, the first Second Division side to win the FA Cup, in 1894.*

SCOTTISH FA CUP 1893-94

FIRST ROUND

Arbroath v Broxburn Shamrock	8-3
St Bernard's v Kilmarnock	3-1
Renton v Grangemouth	7-1
Cambuslang v East Stirlingshire	3-2
Port Glasgow Athletic v Airdrieonians	7-5
Dumbarton v Vale of Leven	2-1
Clyde v King's Park	5-2
Albion Rovers v 2nd Black Watch	6-0
Battlefield v Thistle	3-0
Leith Athletic v Orion	11-2
Queen's Park v Linthouse	5-1
Third Lanark v Inverness Thistle	9-3
Celtic v Hurlford	6-0
Abercorn v 5th KRV	2-1
St Mirren v Heart of Midlothian	1-0
Rangers v Cowlairs	8-0

SECOND ROUND

Abercorn v Battlefield	3-0
Port Glasgow Athletic v Renton	3-1
Queen's Park v Arbroath	3-0
Clyde v Cambuslang	6-0
Rangers v Leith Athletic	2-0
Third Lanark v St Mirren	3-2
Celtic v Albion Rovers	7-0
St Bernard's v Dumbarton	3-1

THIRD ROUND

Third Lanark v Port Glasgow Athletic	2-1
Celtic v St Bernard's	8-1
Clyde v Rangers	0-5
Abercorn v Queen's Park	3-3, 3-3, 0-2

SEMI-FINAL

Third Lanark v Celtic	3-5
Rangers v Queen's Park	1-1, 3-1

FINAL AT HAMPDEN PARK

Rangers v Celtic	3-1

SCOTTISH SECOND DIVISION

		P	W	D	L	F	A	Pts
1	Hibernian	18	13	3	2	83	29	29
2	Cowlairs	18	13	1	4	75	32	27
3	Clyde †	18	11	2	5	51	36	24
4	Motherwell	18	11	1	6	61	46	23
5	Partick	18	10	0	8	56	58	20
6	Port Glasgow	18	9	2	7	52	53	13*
7	Abercorn	18	5	2	11	42	60	12
8	Morton	18	4	1	13	36	62	9
9	Northern	18	3	3	12	29	66	9
10	Thistle	18	2	3	13	31	74	7

*Port Glasgow Athletic had 7 points deducted for fielding an ineligible player
† Clyde promoted to First Division

FIRST DIVISION

		P	W	D	L	F	A	Pts
1	Sunderland	30	21	5	4	80	37	47
2	Everton	30	18	6	6	82	50	42
3	Aston Villa	30	17	5	8	82	43	39
4	Preston	30	15	5	10	62	46	35
5	Blackburn	30	11	10	9	59	49	32
6	Sheff United	30	14	4	12	57	55	32
7	Nottm Forest	30	13	5	12	50	56	31
8	Wednesday	30	12	4	14	50	55	28
9	Burnley	30	11	4	15	44	56	26
10	Bolton	30	9	7	14	61	62	25
11	Wolves	30	9	7	14	43	63	25
12	Small Heath	30	9	7	14	50	74	25
13	WBA	30	10	4	16	51	66	24
14	Stoke	30	9	6	15	50	67	24
15	Derby	30	7	9	14	45	68	23
16	Liverpool	30	7	8	15	51	70	22

SECOND DIVISION

		P	W	D	L	F	A	Pts
1	Bury	30	23	2	5	78	33	48
2	Notts County	30	17	5	8	75	45	39
3	Newton Heath	30	15	8	7	78	44	38
4	Leicester Fosse	30	15	8	7	72	53	38
5	Grimsby	30	18	1	11	79	52	37
6	Darwen	30	16	4	10	74	43	36
7	Burton Wand	30	14	7	9	67	39	35
8	Woolwich A	30	14	6	10	75	58	34
9	Man City	30	14	3	13	82	72	31
10	Newcastle	30	12	3	15	72	84	27
11	Burton Swifts	30	11	3	16	52	74	25
12	Rotherham T	30	11	2	17	55	62	24
13	Lincoln	30	10	0	20	52	92	20
14	Walsall TS	30	10	0	20	47	92	20
15	Burslem PV	30	7	4	19	39	77	18
16	Crewe	30	3	4	23	26	103	10

FA CUP 1894-95

FIRST ROUND

Aston Villa v Derby County	2-1
Newcastle United v Burnley	2-1
Barnsley St Peter's v Liverpool	1-1, 0-4
Southampton St Mary's v Nottingham Forest	1-4
Sunderland v Fairfield	11-1
Luton Town v Preston North End	0-2
Bolton Wanderers v Woolwich Arsenal	1-0
Bury v Leicester Fosse	4-1
Sheffield United v Millwall Athletic	3-1
Small Heath v West Bromwich Albion	1-2
Darwen v Wolverhampton Wanderers	0-0, 0-2
Newton Heath v Stoke	2-3
The Wednesday v Notts County	5-1
Middlesbrough v Chesterfield	4-0
Southport Central v Everton	0-3
Burton Wanderers v Blackburn Rovers	1-2

SECOND ROUND

Aston Villa v Newcastle United	7-1
Liverpool v Nottingham Forest	0-2
Sunderland v Preston North End	2-0
Bolton Wanderers v Bury	1-0
Sheffield United v West Bromwich Albion	1-1, 1-2
Wolverhampton Wanderers v Stoke	2-0
The Wednesday v Middlesbrough	6-1
Everton v Blackburn Rovers	1-1, 3-2

THIRD ROUND

Aston Villa v Nottingham Forest	6-2
Sunderland v Bolton Wanderers	2-1
West Bromwich Albion v Wolverhampton Wanderers	1-0
The Wednesday v Everton	2-0

SEMI-FINAL

Aston Villa v Sunderland	2-1
West Bromwich Albion v The Wednesday	2-0

FINAL AT CRYSTAL PALACE

Aston Villa v West Bromwich Albion	1-0

SCOTTISH FIRST DIVISION

		P	W	D	L	F	A	Pts
1	Hearts	18	15	1	2	50	18	31
2	Celtic	18	11	4	3	52	31	26
3	Rangers	18	10	2	6	41	26	22
4	Third Lanark	18	10	1	7	51	39	21
5	St Mirren	18	9	1	8	34	36	19
6	St Bernard's	18	8	1	9	39	40	17
7	Clyde	18	8	0	10	40	49	16
8	Dundee	18	6	2	10	28	33	14
9	Leith	18	3	1	14	32	64	7
10	Dumbarton	18	3	1	14	27	58	7

SCOTTISH SECOND DIVISION

		P	W	D	L	F	A	Pts
1	Hibernian†	18	14	2	2	92	27	30
2	Motherwell	18	10	2	6	56	39	22
3	Port Glasgow	18	8	4	6	62	56	20
4	Renton*	17	10	0	7	46	44	20
5	Morton	18	9	1	8	59	63	19
6	Airdrieonians	18	8	2	8	68	45	18
7	Partick	18	8	2	8	50	60	18
8	Abercorn	18	7	3	8	48	65	17
9	Dundee Wand*	17	3	1	13	44	86	9*
10	Cowlairs	18	2	3	13	37	77	7

† Hibernian elected to First Division
*Dundee Wanderers and Renton played each other only once. Dundee were awarded two points when Renton failed to turn up for the return fixture.

TEST MATCHES 1894-95

Bury 1 Liverpool 0
Stoke 3 Newton Heath 0
Derby County 2 Notts County 1
Bury promoted. Liverpool relegated.

SCOTTISH FA CUP 1894-95

FIRST ROUND

St Bernard's v Airdrieonians	4-2
Slamannan Rovers v Renton	2-3*, 0-4
Ayr Parkhouse v Polton Vale	5-2
Clyde v Stevenston Thistle	7-2
Rangers v Heart of Midlothian	1-2
Orion v Dundee	1-5
Kilmarnock v East Stirlingshire	5-1
Raith Rovers v 5th KRV	6-3*, 3-4
Celtic v Queen's Park	4-1
Dumbarton v Galston.	2-1
Leith Athletic v Abercorn	5-1*, 1-4
St Mirren v Battlefield	5-0*, 8-1
Annbank v Third Lanark	6-4
Hibernian v Forfar Athletic	6-1
Motherwell v Mossend Swifts	1-2
Lochee United v King's Park	2-5

*These four ties were replayed after various protests. For example the Slamannan crowd was unruly; Raith Rovers failed to provide goal nets.

SECOND ROUND

St Bernard's v Kilmarnock	3-1
Renton v 5th KRV	6-0
Dundee v St Mirren	2-0
Heart of Midlothian v Abercorn	6-1
Clyde v Annbank	4-2
Ayr Parkhouse v Mossend Swifts	3-1
King's Park v Dumbarton	2-1
Hibernian v Celtic	2-0†, 0-2

†Celtic protested that Hibs fielded an ineligible player and a replay was agreed.

THIRD ROUND

St Bernard's v Clyde	2-1
Ayr Parkhouse v Renton	2-3
Dundee v Celtic	1-0
Heart of Midlothian v King's Park	4-2

SEMI-FINAL

Dundee v Renton	1-1, 3-3, 0-3
Heart of Midlothian v St Bernard's	0-0, 0-1

FINAL AT IBROX PARK

St Bernard's v Renton	2-1

The 1895 Cup Final was the first ever to be held at the Crystal Palace, and it got off to a remarkable start. Within 30 seconds a shot from Bob Chatt had ricocheted off John Devey's knee past the helpless West Bromwich goalkeeper Reader and Villa had won the Cup. Because of confusion at the turnstiles—the crowd of 42,000 was then the largest ever seen in London—many spectators missed the game's only goal, which remains the quickest ever scored in a Cup Final. The match was the third Final between Villa and their neighbours in 8 years; Villa had won 2-0 in 1887 and West Brom 3-0 in 1892, so the aggregate was level at three goals each. They remain the only pair of clubs ever to have met each other in three Finals. Yet another oddity to emerge from this game was that both teams, West Bromwich and Aston Villa, lost the Cup. In the winners' case this was the result of its theft, on 11 September, from **below** the window of one William

Shillcock, a boot and shoe manufacturer, who was displaying it to help advertise his wares. The Cup was never recovered and Villa were fined £25, which was used to purchase a replica of the original from Vaughton's of Birmingham. The Monday after the Final, meanwhile, Albion played their last League match needing a five-goal victory to avoid the test matches. They beat Wednesday 6-0; allegations of 'fixing' were never substantiated. In 1958 one Harry Burge, then 83, confessed to having stolen the Cup and having melted it down to make half-crowns. It was probably worth about £20.

League Tables 1895-96

FIRST DIVISION

		P	W	D	L	F	A	Pts
1	Aston Villa	30	20	5	5	78	45	45
2	Derby	30	17	7	6	68	35	41
3	Everton	30	16	7	7	66	43	39
4	Bolton	30	16	5	9	49	37	37
5	Sunderland	30	15	7	8	52	41	37
6	Stoke	30	15	0	15	56	47	30
7	Wednesday	30	12	5	13	44	53	29
8	Blackburn	30	12	5	13	40	50	29
9	Preston	30	11	6	13	44	48	28
10	Burnley	30	10	7	13	48	44	27
11	Bury	30	12	3	15	50	54	27
12	Sheff United	30	10	6	14	40	50	26
13	Nottm Forest	30	11	3	16	42	57	25
14	Wolves	30	10	1	19	61	65	21
15	Small Heath	30	8	4	18	39	79	20
16	WBA	30	6	7	17	30	59	19

Below *Fred Spiksley, the Wednesday left-winger who scored both goals in the 2-1 win over Wolverhampton Wanderers which took the FA Cup to Sheffield for the first time. It was also the first time the new Cup, made after the original had been stolen from a Birmingham shop, had been presented.*

SECOND DIVISION

		P	W	D	L	F	A	Pts
1	Liverpool	30	22	2	6	106	32	46
2	Man City	30	21	4	5	63	38	46
3	Grimsby	30	20	2	8	82	38	42
4	Burton Wand	30	19	4	7	69	40	42
5	Newcastle	30	16	2	12	73	50	34
6	Newton Heath	30	15	3	12	66	57	33
7	Woolwich A	30	14	4	12	59	42	32
8	Leicester Fosse	30	14	4	12	57	44	32
9	Darwen	30	12	6	12	72	67	30
10	Notts County	30	12	2	16	57	54	26
11	Burton Swifts	30	10	4	16	39	69	24
12	Loughborough	30	9	5	16	40	67	23
13	Lincoln	30	9	4	17	53	75	22
14	Burslem PV	30	7	4	19	43	78	18
15	Rotherham Tn	30	7	3	20	34	97	17
16	Crewe	30	5	3	22	30	95	13

SCOTTISH FIRST DIVISION

		P	W	D	L	F	A	Pts
1	Celtic	18	15	0	3	64	25	30
2	Rangers	18	11	4	3	57	39	26
3	Hibernian	18	11	2	5	58	39	24
4	Hearts	18	11	0	7	68	36	22
5	Dundee	18	7	2	9	33	42	16
6	Third Lanark	18	7	1	10	47	51	15
7	St Bernard's	18	7	1	10	36	53	15
8	St Mirren	18	5	3	10	31	51	13
9	Clyde	18	4	3	11	39	59	11
10	Dumbarton	18	4	0	14	36	74	8

SCOTTISH SECOND DIVISION

		P	W	D	L	F	A	Pts
1	Abercorn*	18	12	3	3	55	31	27
2	Leith	18	11	1	6	55	37	23
3	Renton	18	9	3	6	40	28	21
4	Kilmarnock	18	10	1	7	45	45	21
5	Airdrieonians	18	7	4	7	48	44	18
6	Partick	18	8	2	8	44	54	18
7	Port Glasgow	18	6	4	8	40	41	16
8	Motherwell	18	5	3	10	31	47	13
9	Morton	18	4	4	10	32	40	12
10	Linthouse	18	5	1	12	25	48	11

*Abercorn elected to First Division

TEST MATCHES 1895-96

Man City 1 WBA 1   Liverpool 2 WBA 0
Small Heath 0 Liverpool 0   Liverpool 4 Small Heath 0
WBA 6 Man City 1   Small Heath 8 Man City 0
Man City 3 Small Heath 0   WBA 2 Liverpool 0

	P	W	D	L	F	A	Pts
Liverpool	4	2	1	1	6	2	5
WBA	4	2	1	1	9	4	5
Small Heath	4	1	1	2	8	7	3
Man City	4	1	1	2	5	15	3

Liverpool promoted. Small Heath relegated.

FA CUP 1895-96

SECOND ROUND

Wolverhampton Wanderers v Liverpool	2-0
Burnley v Stoke	1-1, 1-7
Derby County v Newton Heath	1-1, 5-1
Grimsby Town v West Bromwich Albion	1-1, 0-3
The Wednesday v Sunderland	2-1
Everton v Sheffield United	3-0
Blackpool v Bolton Wanderers	0-2
Newcastle United v Bury	1-3

THIRD ROUND

Wolverhampton Wanderers v Stoke	3-0
Derby County v West Bromwich Albion	1-0
The Wednesday v Everton	4-0
Bolton Wanderers v Bury	2-0

SEMI-FINAL

Wolverhampton Wanderers v Derby County	2-1
The Wednesday v Bolton Wanderers	1-1, 3-1

FINAL AT CRYSTAL PALACE

The Wednesday v Wolverhampton Wanderers	2-1

SCOTTISH FA CUP 1895-96

FIRST ROUND

Blantyre v Heart of Midlothian	1-12
East Stirlingshire v Hibernian	2-3
St Bernard's v Clackmannan	8-1
Renton v Cowdenbeath	1-0
Lochgelly United v Raith Rovers	2-1*, 2-5
Dumbarton v Rangers	1-1, 1-3
Celtic v Queen's Park	2-4
Third Lanark v Leith Athletic	6-0
Annbank v Kilmarnock	3-2
Ayr v Abercorn	3-2
Port Glasgow Athletic v Arthurlie	4-2
St Mirren v Alloa Athletic	7-0
Arbroath v King's Park	5-0
Morton v Dundee	2-3
Clyde v Polton Vale	3-0
St Johnstone v Dundee Wanderers	4-2

*A Lochgelly player, David 'Anderson', was in fact David McLaren of Lochee United and had already appeared for that club in an earlier round. After a protest from Raith the tie was replayed.

SECOND ROUND

Heart of Midlothian v Ayr	5-1
Hibernian v Raith Rovers	6-1
St Bernard's v Annbank	2-0
Renton v Clyde	2-1
Rangers v St Mirren	5-1
Third Lanark v Dundee	4-1
Queen's Park v Port Glasgow Athletic	8-1
Arbroath v St Johnstone	3-1

THIRD ROUND

Heart of Midlothian v Arbroath	4-0
Hibernian v Rangers	3-2
St Bernard's v Queen's Park	3-2
Renton v Third Lanark	3-3, 2-0

SEMI-FINAL

Heart of Midlothian v St Bernard's	1-0
Hibernian v Renton	2-1

FINAL AT LOGIE GREEN, EDINBURGH

Heart of Midlothian v Hibernian	3-1

Above left *John Reynolds, who played at half-back in the England team which defeated Scotland 3-0 at Everton in 1895. Reynolds, though born in Blackburn, had played five times for Ireland during a spell with Distillery in 1890 and 1891. He then moved to West Bromwich, with whom he won a cap for England against Scotland. He then moved to Villa, with whom he won another seven caps. Only one other player, R E Evans, has been known to play for two of the home countries.*

FIRST DIVISION

	P	W	D	L	F	A	Pts
1 Aston Villa	30	21	5	4	73	38	47
2 Sheff United	30	13	10	7	42	29	36
3 Derby	30	16	4	10	70	50	36
4 Preston	30	11	12	7	55	40	34
5 Liverpool	30	12	9	9	46	38	33
6 Wednesday	30	10	11	9	42	37	31
7 Everton	30	14	3	13	62	57	31
8 Bolton	30	12	6	12	40	43	30
9 Bury	30	10	10	10	39	44	30
10 Wolves	30	11	6	13	45	41	28
11 Nottm Forest	30	9	8	13	44	49	26
12 WBA	30	10	6	14	33	56	26
13 Stoke	30	11	3	16	48	59	25
14 Blackburn	30	11	3	16	35	62	25
15 Sunderland	30	7	9	14	34	47	23
16 Burnley	30	6	7	17	43	61	19

SECOND DIVISION

	P	W	D	L	F	A	Pts
1 Notts County	30	19	4	7	92	43	42
2 Newton Heath	30	17	5	8	56	34	39
3 Grimsby	30	17	4	9	66	45	38
4 Small Heath	30	16	5	9	69	47	37
5 Newcastle	30	17	1	12	56	52	35
6 Man City	30	12	8	10	58	50	32
7 Gainsborough	30	12	7	11	50	47	31
8 Blackpool	30	13	5	12	59	56	31
9 Leicester Fosse	30	13	4	13	59	56	30
10 Woolwich A	30	13	4	13	68	70	30
11 Darwen	30	14	0	16	67	61	28
12 Walsall	30	11	4	15	53	69	26
13 Loughborough	30	12	1	17	50	64	25
14 Burton Swifts	30	9	6	15	46	61	24
15 Burton Wand	30	9	2	19	31	67	20
16 Lincoln	30	5	2	23	27	85	12

TEST MATCHES 1896-97

Notts County 1 Sunderland 0
Newton Heath 2 Burnley 0
Burnley 0 Notts County 1
Sunderland 2 Newton Heath 0
Sunderland 0 Notts County 0
Newton Heath 1 Sunderland 1
Burnley 2 Newton Heath 0
Notts County 1 Burnley 1

	P	W	D	L	F	A	Pts
Notts County	4	2	2	0	3	1	6
Sunderland	4	1	2	1	3	2	4
Burnley	4	1	1	2	3	4	3
Newton Heath	4	1	1	2	3	5	3

Notts County promoted
Burnley relegated

FA CUP 1896-97

FIRST ROUND

Aston Villa v Newcastle United	5-0
Small Heath v Notts County	1-2
Preston North End v Manchester City	6-0
Stoke v Glossop North End	5-2
Burnley v Sunderland	0-1
Nottingham Forest v The Wednesday	1-0
Luton Town v West Bromwich Albion	0-1
Liverpool v Burton Swifts	4-3
Everton v Burton Wanderers	5-2
Stockton v Bury	0-0, 1-12
Blackburn Rovers v Sheffield United	2-1
Millwall Athletic v Wolverhampton Wanderers	1-2
Derby County v Barnsley St Peter's	8-1
Bolton Wanderers v Grimsby Town	0-0, 3-3, 3-2
Heanor Town v Southampton St Mary's	1-1, 0-1
Newton Heath v Kettering	5-1

SECOND ROUND

Aston Villa v Notts County	2-1
Preston North End v Stoke	2-1
Sunderland v Nottingham Forest	1-3
West Bromwich Albion v Liverpool	1-2
Everton v Bury	3-0
Blackburn Rovers v Wolverhampton Wanderers	2-1
Derby County v Bolton Wanderers	4-1
Southampton St Mary's v Newton Heath	1-1, 1-3

THIRD ROUND

Aston Villa v Preston North End	1-1, 0-0, 3-2
Nottingham Forest v Liverpool	1-1, 0-1
Everton v Blackburn Rovers	2-0
Derby County v Newton Heath	2-0

SEMI-FINAL

Aston Villa v Liverpool	3-0
Everton v Derby County	3-2

FINAL AT CRYSTAL PALACE

Aston Villa v Everton	3-2

SCOTTISH FA CUP 1896-97

FIRST ROUND

Arthurlie v Celtic	4-2
Third Lanark v Newton Stewart Athletic	8-1
Heart of Midlothian v Clyde	2-0
St Bernard's v Queen's Park	2-1
St Mirren v Renton	5-1
Partick Thistle v Rangers	2-4
Dumbarton v Raith Rovers	2-1
Duncrab Park v Hibernian	1-10
Motherwell v Kilmarnock	3-3, 2-5
Abercorn v Hurlford	4-0
Falkirk v Orion	2-0
Dundee v Inverness Thistle	7-1
Morton v Johnstone	3-1
Blantyre v Bathgate	5-0
Leith Athletic v Dunblane	5-1
Lochgelly United v King's Park	1-2

SECOND ROUND

Arthurlie v Morton	1-5
Kilmarnock v Falkirk	7-3
Third Lanark v Heart of Midlothian	5-2
Dumbarton v Leith Athletic	4-4, 3-3, 3-2
Rangers v Hibernian	3-0
Dundee v King's Park	5-0
St Bernard's v St Mirren	5-0
Abercorn v Blantyre	4-1

THIRD ROUND

Dumbarton v St Bernard's	2-0
Morton v Abercorn	2-2, 3-2
Dundee v Rangers	0-4
Kilmarnock v Third Lanark	3-1

SEMI-FINAL

Morton v Rangers	2-7
Dumbarton v Kilmarnock	4-3

FINAL AT HAMPDEN PARK

Rangers v Dumbarton	5-1

SCOTTISH FIRST DIVISION

	P	W	D	L	F	A	Pts
1 Hearts	18	13	2	3	47	22	28
2 Hibernian	18	12	2	4	50	20	26
3 Rangers	18	11	3	4	64	30	25
4 Celtic	18	10	4	4	42	18	24
5 Dundee	18	10	2	6	38	30	22
6 St Mirren	18	9	1	8	38	29	19
7 St Bernard's	18	7	0	11	32	40	14
8 Third Lanark	18	5	1	12	29	46	11
9 Clyde	18	4	0	14	27	65	8
10 Abercorn	18	1	1	16	21	88	3

SCOTTISH SECOND DIVISION

	P	W	D	L	F	A	Pts
1 Partick †	18	14	3	1	61	28	31
2 Leith	18	13	1	4	54	28	27
3 Kilmarnock	18	10	1	7	44	33	21
4 Airdrieonians	18	10	1	7	48	39	21
5 Morton	18	7	2	9	38	40	16
6 Renton	18	6	2	10	34	40	14
7 Linthouse	18	8	2	8	44	52	14*
8 Port Glasgow	18	4	5	9	39	50	13
9 Motherwell	18	6	1	11	40	55	13
10 Dumbarton	18	2	2	14	27	64	6

*Four points deducted for fielding an
   ineligible player.
† Partick elected to First Division

Above Footballs from Lancashire, as used in the 1890s.

Left The Aston Villa side that won the double in 1897. Their eleven point margin over the second League club remains a record and the double was not repeated until the Spurs of 64 years later.

FIRST DIVISION

		P	W	D	L	F	A	Pts
1	Sheff United	30	17	8	5	56	31	42
2	Sunderland	30	16	5	9	43	30	37
3	Wolves	30	14	7	9	57	41	35
4	Everton	30	13	9	8	48	39	35
5	Wednesday	30	15	3	12	51	42	33
6	Aston Villa	30	14	5	11	61	51	33
7	WBA	30	11	10	9	44	45	32
8	Nottm Forest	30	11	9	10	47	49	31
9	Liverpool	30	11	6	13	48	45	28
10	Derby	30	11	6	13	57	61	28
11	Bolton	30	11	4	15	28	41	26
12	Preston NE	30	8	8	14	35	43	24
13	Notts County	30	8	8	14	36	46	24
14	Bury	30	8	8	14	39	51	24
15	Blackburn	30	7	10	13	39	54	24
16	Stoke	30	8	8	14	35	55	24

SECOND DIVISION

		P	W	D	L	F	A	Pts
1	Burnley	30	20	8	2	80	24	48
2	Newcastle	30	21	3	6	64	32	45
3	Man City	30	15	9	6	66	36	39
4	Newton Heath	30	16	6	8	64	35	38
5	Woolwich A	30	16	5	9	69	49	37
6	Small Heath	30	16	4	10	58	50	36
7	Leicester Fosse	30	13	7	10	46	35	33
8	Luton	30	13	4	13	68	50	30
9	Gainsborough	30	12	6	12	50	54	30
10	Walsall	30	12	5	13	58	58	29
11	Blackpool	30	10	5	15	49	61	25
12	Grimsby	30	10	4	16	52	62	24
13	Burton Swifts	30	8	5	17	38	69	21
14	Lincoln	30	6	5	19	43	82	17
15	Darwen	30	6	2	22	31	76	14
16	Loughborough	30	6	2	22	24	87	14

SCOTTISH FIRST DIVISION

		P	W	D	L	F	A	Pts
1	Celtic	18	15	3	0	56	13	33
2	Rangers	18	13	3	2	71	15	29
3	Hibernian	18	10	2	6	48	28	22
4	Hearts	18	8	4	6	54	33	20
5	Third Lanark	18	8	2	8	37	38	18
6	St Mirren	18	8	2	8	30	36	18
7	Dundee*	18	5	3	10	29	36	13
8	Partick*	18	6	1	11	34	64	13
9	St Bernard's	18	4	1	13	35	67	9
10	Clyde	18	1	3	14	20	84	5

*Partick Thistle and Dundee played a test match to decide the bottom three and Dundee won 2-0

SCOTTISH SECOND DIVISION

		P	W	D	L	F	A	Pts
1	Kilmarnock	18	14	1	3	64	29	29
2	Port Glasgow	18	12	1	5	66	35	25
3	Morton	18	9	4	5	47	38	22
4	Leith	18	9	2	7	39	38	20
5	Linthouse	18	6	4	8	37	39	16
6	Ayr	18	7	2	9	36	42	16
7	Abercorn	18	6	4	8	33	41	16
8	Airdrieonians	18	6	2	10	44	56	14
9	Hamilton*	18	5	2	11	28	51	12
10	Motherwell	18	3	4	11	31	56	10

*Took the place of Renton, who resigned

Left Ernest 'Nudger' Needham, who led his club, Sheffield United, to the League Championship, the first honour in their history.

Below Harry Linacre, the Nottingham Forest goalkeeper and an England cap in the early part of the twentieth century. Linacre came from a great footballing family in Aston-on-Trent, near Derby. His two uncles, Frank and Fred Forman, played in all the 1898-99 season internationals for England and remain the only brothers from the same professional club to have played together for England. They were also Forest regulars, like their nephew, and Frank Forman was captain of the Forest team that won the club's first honour with the FA Cup in 1898. Five days before the Final their opponents and local rivals Derby County had thrashed them 5-0 in a League match. But, despite this and a crippling injury to wing-half Wragg, Forest won the Final 3-1.

COLORSPORT

FA CUP 1897-98

FIRST ROUND

Southampton St Mary's v Leicester Fosse	2-1
Preston North End v Newcastle United	1-2
Luton Town v Bolton Wanderers	0-1
Manchester City v Wigan County	2-1
West Bromwich Albion v New Brighton Tower	2-0
Sunderland v The Wednesday	0-1
Nottingham Forest v Grimsby Town	4-0
Long Eaton Rangers v Gainsborough Trinity	0-1
Liverpool v Hucknall St John's	2-0
Newton Heath v Walsall	1-0
Notts County v Wolverhampton Wanderers	0-1
Derby County v Aston Villa	1-0
Burnley v Woolwich Arsenal	3-1
Burslem Port Vale v Sheffield United	1-1, 2-1
Everton v Blackburn Rovers	1-0
Bury v Stoke	1-2

SECOND ROUND

Southampton St Mary's v Newcastle United	1-0
Bolton Wanderers v Manchester City	1-0
West Bromwich Albion v The Wednesday	1-0
Nottingham Forest v Gainsborough Trinity	4-0
Liverpool v Newton Heath	0-0, 2-1
Wolverhampton Wanderers v Derby County	0-1
Burnley v Burslem Port Vale	3-0
Everton v Stoke	0-0, 5-1

THIRD ROUND

Southampton St Mary's v Bolton Wanderers	0-0, 4-0
West Bromwich Albion v Nottingham Forest	2-3
Liverpool v Derby County	1-1, 1-5
Burnley v Everton	1-3

SEMI-FINAL

Southampton St Mary's v Nottingham Forest	1-1, 0-2
Derby County v Everton	3-1

FINAL AT CRYSTAL PALACE

Nottingham Forest v Derby County	3-1

SCOTTISH FA CUP 1897-98

SECOND ROUND

Dundee v St Mirren	2-0
Rangers v Cartvale	12-0
Third Lanark v Celtic	3-2
Kilmarnock v Leith Athletic	9-2
Dundee Wanderers v Ayr Parkhouse	3-6
Hibernian v East Stirlingshire	3-1
Heart of Midlothian v Morton	4-1
St Bernard's v Queen's Park	0-5

THIRD ROUND

Queen's Park v Rangers	1-3
Third Lanark v Hibernian	2-0
Ayr Parkhouse v Kilmarnock	2-7
Dundee v Heart of Midlothian	3-0

SEMI-FINAL

Rangers v Third Lanark	1-1, 2-2, 2-0
Kilmarnock v Dundee	3-2

FINAL AT HAMPDEN PARK

Rangers v Kilmarnock	2-0

TEST MATCHES 1897-98

Newcastle 2 Stoke 1	Blackburn 1 Burnley 3
Burnley 2 Blackburn 0	Stoke 1 Newcastle 0
Newcastle 4 Blackburn 0	Blackburn 4 Newcastle 3
Burnley 0 Stoke 2	Stoke 0 Burnley 0

	P	W	D	L	F	A	Pts
Stoke	4	2	1	1	4	2	5
Burnley	4	2	1	1	5	3	5
Newcastle	4	2	0	2	9	6	4
Blackburn	4	1	0	3	5	12	2

Burnley and Newcastle promoted
No clubs relegated

FIRST DIVISION

		P	W	D	L	F	A	Pts
1	Aston Villa	34	19	7	8	76	40	45
2	Liverpool	34	19	5	10	49	33	43
3	Burnley	34	15	9	10	45	47	39
4	Everton	34	15	8	11	48	41	38
5	Notts County	34	12	13	9	47	51	37
6	Blackburn	34	14	8	12	60	52	36
7	Sunderland	34	15	6	13	41	41	36
8	Wolves	34	14	7	13	54	48	35
9	Derby	34	12	11	11	62	57	35
10	Bury	34	14	7	13	48	49	35
11	Nottm Forest	34	11	11	12	42	42	33
12	Stoke	34	13	7	14	47	52	33
13	Newcastle	34	11	8	15	49	48	30
14	WBA	34	12	6	16	42	57	30
15	Preston	34	10	9	15	44	47	29
16	Sheff United	34	9	11	14	45	51	29
17	Bolton	34	9	7	18	37	51	25
18	Wednesday	34	8	8	18	32	61	24

SECOND DIVISION

		P	W	D	L	F	A	Pts
1	Man City	34	23	5	6	92	35	52
2	Glossop NE	34	20	6	8	76	38	46
3	Leicester Fosse	34	18	9	7	64	42	45
4	Newton Heath	34	19	5	10	67	43	43
5	New Brighton	34	18	7	9	71	52	43
6	Walsall	34	15	12	7	79	36	42
7	Woolwich A	34	18	5	11	72	41	41
8	Small Heath	34	17	7	10	85	50	41
9	Burslem PV	34	17	5	12	56	34	39
10	Grimsby	34	15	5	14	71	60	35
11	Barnsley	34	12	7	15	52	56	31
12	Lincoln	34	12	7	15	51	56	31
13	Burton Swifts	34	10	8	16	51	70	28
14	Gainsborough	34	10	5	19	56	72	25
15	Luton	34	10	3	21	51	95	23
16	Blackpool	34	8	4	22	49	90	20
17	Loughborough	34	6	6	22	38	92	18
18	Darwen	34	2	5	27	22	141	9

SCOTTISH FIRST DIVISION

		P	W	D	L	F	A	Pts
1	Rangers	18	18	0	0	79	18	36
2	Hearts	18	12	2	4	56	30	26
3	Celtic	18	11	2	5	51	33	24
4	Hibernian	18	10	3	5	42	43	23
5	St Mirren	18	8	4	6	46	32	20
6	Third Lanark	18	7	3	8	33	38	17
7	St Bernard's	18	4	4	10	30	37	12
8	Clyde	18	4	4	10	23	48	12
9	Partick	18	2	2	14	19	58	6
10	Dundee	18	1	2	15	23	65	4

SCOTTISH SECOND DIVISION

		P	W	D	L	F	A	Pts
1	Kilmarnock*	18	14	4	0	73	24	32
2	Leith	18	12	3	3	63	38	27
3	Port Glasgow	18	12	1	5	75	51	25
4	Motherwell	18	7	6	5	41	40	20
5	Hamilton	18	7	1	10	48	58	15
6	Airdrieonians	18	6	3	9	35	46	15
7	Morton	18	6	1	11	36	41	13
8	Ayr	18	5	3	10	35	51	13
9	Linthouse	18	5	1	12	29	62	11
10	Abercorn	18	4	1	13	41	65	9

*Kilmarnock elected to First Division

Below *The Aston Villa side which won the First Division Championship in 1899.*

Second Division Darwen are the only side to have suffered three 10-goal defeats in a single season. In 1898-99 they lost 10-0 to Manchester City, Walsall and Loughborough, all in the space of six weeks. Their 141 goals against was also a record.

Season 1898-99 provided one unique record. Glasgow Rangers won every single game they played in the Scottish League, the only time that this feat has been performed by a British club. Their only defeat in 1898-99 in fact was a shock collapse, 2-0, to Glasgow rivals Celtic in the Scottish Cup final. Only three other clubs — Celtic, Preston and Liverpool — have gone a League season without defeat.

FA CUP 1898-99

FIRST ROUND

Everton v Jarrow	3-1
Nottingham Forest v Aston Villa	2-1
Sheffield United v Burnley	2-2, 2-1
Preston North End v Grimsby Town	7-0
West Bromwich Albion v South Shore	8-0
Heanor Town v Bury	0-3
Liverpool v Blackburn Rovers	2-0
Glossop North End v Newcastle United	0-1
Notts County v Kettering Town	2-0
New Brompton v Southampton	0-1
Woolwich Arsenal v Derby County	0-6
Bolton Wanderers v Wolverhampton Wanderers	0-0, 0-1
Small Heath v Manchester City	3-2
Stoke v The Wednesday	2-2, 2-0
Newton Heath v Tottenham Hotspur	1-1, 3-5
Bristol City v Sunderland	2-4

SECOND ROUND

Everton v Nottingham Forest	0-1
Sheffield United v Preston North End	2-2, 2-1
West Bromwich Albion v Bury	2-1
Liverpool v Newcastle United	3-1
Notts County v Southampton	0-1
Derby County v Wolverhampton Wanderers	2-1
Small Heath v Stoke	2-2, 1-2
Tottenham Hotspur v Sunderland	2-1

THIRD ROUND

Nottingham Forest v Sheffield United	0-1
West Bromwich Albion v Liverpool	0-2
Southampton v Derby County	1-2
Stoke v Tottenham Hotspur	4-1

SEMI-FINAL

Sheffield United v Liverpool	2-2, 4-4, 0-1*, 1-0
Derby County v Stoke	3-1

*abandoned

FINAL AT CRYSTAL PALACE

Sheffield United v Derby County	4-1

SCOTTISH FA CUP 1898-99

FIRST ROUND

Queen's Park v Kilsyth Wanderers	4-0
Hibernian v Royal Albert	2-1
6th G R V v Celtic	1-8
St Bernard's v Bo'ness	3-3, 4-2
Port Glasgow Athletic v Renton	3-2
Forfar Athletic v West Calder Swifts	4-5
Irvine v Partick Thistle	0-5
Morton v Annbank	3-1
St Mirren v Leith Athletic	7-1
Third Lanark v Arthurlie	4-1
Orion v Kilmarnock	0-2
East Stirlingshire v Dumbarton	4-1
Rangers v Heart of Midlothian	4-1
Ayr Parkhouse v Dundee	3-1
Clyde v Wishaw Thistle	3-0
Airdrieonians v Arbroath	3-3, 2-3

SECOND ROUND

Queen's Park v Hibernian	5-1
Celtic v St Bernard's	3-0
Port Glasgow Athletic v West Calder Swifts	3-1
Morton v Partick Thistle	2-2, 1-2
Third Lanark v St Mirren	1-2
East Stirlingshire v Kilmarnock	1-1, 0-0, 2-4
Ayr Parkhouse v Rangers	1-4
Clyde v Arbroath	3-1

THIRD ROUND

Celtic v Queen's Park	4-2*, 2-1
Port Glasgow Athletic v Partick Thistle	7-3
Kilmarnock v St Mirren	1-2
Rangers v Clyde	4-0

*abandoned

SEMI-FINAL

Celtic v Port Glasgow Athletic	4-2
St Mirren v Rangers	1-2

FINAL AT HAMPDEN PARK

Celtic v Rangers	2-0

FIRST DIVISION

		P	W	D	L	F	A	Pts
1	Aston Villa	34	22	6	6	77	35	50
2	Sheff United	34	18	12	4	63	33	48
3	Sunderland	34	19	3	12	50	35	41
4	Wolves	34	15	9	10	48	37	39
5	Newcastle	34	13	10	11	53	43	36
6	Derby	34	14	8	12	45	43	36
7	Man City	34	13	8	13	50	44	34
8	Nottm Forest	34	13	8	13	56	55	34
9	Stoke	34	10	10	14	37	45	34
10	Liverpool	34	14	5	15	49	45	33
11	Everton	34	13	7	14	47	49	33
12	Bury	34	13	6	15	40	44	32
13	WBA	34	11	8	15	43	51	30
14	Blackburn	34	13	4	17	49	61	30
15	Notts County	34	9	11	14	46	60	29
16	Preston	34	12	4	18	38	48	28
17	Burnley	34	11	5	18	34	54	27
18	Glossop NE	34	4	10	20	31	74	18

SECOND DIVISION

		P	W	D	L	F	A	Pts
1	Wednesday	34	25	4	5	84	22	54
2	Bolton	34	22	8	4	79	25	52
3	Small Heath	34	20	6	8	78	38	46
4	Newton Heath	34	20	4	10	63	27	44
5	Leicester Fosse	34	17	9	8	53	36	43
6	Grimsby	34	17	6	11	67	46	40
7	Chesterfield	34	16	6	12	65	60	38
8	Woolwich A	34	16	4	14	61	43	36
9	Lincoln	34	14	8	12	46	43	36
10	New Brighton	34	13	9	12	66	58	35
11	Burslem PV	34	14	6	14	39	49	34
12	Walsall	34	12	8	14	50	55	32
13	Gainsborough	34	9	7	18	47	75	25
14	Middlesbrough	34	8	8	18	39	69	24
15	Burton Swifts	34	9	6	19	43	84	24
16	Barnsley	34	8	7	19	46	79	23
17	Luton	34	5	8	21	40	75	18
18	Loughborough	34	1	6	27	18	100	8

SCOTTISH FIRST DIVISION

		P	W	D	L	F	A	Pts
1	Rangers	18	15	2	1	68	27	32
2	Celtic	18	9	7	2	46	27	25
3	Hibernian	18	9	6	3	43	24	24
4	Hearts	18	10	3	5	41	24	23
5	Kilmarnock	18	6	6	6	30	37	18
6	Dundee	18	4	7	7	36	40	15
7	Third Lanark	18	5	5	8	31	37	15
8	St Mirren	18	3	6	9	30	46	12
9	St Bernard's	18	4	4	10	29	47	12
10	Clyde	18	2	0	16	25	70	4

SCOTTISH SECOND DIVISION

		P	W	D	L	F	A	Pts
1	Partick*	18	14	1	3	56	26	29
2	Morton*	18	14	0	4	66	25	28
3	Port Glasgow	18	10	0	8	50	41	20
4	Motherwell	18	9	1	8	38	36	19
5	Leith	18	9	1	8	32	37	19
6	Abercorn	18	7	2	9	46	39	16
7	Hamilton	18	7	1	10	33	46	15
8	Ayr	18	6	2	10	39	48	14
9	Airdrieonians	18	4	3	11	27	49	11
10	Linthouse	18	2	5	11	28	68	9

*Partick Thistle and Morton were elected to the First Division.

The Manchester City keeper, C Williams, scored with a goal-kick against Sunderland on 14 April 1900 when his opposite number, Ned Doig, touched the ball on its way into the net. At that time full-backs used to tap goal-kicks into the keeper's hands and he would punt the ball from the 6-yard semi-circle.

Below *Part of the huge crowd at the 1900 Cup Final at Crystal Palace.*

FA CUP 1899-1900

FIRST ROUND
Preston North End v Tottenham Hotspur	1-0
Blackburn Rovers v Portsmouth	0-0, 1-1, 5-0
Nottingham Forest v Grimsby Town	3-0
Sunderland v Derby County	2-2, 3-0
The Wednesday v Bolton Wanderers	1-0
Sheffield United v Leicester Fosse	1-0
Notts County v Chorley	6-0
Burnley v Bury	0-1
Southampton v Everton	3-0
Newcastle United v Reading	2-1
West Bromwich Albion v Walsall	1-1, 6-0
Liverpool v Stoke	0-0, 1-0
Wolverhampton Wanderers v Queen's Park Rangers	1-1, 0-1
Jarrow v Millwall Athletic	0-2
Aston Villa v Manchester City	1-1, 3-1
Bristol City v Stalybridge Rovers	2-1

SECOND ROUND
Preston North End v Blackburn Rovers	1-0
Nottingham Forest v Sunderland	3-0
The Wednesday v Sheffield United	1-1, 0-2
Notts County v Bury	0-0, 0-2
Southampton v Newcastle United	4-1
West Bromwich Albion v Liverpool	1-1, 2-1
Queen's Park Rangers v Millwall Athletic	0-2
Aston Villa v Bristol City	5-1

THIRD ROUND
Preston North End v Nottingham Forest	0-0, 0-1
Sheffield United v Bury	2-2, 0-2
Southampton v West Bromwich Albion	2-1
Millwall Athletic v Aston Villa	1-1, 0-0, 2-1

SEMI-FINAL
Nottingham Forest v Bury	1-1, 2-3
Southampton v Millwall Athletic	0-0, 3-0

FINAL AT CRYSTAL PALACE
Bury v Southampton	4-0

SCOTTISH FA CUP 1899-1900

FIRST ROUND
Rangers v Morton	4-2
Celtic v Bo'ness	7-1
Third Lanark v Raith Rovers	5-1
Heart of Midlothian v St Mirren	0-0, 3-0
Kilmarnock v East Stirlingshire	2-0
Hamilton Academicals v Hibernian	2-3
St Bernard's v Arbroath	1-0
Galston v Partick Thistle	1-2
Forfar Athletic v Motherwell	3-4
Abercorn v Ayr Parkhouse	5-2
Port Glasgow Athletic v Falkirk	7-1
Dundee v Douglas Wanderers	8-0
Maybole v Wishaw Thistle	3-2
Forres Mechanics v Orion	1-1, 1-4
Queen's Park v Leith Athletic	3-0
Airdrieonians v Clyde	0-1

SECOND ROUND
Heart of Midlothian v Hibernian	1-1, 2-1
Dundee v Clyde	3-3, 3-0
Queen's Park v Abercorn	5-1
Rangers v Maybole	12-0
Kilmarnock v Orion	10-0
Partick Thistle v St Bernard's	2-1
Third Lanark v Motherwell	2-1
Port Glasgow Athletic v Celtic	1-5

THIRD ROUND
Rangers v Partick Thistle	6-1
Celtic v Kilmarnock	4-0
Queen's Park v Dundee	1-0
Third Lanark v Heart of Midlothian	1-2

SEMI-FINAL
Rangers v Celtic	1-1, 0-4
Queen's Park v Heart of Midlothian	2-1

FINAL AT IBROX PARK
Celtic v Queen's Park	4-3

FIRST DIVISION

	P	W	D	L	F	A	Pts
1 Liverpool	34	19	7	8	59	35	45
2 Sunderland	34	15	13	6	57	26	43
3 Notts County	34	18	4	12	54	46	40
4 Nottm Forest	34	16	7	11	53	36	39
5 Bury	34	16	7	11	53	37	39
6 Newcastle	34	14	10	10	42	37	38
7 Everton	34	16	5	13	55	42	37
8 Wednesday	34	13	10	11	52	42	36
9 Blackburn	34	12	9	13	39	47	33
10 Bolton	34	13	7	14	39	55	33
11 Man City	34	13	6	15	48	58	32
12 Derby	34	12	7	15	55	42	31
13 Wolves	34	9	13	12	39	55	31
14 Sheff United	34	12	7	15	35	52	31
15 Aston Villa	34	10	10	14	45	51	30
16 Stoke	34	11	5	18	46	57	27
17 Preston	34	9	7	18	49	75	25
18 WBA	34	7	8	19	35	62	22

SECOND DIVISION

	P	W	D	L	F	A	Pts
1 Grimsby	34	20	9	5	60	33	49
2 Small Heath	34	19	10	5	57	24	48
3 Burnley	34	20	4	10	53	29	44
4 New Brighton	34	17	8	9	57	38	42
5 Glossop NE	34	15	8	11	51	33	38
6 Middlesbrough	34	15	7	12	50	40	37
7 Woolwich A	34	15	6	13	39	35	36
8 Lincoln	34	13	7	14	43	39	33
9 Burslem PV	34	11	11	12	45	47	33
10 Newton Heath	34	14	4	16	42	38	32
11 Leicester Fosse	34	11	10	13	39	37	32
12 Blackpool	34	12	7	15	33	58	31
13 Gainsborough	34	10	10	14	45	60	30
14 Chesterfield	34	9	10	15	46	58	28
15 Barnsley	34	11	5	18	47	60	27
16 Walsall	34	7	13	14	40	56	27
17 Stockport	34	11	3	20	38	68	25
18 Burton Swifts	34	8	4	22	34	66	20

SCOTTISH FIRST DIVISION

	P	W	D	L	F	A	Pts
1 Rangers	20	17	1	2	60	25	35
2 Celtic	20	13	3	4	49	28	29
3 Hibernian	20	9	7	4	29	22	25
4 Morton	20	9	3	8	40	40	21
5 Kilmarnock	20	7	4	9	35	47	18
6 Third Lanark	20	6	6	8	20	29	18
7 Dundee	20	6	5	9	36	35	17
8 Queen's Park	20	7	3	10	33	37	17
9 St Mirren	20	5	6	9	33	43	16
10 Hearts	20	5	4	11	22	30	14
11 Partick	20	4	2	14	28	49	10

SCOTTISH SECOND DIVISION

	P	W	D	L	F	A	Pts
1 St Bernard's	18	10	5	3	41	26	25
2 Airdrieonians	18	11	1	6	46	35	23
3 Abercorn	18	9	3	6	37	33	21
4 Clyde	18	9	2	7	43	35	20
5 Port Glasgow	18	9	1	8	45	44	19
6 Ayr	18	9	0	9	32	34	18
7 E Stirlingshire	18	7	4	7	35	39	18
8 Leith	18	5	3	10	23	33	13
9 Hamilton	18	4	4	10	44	51	12
10 Motherwell	18	4	3	11	26	42	11

Below *The legendary Fatty Foulke, Sheffield United's goalkeeper, fishes the ball out of the net after one of two goals scored against his team in the 1901 Cup Final by Sandy Brown of Tottenham Hotspur. Brown's goals earned the Londoners a 2-2 draw and won him a place in the record books. For Brown had become the first man to score in every round of the competition and the centre-forward's tally of 15 goals—including the one he got in the replay at Bolton—remains a record. Spurs were then members of the Southern League and are the only non-League club to have won the Cup since 1888.*

FA CUP 1900-01

FIRST ROUND

Bolton Wanderers v Derby County	1-0
Reading v Bristol Rovers	2-0
Tottenham Hotspur v Preston North End	1-1, 4-2
The Wednesday v Bury	0-1
Middlesbrough v Newcastle United	3-1
Kettering Town v Chesterfield Town	1-1, 2-1
Woolwich Arsenal v Blackburn Rovers	2-0
West Bromwich Albion v Manchester City	1-0
Notts County v Liverpool	2-0
Wolverhampton Wanderers v New Brighton Tower	5-1
Sunderland v Sheffield United	1-2
Southampton v Everton	1-3
Stoke v Small Heath	1-1, 1-2
Newton Heath v Burnley	0-0, 1-7
Aston Villa v Millwall Athletic	5-0
Nottingham Forest v Leicester Fosse	5-1

SECOND ROUND

Bolton Wanderers v Reading	0-1
Tottenham Hotspur v Bury	2-1
Middlesbrough v Kettering Town	5-0
Woolwich Arsenal v West Bromwich Albion	0-1
Notts County v Wolverhampton Wanderers	2-3
Sheffield United v Everton	2-0
Small Heath v Burnley	1-0
Aston Villa v Nottingham Forest	0-0, 3-1

THIRD ROUND

Reading v Tottenham Hotspur	1-1, 0-3
Middlesbrough v West Bromwich Albion	0-1
Wolverhampton Wanderers v Sheffield United	0-4
Small Heath v Aston Villa	0-0, 0-1

SEMI-FINAL

Tottenham Hotspur v West Bromwich Albion	4-0
Sheffield United v Aston Villa	2-2, 3-0

FINAL AT CRYSTAL PALACE

Tottenham Hotspur v Sheffield United	2-2, 3-1*

*replay at Bolton

SCOTTISH FA CUP 1900-01

FIRST ROUND

Dundee Wanderers v Abercorn	0-3
Celtic v Rangers	1-0
Third Lanark v Douglas Wanderers	5-0
Kilmarnock v Airdrieonians	3-2
St Mirren v Kilwinning Eglinton	10-0
Morton v Bo'ness	10-0
Dundee v Arthurlie	3-1
Stenhousemuir v Queen's Park	1-3
St Bernard's v Partick Thistle	5-0
Heart of Midlothian v Mossend Swifts	7-0
Ayr v Orion	2-2, 3-1
Port Glasgow Athletic v Newton Stewart Athletic	9-1
Hibernian v Dumbarton	7-0
Royal Albert v St Johnstone	1-1, 2-2, 2-0
Forfar Athletic v Leith Athletic	0-4
Clyde v East Stirlingshire	6-0

SECOND ROUND

Clyde v Dundee	3-5
Heart of Midlothian v Queen's Park	2-1
Royal Albert v Hibernian	1-1, 0-1
Ayr v St Mirren	1-3
Celtic v Kilmarnock	6-0
Third Lanark v Abercorn	1-1, 1-0
Morton v St Bernard's	3-1
Leith Athletic v Port Glasgow Athletic	0-3

THIRD ROUND

Dundee v Celtic	0-1
St Mirren v Third Lanark	0-0, 1-1, 3-3, 1-0
Port Glasgow Athletic v Heart of Midlothian	1-5
Hibernian v Morton	2-0

SEMI-FINAL

Heart of Midlothian v Hibernian	1-1, 2-1
St Mirren v Celtic	0-1

FINAL AT IBROX PARK

Heart of Midlothian v Celtic	4-3

FIRST DIVISION

		P	W	D	L	F	A	Pts
1	Sunderland	34	19	6	9	50	35	44
2	Everton	34	17	7	10	53	35	41
3	Newcastle	34	14	9	11	48	34	37
4	Blackburn	34	15	6	13	52	48	36
5	Nottm Forest	34	13	9	12	43	43	35
6	Derby	34	13	9	12	39	41	35
7	Bury	34	13	8	13	44	38	34
8	Aston Villa	34	13	8	13	42	40	34
9	Wednesday	34	13	8	13	48	52	34
10	Sheff United	34	13	7	14	53	48	33
11	Liverpool	34	10	12	12	42	38	32
12	Bolton	34	12	8	14	51	56	32
13	Notts County	34	14	4	16	51	57	32
14	Wolves	34	13	6	15	46	57	32
15	Grimsby	34	13	6	15	44	60	32
16	Stoke	34	11	9	14	45	55	31
17	Small Heath	34	11	8	15	47	45	30
18	Man City	34	11	6	17	42	58	28

SECOND DIVISION

		P	W	D	L	F	A	Pts
1	WBA	34	25	5	4	82	29	55
2	Middlesbrough	34	23	5	6	90	24	51
3	Preston NE	34	18	6	10	71	32	42
4	Woolwich A	34	18	6	10	50	26	42
5	Lincoln	34	14	13	7	45	35	41
6	Bristol City	34	17	6	11	52	35	40
7	Doncaster	34	13	8	13	49	58	34
8	Glossop NE	34	10	12	12	36	40	32
9	Burnley	34	10	10	14	41	45	30
10	Burton United	34	11	8	15	46	54	30
11	Barnsley	34	12	6	16	51	63	30
12	Burslem PV	34	10	9	15	43	59	29
13	Blackpool	34	11	7	16	40	56	29
14	Leicester Fosse	34	12	5	17	38	56	29
15	Newton Heath	34	11	6	17	38	53	28
16	Chesterfield	34	11	6	17	47	68	28
17	Stockport	34	8	7	19	36	72	23
18	Gainsborough	34	4	11	19	30	80	19

SCOTTISH FIRST DIVISION

		P	W	D	L	F	A	Pts
1	Rangers	18	13	2	3	43	29	28
2	Celtic	18	11	4	3	38	28	26
3	Hearts	18	10	2	6	32	21	22
4	Third Lanark	18	7	5	6	30	26	19
5	St Mirren	18	8	3	7	29	28	19
6	Hibernian	18	6	4	8	36	24	16
7	Kilmarnock	18	5	6	7	21	25	16
8	Queen's Park	18	5	4	9	21	32	14
9	Dundee	18	4	5	9	16	31	13
10	Morton	18	1	5	12	18	40	7

SCOTTISH SECOND DIVISION

		P	W	D	L	F	A	Pts
1	Port Glasgow*	22	14	4	4	71	31	32
2	Partick*	22	14	3	5	55	26	31
3	Motherwell	22	12	2	8	50	44	26
4	Airdrieonians	22	10	5	7	40	32	25
5	Hamilton	22	11	3	8	45	40	25
6	St Bernard's	22	10	2	10	30	30	22
7	Leith	22	9	3	10	34	38	21
8	Ayr	22	8	5	9	27	33	21
9	E Stirlingshire	22	8	3	11	36	46	19
10	Arthurlie	22	6	5	11	32	42	17
11	Abercorn	22	4	5	13	27	57	13
12	Clyde	22	5	3	14	22	50	13

*Elected to First Division

On 5 April 1902, England met Scotland in an International Championship match at Ibrox Park, Glasgow. The day produced the worst disaster the game had known.

The ground was full by kick-off time, and latecomers, anxious not to miss too much of the game, made a dash from the packed East terrace to the West terrace. They charged up the staircases to the top, and settled to watch the match. Heavy rain was falling. Suddenly, rows of steel pylons at the back and front of the terrace shook and a yawning gap 70 feet by 14 feet wide appeared. People literally dropped through to the ground below, and others followed and fell

on top of them. Officially, 25 were killed, 24 dangerously injured, 153 injured, and 172 slightly injured. The match ended 1-1, but was deleted from international records, and later replayed at Birmingham.

Top The Aston Villa forwards attack Sunderland's goal in March 1902. Before the start of the following season, the curved line marking the goal area was replaced by the six-yard box.

Bottom 'Fatty' Foulke, Sheffield United's 21-stone goalkeeper, prepares to gather a tentative shot from the old-style lines during the 1902 Cup Final.

FA CUP 1901-02

FIRST ROUND

Tottenham Hotspur v Southampton	1-1, 2-2, 1-2
Liverpool v Everton	2-2, 2-0
Bury v West Bromwich Albion	5-1
Walsall v Burnley	1-0
Glossop North End v Nottingham Forest	0-2
Manchester City v Preston North End	1-1, 0-0, 4-2*
Stoke v Aston Villa	2-2, 2-1
Bristol Rovers v Middlesbrough	1-1, 1-0
Northampton Town v Sheffield United	0-2
Wolverhampton Wanderers v Bolton Wanderers	0-2
Woolwich Arsenal v Newcastle United	0-2
The Wednesday v Sunderland	0-1
Blackburn Rovers v Derby County	0-2
Lincoln City v Oxford City	0-0, 4-0
Portsmouth v Grimsby Town	1-1, 2-0
Notts County v Reading	1-2

*At Preston. Preston won the toss for choice of ground.

SECOND ROUND

Southampton v Liverpool	4-1
Walsall v Bury	0-5
Manchester City v Nottingham Forest	0-2
Bristol Rovers v Stoke	0-1
Sheffield United v Bolton Wanderers	2-1
Newcastle United v Sunderland	1-0
Lincoln City v Derby County	1-3
Reading v Portsmouth	0-1

THIRD ROUND

Bury v Southampton	2-3
Nottingham Forest v Stoke	2-0
Newcastle United v Sheffield United	1-1, 1-2
Derby County v Portsmouth	0-0, 6-3

SEMI-FINAL

Southampton v Nottingham Forest	3-1
Sheffield United v Derby County	1-1, 1-1, 1-0

FINAL AT CRYSTAL PALACE

Sheffield United v Southampton	1-1, 2-1†

†replay at Crystal Palace

SCOTTISH FA CUP 1901-02

FIRST ROUND

Arbroath v Kilwinning Eglinton (scratched)	wo
Third Lanark v Morton	0-0, 3-2
St Mirren v Airdrieonians	1-0
Ayr v Dundee	0-0, 0-2
Arthurlie v Port Glasgow Athletic	1-1, 1-3
Celtic v Thornliebank	3-0
Rangers v Johnstone	6-1
Queen's Park v Maxwelltown Volunteers	7-0
Partick Thistle v Kilmarnock	0-4
Falkirk	bye
Forfar Athletic	bye
Heart of Midlothian	bye
Hibernian	bye
Inverness Caledonian	bye
St Bernard's	bye
Stenhousemuir	bye

SECOND ROUND

Heart of Midlothian v Third Lanark	4-1
St Mirren v Stenhousemuir	6-0
Arbroath v Celtic	2-3
Rangers v Inverness Caledonian	5-1
Kilmarnock v Dundee	2-0
Falkirk v St Bernard's	2-0
Forfar Athletic v Queen's Park	1-4
Port Glasgow Athletic v Hibernian	1-5

THIRD ROUND

Falkirk v St Mirren	0-1
Heart of Midlothian v Celtic	1-1, 1-2
Hibernian v Queen's Park	7-1
Rangers v Kilmarnock	2-0

SEMI-FINAL

Rangers v Hibernian	0-2
St Mirren v Celtic	2-3

FINAL AT CELTIC PARK

Hibernian v Celtic	1-0

FIRST DIVISION

		P	W	D	L	F	A	Pts
1	Wednesday	34	19	4	11	54	36	42
2	Aston Villa	34	19	3	12	61	40	41
3	Sunderland	34	16	9	9	51	36	41
4	Sheff United	34	17	5	12	58	44	39
5	Liverpool	34	17	4	13	68	49	38
6	Stoke	34	15	7	12	46	38	37
7	WBA	34	16	4	14	54	53	36
8	Bury	34	16	3	15	54	43	35
9	Derby	34	16	3	15	50	47	35
10	Nottm Forest	34	14	7	13	49	47	35
11	Wolves	34	14	5	15	48	57	33
12	Everton	34	13	6	15	45	47	32
13	Middlesbrough	34	14	4	16	41	50	32
14	Newcastle	34	14	4	16	41	51	32
15	Notts County	34	12	7	15	41	49	31
16	Blackburn	34	12	5	17	44	63	29
17	Grimsby	34	8	9	17	43	62	25
18	Bolton	34	8	3	23	37	73	19

SECOND DIVISION

		P	W	D	L	F	A	Pts
1	Man City	34	25	4	5	95	29	54
2	Small Heath	34	24	3	7	74	36	51
3	Woolwich A	34	20	8	6	66	30	48
4	Bristol City	34	17	8	9	59	38	42
5	Man United	34	15	8	11	53	38	38
6	Chesterfield	34	14	9	11	67	40	37
7	Preston	34	13	10	11	56	40	36
8	Barnsley	34	13	8	13	55	51	34
9	Burslem PV	34	13	8	13	57	62	34
10	Lincoln	34	12	6	16	46	53	30
11	Glossop NE	34	11	7	16	43	58	29
12	Gainsborough	34	11	7	16	41	59	29
13	Burton United	34	11	7	16	39	59	29
14	Blackpool	34	9	10	15	44	59	28
15	Leicester Fosse	34	10	8	16	41	65	28
16	Doncaster	34	9	7	18	35	72	25
17	Stockport	34	7	6	21	39	74	20
18	Burnley	34	6	8	20	30	77	20

SCOTTISH FIRST DIVISION

		P	W	D	L	F	A	Pts
1	Hibernian	22	16	5	1	48	18	37
2	Dundee	22	13	5	4	31	12	31
3	Rangers	22	12	5	5	56	30	29
4	Hearts	22	11	6	5	46	27	28
5	Celtic	22	8	10	4	36	30	26
6	St Mirren	22	7	8	7	39	40	22
7	Third Lanark	22	8	5	9	34	27	21
8	Partick	22	6	7	9	34	50	19
9	Kilmarnock	22	6	4	12	24	43	16
10	Queen's Park	22	5	5	12	33	48	15
11	Port Glasgow	22	3	5	14	26	49	11
12	Morton	22	2	5	15	22	55	9

SCOTTISH SECOND DIVISION

		P	W	D	L	F	A	Pts
1	Airdrieonians*	22	15	5	2	43	19	35
2	Motherwell*	22	12	4	6	44	35	28
3	Ayr	22	12	3	7	34	24	27
4	Leith	22	11	5	6	43	41	27
5	St Bernard's	22	12	2	8	45	32	26
6	Hamilton	22	11	1	10	44	35	23
7	Falkirk	22	8	7	7	39	37	23
8	E Stirlingshire	22	9	3	10	46	41	21
9	Arthurlie	22	6	8	8	34	46	20
10	Abercorn	22	5	2	15	35	58	12
11	Raith	22	3	5	14	34	55	11
12	Clyde	22	2	7	13	22	40	11

*elected to First Division

Bury on the attack against Derby County on their way to the record win, 6-0, in an FA Cup Final.

FA CUP 1902-03

FIRST ROUND

Tottenham Hotspur v West Bromwich Albion	0-0, 2-0
Bolton Wanderers v Bristol City	0-5
Aston Villa v Sunderland	4-1
Barnsley v Lincoln City	2-0
Woolwich Arsenal v Sheffield United	1-3
Bury v Wolverhampton Wanderers	1-0
Grimsby Town v Newcastle United	2-1
Notts County v Southampton	0-0, 2-2, 2-1
Derby County v Small Heath	2-1
Blackburn Rovers v The Wednesday	0-0, 1-0
Nottingham Forest v Reading	0-0, 6-3
Glossop North End v Stoke	2-3
Millwall Athletic v Luton Town	3-0
Preston North End v Manchester City	3-1
Everton v Portsmouth	5-0
Manchester United v Liverpool	2-1

SECOND ROUND

Tottenham Hotspur v Bristol City	1-0
Aston Villa v Barnsley	4-1
Sheffield United v Bury	0-1
Grimsby Town v Notts County	0-2
Derby County v Blackburn Rovers	2-0
Nottingham Forest v Stoke	0-0, 0-2
Millwall Athletic v Preston North End	4-1
Everton v Manchester United	3-1

THIRD ROUND

Tottenham Hotspur v Aston Villa	2-3
Bury v Notts County	1-0
Derby County v Stoke	3-0
Millwall Athletic v Everton	1-0

SEMI-FINAL

Aston Villa v Bury	0-3
Derby County v Millwall Athletic	3-0

FINAL AT CRYSTAL PALACE

Bury v Derby County	6-0

SCOTTISH FA CUP 1902-03

FIRST ROUND

Celtic v St Mirren	0-0, 1-1, 4-0
St Johnstone v Third Lanark	1-10
Nithsdale Wanderers v Orion	1-0
Queen's Park v Motherwell	1-2
Abercorn v Douglas Wanderers	2-2, 1-3
Vale of Leven v Partick Thistle	0-4
Hamilton Academicals v Airdrieonians	5-0
Arbroath v Kilmarnock	1-3
Leith Athletic v Broxburn United	4-1
St Bernard's v Port Glasgow Athletic	1-2
Rangers v Auchterarder Thistle	7-0
Clyde v Heart of Midlothian	1-2
Hibernian v Morton	7-0
Ayr v Camelon	2-0
Dundee v Barholm Rovers	wo
Stenhousemuir v Inverness Caledonian	wo

SECOND ROUND

Celtic v Port Glasgow Athletic	2-0
Hamilton Academicals v Third Lanark	2-2, 1-3
Stenhousemuir v Douglas Wanderers	6-1
Motherwell v Partick Thistle	0-2
Dundee v Nithsdale Wanderers	7-0
Rangers v Kilmarnock	4-0
Ayr v Heart of Midlothian	2-4
Hibernian v Leith Athletic	4-1

THIRD ROUND

Celtic v Rangers	0-3
Dundee v Hibernian	0-0, 0-0, 1-0
Heart of Midlothian v Third Lanark	2-1
Stenhousemuir v Partick Thistle	3-0

SEMI-FINAL

Stenhousemuir v Rangers	1-4
Dundee v Heart of Midlothian	0-0, 0-1

FINAL AT CELTIC PARK

Rangers v Heart of Midlothian	1-1, 0-0, 2-0

CONWAY PICTURE LIBRARY

FIRST DIVISION

		P	W	D	L	F	A	Pts
1	Wednesday	34	20	7	7	48	28	47
2	Man City	34	19	6	9	71	45	44
3	Everton	34	19	5	10	59	32	43
4	Newcastle	34	18	6	10	58	45	42
5	Aston Villa	34	17	7	10	70	48	41
6	Sunderland	34	17	5	12	63	49	39
7	Sheff United	34	15	8	11	62	57	38
8	Wolves	34	14	8	12	44	66	36
9	Nottm Forest	34	11	9	14	57	57	31
10	Middlesbrough	34	9	12	13	46	47	30
11	Small Heath	34	11	8	15	39	52	30
12	Bury	34	7	15	12	40	53	29
13	Notts County	34	12	5	17	37	61	29
14	Derby	34	9	10	15	58	60	28
15	Blackburn	34	11	6	17	48	60	28
16	Stoke	34	10	7	17	54	57	27
17	Liverpool	34	9	8	17	49	62	26
18	WBA	34	7	10	17	36	60	24

SECOND DIVISION

		P	W	D	L	F	A	Pts
1	Preston	34	20	10	4	62	24	50
2	Woolwich A	34	21	7	6	91	22	49
3	Man United	34	20	8	6	65	33	48
4	Bristol City	34	18	6	10	73	41	42
5	Burnley	34	15	9	10	50	55	39
6	Grimsby	34	14	8	12	50	49	36
7	Bolton	34	12	10	12	59	41	34
8	Barnsley	34	11	10	13	38	57	32
9	Gainsborough	34	14	3	17	53	60	31
10	Bradford City	34	12	7	15	45	59	31
11	Chesterfield	34	11	8	15	37	45	30
12	Lincoln	34	11	8	15	41	58	30
13	Burslem PV	34	10	9	15	54	52	29
14	Burton United	34	11	7	16	45	61	29
15	Blackpool	34	11	5	18	40	67	27
16	Stockport	34	8	11	15	40	72	27
17	Glossop NE	34	10	6	18	57	64	26
18	Leicester Fosse	34	6	10	18	42	82	22

SCOTTISH FIRST DIVISION

		P	W	D	L	F	A	Pts
1	Third Lanark	26	20	3	3	61	26	43
2	Hearts	26	18	3	5	62	34	39
3	Celtic	26	18	2	6	68	27	38
4	Rangers	26	16	6	4	80	33	38
5	Dundee	26	13	2	11	54	45	28
6	St Mirren	26	11	5	10	45	38	27
7	Partick	26	10	7	9	46	41	27
8	Queen's Park	26	6	9	11	28	47	21
9	Port Glasgow	26	8	4	14	32	49	20
10	Hibernian	26	7	5	14	29	40	19
11	Morton	26	7	4	15	32	53	18
12	Airdrieonians	26	7	4	15	32	62	18
13	Motherwell	26	6	3	17	26	61	15
14	Kilmarnock	26	4	5	17	24	63	13

SCOTTISH SECOND DIVISION

		P	W	D	L	F	A	Pts
1	Hamilton	22	16	5	1	56	19	37
2	Clyde	22	12	5	5	51	36	29
3	Ayr	22	11	6	5	33	30	28
4	Falkirk	22	11	4	7	50	34	26
5	Raith	22	8	5	9	40	38	21
6	E Stirlingshire	22	8	5	9	35	40	21
7	Leith	22	8	4	10	42	40	20
8	St Bernard's	22	9	2	11	31	43	20
9	Albion*	22	8	5	9	47	37	19
10	Abercorn	22	6	4	12	38	55	16
11	Arthurlie	22	5	5	12	37	50	15
12	Ayr Parkhouse	22	3	4	15	23	61	10

*Two points deducted for fielding an unregistered player.

Below *The Manchester City side that won the FA Cup in 1903-04. Seated in the centre is the captain and great Welsh right-winger, Billy Meredith of Chirk.*

At Bradford, Sheffield FC, the oldest football club in the world, won their first and only honour when they beat Ealing 3-1 in the 1904 Amateur Cup final.

FA CUP 1903-04

FIRST ROUND
Manchester City v Sunderland	3-2
Woolwich Arsenal v Fulham	1-0
Millwall Athletic v Middlesbrough	0-2
Preston North End v Grimsby Town	1-0
Plymouth Argyle v The Wednesday	2-2, 0-2
Notts County v Manchester United	3-3, 1-2
Everton v Tottenham Hotspur	1-2
Stoke v Aston Villa	2-3
Reading v Bolton Wanderers	1-1, 2-3
Southampton v Burslem Port Vale	3-0
Bristol City v Sheffield United	1-3
Bury v Newcastle United	2-1
Portsmouth v Derby County	2-5
Stockton v Wolverhampton Wanderers	1-4
Blackburn Rovers v Liverpool	3-1
West Bromwich Albion v Nottingham Forest	1-1, 1-3

SECOND ROUND
Woolwich Arsenal v Manchester City	0-2
Preston North End v Middlesbrough	0-3
The Wednesday v Manchester United	6-0
Tottenham Hotspur v Aston Villa	0-1*, 1-0
Bolton Wanderers v Southampton	4-1
Bury v Sheffield United	1-2
Derby County v Wolverhampton Wanderers	2-2, 2-2, 1-0
Blackburn Rovers v Nottingham Forest	3-1

*The Tottenham crowd invaded the pitch when Villa were leading 1-0 and the game was abandoned. Tottenham were fined £350 and the FA ordered the return to be played at Villa Park.

THIRD ROUND
Manchester City v Middlesbrough	0-0, 3-1
Tottenham Hotspur v The Wednesday	1-1, 0-2
Sheffield United v Bolton Wanderers	0-2
Derby County v Blackburn Rovers	2-1

SEMI-FINAL
Manchester City v The Wednesday	3-0
Bolton Wanderers v Derby County	1-0

FINAL AT CRYSTAL PALACE
Manchester City v Bolton Wanderers	1-0

SCOTTISH FA CUP 1903-04

FIRST ROUND
Abercorn v Maxwelltown Volunteers	2-2, 1-1, 2-1
Nithsdale Wanderers v Kilmarnock	2-2, 1-1, 1-2
Clyde v Arbroath	2-2, 0-4
Rangers v Heart of Midlothian	3-2
Dundee v Queen's Park	3-0
Hibernian v Airdrieonians	2-1
Motherwell v Partick Thistle	2-1
Ayr v St Mirren	0-2
St Johnstone v Hearts of Beath	2-0
Albion Rovers v Kilwinning Eglinton	2-1
St Bernard's v West Calder Swifts	1-1, 3-3, 2-1
Port Glasgow Athletic v Leith Athletic	1-2
Alloa Athletic v Aberdour	2-1
Third Lanark v Newton Stewart Athletic (scratched)	wo
Celtic v Stanley (scratched)	wo
Morton v Dalbeattie Star (scratched)	wo

SECOND ROUND
Kilmarnock v Albion Rovers	2-2, 1-0
St Bernard's v Celtic	0-4
Dundee v Abercorn	4-0
Third Lanark v Alloa Athletic	3-1
Hibernian v Rangers	1-2
Leith Athletic v Motherwell	3-1
Morton v Arbroath	2-0
St Mirren v St Johnstone	4-0

THIRD ROUND
Celtic v Dundee	1-1, 0-0, 5-0
Third Lanark v Kilmarnock	3-0
St Mirren v Rangers	0-1
Leith Athletic v Morton	1-3

SEMI-FINAL
Celtic v Third Lanark	2-1
Rangers v Morton	3-0

FINAL AT HAMPDEN PARK
Celtic v Rangers	3-2

MANCHESTER CITY FOOTBALL CLUB.

WINNERS OF ENGLISH CUP, 1903-4.
RUNNERS-UP, FOOTBALL LEAGUE, 1903-4. ♦ JOINT HOLDERS MANCHESTER CUP, 1903-4.

RADIO TIMES HULTON PICTURE LIBRARY

League Tables 1904-05

FIRST DIVISION

		P	W	D	L	F	A	Pts
1	Newcastle	34	23	2	9	72	33	48
2	Everton	34	21	5	8	63	36	47
3	Man City	34	20	6	8	66	37	46
4	Aston Villa	34	19	4	11	63	43	42
5	Sunderland	34	16	8	10	60	44	40
6	Sheff United	34	19	2	13	64	56	40
7	Small Heath	34	17	5	12	54	38	39
8	Preston	34	13	10	11	42	37	36
9	Wednesday	34	14	5	15	61	57	33
10	Woolwich A	34	12	9	13	36	40	33
11	Derby	34	12	8	14	37	48	32
12	Stoke	34	13	4	17	40	58	30
13	Blackburn	34	11	5	18	40	51	27
14	Wolves	34	11	4	19	47	73	26
15	Middlesbrough	34	9	8	17	36	56	26
16	Nottm Forest	34	9	7	18	40	61	25
17	Bury	34	10	4	20	47	67	24
18	Notts County	34	5	8	21	36	69	18

SECOND DIVISION

		P	W	D	L	F	A	Pts
1	Liverpool	34	27	4	3	93	25	58
2	Bolton	34	27	2	5	87	32	56
3	Man United	34	24	5	5	81	30	53
4	Bristol City	34	19	4	11	66	45	42
5	Chesterfield	34	14	11	9	44	35	39
6	Gainsborough	34	14	8	12	61	58	36
7	Barnsley	34	14	5	15	38	56	33
8	Bradford City	34	12	8	14	45	49	32
9	Lincoln	34	12	7	15	42	40	31
10	WBA	34	13	4	17	56	48	30
11	Burnley	34	12	6	16	43	52	30
12	Glossop NE	34	10	10	14	37	46	30
13	Grimsby	34	11	8	15	33	46	30
14	Leicester Fosse	34	11	7	16	40	55	29
15	Blackpool	34	9	10	15	36	48	28
16	Burslem PV	34	10	7	17	47	72	27
17	Burton United	34	8	4	22	30	84	20
18	Doncaster	34	3	2	29	23	81	8

SCOTTISH FIRST DIVISION

		P	W	D	L	F	A	Pts
1	Celtic*	26	19	3	4	83	28	41
2	Rangers	26	18	5	3	68	31	41
3	Third Lanark	26	14	7	5	60	28	35
4	Airdrieonians	26	11	5	10	38	45	27
5	Hibernian	26	9	8	9	39	39	26
6	Partick	26	12	2	12	36	56	26
7	Dundee	26	10	5	11	38	32	25
8	Hearts	26	11	3	12	46	44	25
9	Kilmarnock	26	9	5	12	29	45	23
10	St Mirren	26	9	4	13	33	36	22
11	Port Glasgow	26	8	5	13	30	51	21
12	Queen's Park	26	6	8	12	28	45	20
13	Morton	26	7	4	15	27	50	18
14	Motherwell	26	6	2	18	28	53	14

*Celtic won a deciding match against Rangers

SCOTTISH SECOND DIVISION

		P	W	D	L	F	A	Pts
1	Clyde	22	13	6	3	38	22	32
2	Falkirk*	22	12	4	6	31	25	28
3	Hamilton	22	12	3	7	40	22	27
4	Leith	22	10	4	8	36	26	24
5	Ayr	22	11	1	10	46	37	23
6	Arthurlie	22	9	5	8	37	42	23
7	Aberdeen*	22	7	7	8	36	26	21
8	Albion	22	8	4	10	38	53	20
9	E Stirlingshire	22	7	5	10	38	38	19
10	Raith	22	9	1	12	30	34	19
11	Abercorn	22	8	1	13	31	45	17
12	St Bernard's	22	3	5	14	23	54	11

*Aberdeen and Falkirk were elected to the First Division

FA CUP 1904-05

FIRST ROUND

Lincoln City v Manchester City	1-2
Bolton Wanderers v Bristol Rovers	1-1, 3-0
Middlesbrough v Tottenham Hotspur	1-1, 0-1
Newcastle United v Plymouth Argyle	1-1, 1-1, 2-0
Woolwich Arsenal v Bristol City	0-0, 0-1
Derby County v Preston North End	0-2
Blackburn Rovers v The Wednesday	1-2
Small Heath v Portsmouth	0-2
Stoke v Grimsby Town	2-0
Liverpool v Everton	1-1, 1-2
Sunderland v Wolverhampton Wanderers	1-1, 0-1
Southampton v Millwall Athletic	3-1
Aston Villa v Leicester Fosse	5-1
Bury v Notts County	1-0
Fulham v Reading	0-0, 0-0, 1-0
Nottingham Forest v Sheffield United	2-0

SECOND ROUND

Manchester City v Bolton Wanderers	1-2
Tottenham Hotspur v Newcastle United	1-1, 0-4
Bristol City v Preston North End	0-0, 0-1
The Wednesday v Portsmouth	2-1
Stoke v Everton	0-4
Wolverhampton Wanderers v Southampton	2-3
Aston Villa v Bury	3-2
Fulham v Nottingham Forest	1-0

THIRD ROUND

Bolton Wanderers v Newcastle United	0-2
Preston North End v The Wednesday	1-1, 0-3
Everton v Southampton	4-0
Aston Villa v Fulham	5-0

SEMI-FINAL

Newcastle United v The Wednesday	1-0
Everton v Aston Villa	1-1, 1-2

FINAL AT CRYSTAL PALACE

Aston Villa v Newcastle United	2-0

SCOTTISH FA CUP 1904-05

FIRST ROUND

Rangers v Ayr	2-1
Dundee v Heart of Midlothian	1-3
Dumfries v Celtic	1-2
Port Glasgow Athletic v Stranraer	3-0
Airdrieonians v St Johnstone	7-0
Aberdeen v Queen's Park	2-1
St Mirren v Clyde	1-0
Third Lanark v Leith Athletic	4-1
Morton v Renton	2-0
Kilmarnock v Beith	2-2, 1-3
Bathgate v Arbroath	2-1
Arthurlie v Motherwell	0-0, 0-1
Hibernian v Partick Thistle	1-1, 2-4
Kirkcaldy United v Crieff Morrisonians	3-1
Cowdenbeath v 6th GRV	6-0
Lochgelly United v Inverness Caledonian	5-1

SECOND ROUND

Celtic v Lochgelly United	3-0
Aberdeen v Bathgate	1-1, 6-1
Kirkcaldy United v Partick Thistle	0-1
Morton v Rangers	0-6
Airdrieonians v Port Glasgow Athletic	3-0
Motherwell v Third Lanark	0-1
St Mirren v Heart of Midlothian	1-0
Beith v Cowdenbeath	4-0

THIRD ROUND

St Mirren v Airdrieonians	0-0, 1-3
Rangers v Beith	5-1
Celtic v Partick Thistle	3-0
Third Lanark v Aberdeen	4-1

SEMI-FINAL

Celtic v Rangers	0-2
Airdrieonians v Third Lanark	1-2

FINAL AT HAMPDEN PARK

Third Lanark v Rangers	0-0, 3-1

Doncaster Rovers had a disastrous spell in the Second Division and were voted out of the League in 1905 after gaining the fewest number of points (8) ever won by a League club in a single season. Not one of those 8 was won away from home. This equalled Loughborough Town's dreadful 1899-1900 season when they also accumulated just 8 points. Loughborough, however, established a record by winning only one of their 34 League games.

Below The only known panoramic view of Crystal Palace during a Cup Final. The event was played there from 1895 to 1914 but, apart from the small stands on the right, there was little accommodation available. The Crystal Palace itself, which had been moved from Hyde Park after the Great Exhibition of the 1850s, was on the hill above the funfair to the right. The 1905 Final attracted over 100,000 spectators, only the second time in history an English football match had drawn a six-figure crowd. Some fans can be seen clinging on to trees on the left as Aston Villa play Newcastle United.

FIRST DIVISION

		P	W	D	L	F	A	Pts
1	Liverpool	38	23	5	10	79	46	51
2	Preston NE	38	17	13	8	54	39	47
3	Wednesday	38	18	8	12	63	52	44
4	Newcastle	38	18	7	13	74	48	43
5	Man City	38	19	5	14	73	54	43
6	Bolton	38	17	7	14	81	67	41
7	Birmingham	38	17	7	14	65	59	41
8	Aston Villa	38	17	6	15	72	56	40
9	Blackburn	38	16	8	14	54	52	40
10	Stoke	38	16	7	15	54	55	39
11	Everton	38	15	7	16	70	66	37
12	Woolwich A	38	15	7	16	62	64	37
13	Sheff United	38	15	6	17	57	62	36
14	Sunderland	38	15	5	18	61	70	35
15	Derby	38	14	7	17	39	58	35
16	Notts County	38	11	12	15	55	71	34
17	Bury	38	11	10	17	57	74	32
18	Middlesbrough	38	10	11	17	56	71	31
19	Nottm Forest	38	13	5	20	58	79	31
20	Wolves	38	8	7	23	58	99	23

SECOND DIVISION

		P	W	D	L	F	A	Pts
1	Bristol City	38	30	6	2	83	28	66
2	Man United	38	28	6	4	90	28	62
3	Chelsea	38	22	9	7	90	37	53
4	WBA	38	22	8	8	79	36	52
5	Hull	38	19	6	13	67	54	44
6	Leeds City	38	17	9	12	59	47	43
7	Leicester Fosse	38	15	12	11	53	48	42
8	Grimsby	38	15	10	13	46	46	40
9	Burnley	38	15	8	15	42	53	38
10	Stockport	38	13	9	16	44	56	35
11	Bradford City	38	13	8	17	46	60	34
12	Barnsley	38	12	9	17	60	62	33
13	Lincoln	38	12	6	20	69	72	30
14	Blackpool	38	10	9	19	37	62	29
15	Gainsborough	38	12	4	22	44	57	28
16	Glossop NE	38	10	8	20	49	71	28
17	Burslem PV	38	12	4	22	49	82	28
18	Chesterfield	38	10	8	20	40	72	28
19	Burton United	38	10	6	22	34	67	26
20	Clapton Orient	38	7	7	24	35	78	21

SCOTTISH FIRST DIVISION

		P	W	D	L	F	A	Pts
1	Celtic	30	24	1	5	76	19	49
2	Hearts	30	18	7	5	64	27	43
3	Airdrieonians	30	15	8	7	53	31	38
4	Rangers	30	15	7	8	58	48	37
5	Partick	30	15	6	9	44	40	36
6	Third Lanark	30	16	2	12	62	39	34
7	Dundee	30	11	12	7	40	33	34
8	St Mirren	30	13	5	12	41	37	31
9	Motherwell	30	9	8	13	50	62	26
10	Morton	30	10	6	14	35	54	26
11	Hibernian	30	10	5	15	35	40	25
12	Aberdeen	30	8	8	14	36	48	24
13	Falkirk	30	9	5	16	52	68	23
14	Kilmarnock	30	8	4	18	46	68	20
15	Port Glasgow	30	6	8	16	38	68	20
16	Queen's Park	30	5	4	21	39	87	14

SCOTTISH SECOND DIVISION

		P	W	D	L	F	A	Pts
1	Leith	22	15	4	3	46	21	34
2	Clyde*	22	11	9	2	37	21	31
3	Albion	22	12	3	7	48	29	27
4	Hamilton*	22	12	2	8	45	34	26
5	St Bernard's	22	9	4	9	42	34	22
6	Arthurlie	22	10	2	10	42	43	22
7	Ayr	22	9	3	10	43	51	21
8	Raith	22	6	7	9	36	42	19
9	Cowdenbeath	22	7	3	12	27	39	17
10	Abercorn	22	6	5	11	29	45	17
11	Vale of Leven	22	6	4	12	34	49	16
12	E Stirlingshire	22	1	10	11	26	47	12

*Elected to First Division

Below *The Everton team that won the club's first ever FA Cup in 1906.*

FA CUP 1905-06

SECOND ROUND

Woolwich Arsenal v Watford	3-0
Sunderland v Gainsborough Trinity	1-1, 3-0
Manchester United v Norwich City	3-0
Aston Villa v Plymouth Argyle	0-0, 5-1
Derby County v Newcastle United	0-0, 1-2
Blackpool v Sheffield United	2-1
Tottenham Hotspur v Reading	3-2
Stoke v Birmingham	0-1
Chesterfield Town v Everton	0-3
Bradford City v Wolverhampton Wanderers	5-0
The Wednesday v Millwall Athletic	1-1, 3-0
Fulham v Nottingham Forest	1-3
Barnsley v Liverpool	0-1
Brentford v Lincoln City	3-0
New Brompton v Southampton	0-0, 0-1
Brighton v Middlesbrough	1-1, 1-1, 1-3

THIRD ROUND

Woolwich Arsenal v Sunderland	5-0
Manchester United v Aston Villa	5-1
Newcastle United v Blackpool	5-0
Tottenham Hotspur v Birmingham	1-1, 0-2
Everton v Bradford City	1-0
The Wednesday v Nottingham Forest	4-1
Liverpool v Brentford	2-0
Southampton v Middlesbrough	6-1

FOURTH ROUND

Manchester United v Woolwich Arsenal	2-3
Birmingham v Newcastle United	2-2, 0-3
Everton v The Wednesday	4-3
Liverpool v Southampton	3-0

SEMI-FINAL

Woolwich Arsenal v Newcastle United	0-2
Everton v Liverpool	2-0

FINAL AT CRYSTAL PALACE

Everton v Newcastle United	1-0

SCOTTISH FA CUP 1905-06

FIRST ROUND

Dundee v Celtic	1-2
Kilmarnock v Clyde	2-1
Beith v Inverness Thistle	2-0
Third Lanark v Galston	5-0
Forfar Athletic v Queen's Park	0-4
Falkirk v Hibernian	1-2
Leith Athletic v Partick Thistle	1-2
Heart of Midlothian v Nithsdale Wanderers	4-1
Motherwell v Hamilton Academicals	2-3
Airdrieonians v Maxwelltown Volunteers	9-2
Aberdeen v Dunfermline Athletic	3-0
Morton v Lochgelly United	4-3
St Mirren v Black Watch	7-2
Arthurlie v Rangers	1-7
Arbroath v Bo'ness	1-4
Port Glasgow Athletic v Dunblane	6-1

SECOND ROUND

Aberdeen v Rangers	2-3
Hibernian v Partick Thistle	1-1, 1-1, 2-1
Beith v Heart of Midlothian	0-3
Celtic v Bo'ness	3-0
Third Lanark v Hamilton Academicals	2-2, 3-1
St Mirren v Morton	3-1
Kilmarnock v Port Glasgow Athletic	2-2, 0-0, 0-0, 0-1
Queen's Park v Airdrieonians	1-2

THIRD ROUND

Celtic v Heart of Midlothian	1-2
Airdrieonians v St Mirren	0-0, 0-2
Port Glasgow Athletic v Rangers	1-0
Hibernian v Third Lanark	1-2

SEMI-FINAL

St Mirren v Third Lanark	1-1, 0-0, 0-1
Port Glasgow Athletic v Heart of Midlothian	0-2

FINAL AT IBROX PARK

Heart of Midlothian v Third Lanark	1-0

COLORSPORT

League Tables 1906-07

FIRST DIVISION

		P	W	D	L	F	A	Pts
1	Newcastle	38	22	7	9	74	46	51
2	Bristol City	38	20	8	10	66	47	48
3	Everton	38	20	5	13	70	46	45
4	Sheff United	38	17	11	10	57	55	45
5	Aston Villa	38	19	6	13	78	52	44
6	Bolton	38	18	8	12	59	47	44
7	Woolwich A	38	20	4	14	66	59	44
8	Man United	38	17	8	13	53	56	42
9	Birmingham	38	15	8	15	52	52	38
10	Sunderland	38	14	9	15	65	66	37
11	Middlesbrough	38	15	6	17	56	63	36
12	Blackburn	38	14	7	17	56	59	35
13	Wednesday	38	12	11	15	49	60	35
14	Preston	38	14	7	17	44	57	35
15	Liverpool	38	13	7	18	64	65	33
16	Bury	38	13	6	19	58	68	32
17	Man City	38	10	12	16	53	77	32
18	Notts County	38	8	15	15	46	50	31
19	Derby	38	9	9	20	41	59	27
20	Stoke	38	8	10	20	41	64	26

SECOND DIVISION

		P	W	D	L	F	A	Pts
1	Nottm Forest	38	28	4	6	74	36	60
2	Chelsea	38	26	5	7	80	34	57
3	Leicester Fosse	38	20	8	10	62	39	48
4	WBA	38	21	5	12	83	45	47
5	Bradford City	38	21	5	12	70	53	47
6	Wolves	38	17	7	14	66	53	41
7	Burnley	38	17	6	15	62	47	40
8	Barnsley	38	15	8	15	73	55	38
9	Hull	38	15	7	16	65	57	37
10	Leeds City	38	13	10	15	55	63	36
11	Grimsby	38	16	3	19	57	62	35
12	Stockport	38	12	11	15	42	52	35
13	Blackpool	38	11	11	16	33	51	33
14	Gainsborough	38	14	5	19	45	72	33
15	Glossop NE	38	13	6	19	53	79	32
16	Burslem PV	38	12	7	19	60	83	31
17	Clapton Orient	38	11	8	19	45	67	30
18	Chesterfield	38	11	7	20	50	66	29
19	Lincoln	38	12	4	22	46	73	28
20	Burton United	38	8	7	23	34	68	23

SCOTTISH FIRST DIVISION

		P	W	D	L	F	A	Pts
1	Celtic	34	23	9	2	80	30	55
2	Dundee	34	18	12	4	53	26	48
3	Rangers	34	19	7	8	69	33	45
4	Airdrieonians	34	18	6	10	59	44	42
5	Falkirk	34	17	7	10	73	58	41
6	Third Lanark	34	15	9	10	57	48	39
7	St Mirren	34	12	13	9	50	44	37
8	Clyde	34	15	6	13	47	52	36
9	Hearts	34	11	13	10	47	43	35
10	Motherwell	34	12	9	13	45	49	33
11	Aberdeen	34	10	10	14	48	55	30
12	Hibernian	34	10	10	14	40	49	30
13	Morton	34	11	6	17	41	50	28
14	Partick Thistle	34	9	8	17	40	60	26
15	Queen's Park	34	9	6	19	51	66	24
16	Hamilton	34	8	5	21	40	64	21
17	Kilmarnock	34	8	5	21	40	72	21
18	Port Glasgow	34	7	7	20	30	67	21

SCOTTISH SECOND DIVISION

		P	W	D	L	F	A	Pts
1	St Bernard's	22	14	4	4	41	24	32
2	Vale of Leven	22	13	1	8	54	35	27
3	Arthurlie	22	12	3	7	50	39	27
4	Dumbarton	22	11	3	8	52	35	25
5	Leith	22	10	4	8	40	35	24
6	Albion	22	10	3	9	43	36	23
7	Cowdenbeath	22	10	5	7	36	39	23*
8	Ayr	22	7	6	9	34	38	20
9	Abercorn	22	5	7	10	29	47	17
10	Raith	22	6	4	12	39	47	16
11	E Stirlingshire	22	6	4	12	37	48	16
12	Ayr Parkhouse	22	5	2	15	32	64	12

*two points deducted for an irregularity

Below A plate produced by The Wednesday to commemorate winning the Cup in 1907.

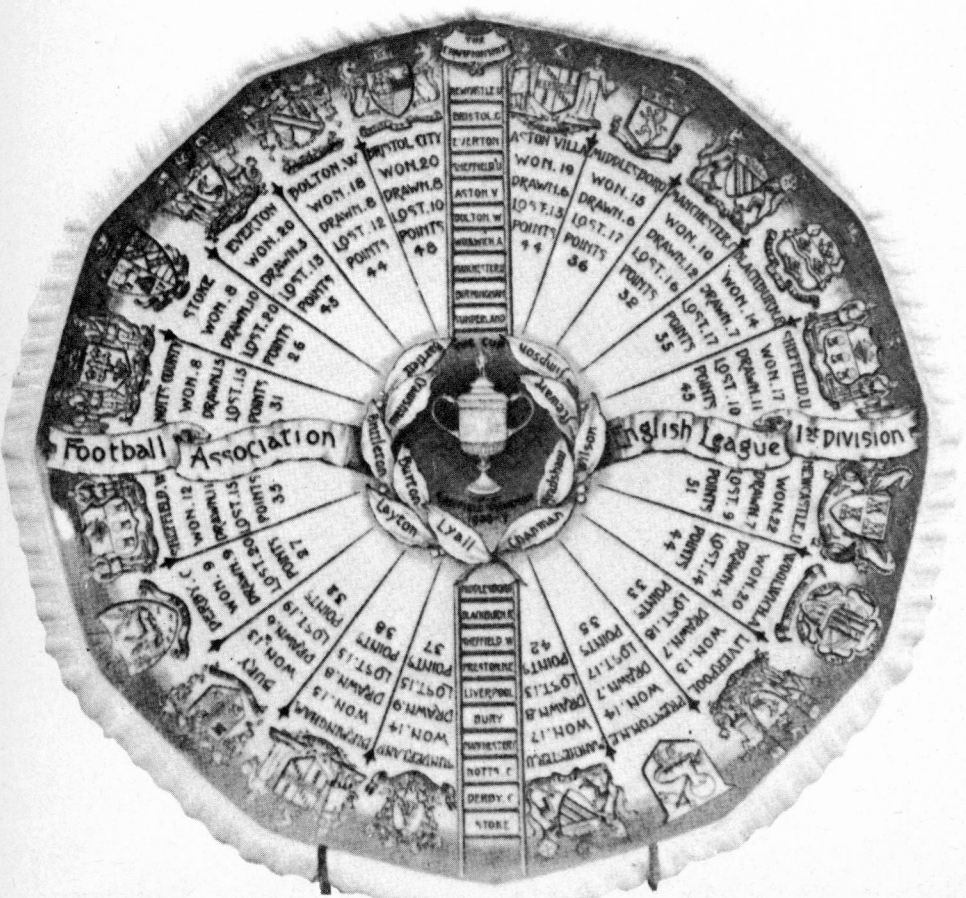

C PROCTOR: COURTESY OF J DANIELS, 20 SILVERTHORNE ROAD, S.W.8

FA CUP 1906-07

SECOND ROUND

Burslem Port Vale v Notts County	2-2, 0-5
Blackburn Rovers v Tottenham Hotspur	1-1, 1-1, 1-2
West Bromwich Albion v Norwich City	1-0
Derby County v Lincoln City	1-0
Fulham v Crystal Palace	0-0, 0-1
Brentford v Middlesbrough	1-0
West Ham United v Everton	1-2
Bolton Wanderers v Aston Villa	2-0
Woolwich Arsenal v Bristol City	2-1
Bristol Rovers v Millwall	3-0
Barnsley v Portsmouth	1-0
Bury v New Brompton	1-0
Oldham Athletic v Liverpool	0-1
Bradford City v Accrington Stanley	1-0
Southampton v The Wednesday	1-1, 1-3
Luton Town v Sunderland	0-0, 0-1

THIRD ROUND

Notts County v Tottenham Hotspur	4-0
West Bromwich Albion v Derby County	2-0
Crystal Palace v Brentford	1-1, 1-0
Everton v Bolton Wanderers	0-0, 3-0
Woolwich Arsenal v Bristol Rovers	1-0
Barnsley v Bury	1-0
Liverpool v Bradford City	1-0
The Wednesday v Sunderland	0-0, 1-0

FOURTH ROUND

West Bromwich Albion v Notts County	3-1
Crystal Palace v Everton	1-1, 0-4
Barnsley v Woolwich Arsenal	1-2
The Wednesday v Liverpool	1-0

SEMI-FINAL

West Bromwich Albion v Everton	1-2
Woolwich Arsenal v The Wednesday	1-3

FINAL AT CRYSTAL PALACE

The Wednesday v Everton	2-1

SCOTTISH FA CUP 1906-07

FIRST ROUND

Third Lanark v St Johnstone	4-1
Falkirk v Rangers	1-2
Heart of Midlothian v Airdrieonians	0-0, 2-0
Dumfries v Port Glasgow Athletic	2-2, 0-2
Maxwelltown Volunteers v Morton	0-3
Ayr v Cowdenbeath	2-0
Raith Rovers v Aberdeen University	5-1
Arbroath v Queen's Park	1-1, 0-4
Renton v St Bernard's	0-0, 1-1, 2-0
Aberdeen v Johnstone	0-0, 1-2
Celtic v Clyde	2-1
Arthurlie v St Mirren	1-2
Partick Thistle v Dundee	2-2, 1-5
Galston v Motherwell	2-1
Kilmarnock v Clachnacuddin	4-0

SECOND ROUND

Queen's Park v Third Lanark	3-1
Raith Rovers v Ayr	4-0
St Mirren v Port Glasgow Athletic	4-1
Morton v Celtic	0-0, 1-1, 1-2
Hibernian v Johnstone	1-1, 5-0
Galston v Rangers	0-4
Kilmarnock v Heart of Midlothian	0-0, 1-2
Renton v Dundee	1-0

THIRD ROUND

Rangers v Celtic	0-3
St Mirren v Hibernian	1-1, 0-2
Queen's Park v Renton	4-1
Heart of Midlothian v Raith Rovers	2-2, 1-0

SEMI-FINAL

Celtic v Hibernian	0-0, 0-0, 3-0
Heart of Midlothian v Queen's Park	1-0

FINAL AT HAMPDEN PARK

Celtic v Heart of Midlothian	3-0

League Tables 1907-08

FIRST DIVISION

		P	W	D	L	F	A	Pts
1	Man United	38	23	6	9	81	48	52
2	Aston Villa	38	17	9	12	77	59	43
3	Man City	38	16	11	11	62	54	43
4	Newcastle	38	15	12	11	65	54	42
5	Wednesday	38	19	4	15	73	64	42
6	Middlesbrough	38	17	7	14	54	45	41
7	Bury	38	14	11	13	58	61	39
8	Liverpool	38	16	6	16	68	61	38
9	Nottm Forest	38	13	11	14	59	62	37
10	Bristol City	38	12	12	14	58	61	36
11	Everton	38	15	6	17	58	64	36
12	Preston	38	12	12	14	47	53	36
13	Chelsea	38	14	8	16	53	62	36
14	Blackburn*	38	12	12	14	51	63	36
15	Woolwich A*	38	12	12	14	51	63	36
16	Sunderland	38	16	3	19	78	75	35
17	Sheff United	38	12	11	15	52	58	35
18	Notts County	38	13	8	17	39	51	34
19	Bolton	38	14	5	19	52	58	33
20	Birmingham	38	9	12	17	40	60	30

*equal

SECOND DIVISION

		P	W	D	L	F	A	Pts
1	Bradford City	38	24	6	8	90	42	54
2	Leicester Fosse	38	21	10	7	72	47	52
3	Oldham	38	22	6	10	76	42	50
4	Fulham	38	22	5	11	82	49	49
5	WBA	38	19	9	10	61	39	47
6	Derby	38	21	4	13	77	45	46
7	Burnley	38	20	6	12	67	50	46
8	Hull	38	21	4	13	73	62	46
9	Wolves	38	15	7	16	50	45	37
10	Stoke	38	16	5	17	57	52	37
11	Gainsborough	38	14	7	17	47	71	35
12	Leeds City	38	12	8	18	53	65	32
13	Stockport	38	12	8	18	48	67	32
14	Clapton Orient	38	11	10	17	40	65	32
15	Blackpool	38	11	9	18	51	58	31
16	Barnsley	38	12	6	20	54	68	30
17	Glossop NE	38	11	8	19	54	74	30
18	Grimsby	38	11	8	19	43	71	30
19	Chesterfield	38	6	11	21	46	92	23
20	Lincoln	38	9	3	26	46	83	21

SCOTTISH FIRST DIVISION

		P	W	D	L	F	A	Pts
1	Celtic	34	24	7	3	86	27	55
2	Falkirk	34	22	7	5	102	40	51
3	Rangers	34	21	8	5	74	40	50
4	Dundee	34	20	8	6	70	27	48
5	Hibernian	34	17	8	9	55	42	42
6	Airdrieonians	34	18	5	11	58	41	41
7	St Mirren	34	13	10	11	50	59	36
8	Aberdeen	34	13	9	12	45	44	35
9	Third Lanark	34	13	7	14	45	50	33
10	Motherwell	34	12	7	15	61	53	31
11	Hamilton	34	10	8	16	54	65	28
12	Hearts	34	11	6	17	50	62	28
13	Morton	34	9	9	16	43	66	27
14	Kilmarnock	34	6	13	15	38	61	25
15	Partick	34	8	9	17	43	69	25
16	Queen's Park	34	7	8	19	54	84	22
17	Clyde	34	5	8	21	36	75	18
18	Port Glasgow	34	5	7	22	39	98	17

SCOTTISH SECOND DIVISION

		P	W	D	L	F	A	Pts
1	Raith	22	14	2	6	37	23	30
2	Dumbarton	22	12	5	5	49	32	27*
3	Ayr	22	11	5	6	40	33	27
4	Abercorn	22	9	5	8	33	30	23
5	E Stirlingshire	22	9	5	8	30	32	23
6	Ayr Parkhouse	22	11	0	11	38	38	22
7	Leith	22	8	5	9	41	40	21
8	St Bernard's	22	8	5	9	31	32	21
9	Albion	22	7	5	10	36	48	19
10	Vale of Leven	22	5	8	9	25	31	18
11	Arthurlie	22	6	5	11	33	45	17
12	Cowdenbeath	22	5	4	13	26	35	14

*Two points deducted for a registration irregularity

Below Wednesday goalkeeper Lyell, well backed up by his defence, repulses a Chelsea attack in a First Division match. It was Chelsea's first ever season in the First Division.

RADIO TIMES HULTON PICTURE LIBRARY

FA CUP 1907-08

SECOND ROUND
Wolverhampton Wanderers v Bury	2-0
Swindon Town v Queen's Park Rangers	2-1
Stoke v Gainsborough Trinity	1-1, 2-2, 3-1
Portsmouth v Leicester Fosse	1-0
Notts County v Bolton Wanderers	1-1, 1-2
Oldham Athletic v Everton	0-0, 1-6
Southampton v West Bromwich Albion	1-0
Bristol Rovers v Chesterfield Town	2-0
Newcastle United v West Ham United	1-2, 0-0
Liverpool v Brighton	1-1, 3-0
Grimsby Town v Carlisle United	6-2
Plymouth Argyle v Crystal Palace	2-3
Manchester City v New Brompton	1-1, 2-1
Norwich City v Fulham	1-2
Manchester United v Chelsea	1-0
Aston Villa v Hull City	3-0

THIRD ROUND
Wolverhampton Wanderers v Swindon Town	2-0
Portsmouth v Stoke	0-1
Bolton Wanderers v Everton	3-3, 1-3
Southampton v Bristol Rovers	2-0
Newcastle United v Liverpool	3-1
Grimsby Town v Crystal Palace	1-0
Manchester City v Fulham	1-1, 1-3
Aston Villa v Manchester United	0-2

FOURTH ROUND
Stoke v Wolverhampton Wanderers	0-1
Everton v Southampton	0-0, 2-3
Newcastle United v Grimsby Town	5-1
Fulham v Manchester United	2-1

SEMI-FINAL
Wolverhampton Wanderers v Southampton	2-0
Newcastle United v Fulham	6-0

FINAL AT CRYSTAL PALACE
Wolverhampton Wanderers v Newcastle United	3-1

SCOTTISH FA CUP 1907-08

FIRST ROUND
Falkirk v Rangers	2-2, 1-4
Heart of Midlothian v St Johnstone	2-1
Celtic v Peebles Rovers	4-0
Hibernian v Abercorn	5-1
St Bernard's v Queen's Park	1-1, 1-1, 0-1
Aberdeen v Albion Rovers	3-0
Dumfries v Motherwell	0-4
Partick Thistle v Bo'ness	4-0
Port Glasgow Athletic v Ayr Parkhouse	7-1
Dunblane v Elgin City	8-3
Kilmarnock v Hamilton Academicals	2-1
Raith Rovers v Inverness Thistle	2-0
Galston v Uphall	wo
St Mirren v Third Lanark	3-1
Morton v Vale of Atholl	7-1
Airdrieonians v Dundee	0-1

SECOND ROUND
Motherwell v St Mirren	2-2, 0-2
Heart of Midlothian v Port Glasgow Athletic	4-0
Rangers v Celtic	1-2
Partick Thistle v Raith Rovers	1-1, 1-2
Queen's Park v Galston	6-2
Kilmarnock v Dunblane	3-0
Hibernian v Morton	3-0
Aberdeen v Dundee	0-0, 2-2, 3-1

THIRD ROUND
Aberdeen v Queen's Park	3-1
Raith Rovers v Celtic	0-3
Hibernian v Kilmarnock	0-1
St Mirren v Heart of Midlothian	1-0*, 3-1

*abandoned

SEMI-FINAL
Aberdeen v Celtic	0-1
Kilmarnock v St Mirren	0-0, 0-2

FINAL AT HAMPDEN PARK
Celtic v St Mirren	5-1

League Tables 1908-09

FIRST DIVISION

		P	W	D	L	F	A	Pts
1	Newcastle	38	24	5	9	65	41	53
2	Everton	38	18	10	10	82	57	46
3	Sunderland	38	21	2	15	78	63	44
4	Blackburn	38	14	13	11	61	50	41
5	Wednesday	38	17	6	15	67	61	40
6	Woolwich A	38	14	10	14	52	49	38
7	Aston Villa	38	14	10	14	58	56	38
8	Bristol City	38	13	12	13	45	58	38
9	Middlesbrough	38	14	9	15	59	53	37
10	Preston	38	13	11	14	48	44	37
11	Chelsea	38	14	9	15	56	61	37
12	Sheff United	38	14	9	15	51	59	37
13	Man United	38	15	7	16	58	68	37
14	Nottm Forest	38	14	8	16	66	57	36
15	Notts County	38	14	8	16	51	48	36
16	Liverpool	38	15	6	17	57	65	36
17	Bury	38	14	8	16	63	77	36
18	Bradford City	38	12	10	16	47	47	34
19	Man City	38	15	4	19	67	69	34
20	Leicester Fosse	38	8	9	21	54	102	25

SECOND DIVISION

		P	W	D	L	F	A	Pts
1	Bolton	38	24	4	10	59	28	52
2	Tottenham	38	20	11	7	67	32	51
3	WBA	38	19	13	6	56	27	51
4	Hull	38	19	6	13	63	39	44
5	Derby	38	16	11	11	55	41	43
6	Oldham	38	17	6	15	55	43	40
7	Wolves	38	14	11	13	56	48	39
8	Glossop NE	38	15	8	15	57	53	38
9	Gainsborough	38	15	8	15	49	70	38
10	Fulham	38	13	11	14	58	48	37
11	Birmingham	38	14	9	15	58	61	37
12	Leeds City	38	14	7	17	43	53	35
13	Grimsby	38	14	7	17	41	54	35
14	Burnley	38	13	7	18	51	58	33
15	Clapton Orient	38	12	9	17	37	49	33
16	Bradford PA	38	13	6	19	51	59	32
17	Barnsley	38	11	10	17	48	57	32
18	Stockport	38	14	3	21	39	71	31
19	Chesterfield	38	11	8	19	37	67	30
20	Blackpool	38	9	11	18	46	68	29

SCOTTISH FIRST DIVISION

		P	W	D	L	F	A	Pts
1	Celtic	34	23	5	6	71	24	51
2	Dundee	34	22	6	6	70	32	50
3	Clyde	34	21	6	7	61	37	48
4	Rangers	34	19	7	8	91	38	45
5	Airdrieonians	34	16	9	9	67	46	41
6	Hibernian	34	16	7	11	40	32	39
7	St Mirren	34	15	6	13	53	45	36
8	Aberdeen	34	15	6	13	61	53	36
9	Falkirk	34	13	7	14	58	56	33
10	Kilmarnock	34	13	7	14	47	61	33
11	Third Lanark	34	11	10	13	56	49	32
12	Hearts	34	12	8	14	54	49	32
13	Port Glasgow	34	10	8	16	39	52	28
14	Motherwell	34	11	6	17	47	73	28
15	Queen's Park	34	6	13	15	42	65	25
16	Hamilton	34	6	12	16	42	72	24
17	Morton	34	8	7	19	39	90	23
18	Partick	34	2	4	28	38	102	8

SCOTTISH SECOND DIVISION

		P	W	D	L	F	A	Pts
1	Abercorn	22	13	5	4	40	18	31
2	Raith	22	11	6	5	46	22	28
3	Vale of Leven	22	12	4	6	39	25	28
4	Dumbarton	22	10	5	7	34	34	25
5	Ayr	22	10	3	9	43	36	23
6	Leith	22	10	3	9	37	33	23
7	Ayr Parkhouse	22	8	5	9	29	31	21
8	St Bernard's	22	9	3	10	34	37	21
9	E Stirlingshire	22	9	3	10	28	34	21
10	Albion	22	9	2	11	37	48	20
11	Cowdenbeath	22	4	4	14	19	42	12
12	Arthurlie	22	5	1	16	29	55	11

Below After a 1-1 draw, 1908 League Champions Manchester United, beat Queen's Park Rangers, the Southern League winners, 4-0 in September to become the first holders of inset the Charity Shield.

FA CUP 1908-09

SECOND ROUND

Manchester United v Everton	1-0
Blackburn Rovers v Chelsea	2-1
Tottenham Hotspur v Fulham	1-0
Crystal Palace v Burnley	0-0, 0-9
Newcastle United v Blackpool	2-1
Leeds City v West Ham United	1-1, 1-2
Preston North End v Sunderland	1-2
West Bromwich Albion v Bradford City	1-2
Bristol City v Bury	2-2, 1-0
Liverpool v Norwich City	2-3
Stockport County v Glossop North End	1-1, 0-1
Portsmouth v The Wednesday	2-2, 0-3
Leicester Fosse v Derby County	0-2
Plymouth Argyle v Exeter City	2-0
Nottingham Forest v Brentford	1-0
Woolwich Arsenal v Millwall Athletic	1-1, 0-1

THIRD ROUND

Manchester United v Blackburn Rovers	6-1
Tottenham Hotspur v Burnley	0-0, 1-3
West Ham United v Newcastle United	0-0, 1-2
Bradford City v Sunderland	0-1
Bristol City v Norwich City	2-0
The Wednesday v Glossop North End	0-1
Derby County v Plymouth Argyle	1-0
Nottingham Forest v Millwall Athletic	3-1

FOURTH ROUND

Burnley v Manchester United	1-0*, 2-3
Newcastle United v Sunderland	2-2, 3-0
Glossop North End v Bristol City	0-0, 0-1
Derby County v Nottingham Forest	3-0

*abandoned

SEMI-FINAL

Manchester United v Newcastle United	1-0
Bristol City v Derby County	1-1, 2-1

FINAL AT CRYSTAL PALACE

Manchester United v Bristol City	1-0

SCOTTISH FA CUP 1908-09

SECOND ROUND

Third Lanark v Aberdeen	4-1
Clyde v Hibernian	1-0
Airdrieonians v Heart of Midlothian	2-0
St Mirren v Beith	3-0
Dundee v Rangers	0-0, 0-1
Queen's Park v Partick Thistle	3-0
Motherwell v Falkirk	1-3
Celtic v Port Glasgow Athletic	4-0

THIRD ROUND

Celtic v Airdrieonians	3-1
Third Lanark v Falkirk	1-2
Clyde v St Mirren	3-1
Rangers v Queen's Park	1-0

SEMI-FINAL

Falkirk v Rangers	0-1
Celtic v Clyde	0-0, 2-0

FINAL AT HAMPDEN PARK

Rangers v Celtic	2-2, 1-1†

†Some newspapers had suggested that, if the first replay ended level, extra-time would be played. The rules, in fact, stated that extra-time could only be played after a third game. When the players left the field some sections of the crowd obviously felt cheated and started protesting. This led to a full-scale riot with pay-boxes burned and hundreds injured. Rangers and Celtic both refused to play a third game as a result, threatening that one or other would simply scratch, and the Scottish FA agreed that the Cup would be withheld.

RADIO TIMES HULTON PICTURE LIBRARY

In April 1909 Leicester Fosse, already relegated to the Second Division, were beaten 12-0 by neighbours Nottingham Forest in one of the last games of the season. As this was a record Division One score, and as those two points confirmed Forest's place in the First Division, a League Commission inquiry examined the circumstances surrounding the match. Their finding was quite simply that the Leicester Fosse players had been celebrating the wedding of a colleague the day before the game was played.

Broxburn and Beith met five times in a first-round Scottish Cup tie. The last three games were played on three consecutive days, Beith finally winning 4-2 on a Friday. The following day they met St Mirren in the next round, their fourth game in four days. They lost . . .

FIRST DIVISION

		P	W	D	L	F	A	Pts
1	Aston Villa	38	23	7	8	84	42	53
2	Liverpool	38	21	6	11	78	57	48
3	Blackburn	38	18	9	11	73	55	45
4	Newcastle	38	19	7	12	70	56	45
5	Man United	38	19	7	12	69	61	45
6	Sheff United	38	16	10	12	62	41	42
7	Bradford City	38	17	8	13	64	47	42
8	Sunderland	38	18	5	15	66	51	41
9	Notts County	38	15	10	13	67	59	40
10	Everton	38	16	8	14	51	56	40
11	Wednesday	38	15	9	14	60	63	39
12	Preston	38	15	5	18	52	58	35
13	Bury	38	12	9	17	62	66	33
14	Nottm Forest	38	11	11	16	54	72	33
15	Tottenham	38	11	10	17	53	69	32
16	Bristol City	38	12	8	18	45	60	32
17	Middlesbrough	38	11	9	18	56	73	31
18	Woolwich A	38	11	9	18	37	67	31
19	Chelsea	38	11	7	20	47	70	29
20	Bolton	38	9	6	23	44	71	24

SECOND DIVISION

		P	W	D	L	F	A	Pts
1	Man City	38	23	8	7	81	40	54
2	Oldham	38	23	7	8	79	39	53
3	Hull City	38	23	7	8	80	46	53
4	Derby	38	22	9	7	72	47	53
5	Leicester Fosse	38	20	4	14	79	58	44
6	Glossop NE	38	18	7	13	64	57	43
7	Fulham	38	14	13	11	51	43	41
8	Wolves	38	17	6	15	64	63	40
9	Barnsley	38	16	7	15	62	59	39
10	Bradford PA	38	17	4	17	64	59	38
11	WBA	38	16	5	17	58	56	37
12	Blackpool	38	14	8	16	50	52	36
13	Stockport	38	13	8	17	50	47	34
14	Burnley	38	14	6	18	62	61	34
15	Lincoln	38	10	11	17	42	69	31
16	Clapton Orient	38	12	6	20	37	60	30
17	Leeds City	38	10	7	21	46	80	27
18	Gainsborough	38	10	6	22	33	75	26
19	Grimsby	38	9	6	23	50	77	24
20	Birmingham	38	8	7	23	42	78	23

SCOTTISH FIRST DIVISION

		P	W	D	L	F	A	Pts
1	Celtic	34	24	6	4	63	22	54
2	Falkirk	34	22	8	4	71	28	52
3	Rangers	34	20	6	8	70	35	46
4	Aberdeen	34	16	8	10	44	29	40
5	Clyde	34	14	9	11	47	40	37
6	Dundee	34	14	8	12	52	44	36
7	Third Lanark	34	13	8	13	62	44	34
8	Hibernian	34	14	6	14	33	40	34
9	Airdrieonians	34	12	9	13	46	57	33
10	Motherwell	34	12	8	14	59	60	32
11	Kilmarnock	34	12	8	14	53	60	32
12	Hearts	34	12	7	15	59	50	31
13	St Mirren	34	13	5	16	49	58	31
14	Queen's Park	34	12	6	16	54	74	30
15	Hamilton	34	11	6	17	50	67	28
16	Partick	34	8	10	16	47	59	26
17	Morton	34	11	3	20	38	60	25
18	Port Glasgow	34	3	5	26	25	95	11

SCOTTISH SECOND DIVISION

		P	W	D	L	F	A	Pts
1	Leith	22	13	7	2	44	19	33
2	Raith*	22	14	5	3	36	21	33
3	St Bernard's	22	12	3	7	43	31	27
4	Dumbarton	22	9	5	8	44	38	23
5	Abercorn	22	7	8	7	38	40	22
6	Vale of Leven	22	8	5	9	36	38	21
7	Ayr	22	9	3	10	37	40	21
8	E Stirlingshire	22	9	2	11	38	43	20
9	Albion	22	7	5	10	34	39	19
10	Arthurlie	22	6	5	11	34	47	17
11	Cowdenbeath	22	7	3	12	22	34	17
12	Ayr Parkhouse	22	4	3	15	27	43	11

*Elected to First Division

Below *In 1910 Newcastle were the last club to win the second FA Cup. The design had been pirated for a minor competition and the old Cup was presented to Lord Kinnaird.*

FA CUP 1909-10

SECOND ROUND

Newcastle United v Fulham	4-0
Bradford City v Blackburn Rovers	1-2
Leicester Fosse v Bury	3-2
Stockport County v Leyton	0-2
Swindon Town v Burnley	2-0
Chelsea v Tottenham Hotspur	0-1
Southampton v Manchester City	0-5
Aston Villa v Derby County	6-1
Bristol Rovers v Barnsley	0-4
Bristol City v West Bromwich Albion	1-1, 2-4
Southend United v Queen's Park Rangers	0-0, 2-3
Wolverhampton Wanderers v West Ham United	1-5
Everton v Woolwich Arsenal	5-0
Sunderland v Bradford Park Avenue	3-1
Portsmouth v Coventry City	0-1
Northampton Town v Nottingham Forest	0-0, 0-1

THIRD ROUND

Newcastle United v Blackburn Rovers	3-1
Leicester Fosse v Leyton	1-0
Swindon Town v Tottenham Hotspur	3-2
Aston Villa v Manchester City	1-2
Barnsley v West Bromwich Albion	1-0
Queen's Park Rangers v West Ham United	1-1, 1-0
Everton v Sunderland	2-0
Coventry City v Nottingham Forest	3-1

FOURTH ROUND

Newcastle United v Leicester Fosse	3-0
Swindon Town v Manchester City	2-0
Barnsley v Queen's Park Rangers	1-0
Coventry City v Everton	0-2

SEMI-FINAL

Newcastle United v Swindon Town	2-0
Barnsley v Everton	0-0, 3-0

FINAL AT CRYSTAL PALACE

Newcastle United v Barnsley	1-1, 2-0*

*Replay at Goodison Park

SCOTTISH FA CUP 1909-10

FIRST ROUND

Rangers v Inverness Thistle	3-1
Queen's Park v Kirkcaldy United	0-0, 6-0
St Mirren v Elgin City	8-0
Kilmarnock v Third Lanark	0-0, 0-2
Dumbarton v Celtic	1-2
Morton v Partick Thistle	4-3
Airdrieonians v Douglas Wanderers	6-0
Leith Athletic v Clyde	0-1
Motherwell v Forfar Athletic	1-0
Bathgate v Heart of Midlothian	0-4
Hamilton v Hibernian	0-0, 0-2
Falkirk v Port Glasgow Athletic	3-0
Dundee v Beith	1-1, 1-0
Ayr v Alloa Athletic	3-2
Aberdeen v Bo'ness	3-0
East Fife v Hurlford	4-1

SECOND ROUND

Motherwell v Morton	3-0
Dundee v Falkirk	3-0
Clyde v Rangers	2-0
St Mirren v Heart of Midlothian	2-2, 0-0, 0-4
Ayr v Hibernian	0-1
Celtic v Third Lanark	3-1
Aberdeen v Airdrieonians	3-0
East Fife v Queen's Park	2-3

THIRD ROUND

Hibernian v Heart of Midlothian	0-1*, 1-0
Celtic v Aberdeen	2-1
Queen's Park v Clyde	2-2, 2-2, 1-2
Motherwell v Dundee	1-3

*abandoned

SEMI-FINAL

Clyde v Celtic	3-1
Hibernian v Dundee	0-0, 0-0, 0-1

FINAL AT IBROX PARK

Dundee v Clyde	2-2, 0-0, 2-1

League Tables 1910-11

FIRST DIVISION

		P	W	D	L	F	A	Pts
1	Man United	38	22	8	8	72	40	52
2	Aston Villa	38	22	7	9	69	41	51
3	Sunderland	38	15	15	8	67	48	45
4	Everton	38	19	7	12	50	36	45
5	Bradford City	38	20	5	13	51	42	45
6	Wednesday	38	17	8	13	47	48	42
7	Oldham	38	16	9	13	44	41	41
8	Newcastle	38	15	10	13	61	43	40
9	Sheff United	38	15	8	15	49	43	38
10	Woolwich A	38	13	12	13	41	49	38
11	Notts County	38	14	10	14	37	45	38
12	Blackburn	38	13	11	14	62	54	37
13	Liverpool	38	15	7	16	53	53	37
14	Preston	38	12	11	15	40	49	35
15	Tottenham	38	13	6	19	52	63	32
16	Middlesbrough	38	11	10	17	49	63	32
17	Man City	38	9	13	16	43	58	31
18	Bury	38	9	11	18	43	71	29
19	Bristol City	38	11	5	22	43	66	27
20	Nottm Forest	38	9	7	22	55	75	25

SECOND DIVISION

		P	W	D	L	F	A	Pts
1	WBA	38	22	9	7	67	41	53
2	Bolton	38	21	9	8	69	40	51
3	Chelsea	38	20	9	9	71	35	49
4	Clapton Orient	38	19	7	12	44	35	45
5	Hull	38	14	16	8	55	39	44
6	Derby	38	17	8	13	73	52	42
7	Blackpool	38	16	10	12	49	38	42
8	Burnley	38	13	15	10	45	45	41
9	Wolves	38	15	8	15	51	52	38
10	Fulham	38	15	7	16	52	48	37
11	Leeds City	38	15	7	16	58	56	37
12	Bradford PA	38	14	9	15	53	55	37
13	Huddersfield	38	13	8	17	57	58	34
14	Glossop NE	38	13	8	17	48	62	34
15	Leicester Fosse	38	14	5	19	52	62	33
16	Birmingham	38	12	8	18	42	64	32
17	Stockport	38	11	8	19	47	79	30
18	Gainsborough	38	9	11	18	37	55	29
19	Barnsley	38	7	14	17	52	62	28
20	Lincoln	38	7	10	21	28	72	24

SCOTTISH FIRST DIVISION

		P	W	D	L	F	A	Pts
1	Rangers	34	23	6	5	90	34	52
2	Aberdeen	34	19	10	5	53	28	48
3	Falkirk	34	17	10	7	65	42	44
4	Partick	34	17	8	9	50	41	42
5	Celtic	34	15	11	8	48	18	41
6	Dundee	34	18	5	11	54	42	41
7	Clyde	34	14	11	9	45	36	39
8	Third Lanark	34	16	7	11	59	53	39
9	Hibernian	34	15	6	13	44	48	36
10	Kilmarnock	34	12	10	12	43	45	34
11	Airdrieonians	34	12	9	13	49	53	33
12	St Mirren	34	12	7	15	46	57	31
13	Morton	34	9	11	14	49	51	29
14	Hearts	34	8	8	18	42	59	24
15	Raith	34	7	10	17	36	56	24
16	Hamilton	34	8	5	21	31	60	21
17	Motherwell	34	8	4	22	37	66	20
18	Queen's Park	34	5	4	25	28	80	14

SCOTTISH SECOND DIVISION

		P	W	D	L	F	A	Pts
1	Dumbarton	22	15	1	6	55	31	31
2	Ayr	22	12	3	7	52	36	27
3	Albion	22	10	5	7	27	21	25
4	Leith	22	9	6	7	42	43	24
5	Cowdenbeath	22	9	5	8	31	27	23
6	St Bernard's	22	10	2	10	36	39	22
7	E Stirlingshire	22	7	6	9	28	35	20
8	Port Glasgow	22	8	3	11	27	32	19
9	Dundee Hibs	22	7	5	10	29	36	19
10	Arthurlie	22	7	5	10	26	33	19
11	Abercorn	22	9	1	12	39	50	19
12	Vale of Leven	22	4	8	10	22	31	16

Below *Bradford City defend in depth as Newcastle threaten their goal in the 1911 Cup Final at Crystal Palace. The game, which ended 0-0, was the Tynesiders' fifth appearance at Crystal Palace in seven years.*

RADIO TIMES HULTON PICTURE LIBRARY

FA CUP 1910-11

SECOND ROUND
Bradford City v Norwich City	2-1
Crewe Alexandra v Grimsby Town	1-5
Burnley v Barnsley	2-0
Brighton v Coventry City	0-0, 0-2
Blackburn Rovers v Tottenham Hotspur	0-0, 2-0
Middlesbrough v Leicester Fosse	0-0, 2-1
West Ham United v Preston North End	3-0
Manchester United v Aston Villa	2-1
Newcastle United v Northampton Town	1-1, 1-0 †
Hull City v Oldham Athletic	1-0
Derby County v West Bromwich Albion	2-0
Everton v Liverpool	2-1
Chesterfield Town v Chelsea	1-4
Wolverhampton Wanderers v Manchester City	1-0
Swindon Town v Woolwich Arsenal	1-0
Darlington v Bradford Park Avenue	2-1

† Both games played at Newcastle. Northampton sold their rights to a replay at home for £900.

THIRD ROUND
Bradford City v Grimsby Town	1-0
Burnley v Coventry City	5-0
Middlesbrough v Blackburn Rovers	0-3
West Ham United v Manchester United	2-1
Newcastle United v Hull City	3-2
Derby County v Everton	5-0
Wolverhampton Wanderers v Chelsea	0-2
Darlington v Swindon Town	0-3

FOURTH ROUND
Bradford City v Burnley	1-0
West Ham United v Blackburn Rovers	2-3
Newcastle United v Derby County	4-0
Chelsea v Swindon Town	3-1

SEMI-FINAL
Bradford City v Blackburn Rovers	3-0
Newcastle United v Chelsea	3-0

FINAL AT CRYSTAL PALACE
Bradford City v Newcastle United	0-0, 1-0*

*Replay at Old Trafford

SCOTTISH FA CUP 1910-11

FIRST ROUND
Aberdeen v Brechin City	3-0
Airdrieonians v Bo'ness	2-0
Celtic v St Mirren	2-0
Heart of Midlothian v Clyde	1-1, 0-1
Dundee v Hibernian	2-1
Leith Athletic v Falkirk	2-2, 1-4
Forfar Athletic v 5th KOSB	3-0
Galston v Lochgelly United	8-0
Rangers v Kilmarnock	2-1
East Stirlingshire v Morton	1-4
Third Lanark v Hamilton Academicals	0-1
Inverness Thistle v Johnstone	0-1
Motherwell v Annbank	5-0
Nithsdale Wanderers v Inverness Caledonian	3-1
Partick Thistle v St Bernard's	7-2
Stanley v Queen's Park	1-6

SECOND ROUND
Aberdeen v Airdrieonians	1-0
Clyde v Queen's Park	4-1
Partick Thistle v Dundee	0-3
Forfar Athletic v Falkirk	2-0
Celtic v Galston	1-0
Rangers v Morton	3-0
Hamilton Academicals v Johnstone	1-1, 3-1
Nithsdale Wanderers v Motherwell	0-0, 0-1

THIRD ROUND
Aberdeen v Forfar Athletic	6-0
Celtic v Clyde	1-0
Dundee v Rangers	2-1
Hamilton Academicals v Motherwell	2-1

SEMI-FINAL
Celtic v Aberdeen	1-0
Hamilton Academicals v Dundee	3-2

FINAL AT IBROX PARK
Celtic v Hamilton Academicals	0-0, 2-1

FIRST DIVISION

		P	W	D	L	F	A	Pts
1	Blackburn	38	20	9	9	60	43	49
2	Everton	38	20	6	12	46	42	46
3	Newcastle	38	18	8	12	64	50	44
4	Bolton	38	20	3	15	54	43	43
5	Wednesday	38	16	9	13	69	49	41
6	Aston Villa	38	17	7	14	76	63	41
7	Middlesbrough	38	16	8	14	56	45	40
8	Sunderland	38	14	11	13	58	51	39
9	WBA	38	15	9	14	43	47	39
10	Woolwich A	38	15	8	15	55	59	38
11	Bradford City	38	15	8	15	46	50	38
12	Tottenham	38	14	9	15	53	53	37
13	Man United	38	13	11	14	45	60	37
14	Sheff United	38	13	10	15	63	56	36
15	Man City	38	13	9	16	56	58	35
16	Notts County	38	14	7	17	46	63	35
17	Liverpool	38	12	10	16	49	55	34
18	Oldham	38	12	10	16	46	54	34
19	Preston	38	13	7	18	40	57	33
20	Bury	38	6	9	23	32	59	21

SECOND DIVISION

		P	W	D	L	F	A	Pts
1	Derby	38	23	8	7	74	28	54
2	Chelsea	38	24	6	8	64	34	54
3	Burnley	38	22	8	8	77	41	52
4	Clapton Orient	38	21	3	14	61	44	45
5	Wolves	38	16	10	12	57	33	42
6	Barnsley	38	15	12	11	45	42	42
7	Hull	38	17	8	13	54	51	42
8	Fulham	38	16	7	15	66	58	39
9	Grimsby	38	15	9	14	48	55	39
10	Leicester Fosse	38	15	7	16	49	66	37
11	Bradford PA	38	13	9	16	44	45	35
12	Birmingham	38	14	6	18	55	59	34
13	Bristol City	38	14	6	18	41	60	34
14	Blackpool	38	13	8	17	32	52	34
15	Nottm Forest	38	13	7	18	46	48	33
16	Stockport	38	11	11	16	47	54	33
17	Huddersfield	38	13	6	19	50	64	32
18	Glossop NE	38	8	12	18	42	56	28
19	Leeds City	38	10	8	20	50	78	28
20	Gainsborough	38	5	13	20	30	64	23

SCOTTISH FIRST DIVISION

		P	W	D	L	F	A	Pts
1	Rangers	34	24	3	7	86	34	51
2	Celtic	34	17	11	6	58	33	45
3	Clyde	34	19	4	11	56	32	42
4	Hearts	34	16	8	10	54	40	40
5	Partick	34	16	8	10	47	40	40
6	Morton	34	14	9	11	44	44	37
7	Falkirk	34	15	6	13	46	43	36
8	Dundee	34	13	9	12	52	41	35
9	Aberdeen	34	14	7	13	44	44	35
10	Airdrieonians	34	12	8	14	40	41	32
11	Third Lanark	34	12	7	15	40	57	31
12	Hamilton	34	11	8	15	32	44	30
13	Hibernian	34	12	5	17	44	47	29
14	Motherwell	34	11	5	18	34	44	27
15	Raith	34	9	9	16	39	59	27
16	Kilmarnock	34	11	4	19	38	60	26
17	Queen's Park	34	8	9	17	29	53	25
18	St Mirren	34	7	10	17	32	59	24

SCOTTISH SECOND DIVISION

		P	W	D	L	F	A	Pts
1	Ayr	22	16	3	3	54	24	35
2	Abercorn	22	13	4	5	43	22	30
3	Dumbarton	22	13	1	8	47	31	27
4	Cowdenbeath	22	12	2	8	39	31	26
5	St Johnstone	22	10	4	8	29	27	24
6	St Bernard's	22	9	5	8	38	36	23
7	Leith	22	9	4	9	31	34	22
8	Arthurlie	22	7	5	10	26	30	19
9	E Stirlingshire	22	7	3	12	21	31	17
10	Dundee Hibs	22	5	5	12	21	41	15
11	Vale of Leven	22	6	1	15	19	37	13
12	Albion	22	6	1	15	26	50	13

Below *Spurs entertain the Football League champions, Blackburn Rovers, at White Hart Lane. Bob Crompton (right of goalkeeper), Blackburn's captain, watches anxiously as his keeper is challenged by a Tottenham forward.*

FA CUP 1911-12

SECOND ROUND

Coventry City v Manchester United	1-5
Aston Villa v Reading	1-1, 0-1
Derby County v Blackburn Rovers	1-2
Wolverhampton Wanderers v Lincoln City	2-1
Leeds City v West Bromwich Albion	0-1
Crystal Palace v Sunderland	0-0, 0-1
Fulham v Liverpool	3-0
Darlington v Northampton Town	1-1, 0-2
Swindon Town v Notts County	2-0
Middlesbrough v West Ham United	1-1, 1-2
Everton v Bury	1-1, 6-0
Manchester City v Oldham Athletic	0-1
Bradford City v Chelsea	2-0
Bradford Park Avenue v Portsmouth	2-0
Barnsley v Leicester Fosse	1-0
Bolton Wanderers v Blackpool	1-0

THIRD ROUND

Reading v Manchester United	1-1, 0-3
Blackburn Rovers v Wolverhampton Wanderers	3-2
Sunderland v West Bromwich Albion	1-2
Fulham v Northampton Town	2-1
West Ham United v Swindon Town	1-1, 0-4
Oldham Athletic v Everton	0-2
Bradford Park Avenue v Bradford City	0-1
Bolton Wanderers v Barnsley	1-2

FOURTH ROUND

Manchester United v Blackburn Rovers	1-1, 2-4
West Bromwich Albion v Fulham	3-0
Swindon Town v Everton	2-1
Barnsley v Bradford City	0-0, 0-0, 0-0, 3-2

SEMI-FINAL

Blackburn Rovers v West Bromwich Albion	0-0, 0-1
Swindon Town v Barnsley	0-0, 0-1

FINAL AT CRYSTAL PALACE

Barnsley v West Bromwich Albion	0-0, 1-0✳

✳Replay at Bramall Lane

SCOTTISH FA CUP 1911-12

FIRST ROUND

St Mirren v Aberdeen	3-3, 0-4
Raith Rovers v Airdrieonians	0-0, 1-3
Armadale v Peterhead	2-1
Broxburn Athletic v Beith	6-0
Celtic v Dunfermline Athletic	1-0
Clyde v Abercorn	2-0
Partick Thistle v Dundee	2-2, 0-3
East Stirlingshire v Dumbarton	3-1
Falkirk v King's Park	2-2, 6-1
Rangers v Stenhousemuir	3-0
Morton v Clachnacuddin	2-0
Hibernian v Heart of Midlothian	1-1, 0-0, 1-2
Kilmarnock v Hamilton Academicals	1-0
Leith v Ayr United	3-0
St Johnstone v Motherwell	0-2
Third Lanark v Renton	5-0

SECOND ROUND

Aberdeen v Armadale	3-0
Celtic v East Stirlingshire	3-0
Clyde v Rangers	3-1
Heart of Midlothian v Dundee	1-0
Leith Athletic v Kilmarnock	0-2
Falkirk v Morton	0-0, 1-3
Motherwell v Airdrieonians	5-1
Third Lanark v Broxburn Athletic	6-1

THIRD ROUND

Aberdeen v Celtic	2-2, 0-2
Kilmarnock v Clyde	1-6
Morton v Heart of Midlothian	0-1
Third Lanark v Motherwell	3-1

SEMI-FINAL

Celtic v Heart of Midlothian	3-0
Clyde v Third Lanark	3-1

FINAL AT IBROX PARK

Celtic v Clyde	2-0

FIRST DIVISION

		P	W	D	L	F	A	Pts
1	Sunderland	38	25	4	9	86	43	54
2	Aston Villa	38	19	12	7	86	52	50
3	Wednesday	38	21	7	10	75	55	49
4	Man United	38	19	8	11	69	43	46
5	Blackburn	38	16	13	9	79	43	45
6	Man City	38	18	8	12	53	37	44
7	Derby	38	17	8	13	69	66	42
8	Bolton	38	16	10	12	62	63	42
9	Oldham	38	14	14	10	50	55	42
10	WBA	38	13	12	13	57	50	38
11	Everton	38	15	7	16	48	54	37
12	Liverpool	38	16	5	17	61	71	37
13	Bradford City	38	12	11	15	50	60	35
14	Newcastle	38	13	8	17	47	47	34
15	Sheff United	38	14	6	18	56	70	34
16	Middlesbrough	38	11	10	17	55	69	32
17	Tottenham	38	12	6	20	45	72	30
18	Chelsea	38	11	6	21	51	73	28
19	Notts County	38	7	9	22	28	56	23
20	Woolwich A	38	3	12	23	26	74	18

SECOND DIVISION

		P	W	D	L	F	A	Pts
1	Preston	38	19	15	4	56	33	53
2	Burnley	38	21	8	9	88	53	50
3	Birmingham	38	18	10	10	59	44	46
4	Barnsley	38	19	7	12	57	47	45
5	Huddersfield	38	17	9	12	66	40	43
6	Leeds City	38	15	10	13	70	64	40
7	Grimsby	38	15	10	13	51	50	40
8	Lincoln	38	15	10	13	50	52	40
9	Fulham	38	17	5	16	65	55	39
10	Wolves	38	14	10	14	56	54	38
11	Bury	38	15	8	15	53	57	38
12	Hull	38	15	6	17	60	56	36
13	Bradford PA	38	14	8	16	60	60	36
14	Clapton Orient	38	10	14	14	34	47	34
15	Leicester Fosse	38	13	7	18	50	65	33
16	Bristol City	38	9	15	14	46	72	33
17	Nottm Forest	38	12	8	18	58	59	32
18	Glossop NE	38	12	8	18	49	68	32
19	Stockport	38	8	10	20	56	78	26
20	Blackpool	38	9	8	21	39	69	26

SCOTTISH FIRST DIVISION

		P	W	D	L	F	A	Pts
1	Rangers	34	24	5	5	76	41	53
2	Celtic	34	22	5	7	53	28	49
3	Hearts	34	17	7	10	71	43	41
4	Airdrieonians	34	15	11	8	64	46	41
5	Falkirk	34	14	12	8	56	38	40
6	Hibernian	34	16	5	13	63	54	37
7	Motherwell	34	12	13	9	47	39	37
8	Aberdeen	34	14	9	11	47	40	37
9	Clyde	34	13	9	12	41	44	35
10	Hamilton	34	12	8	14	44	47	32
11	Kilmarnock	34	10	11	13	37	54	31
12	St Mirren	34	10	10	14	50	60	30
13	Morton	34	11	7	16	50	59	29
14	Dundee	34	8	13	13	33	46	29
15	Third Lanark	34	8	12	14	31	41	28
16	Raith	34	8	10	16	46	60	26
17	Partick	34	10	4	20	40	55	24
18	Queen's Park	34	5	3	26	34	88	13

SCOTTISH SECOND DIVISION

		P	W	D	L	F	A	Pts
1	Ayr*	26	13	8	5	45	19	34
2	Dunfermline	26	13	7	6	45	27	33
3	E Stirlingshire	26	12	8	6	43	27	32
4	Abercorn	26	12	7	7	33	31	31
5	Cowdenbeath	26	12	6	8	36	27	30
6	Dumbarton*	26	12	5	9	39	30	29
7	St Bernard's	26	12	3	11	36	34	27
8	Johnstone	26	9	6	11	31	43	24
9	Albion	26	10	3	13	38	40	23
10	Dundee Hibs	26	6	10	10	34	43	22
11	St Johnstone	26	7	7	12	29	38	21
12	Vale of Leven	26	8	5	13	28	45	21
13	Arthurlie	26	7	5	14	37	49	19
14	Leith	26	5	8	13	26	47	18

*Ayr United and Dumbarton were elected to the First Division. Nevertheless, no clubs were demoted from the First Division.

FA CUP 1912-13

SECOND ROUND

Aston Villa v West Ham United	5-0
Crystal Palace v Bury	2-0
Bradford Park Avenue v Wolverhampton Wanderers	3-0
Chelsea v The Wednesday	1-1, 0-6
Oldham Athletic v Nottingham Forest	5-1
Plymouth Argyle v Manchester United	0-2
Brighton v Everton	0-0, 0-1
Bristol Rovers v Norwich City	1-1, 2-2, 1-0
Sunderland v Manchester City	2-0
Huddersfield Town v Swindon Town	1-2
Hull City v Newcastle United	0-0, 0-3
Woolwich Arsenal v Liverpool	1-4
Burnley v Gainsborough Trinity	4-1
Middlesbrough v Queen's Park Rangers	3-2
Barnsley v Blackburn Rovers	2-3
Reading v Tottenham Hotspur	1-0

THIRD ROUND

Aston Villa v Crystal Palace	5-0
Bradford Park Avenue v The Wednesday	2-1
Oldham Athletic v Manchester United	0-0, 2-1
Bristol Rovers v Everton	0-4
Sunderland v Swindon Town	4-2
Liverpool v Newcastle United	1-1, 0-1
Burnley v Middlesbrough	3-1
Reading v Blackburn Rovers	1-2

FOURTH ROUND

Bradford Park Avenue v Aston Villa	0-5
Everton v Oldham Athletic	0-1
Sunderland v Newcastle United	0-0, 2-2, 3-0
Blackburn Rovers v Burnley	0-1

SEMI-FINAL

Aston Villa v Oldham Athletic	1-0
Sunderland v Burnley	0-0, 3-2

FINAL AT CRYSTAL PALACE

Aston Villa v Sunderland	1-0

SCOTTISH FA CUP 1912-13

SECOND ROUND

Ayr United v Airdrieonians	0-2
Celtic v Arbroath	4-0
East Stirlingshire v Clyde	1-1, 0-0, 0-1
Dumbarton v Aberdeen	2-1
Dundee v Thornhill	5-0
Morton v Falkirk	2-2, 1-3
Hamilton Academicals v Rangers	1-1, 0-2
Heart of Midlothian v Dunfermline Athletic	3-1
Hibernian v Motherwell	0-0, 1-1, 2-1
Kilmarnock v Abercorn	5-1
Partick Thistle v Inverness Caledonian	4-1
Aberdeen University v Peebles Rovers	0-3
Queen's Park v Dundee Hibernians	4-2
Raith Rovers v Broxburn United	5-0
St Johnstone v East Fife	3-0
St Mirren v Third Lanark	0-0, 2-0

THIRD ROUND

Celtic v Peebles Rovers	3-0
Clyde v Queen's Park	1-0
Dumbarton v St Johnstone	1-0
Partick Thistle v Dundee	0-1
Rangers v Falkirk	1-3
Kilmarnock v Heart of Midlothian	0-2
Raith Rovers v Hibernian	2-2, 1-0
St Mirren v Airdrieonians	1-0

FOURTH ROUND

Clyde v Dundee	1-1, 0-0, 2-1
Falkirk v Dumbarton	1-0
Celtic v Heart of Midlothian	0-1
Raith Rovers v St Mirren	2-1

SEMI-FINAL

Falkirk v Heart of Midlothian	1-0
Raith Rovers v Clyde	1-1, 1-0

FINAL AT CELTIC PARK

Falkirk v Raith Rovers	2-0

Above Aston Villa's one goal victory over Oldham in the semi-final of the FA Cup meant that for the only time in the history of the competition the Finalists — Villa and Sunderland — were also the clubs that finished first and second in the League. Here, a Villa attack against Oldham comes to nothing but Villa did win the Cup, 1-0.

FIRST DIVISION

		P	W	D	L	F	A	Pts
1	Blackburn	38	20	11	7	78	42	51
2	Aston Villa	38	19	6	13	65	50	44
3	Oldham	38	17	9	12	55	45	43
4	Middlesbrough	38	19	5	14	77	60	43
5	WBA	38	15	13	10	46	42	43
6	Bolton	38	16	10	12	65	52	42
7	Sunderland	38	17	6	15	63	52	40
8	Chelsea	38	16	7	15	46	55	39
9	Bradford City	38	12	14	12	40	40	38
10	Sheff United	38	16	5	17	63	60	37
11	Newcastle	38	13	11	14	39	48	37
12	Burnley	38	12	12	14	61	53	36
13	Man City	38	14	8	16	51	53	36
14	Man United	38	15	6	17	52	62	36
15	Everton	38	12	11	15	46	55	35
16	Liverpool	38	14	7	17	46	62	35
17	Tottenham	38	12	10	16	50	62	34
18	Wednesday	38	13	8	17	53	70	34
19	Preston	38	12	6	20	52	69	30
20	Derby	38	8	11	19	55	71	27

SECOND DIVISION

		P	W	D	L	F	A	Pts
1	Notts County	38	23	7	8	77	36	53
2	Bradford PA	38	23	3	12	71	47	49
3	Arsenal	38	20	9	9	54	38	49
4	Leeds City	38	20	7	11	76	46	47
5	Barnsley	38	19	7	12	51	45	45
6	Clapton Orient	38	16	11	11	47	35	43
7	Hull	38	16	9	13	53	37	41
8	Bristol City	38	16	9	13	52	50	41
9	Wolves	38	18	5	15	51	52	41
10	Bury	38	15	10	13	39	40	40
11	Fulham	38	16	6	16	46	43	38
12	Stockport	38	13	10	15	55	57	36
13	Huddersfield	38	13	8	17	47	53	34
14	Birmingham	38	12	10	16	48	60	34
15	Grimsby	38	13	8	17	42	58	34
16	Blackpool	38	9	14	15	33	44	32
17	Glossop NE	38	11	6	21	51	67	28
18	Leicester Fosse	38	11	4	23	45	61	26
19	Lincoln	38	10	6	22	36	66	26
20	Nottm Forest	38	7	9	22	37	76	23

SCOTTISH FIRST DIVISION

		P	W	D	L	F	A	Pts
1	Celtic	38	30	5	3	81	14	65
2	Rangers	38	27	5	6	79	31	59
3	Hearts	38	23	8	7	70	29	54
4	Morton	38	26	2	10	76	51	54
5	Falkirk	38	20	9	9	69	51	49
6	Airdrieonians	38	18	12	8	72	43	48
7	Dundee	38	19	5	14	64	53	43
8	Third Lanark	38	13	10	15	42	51	36
9	Clyde	38	11	11	16	46	46	33
10	Ayr	38	13	7	18	58	74	33
11	Raith	38	13	6	19	56	57	32
12	Kilmarnock	38	11	9	18	48	68	31
13	Hibernian	38	12	6	20	58	75	30
14	Aberdeen	38	10	10	18	38	55	30
15	Partick	38	10	9	19	37	51	29
16	Queen's Park	38	10	9	19	52	84	29
17	Motherwell	38	11	6	21	49	66	28
18	Hamilton	38	11	6	21	46	65	28
19	Dumbarton	38	10	7	21	45	87	27
20	St Mirren	38	8	6	24	38	73	22

SCOTTISH SECOND DIVISION

		P	W	D	L	F	A	Pts
1	Cowdenbeath	22	13	5	4	34	17	31
2	Albion	22	10	7	5	38	33	27
3	Dunfermline	22	11	4	7	46	28	26
4	Dundee Hibs	22	11	4	7	36	31	26
5	St Johnstone	22	9	5	8	48	38	23
6	Abercorn	22	10	3	9	32	32	23
7	St Bernard's	22	8	6	8	39	31	22
8	E Stirlingshire	22	7	8	7	40	36	22
9	Arthurlie	22	8	4	10	35	37	20
10	Leith	22	5	9	8	31	37	19
11	Vale of Leven	22	5	3	14	23	47	13
12	Johnstone	22	4	4	14	20	55	12

Below *September 1913 and Woolwich Arsenal play Hull at Highbury. It had been a rush removal to what were then the grounds of a theological college, and in Arsenal's first match there, earlier in the month, the players washed in bowls of water, while an injured player was taken away on a milk-cart.*

FA CUP 1913-14

SECOND ROUND
Sheffield United v Bradford Park Avenue	3-1
Millwall Athletic v Bradford City	1-0
Manchester City v Tottenham Hotspur	2-1
Blackburn Rovers v Bury	2-0
Burnley v Derby County	3-2
Bolton Wanderers v Swindon Town	4-2
Sunderland v Plymouth Argyle	2-1
Glossop North End v Preston North End	0-1
Exeter City v Aston Villa	1-2
Leeds City v West Bromwich Albion	0-2
Wolverhampton Wanderers v The Wednesday	1-1, 0-1
Brighton v Clapton Orient	3-1
Liverpool v Gillingham	2-0
West Ham United v Crystal Palace	2-0
Swansea Town v Queen's Park Rangers	1-2
Birmingham v Huddersfield Town	1-0

THIRD ROUND
Millwall Athletic v Sheffield United	0-4
Blackburn Rovers v Manchester City	1-2
Burnley v Bolton Wanderers	3-0
Sunderland v Preston North End	2-0
Aston Villa v West Bromwich Albion	2-1
The Wednesday v Brighton	3-0
West Ham United v Liverpool	1-1, 1-5
Birmingham v Queen's Park Rangers	1-2

FOURTH ROUND
Manchester City v Sheffield United	0-0, 0-0, 0-1
Sunderland v Burnley	0-0, 1-2
The Wednesday v Aston Villa	0-1
Liverpool v Queen's Park Rangers	2-1

SEMI-FINAL
Sheffield United v Burnley	0-0, 0-1
Aston Villa v Liverpool	0-2

FINAL AT CRYSTAL PALACE
Burnley v Liverpool	1-0

SCOTTISH FA CUP 1913-14

SECOND ROUND
Aberdeen v Albion Rovers	4-1
Airdrieonians v Dundee Hibernian	5-0
Broxburn United v Dumfries	5-1
Celtic v Clyde	0-0, 2-0
Morton v Hibernian	1-1, 1-2
East Stirlingshire v Forfar Athletic	1-1, 0-2
Kilmarnock v Hamilton Academicals	3-1
Leith Athletic v Motherwell	1-1, 2-5
Partick Thistle v Nithsdale Wanderers	1-0
Forres Mechanics v Peebles Rovers	0-4
Queen's Park v Arthurlie	1-0
Raith Rovers v Heart of Midlothian	2-0
Rangers v Alloa Athletic	5-0
St Mirren v Dundee	2-1
Kirkcaldy United v Stevenston United	0-4
Third Lanark v Dumbarton	2-0

THIRD ROUND
Forfar Athletic v Celtic	0-5
Hibernian v Rangers	2-1
Broxburn United v Motherwell	0-2
Kilmarnock v Partick Thistle	1-4
Airdrieonians v Queen's Park	1-1, 1-2
Aberdeen v St Mirren	1-2
Stevenston United v Peebles Rovers	3-2
Third Lanark v Raith Rovers	4-1

FOURTH ROUND
Motherwell v Celtic	1-3
Queen's Park v Hibernian	1-3
St Mirren v Partick Thistle	1-0
Third Lanark v Stevenston United	1-1, 0-0, 1-0

SEMI-FINAL
Celtic v Third Lanark	2-0
Hibernian v St Mirren	3-1

FINAL AT IBROX PARK
Celtic v Hibernian	0-0, 4-1

FIRST DIVISION 1914-15

		P	W	D	L	F	A	Pts
1	Everton	38	19	8	11	76	47	46
2	Oldham	38	17	11	10	70	56	45
3	Blackburn	38	18	7	13	83	61	43
4	Burnley	38	18	7	13	61	47	43
5	Man City	38	15	13	10	49	39	43
6	Sheff United	38	15	13	10	49	41	43
7	Wednesday	38	15	13	10	61	54	43
8	Sunderland	38	18	5	15	81	72	41
9	Bradford PA	38	17	7	14	69	65	41
10	Bradford City	38	13	14	11	55	49	40
11	WBA	38	15	10	13	49	43	40
12	Middlesbrough	38	13	12	13	62	74	38
13	Aston Villa	38	13	11	14	62	72	37
14	Liverpool*	38	14	9	15	65	75	37
15	Newcastle	38	11	10	17	46	48	32
16	Notts County	38	9	13	16	41	57	31
17	Bolton	38	11	8	19	68	84	30
18	Man United*	38	9	12	17	46	62	30
19	Chelsea	38	8	13	17	51	65	29
20	Tottenham	38	8	12	18	57	90	28

*A commission concluded that the Manchester United–Liverpool game on 2 April 1915 had been 'fixed' but the result (2-0) was allowed to stand. No points were deducted.

SCOTTISH DIVISION 'A' 1914-15

		P	W	D	L	F	A	Pts
1	Celtic	38	30	5	3	91	25	65
2	Hearts	38	27	7	4	83	32	61
3	Rangers	38	23	4	11	74	47	50
4	Morton	38	18	12	8	74	48	48
5	Ayr	38	20	8	10	55	40	48
6	Falkirk	38	16	7	15	48	48	39
7	Hamilton	38	16	6	16	60	55	38
8	Partick	38	15	8	15	56	58	38
9	St Mirren	38	14	8	16	56	65	36
10	Airdrieonians	38	14	7	17	54	60	35
11	Hibernian	38	12	11	15	59	66	35
12	Kilmarnock	38	15	4	19	55	59	34
13	Dumbarton	38	13	8	17	51	66	34
14	Aberdeen	38	11	11	16	39	52	33
15	Dundee	38	12	9	17	43	61	33
16	Third Lanark	38	10	12	16	51	57	32
17	Clyde	38	12	6	20	44	59	30
18	Motherwell	38	10	10	18	49	66	30
19	Raith	38	9	10	19	53	68	28
20	Queen's Park	38	4	5	29	27	90	13

SECOND DIVISION 1914-15

		P	W	D	L	F	A	Pts
1	Derby	38	23	7	8	71	33	53
2	Preston	38	20	10	8	61	42	50
3	Barnsley	38	22	3	13	51	51	47
4	Wolves	38	19	7	12	77	52	45
5	Birmingham	38	17	9	12	62	39	43
6	Arsenal	38	19	5	14	69	41	43
7	Hull	38	19	5	14	65	54	43
8	Huddersfield	38	17	8	13	61	42	42
9	Clapton Orient	38	16	9	13	50	48	41
10	Blackpool	38	17	5	16	58	57	39
11	Bury	38	15	8	15	61	56	38
12	Fulham	38	15	7	16	53	47	37
13	Bristol City	38	15	7	16	62	56	37
14	Stockport	38	15	7	16	54	60	37
15	Leeds City	38	14	4	20	65	64	32
16	Lincoln	38	11	9	18	46	65	31
17	Grimsby	38	11	9	18	48	76	31
18	Nottm Forest	38	10	9	19	43	77	29
19	Leicester Fosse	38	10	4	24	47	88	24
20	Glossop NE	38	6	6	26	31	87	18

SCOTTISH DIVISION 'B' 1914-15

		P	W	D	L	F	A	Pts
1	Cowdenbeath	26	16	5	5	49	17	37
2	Leith	26	15	7	4	54	31	37
3	St Bernard's	26	18	1	7	66	34	37
4	E Stirlingshire	26	13	5	8	53	46	31
5	Clydebank	26	13	4	9	68	37	30
6	Dunfermline	26	13	2	11	49	39	28
7	Johnstone	26	11	5	10	41	52	27
8	St Johnstone	26	10	6	10	56	53	26
9	Albion	26	9	7	10	37	42	25
10	Lochgelly	26	9	3	14	44	60	21
11	Dundee Hibs	26	8	3	15	48	61	19
12	Abercorn	26	5	7	14	35	65	17
13	Arthurlie	26	6	4	16	36	66	16
14	Vale of Leven	26	4	5	17	33	66	13

WINNERS 1914-15

Southern League Watford
Central League Huddersfield Town
Irish Cup Linfield
Irish League Belfast Celtic
Welsh Cup Wrexham

FA CUP 1914-15

FIRST ROUND

Blackpool v Sheffield United	1-2
Liverpool v Stockport County	3-0
Bradford Park Avenue v Portsmouth	1-0
Bury v Plymouth Argyle	1-1, 2-1
Croydon Common v Oldham Athletic	0-3
Rochdale v Gillingham	2-0
Birmingham v Crystal Palace	2-2, 3-0
Brighton v Lincoln City	2-1
Bolton Wanderers v Notts County	2-1
Millwall Athletic v Clapton Orient	2-1
Burnley v Huddersfield Town	3-1
Bristol Rovers v Southend United	0-0, 0-3
Hull City v West Bromwich Albion	1-0
Grimsby Town v Northampton Town	0-3
Southampton v Luton Town	3-0
South Shields v Fulham	1-2
Chelsea v Swindon	1-1, 5-2
Arsenal v Merthyr Town	3-0
Preston North End v Manchester City	0-0, 0-3
Aston Villa v Exeter City	2-0
West Ham United v Newcastle United	2-2, 2-3
Swansea Town v Blackburn Rovers	1-0
The Wednesday v Manchester United	1-0
Reading v Wolverhampton Wanderers	0-1
Everton v Barnsley	3-0
Bristol City v Cardiff City	2-0
Queen's Park Rangers v Glossop North End	2-1
Derby County v Leeds City	1-2
Darlington v Bradford City	0-1
Middlesbrough v Goole Town	9-3
Nottingham Forest v Norwich City	1-4
Tottenham Hotspur v Sunderland	2-1

SECOND ROUND

Sheffield United v Liverpool	1-0
Bury v Bradford Park Avenue	0-1
Oldham Athletic v Rochdale	3-0
Brighton v Birmingham	0-0*, 0-3
Bolton Wanderers v Millwall Athletic	0-0*, 2-2*, 4-1
Burnley v Southend United	6-0
Hull City v Northampton Town	2-1
Fulham v Southampton	2-3*
Chelsea v Arsenal	1-0
Manchester City v Aston Villa	1-0
Newcastle United v Swansea Town	1-1*, 2-0
The Wednesday v Wolverhampton Wanderers	2-0
Everton v Bristol City	4-0
Queen's Park Rangers v Leeds City	1-0
Bradford City v Middlesbrough	1-0
Norwich City v Tottenham Hotspur	3-2

THIRD ROUND

Sheffield United v Bradford Park Avenue	1-0*
Birmingham v Oldham Athletic	2-3
Bolton Wanderers v Burnley	2-1*
Southampton v Hull City	2-2*, 0-4
Manchester City v Chelsea	0-1
The Wednesday v Newcastle United	1-2
Queen's Park Rangers v Everton	1-2
Bradford City v Norwich City	1-1*, 0-0*, 2-0

FOURTH ROUND

Oldham Athletic v Sheffield United	0-0*, 0-3
Bolton Wanderers v Hull City	4-2
Chelsea v Newcastle United	1-1*, 1-0
Bradford City v Everton	0-2

SEMI-FINAL

Sheffield United v Bolton Wanderers	2-1
Chelsea v Everton	2-0

FINAL AT OLD TRAFFORD

Sheffield United v Chelsea	3-0

* Extra time played

Left *A heatwave in London during August 1914 prompts this St John's Ambulance man to supply the crowd with drinking water.*

There was such a rush of games at the end of season 1915-16 that Celtic played two League games on 15 April. They beat Raith Rovers 6-0 and, in the evening, Motherwell 3-1.

WINNERS 1915-16

Lancashire Regional Tournament Manchester City
Lancashire Tournament Northern Division Burnley
Lancashire Tournament Southern Division Manchester City
Midland Regional Tournament Nottingham Forest
Midland Tournament Southern Division Nottingham Forest
Midland Tournament Northern Division Leeds City
Midland Tournament Midland Division Grimsby Town
London Combination Chelsea
London Supplementary Tournament 'A' Chelsea
London Supplementary Tournament 'B' West Ham United
South Western Combination Portsmouth
Irish Cup Linfield

WINNERS 1916-17

Lancashire Regional Tournament Liverpool
Lancashire Subsidiary Tournament Rochdale
Midland Regional Tournament Leeds City
Midland Subsidiary Tournament Bradford PA
London Combination West Ham United
Irish Cup Glentoran
Belfast and District League Glentoran

WINNERS 1917-18

Lancashire Regional Tournament Stoke
Lancashire Subsidiary Tournament Liverpool
Midland Regional Tournament Leeds City
Midland Subsidiary Tournament Grimsby Town
League Championship Play-off Leeds City
London Combination Chelsea
Irish Cup Belfast Celtic
Belfast and District League Linfield

WINNERS 1918-19

Lancashire Regional Tournament Everton
Lancashire Subsidiary Tournament 'A' Blackpool
Lancashire Subsidiary Tournament 'B' Oldham Athletic
Lancashire Subsidiary Tournament 'C' Manchester City
Lancashire Subsidiary Tournament 'D' Liverpool
Midland Regional Tournament Nottingham Forest
Midland Subsidiary Tournament 'A' Sheffield United
Midland Subsidiary Tournament 'B' Birmingham
Midland Subsidiary Tournament 'C' Bradford PA
Midland Subsidiary Tournament 'D' Hull City
League Championship Play-off Nottingham Forest
London Combination Brentford
Irish Cup Linfield

Right *George Utley leads Sheffield United out for their semi-final FA Cup tie with Bolton Wanderers in 1915. United won 2-1, going on to the only Final this century initially played outside London. That Final, in which they beat Chelsea 3-0, was played at Old Trafford, and has always been known as the 'Khaki Final' because of the large number of soldiers in the crowd.*

The only first-class game in English football played without spectators was the 1915 Bradford City-Norwich second Cup replay. Questions had been raised in the Commons about British-made shells failing to explode in France. The Government decided that the people making the shells were being distracted, and banned football matches during working hours in the vicinity of munitions factories. The game, at Lincoln, was played behind locked doors.

SCOTTISH LEAGUE 1915-16

		P	W	D	L	F	A	Pts
1	Celtic	38	32	3	3	116	23	67
2	Rangers	38	25	6	7	87	39	56
3	Morton*	37	22	7	8	83	35	51
4	Ayr	38	20	8	10	72	45	48
5	Partick	38	19	8	11	65	41	46
6	Hearts*	37	20	6	11	66	45	46
7	Hamilton	38	19	3	16	68	76	41
8	Dundee	38	18	4	16	57	49	40
9	Dumbarton	38	13	11	14	53	64	37
10	Kilmarnock	38	12	11	15	46	49	35
11	Aberdeen	38	11	12	15	51	64	34
12	Falkirk	38	12	9	17	45	61	33
13	St Mirren	38	13	4	21	50	67	30
14	Motherwell	38	11	8	19	55	81	30
15	Airdrieonians	38	11	8	19	44	71	30
16	Clyde	38	11	7	20	49	71	29
17	Third Lanark	38	9	11	18	38	56	29
18	Queen's Park	38	11	6	21	53	100	28
19	Hibernian	38	9	7	22	44	70	25
20	Raith	38	9	5	24	30	65	23

*Morton and Hearts only played each other once.

SCOTTISH LEAGUE 1916-17

		P	W	D	L	F	A	Pts
1	Celtic	38	27	10	1	77	17	64
2	Morton	38	24	6	8	72	39	54
3	Rangers	38	24	5	9	68	32	53
4	Airdrieonians	38	21	8	9	71	38	50
5	Third Lanark	38	19	11	8	53	37	49
6	Kilmarnock	38	18	7	13	69	45	43
7	St Mirren	38	15	10	13	49	43	40
8	Motherwell	38	16	6	16	57	58	38
9	Partick	38	14	7	17	44	43	35
10	Dumbarton	38	12	11	15	56	73	35
11	Hamilton	38	13	9	16	54	73	35
12	Falkirk	38	12	10	16	57	57	34
13	Clyde	38	10	14	14	41	51	34
14	Hearts	38	14	4	20	44	59	32
15	Ayr	38	12	7	19	46	59	31
16	Dundee	38	13	4	21	58	71	30
17	Hibernian	38	10	10	18	57	72	30
18	Queen's Park	38	11	7	20	56	81	29
19	Raith	38	8	7	23	42	91	23
20	Aberdeen	38	7	7	24	36	68	21

SCOTTISH LEAGUE 1917-18

		P	W	D	L	F	A	Pts
1	Rangers	34	25	6	3	66	24	56
2	Celtic	34	24	7	3	66	26	55
3	Kilmarnock	34	19	5	10	69	41	43
4	Morton	34	17	9	8	53	42	43
5	Motherwell	34	16	9	9	70	51	41
6	Partick	34	14	12	8	51	37	40
7	Queen's Park	34	14	6	14	64	63	34
8	Dumbarton	34	13	8	13	48	49	34
9	Clydebank	34	14	5	15	55	56	33
10	Hearts	34	14	4	16	41	58	32
11	St Mirren	34	11	7	16	42	50	29
12	Hamilton	34	11	6	17	52	63	28
13	Third Lanark	34	10	7	17	56	62	27
14	Falkirk	34	9	9	16	38	58	27
15	Airdrieonians	34	10	6	18	46	58	26
16	Hibernian	34	8	9	17	42	57	25
17	Clyde	34	9	2	23	37	72	20
18	Ayr	34	5	9	20	32	61	19

SCOTTISH LEAGUE 1918-19

		P	W	D	L	F	A	Pts
1	Celtic	34	26	6	2	70	22	58
2	Rangers	34	26	5	3	86	16	57
3	Morton	34	18	11	5	76	38	47
4	Partick	34	17	7	10	62	43	41
5	Motherwell	34	14	10	10	51	40	38
6	Hearts	34	14	9	11	59	52	37
7	Ayr	34	15	7	11	57	53	37
8	Queen's Park	34	15	5	14	59	57	35
9	Kilmarnock	34	14	7	13	61	59	35
10	Clydebank	34	12	8	14	52	65	32
11	St Mirren	34	10	12	12	43	55	32
12	Third Lanark	34	11	9	14	60	60	31
13	Airdrieonians	34	9	11	14	45	54	29
14	Hamilton	34	11	5	18	49	75	27
15	Dumbarton	34	7	8	19	31	57	22
16	Falkirk	34	6	8	20	46	72	20
17	Clyde	34	7	6	21	45	75	20
18	Hibernian	34	5	4	25	28	87	14

FIRST DIVISION

		P	W	D	L	F	A	Pts
1	WBA	42	28	4	10	104	47	60
2	Burnley	42	21	9	12	65	59	51
3	Chelsea	42	22	5	15	56	51	49
4	Liverpool	42	19	10	13	59	44	48
5	Sunderland	42	22	4	16	72	59	48
6	Bolton	42	19	9	14	72	65	47
7	Man City	42	18	9	15	71	62	45
8	Newcastle	42	17	9	16	44	39	43
9	Aston Villa	42	18	6	18	75	73	42
10	Arsenal	42	15	12	15	56	58	42
11	Bradford PA	42	15	12	15	60	63	42
12	Man United	42	13	14	15	54	50	40
13	Middlesbrough	42	15	10	17	61	65	40
14	Sheff United	42	16	8	18	59	69	40
15	Bradford City	42	14	11	17	54	63	39
16	Everton	42	12	14	16	69	68	38
17	Oldham	42	15	8	19	49	52	38
18	Derby	42	13	12	17	47	57	38
19	Preston	42	14	10	18	57	73	38
20	Blackburn	42	13	11	18	64	77	37
21	Notts County	42	12	12	18	56	74	36
22	Wednesday	42	7	9	26	28	64	23

SECOND DIVISION

		P	W	D	L	F	A	Pts
1	Tottenham	42	32	6	4	102	32	70
2	Huddersfield	42	28	8	6	97	38	64
3	Birmingham	42	24	8	10	85	34	56
4	Blackpool	42	21	10	11	65	47	52
5	Bury	42	20	8	14	60	44	48
6	Fulham	42	19	9	14	61	50	47
7	West Ham	42	19	9	14	47	40	47
8	Bristol City	42	13	17	12	46	43	43
9	South Shields	42	15	12	15	58	48	42
10	Stoke	42	18	6	18	60	54	42
11	Hull	42	18	6	18	78	72	42
12	Barnsley	42	15	10	17	61	55	40
13	Port Vale*	42	16	8	18	59	62	40
14	Leicester	42	15	10	17	41	61	40
15	Clapton Orient	42	16	6	20	51	59	38
16	Stockport	42	14	9	19	52	61	37
17	Rotherham Co	42	13	8	21	51	83	34
18	Nottm Forest	42	11	9	22	43	73	31
19	Wolves	42	10	10	22	55	80	30
20	Coventry	42	9	11	22	35	73	29
21	Lincoln	42	9	9	24	44	101	27
22	Grimsby	42	10	5	27	34	75	25

*Leeds City were expelled from the League on 4 October 1919, when their record was P8 W4 D2 L2 F17 A10 Pts10. Port Vale took over their remaining fixtures

SCOTTISH LEAGUE

		P	W	D	L	F	A	Pts
1	Rangers	42	31	9	2	106	25	71
2	Celtic	42	29	10	3	89	31	68
3	Motherwell	42	23	11	8	73	53	57
4	Dundee	42	22	6	14	79	65	50
5	Clydebank	42	20	8	14	78	54	48
6	Morton	42	16	13	13	71	48	45
7	Airdrieonians	42	17	10	15	57	43	44
8	Third Lanark	42	16	11	15	57	62	43
9	Kilmarnock	42	20	3	19	59	74	43
10	Ayr	42	15	10	17	72	69	40
11	Dumbarton	42	13	13	16	57	65	39
12	Queen's Park	42	14	10	18	67	73	38
13	Partick	42	13	12	17	51	62	38
14	St Mirren	42	15	8	19	63	81	38
15	Hearts	42	14	9	19	57	72	37
16	Clyde	42	14	9	19	64	71	37
17	Aberdeen	42	11	13	18	46	64	35
18	Hibernian	42	13	7	22	60	79	33
19	Raith	42	11	10	21	61	82	32
20	Falkirk	42	10	11	21	45	74	31
21	Hamilton	42	11	7	24	56	86	29
22	Albion	42	10	7	25	42	77	27

SCOTTISH FA CUP 1919-20

FIRST ROUND

Cowdenbeath v Aberdeen	0-1
Albion Rovers v Dykehead	0-0, 2-1
Dunfermline Harp v Alloa Athletic	0-0, 0-1
Armadale v Clyde	1-0
Dundee v Airdrieonians	1-0
East Fife v Arthurlie	4-0
East Stirlingshire v Thornhill	6-0
St Bernard's v Bathgate	2-0
Heart of Midlothian v Nithsdale Wanderers	5-1
Galston v Hibernian	0-0, 1-2
Lochgelly United v Clachnacuddin	2-0
Morton v Forfar Athletic	4-0
Partick Thistle v Motherwell	3-1
Queen's Park v Hamilton Academicals	2-0
Rangers v Dumbarton	0-0, 1-0
Royal Albert v Forres Mechanics	7-0
Stevenston United v St Mirren	1-2
Third Lanark v Inverness Caledonian	4-1

SECOND ROUND

Aberdeen v Gala Fairydean	2-0
Albion Rovers v Huntingtower (scratched)	w o
Armadale v Hibernian	1-0
Ayr United v St Mirren	2-1
Broxburn United v Queen of the South Wanderers	1-0
Dundee v Celtic	1-3
St Bernard's v Bathgate	2-0
Heart of Midlothian v Falkirk	2-0
Alloa Athletic v Kilmarnock	0-2
Lochgelly United v Royal Albert	2-1
St Johnstone v Morton	1-1, 3-5
Partick Thistle v East Fife	5-0
Queen's Park v Vale of Leithen	3-0
Raith Rovers v East Stirlingshire	0-0, 1-1, 0-0, 4-0
Rangers v Arbroath	5-0
Third Lanark v Vale of Leven	2-1

THIRD ROUND

Aberdeen v Heart of Midlothian	1-0
St Bernard's v Albion Rovers	1-1, 1-4
Ayr United v Armadale	1-1, 0-1
Celtic v Partick Thistle	2-0
Kilmarnock v Queen's Park	4-1
Raith Rovers v Morton	2-2, 0-3
Rangers v Broxburn United	3-0
Lochgelly United v Third Lanark	0-3

FOURTH ROUND

Albion Rovers v Aberdeen	2-1
Morton v Third Lanark	3-0
Armadale v Kilmarnock	1-2
Rangers v Celtic	1-0

SEMI-FINAL

Kilmarnock v Morton	3-2
Albion Rovers v Rangers	0-0, 1-1, 2-0

FINAL AT HAMPDEN PARK

Kilmarnock v Albion Rovers	3-2

FA CUP 1919-20

FIRST ROUND

Aston Villa v Queen's Park Rangers	2-1
Port Vale v Manchester United	1-2
Sunderland v Hull City	6-2
Thorneycroft's Wanderers v Burnley	0-0, 0-5
Bristol Rovers v Tottenham Hotspur	1-4
West Stanley v Gillingham	3-1
Southampton v West Ham United	0-0, 1-3
Bury v Stoke	2-0
Bolton Wanderers v Chelsea	0-1
Fulham v Swindon Town	1-2
Newport County v Leicester City	0-0, 0-2
Manchester City v Clapton Orient	4-1
Bradford Park Avenue v Nottingham Forest	3-0
Castleford Town v Hednesford Town	2-0
Notts County v Millwall Athletic	2-0
Middlesbrough v Lincoln City	4-1
Grimsby Town v Bristol City	1-2
Arsenal v Rochdale	4-2
Cardiff City v Oldham Athletic	2-0
Blackburn Rovers v Wolverhampton Wanderers	2-2, 0-1
Bradford City v Portsmouth	2-2*, 2-0
Sheffield United v Southend United	3-0
Preston North End v Stockport County	3-1
Blackpool v Derby County	0-0, 4-1
Huddersfield Town v Brentford	5-1
Newcastle United v Crystal Palace	2-0
Plymouth Argyle v Reading	2-0
West Bromwich Albion v Barnsley	0-1
South Shields v Liverpool	1-1, 0-2
Luton Town v Coventry City	2-2, 1-0
Birmingham v Everton	2-0
Darlington v The Wednesday	0-0, 2-0

*abandoned

SECOND ROUND

Manchester United v Aston Villa	1-2
Burnley v Sunderland	1-1, 0-2
Tottenham Hotspur v West Stanley	4-0
West Ham United v Bury	6-0
Chelsea v Swindon Town	4-0
Leicester City v Manchester City	3-0
Bradford Park Avenue v Castleford Town	3-2
Notts County v Middlesbrough	1-0
Bristol City v Arsenal	1-0
Wolverhampton Wanderers v Cardiff City	1-2
Bradford City v Sheffield United	2-1
Preston North End v Blackpool	2-1
Newcastle United v Huddersfield Town	0-1
Plymouth Argyle v Barnsley	4-1
Luton Town v Liverpool	0-2
Birmingham v Darlington	4-0

THIRD ROUND

Aston Villa v Sunderland	1-0
Tottenham Hotspur v West Ham United	3-0
Chelsea v Leicester City	3-0
Notts County v Bradford Park Avenue	3-4
Bristol City v Cardiff City	2-1
Preston North End v Bradford City	0-3
Huddersfield Town v Plymouth Argyle	3-1
Liverpool v Birmingham	2-0

FOURTH ROUND

Tottenham Hotspur v Aston Villa	0-1
Chelsea v Bradford Park Avenue	4-1
Bristol City v Bradford City	2-0
Huddersfield Town v Liverpool	2-1

SEMI-FINAL

Aston Villa v Chelsea	3-1
Huddersfield Town v Bristol City	2-1

FINAL AT STAMFORD BRIDGE

Aston Villa v Huddersfield Town	1-0

Far left *Billy Walker, the Aston Villa forward whose two goals in Villa's 3-1 win over Chelsea in the FA Cup semi-final saved the Football Association an embarrassing situation. If Chelsea had won they would have played the Final on their own ground, Stamford Bridge. This was against the rules of the competition but arrangements were too far advanced to be changed.*

FIRST DIVISION

		P	W	D	L	F	A	Pts
1	Burnley	42	23	13	6	79	36	59
2	Man City	42	24	6	12	70	50	54
3	Bolton	42	19	14	9	77	53	52
4	Liverpool	42	18	15	9	63	35	51
5	Newcastle	42	20	10	12	66	45	50
6	Tottenham	42	19	9	14	70	48	47
7	Everton	42	17	13	12	66	55	47
8	Middlesbrough	42	17	12	13	53	53	46
9	Arsenal	42	15	14	13	59	63	44
10	Aston Villa	42	18	7	17	63	70	43
11	Blackburn	42	13	15	14	57	59	41
12	Sunderland	42	14	13	15	57	60	41
13	Man United	42	15	10	17	64	68	40
14	WBA	42	13	14	15	54	58	40
15	Bradford City	42	12	15	15	61	63	39
16	Preston	42	15	9	18	61	65	39
17	Huddersfield	42	15	9	18	42	49	39
18	Chelsea	42	13	13	16	48	58	39
19	Oldham	42	9	15	18	49	86	33
20	Sheff United	42	6	18	18	42	68	30
21	Derby	42	5	16	21	32	58	26
22	Bradford PA	42	8	8	26	43	76	24

SECOND DIVISION

		P	W	D	L	F	A	Pts
1	Birmingham	42	24	10	8	79	38	58
2	Cardiff	42	24	10	8	59	32	58
3	Bristol City	42	19	13	10	49	29	51
4	Blackpool	42	20	10	12	54	42	50
5	West Ham	42	19	10	13	51	30	48
6	Notts County	42	18	11	13	55	40	47
7	Clapton Orient	42	16	13	13	43	42	45
8	South Shields	42	17	10	15	61	46	44
9	Fulham	42	16	10	16	43	47	42
10	Wednesday	42	15	11	16	48	48	41
11	Bury	42	15	10	17	45	49	40
12	Leicester	42	12	16	14	39	46	40
13	Hull	42	10	20	12	43	53	40
14	Leeds	42	14	10	18	40	45	38
15	Wolves	42	16	6	20	49	66	38
16	Barnsley	42	10	16	16	48	50	36
17	Port Vale	42	11	14	17	43	49	36
18	Nottm Forest	42	12	12	18	48	55	36
19	Rotherham Co	42	12	12	18	37	53	36
20	Stoke	42	12	11	19	46	56	35
21	Coventry	42	12	11	19	39	70	35
22	Stockport	42	9	12	21	42	75	30

THIRD DIVISION

		P	W	D	L	F	A	Pts
1	Crystal Palace	42	24	11	7	70	34	59
2	Southampton	42	19	16	7	64	28	54
3	QPR	42	22	9	11	61	32	53
4	Swindon	42	21	10	11	73	49	52
5	Swansea	42	18	15	9	56	45	51
6	Watford	42	20	8	14	59	44	48
7	Millwall Ath	42	18	11	13	42	30	47
8	Merthyr Town	42	15	15	12	60	49	45
9	Luton	42	16	12	14	61	56	44
10	Bristol Rovers	42	18	7	17	68	57	43
11	Plymouth	42	11	21	10	35	34	43
12	Portsmouth	42	12	15	15	46	48	39
13	Grimsby	42	15	9	18	49	59	39
14	Northampton	42	15	8	19	59	75	38
15	Newport	42	14	9	19	43	64	37
16	Norwich	42	10	16	16	44	53	36
17	Southend	42	14	8	20	44	61	36
18	Brighton	42	14	8	20	42	61	36
19	Exeter	42	10	15	17	39	54	35
20	Reading	42	12	7	23	42	59	31
21	Brentford	42	9	12	21	42	67	30
22	Gillingham	42	8	12	22	34	74	28

SCOTTISH LEAGUE

		P	W	D	L	F	A	Pts
1	Rangers	42	35	6	1	91	24	76
2	Celtic	42	30	6	6	86	35	66
3	Hearts	42	20	10	12	74	49	50
4	Dundee	42	19	11	12	54	48	49
5	Motherwell	42	19	10	13	75	51	48
6	Partick	42	17	12	13	53	39	46
7	Clyde	42	21	3	18	63	62	45
8	Third Lanark	42	19	6	17	74	61	44
9	Morton	42	15	14	13	66	58	44
10	Airdrieonians	42	17	9	16	71	64	43
11	Aberdeen	42	14	14	14	53	54	42
12	Kilmarnock	42	17	8	17	62	68	42
13	Hibernian	42	16	9	17	58	57	41
14	Ayr	42	14	12	16	62	69	40
15	Hamilton	42	14	12	16	44	57	40
16	Raith	42	16	5	21	54	58	37
17	Albion	42	11	12	19	57	68	34
18	Falkirk	42	11	12	19	54	72	34
19	Queen's Park	42	11	11	20	45	80	33
20	Clydebank	42	7	14	21	47	72	28
21	Dumbarton	42	10	4	28	41	89	24
22	St Mirren	42	7	4	31	43	92	18

FA CUP 1920-21

SECOND ROUND

Southend United v Blackpool	1-0
Tottenham Hotspur v Bradford City	4-0
Notts County v Aston Villa	0-0, 0-1
Bradford Park Avenue v Huddersfield Town	0-1
Crystal Palace v Hull City	0-2
Burnley v Queen's Park Rangers	4-2
South Shields v Luton Town	0-4
Preston North End v Watford	4-1
Everton v The Wednesday	1-1, 1-0
Newcastle United v Liverpool	1-0
Lincoln City v Fulham	0-0, 0-1
Derby County v Wolverhampton Wanderers	1-1, 0-1
Grimsby Town v Southampton	1-3
Brighton v Cardiff City	0-0, 0-1
Swansea Town v Plymouth Argyle	1-2
Swindon Town v Chelsea	0-2

THIRD ROUND

Southend United v Tottenham Hotspur	1-4
Aston Villa v Huddersfield Town	2-0
Hull City v Burnley	3-0
Luton Town v Preston North End	2-3
Everton v Newcastle United	3-0
Fulham v Wolverhampton Wanderers	0-1
Southampton v Cardiff City	0-1
Plymouth Argyle v Chelsea	0-0, 0-0, 1-2

FOURTH ROUND

Tottenham Hotspur v Aston Villa	1-0
Hull City v Preston North End	0-0, 0-1
Everton v Wolverhampton Wanderers	0-1
Cardiff City v Chelsea	1-0

SEMI-FINAL

Tottenham Hotspur v Preston North End	2-1
Wolverhampton Wanderers v Cardiff City	0-0, 3-1

FINAL AT STAMFORD BRIDGE

Tottenham Hotspur v Wolverhampton Wanderers 1-0

SCOTTISH FA CUP 1920-21

SECOND ROUND

Kilmarnock v Aberdeen	1-2
Albion Rovers v Mid-Annandale	3-1
Clydebank v Alloa Athletic	0-0, 1-1, 0-1
Bo'ness v Armadale	0-0, 0-2
Ayr United v Dykehead	4-0
Vale of Leven v Celtic	0-3
Dumbarton v Elgin City	3-0
Dundee v Stenhousemuir	1-0
Stevenston United v East Fife	0-0, 1-2
East Stirlingshire v Solway Star	5-1
Broxburn United v Hamilton Academicals	1-2
Clyde v Heart of Midlothian	0-0, 1-1, 2-3
Motherwell v Renton	3-0
Queen of the South v Nithsdale Wanderers	1-3
Partick Thistle v Hibernian	0-0, 0-0, 1-0
Rangers v Morton	2-0

THIRD ROUND

Armadale v Albion Rovers	0-0, 0-0, 2-2, 0-2
East Fife v Celtic	1-3
Dumbarton v Nithsdale Wanderers	5-0
Aberdeen v Dundee	1-1, 0-0, 0-2
Hamilton Academicals v Heart of Midlothian	0-1
Motherwell v Ayr United	1-1, 1-1, 3-1
East Stirlingshire v Partick Thistle	1-2
Rangers v Alloa Athletic	0-0, 4-1

FOURTH ROUND

Dundee v Albion Rovers	0-2
Celtic v Heart of Midlothian	1-2
Partick Thistle v Motherwell	0-0, 2-2, 2-1
Dumbarton v Rangers	0-3

SEMI-FINAL

Partick v Heart of Midlothian	0-0, 0-0, 2-0
Rangers v Albion Rovers	4-1

FINAL AT CELTIC PARK

Partick Thistle v Rangers 1-0

Burnley's Championship side which went 30 games without defeat in 1920-21.

RADIO TIMES HULTON PICTURE LIBRARY

FIRST DIVISION

	P	W	D	L	F	A	Pts
1 Liverpool	42	22	13	7	63	36	57
2 Tottenham	42	21	9	12	65	39	51
3 Burnley	42	22	5	15	72	54	49
4 Cardiff	42	19	10	13	61	53	48
5 Aston Villa	42	22	3	17	74	55	47
6 Bolton	42	20	7	15	68	59	47
7 Newcastle	42	18	10	14	59	45	46
8 Middlesbrough	42	16	14	12	79	69	46
9 Chelsea	42	17	12	13	40	43	46
10 Man City	42	18	9	15	65	70	45
11 Sheff United	42	15	10	17	59	54	40
12 Sunderland	42	16	8	18	60	62	40
13 WBA	42	15	10	17	51	63	40
14 Huddersfield	42	15	9	18	53	54	39
15 Blackburn	42	13	12	17	54	57	38
16 Preston	42	13	12	17	42	65	38
17 Arsenal	42	15	7	20	47	56	37
18 Birmingham	42	15	7	20	48	60	37
19 Oldham	42	13	11	18	38	50	37
20 Everton	42	12	12	18	57	55	36
21 Bradford City	42	11	10	21	48	72	32
22 Man United	42	8	12	22	41	73	28

SECOND DIVISION

	P	W	D	L	F	A	Pts
1 Nottm Forest	42	22	12	8	51	30	56
2 Stoke	42	18	16	8	60	44	52
3 Barnsley	42	22	8	12	67	52	52
4 West Ham	42	20	8	14	52	39	48
5 Hull	42	19	10	13	51	41	48
6 South Shields	42	17	12	13	43	38	46
7 Fulham	42	18	9	15	57	38	45
8 Leeds	42	16	13	13	48	38	45
9 Leicester	42	14	17	11	39	34	45
10 Wednesday	42	15	14	13	47	50	44
11 Bury	42	15	10	17	54	55	40
12 Derby	42	15	9	18	60	64	39
13 Notts County	42	12	15	15	47	51	39
14 Crystal Palace	42	13	13	16	45	51	39
15 Clapton Orient	42	15	9	18	43	50	39
16 Rotherham Co	42	14	11	17	32	43	39
17 Wolves	42	13	11	18	44	49	37
18 Port Vale	42	14	8	20	43	57	36
19 Blackpool	42	15	5	22	44	57	35
20 Coventry	42	12	10	20	51	60	34
21 Bristol City	42	12	9	21	37	58	33
22 Bradford PA	42	12	9	21	46	62	33

THIRD DIVISION (NORTH)

	P	W	D	L	F	A	Pts
1 Stockport	38	24	8	6	60	21	56
2 Darlington	38	22	6	10	81	37	50
3 Grimsby	38	21	8	9	72	47	50
4 Hartlepools	38	17	8	13	52	39	42
5 Accrington	38	19	3	16	73	57	41
6 Crewe	38	18	5	15	60	56	41
7 Stalybridge Cel	38	18	5	15	62	63	41
8 Walsall	38	18	3	17	66	65	39
9 Southport	38	14	10	14	55	44	38
10 Ashington	38	17	4	17	59	66	38
11 Durham City	38	17	3	18	68	67	37
12 Wrexham	38	14	9	15	51	56	37
13 Chesterfield	38	16	3	19	48	67	35
14 Lincoln	38	14	6	18	48	59	34
15 Barrow	38	14	5	19	42	54	33
16 Nelson	38	13	7	18	48	66	33
17 Wigan Borough	38	11	9	18	46	72	31
18 Tranmere	38	9	11	18	51	61	29
19 Halifax	38	10	9	19	56	76	29
20 Rochdale	38	11	4	23	52	77	26

THIRD DIVISION (SOUTH)

	P	W	D	L	F	A	Pts
1 Southampton	42	23	15	4	68	21	61
2 Plymouth	42	25	11	6	63	24	61
3 Portsmouth	42	18	17	7	62	39	53
4 Luton	42	22	8	12	64	35	52
5 QPR	42	18	13	11	53	44	49
6 Swindon	42	16	13	13	72	60	45
7 Watford	42	13	18	11	54	48	44
8 Aberdare Ath	42	17	10	15	57	51	44
9 Brentford	42	16	11	15	52	43	43
10 Swansea	42	13	15	14	50	47	41
11 Merthyr Town	42	17	6	19	45	56	40
12 Millwall Ath	42	10	18	14	38	42	38
13 Reading	42	14	18	10	40	47	38
14 Bristol Rovers	42	14	10	18	52	67	38
15 Norwich	42	12	13	17	50	62	37
16 Charlton	42	13	11	18	43	56	37
17 Northampton	42	13	11	18	47	71	37
18 Gillingham	42	14	8	20	47	60	36
19 Brighton	42	13	9	20	45	51	35
20 Newport	42	11	12	19	44	61	34
21 Exeter	42	11	12	19	38	59	34
22 Southend	42	8	11	23	34	74	27

SCOTTISH FIRST DIVISION

	P	W	D	L	F	A	Pts
1 Celtic	42	27	13	2	83	20	67
2 Rangers	42	28	10	4	83	26	66
3 Raith	42	19	13	10	66	43	51
4 Dundee	42	19	11	12	57	40	49
5 Falkirk	42	16	17	9	48	38	49
6 Partick	42	20	8	14	57	53	48
7 Hibernian	42	16	14	12	55	44	46
8 St Mirren	42	17	12	13	71	61	46
9 Third Lanark	42	17	12	13	58	52	46
10 Clyde	42	16	12	14	60	51	44
11 Albion	42	17	10	15	55	51	44
12 Morton	42	16	10	16	58	57	42
13 Motherwell	42	16	7	19	63	58	39
14 Ayr	42	13	12	17	55	63	38
15 Aberdeen	42	13	9	20	48	54	35
16 Airdrieonians	42	12	11	19	46	56	35
17 Kilmarnock	42	13	9	20	56	83	35
18 Hamilton	42	9	16	17	51	62	34
19 Hearts	42	11	10	21	50	60	32
20 Dumbarton*	42	10	10	22	46	81	30
21 Queen's Park*	42	9	10	23	38	82	28
22 Clydebank*	42	6	8	28	34	103	20

* Three clubs relegated to Second Division

SCOTTISH SECOND DIVISION

	P	W	D	L	F	A	Pts
1 Alloa*	38	26	8	4	81	32	60
2 Cowdenbeath	38	19	9	10	56	30	47
3 Armadale	38	20	5	13	64	49	45
4 Vale of Leven	38	17	10	11	56	43	44
5 Bathgate	38	16	11	11	56	41	43
6 Bo'ness	38	16	7	15	57	49	39
7 Broxburn	38	14	11	13	43	43	39
8 Dunfermline	38	14	10	14	56	42	38
9 St Bernard's	38	15	8	15	50	49	38
10 Stenhousemuir	38	14	10	14	50	51	38
11 Johnstone	38	14	10	14	46	59	38
12 East Fife	38	15	7	16	55	54	37
13 St Johnstone	38	12	11	15	41	52	35
14 Forfar	38	11	12	15	44	53	34
15 E Stirlingshire	38	12	10	16	43	60	34
16 Arbroath	38	11	11	16	45	56	33
17 King's Park	38	10	12	16	47	65	32
18 Lochgelly Utd	38	11	9	18	46	56	31
19 Dundee Hibs	38	10	8	20	47	65	28
20 Clackmannan	38	10	7	21	41	75	27

* Only Alloa promoted

FA CUP 1921-22

SECOND ROUND

Crystal Palace v Millwall Athletic	0-0, 0-2
Southend United v Swansea Town	0-1
Swindon Town v Blackburn Rovers	0-1
Brighton v Huddersfield Town	0-0, 0-2
Aston Villa v Luton Town	1-0
Northampton Town v Stoke	2-2, 0-3
Liverpool v West Bromwich Albion	0-1
Bradford City v Notts County	1-1, 1-1, 0-1
Bradford Park Avenue v Arsenal	2-3
Leicester City v Fulham	2-0
Barnsley v Oldham Athletic	3-1
Preston North End v Newcastle United	3-1
Southampton v Cardiff City	1-1, 0-2
Nottingham Forest v Hull City	3-0
Bolton Wanderers v Manchester City	1-3
Tottenham Hotspur v Watford	1-0

THIRD ROUND

Millwall Athletic v Swansea Town	4-0
Blackburn Rovers v Huddersfield Town	1-1, 0-5
Stoke v Aston Villa	0-0, 0-4
West Bromwich Albion v Notts County	1-1, 0-2
Arsenal v Leicester City	3-0
Barnsley v Preston North End	1-1, 0-3
Cardiff City v Nottingham Forest	4-1
Tottenham Hotspur v Manchester City	2-1

FOURTH ROUND

Huddersfield Town v Millwall Athletic	3-0
Notts County v Aston Villa	2-2, 4-3
Arsenal v Preston North End	1-1, 1-2
Cardiff City v Tottenham Hotspur	1-1, 1-2

SEMI-FINAL

Huddersfield Town v Notts County	3-1
Preston North End v Tottenham Hotspur	2-1

FINAL AT STAMFORD BRIDGE

Huddersfield Town v Preston North End	1-0

SCOTTISH FA CUP 1921-22

SECOND ROUND

Aberdeen v Queen's Park	1-1, 2-1
Cowdenbeath v Airdrieonians	0-0, 1-4
Vale of Leven v Alloa Athletic	0-0, 0-1
Bathgate v Falkirk	1-0
Celtic v Third Lanark	1-0
Clyde v Bo'ness	5-1
Royal Albert v Dundee	0-1
East Stirlingshire v Dunfermline Athletic	2-1
Morton v Clydebank	1-1, 3-1
Hamilton Academicals v King's Park	4-1
Broxburn United v Heart of Midlothian	2-2, 2-2, 1-3
Motherwell v Hibernian	3-2
Ayr United v Partick Thistle	0-1
Inverness Citadel v Queen of the South	2-2, 1-2
Albion Rovers v Rangers	1-1, 0-4
Kilmarnock v St Mirren	1-4

THIRD ROUND

Aberdeen v Dundee	3-0
Morton v Clyde	4-1
Celtic v Hamilton Academicals	1-3
Motherwell v Alloa Athletic	1-0
Partick Thistle v Bathgate	3-0
Queen of the South v East Stirlingshire	2-0
Heart of Midlothian v Rangers	0-4
St Mirren v Airdrieonians	3-0

FOURTH ROUND

Hamilton Academicals v Aberdeen	0-0, 0-2
Motherwell v Morton	1-2
Partick Thistle v Queen of the South	1-0
Rangers v St Mirren	1-1, 2-0

SEMI-FINAL

Morton v Aberdeen	3-1
Rangers v Partick Thistle	2-0

FINAL AT HAMPDEN PARK

Morton v Rangers	1-0

On Boxing Day 1921, Aston Villa's winning goal in their Division One fixture with Sheffield United was a spectacular 30-yard header. Frank Barson, Villa's centre-half, was the man responsible. Another Villa player, Billy Walker, had also done the unusual in a League match that season. In November, he had scored three penalties against Bradford City—a record for one game.

Jimmy Evans, Southend United's full-back, scored a total of 10 goals in the Third Division South in 1921-22. All were from penalties, and meant that Evans became the first full-back to finish a season as a club's top League scorer.

The Scottish Second Division restarted in 1921-22, with promotion by position.

FIRST DIVISION

		P	W	D	L	F	A	Pts
1	Liverpool	42	26	8	8	70	31	60
2	Sunderland	42	22	10	10	72	54	54
3	Huddersfield	42	21	11	10	60	32	53
4	Newcastle	42	18	12	12	45	37	48
5	Everton	42	20	7	15	63	59	47
6	Aston Villa	42	18	10	14	64	51	46
7	WBA	42	17	11	14	58	49	45
8	Man City	42	17	11	14	50	49	45
9	Cardiff	42	18	7	17	73	59	43
10	Sheff United	42	16	10	16	68	64	42
11	Arsenal	42	16	10	16	61	62	42
12	Tottenham	42	17	7	18	50	50	41
13	Bolton	42	14	12	16	50	58	40
14	Blackburn	42	14	12	16	47	62	40
15	Burnley	42	16	6	20	58	59	38
16	Preston	42	13	11	18	60	64	37
17	Birmingham	42	13	11	18	41	57	37
18	Middlesbrough	42	13	10	19	57	63	36
19	Chelsea	42	9	18	15	45	53	36
20	Nottm Forest	42	13	8	21	41	70	34
21	Stoke	42	10	10	22	47	67	30
22	Oldham	42	10	10	22	35	65	30

SECOND DIVISION

		P	W	D	L	F	A	Pts
1	Notts County	42	23	7	12	46	34	53
2	West Ham	42	20	11	11	63	38	51
3	Leicester	42	21	9	12	65	44	51
4	Man United	42	17	14	11	51	36	48
5	Blackpool	42	18	11	13	60	43	47
6	Bury	42	18	11	13	55	46	47
7	Leeds	42	18	11	13	43	36	47
8	Wednesday	42	17	12	13	54	47	46
9	Barnsley	42	17	11	14	62	51	45
10	Fulham	42	16	12	14	43	32	44
11	Southampton	42	14	14	14	40	40	42
12	Hull	42	14	14	14	43	45	42
13	South Shields	42	15	10	17	35	44	40
14	Derby	42	14	11	17	46	50	39
15	Bradford City	42	12	13	17	41	45	37
16	Crystal Palace	42	13	11	18	54	62	37
17	Port Vale	42	14	9	19	39	51	37
18	Coventry	42	15	7	20	46	63	37
19	Clapton Orient	42	12	12	18	40	50	36
20	Stockport	42	14	8	20	43	58	36
21	Rotherham Co	42	13	9	20	44	63	35
22	Wolves	42	9	9	24	42	77	27

FA CUP 1922-23

SECOND ROUND

Bolton Wanderers v Leeds United	3-1
Millwall Athletic v Huddersfield Town	0-0, 0-3
Charlton Athletic v Preston North End	2-0
West Bromwich Albion v Sunderland	2-1
Middlesbrough v Sheffield United	1-1, 0-3
Wolverhampton Wanderers v Liverpool	0-2
Wigan Borough v Queen's Park Rangers	2-4
South Shields v Blackburn Rovers	0-0, 1-0
Bury v Stoke	3-1
Chelsea v Southampton	0-0, 0-1
Brighton v West Ham United	1-1, 0-1
Plymouth Argyle v Bradford Park Avenue	4-1
Bristol City v Derby County	0-3
The Wednesday v Barnsley	2-1
Tottenham Hotspur v Manchester United	4-0
Leicester City v Cardiff City	0-1

THIRD ROUND

Huddersfield Town v Bolton Wanderers	1-1, 0-1
Charlton Athletic v West Bromwich Albion	1-0
Liverpool v Sheffield United	1-2
Queen's Park Rangers v South Shields	3-0
Bury v Southampton	0-0, 0-1
West Ham United v Plymouth Argyle	2-0
Derby County v The Wednesday	1-0
Cardiff City v Tottenham Hotspur	2-3

FOURTH ROUND

Charlton Athletic v Bolton Wanderers	0-1
Queen's Park Rangers v Sheffield United	0-1
Southampton v West Ham United	1-1, 1-1, 0-1
Tottenham Hotspur v Derby County	0-1

SEMI-FINAL

Bolton Wanderers v Sheffield United	1-0
West Ham United v Derby County	5-2

FINAL

Bolton Wanderers v West Ham United	2-0

THIRD DIVISION (SOUTH)

		P	W	D	L	F	A	Pts
1	Bristol City	42	24	11	7	66	40	59
2	Plymouth	42	23	7	12	61	29	53
3	Swansea	42	22	9	11	78	45	53
4	Brighton	42	20	11	11	52	34	51
5	Luton	42	21	7	14	68	49	49
6	Portsmouth	42	19	8	15	58	52	46
7	Millwall Ath	42	14	18	10	45	40	46
8	Northampton	42	17	11	14	54	44	45
9	Swindon	42	17	11	14	62	56	45
10	Watford	42	17	10	15	57	54	44
11	QPR	42	16	10	16	54	49	42
12	Charlton	42	14	14	14	55	51	42
13	Bristol Rovers	42	13	16	13	35	36	42
14	Brentford	42	13	12	17	41	51	38
15	Southend	42	12	13	17	49	54	37
16	Gillingham	42	15	7	20	51	59	37
17	Merthyr Town	42	11	14	17	39	48	36
18	Norwich	42	13	10	19	51	71	36
19	Reading	42	10	14	18	36	55	34
20	Exeter	42	13	7	22	47	84	33
21	Aberdare Ath	42	9	11	22	42	70	29
22	Newport	42	8	11	23	40	70	27

THIRD DIVISION (NORTH)

		P	W	D	L	F	A	Pts
1	Nelson	38	24	3	11	61	41	51
2	Bradford PA	38	19	9	10	67	38	47
3	Walsall	38	19	8	11	51	44	46
4	Chesterfield	38	19	7	12	68	52	45
5	Wigan Borough	38	18	8	12	64	39	44
6	Crewe	38	17	9	12	48	38	43
7	Halifax	38	17	7	14	53	46	41
8	Accrington	38	17	7	14	59	65	41
9	Darlington	38	15	10	13	59	46	40
10	Wrexham	38	14	10	14	38	48	38
11	Stalybridge Cel	38	15	6	17	42	47	36
12	Rochdale	38	13	10	15	42	53	36
13	Lincoln	38	13	10	15	39	55	36
14	Grimsby	38	14	5	19	55	52	33
15	Hartlepools	38	10	12	16	48	54	32
16	Tranmere	38	12	8	18	49	59	32
17	Southport	38	12	7	19	32	46	31
18	Barrow	38	13	4	21	50	60	30
19	Ashington	38	11	8	19	51	77	30
20	Durham City	38	9	10	19	43	59	28

SCOTTISH FA CUP 1922-23

SECOND ROUND

Airdrieonians v Aberdeen	1-1, 0-2
Ayr United v Rangers	2-0
Bo'ness v Heart of Midlothian	3-2
Celtic v Hurlford	4-0
Dundee v St Bernard's	0-0, 3-2
Dunfermline Athletic v Clydebank	1-0
Hibernian v Peebles Rovers	0-0, 3-0
Kilmarnock v East Fife	1-1, 0-1
Johnstone v Falkirk	0-1
Hamilton Academicals v King's Park	1-0
Motherwell v St Mirren	2-1
Dundee Hibernians v Nithsdale Wanderers	0-1
Peterhead v Galston	1-0
Queen's Park v Bathgate	1-1, 2-0
Raith Rovers v Cowdenbeath	2-0
Vale of Leven v Third Lanark	2-2, 1-2

THIRD ROUND

Aberdeen v Peterhead	13-0
Bo'ness v Nithsdale Wanderers	2-0
Celtic v East Fife	2-1
Dundee v Hamilton Academicals	0-0, 1-0
Hibernian v Queen's Park	2-0
Motherwell v Falkirk	3-0
Dunfermline Athletic v Raith Rovers	0-3
Third Lanark v Ayr United	2-0

FOURTH ROUND

Celtic v Raith Rovers	1-0
Hibernian v Aberdeen	2-0
Motherwell v Bo'ness	4-2
Dundee v Third Lanark	0-0, 1-1, 0-1

SEMI-FINAL

Celtic v Motherwell	2-0
Hibernian v Third Lanark	1-0

FINAL AT HAMPDEN PARK

Celtic v Hibernian	1-0

SCOTTISH FIRST DIVISION

		P	W	D	L	F	A	Pts
1	Rangers	38	23	9	6	67	29	55
2	Airdrieonians	38	20	10	8	58	38	50
3	Celtic	38	19	8	11	52	39	46
4	Falkirk	38	14	17	7	44	32	45
5	Aberdeen	38	15	12	11	46	34	42
6	St Mirren	38	15	12	11	54	44	42
7	Dundee	38	17	7	14	51	45	41
8	Hibernian	38	17	7	14	45	40	41
9	Raith	38	13	13	12	31	43	39
10	Ayr	38	13	12	13	43	44	38
11	Partick	38	14	9	15	51	48	37
12	Hearts	38	11	15	12	51	50	37
13	Motherwell	38	13	10	15	59	60	36
14	Morton	38	12	11	15	44	47	35
15	Kilmarnock	38	14	7	17	57	66	35
16	Clyde	38	12	9	17	36	44	33
17	Third Lanark	38	11	8	19	40	59	30
18	Hamilton	38	11	7	20	43	59	29
19	Albion	38	8	10	20	38	64	26
20	Alloa	38	6	11	21	27	52	23

SCOTTISH SECOND DIVISION

		P	W	D	L	F	A	Pts
1	Queen's Park	38	24	9	5	73	31	57
2	Clydebank	38	21	10	7	69	29	52
3	St Johnstone	38	19	12	7	60	39	48*
4	Dumbarton	38	17	8	13	61	40	42
5	Bathgate	38	16	9	13	67	55	41
6	Armadale	38	15	11	12	63	52	41
7	Bo'ness	38	12	17	9	48	46	41
8	Broxburn	38	14	12	12	40	43	40
9	East Fife	38	16	7	15	48	42	39
10	Lochgelly	38	16	5	17	41	64	37
11	Cowdenbeath	38	16	6	16	56	52	36*
12	King's Park	38	14	6	18	46	60	34
13	Dunfermline	38	11	11	16	47	44	33
14	Stenhousemuir	38	13	7	18	53	67	33
15	Forfar	38	13	7	18	51	73	33
16	Johnstone	38	13	6	19	41	62	32
17	Vale of Leven	38	11	8	19	50	59	30
18	St Bernard's	38	8	15	15	39	50	29*
19	E Stirlingshire	38	10	8	20	48	69	28
20	Arbroath	38	8	12	18	45	69	28

*Two points deducted for fielding an ineligible player.

In Division Two, 1922-23, Southampton had an uneventful season, finishing in the middle of the table. But their final record is something of a curiosity. It reads, P42, W14, D14, L14, F40, A40, Pts42.

Liverpool won the League Championship for the second successive season.

The most goals a player has scored in an FA Cup game and yet finished on the losing side is seven. Billy Minter of St Albans City scored seven times against Dulwich Hamlet in a replayed Fourth Round qualifying tie on 22 November 1922. But despite poor Minter's monumental contribution, his side eventually lost the match 8-7.

FIRST DIVISION

		P	W	D	L	F	A	Pts
1	Huddersfield	42	23	11	8	60	33	57
2	Cardiff	42	22	13	7	61	34	57
3	Sunderland	42	22	9	11	71	54	53
4	Bolton	42	18	14	10	68	34	50
5	Sheff United	42	19	12	11	69	49	50
6	Aston Villa	42	18	13	11	52	37	49
7	Everton	42	18	13	11	62	53	49
8	Blackburn	42	17	11	14	54	50	45
9	Newcastle	42	17	10	15	60	54	44
10	Notts County	42	14	14	14	44	49	42
11	Man City	42	15	12	15	54	71	42
12	Liverpool	42	15	11	16	49	48	41
13	West Ham	42	13	15	14	40	43	41
14	Birmingham	42	13	13	16	41	49	39
15	Tottenham	42	12	14	16	50	56	38
16	WBA	42	12	14	16	51	62	38
17	Burnley	42	12	12	18	55	60	36
18	Preston	42	12	10	20	52	67	34
19	Arsenal	42	12	9	21	40	63	33
20	Nottm Forest	42	10	12	20	42	64	32
21	Chelsea	42	9	14	19	31	53	32
22	Middlesbrough	42	7	8	27	37	60	22

SECOND DIVISION

		P	W	D	L	F	A	Pts
1	Leeds	42	21	12	9	61	35	54
2	Bury	42	21	9	12	63	35	51
3	Derby	42	21	9	12	75	42	51
4	Blackpool	42	18	13	11	72	47	49
5	Southampton	42	17	14	11	52	31	48
6	Stoke	42	14	18	10	44	42	46
7	Oldham	42	14	17	11	45	52	45
8	Wednesday	42	16	12	14	54	51	44
9	South Shields	42	17	10	15	49	50	44
10	Clapton Orient	42	14	15	13	40	36	43
11	Barnsley	42	16	11	15	57	61	43
12	Leicester	42	17	8	17	64	54	42
13	Stockport	42	13	16	13	44	52	42
14	Man United	42	13	14	15	52	44	40
15	Crystal Palace	42	13	13	16	53	65	39
16	Port Vale	42	13	12	17	50	66	38
17	Hull	42	10	17	15	46	51	37
18	Bradford City	42	11	15	16	35	48	37
19	Coventry	42	11	13	18	52	68	35
20	Fulham	42	10	14	18	45	56	34
21	Nelson	42	10	13	19	40	74	33
22	Bristol City	42	7	15	20	32	65	29

FA CUP 1923-24

SECOND ROUND

Derby County v Newcastle United	2-2, 2-2, 2-2, 3-5
Exeter City v Watford	0-0, 0-1
Southampton v Blackpool	3-1
Bolton Wanderers v Liverpool	1-4
Manchester City v Halifax Town	2-2, 0-0, 3-0
Brighton v Everton	5-2
Cardiff City v Arsenal	1-0
The Wednesday v Bristol City	1-1, 0-2
Swansea Town v Aston Villa	0-2
West Ham United v Leeds United	1-1, 0-1
West Bromwich Albion v Corinthians	5-0
Charlton Athletic v Wolverhampton Wanderers	0-0, 0-1
Swindon Town v Oldham Athletic	2-0
Crystal Palace v Notts County	0-0, 0-0, 0-0, 2-1
Burnley v Fulham	0-0, 1-0
Manchester United v Huddersfield Town	0-3

THIRD ROUND

Watford v Newcastle United	0-1
Southampton v Liverpool	0-0, 0-2
Brighton v Manchester City	1-5
Cardiff City v Bristol City	3-0
Aston Villa v Leeds United	3-0
West Bromwich Albion v Wolverhampton Wanderers	1-1, 2-0
Crystal Palace v Swindon Town	1-2
Burnley v Huddersfield Town	1-0

FOURTH ROUND

Newcastle United v Liverpool	1-0
Manchester City v Cardiff City	0-0, 1-0
West Bromwich Albion v Aston Villa	0-2
Swindon Town v Burnley	1-1, 1-3

SEMI-FINAL

Newcastle United v Manchester City	2-0
Aston Villa v Burnley	3-0

FINAL

Newcastle United v Aston Villa	2-0

THIRD DIVISION (SOUTH)

		P	W	D	L	F	A	Pts
1	Portsmouth	42	24	11	7	87	30	59
2	Plymouth	42	23	9	10	70	34	55
3	Millwall Ath	42	22	10	10	64	38	54
4	Swansea	42	22	8	12	60	48	52
5	Brighton	42	21	9	12	68	37	51
6	Swindon	42	17	13	12	58	44	47
7	Luton	42	16	14	12	50	44	46
8	Northampton	42	17	11	14	64	47	45
9	Bristol Rovers	42	15	13	14	52	46	43
10	Newport	42	17	9	16	56	64	43
11	Norwich	42	16	8	18	60	59	40
12	Aberdare Ath	42	12	14	16	45	58	38
13	Merthyr Town	42	11	16	15	45	65	38
14	Charlton	42	11	15	16	38	45	37
15	Gillingham	42	12	13	17	43	58	37
16	Exeter	42	15	7	20	37	52	37
17	Brentford	42	14	8	20	54	71	36
18	Reading	42	13	9	20	51	57	35
19	Southend	42	12	10	20	53	84	34
20	Watford	42	9	15	18	45	54	33
21	Bournemouth	42	11	11	20	40	65	33
22	QPR	42	11	9	22	37	77	31

THIRD DIVISION (NORTH)

		P	W	D	L	F	A	Pts
1	Wolves	42	24	15	3	76	27	63
2	Rochdale	42	25	12	5	60	26	62
3	Chesterfield	42	22	10	10	70	39	54
4	Rotherham Co	42	23	6	13	70	43	52
5	Bradford PA	42	21	10	11	69	43	52
6	Darlington	42	20	8	14	70	53	48
7	Southport	42	16	14	12	44	42	46
8	Ashington	42	18	8	16	59	61	44
9	Doncaster	42	15	12	15	59	53	42
10	Wigan Borough	42	14	14	14	55	53	42
11	Grimsby	42	14	13	15	49	47	41
12	Tranmere	42	13	15	14	51	60	41
13	Accrington	42	16	8	18	48	61	40
14	Halifax	42	15	10	17	42	59	40
15	Durham City	42	15	9	18	59	60	39
16	Wrexham	42	10	18	14	37	44	38
17	Walsall	42	14	8	20	44	59	36
18	New Brighton	42	11	13	18	40	53	35
19	Lincoln	42	10	12	20	48	59	32
20	Crewe	42	7	13	22	32	58	27
21	Hartlepools	42	7	11	24	33	70	25
22	Barrow	42	8	9	25	35	80	25

SCOTTISH FIRST DIVISION

		P	W	D	L	F	A	Pts
1	Rangers	38	25	9	4	72	22	59
2	Airdrieonians	38	20	10	8	72	46	50
3	Celtic	38	17	12	9	56	33	46
4	Raith	38	18	7	13	56	38	43
5	Dundee	38	15	13	10	70	57	43
6	St Mirren	38	15	12	11	53	45	42
7	Hibernian	38	15	11	12	66	52	41
8	Partick	38	15	9	14	58	55	39
9	Hearts	38	14	10	14	61	50	38
10	Motherwell	38	15	7	16	58	63	37
11	Morton	38	16	5	17	48	54	37
12	Hamilton	38	15	6	17	52	57	36
13	Aberdeen	38	13	10	15	37	41	36
14	Ayr	38	12	10	16	38	60	34
15	Falkirk	38	13	6	19	46	53	32
16	Kilmarnock	38	12	8	18	48	65	32
17	Queen's Park	38	11	9	18	43	60	31
18	Third Lanark	38	11	8	19	54	78	30
19	Clyde	38	10	9	19	40	70	29
20	Clydebank	38	10	5	23	42	71	25

SCOTTISH SECOND DIVISION

		P	W	D	L	F	A	Pts
1	St Johnstone	38	22	12	4	79	33	56
2	Cowdenbeath	38	23	9	6	78	33	55
3	Bathgate	38	16	12	10	58	49	44
4	Stenhousemuir	38	16	11	11	58	45	43
5	Albion	38	15	12	11	67	53	42
6	King's Park	38	16	10	12	67	56	42
7	Dunfermline	38	14	11	13	52	45	39
8	Johnstone	38	16	7	15	60	56	39
9	Dundee United	38	12	15	11	41	41	39
10	Dumbarton	38	17	5	16	55	58	39
11	Armadale	38	16	6	16	56	63	38
12	Bo'ness	38	13	11	14	45	52	37
13	East Fife	38	14	9	15	54	47	37
14	Forfar	38	14	7	17	43	68	35
15	Broxburn	38	13	8	17	50	56	34
16	Alloa	38	14	6	18	44	53	34
17	Arbroath	38	12	8	18	49	51	32
18	St Bernard's	38	11	10	17	49	54	32
19	Vale of Leven	38	11	9	18	41	67	31
20	Lochgelly	38	4	4	30	20	86	12

SCOTTISH FA CUP 1923-24

SECOND ROUND

Airdrieonians v St Johnstone	4-0
Forfar Athletic v Motherwell	1-3
Ayr United v Kilmarnock	1-0
Clydebank v Arbroath	4-0
Falkirk v East Fife	2-0
Queen's Park v Armadale	3-1
Heart of Midlothian v Galston	6-0
Clyde v Vale of Leven	2-0
Cowdenbeath v Aberdeen	0-2
East Stirlingshire v Mid-Annandale	1-0
St Bernard's v Stenhousemuir	0-0, 0-0, 2-0
Dundee v Raith Rovers	0-0, 0-1
Hibernian v Alloa Athletic	1-1, 5-0
St Mirren v Rangers	0-1
Partick Thistle v Bo'ness	3-0
Hamilton Academicals v Queen of the South	2-1

THIRD ROUND

Motherwell v Airdrieonians	0-5
Clydebank v Ayr United	2-3
Falkirk v Queen's Park	0-0, 2-0
Heart of Midlothian v Clyde	3-1
Aberdeen v East Stirlingshire	2-0
Raith Rovers v St Bernard's	0-1
Rangers v Hibernian	1-2
Partick Thistle v Hamilton Academicals	1-1, 2-1

FOURTH ROUND

Airdrieonians v Ayr United	1-1, 0-0, 1-0
Heart of Midlothian v Falkirk	1-2
Aberdeen v St Bernard's	3-0
Hibernian v Partick Thistle	2-2, 1-1, 2-1

SEMI-FINAL

Airdrieonians v Falkirk	2-1
Aberdeen v Hibernian	0-0, 0-0, 0-1

FINAL AT IBROX PARK

Airdrieonians v Hibernian	2-0

The first player to have scored two goals for each side in a single Football League game is Sammy Wynne of Oldham. In the Division Two match with Manchester United on 6 October 1923, Wynne scored for his own side with a free-kick and a penalty, but also put two through his own goal. Those four goals probably give poor Wynne the dubious record for the most goals scored by a full-back in one League game.

A Birch, Chesterfield's goalkeeper, set a League goalscoring record for a keeper in 1923-24. Birch, who played in every one of his club's Division Three North fixtures, scored from five penalties.

During the Third Division North match between Crewe and Bradford Park Avenue on 8 March 1924, four penalties were awarded in five minutes, a League record.

FIRST DIVISION

		P	W	D	L	F	A	Pts
1	Huddersfield	42	21	16	5	69	28	58
2	WBA	42	23	10	9	58	34	56
3	Bolton	42	22	11	9	76	34	55
4	Liverpool	42	20	10	12	63	55	50
5	Bury	42	17	15	10	54	51	49
6	Newcastle	42	16	16	10	61	42	48
7	Sunderland	42	19	10	13	64	51	48
8	Birmingham	42	17	12	13	49	53	46
9	Notts County	42	16	13	13	42	31	45
10	Man City	42	17	9	16	76	68	43
11	Cardiff	42	16	11	15	56	51	43
12	Tottenham	42	15	12	15	52	43	42
13	West Ham	42	15	12	15	62	60	42
14	Sheff United	42	13	13	16	55	63	39
15	Aston Villa	42	13	13	16	58	71	39
16	Blackburn	42	11	13	18	53	66	35
17	Everton	42	12	11	19	40	60	35
18	Leeds	42	11	12	19	46	59	34
19	Burnley	42	11	12	19	46	75	34
20	Arsenal	42	14	5	23	46	58	33
21	Preston	42	10	6	26	37	74	26
22	Nottm Forest	42	6	12	24	29	65	24

SECOND DIVISION

		P	W	D	L	F	A	Pts
1	Leicester	42	24	11	7	90	32	59
2	Man United	42	23	11	8	57	23	57
3	Derby	42	22	11	9	71	36	55
4	Portsmouth	42	15	18	9	58	50	48
5	Chelsea	42	16	15	11	51	37	47
6	Wolves	42	20	6	16	55	51	46
7	Southampton	42	13	18	11	40	36	44
8	Port Vale	42	17	8	17	48	56	42
9	South Shields	42	12	17	13	42	38	41
10	Hull	42	15	11	16	50	49	41
11	Clapton Orient	42	14	12	16	42	42	40
12	Fulham	42	15	10	17	41	56	40
13	Middlesbrough	42	10	19	13	36	44	39
14	Wednesday	42	15	8	19	50	56	38
15	Barnsley	42	13	12	17	46	59	38
16	Bradford City	42	13	12	17	37	50	38
17	Blackpool	42	14	9	19	65	61	37
18	Oldham	42	13	11	18	35	51	37
19	Stockport	42	13	11	18	37	57	37
20	Stoke	42	12	11	19	34	46	35
21	Crystal Palace	42	12	10	20	38	54	34
22	Coventry	42	11	9	22	45	84	31

FA CUP 1924-25

SECOND ROUND

Cardiff City v Fulham	1-0
Notts County v Norwich City	4-0
Hull City v Crystal Palace	3-2
Newcastle United v Leicester City	2-2, 0-1
Bradford Park Avenue v Blackpool	1-1, 1-2
Nottingham Forest v West Ham United	0-2
Tottenham Hotspur v Bolton Wanderers	1-1, 1-0
Blackburn Rovers v Portsmouth	0-0, 0-0, 1-0
Southampton v Brighton	1-0
Barnsley v Bradford City	0-3
Birmingham v Stockport County	1-0
Bristol City v Liverpool	0-1
West Bromwich Albion v Preston North End	2-0
Swansea Town v Aston Villa	1-3
Sunderland v Everton	0-0, 1-2
Sheffield United v The Wednesday	3-2

THIRD ROUND

Notts County v Cardiff City	0-2
Hull City v Leicester City	1-1, 1-3
West Ham United v Blackpool	1-1, 1-0
Tottenham Hotspur v Blackburn Rovers	2-2, 1-3
Southampton v Bradford City	2-0
Liverpool v Birmingham	2-1
West Bromwich Albion v Aston Villa	1-1, 2-1
Sheffield United v Everton	1-0

FOURTH ROUND

Cardiff City v Leicester City	2-1
Blackburn Rovers v Blackpool	1-0
Southampton v Liverpool	1-0
Sheffield United v West Bromwich Albion	2-0

SEMI-FINAL

Cardiff City v Blackburn Rovers	3-1
Sheffield United v Southampton	2-0

FINAL

Sheffield United v Cardiff City	1-0

THIRD DIVISION (SOUTH)

		P	W	D	L	F	A	Pts
1	Swansea	42	23	11	8	68	35	57
2	Plymouth	42	23	10	9	77	38	56
3	Bristol City	42	22	9	11	60	41	53
4	Swindon	42	20	11	11	66	38	51
5	Millwall Ath	42	18	13	11	58	38	49
6	Newport	42	20	9	13	62	42	49
7	Exeter	42	19	9	14	59	48	47
8	Brighton	42	19	8	15	59	45	46
9	Northampton	42	20	6	16	51	44	46
10	Southend	42	19	5	18	51	61	43
11	Watford	42	17	9	16	38	47	43
12	Norwich	42	14	13	15	53	51	41
13	Gillingham	42	13	14	15	35	44	40
14	Reading	42	14	10	18	37	38	38
15	Charlton	42	13	12	17	46	48	38
16	Luton	42	10	17	15	49	57	37
17	Bristol Rovers	42	12	13	17	42	49	37
18	Aberdare Ath	42	14	9	19	54	67	37
19	QPR	42	14	8	20	42	63	36
20	Bournemouth	42	13	8	21	40	58	34
21	Brentford	42	9	7	26	38	91	25
22	Merthyr Town	42	8	5	29	35	77	21

THIRD DIVISION (NORTH)

		P	W	D	L	F	A	Pts
1	Darlington	42	24	10	8	78	33	58
2	Nelson	42	23	7	12	79	50	53
3	New Brighton	42	23	7	12	75	50	53
4	Southport	42	22	7	13	59	37	51
5	Bradford PA	42	19	12	11	84	42	50
6	Rochdale	42	21	7	14	75	53	49
7	Chesterfield	42	17	11	14	60	44	45
8	Lincoln	42	18	8	16	53	58	44
9	Halifax	42	16	11	15	56	52	43
10	Ashington	42	16	10	16	68	76	42
11	Wigan Borough	42	15	11	16	62	65	41
12	Grimsby	42	15	9	18	60	60	39
13	Durham City	42	13	13	16	50	68	39
14	Barrow	42	16	7	19	51	74	39
15	Crewe	42	13	13	16	53	78	39
16	Wrexham	42	15	8	19	53	61	38
17	Accrington	42	15	8	19	60	72	38
18	Doncaster	42	14	10	18	54	65	38
19	Walsall	42	13	11	18	44	53	37
20	Hartlepools	42	12	11	19	45	63	35
21	Tranmere	42	14	4	24	59	78	32
22	Rotherham Co	42	7	7	28	42	88	21

SCOTTISH FA CUP 1924-25

SECOND ROUND

Celtic v Alloa Athletic	2-1
Vale of Leven v Solway Star	2-2, 3-3, 1-2
St Mirren v Ayr United	1-0
Partick Thistle v Dundee United	5-1
Montrose v Rangers	0-2
Arbroath v Clyde	3-0
Kilmarnock v Heart of Midlothian	2-1
Dykehead v Peebles Rovers	3-1
Dundee v Lochgelly United	2-1
Airdrieonians v Queen's Park	4-0
Royal Albert v Broxburn United	1-3
Falkirk v Dumbarton	2-0
Hamilton Academicals v East Stirlingshire	4-0
Raith Rovers v Bo'ness	0-0, 3-1
Armadale v Aberdeen	1-1, 0-2
Motherwell v Arthurlie	2-0

THIRD ROUND

Celtic v Solway Star	2-0
St Mirren v Partick Thistle	2-0
Rangers v Arbroath	5-3
Kilmarnock v Dykehead	5-3
Dundee v Airdrieonians	3-1
Broxburn United v Falkirk	2-1
Hamilton Academicals v Raith Rovers	1-0
Aberdeen v Motherwell	0-0, 2-1

FOURTH ROUND

St Mirren v Celtic	0-0, 1-1, 0-1
Kilmarnock v Rangers	1-2
Dundee v Broxburn United	1-0
Aberdeen v Hamilton Academicals	0-2

SEMI-FINAL

Celtic v Rangers	5-0
Dundee v Hamilton Academicals	1-1, 2-0

FINAL

Celtic v Dundee	2-1

SCOTTISH FIRST DIVISION

		P	W	D	L	F	A	Pts
1	Rangers	38	25	10	3	77	27	60
2	Airdrieonians	38	25	7	6	85	31	57
3	Hibernian	38	22	8	8	78	43	52
4	Celtic	38	18	8	12	76	43	44
5	Cowdenbeath	38	16	10	12	76	65	42
6	St Mirren	38	18	4	16	65	63	40
7	Partick	38	14	10	14	60	61	38
8	Dundee	38	14	8	16	48	55	36
9	Raith	38	14	8	16	52	60	36
10	Hearts	38	12	11	15	65	69	35
11	St Johnstone	38	12	11	15	56	71	35
12	Kilmarnock	38	12	9	17	53	64	33
13	Hamilton	38	15	3	20	50	63	33
14	Morton	38	12	9	17	46	69	33
15	Aberdeen	38	11	10	17	46	56	32
16	Falkirk	38	12	8	18	44	54	32
17	Queen's Park	38	12	8	18	50	71	32
18	Motherwell	38	10	10	18	55	64	30
19	Ayr	38	11	8	19	43	65	30
20	Third Lanark	38	11	8	19	53	84	30

SCOTTISH SECOND DIVISION

		P	W	D	L	F	A	Pts
1	Dundee United	38	20	10	8	58	44	50
2	Clydebank	38	20	8	10	65	42	48
3	Clyde	38	20	7	11	72	39	47
4	Alloa	38	17	11	10	57	33	45
5	Arbroath	38	16	10	12	47	46	42
6	Bo'ness	38	16	9	13	71	48	41
7	Broxburn	38	16	9	13	48	54	41
8	Dumbarton	38	15	10	13	45	44	40
9	East Fife	38	17	5	16	66	58	39
10	King's Park	38	15	8	15	54	46	38
11	Stenhousemuir	38	15	7	16	51	58	37
12	Arthurlie	38	14	8	16	56	60	36
13	Dunfermline	38	14	7	17	62	57	35
14	Armadale	38	15	5	18	55	62	35
15	Albion	38	15	5	18	46	61	35
16	Bathgate	38	12	10	16	58	74	34
17	St Bernard's	38	14	4	20	52	70	32
18	E Stirlingshire	38	11	8	19	58	72	30
19	Johnstone	38	12	4	22	53	85	28
20	Forfar	38	10	7	21	46	67	27

Merthyr Town, who finished bottom of the Third Division South, suffered 29 defeats in their 42 matches, the greatest number ever lost in a single season in that division.

Manchester United conceded only 23 goals in their 42 Second Division matches. This is the lowest number of goals ever recorded against a club in that division.

Arthur Chandler, of Second Division champions Leicester City, not only led that division's scoring lists with 33 goals, but also established a record by finding the net in sixteen consecutive League games.

Huddersfield, in winning their second consecutive Championship, did not concede more than two goals in any League game.

FIRST DIVISION

		P	W	D	L	F	A	Pts
1	Huddersfield	42	23	11	8	92	60	57
2	Arsenal	42	22	8	12	87	63	52
3	Sunderland	42	21	6	15	96	80	48
4	Bury	42	20	7	15	85	77	47
5	Sheff United	42	19	8	15	102	82	46
6	Aston Villa	42	16	12	14	86	76	44
7	Liverpool	42	14	16	12	70	63	44
8	Bolton	42	17	10	15	75	76	44
9	Man United	42	19	6	17	66	73	44
10	Newcastle	42	16	10	16	84	75	42
11	Everton	42	12	18	12	72	70	42
12	Blackburn	42	15	11	16	91	80	41
13	WBA	42	16	8	18	79	78	40
14	Birmingham	42	16	8	18	66	81	40
15	Tottenham	42	15	9	18	66	79	39
16	Cardiff	42	16	7	19	61	76	39
17	Leicester	42	14	10	18	70	80	38
18	West Ham	42	15	7	20	63	76	37
19	Leeds	42	14	8	20	64	76	36
20	Burnley	42	13	10	19	85	108	36
21	Man City	42	12	11	19	89	100	35
22	Notts County	42	13	7	22	54	74	33

SECOND DIVISION

		P	W	D	L	F	A	Pts
1	Wednesday	42	27	6	9	88	48	60
2	Derby	42	25	7	10	77	42	57
3	Chelsea	42	19	14	9	76	49	52
4	Wolves	42	21	7	14	84	60	49
5	Swansea	42	19	11	12	77	57	49
6	Blackpool	42	17	11	14	76	69	45
7	Oldham	42	18	8	16	74	62	44
8	Port Vale	42	19	6	17	79	69	44
9	South Shields	42	18	8	16	74	65	44
10	Middlesbrough	42	21	2	19	77	68	44
11	Portsmouth	42	17	10	15	79	74	44
12	Preston	42	18	7	17	71	84	43
13	Hull	42	16	9	17	63	61	41
14	Southampton	42	15	8	19	63	63	38
15	Darlington	42	14	10	18	72	77	38
16	Bradford City	42	13	10	19	47	66	36
17	Nottm Forest	42	14	8	20	51	73	36
18	Barnsley	42	12	12	18	58	84	36
19	Fulham	42	11	12	19	46	77	34
20	Clapton Orient	42	12	9	21	50	65	33
21	Stoke	42	12	8	22	54	77	32
22	Stockport	42	8	9	25	51	97	25

FOURTH ROUND

Bournemouth v Bolton Wanderers	2-2, 2-6
South Shields v Birmingham	2-1
Nottingham Forest v Swindon Town	2-0
Southend United v Derby County	4-1
Swansea Town v Stoke City	6-3
Bury v Millwall	3-3, 0-2
Arsenal v Blackburn Rovers	3-1
West Bromwich Albion v Aston Villa	1-2
Manchester City v Huddersfield Town	4-0
Crystal Palace v Chelsea	2-1
Clapton Orient v Middlesbrough	4-2
Cardiff City v Newcastle United	0-2
Tottenham Hotspur v Manchester United	2-2, 0-2
Sheffield United v Sunderland	1-2
Fulham v Liverpool	3-1
Notts County v New Brighton	2-0

FIFTH ROUND

Bolton Wanderers v South Shields	3-0
Southend United v Nottingham Forest	0-1
Millwall v Swansea Town	0-1
Aston Villa v Arsenal	1-1, 0-2
Manchester City v Crystal Palace	11-4
Clapton Orient v Newcastle United	2-0
Sunderland v Manchester United	3-3, 1-2
Notts County v Fulham	0-1

SIXTH ROUND

Nottingham Forest v Bolton Wanderers	2-2, 0-0, 0-1
Swansea Town v Arsenal	2-1
Clapton Orient v Manchester City	1-6
Fulham v Manchester United	1-2

SEMI-FINAL

Bolton Wanderers v Swansea Town	3-0
Manchester City v Manchester United	3-0

FINAL

Bolton Wanderers v Manchester City	1-0

THIRD DIVISION (NORTH)

		P	W	D	L	F	A	Pts
1	Grimsby	42	26	9	7	91	40	61
2	Bradford PA	42	26	8	8	101	43	60
3	Rochdale	42	27	5	10	104	58	59
4	Chesterfield	42	25	5	12	100	54	55
5	Halifax	42	17	11	14	53	50	45
6	Hartlepools	42	18	8	16	82	73	44
7	Tranmere	42	19	6	17	73	83	44
8	Nelson	42	16	11	15	89	71	43
9	Ashington	42	16	11	15	70	62	43
10	Doncaster	42	16	11	15	80	72	43
11	Crewe	42	17	9	16	63	61	43
12	New Brighton	42	17	8	17	69	67	42
13	Durham City	42	18	6	18	63	70	42
14	Rotherham	42	17	7	18	69	92	41
15	Lincoln	42	17	5	20	66	82	39
16	Coventry	42	16	6	20	73	82	38
17	Wigan Borough	42	13	11	18	68	74	37
18	Accrington	42	17	3	22	81	105	37
19	Wrexham	42	11	10	21	63	92	32
20	Southport	42	11	10	21	62	92	32
21	Walsall	42	10	6	26	58	107	26
22	Barrow	42	7	4	31	50	98	18

THIRD DIVISION (SOUTH)

		P	W	D	L	F	A	Pts
1	Reading	42	23	11	8	77	52	57
2	Plymouth	42	24	8	10	107	67	56
3	Millwall	42	21	11	10	73	39	53
4	Bristol City	42	21	9	12	72	51	51
5	Brighton	42	19	9	14	84	73	47
6	Swindon	42	20	6	16	69	64	46
7	Luton	42	18	7	17	80	75	43
8	Bournemouth	42	17	9	16	75	91	43
9	Aberdare	42	17	8	17	74	66	42
10	Gillingham	42	17	8	17	53	49	42
11	Southend	42	19	4	19	78	73	42
12	Northampton	42	17	7	18	82	80	41
13	Crystal Palace	42	19	3	20	75	79	41
14	Merthyr Town	42	14	11	17	69	75	39
15	Watford	42	15	9	18	73	89	39
16	Norwich	42	15	9	18	58	73	39
17	Newport	42	14	10	18	64	74	38
18	Brentford	42	16	6	20	69	94	38
19	Bristol Rovers	42	15	6	21	66	69	36
20	Exeter	42	15	5	22	72	70	35
21	Charlton	42	11	13	18	48	68	35
22	QPR	42	6	9	27	37	84	21

SECOND ROUND

Arbroath v St Mirren	0-0, 0-3
Partick Thistle v King's Park	4-1
Hibernian v Airdrieonians	2-3
Bo'ness v Bathgate	1-1, 1-3
Rangers v Stenhousemuir	1-0
Falkirk v Montrose	5-1
Morton v Raith Rovers	3-1
Albion Rovers v Peebles Rovers	1-1, 4-0
Celtic v Hamilton Academicals	4-0
Alloa Athletic v Heart of Midlothian	2-5
Forfar Athletic v Dumbarton	2-2, 1-4
Arthurlie v Clyde	2-2, 0-1
Aberdeen v Dundee	0-0, 3-0
St Johnstone v Queen's Park	7-2
Third Lanark v Leith Athletic	6-1
Solway Star v Brechin City	0-3

THIRD ROUND

St Mirren v Partick Thistle	2-1
Bathgate v Airdrieonians	2-5
Falkirk v Rangers	0-2
Morton v Albion Rovers	1-0
Heart of Midlothian v Celtic	0-4
Dumbarton v Clyde	3-0
Aberdeen v St Johnstone	2-2, 1-0
Third Lanark v Brechin City	4-0

FOURTH ROUND

St Mirren v Airdrieonians	2-0
Morton v Rangers	0-4
Celtic v Dumbarton	6-1
Third Lanark v Aberdeen	1-1, 0-3

SEMI-FINAL

St Mirren v Rangers	1-0
Celtic v Aberdeen	1-0

FINAL

St Mirren v Celtic	2-0

SCOTTISH FIRST DIVISION

		P	W	D	L	F	A	Pts
1	Celtic	38	25	8	5	97	40	58
2	Airdrieonians	38	23	4	11	95	54	50
3	Hearts	38	21	8	9	87	56	50
4	St Mirren	38	20	7	11	62	52	47
5	Motherwell	38	19	8	11	67	46	46
6	Rangers	38	19	6	13	79	55	44
7	Cowdenbeath	38	18	6	14	87	68	42
8	Falkirk	38	14	14	10	61	57	42
9	Kilmarnock	38	17	7	14	79	77	41
10	Dundee	38	14	9	15	47	59	37
11	Aberdeen	38	13	10	15	49	54	36
12	Hamilton	38	13	9	16	68	79	35
13	Queen's Park	38	15	4	19	70	81	34
14	Partick	38	10	13	15	64	73	33
15	Morton	38	12	7	19	57	84	31
16	Hibernian	38	12	6	20	72	77	30
17	Dundee United	38	11	6	21	52	74	28
18	St Johnstone	38	9	10	19	43	78	28
19	Raith	38	11	4	23	46	81	26
20	Clydebank	38	7	8	23	55	92	22

SCOTTISH SECOND DIVISION

		P	W	D	L	F	A	Pts
1	Dunfermline	38	26	7	5	109	43	59
2	Clyde	38	24	5	9	87	51	53
3	Ayr	38	20	12	6	77	39	52
4	East Fife	38	20	9	9	98	73	49
5	Stenhousemuir	38	19	10	9	74	52	48
6	Third Lanark	38	19	8	11	72	47	46
7	Arthurlie	38	17	5	16	81	75	39
8	Bo'ness	38	17	5	16	65	70	39
9	Albion	38	16	6	16	78	71	38
10	Arbroath	38	17	4	17	80	73	38
11	Dumbarton	38	14	10	14	54	78	38
12	Nithsdale	38	15	7	16	79	82	37
13	King's Park	38	14	9	15	67	73	37
14	St Bernard's	38	15	5	18	86	82	35
15	Armadale	38	14	5	19	82	101	33
16	Alloa	38	11	8	19	54	63	30
17	Queen of the S	38	10	8	20	64	88	28
18	E Stirlingshire	38	10	7	21	59	89	27
19	Bathgate	38	7	6	25	60	105	20
20	Broxburn	38	4	6	28	55	126	14

Manchester City had a distressing end to the 1925-26 season. After losing the Cup Final 1-0 to Bolton, City went to Newcastle for their last League game. They missed a penalty, lost 3-2, and were relegated. Had they scored from the penalty they would have remained in the First Division. City thus became the first club to reach the Cup Final and be relegated in the same season.

Huddersfield created a League record by playing 18 consecutive First Division games away from home without defeat. This run lasted from 15 November 1924 to 14 November 1925 and included 12 wins.

Louis Page scored a double hat-trick in his first game as centre-forward for Burnley, against Birmingham, on 10 April 1926.

FIRST DIVISION

		P	W	D	L	F	A	Pts
1	Newcastle	42	25	6	11	96	58	56
2	Huddersfield	42	17	17	8	76	60	51
3	Sunderland	42	21	7	14	98	70	49
4	Bolton	42	19	10	13	84	62	48
5	Burnley	42	19	9	14	91	80	47
6	West Ham	42	19	8	15	86	70	46
7	Leicester	42	17	12	13	85	70	46
8	Sheff United	42	17	10	15	74	86	44
9	Liverpool	42	18	7	17	69	61	43
10	Aston Villa	42	18	7	17	81	83	43
11	Arsenal	42	17	9	16	77	86	43
12	Derby	42	17	7	18	86	73	41
13	Tottenham	42	16	9	17	76	78	41
14	Cardiff	42	16	9	17	55	65	41
15	Man United	42	13	14	15	52	64	40
16	Wednesday	42	15	9	18	75	92	39
17	Birmingham	42	17	4	21	64	73	38
18	Blackburn	42	15	8	19	77	96	38
19	Bury	42	12	12	18	68	77	36
20	Everton	42	12	10	20	64	90	34
21	Leeds	42	11	8	23	69	88	30
22	WBA	42	11	8	23	65	86	30

SECOND DIVISION

		P	W	D	L	F	A	Pts
1	Middlesbrough	42	27	8	7	122	60	62
2	Portsmouth	42	23	8	11	87	49	54
3	Man City	42	22	10	10	108	61	54
4	Chelsea	42	20	12	10	62	52	52
5	Nottm Forest	42	18	14	10	80	55	50
6	Preston	42	20	9	13	63	52	49
7	Hull	42	20	7	15	63	52	47
8	Port Vale	42	16	13	13	88	78	45
9	Blackpool	42	18	8	16	95	80	44
10	Oldham	42	19	6	17	74	84	44
11	Barnsley	42	17	9	16	88	87	43
12	Swansea	42	16	11	15	68	72	43
13	Southampton	42	15	12	15	60	62	42
14	Reading	42	16	8	18	64	72	40
15	Wolves	42	14	7	21	73	75	35
16	Notts County	42	15	5	22	70	96	35
17	Grimsby	42	11	12	19	74	91	34
18	Fulham	42	13	8	21	58	92	34
19	South Shields	42	11	11	20	71	96	33
20	Clapton Orient	42	12	7	23	60	96	31
21	Darlington	42	12	6	24	79	98	30
22	Bradford City	42	7	9	26	50	88	23

FA CUP 1926-27

FOURTH ROUND

Chelsea v Accrington Stanley	7-2
Fulham v Burnley	0-4
Leeds United v Bolton Wanderers	0-0, 0-3
Darlington v Cardiff City	0-2
The Wednesday v South Shields	1-1, 0-1
Barnsley v Swansea Town	1-3
Reading v Portsmouth	3-1
West Ham United v Brentford	1-1, 0-2
Port Vale v Arsenal	2-2, 0-1
Liverpool v Southport	3-1
Wolverhampton Wanderers v Nottingham Forest	2-0
Hull City v Everton	1-1, 2-2, 3-2
Derby County v Millwall	0-2
Preston North End v Middlesbrough	0-3
Southampton v Birmingham	4-1
Corinthians v Newcastle United	1-3

FIFTH ROUND

Chelsea v Burnley	2-1
Bolton Wanderers v Cardiff City	0-2
South Shields v Swansea Town	2-2, 1-2
Reading v Brentford	1-0
Arsenal v Liverpool	2-0
Wolverhampton Wanderers v Hull City	1-0
Millwall v Middlesbrough	3-2
Southampton v Newcastle United	2-1

SIXTH ROUND

Chelsea v Cardiff City	0-0, 2-3
Swansea Town v Reading	1-3
Arsenal v Wolverhampton Wanderers	2-1
Millwall v Southampton	0-0, 0-2

SEMI-FINAL

Cardiff City v Reading	3-0
Arsenal v Southampton	2-1

FINAL

Cardiff City v Arsenal	1-0

THIRD DIVISION (NORTH)

		P	W	D	L	F	A	Pts
1	Stoke	42	27	9	6	92	40	63
2	Rochdale	42	26	6	10	105	65	58
3	Bradford PA	42	24	7	11	101	59	55
4	Halifax	42	21	11	10	70	53	53
5	Nelson	42	22	7	13	104	75	51
6	Stockport	42	22	7	13	93	69	49*
7	Chesterfield	42	21	5	16	92	68	47
8	Doncaster	42	18	11	13	81	65	47
9	Tranmere	42	19	8	15	85	67	46
10	New Brighton	42	18	10	14	79	67	46
11	Lincoln	42	15	12	15	90	78	42
12	Southport	42	15	9	18	80	85	39
13	Wrexham	42	14	10	18	65	73	38
14	Walsall	42	14	10	18	68	81	38
15	Crewe	42	14	9	19	71	81	37
16	Ashington	42	12	12	18	60	90	36
17	Hartlepools	42	14	6	22	66	81	34
18	Wigan Borough	42	11	10	21	66	83	32
19	Rotherham	42	10	12	20	70	92	32
20	Durham City	42	12	6	24	58	105	30
21	Accrington	42	10	7	25	62	98	27
22	Barrow	42	7	8	27	34	117	22

*Two points deducted for fielding Joe Smith without FA permission on 26 March 1927.

THIRD DIVISION (SOUTH)

		P	W	D	L	F	A	Pts
1	Bristol City	42	27	8	7	104	54	62
2	Plymouth	42	25	10	7	95	61	60
3	Millwall	42	23	10	9	89	51	56
4	Brighton	42	21	11	10	79	50	53
5	Swindon	42	21	9	12	100	85	51
6	Crystal Palace	42	18	9	15	84	81	45
7	Bournemouth	42	18	8	16	78	66	44
8	Luton	42	15	14	13	68	66	44
9	Newport	42	19	6	17	57	71	44
10	Bristol Rovers	42	16	9	17	78	80	41
11	Brentford	42	13	14	15	70	61	40
12	Exeter	42	15	10	17	76	73	40
13	Charlton	42	16	8	18	60	61	40
14	QPR	42	15	9	18	65	71	39
15	Coventry	42	15	7	20	71	86	37
16	Norwich	42	12	11	19	59	71	35
17	Merthyr Town	42	13	9	20	63	80	35
18	Northampton	42	15	5	22	59	83	35
19	Southend	42	14	6	22	64	77	34
20	Gillingham	42	11	10	21	54	72	32
21	Watford	42	12	8	22	57	87	32
22	Aberdare Ath	42	9	7	26	62	101	25

SCOTTISH FIRST DIVISION

		P	W	D	L	F	A	Pts
1	Rangers	38	23	10	5	85	41	56
2	Motherwell	38	23	5	10	81	52	51
3	Celtic	38	21	7	10	101	55	49
4	Airdrieonians	38	18	9	11	97	64	45
5	Dundee	38	17	9	12	77	51	43
6	Falkirk	38	16	10	12	77	60	42
7	Cowdenbeath	38	18	6	14	74	60	42
8	Aberdeen	38	13	14	11	73	72	40
9	Hibernian	38	16	7	15	62	71	39
10	St Mirren	38	16	5	17	78	76	37
11	Partick	38	15	6	17	89	74	36
12	Queen's Park	38	15	6	17	74	84	36
13	Hearts	38	12	11	15	65	64	35
14	St Johnstone	38	13	9	16	55	69	35
15	Hamilton	38	13	9	16	60	85	35
16	Kilmarnock	38	12	8	18	54	71	32
17	Clyde	38	10	9	19	54	85	29
18	Dunfermline	38	10	8	20	53	85	28
19	Morton	38	12	4	22	56	101	28
20	Dundee United	38	7	8	23	56	101	22

The highest number of goals scored by a recognized half-back in a League match is three. T McDonald of Newcastle grabbed a hat-trick against Cardiff on Christmas Day 1926.

SCOTTISH SECOND DIVISION

		P	W	D	L	F	A	Pts
1	Bo'ness	38	23	10	5	86	41	56
2	Raith	38	21	7	10	92	52	49
3	Clydebank	38	18	9	11	94	75	45
4	Third Lanark	38	17	10	11	67	48	44
5	E Stirlingshire	38	18	8	12	93	75	44
6	East Fife	38	19	4	15	103	91	42
7	Arthurlie	38	18	5	15	90	83	41
8	Ayr	38	13	15	10	67	68	41
9	Forfar	38	15	7	16	66	79	37
10	Stenhousemuir	38	12	12	14	69	75	36
11	Queen of the S	38	16	4	18	72	80	36
12	King's Park	38	13	9	16	76	75	35
13	St Bernard's	38	14	6	18	70	77	34
14	Armadale	38	12	10	16	69	78	34
15	Alloa	38	11	11	16	70	78	33
16	Albion	38	11	11	16	74	87	33
17	Bathgate	38	13	7	18	76	98	33
18	Dumbarton	38	13	6	19	69	84	32
19	Arbroath	38	13	6	19	64	82	32
20	Nithsdale	38	7	9	22	59	100	23

Middlesbrough's George Camsell established an individual scoring record with his 59 Second Division goals in 1926-27. William Dean beat it by just one the following season, 1927-28. Camsell also established a record for the number of League hat-tricks in a season with his nine in 1926-27.

SCOTTISH FA CUP 1926-27

SECOND ROUND

Buckie Thistle v Beith	2-0
Bo'ness v Cowdenbeath	2-1
Kilmarnock v Dundee	1-1, 1-5
Brechin City v Celtic	3-6
Falkirk v Queen's Park	6-3
Mid-Annandale v Forfar Athletic	3-0
Rangers v St Mirren	6-0
Hamilton Academicals v Clydebank	5-1
Alloa Athletic v Dumbarton	1-1, 4-0
St Bernard's v Arthurlie	0-3
East Fife v Aberdeen	1-1, 2-1
Dunfermline Athletic v Airdrieonians	2-1
Elgin City v Clyde	2-4
Partick Thistle v King's Park	4-2
Dundee United v Vale of Leven	4-1
Broxburn United v Montrose	2-2, 0-1

THIRD ROUND

Buckie Thistle v Bo'ness	0-3
Dundee v Celtic	2-4
Falkirk v Mid-Annandale	3-0
Rangers v Hamilton Academicals	4-0
Alloa Athletic v Arthurlie	0-0, 0-3
East Fife v Dunfermline Athletic	2-0
Clyde v Partick Thistle	0-1
Dundee United v Montrose	2-2, 3-1

FOURTH ROUND

Bo'ness v Celtic	2-5
Falkirk v Rangers	2-2, 1-0
Arthurlie v East Fife	0-3
Partick Thistle v Dundee United	5-0

SEMI-FINAL

Celtic v Falkirk	1-0
East Fife v Partick Thistle	2-1

FINAL

Celtic v East Fife	3-1

FIRST DIVISION

		P	W	D	L	F	A	Pts
1	Everton	42	20	13	9	102	66	53
2	Huddersfield	42	22	7	13	91	68	51
3	Leicester	42	18	12	12	96	72	48
4	Derby	42	17	10	15	96	83	44
5	Bury	42	20	4	18	80	80	44
6	Cardiff	42	17	10	15	70	80	44
7	Bolton	42	16	11	15	81	66	43
8	Aston Villa	42	17	9	16	78	73	43
9	Newcastle	42	15	13	14	79	81	43
10	Arsenal	42	13	15	14	82	86	41
11	Birmingham	42	13	15	14	70	75	41
12	Blackburn	42	16	9	17	66	78	41
13	Sheff United	42	15	10	17	79	86	40
14	Wednesday	42	13	13	16	81	78	39
15	Sunderland	42	15	9	18	74	76	39
16	Liverpool	42	13	13	16	84	87	39
17	West Ham	42	14	11	17	81	88	39
18	Burnley	42	16	7	19	82	98	39
19	Man United	42	16	7	19	72	80	39
20	Portsmouth	42	16	7	19	66	90	39
21	Tottenham	42	15	8	19	74	86	38
22	Middlesbrough	42	11	15	16	81	88	37

SECOND DIVISION

		P	W	D	L	F	A	Pts
1	Man City	42	25	9	8	100	59	59
2	Leeds	42	25	7	10	98	49	57
3	Chelsea	42	23	8	11	75	45	54
4	Preston	42	22	9	11	100	66	53
5	Stoke	42	22	8	12	78	59	52
6	Swansea	42	18	12	12	75	63	48
7	Oldham	42	19	8	15	75	51	46
8	WBA	42	17	12	13	90	70	46
9	Port Vale	42	18	8	16	68	57	44
10	Nottm Forest	42	15	10	17	83	84	40
11	Grimsby	42	14	12	16	69	83	40
12	Bristol City	42	15	9	18	76	79	39
13	Hull	42	12	15	15	41	54	39
14	Barnsley	42	14	11	17	65	85	39
15	Notts County	42	13	12	17	68	74	38
16	Wolves	42	13	10	19	63	91	36
17	Southampton	42	14	7	21	68	77	35
18	Reading	42	11	13	18	53	75	35
19	Blackpool	42	13	8	21	83	101	34
20	Clapton Orient	42	11	12	19	55	85	34
21	Fulham	42	13	7	22	68	89	33
22	South Shields	42	7	9	26	56	111	23

THIRD DIVISION (SOUTH)

		P	W	D	L	F	A	Pts
1	Millwall	42	30	5	7	127	50	65
2	Northampton	42	23	9	10	102	64	55
3	Plymouth	42	23	7	12	85	54	53
4	Brighton	42	19	10	13	81	69	48
5	Crystal Palace	42	18	12	12	79	72	48
6	Swindon	42	19	9	14	90	69	47
7	Southend	42	20	6	16	80	64	46
8	Exeter	42	17	12	13	70	60	46
9	Newport	42	18	9	15	81	84	45
10	QPR	42	17	9	16	72	71	43
11	Charlton	42	15	13	14	60	70	43
12	Brentford	42	16	8	18	76	74	40
13	Luton	42	16	7	19	94	87	39
14	Bournemouth	42	13	12	17	72	79	38
15	Watford	42	14	10	18	68	78	38
16	Gillingham	42	13	11	18	62	81	37
17	Norwich	42	10	16	16	66	70	36
18	Walsall	42	12	9	21	75	101	33
19	Bristol Rovers	42	14	4	24	67	93	32
20	Coventry	42	11	9	22	67	96	31
21	Merthyr Town	42	9	13	20	53	91	31
22	Torquay	42	8	14	20	53	103	30

THIRD DIVISION (NORTH)

		P	W	D	L	F	A	Pts
1	Bradford PA	42	27	9	6	101	45	63
2	Lincoln	42	24	7	11	91	64	55
3	Stockport	42	23	8	11	89	51	54
4	Doncaster	42	23	7	12	80	44	53
5	Tranmere	42	22	9	11	105	72	53
6	Bradford City	42	18	12	12	85	60	48
7	Darlington	42	21	5	16	89	74	47
8	Southport	42	20	5	17	79	70	45
9	Accrington	42	18	8	16	76	67	44
10	New Brighton	42	14	14	14	72	62	42
11	Wrexham	42	18	6	18	64	67	42
12	Halifax	42	13	15	14	73	71	41
13	Rochdale	42	17	7	18	74	77	41
14	Rotherham	42	14	11	17	65	69	39
15	Hartlepools	42	16	6	20	69	81	38
16	Chesterfield	42	13	10	19	71	78	36
17	Crewe	42	12	10	20	77	86	34
18	Ashington	42	11	11	20	77	103	33
19	Barrow	42	10	11	21	54	102	31
20	Wigan Borough	42	10	10	22	56	97	30
21	Durham City	42	11	7	24	53	100	29
22	Nelson	42	10	6	26	76	136	26

SCOTTISH FIRST DIVISION

		P	W	D	L	F	A	Pts
1	Rangers	38	26	8	4	109	36	60
2	Celtic	38	23	9	6	93	39	55
3	Motherwell	38	23	9	6	92	46	55
4	Hearts	38	20	7	11	89	50	47
5	St Mirren	38	18	8	12	77	76	44
6	Partick	38	18	7	13	85	67	43
7	Aberdeen	38	19	5	14	71	61	43
8	Kilmarnock	38	15	10	13	68	78	40
9	Cowdenbeath	38	16	7	15	66	68	39
10	Falkirk	38	16	5	17	76	69	37
11	St Johnstone	38	14	8	16	66	67	36
12	Hibernian	38	13	9	16	73	75	35
13	Airdrieonians	38	12	11	15	59	69	35
14	Dundee	38	14	7	17	65	80	35
15	Clyde	38	10	11	17	46	72	31
16	Queen's Park	38	12	6	20	69	80	30
17	Raith	38	11	7	20	60	89	29
18	Hamilton	38	11	6	21	67	86	28
19	Bo'ness	38	9	8	21	48	86	26
20	Dunfermline	38	4	4	30	41	126	12

SCOTTISH SECOND DIVISION

		P	W	D	L	F	A	Pts
1	Ayr	38	24	6	8	117	60	54
2	Third Lanark	38	18	9	11	99	66	45
3	King's Park	38	16	12	10	84	68	44
4	East Fife	38	18	7	13	87	73	43
5	Forfar	38	18	7	13	83	73	43
6	Dundee United	38	17	9	12	81	73	43
7	Arthurlie	38	18	4	16	84	90	40
8	Albion	38	17	4	17	79	69	38
9	E Stirlingshire	38	14	10	14	84	76	38
10	Arbroath	38	16	4	18	84	86	36
11	Dumbarton	38	16	4	18	66	72	36
12	Queen of the S	38	15	6	17	92	106	36
13	Leith	38	13	9	16	76	71	35
14	Clydebank	38	16	3	19	78	80	35
15	Alloa	38	12	11	15	72	76	35
16	Stenhousemuir	38	15	5	18	75	81	35
17	St Bernard's	38	15	5	18	75	101	35
18	Morton	38	13	8	17	65	82	34
19	Bathgate	38	10	11	17	62	81	31
20	Armadale	38	8	8	22	53	112	24

FA CUP 1927-28

FOURTH ROUND

Exeter City v Blackburn Rovers	2-2, 1-3
Port Vale v New Brighton	3-0
Bury v Manchester United	1-1, 0-1
Wrexham v Birmingham	1-3
Arsenal v Everton	4-3
Aston Villa v Crewe Alexandra	3-0
Sunderland v Manchester City	1-2
Stoke City v Bolton Wanderers	4-2
Huddersfield Town v West Ham United	2-1
Southport v Middlesbrough	0-3
Reading v Leicester City	0-1
Tottenham Hotspur v Oldham Athletic	3-0
Sheffield United v Wolverhampton Wanderers	3-1
Swindon Town v The Wednesday	1-2
Derby County v Nottingham Forest	0-0, 0-2
Cardiff City v Liverpool	2-1

FIFTH ROUND

Blackburn Rovers v Port Vale	2-1
Manchester United v Birmingham	1-0
Arsenal v Aston Villa	4-1
Manchester City v Stoke City	0-1
Huddersfield Town v Middlesbrough	4-0
Leicester City v Tottenham Hotspur	0-3
The Wednesday v Sheffield United	1-1, 1-4
Nottingham Forest v Cardiff City	2-1

SIXTH ROUND

Blackburn Rovers v Manchester United	2-0
Arsenal v Stoke City	4-1
Huddersfield Town v Tottenham Hotspur	6-1
Sheffield United v Nottingham Forest	3-0

SEMI-FINAL

Blackburn Rovers v Arsenal	1-0
Huddersfield Town v Sheffield United	2-2, 0-0, 1-0

FINAL

Blackburn Rovers v Huddersfield Town	3-1

SCOTTISH FA CUP 1927-28

SECOND ROUND

Rangers v Cowdenbeath	4-2
Armadale v King's Park	2-4
Brechin City v Albion Rovers	1-4
Airdrieonians v Hamilton Academicals	2-1
Third Lanark v Hibernian	0-2
Ayr United v Falkirk	2-4
Dunfermline Athletic v Leith Amateurs	3-1
Dundee United v Dundee	3-3, 0-1
Keith v Celtic	1-6
Stenhousemuir v Alloa Athletic	1-2
Motherwell v Raith Rovers	2-2, 2-1
Heart of Midlothian v Forres Mechanics	7-0
Queen's Park v Morton	4-1
Forfar Athletic v Kilmarnock	1-2
Partick Thistle v Nithsdale Wanderers	4-0
St Mirren v Vale of Atholl	5-1

THIRD ROUND

Rangers v King's Park	3-1
Albion Rovers v Airdrieonians	3-1
Hibernian v Falkirk	0-0, 1-0
Dundee v Dunfermline Athletic	1-2
Celtic v Alloa Athletic	2-0
Heart of Midlothian v Motherwell	1-2
Kilmarnock v Queen's Park	4-4, 0-1
St Mirren v Partick Thistle	0-5

FOURTH ROUND

Albion Rovers v Rangers	0-1
Dunfermline Athletic v Hibernian	0-4
Motherwell v Celtic	0-2
Queen's Park v Partick Thistle	1-0

SEMI-FINAL

Rangers v Hibernian	3-0
Celtic v Queen's Park	2-1

FINAL

Rangers v Celtic	4-0

On 3 March 1928 Ronnie Dix became the youngest person to score in the League. Dix, aged 15 years and 180 days, scored for Bristol Rovers against Norwich in a Division Three South match. Dix had made his League debut just seven days earlier against Charlton.

Dixie Dean's 60 goals in 39 League games for Everton set a League scoring record.

1927-28 saw the keenest relegation struggle in the League's history. Of the last nine clubs in Division One, seven finished the season with 39 points, one had 38, and one 37. Spurs and Middlesbrough were demoted. Spurs' 38 points meant that they were relegated with the highest number of points ever secured by a club removed from either the First or Second Division.

FIRST DIVISION

		P	W	D	L	F	A	Pts
1	Wednesday	42	21	10	11	86	62	52
2	Leicester	42	21	9	12	96	67	51
3	Aston Villa	42	23	4	15	98	81	50
4	Sunderland	42	20	7	15	93	75	47
5	Liverpool	42	17	12	13	90	64	46
6	Derby	42	18	10	14	86	71	46
7	Blackburn	42	17	11	14	72	63	45
8	Man City	42	18	9	15	95	86	45
9	Arsenal	42	16	13	13	77	72	45
10	Newcastle	42	19	6	17	70	72	44
11	Sheff United	42	15	11	16	86	85	41
12	Man United	42	14	13	15	66	76	41
13	Leeds	42	16	9	17	71	84	41
14	Bolton	42	14	12	16	73	80	40
15	Birmingham	42	15	10	17	68	77	40
16	Huddersfield	42	14	11	17	70	61	39
17	West Ham	42	15	9	18	86	96	39
18	Everton	42	17	4	21	63	75	38
19	Burnley	42	15	8	19	81	103	38
20	Portsmouth	42	15	6	21	56	80	36
21	Bury	42	12	7	23	62	99	31
22	Cardiff	42	8	13	21	43	59	29

SECOND DIVISION

		P	W	D	L	F	A	Pts
1	Middlesbrough	42	22	11	9	92	57	55
2	Grimsby	42	24	5	13	82	61	53
3	Bradford PA	42	22	4	16	88	70	48
4	Southampton	42	17	14	11	74	60	48
5	Notts County	42	19	9	14	78	65	47
6	Stoke	42	17	12	13	74	51	46
7	WBA	42	19	8	15	80	79	46
8	Blackpool	42	19	7	16	92	76	45
9	Chelsea	42	17	10	15	64	65	44
10	Tottenham	42	17	9	16	75	81	43
11	Nottm Forest	42	15	12	15	71	70	42
12	Hull	42	13	14	15	58	63	40
13	Preston	42	15	9	18	78	79	39
14	Millwall	42	16	7	19	71	86	39
15	Reading	42	15	9	18	63	86	39
16	Barnsley	42	16	6	20	69	66	38
17	Wolves	42	15	7	20	77	81	37
18	Oldham	42	16	5	21	54	75	37
19	Swansea	42	13	10	19	62	75	36
20	Bristol City	42	13	10	19	58	72	36
21	Port Vale	42	15	4	23	71	86	34
22	Clapton Orient	42	12	8	22	45	72	32

THIRD DIVISION (SOUTH)

		P	W	D	L	F	A	Pts
1	Charlton	42	23	8	11	86	60	54
2	Crystal Palace	42	23	8	11	81	67	54
3	Northampton	42	20	12	10	96	57	52
4	Plymouth	42	20	12	10	83	51	52
5	Fulham	42	21	10	11	101	71	52
6	QPR	42	19	14	9	82	61	52
7	Luton	42	19	11	12	89	73	49
8	Watford	42	19	10	13	79	74	48
9	Bournemouth	42	19	9	14	84	77	47
10	Swindon	42	15	13	14	75	72	43
11	Coventry	42	14	14	14	62	57	42
12	Southend	42	15	11	16	80	75	41
13	Brentford	42	14	10	18	56	60	38
14	Walsall	42	13	12	17	73	79	38
15	Brighton	42	16	6	20	58	76	38
16	Newport	42	13	9	20	69	86	35
17	Norwich	42	14	6	22	69	81	34
18	Torquay	42	14	6	22	66	84	34
19	Bristol Rovers	42	13	7	22	60	79	33
20	Merthyr Town	42	11	8	23	55	103	30
21	Exeter	42	9	11	22	67	88	29
22	Gillingham	42	10	9	23	43	83	29

THIRD DIVISION (NORTH)

		P	W	D	L	F	A	Pts
1	Bradford City	42	27	9	6	128	43	63
2	Stockport	42	28	6	8	111	58	62
3	Wrexham	42	21	10	11	91	69	52
4	Wigan Borough	42	21	9	12	82	49	51
5	Doncaster	42	20	10	12	76	66	50
6	Lincoln	42	21	6	15	91	67	48
7	Tranmere	42	22	3	17	79	77	47
8	Carlisle	42	19	8	15	86	77	46
9	Crewe	42	18	8	16	80	68	44
10	South Shields	42	18	8	16	83	74	44
11	Chesterfield	42	18	5	19	71	77	41
12	Southport	42	16	8	18	75	85	40
13	Halifax	42	13	13	16	63	62	39
14	New Brighton	42	15	9	18	64	71	39
15	Nelson	42	17	5	20	77	90	39
16	Rotherham	42	15	9	18	60	77	39
17	Rochdale	42	13	10	19	79	96	36
18	Accrington	42	13	8	21	68	82	34
19	Darlington	42	13	7	22	64	88	33
20	Barrow	42	10	8	24	64	93	28
21	Hartlepools	42	10	6	26	59	112	26
22	Ashington	42	8	7	27	45	115	23

SCOTTISH FIRST DIVISION

		P	W	D	L	F	A	Pts
1	Rangers	38	30	7	1	107	32	67
2	Celtic	38	22	7	9	67	44	51
3	Motherwell	38	20	10	8	85	66	50
4	Hearts	38	19	9	10	91	57	47
5	Queen's Park	38	18	7	13	100	69	43
6	Partick Thistle	38	17	7	14	91	70	41
7	Aberdeen	38	16	8	14	81	69	40
8	St Mirren	38	16	8	14	78	74	40
9	St Johnstone	38	14	10	14	57	70	38
10	Kilmarnock	38	14	8	16	79	74	36
11	Falkirk	38	14	8	16	68	86	36
12	Hamilton	38	13	9	16	58	83	35
13	Cowdenbeath	38	14	5	19	55	69	33
14	Hibernian	38	13	6	19	54	62	32
15	Airdrieonians	38	12	7	19	56	65	31
16	Ayr	38	12	7	19	65	84	31
17	Clyde	38	12	6	20	47	71	30
18	Dundee	38	9	11	18	58	68	29
19	Third Lanark	38	10	6	22	71	102	26
20	Raith	38	9	6	23	52	105	24

SCOTTISH SECOND DIVISION

		P	W	D	L	F	A	Pts
1	Dundee United	36	24	3	9	99	55	51
2	Morton	36	21	8	7	85	49	50
3	Arbroath	36	19	9	8	90	60	47
4	Albion	36	18	8	10	95	67	44
5	Leith	36	18	7	11	78	56	43
6	St Bernard's	36	16	9	11	77	55	41
7	Forfar	35	14	10	11	69	75	38
8	East Fife	35	15	6	14	88	77	36
9	Queen of the S	36	16	4	16	86	79	36
10	Bo'ness	35	15	5	15	62	62	35
11	Dunfermline	36	13	7	16	66	72	33
12	E Stirlingshire	36	14	4	18	71	75	32
13	Alloa	36	12	7	17	64	77	31
14	Dumbarton	36	11	9	16	59	78	31
15	King's Park	36	8	13	15	60	84	29
16	Clydebank	36	11	5	20	70	86	27
17	Arthurlie *	32	9	7	16	51	73	25
18	Stenhousemuir	35	9	6	20	52	90	24
19	Armadale	36	8	7	21	47	99	23

*Arthurlie resigned towards the end of the season—but their record was allowed to stand.

FA CUP 1928-29

FOURTH ROUND

Blackburn Rovers v Derby County	1-1, 3-0
Manchester United v Bury	0-1
Leicester City v Swansea Town	1-0
Liverpool v Bolton Wanderers	0-0, 2-5
West Bromwich Albion v Middlesbrough	1-0
Plymouth Argyle v Bradford Park Avenue	0-1
Huddersfield Town v Leeds United	3-0
Millwall v Crystal Palace	0-0, 3-5
Chelsea v Birmingham	1-0
Portsmouth v Bradford City	2-0
Bournemouth v Watford	6-4
West Ham United v Corinthians	3-0
Reading v The Wednesday	1-0
Aston Villa v Clapton Orient	0-0, 8-0
Burnley v Swindon Town	3-3, 2-3
Arsenal v Mansfield Town	2-0

FIFTH ROUND

Blackburn Rovers v Bury	1-0
Leicester City v Bolton Wanderers	1-2
West Bromwich Albion v Bradford Park Avenue	6-0
Huddersfield Town v Crystal Palace	5-2
Chelsea v Portsmouth	1-1, 0-1
Bournemouth v West Ham United	1-1, 1-3
Reading v Aston Villa	1-3
Swindon Town v Arsenal	0-0, 0-1

SIXTH ROUND

Blackburn Rovers v Bolton Wanderers	1-1, 1-2
West Bromwich Albion v Huddersfield Town	1-1, 1-2
Portsmouth v West Ham United	3-2
Aston Villa v Arsenal	1-0

SEMI-FINAL

Bolton Wanderers v Huddersfield Town	3-1
Portsmouth v Aston Villa	1-0

FINAL

Bolton Wanderers v Portsmouth	2-0

SCOTTISH FA CUP 1928-29

SECOND ROUND

Celtic v East Stirlingshire	3-0
Murrayfield Amateurs v Arbroath	1-1, 2-5
Cowdenbeath v Airdrieonians	0-0, 2-3
St Johnstone v Motherwell	2-3
Bathgate v Raith Rovers	1-1, 2-5
Fraserburgh v Dumbarton	0-3
Albion Rovers v Clackmannan	8-1
Kilmarnock v Bo'ness	3-2
Rangers v Partick Thistle	5-1
Clyde v Hamilton Academicals	1-1, 2-1
Dundee v Brechin City	6-1
Stenhousemuir v Dundee United	1-1, 0-2
Aberdeen v Queen's Park	4-0
Queen of the South v Falkirk	1-2
Ayr United v Armadale	5-1
Third Lanark v St Mirren	0-1

THIRD ROUND

Celtic v Arbroath	4-1
Airdrieonians v Motherwell	1-1, 1-3
Raith Rovers v Dumbarton	3-2
Albion Rovers v Kilmarnock	0-1
Clyde v Rangers	0-2
Dundee v Dundee United	1-1, 0-1
Falkirk v Aberdeen	3-5
Ayr United v St Mirren	0-2

FOURTH ROUND

Celtic v Motherwell	0-0, 2-1
Raith Rovers v Kilmarnock	2-3
Rangers v Dundee United	3-1
St Mirren v Aberdeen	4-3

SEMI-FINAL

Celtic v Kilmarnock	0-1
Rangers v St Mirren	3-2

FINAL

Kilmarnock v Rangers	2-0

The worst kind of record

During the 1928-29 season, Rotherham United became only the second side to have had at least 10 goals scored against them in more than one Football League game in the same season. Rotherham, of Division Three North, first lost 11-1 at Bradford City on 25 August 1928, and then 10-1 away to South Shields on 16 March 1929.

The Scottish team in the Football League

In the First Division, the record for fielding a side containing the most Scotsmen belongs to Newcastle United. In the Newcastle side that faced Leeds United on 6 October 1928, only Wood, the centre-half, came from outside Scotland. In 1955-56 Accrington went one better by fielding a team of 11 Scots in several Third Division North fixtures.

League Tables 1929-30

FIRST DIVISION

		P	W	D	L	F	A	Pts
1	Sheff Wed	42	26	8	8	105	57	60
2	Derby	42	21	8	13	90	82	50
3	Man City	42	19	9	14	91	81	47
4	Aston Villa	42	21	5	16	92	83	47
5	Leeds	42	20	6	16	79	63	46
6	Blackburn	42	19	7	16	99	93	45
7	West Ham	42	19	5	18	86	79	43
8	Leicester	42	17	9	16	86	90	43
9	Sunderland	42	18	7	17	76	80	43
10	Huddersfield	42	17	9	16	63	69	43
11	Birmingham	42	16	9	17	67	62	41
12	Liverpool	42	16	9	17	63	79	41
13	Portsmouth	42	15	19	17	66	62	40
14	Arsenal	42	14	11	17	78	66	39
15	Bolton	45	15	9	18	74	74	39
16	Middlesbrough	42	16	6	20	82	84	38
17	Man United	42	15	8	19	67	88	38
18	Grimsby	42	15	7	20	73	89	37
19	Newcastle	42	15	7	20	71	92	37
20	Sheff United	42	15	6	21	91	96	36
21	Burnley	42	14	8	20	79	97	36
22	Everton	42	12	11	19	80	92	35

SECOND DIVISION

		P	W	D	L	F	A	Pts
1	Blackpool	42	27	4	11	98	67	58
2	Chelsea	42	22	11	9	74	46	55
3	Oldham	42	21	11	10	90	51	53
4	Bradford PA	42	19	12	11	91	70	50
5	Bury	42	22	5	15	78	67	49
6	WBA	42	21	5	16	105	73	47
7	Southampton	42	17	11	14	77	76	45
8	Cardiff	42	18	8	16	61	59	44
9	Wolves	42	16	9	17	77	79	41
10	Nottm Forest	42	13	15	14	55	69	41
11	Stoke	42	16	8	18	74	72	40
12	Tottenham	42	15	9	18	59	61	39
13	Charlton	42	14	11	17	59	63	39
14	Millwall	42	12	15	15	57	73	39
15	Swansea	42	14	9	19	57	61	37
16	Preston	42	13	11	18	65	80	37
17	Barnsley	42	14	8	20	56	71	36
18	Bradford City	42	12	12	18	60	77	36
19	Reading	42	12	11	19	54	67	35
20	Bristol City	42	13	9	20	61	83	35
21	Hull	42	14	7	21	51	78	35
22	Notts County	42	9	15	18	54	70	33

THIRD DIVISION (SOUTH)

		P	W	D	L	F	A	Pts
1	Plymouth	42	30	8	4	98	38	68
2	Brentford	42	28	5	9	94	44	61
3	QPR	42	21	9	12	80	68	51
4	Northampton	42	21	8	13	82	58	50
5	Brighton	42	21	8	13	87	63	50
6	Coventry	42	19	9	14	88	73	47
7	Fulham	42	18	11	13	87	83	47
8	Norwich	42	18	10	14	88	77	46
9	Crystal Palace	42	17	12	13	81	74	46
10	Bournemouth	42	15	13	14	72	61	43
11	Southend	42	15	13	14	69	59	43
12	Clapton Orient	42	14	13	15	55	62	41
13	Luton	42	14	12	16	64	78	40
14	Swindon	42	13	12	17	73	83	38
15	Watford	42	15	8	19	60	73	38
16	Exeter	42	12	11	19	67	73	35
17	Walsall	42	13	8	21	71	78	34
18	Newport	42	12	10	20	74	85	34
19	Torquay	42	10	11	21	64	94	31
20	Bristol Rovers	42	11	8	23	67	93	30
21	Gillingham	42	11	8	23	51	80	30
22	Merthyr Town	42	6	9	27	60	135	21

THIRD DIVISION (NORTH)

		P	W	D	L	F	A	Pts
1	Port Vale	42	30	7	5	103	37	67
2	Stockport	42	28	7	7	106	44	63
3	Darlington	42	22	6	14	108	73	50
4	Chesterfield	42	22	6	14	76	56	50
5	Lincoln	42	17	14	11	83	61	48
6	York	42	15	16	11	77	64	46
7	South Shields	42	18	10	14	77	74	46
8	Hartlepools	42	17	11	14	81	74	45
9	Southport	42	15	13	14	81	74	43
10	Rochdale	42	18	7	17	89	91	43
11	Crewe	42	17	8	17	82	71	42
12	Tranmere	42	16	9	17	83	86	41
13	New Brighton	42	16	8	18	69	79	40
14	Doncaster	42	15	9	18	62	69	39
15	Carlisle	42	16	7	19	90	101	39
16	Accrington	42	14	9	19	84	81	37
17	Wrexham	42	13	8	21	67	88	34
18	Wigan Borough	42	13	7	22	60	88	33
19	Nelson	42	13	7	22	51	80	33
20	Rotherham	42	11	8	23	67	113	30
21	Halifax	42	10	8	24	44	79	28
22	Barrow	42	11	5	26	41	98	27

SCOTTISH FIRST DIVISION

		P	W	D	L	F	A	Pts
1	Rangers	38	28	4	6	94	32	60
2	Motherwell	38	25	5	8	104	48	55
3	Aberdeen	38	23	7	8	85	61	53
4	Celtic	38	22	5	11	88	46	49
5	St Mirren	38	18	5	15	73	56	41
6	Partick	38	16	9	13	72	61	41
7	Falkirk	38	16	9	13	62	64	41
8	Kilmarnock	38	15	9	14	77	73	39
9	Ayr	38	16	6	16	70	92	38
10	Hearts	38	14	9	15	69	69	37
11	Clyde	38	13	11	14	64	69	37
12	Airdrieonians	38	16	4	18	60	66	36
13	Hamilton	38	14	7	17	76	81	35
14	Dundee	38	14	6	18	51	58	34
15	Queen's Park	38	15	4	19	67	80	34
16	Cowdenbeath	38	13	7	18	64	74	33
17	Hibernian	38	9	11	18	45	62	29
18	Morton	38	10	7	21	67	95	27
19	Dundee United	38	7	8	23	56	109	22
20	St Johnstone	38	6	7	25	48	96	19

SCOTTISH SECOND DIVISION

		P	W	D	L	F	A	Pts
1	Leith Athletic	38	23	11	4	92	42	57
2	East Fife	38	26	5	7	114	58	57
3	Albion	38	24	6	8	101	60	54
4	Third Lanark	38	23	6	9	92	53	52
5	Raith	38	18	8	12	94	67	44
6	King's Park	38	17	8	13	109	80	42
7	Queen of the S	38	18	6	14	65	63	42
8	Forfar	38	18	5	15	98	95	41
9	Arbroath	38	16	7	15	83	87	39
10	Dunfermline	38	16	6	16	99	85	38
11	Montrose	38	14	10	14	79	87	38
12	E Stirlingshire	38	16	4	18	83	75	36
13	Bo'ness	38	15	4	19	67	95	34
14	St Bernard's	38	13	6	19	65	65	32
15	Armadale	38	13	5	20	56	91	31
16	Dumbarton	38	14	2	22	77	95	30
17	Stenhousemuir	38	11	5	22	75	108	27
18	Clydebank	38	7	10	21	66	92	24
19	Alloa	38	9	6	23	55	104	24
20	Brechin	38	7	4	27	57	125	18

FA CUP 1929-30

FOURTH ROUND
West Ham United v Leeds United	4-1
Millwall v Doncaster Rovers	4-0
Arsenal v Birmingham	2-2, 1-0
Middlesbrough v Charlton Athletic	1-1, 1-1, 1-0
Hull City v Blackpool	3-1
Swindon Town v Manchester City	1-1, 1-10
Newcastle United v Clapton Orient	3-1
Portsmouth v Brighton	0-1
Aston Villa v Walsall	3-1
Blackburn Rovers v Everton	4-1
Huddersfield Town v Sheffield United	2-1
Wrexham v Bradford City	0-0, 1-2
Nottingham Forest v Fulham	2-1
Sunderland v Cardiff City	2-1
Oldham Athletic v Sheffield Wednesday	3-4
Derby County v Bradford Park Avenue	1-1, 1-2

FIFTH ROUND
West Ham United v Millwall	4-1
Middlesbrough v Arsenal	0-2
Manchester City v Hull City	1-2
Newcastle United v Brighton	3-0
Aston Villa v Blackburn Rovers	4-1
Huddersfield Town v Bradford City	2-1
Sunderland v Nottingham Forest	2-2, 1-3
Sheffield Wednesday v Bradford Park Avenue	5-1

SIXTH ROUND
West Ham United v Arsenal	0-3
Newcastle United v Hull City	1-1, 0-1
Aston Villa v Huddersfield Town	1-2
Nottingham Forest v Sheffield Wednesday	2-2, 1-3

SEMI-FINAL
Arsenal v Hull City	2-2, 1-0
Huddersfield Town v Sheffield Wednesday	2-1

FINAL
Arsenal v Huddersfield Town	2-0

SCOTTISH FA CUP 1929-30

SECOND ROUND
Rangers v Cowdenbeath	2-2, 3-0
Motherwell v Clyde	3-0
Montrose v Citadel	3-1
Albion Rovers v Beith	2-1
Dundee v St Johnstone	4-1
Airdrieonians v Murrayfield Amateurs	8-3
Heart of Midlothian v St Bernard's	0-0, 5-1
Ayr United v Hibernian	1-3
Forfar Athletic v St Mirren	0-0, 0-3
Celtic v Arbroath	5-0
Hamilton Academicals v Kilmarnock	4-2
Vale of Leithen v King's Park	2-7
Falkirk v Queen of the South	1-1, 4-3
Leith Athletic v Clachnacuddin	2-0
Dundee United v Partick Thistle	0-3
Aberdeen v Nithsdale Wanderers	5-1

THIRD ROUND
Motherwell v Rangers	2-5
Albion Rovers v Montrose	2-2, 1-3
Dundee v Airdrieonians	0-0, 0-0, 1-0
Hibernian v Heart of Midlothian	1-3
Celtic v St Mirren	1-3
Hamilton Academicals v King's Park	4-0
Falkirk v Leith Athletic	0-0, 1-1, 1-1, 1-0
Partick Thistle v Aberdeen	3-2

FOURTH ROUND
Rangers v Montrose	3-0
Dundee v Heart of Midlothian	2-2, 0-4
St Mirren v Hamilton Academicals	3-4
Partick Thistle v Falkirk	3-1

SEMI-FINAL
Rangers v Heart of Midlothian	4-1
Partick Thistle v Hamilton Academicals	3-1

FINAL
Rangers v Partick Thistle	0-0, 2-1

Jim Barrett of West Ham United made his international debut for England against Northern Ireland on 19 October 1929. After only eight minutes he was injured and carried off, and as he never played for England again, his became the shortest international career on record.

Sheffield Wednesday won the League Championship for the second successive season.

Albert Geldard of Bradford Park Avenue became the youngest footballer to play in the League when, aged 15 years and 156 days, he played against Millwall in a Division Two match on 16 September 1929.

Joe Bambrick's six goals in Northern Ireland's 7-0 win over Wales in February 1930 made him the highest individual scorer in an international match between Home Countries.

FIRST DIVISION

		P	W	D	L	F	A	Pts
1	Arsenal	42	28	10	4	127	59	66
2	Aston Villa	42	25	9	8	128	78	59
3	Sheff Wed	42	22	8	12	102	75	52
4	Portsmouth	42	18	13	11	84	67	49
5	Huddersfield	42	18	12	12	81	65	48
6	Derby	42	18	10	14	94	79	46
7	Middlesbrough	42	19	8	15	98	90	46
8	Man City	42	18	10	14	75	70	46
9	Liverpool	42	15	12	15	86	85	42
10	Blackburn	42	17	8	17	83	84	42
11	Sunderland	42	16	9	17	89	85	41
12	Chelsea	42	15	10	17	64	67	40
13	Grimsby	42	17	5	20	82	87	39
14	Bolton	42	15	9	18	68	81	39
15	Sheff United	42	14	10	18	78	84	38
16	Leicester	42	16	6	20	80	95	38
17	Newcastle	42	15	6	21	78	87	36
18	West Ham	42	14	8	20	79	94	36
19	Birmingham	42	13	10	19	55	70	36
20	Blackpool	42	11	10	21	71	125	32
21	Leeds	42	12	7	23	68	81	31
22	Man United	42	7	8	27	53	115	22

SECOND DIVISION

		P	W	D	L	F	A	Pts
1	Everton	42	28	5	9	121	66	61
2	WBA	42	22	10	10	83	49	54
3	Tottenham	42	22	7	13	88	55	51
4	Wolves	42	21	5	16	84	67	47
5	Port Vale	42	21	5	16	67	61	47
6	Bradford PA	42	18	10	14	97	66	46
7	Preston	42	17	11	14	83	64	45
8	Burnley	42	17	11	14	81	77	45
9	Southampton	42	19	6	17	74	62	44
10	Bradford City	42	17	10	15	61	63	44
11	Stoke	42	17	10	15	64	71	44
12	Oldham	42	16	10	16	61	72	42
13	Bury	42	19	3	20	75	82	41
14	Millwall	42	16	7	19	71	80	39
15	Charlton	42	15	9	18	59	86	39
16	Bristol City	42	15	8	19	54	82	38
17	Nottm Forest	42	14	9	19	80	85	37
18	Plymouth	42	14	8	20	76	84	36
19	Barnsley	42	13	9	20	59	79	35
20	Swansea	42	12	10	20	51	74	34
21	Reading	42	12	6	24	72	96	30
22	Cardiff	42	8	9	25	47	87	25

THIRD DIVISION (SOUTH)

		P	W	D	L	F	A	Pts
1	Notts County	42	24	11	7	97	46	59
2	Crystal Palace	42	22	7	13	107	71	51
3	Brentford	42	22	6	14	90	64	50
4	Brighton	42	17	15	10	68	53	49
5	Southend	42	22	5	15	76	60	49
6	Northampton	42	18	12	12	77	59	48
7	Luton	42	19	8	15	76	51	46
8	QPR	42	20	3	19	82	75	43
9	Fulham	42	18	7	17	77	75	43
10	Bournemouth	42	15	13	14	72	73	43
11	Torquay	42	17	9	16	80	84	43
12	Swindon	42	18	6	18	89	94	42
13	Exeter	42	17	8	17	84	90	42
14	Coventry	42	16	9	17	75	65	41
15	Bristol Rovers	42	16	8	18	75	92	40
16	Gillingham	42	14	10	18	61	76	38
17	Walsall	42	14	9	19	78	95	37
18	Watford	42	14	7	21	72	75	35
19	Clapton Orient	42	14	7	21	63	91	35
20	Thames	42	13	8	21	54	93	34
21	Norwich	42	10	8	24	47	76	28
22	Newport	42	11	6	25	69	111	28

THIRD DIVISION (NORTH)

		P	W	D	L	F	A	Pts
1	Chesterfield	42	26	6	10	102	57	58
2	Lincoln	42	25	7	10	102	59	57
3	Tranmere	42	24	6	12	111	74	54
4	Wrexham	42	21	12	9	94	62	54
5	Southport	42	22	9	11	88	56	53
6	Hull	42	20	10	12	99	55	50
7	Stockport	42	20	9	13	77	61	49
8	Carlisle	42	20	5	17	98	81	45
9	Gateshead	42	16	13	13	71	73	45
10	Wigan Borough	42	19	5	18	76	86	43
11	Darlington	42	16	10	16	71	59	42
12	York	42	18	6	18	85	82	42
13	Accrington	42	15	9	18	84	108	39
14	Rotherham	42	13	12	17	81	83	38
15	Doncaster	42	13	11	18	65	65	37
16	Barrow	42	15	7	20	68	89	37
17	Halifax	42	13	9	20	55	89	35
18	Crewe	42	14	6	22	66	93	34
19	New Brighton	42	13	7	22	49	76	33
20	Hartlepools	42	12	6	24	67	86	30
21	Rochdale	42	12	6	24	62	107	30
22	Nelson	42	6	7	29	43	113	19

SCOTTISH FIRST DIVISION

		P	W	D	L	F	A	Pts
1	Rangers	38	27	6	5	96	29	60
2	Celtic	38	24	10	4	101	34	58
3	Motherwell	38	24	8	6	102	42	56
4	Partick	38	24	5	9	76	44	53
5	Hearts	38	19	6	13	90	63	44
6	Aberdeen	38	17	7	14	79	63	41
7	Cowdenbeath	38	17	7	14	58	65	41
8	Dundee	38	17	5	16	65	63	39
9	Airdrieonians	38	17	5	16	59	66	39
10	Hamilton	38	16	5	17	59	57	37
11	Kilmarnock	38	15	5	18	59	60	35
12	Clyde	38	15	4	19	60	87	34
13	Queen's Park	38	13	7	18	71	72	33
14	Falkirk	38	14	4	20	77	87	32
15	St Mirren	38	11	8	19	49	72	30
16	Morton	38	11	7	20	58	83	29
17	Leith	38	8	11	19	52	85	27
18	Ayr	38	8	11	19	53	92	27
19	Hibernian	38	9	7	22	49	81	25
20	East Fife	38	8	4	26	45	113	20

SCOTTISH SECOND DIVISION

		P	W	D	L	F	A	Pts
1	Third Lanark	38	27	7	4	107	42	61
2	Dundee United	38	21	8	9	93	54	50
3	Dunfermline	38	20	7	11	83	50	47
4	Raith	38	20	6	12	93	72	46
5	Queen of the S	38	18	6	14	83	66	42
6	St Johnstone	38	18	6	14	76	64	42
7	E Stirlingshire	38	17	7	14	85	74	41
8	Montrose	38	19	3	16	75	90	41
9	Albion	38	14	11	13	80	83	39
10	Dumbarton	38	15	8	15	73	72	38
11	St Bernard's	38	14	9	15	85	66	37
12	Forfar	38	15	6	17	78	83	36
13	Alloa	38	15	5	18	65	87	35
14	King's Park	38	14	6	18	78	70	34
15	Arbroath	38	15	4	19	83	94	34
16	Brechin	38	13	7	18	52	84	33
17	Stenhousemuir	38	13	6	19	78	98	32
18	Armadale	38	13	2	23	74	99	28
19	Clydebank	38	10	2	26	61	108	22
20	Bo'ness	38	9	4	25	54	100	22

FA CUP 1930-31

FOURTH ROUND

Birmingham v Port Vale	2-0
Watford v Brighton	2-0
Chelsea v Arsenal	2-1
Blackburn Rovers v Bristol Rovers	5-1
Bolton Wanderers v Sunderland	1-1, 1-3
Sheffield United v Notts County	4-1
Bury v Exeter City	1-2
Leeds United v Newcastle United	4-1
Crystal Palace v Everton	0-6
Grimsby Town v Manchester United	1-0
Southport v Blackpool	2-1
Bradford Park Avenue v Burnley	2-0
Brentford v Portsmouth	0-1
West Bromwich Albion v Tottenham Hotspur	1-0
Barnsley v Sheffield Wednesday	2-1
Bradford City v Wolverhampton Wanderers	0-0, 2-4

FIFTH ROUND

Birmingham v Watford	3-0
Chelsea v Blackburn Rovers	3-0
Sunderland v Sheffield United	2-1
Exeter City v Leeds United	3-1
Everton v Grimsby Town	5-3
Southport v Bradford Park Avenue	1-0
Portsmouth v West Bromwich Albion	0-1
Barnsley v Wolverhampton Wanderers	1-3

SIXTH ROUND

Birmingham v Chelsea	2-2, 3-0
Sunderland v Exeter City	1-1, 4-2
Everton v Southport	9-1
West Bromwich Albion v Wolverhampton Wanderers	1-1, 2-1

SEMI-FINAL

Birmingham v Sunderland	2-0
Everton v West Bromwich Albion	0-1

FINAL

West Bromwich Albion v Birmingham	2-1

SCOTTISH FA CUP 1930-31

SECOND ROUND

Dundee United v Celtic	2-3
Queen's Park v Morton	0-1
Aberdeen v Partick Thistle	1-1, 3-0
Rangers v Dundee	1-2
Kilmarnock v Heart of Midlothian	3-2
Montrose v Civil Service Strollers	2-0
Bo'ness v Alloa Athletic	4-2
Murrayfield Amateurs v Ayr United	0-1
Motherwell v Albion Rovers	4-1
Hamilton Academicals v Hibernian	2-2, 2-5
Cowdenbeath v St Johnstone	1-1, 4-0
King's Park v St Bernard's	1-1, 0-1
St Mirren v Clyde	3-1
Inverness Caledonian v Falkirk	2-7
Third Lanark v Airdrieonians	1-0
Arbroath v Edinburgh City	1-0

THIRD ROUND

Morton v Celtic	1-4
Dundee v Aberdeen	1-1, 0-2
Montrose v Kilmarnock	0-3
Bo'ness v Ayr United	1-0
Hibernian v Motherwell	0-3
Cowdenbeath v St Bernard's	3-0
St Mirren v Falkirk	2-0
Third Lanark v Arbroath	4-2

FOURTH ROUND

Celtic v Aberdeen	4-0
Bo'ness v Kilmarnock	1-1, 0-5
Cowdenbeath v Motherwell	0-1
Third Lanark v St Mirren	1-1, 0-3

SEMI-FINAL

Celtic v Kilmarnock	3-0
Motherwell v St Mirren	1-0

FINAL

Celtic v Motherwell	2-2, 4-2

The outstanding example of each member of a forward line scoring in a single game was when all five Everton forwards scored against Charlton Athletic at the Valley in an 18 minute spell. The Everton forwards were Stein, Dean, Dunn, Critchley and Johnson. The match, a Division Two League fixture played on 7 February 1931, ended as a convincing 7-0 victory for the Merseysiders, who went on to win the Division Two Championship.

The famous occasion when a referee was 'sent off' occurred in the annual Sheffield versus Glasgow match on 22 September 1930. Sheffield were playing in white shirts and black shorts, and the referee, Mr J Thomson of Burnbank, wore a white shirt without a jacket. When Sheffield's captain, Jimmy Seed, found that he was passing to the referee in error, he asked him to stop the game and put on a jacket. Mr Thomson obliged.

FIRST DIVISION

	P	W	D	L	F	A	Pts
1 Everton	42	26	4	12	116	64	56
2 Arsenal	42	22	10	10	90	48	54
3 Sheff Wed	42	22	6	14	96	82	50
4 Huddersfield	42	19	10	13	80	63	48
5 Aston Villa	42	19	8	15	104	72	46
6 WBA	42	20	6	16	77	55	46
7 Sheff United	42	20	6	16	80	75	46
8 Portsmouth	42	19	7	16	62	62	45
9 Birmingham	42	18	8	16	78	67	44
10 Liverpool	42	19	6	17	81	93	44
11 Newcastle	42	18	6	18	80	87	42
12 Chelsea	42	16	8	18	69	73	40
13 Sunderland	42	15	10	17	67	73	40
14 Man City	42	13	12	17	83	73	38
15 Derby	42	14	10	18	71	75	38
16 Blackburn	42	16	6	20	89	95	38
17 Bolton	42	17	4	21	72	80	38
18 Middlesbrough	42	15	8	19	64	89	38
19 Leicester	42	15	7	20	74	94	37
20 Blackpool	42	12	9	21	65	102	33
21 Grimsby	42	13	6	23	67	98	32
22 West Ham	42	12	7	23	62	107	31

SECOND DIVISION

	P	W	D	L	F	A	Pts
1 Wolves	42	24	8	10	115	49	56
2 Leeds	42	22	10	10	78	54	54
3 Stoke	42	19	14	9	69	48	52
4 Plymouth	42	20	9	13	100	66	49
5 Bury	42	21	7	14	70	58	49
6 Bradford PA	42	21	7	14	72	63	49
7 Bradford City	42	16	13	13	80	61	45
8 Tottenham	42	16	11	15	87	78	43
9 Millwall	42	17	9	16	61	61	43
10 Charlton	42	17	9	16	61	66	43
11 Nottm Forest	42	16	10	16	77	72	42
12 Man United	42	17	8	17	71	72	42
13 Preston	42	16	10	16	75	77	42
14 Southampton	42	17	7	18	66	77	41
15 Swansea	42	16	7	19	73	75	39
16 Notts County	42	13	12	17	75	75	38
17 Chesterfield	42	13	11	18	64	86	37
18 Oldham	42	13	10	19	62	84	36
19 Burnley	42	13	9	20	59	87	35
20 Port Vale	42	13	7	22	58	89	33
21 Barnsley	42	12	9	21	55	91	33
22 Bristol City	42	6	11	25	39	78	23

THIRD DIVISION (SOUTH)

	P	W	D	L	F	A	Pts
1 Fulham	42	24	9	9	111	62	57
2 Reading	42	23	9	10	97	67	55
3 Southend	42	21	11	10	77	53	53
4 Crystal Palace	42	20	11	11	74	63	51
5 Brentford	42	19	10	13	68	52	48
6 Luton	42	20	7	15	95	70	47
7 Exeter	42	20	7	15	77	62	47
8 Brighton	42	17	12	13	73	58	46
9 Cardiff	42	19	8	15	87	73	46
10 Norwich	42	17	12	13	76	67	46
11 Watford	42	19	8	15	81	79	46
12 Coventry	42	18	8	16	108	97	44
13 QPR	42	15	12	15	79	73	42
14 Northampton	42	16	7	19	69	69	39
15 Bournemouth	42	13	12	17	70	78	38
16 Clapton Orient	42	12	11	19	77	90	35
17 Swindon	42	14	6	22	70	84	34
18 Bristol Rovers	42	13	8	21	65	92	34
19 Torquay	42	12	9	21	72	106	33
20 Mansfield	42	11	10	21	75	108	32
21 Gillingham	42	10	8	24	40	82	28
22 Thames	42	7	9	26	53	109	23

THIRD DIVISION (NORTH)

	P	W	D	L	F	A	Pts
1 Lincoln	40	26	5	9	106	47	57
2 Gateshead	40	25	7	8	94	48	57
3 Chester	40	21	8	11	78	60	50
4 Tranmere	40	19	11	10	107	58	49
5 Barrow	40	24	1	15	86	59	49
6 Crewe	40	21	6	13	95	66	48
7 Southport	40	18	10	12	58	53	46
8 Hull	40	20	5	15	82	53	45
9 York	40	18	7	15	76	81	43
10 Wrexham	40	18	7	15	64	69	43
11 Darlington	40	17	4	19	66	69	38
12 Stockport	40	13	11	16	55	53	37
13 Hartlepools	40	16	5	19	78	100	37
14 Accrington	40	15	6	19	75	80	36
15 Doncaster	40	16	4	20	59	80	36
16 Walsall	40	16	3	21	57	85	35
17 Halifax	40	13	8	19	61	87	34
18 Carlisle	40	11	11	18	64	79	33
19 Rotherham	40	14	4	22	63	72	32
20 New Brighton	40	8	8	24	38	76	24
21 Rochdale	40	4	3	33	48	135	11
22 Wigan Borough resigned from the League							

SCOTTISH FIRST DIVISION

	P	W	D	L	F	A	Pts
1 Motherwell	38	30	6	2	119	31	66
2 Rangers	38	28	5	5	118	42	61
3 Celtic	38	20	8	10	94	50	48
4 Third Lanark	38	21	4	13	92	81	46
5 St Mirren	38	20	4	14	77	56	44
6 Partick	38	19	4	15	58	59	42
7 Aberdeen	38	16	9	13	57	49	41
8 Hearts	38	17	5	16	63	61	39
9 Kilmarnock	38	16	7	15	68	70	39
10 Hamilton	38	16	6	16	84	65	38
11 Dundee	38	14	10	14	61	72	38
12 Cowdenbeath	38	15	8	15	66	78	38
13 Clyde	38	13	9	16	58	70	35
14 Airdrieonians	38	13	6	19	74	81	32
15 Morton	38	12	7	19	78	87	31
16 Queen's Park	38	13	5	20	59	79	31
17 Ayr	38	11	7	20	70	90	29
18 Falkirk	38	11	5	22	70	76	27
19 Dundee United	38	6	7	25	40	118	19
20 Leith	38	6	4	28	46	137	16

SCOTTISH SECOND DIVISION

	P	W	D	L	F	A	Pts
1 E Stirlingshire	38	26	3	9	111	55	55
2 St Johnstone	38	24	7	7	102	52	55
3 Raith	38	20	6	12	83	65	46
4 Stenhousemuir	38	19	8	11	88	76	46
5 St Bernard's	38	19	7	12	81	62	45
6 Forfar	38	19	7	12	90	79	45
7 Hibernian	38	18	8	12	73	52	44
8 East Fife	38	18	5	15	107	77	41
9 Queen of the S	38	18	5	15	99	91	41
10 Dunfermline	38	17	6	15	78	73	40
11 Arbroath	38	17	5	16	82	78	39
12 Dumbarton	38	14	10	14	70	68	38
13 Alloa	38	14	7	17	73	74	35
14 Bo'ness	38	15	4	19	70	103	34
15 King's Park	38	14	5	19	97	93	33
16 Albion	38	13	2	23	81	104	28
17 Montrose	38	11	6	21	60	96	28
18 Armadale	38	10	5	23	68	102	25
19 Brechin	38	9	7	22	52	97	25
20 Edinburgh City	38	5	7	26	78	146	17

FA CUP 1931-32

FOURTH ROUND

Huddersfield Town v Queen's Park Rangers	5-0
Preston North End v Wolverhampton Wanderers	2-0
Portsmouth v Aston Villa	1-1, 1-0
Arsenal v Plymouth Argyle	4-2
Bury v Sheffield United	3-1
Sunderland v Stoke City	1-1, 1-1, 1-2
Manchester City v Brentford	6-1
Derby County v Blackburn Rovers	3-2
Chesterfield v Liverpool	2-4
Grimsby Town v Birmingham	2-1
Sheffield Wednesday v Bournemouth	7-0
Chelsea v West Ham United	3-1
Newcastle United v Southport	1-1, 1-1, 9-0
Port Vale v Leicester City	1-2
Watford v Bristol City	2-1
Bradford Park Avenue v Northampton Town	4-2

FIFTH ROUND

Huddersfield Town v Preston North End	4-0
Portsmouth v Arsenal	0-2
Bury v Stoke City	3-0
Manchester City v Derby County	3-0
Liverpool v Grimsby Town	1-0
Sheffield Wednesday v Chelsea	1-1, 0-2
Newcastle United v Leicester City	3-1
Watford v Bradford Park Avenue	1-0

SIXTH ROUND

Huddersfield Town v Arsenal	0-1
Bury v Manchester City	3-4
Liverpool v Chelsea	0-2
Newcastle United v Watford	5-0

SEMI-FINAL

Arsenal v Manchester City	1-0
Chelsea v Newcastle United	1-2

FINAL

Newcastle United v Arsenal	2-1

SCOTTISH FA CUP 1931-32

SECOND ROUND

Raith Rovers v Rangers	0-5
Heart of Midlothian v Cowdenbeath	4-1
Queen's Park v Motherwell	0-2
St Johnstone v Celtic	2-4
Hamilton Academicals v Armadale	5-2
Clyde v Arbroath	1-0
Edinburgh City v St Bernard's	2-3
Kilmarnock v Albion Rovers	2-0
Queen of the South v Dundee United	2-2, 1-1, 1-2
Dunfermline Athletic v Dundee	1-0
Airdrieonians v King's Park	2-2, 3-1
Bo'ness v Partick Thistle	2-2, 1-5

THIRD ROUND

Heart of Midlothian v Rangers	0-1
Motherwell v Celtic	2-0
Clyde v St Bernard's	2-0
Dundee United v Kilmarnock	1-1, 0-3
Hamilton Academicals	bye
Dunfermline Athletic	bye
Airdrieonians	bye
Partick Thistle	bye

FOURTH ROUND

Rangers v Motherwell	2-0
Clyde v Hamilton Academicals	0-2
Dunfermline Athletic v Kilmarnock	1-3
Airdrieonians v Partick Thistle	4-1

SEMI-FINAL

Rangers v Hamilton Academicals	5-2
Kilmarnock v Airdrieonians	3-2

FINAL

Rangers v Kilmarnock	1-1, 3-0

There is thought to have been only one League game without a corner kick. That was a Division One match between Newcastle United and Portsmouth, 5 December 1931, which ended as it began, 0-0.

On 26 October 1931, Wigan Borough became the first League club to resign during a season. Their record was expunged.

Rochdale break all the wrong records
Rochdale had a grim season in Division Three North. They set a League record by losing 17 games in succession: on 7 November 1931, they beat New Brighton 3-2, but then failed to gain another point until their 1-1 draw with the same team on 9 March 1932. Their 33 defeats in 40 matches were also a record for the division.

FIRST DIVISION

		P	W	D	L	F	A	Pts
1	Arsenal	42	25	8	9	118	61	58
2	Aston Villa	42	23	8	11	92	67	54
3	Sheff Wed	42	21	9	12	80	68	51
4	WBA	42	20	9	13	83	70	49
5	Newcastle	42	22	5	15	71	63	49
6	Huddersfield	42	18	11	13	66	53	47
7	Derby	42	15	14	13	76	69	44
8	Leeds	42	15	14	13	59	62	44
9	Portsmouth	42	18	7	17	74	76	43
10	Sheff United	42	17	9	16	74	80	43
11	Everton	42	16	9	17	81	74	41
12	Sunderland	42	15	10	17	63	80	40
13	Birmingham	42	14	11	17	57	57	39
14	Liverpool	42	14	11	17	79	84	39
15	Blackburn	42	14	10	18	76	102	38
16	Man City	42	16	5	21	68	71	37
17	Middlesbrough	42	14	9	19	63	73	37
18	Chelsea	42	14	7	21	63	73	35
19	Leicester	42	11	13	18	75	89	35
20	Wolves	42	13	9	20	80	96	35
21	Bolton	42	12	9	21	78	92	33
22	Blackpool	42	14	5	23	69	85	33

SECOND DIVISION

		P	W	D	L	F	A	Pts
1	Stoke	42	25	6	11	78	39	56
2	Tottenham	42	20	15	7	96	51	55
3	Fulham	42	20	10	12	78	65	50
4	Bury	42	20	9	13	84	59	49
5	Nottm Forest	42	17	15	10	67	59	49
6	Man United	42	15	13	14	71	68	43
7	Millwall	42	16	11	15	59	57	43
8	Bradford PA	42	17	8	17	77	71	42
9	Preston	42	16	10	16	74	70	42
10	Swansea	42	19	4	19	50	54	42
11	Bradford City	42	14	13	15	65	61	41
12	Southampton	42	18	5	19	66	66	41
13	Grimsby	42	14	13	15	79	84	41
14	Plymouth	42	16	9	17	63	67	41
15	Notts County	42	15	10	17	67	78	40
16	Oldham	42	15	8	19	67	80	38
17	Port Vale	42	14	10	18	66	79	38
18	Lincoln	42	12	13	17	72	87	37
19	Burnley	42	11	14	17	67	79	36
20	West Ham	42	13	9	20	75	93	35
21	Chesterfield	42	12	10	20	61	84	34
22	Charlton	42	12	7	23	60	91	31

THIRD DIVISION (SOUTH)

		P	W	D	L	F	A	Pts
1	Brentford	42	26	10	6	90	49	62
2	Exeter	42	24	10	8	88	48	58
3	Norwich	42	22	13	7	88	55	57
4	Reading	42	19	13	10	103	71	51
5	Crystal Palace	42	19	8	15	78	64	46
6	Coventry	42	19	6	17	106	77	44
7	Gillingham	42	18	8	16	72	61	44
8	Northampton	42	18	8	16	76	66	44
9	Bristol Rovers	42	15	14	13	61	56	44
10	Torquay	42	16	12	14	72	67	44
11	Watford	42	16	12	14	66	63	44
12	Brighton	42	17	8	17	66	65	42
13	Southend	42	15	11	16	65	82	41
14	Luton	42	13	13	16	78	78	39
15	Bristol City	42	12	13	17	83	90	37
16	QPR	42	13	11	18	72	87	37
17	Aldershot	42	13	10	19	61	72	36
18	Bournemouth	42	12	12	18	60	81	36
19	Cardiff	42	12	7	23	69	99	31
20	Clapton Orient	42	8	13	21	59	93	29
21	Newport	42	11	7	24	61	105	29
22	Swindon	42	9	11	22	60	105	29

THIRD DIVISION (NORTH)

		P	W	D	L	F	A	Pts
1	Hull	42	26	7	9	100	45	59
2	Wrexham	42	24	9	9	106	51	57
3	Stockport	42	21	12	9	99	58	54
4	Chester	42	22	8	12	94	66	52
5	Walsall	42	19	10	13	75	58	48
6	Doncaster	42	17	14	11	77	79	48
7	Gateshead	42	19	9	14	78	67	47
8	Barnsley	42	19	8	15	92	80	46
9	Barrow	42	18	7	17	60	60	43
10	Crewe	42	20	3	19	80	84	43
11	Tranmere	42	17	8	17	70	66	42
12	Southport	42	17	7	18	70	67	41
13	Accrington	42	15	10	17	78	76	40
14	Hartlepools	42	16	7	19	87	116	39
15	Halifax	42	15	8	19	71	90	38
16	Mansfield	42	14	7	21	84	100	35
17	Rotherham	42	14	6	22	60	84	34
18	Rochdale	42	13	7	22	58	80	33
19	Carlisle	42	13	7	22	51	75	33
20	York	42	13	6	23	72	92	32
21	New Brighton	42	11	10	21	63	88	32
22	Darlington	42	10	8	24	66	109	28

SCOTTISH FIRST DIVISION

		P	W	D	L	F	A	Pts
1	Rangers	38	26	10	2	113	43	62
2	Motherwell	38	27	5	6	114	53	59
3	Hearts	38	21	8	9	84	51	50
4	Celtic	38	20	8	10	75	44	48
5	St Johnstone	38	17	10	11	70	57	44
6	Aberdeen	38	18	6	14	85	58	42
7	St Mirren	38	18	6	14	73	60	42
8	Hamilton	38	18	6	14	92	78	42
9	Queen's Park	38	17	7	14	78	79	41
10	Partick	38	17	6	15	75	55	40
11	Falkirk	38	15	6	17	70	70	36
12	Clyde	38	15	5	18	69	75	35
13	Third Lanark	38	14	7	17	70	80	35
14	Kilmarnock	38	13	9	16	72	86	35
15	Dundee	38	12	9	17	58	74	33
16	Ayr	38	13	4	21	62	96	30
17	Cowdenbeath	38	10	5	23	65	111	25
18	Airdrieonians	38	10	3	25	55	102	23
19	Morton	38	6	9	23	49	97	21
20	E Stirlingshire	38	7	3	28	55	115	17

SCOTTISH SECOND DIVISION

		P	W	D	L	F	A	Pts
1	Hibernian	34	25	4	5	80	29	54
2	Queen of the S	34	20	9	5	93	59	49
3	Dunfermline	34	20	7	7	89	44	47
4	Stenhousemuir	34	18	6	10	67	58	42
5	Albion	34	19	2	13	82	57	40
6	Raith	34	16	4	14	83	67	36
7	East Fife	34	15	4	15	85	71	34
8	King's Park	34	13	8	13	85	80	34
9	Dumbarton	34	14	6	14	69	67	34
10	Arbroath	34	14	5	15	65	62	33
11	Alloa	34	14	5	15	60	58	33
12	St Bernard's	34	13	6	15	67	64	32
13	Dundee United	34	14	4	16	65	67	32
14	Forfar	34	12	4	18	68	87	28
15	Brechin	34	11	4	19	65	95	26
16	Leith	34	10	5	19	43	81	25
17	Montrose	34	8	5	21	63	89	21
18	Edinburgh City	34	4	4	26	39	133	12

FA CUP 1932-33

FOURTH ROUND

Burnley v Sheffield United	3-1
Darlington v Chesterfield	0-2
Bolton Wanderers v Grimsby Town	2-1
Manchester City v Walsall	2-0
Southend United v Derby County	2-3
Aldershot v Millwall	1-0
Aston Villa v Sunderland	0-3
Blackpool v Huddersfield Town	2-0
Everton v Bury	3-1
Tranmere Rovers v Leeds United	0-0, 0-4
Chester v Halifax Town	0-0, 2-3
Luton Town v Tottenham Hotspur	2-0
Brighton v Bradford Park Avenue	2-1
West Ham United v West Bromwich Albion	2-0
Middlesbrough v Stoke City	4-1
Birmingham v Blackburn Rovers	3-0

FIFTH ROUND

Burnley v Chesterfield	1-0
Bolton Wanderers v Manchester City	2-4
Derby County v Aldershot	2-0
Sunderland v Blackpool	1-0
Everton v Leeds United	2-0
Halifax Town v Luton Town	0-2
Brighton v West Ham United	2-2, 0-1
Middlesbrough v Birmingham	0-0, 0-3

SIXTH ROUND

Burnley v Manchester City	0-1
Derby County v Sunderland	4-4, 1-0
Everton v Luton Town	6-0
West Ham United v Birmingham	4-0

SEMI-FINAL

Manchester City v Derby County	3-2
Everton v West Ham United	2-1

FINAL

Everton v Manchester City	3-0

SCOTTISH FA CUP 1932-33

SECOND ROUND

Celtic v Falkirk	2-0
Partick Thistle v Ayr United	1-1, 2-0
Albion Rovers v Dumbarton	2-1
Heart of Midlothian v Airdrieonians	6-1
St Johnstone v Dundee United	4-3
Hibernian v Aberdeen	1-1, 1-0
Motherwell v Montrose	7-1
Dundee v Bo'ness	4-0
Kilmarnock v St Mirren	1-0
Rangers v Queen's Park	1-1, 1-1, 3-1
Clyde v Leith Athletic	1-1, 5-0
Stenhousemuir v Third Lanark	2-0

THIRD ROUND

Celtic v Partick Thistle	2-1
Heart of Midlothian v St Johnstone	2-0
Motherwell v Dundee	5-0
Kilmarnock v Rangers	1-0
Albion Rovers	bye
Hibernian	bye
Clyde	bye
Stenhousemuir	bye

FOURTH ROUND

Celtic v Albion Rovers	1-1, 3-1
Heart of Midlothian v Hibernian	2-0
Motherwell v Kilmarnock	3-3, 8-3
Clyde v Stenhousemuir	3-2

SEMI-FINAL

Celtic v Heart of Midlothian	0-0, 2-1
Motherwell v Clyde	2-0

FINAL

Celtic v Motherwell	1-0

Reduced to ten men after 10 minutes, Wales did well to beat Scotland 5-2 at Tynecastle, Edinburgh, in October 1932. It was their first win on Scottish soil since 1906.

Everton capped a memorable three seasons by winning the FA Cup. In 1931-32, they were League champions, the season before, they had won the Second Division Championship.

The international Rangers

Towards the end of 1932-33, Glasgow Rangers had 13 internationals on their books. They were: Archibald, Brown, Craig, Fleming, Gray, T Hamilton, McPhail, Marshall, Meiklejohn and Morton, all Scotsmen, and English, R Hamilton and McDonald, who were Irish internationals. This considerable array of Scots and Irish talent helped Rangers finish the season at the top of the Scottish First Division, three points clear of Motherwell.

FIRST DIVISION

		P	W	D	L	F	A	Pts
1	Arsenal	42	25	9	8	75	47	59
2	Huddersfield	42	23	10	9	90	61	56
3	Tottenham	42	21	7	14	79	56	49
4	Derby	42	17	11	14	68	54	45
5	Man City	42	17	11	14	65	72	45
6	Sunderland	42	16	12	14	81	56	44
7	WBA	42	17	10	15	78	70	44
8	Blackburn	42	18	7	17	74	81	43
9	Leeds	42	17	8	17	75	66	42
10	Portsmouth	42	15	12	15	52	55	42
11	Sheff Wed	42	16	9	17	62	67	41
12	Stoke	42	15	11	16	58	71	41
13	Aston Villa	42	14	12	16	78	75	40
14	Everton	42	12	16	14	62	63	40
15	Wolves	42	14	12	16	74	86	40
16	Middlesbrough	42	16	7	19	68	80	39
17	Leicester	42	14	11	17	59	74	39
18	Liverpool	42	14	10	18	79	87	38
19	Chelsea	42	14	8	20	67	69	36
20	Birmingham	42	12	12	18	54	56	36
21	Newcastle	42	10	14	18	68	77	34
22	Sheff United	42	12	7	23	58	101	31

SECOND DIVISION

		P	W	D	L	F	A	Pts
1	Grimsby	42	27	5	10	103	59	59
2	Preston	42	23	6	13	71	52	52
3	Bolton	42	21	9	12	79	55	51
4	Brentford	42	22	7	13	85	60	51
5	Bradford PA	42	23	3	16	86	67	49
6	Bradford City	42	20	6	16	73	67	46
7	West Ham	42	17	11	14	78	70	45
8	Port Vale	42	19	7	16	60	55	45
9	Oldham	42	17	10	15	72	60	44
10	Plymouth	42	15	13	14	69	70	43
11	Blackpool	42	15	13	14	62	64	43
12	Bury	42	17	9	16	70	73	43
13	Burnley	42	18	6	18	60	72	42
14	Southampton	42	15	8	19	54	58	38
15	Hull	42	13	12	17	52	68	38
16	Fulham	42	15	7	20	48	67	37
17	Nottm Forest	42	13	9	20	73	74	35
18	Notts County	42	12	11	19	53	62	35
19	Swansea	42	10	15	17	51	60	35
20	Man United	42	14	6	22	59	85	34
21	Millwall	42	11	11	20	39	68	33
22	Lincoln	42	9	8	25	44	75	26

THIRD DIVISION (NORTH)

		P	W	D	L	F	A	Pts
1	Barnsley	42	27	8	7	118	61	62
2	Chesterfield	42	27	7	8	86	43	61
3	Stockport	42	24	11	7	115	52	59
4	Walsall	42	23	7	12	97	60	53
5	Doncaster	42	22	9	11	83	61	53
6	Wrexham	42	23	5	14	102	73	51
7	Tranmere	42	20	7	15	84	63	47
8	Barrow	42	19	9	14	116	94	47
9	Halifax	42	20	4	18	80	91	44
10	Chester	42	17	6	19	89	86	40
11	Hartlepools	42	16	7	19	89	93	39
12	York	42	15	8	19	71	74	38
13	Carlisle	42	15	8	19	66	81	38
14	Crewe	42	15	6	21	81	97	36
15	New Brighton	42	14	8	20	62	87	36
16	Darlington	42	13	9	20	70	101	35
17	Mansfield	42	11	12	19	81	88	34
18	Southport	42	8	17	17	63	90	33
19	Gateshead	42	12	9	21	76	110	33
20	Accrington	42	13	7	22	65	101	33
21	Rotherham	42	10	8	24	53	91	28
22	Rochdale	42	9	6	27	53	103	24

THIRD DIVISION (SOUTH)

		P	W	D	L	F	A	Pts
1	Norwich	42	25	11	6	88	49	61
2	Coventry	42	21	12	9	100	54	54
3	Reading	42	21	12	9	82	50	54
4	QPR	42	24	6	12	70	51	54
5	Charlton	42	22	8	12	83	56	52
6	Luton	42	21	10	11	83	61	52
7	Bristol Rovers	42	20	11	11	77	47	51
8	Swindon	42	17	11	14	64	68	45
9	Exeter	42	16	11	15	68	57	43
10	Brighton	42	15	13	14	68	60	43
11	Clapton Orient	42	16	10	16	75	69	42
12	Crystal Palace	42	16	9	17	71	67	41
13	Northampton	42	14	12	16	71	78	40
14	Aldershot	42	13	12	17	52	71	38
15	Watford	42	15	7	20	71	63	37
16	Southend	42	12	10	20	51	74	34
17	Gillingham	42	11	11	20	75	96	33
18	Newport	42	8	17	17	49	70	33
19	Bristol City	42	10	13	19	58	85	33
20	Torquay	42	13	7	22	53	93	33
21	Bournemouth	42	9	9	24	60	102	27
22	Cardiff	42	9	6	27	57	105	24

SCOTTISH FIRST DIVISION

		P	W	D	L	F	A	Pts
1	Rangers	38	30	6	2	118	41	66
2	Motherwell	38	29	4	5	97	45	62
3	Celtic	38	18	11	9	78	53	47
4	Queen of the S	38	21	3	14	75	78	45
5	Aberdeen	38	18	8	12	90	57	44
6	Hearts	38	17	10	11	86	59	44
7	Kilmarnock	38	17	9	12	73	64	43
8	Ayr	38	16	10	12	87	92	42
9	St Johnstone	38	17	6	15	74	53	40
10	Falkirk	38	16	6	16	73	68	38
11	Hamilton	38	15	8	15	65	79	38
12	Dundee	38	15	6	17	68	64	36
13	Partick	38	14	5	19	73	78	33
14	Clyde	38	10	11	17	56	70	31
15	Queen's Park	38	13	5	20	65	85	31
16	Hibernian	38	12	3	23	51	69	27
17	St Mirren	38	9	9	20	46	75	27
18	Airdrieonians	38	10	6	22	59	103	26
19	Third Lanark	38	8	9	21	62	103	25
20	Cowdenbeath	38	5	5	28	58	118	15

SCOTTISH SECOND DIVISION

		P	W	D	L	F	A	Pts
1	Albion	34	20	5	9	74	47	45
2	Dunfermline	34	20	4	10	90	52	44
3	Arbroath	34	20	4	10	83	53	44
4	Stenhousemuir	34	18	4	12	70	73	40
5	Morton	34	17	5	12	67	64	39
6	Dumbarton	34	17	3	14	67	68	37
7	King's Park	34	14	8	12	78	70	36
8	Raith	34	15	5	14	71	55	35
9	E Stirlingshire	34	14	7	13	65	74	35
10	St Bernard's	34	15	4	15	75	56	34
11	Forfar	34	13	7	14	77	71	33
12	Leith	34	12	8	14	63	60	32
13	East Fife	34	12	8	14	71	76	32
14	Brechin	34	13	5	16	60	70	31
15	Alloa	34	11	9	14	55	68	31
16	Montrose	34	11	4	19	53	81	26
17	Dundee United	34	10	4	20	81	88	24
18	Edinburgh City	34	4	6	24	37	111	14

The record number of goals scored by a conventional half-back in a Football League game is three. The record was set in 1926 by a Newcastle player, T McDonald, and equalled against Wolves on 21 April 1934 by another Newcastle player, W Imrie.

In June 1934, Stanley Rous was appointed secretary of the Football Association.

S Milton had surely one of the unhappiest Football League debuts on record. A goal-keeper, Milton was picked to play in that position for Halifax Town against Stockport County in a Third Division North League match on 6 January 1934. Milton was faced with a Stockport attack in fine fettle, and he had to retrieve the ball from his net 13 times, an unenviable record. The score—13-0—also set a record, for the highest score in a League match.

FA CUP 1933-34

FOURTH ROUND

Portsmouth v Grimsby Town	2-0
Bury v Swansea Town	1-1, 0-3
Liverpool v Tranmere Rovers	3-1
Brighton v Bolton Wanderers	1-1, 1-6
Workington v Preston North End	1-2
Huddersfield Town v Northampton Town	0-2
Birmingham v Charlton Athletic	1-0
Millwall v Leicester City	3-6
Aston Villa v Sunderland	7-2
Tottenham Hotspur v West Ham United	4-1
Derby County v Wolverhampton Wanderers	3-0
Arsenal v Crystal Palace	7-0
Stoke City v Blackpool	3-0
Chelsea v Nottingham Forest	1-1, 3-0
Oldham Athletic v Sheffield Wednesday	1-1, 1-6
Hull City v Manchester City	2-2, 1-4

FIFTH ROUND

Swansea Town v Portsmouth	0-1
Liverpool v Bolton Wanderers	0-3
Preston North End v Northampton Town	4-0
Birmingham v Leicester City	1-2
Tottenham Hotspur v Aston Villa	0-1
Arsenal v Derby County	1-0
Stoke City v Chelsea	3-1
Sheffield Wednesday v Manchester City	2-2, 0-2

SIXTH ROUND

Bolton Wanderers v Portsmouth	0-3
Preston North End v Leicester City	0-1
Arsenal v Aston Villa	1-2
Manchester City v Stoke City	1-0

SEMI-FINAL

Portsmouth v Leicester City	4-1
Manchester City v Aston Villa	6-1

FINAL

Manchester City v Portsmouth	2-1

SCOTTISH FA CUP 1933-34

SECOND ROUND

Third Lanark v Rangers	0-3
Queen's Park v Heart of Midlothian	1-2
Hibernian v Alloa Athletic	6-0
Aberdeen v Dundee	2-0
Vale of Leithen v St Johnstone	1-3
Cowdenbeath v St Bernard's	2-1
Brechin City v St Mirren	0-4
Ayr United v Celtic	2-3
Hamilton Academicals v Falkirk	2-4
Albion Rovers v Kilmarnock	2-1
Ross County v Galston	3-1
Partick Thistle v Motherwell	3-3, 1-2
East Stirlingshire v Arbroath	1-1, 3-0
Queen of the South	bye

THIRD ROUND

Rangers v Heart of Midlothian	0-0, 2-1
Hibernian v Aberdeen	0-1
Queen of the South v Cowdenbeath	3-0
Celtic v Falkirk	3-1
Albion Rovers v Ross County	6-1
Motherwell v East Stirlingshire	5-0
St Johnstone	bye
St Mirren	bye

FOURTH ROUND

Rangers v Aberdeen	1-0
St Johnstone v Queen of the South	2-0
St Mirren v Celtic	2-0
Albion Rovers v Motherwell	1-1, 0-6

SEMI-FINAL

Rangers v St Johnstone	1-0
St Mirren v Motherwell	3-1

FINAL

Rangers v St Mirren	5-0

FIRST DIVISION

		P	W	D	L	F	A	Pts
1	Arsenal	42	23	12	7	115	46	58
2	Sunderland	42	19	16	7	90	51	54
3	Sheff Wed	42	18	13	11	70	64	49
4	Man City	42	20	8	14	82	67	48
5	Grimsby	42	17	11	14	78	60	45
6	Derby	42	18	9	15	81	66	45
7	Liverpool	42	19	7	16	85	88	45
8	Everton	42	16	12	14	89	88	44
9	WBA	42	17	10	15	83	83	44
10	Stoke	42	18	6	18	71	70	42
11	Preston	42	15	12	15	62	67	42
12	Chelsea	42	16	9	17	73	82	41
13	Aston Villa	42	14	13	15	74	88	41
14	Portsmouth	42	15	10	17	71	72	40
15	Blackburn	42	14	11	17	66	78	39
16	Huddersfield	42	14	10	18	76	71	38
17	Wolves	42	15	8	19	88	94	38
18	Leeds	42	13	12	17	75	92	38
19	Birmingham	42	13	10	19	63	81	36
20	Middlesbrough	42	10	14	18	70	91	34
21	Leicester	42	12	9	21	61	86	33
22	Tottenham	42	10	10	22	54	93	30

SECOND DIVISION

		P	W	D	L	F	A	Pts
1	Brentford	42	26	9	7	93	48	61
2	Bolton	42	26	4	12	96	48	56
3	West Ham	42	26	4	12	80	63	56
4	Blackpool	42	21	11	10	79	57	53
5	Man United	42	23	4	15	76	55	50
6	Newcastle	42	22	4	16	89	68	48
7	Fulham	42	17	12	13	76	56	46
8	Plymouth	42	19	8	15	75	64	46
9	Nottm Forest	42	17	8	17	76	70	42
10	Bury	42	19	4	19	62	73	42
11	Sheff United	42	16	9	17	79	70	41
12	Burnley	42	16	9	17	63	73	41
13	Hull	42	16	8	18	63	74	40
14	Norwich	42	14	11	17	71	61	39
15	Bradford PA	42	11	16	15	55	63	38
16	Barnsley	42	13	12	17	60	83	38
17	Swansea	42	14	8	20	56	67	36
18	Port Vale	42	11	12	19	55	74	34
19	Southampton	42	11	12	19	46	75	34
20	Bradford City	42	12	8	22	50	68	32
21	Oldham	42	10	6	26	56	95	26
22	Notts County	42	9	7	26	46	97	25

THIRD DIVISION (SOUTH)

		P	W	D	L	F	A	Pts
1	Charlton	42	27	7	8	103	52	61
2	Reading	42	21	11	10	89	65	53
3	Coventry	42	21	9	12	86	50	51
4	Luton	42	19	12	11	92	60	50
5	Crystal Palace	42	19	10	13	86	64	48
6	Watford	42	19	9	14	76	49	47
7	Northampton	42	19	8	15	65	67	46
8	Bristol Rovers	42	17	10	15	73	77	44
9	Brighton	42	17	9	16	69	62	43
10	Torquay	42	18	6	18	81	75	42
11	Exeter	42	16	9	17	70	75	41
12	Millwall	42	17	7	18	57	62	41
13	QPR	42	16	9	17	63	72	41
14	Clapton Orient	42	15	10	17	65	65	40
15	Bristol City	42	15	9	18	52	68	39
16	Swindon	42	13	12	17	67	78	38
17	Bournemouth	42	15	7	20	54	71	37
18	Aldershot	42	13	10	19	50	75	36
19	Cardiff	42	13	9	20	62	82	35
20	Gillingham	42	11	13	18	55	75	35
21	Southend	42	11	9	22	65	78	31
22	Newport	42	10	5	27	54	112	25

THIRD DIVISION (NORTH)

		P	W	D	L	F	A	Pts
1	Doncaster	42	26	5	11	87	44	57
2	Halifax	42	25	5	12	76	67	55
3	Chester	42	20	14	8	91	58	54
4	Lincoln	42	22	7	13	87	58	51
5	Darlington	42	21	9	12	80	59	51
6	Tranmere	42	20	11	11	74	55	51
7	Stockport	42	22	3	17	90	72	47
8	Mansfield	42	19	9	14	75	62	47
9	Rotherham	42	19	7	16	86	73	45
10	Chesterfield	42	17	10	15	71	52	44
11	Wrexham	42	16	11	15	76	69	43
12	Hartlepools	42	17	7	18	80	78	41
13	Crewe	42	14	11	17	66	86	39
14	Walsall	42	13	10	19	81	72	36
15	York	42	15	6	21	76	82	36
16	New Brighton	42	14	8	20	59	76	36
17	Barrow	42	13	9	20	58	87	35
18	Accrington	42	12	10	20	63	89	34
19	Gateshead	42	13	8	21	58	96	34
20	Rochdale	42	11	11	20	53	71	33
21	Southport	42	10	12	20	55	85	32
22	Carlisle	42	8	7	27	51	102	23

SCOTTISH FIRST DIVISION

		P	W	D	L	F	A	Pts
1	Rangers	38	25	5	8	96	46	55
2	Celtic	38	24	4	10	92	45	52
3	Hearts	38	20	10	8	87	51	50
4	Hamilton	38	19	10	9	87	67	48
5	St Johnstone	38	18	10	10	66	46	46
6	Aberdeen	38	17	10	11	68	54	44
7	Motherwell	38	15	10	13	83	64	40
8	Dundee	38	16	8	14	63	63	40
9	Kilmarnock	38	16	6	16	76	68	38
10	Clyde	38	14	10	14	71	69	38
11	Hibernian	38	14	8	16	59	70	36
12	Queen's Park	38	13	10	15	61	80	36
13	Partick	38	15	5	18	61	68	35
14	Airdrieonians	38	13	7	18	64	72	33
15	Dunfermline	38	13	5	20	56	96	31
16	Albion	38	10	9	19	62	77	29
17	Queen of the S	38	11	7	20	52	72	29
18	Ayr	38	12	5	21	61	112	29
19	St Mirren	38	11	5	22	49	70	27
20	Falkirk	38	9	6	23	58	82	24

SCOTTISH SECOND DIVISION

		P	W	D	L	F	A	Pts
1	Third Lanark	34	23	6	5	94	43	52
2	Arbroath	34	23	4	7	78	42	50
3	St Bernard's	34	20	7	7	103	47	47
4	Dundee United	34	18	6	10	105	65	42
5	Stenhousemuir	34	17	5	12	86	80	39
6	Morton	34	17	4	13	88	64	38
7	King's Park	34	18	2	14	86	71	38
8	Leith	34	16	5	13	69	71	37
9	East Fife	34	16	3	15	79	73	35
10	Alloa	34	12	10	12	68	61	34
11	Forfar	34	13	8	13	77	73	34
12	Cowdenbeath	34	13	6	15	84	75	32
13	Raith	34	13	3	18	68	73	29
14	E Stirlingshire	34	11	7	16	57	76	29
15	Brechin	34	10	6	18	51	98	26
16	Dumbarton	34	9	4	21	60	105	22
17	Montrose	34	7	6	21	58	105	20
18	Edinburgh City	34	3	2	29	45	134	8

FA CUP 1934-35

FOURTH ROUND

Wolverhampton Wanderers v Sheffield Wednesday	1-2
Norwich City v Leeds United	3-3, 2-1
Reading v Millwall	1-0
Leicester City v Arsenal	0-1
Southampton v Birmingham	0-3
Blackburn Rovers v Liverpool	1-0
Nottingham Forest v Manchester United	0-0, 3-0
Burnley v Luton Town	3-1
Plymouth Argyle v Bolton Wanderers	1-4
Tottenham Hotspur v Newcastle United	2-0
Derby County v Swansea Town	3-0
Sunderland v Everton	1-1, 4-6
Swindon Town v Preston North End	0-2
Portsmouth v Bristol City	0-0, 0-2
Bradford City v Stockport County	0-0, 2-3
West Bromwich Albion v Sheffield United	7-1

FIFTH ROUND

Norwich City v Sheffield Wednesday	0-1
Reading v Arsenal	0-1
Blackburn Rovers v Birmingham	1-2
Nottingham Forest v Burnley	0-0, 0-3
Tottenham Hotspur v Bolton Wanderers	1-1, 1-1, 0-2
Everton v Derby County	3-1
Bristol City v Preston North End	0-0, 0-5
Stockport County v West Bromwich Albion	0-5

SIXTH ROUND

Sheffield Wednesday v Arsenal	2-1
Burnley v Birmingham	3-2
Everton v Bolton Wanderers	1-2
West Bromwich Albion v Preston North End	1-0

SEMI-FINAL

Sheffield Wednesday v Burnley	3-0
Bolton Wanderers v West Bromwich Albion	1-1, 0-2

FINAL

Sheffield Wednesday v West Bromwich Albion	4-2

SCOTTISH FA CUP 1934-35

SECOND ROUND

Motherwell v Morton	7-1
Rangers v Third Lanark	2-0
St Mirren v Forfar Athletic	3-0
Airdrieonians v Rosyth Dockyard	1-0
Ayr United v King's Park	1-1, 2-2, 4-4, 1-2
Heart of Midlothian v Kilmarnock	2-0
Dundee United v Queen's Park	6-3
Aberdeen v Albion Rovers	4-0
Hibernian v Clachnacuddin	7-1
Celtic v Partick Thistle	1-1, 3-1
Brechin City v Raith Rovers	1-1, 4-2
Clyde v Hamilton Academicals	3-3, 3-6
St Johnstone v Dumbarton	4-0
Buckie Thistle	bye

THIRD ROUND

Rangers v St Mirren	1-0
Airdrieonians v King's Park	6-2
Heart of Midlothian v Dundee United	2-2, 4-2
Aberdeen v Hibernian	0-0, 1-1, 3-2
Brechin City v Hamilton Academicals	2-4
Buckie Thistle v St Johnstone	0-1
Motherwell	bye
Celtic	bye

FOURTH ROUND

Motherwell v Rangers	1-4
Airdrieonians v Heart of Midlothian	2-3
Aberdeen v Celtic	3-1
Hamilton Academicals v St Johnstone	3-0

SEMI-FINAL

Rangers v Heart of Midlothian	1-1, 2-0
Aberdeen v Hamilton Academicals	1-2

FINAL

Rangers v Hamilton Academicals	2-1

The famous occasion when a player headed a goal from a penalty-kick took place on 5 January 1935. Anfield was the setting for a North-South clash between Liverpool and Arsenal. In the course of the game, Arsenal were awarded a penalty which their full-back, Eddie Hapgood, elected to take. Liverpool's goalkeeper, Riley, fisted Hapgood's spot-kick back out, and Hapgood headed home the rebound. Arsenal won the match 2-0.

The record gate for an English League match was broken on 23 February 1935, when 77,582 people paid to see Manchester City play Arsenal at Maine Road, Manchester. Season-ticket holders brought the total number of spectators present to 80,000.

S Raleigh, Gillingham's centre-forward, died from concussion sustained in a match with Brighton, 1 December 1934.

FIRST DIVISION

		P	W	D	L	F	A	Pts
1	Sunderland	42	25	6	11	109	74	56
2	Derby	42	18	12	12	61	52	48
3	Huddersfield	42	18	12	12	59	56	48
4	Stoke	42	20	7	15	57	57	47
5	Brentford	42	17	12	13	81	60	46
6	Arsenal	42	15	15	12	78	48	45
7	Preston	42	18	8	16	67	64	44
8	Chelsea	42	15	13	14	65	72	43
9	Man City	42	17	8	17	68	60	42
10	Portsmouth	42	17	8	17	54	67	42
11	Leeds	42	15	11	16	66	64	41
12	Birmingham	42	15	11	16	61	63	41
13	Bolton	42	14	13	15	67	76	41
14	Middlesbrough	42	15	10	17	84	70	40
15	Wolves	42	15	10	17	77	76	40
16	Everton	42	13	13	16	89	89	39
17	Grimsby	42	17	5	20	65	73	39
18	WBA	42	16	6	20	89	88	38
19	Liverpool	42	13	12	17	60	64	38
20	Sheff Wed	42	13	12	17	63	77	38
21	Aston Villa	42	13	9	20	81	110	35
22	Blackburn	42	12	9	21	55	96	33

SECOND DIVISION

		P	W	D	L	F	A	Pts
1	Man United	42	22	12	8	85	43	56
2	Charlton	42	22	11	9	85	58	55
3	Sheff United	42	20	12	10	79	50	52
4	West Ham	42	22	8	12	90	68	52
5	Tottenham	42	18	13	11	91	55	49
6	Leicester	42	19	10	13	79	57	48
7	Plymouth	42	20	8	14	71	57	48
8	Newcastle	42	20	6	16	88	79	46
9	Fulham	42	15	14	13	76	52	44
10	Blackpool	42	18	7	17	93	72	43
11	Norwich	42	17	9	16	72	65	43
12	Bradford City	42	15	13	14	55	65	43
13	Swansea	42	15	9	18	67	76	39
14	Bury	42	13	12	17	66	84	38
15	Burnley	42	12	13	17	50	59	37
16	Bradford PA	42	14	9	19	62	84	37
17	Southampton	42	14	9	19	47	65	37
18	Doncaster	42	14	9	19	51	71	37
19	Nottm Forest	42	12	11	19	69	76	35
20	Barnsley	42	12	9	21	54	80	33
21	Port Vale	42	12	8	22	56	106	32
22	Hull	42	5	10	27	47	111	20

THIRD DIVISION (SOUTH)

		P	W	D	L	F	A	Pts
1	Coventry	42	24	9	9	102	45	57
2	Luton	42	22	12	8	81	45	56
3	Reading	42	26	2	14	87	62	54
4	QPR	42	22	9	11	84	53	53
5	Watford	42	20	9	13	80	54	49
6	Crystal Palace	42	22	5	15	96	74	49
7	Brighton	42	18	8	16	70	63	44
8	Bournemouth	42	16	11	15	60	56	43
9	Notts County	42	15	12	15	60	57	42
10	Torquay	42	16	9	17	62	62	41
11	Aldershot	42	14	12	16	53	61	40
12	Millwall	42	14	12	16	58	71	40
13	Bristol City	42	15	10	17	48	59	40
14	Clapton Orient	42	16	6	20	55	61	38
15	Northampton	42	15	8	19	62	90	38
16	Gillingham	42	14	9	19	66	77	37
17	Bristol Rovers	42	14	9	19	69	95	37
18	Southend	42	13	10	19	61	62	36
19	Swindon	42	14	8	20	64	73	36
20	Cardiff	42	13	10	19	60	73	36
21	Newport	42	11	9	22	60	111	31
22	Exeter	42	8	11	23	59	93	27

THIRD DIVISION (NORTH)

		P	W	D	L	F	A	Pts
1	Chesterfield	42	24	12	6	92	39	60
2	Chester	42	22	11	9	100	45	55
3	Tranmere	42	22	11	9	93	58	55
4	Lincoln	42	22	10	8	91	51	53
5	Stockport	42	20	8	14	65	49	48
6	Crewe	42	19	9	14	80	76	47
7	Oldham	42	18	9	15	86	73	45
8	Hartlepools	42	15	12	15	57	61	42
9	Accrington	42	17	8	17	63	72	42
10	Walsall	42	16	9	17	79	59	41
11	Rotherham	42	16	9	17	69	66	41
12	Darlington	42	17	6	19	74	79	40
13	Carlisle	42	14	12	16	56	62	40
14	Gateshead	42	13	14	15	56	76	40
15	Barrow	42	13	12	17	58	65	38
16	York	42	13	12	17	62	95	38
17	Halifax	42	15	7	20	57	61	37
18	Wrexham	42	15	7	20	66	75	37
19	Mansfield	42	14	9	19	80	91	37
20	Rochdale	42	10	13	19	58	88	33
21	Southport	42	11	9	22	48	90	31
22	New Brighton	42	9	6	27	43	102	24

SCOTTISH FIRST DIVISION

		P	W	D	L	F	A	Pts
1	Celtic	38	32	2	4	115	33	66
2	Rangers	38	27	7	4	110	43	61
3	Aberdeen	38	26	9	3	96	50	61
4	Motherwell	38	18	12	8	77	58	48
5	Hearts	38	20	7	11	88	55	47
6	Hamilton	38	15	7	16	77	74	37
7	St Johnstone	38	15	7	16	70	81	37
8	Kilmarnock	38	14	7	17	69	64	35
9	Partick	38	12	10	16	64	72	34
10	Dunfermline	38	13	8	17	73	92	34
11	Third Lanark	38	14	5	19	63	71	33
12	Arbroath	38	11	11	16	46	69	33
13	Dundee	38	11	10	17	67	80	32
14	Queen's Park	38	11	10	17	58	75	32
15	Queen of the S	38	11	9	18	54	72	31
16	Albion	38	13	4	21	69	92	30
17	Hibernian	38	11	7	20	56	82	29
18	Clyde	38	10	8	20	63	84	28
19	Airdrieonians	38	9	9	20	68	91	27
20	Ayr	38	11	3	24	53	98	25

SCOTTISH SECOND DIVISION

		P	W	D	L	F	A	Pts
1	Falkirk	34	28	3	3	132	34	59
2	St Mirren	34	25	2	7	114	41	52
3	Morton	34	21	6	7	117	60	48
4	Alloa	34	19	6	9	65	51	44
5	St Bernard's	34	18	4	12	106	78	40
6	East Fife	34	16	6	12	86	79	38
7	Dundee United	34	16	5	13	108	81	37
8	E Stirlingshire	34	13	8	13	70	75	34
9	Leith	34	15	3	16	67	77	33
10	Cowdenbeath	34	13	5	16	76	77	31
11	Stenhousemuir	34	13	3	18	59	78	29
12	Montrose	34	13	3	18	58	82	29
13	Forfar	34	10	7	17	60	81	27
14	King's Park	34	11	5	18	55	109	27
15	Edinburgh City	34	8	9	17	57	83	25
16	Brechin	34	8	6	20	57	96	22
17	Raith	34	9	3	22	60	96	21
18	Dumbarton	34	5	6	23	52	121	16

FA CUP 1935-36

FOURTH ROUND

Liverpool v Arsenal	0-2
Sheffield Wednesday v Newcastle United	1-1, 1-3
Tranmere Rovers v Barnsley	2-4
Stoke City v Manchester United	0-0, 2-0
Port Vale v Grimsby Town	0-4
Manchester City v Luton Town	2-1
Middlesbrough v Clapton Orient	3-0
Leicester City v Watford	6-3
Fulham v Blackpool	5-2
Chelsea v Plymouth Argyle	4-1
Bradford City v Blackburn Rovers	3-1
Derby County v Nottingham Forest	2-0
Preston North End v Sheffield United	0-0, 0-2
Leeds United v Bury	2-1*, 3-2
Tottenham Hotspur v Huddersfield Town	1-0
Bradford Park Avenue v West Bromwich Albion	1-1, 1-1, 2-0

*abandoned

FIFTH ROUND

Newcastle United v Arsenal	3-3, 0-3
Barnsley v Stoke City	2-1
Grimsby Town v Manchester City	3-2
Middlesbrough v Leicester City	2-1
Chelsea v Fulham	0-0, 2-3
Bradford City v Derby County	0-1
Sheffield United v Leeds United	3-1
Bradford Park Avenue v Tottenham Hotspur	0-0, 1-2

SIXTH ROUND

Arsenal v Barnsley	4-1
Grimsby Town v Middlesbrough	3-1
Fulham v Derby County	3-0
Sheffield United v Tottenham Hotspur	3-1

SEMI-FINAL

Arsenal v Grimsby Town	1-0
Fulham v Sheffield United	1-2

FINAL

Arsenal v Sheffield United	1-0

SCOTTISH FA CUP 1935-36

SECOND ROUND

Aberdeen v King's Park	6-0
Celtic v St Johnstone	1-2
Dalbeattie Star v St Mirren	0-1
Albion Rovers v Rangers	1-3
Clyde v Hibernian	4-1
Dundee v Airdrieonians	2-1
Cowdenbeath v Dundee United	5-3
Motherwell v St Bernard's	3-0
Falkirk v Kilmarnock	1-1, 3-1
Dunfermline Athletic v Galston	5-2
Morton v Stenhousemuir	3-0
Elgin City v Queen of the South	0-3
Third Lanark v Leith Athletic	2-0
Dumbarton	bye

THIRD ROUND

Aberdeen v St Johnstone	1-1, 1-0
St Mirren v Rangers	1-2
Clyde v Dundee	1-1, 3-0
Cowdenbeath v Motherwell	1-3
Morton v Queen of the South	2-0
Third Lanark v Dumbarton	8-0
Falkirk	bye
Dunfermline Athletic	bye

FOURTH ROUND

Aberdeen v Rangers	0-1
Clyde v Motherwell	3-2
Falkirk v Dunfermline Athletic	5-0
Morton v Third Lanark	3-5

SEMI-FINAL

Rangers v Clyde	3-0
Falkirk v Third Lanark	1-3

FINAL

Rangers v Third Lanark	1-0

The loneliness of long-distance football

On Good Friday, 10 April 1936, Swansea Town defeated Plymouth by two goals to one in a Second Division match at Home Park, Plymouth. The following day, Swansea met Newcastle at St James' Park, Newcastle, losing 2-0. Between the two games, Swansea travelled 400 miles, a record distance for a League club to travel between games played on consecutive days.

Footballing fatality

James Thorpe, Sunderland's goalkeeper, died a few days after his team had met Chelsea on 1 February 1936. His death was due to diabetes, but a coroner's jury found that the illness had been accelerated by rough usage of the goalkeeper. They criticized the referee (who was not called as a witness), and urged all referees to exercize stricter control. An FA commission later exonerated the referee, adding that he had acted totally in accordance with his instructions.

FIRST DIVISION

		P	W	D	L	F	A	Pts
1	Man City	42	22	13	7	107	61	57
2	Charlton	42	21	12	9	58	49	54
3	Arsenal	42	18	16	8	80	49	52
4	Derby	42	21	7	14	96	90	49
5	Wolves	42	21	5	16	84	67	47
6	Brentford	42	18	10	14	82	78	46
7	Middlesbrough	42	19	8	15	74	71	46
8	Sunderland	42	19	6	17	89	87	44
9	Portsmouth	42	17	10	15	62	66	44
10	Stoke	42	15	12	15	72	57	42
11	Birmingham	42	13	15	14	64	60	41
12	Grimsby	42	17	7	18	86	81	41
13	Chelsea	42	14	13	15	52	55	41
14	Preston	42	14	13	15	56	67	41
15	Huddersfield	42	12	15	15	62	64	39
16	WBA	42	16	6	20	77	98	38
17	Everton	42	14	9	19	81	78	37
18	Liverpool	42	12	11	19	62	84	35
19	Leeds	42	15	4	23	60	80	34
20	Bolton	42	10	14	18	43	66	34
21	Man United	42	10	12	20	55	78	32
22	Sheff Wed	42	9	12	21	53	69	30

SECOND DIVISION

		P	W	D	L	F	A	Pts
1	Leicester	42	24	8	10	89	57	56
2	Blackpool	42	24	7	11	88	53	55
3	Bury	42	22	8	12	74	55	52
4	Newcastle	42	22	5	15	80	56	49
5	Plymouth	42	18	13	11	71	53	49
6	West Ham	42	19	11	12	73	55	49
7	Sheff United	42	18	10	14	66	54	46
8	Coventry	42	17	11	14	66	54	45
9	Aston Villa	42	16	12	14	82	70	44
10	Tottenham	42	17	9	16	88	66	43
11	Fulham	42	15	13	14	71	61	43
12	Blackburn	42	16	10	16	70	62	42
13	Burnley	42	16	10	16	57	61	42
14	Barnsley	42	16	9	17	50	64	41
15	Chesterfield	42	16	8	18	84	89	40
16	Swansea	42	15	7	20	50	65	37
17	Norwich	42	14	8	20	63	71	36
18	Nottm Forest	42	12	10	20	68	90	34
19	Southampton	42	11	12	19	53	77	34
20	Bradford PA	42	12	9	21	52	88	33
21	Bradford City	42	9	12	21	54	94	30
22	Doncaster	42	7	10	25	30	84	24

THIRD DIVISION (NORTH)

		P	W	D	L	F	A	Pts
1	Stockport	42	23	14	5	84	39	60
2	Lincoln	42	25	7	10	103	57	57
3	Chester	42	22	9	11	87	57	53
4	Oldham	42	20	11	11	77	59	51
5	Hull	42	17	12	13	68	69	46
6	Hartlepools	42	19	7	16	75	69	45
7	Halifax	42	18	9	15	68	63	45
8	Wrexham	42	16	12	14	71	57	44
9	Mansfield	42	18	8	16	91	76	44
10	Carlisle	42	18	8	16	65	68	44
11	Port Vale	42	17	10	15	58	64	44
12	York	42	16	11	15	79	70	43
13	Accrington	42	16	9	17	76	69	41
14	Southport	42	12	13	17	73	87	37
15	New Brighton	42	13	11	18	55	70	37
16	Barrow	42	13	10	19	70	86	36
17	Rotherham	42	14	7	21	78	91	35
18	Rochdale	42	13	9	20	69	86	35
19	Tranmere	42	12	9	21	71	88	33
20	Crewe	42	10	12	20	55	83	32
21	Gateshead	42	11	10	21	63	98	32
22	Darlington	42	8	14	20	66	96	30

THIRD DIVISION (SOUTH)

		P	W	D	L	F	A	Pts
1	Luton	42	27	4	11	103	53	58
2	Notts County	42	23	10	9	74	52	56
3	Brighton	42	24	5	13	74	43	53
4	Watford	42	19	11	12	85	60	49
5	Reading	42	19	11	12	76	60	49
6	Bournemouth	42	20	9	13	65	59	49
7	Northampton	42	20	6	16	85	68	46
8	Millwall	42	18	10	14	64	54	46
9	QPR	42	18	9	15	73	52	45
10	Southend	42	17	11	14	78	67	45
11	Gillingham	42	18	8	16	52	66	44
12	Clapton Orient	42	14	15	13	52	52	43
13	Swindon	42	14	11	17	75	73	39
14	Crystal Palace	42	13	12	17	62	61	38
15	Bristol Rovers	42	16	4	22	71	80	36
16	Bristol City	42	15	6	21	58	70	36
17	Walsall	42	13	10	19	62	84	36
18	Cardiff	42	14	7	21	54	87	35
19	Newport	42	12	10	20	67	98	34
20	Torquay	42	11	10	21	57	80	32
21	Exeter	42	10	12	20	59	88	32
22	Aldershot	42	7	9	26	50	89	23

SCOTTISH FIRST DIVISION

		P	W	D	L	F	A	Pts
1	Rangers	38	26	9	3	88	32	61
2	Aberdeen	38	23	8	7	89	44	54
3	Celtic	38	22	8	8	89	58	52
4	Motherwell	38	22	7	9	96	54	51
5	Hearts	38	24	3	11	99	60	51
6	Third Lanark	38	20	6	12	79	61	46
7	Falkirk	38	19	6	13	98	66	44
8	Hamilton	38	18	5	15	91	96	41
9	Dundee	38	12	15	11	58	69	39
10	Clyde	38	16	6	16	59	70	38
11	Kilmarnock	38	14	9	15	60	70	37
12	St Johnstone	38	14	8	16	74	68	36
13	Partick	38	11	12	15	73	68	34
14	Arbroath	38	13	5	20	57	84	31
15	Queen's Park	38	9	12	17	51	77	30
16	St Mirren	38	11	7	20	68	81	29
17	Hibernian	38	6	13	19	54	83	25
18	Queen of the S	38	8	8	22	49	95	24
19	Dunfermline	38	5	11	22	65	98	21
20	Albion	38	5	6	27	53	116	16

SCOTTISH SECOND DIVISION

		P	W	D	L	F	A	Pts
1	Ayr	34	25	4	5	122	49	54
2	Morton	34	23	5	6	110	42	51
3	St Bernard's	34	22	4	8	102	51	48
4	Airdrieonians	34	18	8	8	85	60	44
5	East Fife	34	15	8	11	76	51	38
6	Cowdenbeath	34	14	10	10	75	59	38
7	E Stirlingshire	34	18	2	14	81	78	38
8	Raith	34	16	4	14	72	66	36
9	Alloa	34	13	7	14	64	65	33
10	Stenhousemuir	34	14	4	16	82	86	32
11	Leith	34	13	5	16	62	65	31
12	Forfar	34	11	8	15	73	89	30
13	Montrose	34	11	6	17	65	100	28
14	Dundee United	34	9	9	16	72	97	27
15	Dumbarton	34	11	5	18	57	83	27
16	Brechin	34	8	9	17	64	98	25
17	King's Park	34	11	3	20	61	106	25
18	Edinburgh City	34	2	3	29	42	120	7

Ted Harston of Mansfield Town set a record for goals scored in a season in Division Three North. In the 41 games he played during the season, Harston found the net 55 times.

On 30 January 1937, there was not one away win in all the 35 FA Cup and League matches played.

On 17 April 1937, 149,547 people watched Scotland beat England 3-1 at Hampden Park in the last match of the Home Championship. This was both a British and a world record attendance. The receipts totalled £24,303. Seven days later, at the same ground, 144,303 people paid £11,000 to watch Celtic triumph 2-1 over Aberdeen in the Scottish Cup final. Both the attendance and the receipts broke all previous records for the Scottish Cup final.

FA CUP 1936-37

FOURTH ROUND

Luton Town v Sunderland	2-2, 1-3
Swansea Town v York City	0-0, 3-1
Grimsby Town v Walsall	5-1
Wolverhampton Wanderers v Sheffield United	2-2, 2-1
Millwall v Chelsea	3-0
Derby County v Brentford	3-0
Bolton Wanderers v Norwich City	1-1, 2-1
Manchester City v Accrington Stanley	2-0
Tottenham Hotspur v Plymouth Argyle	1-0
Everton v Sheffield Wednesday	3-0
Preston North End v Stoke City	5-1
Exeter City v Leicester City	3-1
Coventry City v Chester	2-0
West Bromwich Albion v Darlington	3-2
Burnley v Bury	4-1
Arsenal v Manchester United	5-0

FIFTH ROUND

Sunderland v Swansea Town	3-0
Grimsby Town v Wolverhampton Wanderers	1-1, 2-6
Millwall v Derby County	2-1
Bolton Wanderers v Manchester City	0-5
Everton v Tottenham Hotspur	1-1, 3-4
Preston North End v Exeter City	5-3
Coventry City v West Bromwich Albion	2-3
Burnley v Arsenal	1-7

SIXTH ROUND

Wolverhampton Wanderers v Sunderland	1-1, 2-2, 0-4
Millwall v Manchester City	2-0
Tottenham Hotspur v Preston North End	1-3
West Bromwich Albion v Arsenal	3-1

SEMI-FINAL

Sunderland v Millwall	2-1
Preston North End v West Bromwich Albion	4-1

FINAL

Sunderland v Preston North End	3-1

SCOTTISH FA CUP 1936-37

SECOND ROUND

Inverness Caledonian v East Fife	1-6
Albion Rovers v Celtic	2-5
Duns v Dumbarton	2-0
Falkirk v Motherwell	0-3
St Mirren v Brechin City	1-0
Cowdenbeath v Solway Star	9-1
Clyde v St Johnstone	3-1
Dundee v Queen's Park	2-0
Hamilton Academicals v Hibernian	2-1
Heart of Midlothian v King's Park	15-0
Aberdeen v Third Lanark	4-2
Partick Thistle v Arbroath	4-1
Queen of the South v Airdrieonians	2-0
Morton	bye

THIRD ROUND

East Fife v Celtic	0-3
Duns v Motherwell	2-5
St Mirren v Cowdenbeath	1-0
Clyde v Dundee	0-0, 1-0
Hamilton Academicals v Heart of Midlothian	2-1
Morton v Partick Thistle	1-1, 2-1
Aberdeen	bye
Queen of the South	bye

FOURTH ROUND

Celtic v Motherwell	4-4, 2-1
St Mirren v Clyde	0-3
Hamilton Academicals v Aberdeen	1-2
Morton v Queen of the South	4-1

SEMI-FINAL

Celtic v Clyde	2-0
Aberdeen v Morton	2-0

FINAL

Celtic v Aberdeen	2-1

FIRST DIVISION

		P	W	D	L	F	A	Pts
1	Arsenal	42	21	10	11	77	44	52
2	Wolves	42	20	11	11	72	49	51
3	Preston	42	16	17	9	64	44	49
4	Charlton	42	16	14	12	65	51	46
5	Middlesbrough	42	19	8	15	72	65	46
6	Brentford	42	18	9	15	69	59	45
7	Bolton	42	15	15	12	64	60	45
8	Sunderland	42	14	16	12	55	57	44
9	Leeds	42	14	15	13	64	69	43
10	Chelsea	42	14	13	15	65	65	41
11	Liverpool	42	15	11	16	65	71	41
12	Blackpool	42	16	8	18	61	66	40
13	Derby	42	15	10	17	66	87	40
14	Everton	42	16	7	19	79	75	39
15	Huddersfield	42	17	5	20	55	68	39
16	Leicester	42	14	11	17	54	75	39
17	Stoke	42	13	12	17	58	59	38
18	Birmingham	42	10	18	14	58	62	38
19	Portsmouth	42	13	12	17	62	68	38
20	Grimsby	42	13	12	17	51	68	38
21	Man City	42	14	8	20	80	77	36
22	WBA	42	14	8	20	74	91	36

SECOND DIVISION

		P	W	D	L	F	A	Pts
1	Aston Villa	42	25	7	10	73	35	57
2	Man United	42	22	9	11	82	50	53
3	Sheff United	42	22	9	11	73	56	53
4	Coventry	42	20	12	10	66	45	52
5	Tottenham	42	19	6	17	76	54	44
6	Burnley	42	17	10	15	54	54	44
7	Bradford PA	42	17	9	16	69	56	43
8	Fulham	42	16	11	15	61	57	43
9	West Ham	42	14	14	14	53	52	42
10	Bury	42	18	5	19	63	60	41
11	Chesterfield	42	16	9	17	63	63	41
12	Luton	42	15	10	17	89	86	40
13	Plymouth	42	14	12	16	57	65	40
14	Norwich	42	14	11	17	56	75	39
15	Southampton	42	15	9	18	55	77	39
16	Blackburn	42	14	10	18	71	80	38
17	Sheff Wed	42	14	10	18	49	56	38
18	Swansea	42	13	12	17	45	73	38
19	Newcastle	42	14	8	20	51	58	36
20	Nottm Forest	42	14	8	20	47	60	36
21	Barnsley	42	11	14	17	50	64	36
22	Stockport	42	11	9	22	43	70	31

THIRD DIVISION (NORTH)

		P	W	D	L	F	A	Pts
1	Tranmere	42	23	10	9	81	41	56
2	Doncaster	42	21	12	9	74	49	54
3	Hull	42	20	13	9	80	43	53
4	Oldham	42	19	13	10	67	46	51
5	Gateshead	42	20	11	11	84	59	51
6	Rotherham	42	20	10	12	68	56	50
7	Lincoln	42	19	8	15	66	50	46
8	Crewe	42	18	9	15	71	53	45
9	Chester	42	16	12	14	77	72	44
10	Wrexham	42	16	11	15	58	63	43
11	York	42	16	10	16	70	68	42
12	Carlisle	42	15	9	18	57	67	39
13	New Brighton	42	15	8	19	60	61	38
14	Bradford City	42	14	10	18	66	69	38
15	Port Vale	42	12	14	16	65	73	38
16	Southport	42	12	14	16	53	82	38
17	Rochdale	42	13	11	18	67	78	37
18	Halifax	42	12	12	18	44	66	36
19	Darlington	42	11	10	21	54	79	32
20	Hartlepools	42	10	12	20	53	80	32
21	Barrow	42	11	10	21	41	71	32
22	Accrington	42	11	7	24	45	75	29

THIRD DIVISION (SOUTH)

		P	W	D	L	F	A	Pts
1	Millwall	42	23	10	9	83	37	56
2	Bristol City	42	21	13	8	68	40	55
3	QPR	42	22	9	11	80	47	53
4	Watford	42	21	11	10	73	43	53
5	Brighton	42	21	9	12	64	44	51
6	Reading	42	20	11	11	71	63	51
7	Crystal Palace	42	18	12	12	67	47	48
8	Swindon	42	17	10	15	49	49	44
9	Northampton	42	17	9	16	51	57	43
10	Cardiff	42	15	12	15	67	54	42
11	Notts County	42	16	9	17	50	50	41
12	Southend	42	15	10	17	70	68	40
13	Bournemouth	42	14	12	16	56	57	40
14	Mansfield	42	15	9	18	62	67	39
15	Bristol Rovers	42	13	13	16	46	61	39
16	Newport	42	11	16	15	43	52	38
17	Exeter	42	13	12	17	57	70	38
18	Aldershot	42	15	5	22	39	59	35
19	Clapton Orient	42	13	7	22	42	61	33
20	Torquay	42	9	12	21	38	73	30
21	Walsall	42	11	7	24	52	88	29
22	Gillingham	42	10	6	26	36	77	26

SCOTTISH FIRST DIVISION

		P	W	D	L	F	A	Pts
1	Celtic	38	27	7	4	114	42	61
2	Hearts	38	26	6	6	90	50	58
3	Rangers	38	18	13	7	75	49	49
4	Falkirk	38	19	9	10	82	52	47
5	Motherwell	38	17	10	11	78	69	44
6	Aberdeen	38	15	9	14	74	59	39
7	Partick	38	15	9	14	68	70	39
8	St Johnstone	38	16	7	15	78	81	39
9	Third Lanark	38	11	13	14	68	73	35
10	Hibernian	38	11	13	14	57	65	35
11	Arbroath	38	11	13	14	58	79	35
12	Queen's Park	38	11	12	15	59	74	34
13	Hamilton	38	13	7	18	81	76	33
14	St Mirren	38	14	5	19	58	66	33
15	Clyde	38	10	13	15	68	78	33
16	Queen of the S	38	11	11	16	58	71	33
17	Ayr	38	9	15	14	66	85	33
18	Kilmarnock	38	12	9	17	65	91	33
19	Dundee	38	13	6	19	70	74	32
20	Morton	38	6	3	29	64	127	15

SCOTTISH SECOND DIVISION

		P	W	D	L	F	A	Pts
1	Raith	34	27	5	2	142	54	59
2	Albion	34	20	8	6	97	50	48
3	Airdrieonians	34	21	5	8	100	53	47
4	St Bernard's	34	20	5	9	75	49	45
5	East Fife	34	19	5	10	104	61	43
6	Cowdenbeath	34	17	9	8	115	71	43
7	Dumbarton	34	17	5	12	85	66	39
8	Stenhousemuir	34	17	5	12	87	78	39
9	Dunfermline	34	17	5	12	82	76	39
10	Leith	34	16	5	13	71	56	37
11	Alloa	34	11	4	19	78	106	26
12	King's Park	34	11	4	19	64	96	26
13	E Stirlingshire	34	9	7	18	55	95	25
14	Dundee United	34	9	5	20	69	104	23
15	Forfar	34	8	6	20	67	100	22
16	Montrose	34	7	8	19	56	88	22
17	Edinburgh City	34	7	3	24	77	135	17
18	Brechin	34	5	2	27	53	139	12

During the season, Jimmy Richardson, the Millwall inside-right, appeared in all three divisions of the Football League, playing with Huddersfield, Newcastle and Millwall.

Raith Rovers, with 142 goals from 34 games, amassed the highest aggregate of goals in a League season in British League football. On their way to this record, they set another, by losing only two of their League matches, the fewest number in any post-1919 division.

The only Second Division Scottish club to win the Scottish Cup is East Fife, who achieved this distinction in 1937-38. East Fife, who had two players on loan because of injuries to their regular players, took part in five replays during the course of the competition. This included the final, when after a 1-1 draw, East Fife disposed of Kilmarnock by four goals to two.

FA CUP 1937-38

FOURTH ROUND
Preston North End v Leicester City	2-0
Wolverhampton Wanderers v Arsenal	1-2
Barnsley v Manchester United	2-2, 0-1
Brentford v Portsmouth	2-1
Manchester City v Bury	3-1
Luton Town v Swindon Town	2-1
Charlton Athletic v Leeds United	2-1
Aston Villa v Blackpool	4-0
Everton v Sunderland	0-1
Bradford Park Avenue v Stoke City	1-1, 2-1
Chesterfield v Burnley	3-2
New Brighton v Tottenham Hotspur	0-0, 2-5
York City v West Bromwich Albion	3-2
Nottingham Forest v Middlesbrough	1-3
Sheffield United v Liverpool	1-1, 0-1
Huddersfield Town v Notts County	1-0

FIFTH ROUND
Arsenal v Preston North End	0-1
Brentford v Manchester United	2-0
Luton Town v Manchester City	1-3
Charlton Athletic v Aston Villa	1-1, 2-2, 1-4
Sunderland v Bradford Park Avenue	1-0
Chesterfield v Tottenham Hotspur	2-2, 1-2
York City v Middlesbrough	1-0
Liverpool v Huddersfield Town	0-1

SIXTH ROUND
Brentford v Preston North End	0-3
Aston Villa v Manchester City	3-2
Tottenham Hotspur v Sunderland	0-1
York City v Huddersfield Town	0-0, 1-2

SEMI-FINAL
Preston North End v Aston Villa	2-1
Sunderland v Huddersfield Town	1-3

FINAL
Preston North End v Huddersfield Town	1-0

SCOTTISH FA CUP 1937-38

SECOND ROUND
Rangers v Queen of the South	3-1
Falkirk v St Mirren	3-2
Ross County v Albion Rovers	2-5
Larbert Amateurs v Morton	2-3
Queen's Park v Ayr United	1-1, 1-2
Celtic v Nithsdale Wanderers	5-0
St Bernard's v King's Park	1-1, 4-3
Stenhousemuir v Motherwell	1-1, 1-6
Hamilton Academicals v Forfar Athletic	5-1
Raith Rovers v Edinburgh City	9-2
Partick Thistle v Cowdenbeath	1-0
Aberdeen v St Johnstone	5-1
East Fife v Dundee United	5-0
Kilmarnock	bye

THIRD ROUND
Falkirk v Albion Rovers	4-0
Morton v Ayr United	1-1, 1-4
Celtic v Kilmarnock	1-2
Motherwell v Hamilton Academicals	2-0
Partick Thistle v Raith Rovers	1-2
East Fife v Aberdeen	1-1, 2-1
Rangers	bye
St Bernard's	bye

FOURTH ROUND
Falkirk v Rangers	1-2
Kilmarnock v Ayr United	1-1, 5-0
St Bernard's v Motherwell	3-1
East Fife v Raith Rovers	2-2, 3-2

SEMI-FINAL
Rangers v Kilmarnock	3-4
St Bernard's v East Fife	1-1, 1-1, 1-2

FINAL
Kilmarnock v East Fife	1-1, 2-4

FIRST DIVISION

		P	W	D	L	F	A	Pts
1	Everton	42	27	5	10	88	52	59
2	Wolves	42	22	11	9	88	39	55
3	Charlton	42	22	6	14	75	59	50
4	Middlesbrough	42	20	9	13	93	74	49
5	Arsenal	42	19	9	14	55	41	47
6	Derby	42	19	8	15	66	55	46
7	Stoke	42	17	12	13	71	68	46
8	Bolton	42	15	15	12	67	58	45
9	Preston	42	16	12	14	63	59	44
10	Grimsby	42	16	11	15	61	69	43
11	Liverpool	42	14	14	14	62	63	42
12	Aston Villa	42	15	11	16	71	60	41
13	Leeds	42	16	9	17	59	67	41
14	Man United	42	11	16	15	57	65	38
15	Blackpool	42	12	14	16	56	68	38
16	Sunderland	42	13	12	17	54	67	38
17	Portsmouth	42	12	13	17	47	70	37
18	Brentford	42	14	8	20	53	74	36
19	Huddersfield	42	12	11	19	58	64	35
20	Chelsea	42	12	9	21	64	80	33
21	Birmingham	42	12	8	22	62	84	32
22	Leicester	42	9	11	22	48	82	29

SECOND DIVISION

		P	W	D	L	F	A	Pts
1	Blackburn	42	25	5	12	94	60	55
2	Sheff United	42	20	14	8	69	41	54
3	Sheff Wed	42	21	11	10	88	59	53
4	Coventry	42	21	8	13	62	45	50
5	Man City	42	21	7	14	96	72	49
6	Chesterfield	42	20	9	13	69	52	49
7	Luton	42	22	5	15	82	66	49
8	Tottenham	42	19	9	14	67	62	47
9	Newcastle	42	18	10	14	61	48	46
10	WBA	42	18	9	15	89	72	45
11	West Ham	42	17	10	15	70	52	44
12	Fulham	42	17	10	15	61	55	44
13	Millwall	42	14	14	14	64	53	42
14	Burnley	42	15	9	18	50	56	39
15	Plymouth	42	15	8	19	49	55	38
16	Bury	42	12	13	17	65	74	37
17	Bradford PA	42	12	11	19	61	82	35
18	Southampton	42	13	9	20	56	82	35
19	Swansea	42	11	12	19	50	83	34
20	Nottm Forest	42	10	11	21	49	82	31
21	Norwich	42	13	5	24	50	91	31
22	Tranmere	42	6	5	31	39	99	17

FA CUP 1938-39

FOURTH ROUND

Portsmouth v West Bromwich Albion	2-0
West Ham United v Tottenham Hotspur	3-3, 1-1, 2-1
Preston North End v Aston Villa	2-0
Cardiff City v Newcastle United	0-0, 1-4
Leeds United v Huddersfield Town	2-4
Notts County v Walsall	0-0, 0-4
Middlesbrough v Sunderland	0-2
Blackburn Rovers v Southend United	4-2
Wolverhampton Wanderers v Leicester City	5-1
Liverpool v Stockport County	5-1
Everton v Doncaster Rovers	8-0
Birmingham v Chelmsford City	6-0
Chelsea v Fulham	3-0
Sheffield Wednesday v Chester	1-1, 1-1, 2-0
Sheffield United v Manchester City	2-0
Millwall v Grimsby Town	2-2, 2-3

FIFTH ROUND

Portsmouth v West Ham United	2-0
Newcastle United v Preston North End	1-2
Huddersfield Town v Walsall	3-0
Sunderland v Blackburn Rovers	1-1, 0-0, 0-1
Wolverhampton Wanderers v Liverpool	4-1
Birmingham v Everton	2-2, 1-2
Chelsea v Sheffield Wednesday	1-1, 0-0, 3-1
Sheffield United v Grimsby Town	0-0, 0-1

SIXTH ROUND

Portsmouth v Preston North End	1-0
Huddersfield Town v Blackburn Rovers	1-1, 2-1
Wolverhampton Wanderers v Everton	2-0
Chelsea v Grimsby Town	0-1

SEMI-FINAL

Portsmouth v Huddersfield Town	2-1
Wolverhampton Wanderers v Grimsby Town	5-0

FINAL

Portsmouth v Wolverhampton Wanderers	4-1

THIRD DIVISION (SOUTH)

		P	W	D	L	F	A	Pts
1	Newport	42	22	11	9	58	45	55
2	Crystal Palace	42	20	12	10	71	52	52
3	Brighton	42	19	11	12	68	49	49
4	Watford	42	17	12	13	62	51	46
5	Reading	42	16	14	12	69	59	46
6	QPR	42	15	14	13	68	49	44
7	Ipswich	42	16	12	14	62	52	44
8	Bristol City	42	16	12	14	61	63	44
9	Swindon	42	18	8	16	72	77	44
10	Aldershot	42	16	12	14	53	66	44
11	Notts County	42	17	9	16	59	54	43
12	Southend	42	16	9	17	61	64	41
13	Cardiff	42	15	11	16	61	65	41
14	Exeter	42	13	14	15	65	82	40
15	Bournemouth	42	13	13	16	52	58	39
16	Mansfield	42	12	15	15	44	62	39
17	Northampton	42	15	8	19	51	58	38
18	Port Vale	42	14	9	19	52	58	37
19	Torquay	42	14	9	19	54	70	37
20	Clapton Orient	42	11	13	18	53	55	35
21	Walsall	42	11	11	20	68	69	33
22	Bristol Rovers	42	10	13	19	55	61	33

THIRD DIVISION (NORTH)

		P	W	D	L	F	A	Pts
1	Barnsley	42	30	7	5	94	34	67
2	Doncaster	42	21	14	7	87	47	56
3	Bradford City	42	22	8	12	89	56	52
4	Southport	42	20	10	12	75	54	50
5	Oldham	42	22	5	15	76	59	49
6	Chester	42	20	9	13	88	70	49
7	Hull	42	18	10	14	83	74	46
8	Crewe	42	19	6	17	82	70	44
9	Stockport	42	17	9	16	91	77	43
10	Gateshead	42	14	14	14	74	67	42
11	Rotherham	42	17	8	17	64	64	42
12	Halifax	42	13	16	13	52	54	42
13	Barrow	42	16	9	17	66	65	41
14	Wrexham	42	17	7	18	66	79	41
15	Rochdale	42	15	9	18	92	82	39
16	New Brighton	42	15	9	18	68	73	39
17	Lincoln	42	12	9	21	66	92	33
18	Darlington	42	13	7	22	62	92	33
19	Carlisle	42	13	7	22	64	111	33
20	York	42	12	8	22	66	92	32
21	Hartlepools	42	12	7	23	55	94	31
22	Accrington	42	7	6	29	49	103	20

SCOTTISH FIRST DIVISION

		P	W	D	L	F	A	Pts
1	Rangers	38	25	9	4	112	55	59
2	Celtic	38	20	8	10	99	53	48
3	Aberdeen	38	20	6	12	91	61	46
4	Hearts	38	20	5	13	98	70	45
5	Falkirk	38	19	7	12	73	63	45
6	Queen of the S	38	17	9	12	69	64	43
7	Hamilton	38	18	5	15	67	71	41
8	St Johnstone	38	17	6	15	85	82	40
9	Clyde	38	17	5	16	78	70	39
10	Kilmarnock	38	15	9	14	73	86	39
11	Partick Thistle	38	17	4	17	74	87	38
12	Motherwell	38	16	5	17	82	86	37
13	Hibernian	38	14	7	17	68	69	35
14	Ayr	38	13	9	16	76	83	35
15	Third Lanark	38	12	8	18	80	96	32
16	Albion	38	12	6	20	65	90	30
17	Arbroath	38	11	8	19	54	75	30
18	St Mirren	38	11	7	20	57	80	29
19	Queen's Park	38	11	5	22	57	83	27
20	Raith	38	10	2	26	65	99	22

SCOTTISH SECOND DIVISION

		P	W	D	L	F	A	Pts
1	Cowdenbeath	34	28	4	2	120	45	60
2	Alloa	34	22	4	8	91	46	48
3	East Fife	34	21	6	7	99	61	48
4	Airdrieonians	34	21	5	8	85	57	47
5	Dunfermline	34	18	5	11	99	78	41
6	Dundee	34	15	7	12	99	63	37
7	St Bernard's	34	15	6	13	79	79	36
8	Stenhousemuir	34	15	5	14	74	69	35
9	Dundee United	34	15	3	16	78	69	33
10	Brechin	34	11	9	14	82	106	31
11	Dumbarton	34	9	12	13	68	76	30
12	Morton	34	11	6	17	74	88	28
13	King's Park	34	12	2	20	87	92	26
14	Montrose	34	10	5	19	82	96	25
15	Forfar	34	11	3	20	74	138	25
16	Leith	34	10	4	20	57	83	24
17	E Stirlingshire	34	9	4	21	89	130	22
18	Edinburgh	34	6	4	24	58	119	16

SCOTTISH FA CUP 1938-39

SECOND ROUND

Dundee v Clyde	0-0, 0-1
Rangers v Hamilton Academicals	2-0
Blairgowrie v Buckie Thistle	3-3, 1-4
Third Lanark v Cowdenbeath	3-0
Dunfermline Athletic v Duns	2-0
Hibernian v Kilmarnock	3-1
Falkirk v Airdrieonians	7-0
Aberdeen v Queen's Park	5-1
Queen of the South v Babcock & Wilcox	5-0
Heart of Midlothian v Elgin City	14-1
Montrose v Celtic	1-7
Edinburgh City v St Mirren	1-3
Dundee United v Motherwell	1-5
Alloa Athletic	bye

THIRD ROUND

Rangers v Clyde	1-4
Buckie Thistle v Third Lanark	0-6
Dunfermline Athletic v Alloa Athletic	1-1, 2-3
Falkirk v Aberdeen	2-3
Heart of Midlothian v Celtic	2-2, 1-2
Motherwell v St Mirren	4-2
Hibernian	bye
Queen of the South	bye

FOURTH ROUND

Clyde v Third Lanark	1-0
Hibernian v Alloa Athletic	3-1
Aberdeen v Queen of the South	2-0
Motherwell v Celtic	3-1

SEMI-FINAL

Clyde v Hibernian	1-0
Aberdeen v Motherwell	1-1, 1-3

FINAL

Clyde v Motherwell	4-0

Dixie Dean goes West

On 25 January 1939, Dixie Dean, the most prolific goalscorer of the time, left Notts County and English football to join Sligo Rovers in Eire. In April of that year, he played centre-forward for Sligo in the FA of Ireland Cup final against Shelbourne. The game ended in a 1-1 draw, and Sligo lost the replay 1-0.

1938-39 was the last season when players went unidentified. In 1939-40, players wore numbers in League games for the first time.

In Division Two, Tranmere Rovers lost 31 of their 42 League games, a Division Two record. Wolves set a First Division record in 1938-39 by conceding only 39 goals in 42 games, a record under the new offside rule. Barnsley also set a record—in Division Three North—letting in only 34 goals in 42 games.

The War Years

FIRST DIVISION 1939-40

	P	W	D	L	F	A	Pts
Blackpool	3	3	0	0	5	2	6
Sheff United	3	2	1	0	3	1	5
Arsenal	3	2	1	0	8	4	5
Liverpool	3	2	0	1	6	3	4
Everton	3	1	2	0	5	4	4
Bolton	3	2	0	1	6	5	4
Charlton	3	2	0	1	3	4	4
Derby	3	2	0	1	3	3	4
Man United	3	1	1	1	5	3	3
Chelsea	3	1	1	1	4	4	3
Stoke	3	1	1	1	7	4	3
Brentford	3	1	1	1	3	3	3
Leeds	3	1	1	1	2	4	3
Grimsby	3	1	1	1	2	4	3
Sunderland	3	1	0	2	6	7	2
Aston Villa	3	1	0	2	3	3	2
Wolverhampton	3	0	2	1	3	4	2
Huddersfield	3	1	0	2	2	3	2
Preston	3	0	2	1	0	2	2
Portsmouth	3	1	0	2	3	5	2
Blackburn	3	0	1	2	3	5	1
Middlesbrough	3	0	1	2	3	8	1

SECOND DIVISION 1939-40

	P	W	D	L	F	A	Pts
Luton	3	2	1	0	7	1	5
Birmingham	3	2	1	0	5	1	5
West Ham	3	2	0	1	5	4	4
Coventry	3	1	2	0	8	6	4
Leicester	3	2	0	1	6	5	4
Nottm Forest	3	2	0	1	5	5	4
Plymouth	3	2	0	1	4	3	4
Tottenham	3	1	2	0	6	5	4
WBA	3	1	1	1	8	8	3
Bury	3	1	1	1	4	5	3
Newport	3	1	1	1	5	4	3
Millwall	3	1	1	1	5	4	3
Man City	3	1	1	1	6	5	3
Southampton	3	1	0	2	5	6	2
Swansea	3	1	0	2	5	11	2
Barnsley	3	1	0	2	7	8	2
Chesterfield	2	1	0	1	2	2	2
Newcastle	3	1	0	2	8	6	2
Sheff Wed	3	1	0	2	3	5	2
Bradford	3	0	1	2	2	7	1
Fulham	3	0	1	2	3	6	1
Burnley	2	0	1	1	1	3	1

THIRD DIVISION (NORTH) 1939-40

	P	W	D	L	F	A	Pts
Accrington	3	3	0	0	6	1	6
Halifax	3	2	1	0	6	1	5
Darlington	3	2	1	0	5	2	5
Chester	3	2	1	0	5	2	5
Rochdale	3	2	0	1	2	2	4
New Brighton	3	2	0	1	4	5	4
Tranmere	3	1	1	1	6	6	3
Rotherham	3	1	1	1	5	6	3
Wrexham	3	1	1	1	3	2	3
Lincoln	3	1	1	1	6	7	3
Crewe	2	1	1	0	3	0	3
Oldham	3	1	0	2	3	5	2
Doncaster	3	1	0	2	4	5	2
Gateshead	3	1	0	2	6	7	2
Southport	3	0	2	1	4	5	2
Hull	2	0	2	0	3	3	2
Hartlepools	3	0	2	1	1	4	2
Barrow	3	0	2	1	4	5	2
Carlisle	2	1	0	1	3	3	2
York	3	0	1	2	3	5	1
Bradford City	3	0	1	2	3	6	1
Stockport	2	0	0	2	0	5	0

THIRD DIVISION (SOUTH) 1939-40

	P	W	D	L	F	A	Pts
Reading	3	2	1	0	8	2	5
Exeter	3	2	1	0	5	3	5
Cardiff	3	2	0	1	5	5	4
Crystal Palace	3	2	0	1	8	9	4
Brighton	3	1	2	0	5	4	4
Ipswich	3	1	2	0	5	3	4
Notts County	2	2	0	0	6	3	4
Southend	3	1	1	1	3	3	3
Bristol City	3	1	1	1	5	5	3
Clapton Orient	3	0	3	0	3	3	3
Mansfield	3	1	1	1	8	8	3
Norwich	3	1	1	1	4	4	3
Torquay	3	0	3	0	4	4	3
Bournemouth	3	1	1	1	13	4	3
Walsall	3	1	1	1	3	3	3
Northampton	3	1	0	2	2	12	2
QPR	3	0	2	1	4	5	2
Watford	3	0	2	1	4	5	2
Bristol Rovers	3	0	1	2	2	7	1
Port Vale	2	0	1	1	0	1	1
Aldershot	3	0	1	2	3	4	1
Swindon	3	0	1	2	2	4	1

SCOTTISH DIVISION 'A' 1939-40

	P	W	D	L	F	A	Pts
Rangers	5	4	1	0	14	3	9
Falkirk	5	4	0	1	20	10	8
Aberdeen	5	3	0	2	9	9	6
Celtic	5	3	0	2	7	7	6
Hearts	5	2	2	1	13	9	6
Partick Thistle	5	2	2	1	7	7	6
Motherwell	5	2	1	2	14	12	5
Hamilton	5	2	1	1	7	11	5
Third Lanark	5	2	1	2	9	8	5
Queen of the S	5	2	1	2	10	9	5
Albion	5	2	1	2	12	7	5
St Mirren	5	1	3	1	8	8	5
Kilmarnock	5	2	1	2	10	9	5
Hibernian	5	2	0	3	11	13	4
Alloa	5	2	0	3	8	13	4
Arbroath	5	2	0	3	9	9	4
St Johnstone	5	2	0	3	7	8	4
Ayr	5	2	0	3	10	17	4
Clyde	5	1	0	4	10	14	2
Cowdenbeath	5	1	0	4	6	14	2

SCOTTISH DIVISION 'B' 1939-40

	P	W	D	L	F	A	Pts
Dundee	4	3	1	0	13	5	7
Dunfermline	4	2	2	0	10	5	6
King's Park	4	2	2	0	11	7	6
East Fife	4	2	1	1	12	6	5
Queen's Park	4	1	3	0	7	5	5
Stenhousemuir	4	2	1	1	6	5	5
Dundee United	4	2	1	1	8	7	5
Dumbarton	4	2	1	1	9	9	5
E Stirlingshire	4	1	2	1	7	7	4
St Bernard's	4	1	2	1	7	7	4
Airdrieonians	4	2	0	2	7	8	4
Edinburgh	4	1	1	2	9	8	3
Montrose	4	1	1	2	7	8	3
Raith	4	1	1	2	8	12	3
Morton	4	1	1	2	4	7	3
Leith	4	1	0	3	4	7	2
Brechin	4	0	2	2	3	8	2
Forfar	4	0	0	4	7	18	0

WINNERS 1939-40

League Cup West Ham United
Midland League Wolverhampton Wanderers
North East League Huddersfield Town
North West League Bury
South 'A' League Arsenal
South 'B' League Queen's Park Rangers
South 'C' League Tottenham Hotspur
South 'D' League Crystal Palace
West League Stoke City
South West League Plymouth Argyle
East Midland League Chesterfield
Scottish Emergency Cup Rangers
Scottish Regional League West & South Rangers
Scottish Regional League East & North Falkirk
Irish FA Cup Ballymena United
FA of Ireland Cup (Eire) Shamrock Rovers
League of Ireland (Eire) St James' Gate

WINNERS 1940-41

League Cup Preston North End
Football League South Watford
Northern Regional League Preston North End
Southern Regional League Crystal Palace
London Cup Reading
Lancashire Cup Manchester United
Midland Cup Leicester City
Combined Cities Cup Middlesbrough
Western Regional Cup Bristol City
Scottish Southern League Cup Rangers
Scottish Summer Cup Hibernian
Scottish Southern League Rangers
Irish FA Cup Belfast Celtic
FA of Ireland Cup (Eire) Cork United
League of Ireland (Eire) Cork United

WINNERS 1941-42

League Cup Wolverhampton Wanderers
League North Blackpool
League South Leicester City
London Cup Brentford
London League Arsenal
Scottish Southern League Cup Rangers
Scottish Summer Cup Rangers
Scottish Southern League Rangers
Scottish North Eastern League 1st series Rangers
Scottish North Eastern League 2nd series Aberdeen
Irish FA Cup Linfield
FA of Ireland Cup (Eire) Dundalk
League of Ireland (Eire) Cork United

WINNERS 1942-43

League North Cup Blackpool
League North Blackpool
League South Cup Arsenal
League South Arsenal
League West Cup Swansea Town
League West Lovells Athletic
Scottish Southern League Cup Rangers
Scottish Summer Cup St Mirren
Scottish Southern League Rangers
Scottish North Eastern League 1st series Aberdeen
Scottish North Eastern League 2nd series Aberdeen
Irish FA Cup Belfast Celtic
FA of Ireland Cup (Eire) Drumcondra
League of Ireland (Eire) Cork United

WINNERS 1943-44

League North Cup Aston Villa
League North Blackpool
League South Cup Charlton Athletic
League South Tottenham Hotspur
League West Cup Bath City
League West Lovells Athletic
Scottish Southern League Cup Hibernian
Scottish Summer Cup Motherwell
Scottish Southern League Rangers
Scottish North Eastern League 1st series Raith Rovers
Scottish North Eastern League 2nd series Aberdeen
Irish FA Cup Belfast Celtic
FA of Ireland Cup (Eire) Shamrock Rovers
League of Ireland (Eire) Shelbourne

Above *When War broke out, the 1939-40 football season had hardly got under way. The tables above show the state of each division when the League programme was halted. Goal average has not been calculated, as at such an early stage in the season, the figures presented in these hitherto unpublished tables serve as a guide to each team's performance, rather than a means of listing the teams in order.*

The Englishman who played for Wales
Stanley Mortensen made his war-time international debut against his own country. At Wembley, on 25 September 1943, England played Wales. Mortensen was reserve for England, but when the injured Welsh left-half, Ivor Powell, was unable to resume after the interval, it was agreed by both sides that Mortensen should take Powell's place. The game ended in an 8-3 victory for England.

WINNERS 1944-45

- **League North Cup** Bolton Wanderers
- **League North** Huddersfield Town
- **League South Cup** Chelsea
- **League South** Tottenham Hotspur
- **League West Cup** Bath City
- **League West** Cardiff City
- **Scottish Southern League Cup** Rangers
- **Scottish Summer Cup** Partick Thistle
- **Scottish Southern League** Rangers
- **Scottish North Eastern League 1st series** Dundee
- **Scottish North Eastern League 2nd series** Aberdeen
- **Irish FA Cup** Linfield
- **FA of Ireland Cup (Eire)** Shamrock Rovers
- **League of Ireland (Eire)** Cork United

WINNERS 1945-46

- **League North** Sheffield United
- **League South** Birmingham City
- **League Three North Cup** Rotherham United
- **League Three North (West)** Accrington Stanley
- **League Three North (East)** Rotherham United
- **League Three South Cup** Bournemouth
- **League Three South (North)** Queen's Park Rangers
- **League Three South (South)** Crystal Palace
- **Scottish Southern League 'A'** Rangers
- **Scottish Southern League 'B'** Dundee
- **Scottish Victory Cup** Rangers
- **Irish FA Cup** Linfield
- **FA of Ireland Cup (Eire)** Drumcondra
- **League of Ireland (Eire)** Cork United

SCOTTISH SOUTHERN LEAGUE CUP 1945-46 (LEAGUE CUP)

SECTION WINNERS

Division A	Division B
1 Heart of Midlothian	1 East Fife
2 Rangers	2 Ayr United
3 Aberdeen	3 Airdrieonians
4 Clyde	4 Dundee

QUARTER-FINAL

Aberdeen v Ayr United	2-0
Airdrieonians v Clyde	1-0
Heart of Midlothian v East Fife	3-0
Rangers v Dundee	3-1

SEMI-FINAL

Aberdeen v Airdrieonians	2-2, 5-3
Rangers v Hearts	2-1

FINAL

Aberdeen v Rangers	3-2

LEADING GOALSCORERS (ENGLAND) 1939-46

Albert Stubbins, Newcastle United	226
Jock Dodds, Blackpool	221
Tommy Lawton, Everton, Tranmere Rovers, Aldershot and Chelsea	212

FA CUP 1945-46

THIRD ROUND (two legs)

Stoke City v Burnley	3-1, 1-2
Huddersfield Town v Sheffield United	1-1, 0-2
Mansfield Town v Sheffield Wednesday	0-0, 0-5
Chesterfield v York City	1-1, 2-3
Bolton Wanderers v Blackburn Rovers	1-0, 3-1
Chester v Liverpool	0-2, 1-3
Wrexham v Blackpool	1-4, 1-4
Leeds United v Middlesbrough	4-4, 2-7
Accrington Stanley v Manchester United	2-2, 1-5
Preston North End v Everton	2-1, 2-2
Charlton Athletic v Fulham	3-1, 1-2
Lovells Athletic v Wolverhampton Wanderers	2-4, 1-8
Southampton v Newport County	4-3, 2-1
Queen's Park Rangers v Crystal Palace	0-0, 0-0*, 1-0
Bristol City v Swansea Town	5-1, 2-2
Tottenham Hotspur v Brentford	2-2, 0-2
Chelsea v Leicester City	1-1, 2-0
West Ham United v Arsenal	6-0, 0-1
Northampton Town v Millwall	2-2, 0-3
Coventry City v Aston Villa	2-1, 0-2
Norwich City v Brighton	1-2, 1-4
Aldershot v Plymouth Argyle	2-0, 1-0
Luton Town v Derby County	0-6, 0-3
Cardiff City v West Bromwich Albion	1-1, 0-4
Newcastle United v Barnsley	4-2, 0-3
Rotherham United v Gateshead	2-2, 2-0
Bradford Park Avenue v Port Vale	2-1, 1-1
Manchester City v Barrow	6-2, 2-2
Grimsby Town v Sunderland	1-3, 1-2
Bury v Rochdale	3-3, 4-2
Birmingham City v Portsmouth	1-0, 0-0
Nottingham Forest v Watford	1-1, 1-1*, 0-1

*abandoned

FOURTH ROUND (two legs)

Stoke City v Sheffield United	2-0, 2-3
Sheffield Wednesday v York City	5-1, 6-1
Bolton Wanderers v Liverpool	5-0, 0-2
Blackpool v Middlesbrough	3-2, 2-3, 0-1
Manchester United v Preston North End	1-0, 1-3
Charlton Athletic v Wolverhampton Wanderers	5-2, 1-1
Southampton v Queen's Park Rangers	0-1, 3-4
Bristol City v Brentford	2-1, 0-5
Chelsea v West Ham United	2-0, 0-1
Millwall v Aston Villa	2-4, 1-9
Brighton v Aldershot	3-0, 4-1
Derby County v West Bromwich Albion	1-0, 3-1
Barnsley v Rotherham United	3-0, 1-2
Bradford Park Avenue v Manchester City	1-3, 8-2
Sunderland v Bury	3-1, 4-5
Birmingham City v Watford	5-0, 1-1

FIFTH ROUND (two legs)

Stoke City v Sheffield Wednesday	2-0, 0-0
Bolton Wanderers v Middlesbrough	1-0, 1-1
Preston North End v Charlton Athletic	1-1, 0-6
Queen's Park Rangers v Brentford	1-3, 0-0
Chelsea v Aston Villa	0-1, 0-1
Brighton v Derby County	1-4, 0-6
Barnsley v Bradford Park Avenue	0-1, 1-1
Sunderland v Birmingham City	1-0, 1-3

SIXTH ROUND (two legs)

Stoke City v Bolton Wanderers	0-2, 0-0
Charlton Athletic v Brentford	6-3, 3-1
Aston Villa v Derby County	3-4, 1-1
Bradford Park Avenue v Birmingham City	2-2, 0-6

SEMI-FINAL

Bolton Wanderers v Charlton Athletic	0-2
Derby County v Birmingham City	1-1, 4-0

FINAL

Derby County v Charlton Athletic	4-1

Top *In 1945 Jack Tinn, manager of Portsmouth, proudly shows Field Marshal Montgomery the FA Cup won by Portsmouth six years earlier. There was no FA Cup competition during the War, so Pompey held the Cup until the competition restarted in 1945-46.*

Above *A shot by Duncan, deflected by Charlton's Bert Turner, enters the net for Derby's first goal in the 1946 Cup Final. During this game, the ball burst. Oddly enough, the chances of this happening were discussed in a BBC broadcast shortly before* the game, and the referee, Mr E D Smith of Cumberland, remarked that it was a million-to-one chance. Even more curiously, the ball also burst when Derby played Charlton in a League match just five days after their Wembley meeting.

FIRST DIVISION

	P	W	D	L	F	A	Pts
1 Liverpool	42	25	7	10	84	52	57
2 Man United	42	22	12	8	95	54	56
3 Wolves	42	25	6	11	98	56	56
4 Stoke	42	24	7	11	90	53	55
5 Blackpool	42	22	6	14	71	70	50
6 Sheff United	42	21	7	14	89	75	49
7 Preston	42	18	11	13	76	74	47
8 Aston Villa	42	18	9	15	67	53	45
9 Sunderland	42	18	8	16	65	66	44
10 Everton	42	17	9	16	62	67	43
11 Middlesbrough	42	17	8	17	73	68	42
12 Portsmouth	42	16	9	17	66	60	41
13 Arsenal	42	16	9	17	72	70	41
14 Derby	42	18	5	19	73	79	41
15 Chelsea	42	16	7	19	69	84	39
16 Grimsby	42	13	12	17	61	82	38
17 Blackburn	42	14	8	20	45	53	36
18 Bolton	42	13	8	21	57	69	34
19 Charlton	42	11	12	19	57	71	34
20 Huddersfield	42	13	7	22	53	79	33
21 Brentford	42	9	7	26	45	88	25
22 Leeds	42	6	6	30	45	90	18

SECOND DIVISION

	P	W	D	L	F	A	Pts
1 Man City	42	26	10	6	78	35	62
2 Burnley	42	22	14	6	65	29	58
3 Birmingham	42	25	5	12	74	33	55
4 Chesterfield	42	18	14	10	58	44	50
5 Newcastle	42	19	10	13	95	62	48
6 Tottenham	42	17	14	11	65	53	48
7 WBA	42	20	8	14	88	75	48
8 Coventry	42	16	13	13	66	59	45
9 Leicester	42	18	7	17	69	64	43
10 Barnsley	42	17	8	17	84	86	42
11 Nottm Forest	42	15	10	17	69	74	40
12 West Ham	42	16	8	18	70	76	40
13 Luton	42	16	7	19	71	73	39
14 Southampton	42	15	9	18	69	76	39
15 Fulham	42	15	9	18	63	74	39
16 Bradford PA	42	14	11	17	65	77	39
17 Bury	42	12	12	18	80	78	36
18 Millwall	42	14	8	20	56	79	36
19 Plymouth	42	14	5	23	79	96	33
20 Sheff Wed	42	12	8	22	67	88	32
21 Swansea	42	11	7	24	55	83	29
22 Newport	42	10	3	29	61	133	23

THIRD DIVISION (NORTH)

	P	W	D	L	F	A	Pts
1 Doncaster	42	33	6	3	123	40	72
2 Rotherham	42	29	6	7	114	53	64
3 Chester	42	25	6	11	95	51	56
4 Stockport	42	24	2	16	78	53	50
5 Bradford City	42	20	10	12	62	47	50
6 Rochdale	42	19	10	13	80	64	48
7 Wrexham	42	17	12	13	65	51	46
8 Crewe	42	17	9	16	70	74	43
9 Barrow	42	17	7	18	54	62	41
10 Tranmere	42	17	7	18	66	77	41
11 Hull	42	16	8	18	49	53	40
12 Lincoln	42	17	5	20	86	87	39
13 Hartlepools	42	15	9	18	64	73	39
14 Gateshead	42	16	6	20	62	72	38
15 York	42	14	9	19	67	81	37
16 Carlisle	42	14	9	19	70	93	37
17 Darlington	42	15	6	21	68	80	36
18 New Brighton	42	14	8	20	57	77	36
19 Oldham	42	12	8	22	55	80	32
20 Accrington	42	14	4	24	56	92	32
21 Southport	42	7	11	24	53	85	25
22 Halifax	42	8	6	28	43	92	22

THIRD DIVISION (SOUTH)

	P	W	D	L	F	A	Pts
1 Cardiff	42	30	6	6	93	30	66
2 QPR	42	23	11	8	74	40	57
3 Bristol City	42	20	11	11	94	56	51
4 Swindon	42	19	11	12	84	73	49
5 Walsall	42	17	12	13	74	59	46
6 Ipswich	42	16	14	12	61	53	46
7 Bournemouth	42	18	8	16	72	54	44
8 Southend	42	17	10	15	71	60	44
9 Reading	42	16	11	15	83	74	43
10 Port Vale	42	17	9	16	68	63	43
11 Torquay	42	15	12	15	52	61	42
12 Notts County	42	15	10	17	63	63	40
13 Northampton	42	15	10	17	72	75	40
14 Bristol Rovers	42	16	8	18	59	69	40
15 Exeter	42	15	9	18	60	69	39
16 Watford	42	17	5	20	61	76	39
17 Brighton	42	13	12	17	54	72	38
18 Crystal Palace	42	13	11	18	49	62	37
19 Leyton Orient	42	12	8	22	54	75	32
20 Aldershot	42	10	12	20	48	78	32
21 Norwich	42	10	8	24	64	100	28
22 Mansfield	42	9	10	23	48	96	28

SCOTTISH DIVISION 'A'

	P	W	D	L	F	A	Pts
1 Rangers	30	21	4	5	76	26	46
2 Hibernian	30	19	6	5	69	33	44
3 Aberdeen	30	16	7	7	58	41	39
4 Hearts	30	16	6	8	52	43	38
5 Partick Thistle	30	16	3	11	74	59	35
6 Morton	30	12	10	8	58	45	34
7 Celtic	30	13	6	11	53	55	32
8 Motherwell	30	12	5	13	58	54	29
9 Third Lanark	30	11	6	13	56	64	28
10 Clyde	30	9	9	12	55	65	27
11 Falkirk	30	8	10	12	62	61	26
12 Queen of the S	30	9	8	13	44	69	26
13 Queen's Park	30	8	6	16	47	60	22
14 St Mirren	30	9	4	17	47	65	22
15 Kilmarnock	30	6	9	15	44	66	21
16 Hamilton	30	2	7	21	38	85	11

SCOTTISH DIVISION 'B'

	P	W	D	L	F	A	Pts
1 Dundee	26	21	3	2	113	30	45
2 Airdrieonians	26	19	4	3	78	38	42
3 East Fife	26	12	7	7	58	39	31
4 Albion	26	10	7	9	50	54	27
5 Alloa	26	11	5	10	51	57	27
6 Raith	26	10	6	10	45	52	26
7 Stenhousemuir	26	8	7	11	43	53	23
8 Dunfermline	26	10	3	13	50	72	23
9 St Johnstone	26	9	4	13	45	47	22
10 Dundee United	26	9	4	13	53	60	22
11 Ayr	26	9	2	15	56	73	20
12 Arbroath	26	7	6	13	42	63	20
13 Dumbarton	26	7	4	15	41	54	18
14 Cowdenbeath	26	6	6	14	44	77	18

FA CUP 1946-47

FOURTH ROUND

West Bromwich Albion v Charlton Athletic	1-2
Blackburn Rovers v Port Vale	2-0
Preston North End v Barnsley	6-0
Sheffield Wednesday v Everton	2-1
Newcastle United v Southampton	3-1
Brentford v Leicester City	0-0, 0-0, 1-4
Wolverhampton Wanderers v Sheffield United	0-0, 0-2
Chester v Stoke City	0-0, 2-3
Burnley v Coventry City	2-0
Luton Town v Swansea Town	2-0
Middlesbrough v Chesterfield	2-1
Manchester United v Nottingham Forest	0-2
Liverpool v Grimsby Town	2-0
Chelsea v Derby County	2-2, 0-1
Birmingham City v Portsmouth	1-0
Bolton Wanderers v Manchester City	3-3, 0-1

FIFTH ROUND

Charlton Athletic v Blackburn Rovers	1-0
Sheffield Wednesday v Preston North End	0-2
Newcastle United v Leicester City	1-1, 2-1
Stoke City v Sheffield United	0-1
Luton Town v Burnley	0-0, 0-3
Nottingham Forest v Middlesbrough	2-2, 2-6
Liverpool v Derby County	1-0
Birmingham City v Manchester City	5-0

SIXTH ROUND

Charlton Athletic v Preston North End	2-1
Sheffield United v Newcastle United	0-2
Middlesbrough v Burnley	1-1, 0-1
Liverpool v Birmingham City	4-1

SEMI-FINAL

Charlton Athletic v Newcastle United	4-0
Burnley v Liverpool	0-0, 1-0

FINAL

Charlton Athletic v Burnley	1-0

SCOTTISH FA CUP 1946-47

SECOND ROUND

Aberdeen v Ayr United	8-0
East Fife v East Stirlingshire	5-1
Morton	bye
Dundee	bye
Albion Rovers	bye
Arbroath	bye
Raith Rovers	bye
Heart of Midlothian	bye
Cowdenbeath	bye
Hibernian	bye
Rangers	bye
Dumbarton	bye
Third Lanark	bye
Motherwell	bye
Falkirk	bye
Queen's Park	bye

THIRD ROUND

Morton v Aberdeen	1-1, 1-2
Dundee v Albion Rovers	3-0
Arbroath v Raith Rovers	5-4
Heart of Midlothian v Cowdenbeath	2-0
Rangers v Hibernian	0-0, 0-2
Dumbarton v Third Lanark	2-0
Falkirk v Motherwell	0-0, 0-1
East Fife v Queen's Park	3-1

FOURTH ROUND

Dundee v Aberdeen	1-2
Arbroath v Heart of Midlothian	2-1
Hibernian v Dumbarton	2-0
East Fife v Motherwell	0-2

SEMI-FINAL

Aberdeen v Arbroath	2-0
Hibernian v Motherwell	2-0

FINAL

Aberdeen v Hibernian	2-1

When Italy beat Hungary 3-2 on 11 May 1947, a record ten members of the victorious Italian team came from Juventus.

Hull City used 42 players in the Third Division North, 1946-47. This was only the third time in the history of the League that such a large pool of players had been used in one season by a single club.

Cardiff equalled a Division Three South record by winning 30 of their 42 matches. By contrast, Leeds set a First Division record by losing 30 of their 42 matches.

Doncaster Rovers enjoyed an enormously successful season in winning the Third Division North championship in 1946-47. They set four League records during the course of the season. Their points total (72) was the highest number of points ever won by a club in any division of the League; that total included 37 points won away from home, also a League record. By winning 18 of their 21 away games, Doncaster established a third League record, for the most games won away from home and, in all, Doncaster Rovers won 33 of their 42 Division Three North games to set another League record. They also equalled the record for the division by losing just three matches during the season.

FIRST DIVISION

		P	W	D	L	F	A	Pts
1	Arsenal	42	23	13	6	81	32	59
2	Man United	42	19	14	9	81	48	52
3	Burnley	42	20	12	10	56	43	52
4	Derby	42	19	12	11	77	57	50
5	Wolves	42	19	9	14	83	70	47
6	Aston Villa	42	19	9	14	65	57	47
7	Preston	42	20	7	15	67	68	47
8	Portsmouth	42	19	7	16	68	50	45
9	Blackpool	42	17	10	15	57	41	44
10	Man City	42	15	12	15	52	47	42
11	Liverpool	42	16	10	16	65	61	42
12	Sheff United	42	16	10	16	65	70	42
13	Charlton	42	17	6	19	57	66	40
14	Everton	42	17	6	19	52	66	40
15	Stoke	42	14	10	18	41	55	38
16	Middlesbrough	42	14	9	19	71	73	37
17	Bolton	42	16	5	21	46	58	37
18	Chelsea	42	14	9	19	53	71	37
19	Huddersfield	42	12	12	18	51	60	36
20	Sunderland	42	13	10	19	56	67	36
21	Blackburn	42	11	10	21	54	72	32
22	Grimsby	42	8	6	28	45	111	22

SECOND DIVISION

		P	W	D	L	F	A	Pts
1	Birmingham	42	22	15	5	55	24	59
2	Newcastle	42	24	8	10	72	41	56
3	Southampton	42	21	10	11	71	53	52
4	Sheff Wed	42	20	11	11	66	53	51
5	Cardiff	42	18	11	13	61	58	47
6	West Ham	42	16	14	12	55	53	46
7	WBA	42	18	9	15	63	58	45
8	Tottenham	42	15	14	13	56	43	44
9	Leicester	42	16	11	15	60	57	43
10	Coventry	42	14	13	15	59	52	41
11	Fulham	42	15	10	17	47	46	40
12	Barnsley	42	15	10	17	62	64	40
13	Luton	42	14	12	16	56	59	40
14	Bradford PA	42	16	8	18	68	72	40
15	Brentford	42	13	14	15	44	61	40
16	Chesterfield	42	16	7	19	54	55	39
17	Plymouth	42	9	20	13	40	58	38
18	Leeds	42	14	8	20	62	72	36
19	Nottm Forest	42	12	11	19	54	60	35
20	Bury	42	9	16	17	58	68	34
21	Doncaster	42	9	11	22	40	66	29
22	Millwall	42	9	11	22	44	74	29

FA CUP 1947-48

FOURTH ROUND

Queen's Park Rangers v Stoke City	3-0
Luton Town v Coventry City	3-2
Brentford v Middlesbrough	1-2
Crewe Alexandra v Derby County	0-3
Manchester United v Liverpool	3-0
Charlton Athletic v Stockport County	3-0
Manchester City v Chelsea	2-0
Portsmouth v Preston North End	1-3
Fulham v Bristol Rovers	5-2
Wolverhampton Wanderers v Everton	1-1, 2-3
Blackpool v Chester	4-0
Colchester United v Bradford Park Avenue	3-2
Southampton v Blackburn Rovers	3-2
Swindon Town v Notts County	1-0
Tottenham Hotspur v West Bromwich Albion	3-1
Leicester City v Sheffield Wednesday	2-1

FIFTH ROUND

Queen's Park Rangers v Luton Town	3-1
Middlesbrough v Derby County	1-2
Manchester United v Charlton Athletic	2-0
Manchester City v Preston North End	0-1
Fulham v Everton	1-1, 1-0
Blackpool v Colchester United	5-0
Southampton v Swindon Town	3-0
Tottenham Hotspur v Leicester City	5-2

SIXTH ROUND

Queen's Park Rangers v Derby County	1-1, 0-5
Manchester United v Preston North End	4-1
Fulham v Blackpool	0-2
Southampton v Tottenham Hotspur	0-1

SEMI-FINAL

Derby County v Manchester United	1-3
Blackpool v Tottenham Hotspur	3-1

FINAL

Manchester United v Blackpool	4-2

THIRD DIVISION (SOUTH)

		P	W	D	L	F	A	Pts
1	QPR	42	26	9	7	74	37	61
2	Bournemouth	42	24	9	9	76	35	57
3	Walsall	42	21	9	12	70	40	51
4	Ipswich	42	23	3	16	67	61	49
5	Swansea	42	18	12	12	70	52	48
6	Notts County	42	19	8	15	68	59	46
7	Bristol City	42	18	7	17	77	65	43
8	Port Vale	42	16	11	15	63	54	43
9	Southend	42	15	13	14	51	58	43
10	Reading	42	15	11	16	56	58	41
11	Exeter	42	15	11	16	55	63	41
12	Newport	42	14	13	15	61	73	41
13	Crystal Palace	42	13	13	16	49	49	39
14	Northampton	42	14	11	17	58	72	39
15	Watford	42	14	10	18	57	79	38
16	Swindon	42	10	16	16	41	46	36
17	Leyton Orient	42	13	10	19	51	73	36
18	Torquay	42	11	13	18	63	62	35
19	Aldershot	42	10	15	17	45	67	35
20	Bristol Rovers	42	13	8	21	71	75	34
21	Norwich	42	13	8	21	61	76	34
22	Brighton	42	11	12	19	43	73	34

THIRD DIVISION (NORTH)

		P	W	D	L	F	A	Pts
1	Lincoln	42	26	8	8	81	40	60
2	Rotherham	42	25	9	8	95	49	59
3	Wrexham	42	21	8	13	74	54	50
4	Gateshead	42	19	11	12	75	57	49
5	Hull	42	18	11	13	59	48	47
6	Accrington	42	20	6	16	62	59	46
7	Barrow	42	16	13	13	49	40	45
8	Mansfield	42	17	11	14	57	51	45
9	Carlisle	42	18	7	17	88	77	43
10	Crewe	42	18	7	17	61	63	43
11	Oldham	42	14	13	15	63	64	41
12	Rochdale	42	15	11	16	48	72	41
13	York	42	13	14	15	65	60	40
14	Bradford City	42	15	10	17	65	66	40
15	Southport	42	14	11	17	60	63	39
16	Darlington	42	13	13	16	54	70	39
17	Stockport	42	13	12	17	63	67	38
18	Tranmere	42	16	4	22	54	72	36
19	Hartlepools	42	14	8	20	51	73	36
20	Chester	42	13	9	20	64	67	35
21	Halifax	42	7	13	22	43	76	27
22	New Brighton	42	8	9	25	38	81	25

SCOTTISH FA CUP 1947-48

SECOND ROUND

Rangers v Leith Athletic	4-0
Partick Thistle v Dundee United	4-3
East Fife v St Johnstone	5-1
Peterhead v Dumbarton	1-2
Hibernian v Arbroath	4-0
Nithsdale Wanderers v Aberdeen	0-5
St Mirren v East Stirlingshire	2-0
Clyde v Dunfermline Athletic	2-1
Morton v Falkirk	3-2
Queen's Park v Deveronvale	8-2
Airdrieonians v Heart of Midlothian	2-1
Stirling Albion v Raith Rovers	2-4
Celtic v Cowdenbeath	3-0
Motherwell v Third Lanark	1-0
Montrose v Duns	2-0
Alloa Athletic v Queen of the South	0-1

THIRD ROUND

Rangers v Partick Thistle	3-0
Dumbarton v East Fife	0-1
Hibernian v Aberdeen	4-2
St Mirren v Clyde	2-1
Morton v Queen's Park	3-0
Airdrieonians v Raith Rovers	3-0
Celtic v Motherwell	1-0
Montrose v Queen of the South	2-1

FOURTH ROUND

Rangers v East Fife	1-0
Hibernian v St Mirren	3-1
Airdrieonians v Morton	0-3
Celtic v Montrose	4-0

SEMI-FINAL

Rangers v Hibernian	1-0
Morton v Celtic	1-0

FINAL

Rangers v Morton	1-1, 1-0

SCOTTISH DIVISION 'A'

		P	W	D	L	F	A	Pts
1	Hibernian	30	22	4	4	86	27	48
2	Rangers	30	21	4	5	64	28	46
3	Partick	30	16	4	10	61	42	36
4	Dundee	30	15	3	12	67	51	33
5	St Mirren	30	13	5	12	54	58	31
6	Clyde	30	12	7	11	52	57	31
7	Falkirk	30	10	10	10	55	48	30
8	Motherwell	30	13	3	14	45	47	29
9	Hearts	30	10	8	12	37	42	28
10	Aberdeen	30	10	7	13	45	45	27
11	Third Lanark	30	10	6	14	56	73	26
12	Celtic	30	10	5	15	41	56	25
13	Queen of the S	30	10	5	15	49	74	25
14	Morton	30	9	6	15	47	43	24
15	Airdrieonians	30	7	7	16	39	78	21
16	Queen's Park	30	9	2	19	45	75	20

SCOTTISH DIVISION 'B'

		P	W	D	L	F	A	Pts
1	East Fife	30	25	3	2	103	36	53
2	Albion	30	19	4	7	58	49	42
3	Hamilton	30	17	6	7	75	45	40
4	Raith	30	14	6	10	83	66	34
5	Cowdenbeath	30	12	8	10	56	53	32
6	Kilmarnock	30	13	4	13	72	62	30
7	Dunfermline	30	13	3	14	72	71	29
8	Stirling	30	11	6	13	85	66	28
9	St Johnstone	30	11	5	14	69	63	27
10	Ayr	30	9	9	12	59	61	27
11	Dumbarton	30	9	7	14	66	79	25
12	Alloa	30	10	6	14	53	77	24*
13	Arbroath	30	10	3	17	55	62	23
14	Stenhousemuir	30	6	11	13	53	83	23
15	Dundee United	30	10	2	18	58	88	22
16	Leith	30	6	7	17	45	84	19

*Two points deducted for fielding unregistered players.

In the 1947-48 FA Cup, Manchester United were drawn in turn against six Division One clubs. This was the first instance of this happening to any club. The teams United met were, in order, Aston Villa, Liverpool, Charlton Athletic, Preston North End, and Blackpool, whom they beat 4-2 in the Final.

Quick off the mark
William Sharp, of Partick Thistle, scored against Queen of the South just seven seconds after the Scottish Division 'A' match had kicked off on 20 December 1947.

Tommy Lawton became the first Third Division player since World War Two to represent England in the International Championship. Lawton, of Notts County, played at centre-forward in England's 2-0 win over Scotland at Hampden Park on 10 April 1948.

In January 1948, 83,260 people watched Manchester United play Arsenal in a First Division match at Maine Road, Manchester. This was a record for a League match.

FIRST DIVISION

		P	W	D	L	F	A	Pts
1	Portsmouth	42	25	8	9	84	42	58
2	Man United	42	21	11	10	77	44	53
3	Derby	42	22	9	11	74	55	53
4	Newcastle	42	20	12	10	70	56	52
5	Arsenal	42	18	13	11	74	44	49
6	Wolves	42	17	12	13	79	66	46
7	Man City	42	15	15	12	47	51	45
8	Sunderland	42	13	17	12	49	58	43
9	Charlton	42	15	12	15	63	67	42
10	Aston Villa	42	16	10	16	60	76	42
11	Stoke	42	16	9	17	66	68	41
12	Liverpool	42	13	14	15	53	43	40
13	Chelsea	42	12	14	16	69	68	38
14	Bolton	42	14	10	18	59	68	38
15	Burnley	42	12	14	16	43	50	38
16	Blackpool	42	11	16	15	54	67	38
17	Birmingham	42	11	15	16	36	38	37
18	Everton	42	13	11	18	41	63	37
19	Middlesbrough	42	11	12	19	46	57	34
20	Huddersfield	42	12	10	20	40	69	34
21	Preston	42	11	11	20	62	75	33
22	Sheff United	42	11	11	20	57	78	33

SECOND DIVISION

		P	W	D	L	F	A	Pts
1	Fulham	42	24	9	9	77	37	57
2	WBA	42	24	8	10	69	39	56
3	Southampton	42	23	9	10	69	36	55
4	Cardiff	42	19	13	10	62	47	51
5	Tottenham	42	17	16	9	72	44	50
6	Chesterfield	42	15	17	10	51	45	47
7	West Ham	42	18	10	14	56	58	46
8	Sheff Wed	42	15	13	14	63	56	43
9	Barnsley	42	14	12	16	62	61	40
10	Luton	42	14	12	16	55	57	40
11	Grimsby	42	15	10	17	72	76	40
12	Bury	42	17	6	19	67	76	40
13	QPR	42	14	11	17	44	62	39
14	Blackburn	42	15	8	19	53	63	38
15	Leeds	42	12	13	17	55	63	37
16	Coventry	42	15	7	20	55	64	37
17	Bradford PA	42	13	11	18	65	78	37
18	Brentford	42	11	14	17	42	53	36
19	Leicester	42	10	16	16	62	79	36
20	Plymouth	42	12	12	18	49	64	36
21	Nottm Forest	42	14	7	21	50	54	35
22	Lincoln	42	8	12	22	53	91	28

THIRD DIVISION (SOUTH)

		P	W	D	L	F	A	Pts
1	Swansea	42	27	8	7	87	34	62
2	Reading	42	25	5	12	77	50	55
3	Bournemouth	42	22	8	12	69	48	52
4	Swindon	42	18	15	9	64	56	51
5	Bristol Rovers	42	19	10	13	61	51	48
6	Brighton	42	15	18	9	55	55	48
7	Ipswich	42	18	9	15	78	77	45
8	Millwall	42	17	11	14	63	64	45
9	Torquay	42	17	11	14	65	70	45
10	Norwich	42	16	12	14	67	49	44
11	Notts County	42	19	5	18	102	68	43
12	Exeter	42	15	10	17	63	76	40
13	Port Vale	42	14	11	17	51	54	39
14	Walsall	42	15	8	19	56	64	38
15	Newport	42	14	9	19	68	92	37
16	Bristol City	42	11	14	17	44	62	36
17	Watford	42	10	15	17	41	54	35
18	Southend	42	9	16	17	41	46	34
19	Leyton Orient	42	11	12	19	58	80	34
20	Northampton	42	12	9	21	51	62	33
21	Aldershot	42	11	11	20	48	59	33
22	Crystal Palace	42	8	11	23	38	76	27

THIRD DIVISION (NORTH)

		P	W	D	L	F	A	Pts
1	Hull	42	27	11	4	93	28	65
2	Rotherham	42	28	6	8	90	46	62
3	Doncaster	42	20	10	12	53	40	50
4	Darlington	42	20	6	16	83	74	46
5	Gateshead	42	16	13	13	69	58	45
6	Oldham	42	18	9	15	75	67	45
7	Rochdale	42	18	9	15	55	53	45
8	Stockport	42	16	11	15	61	56	43
9	Wrexham	42	17	9	16	56	62	43
10	Mansfield	42	14	14	14	52	48	42
11	Tranmere	42	13	15	14	46	57	41
12	Crewe	42	16	9	17	52	74	41
13	Barrow	42	14	12	16	41	48	40
14	York	42	15	9	18	74	74	39
15	Carlisle	42	14	11	17	60	77	39
16	Hartlepools	42	14	10	18	45	58	38
17	New Brighton	42	14	8	20	46	58	36
18	Chester	42	11	13	18	57	56	35
19	Halifax	42	12	11	19	45	62	35
20	Accrington	42	12	10	20	55	64	34
21	Southport	42	11	9	22	45	64	31
22	Bradford City	42	10	9	23	48	77	29

SCOTTISH DIVISION 'A'

		P	W	D	L	F	A	Pts
1	Rangers	30	20	6	4	63	32	46
2	Dundee	30	20	5	5	71	48	45
3	Hibernian	30	17	5	8	75	52	39
4	East Fife	30	16	3	11	64	46	35
5	Falkirk	30	12	8	10	70	54	32
6	Celtic	30	12	7	11	48	40	31
7	Third Lanark	30	13	5	12	56	52	31
8	Hearts	30	12	6	12	64	54	30
9	St Mirren	30	13	4	13	51	47	30
10	Queen of the S	30	11	8	11	47	53	30
11	Partick	30	9	9	12	50	63	27
12	Motherwell	30	10	5	15	44	49	25
13	Aberdeen	30	7	11	12	39	48	25
14	Clyde	30	9	6	15	50	67	24
15	Morton	30	7	8	15	39	51	22
16	Albion	30	3	2	25	30	105	8

SCOTTISH DIVISION 'B'

		P	W	D	L	F	A	Pts
1	Raith	30	20	2	8	80	44	42
2	Stirling	30	20	2	8	71	47	42
3	Airdrieonians	30	16	9	5	76	42	41
4	Dunfermline	30	16	9	5	80	58	41
5	Queen's Park	30	14	7	9	66	49	35
6	St Johnstone	30	14	4	12	58	51	32
7	Arbroath	30	12	8	10	62	56	32
8	Dundee United	30	10	7	13	60	67	27
9	Ayr	30	10	7	13	51	70	27
10	Hamilton	30	9	8	13	48	57	26
11	Kilmarnock	30	9	7	14	58	61	25
12	Stenhousemuir	30	8	8	14	50	54	24
13	Cowdenbeath	30	9	5	16	53	58	23
14	Alloa	30	10	3	17	42	85	23
15	Dumbarton	30	8	6	16	52	79	22
16	E Stirlingshire	30	6	6	18	38	67	18

FA CUP 1948-49

FOURTH ROUND

Manchester United v Bradford Park Avenue	1-1, 1-1, 5-0
Yeovil Town v Sunderland	2-1
Hull City v Grimsby Town	3-2
Stoke City v Blackpool	1-1, 1-0
Wolverhampton Wanderers v Sheffield United	3-0
Liverpool v Notts County	1-0
West Bromwich Albion v Gateshead	3-1
Chelsea v Everton	2-0
Leicester City v Preston North End	2-0
Luton Town v Walsall	4-0
Brentford v Torquay United	1-0
Burnley v Rotherham United	1-0
Portsmouth v Sheffield Wednesday	2-1
Newport County v Huddersfield Town	3-3, 3-1
Derby County v Arsenal	1-0
Cardiff City v Aston Villa	2-1

FIFTH ROUND

Manchester United v Yeovil Town	8-0
Hull City v Stoke City	2-0
Wolverhampton Wanderers v Liverpool	3 1
West Bromwich Albion v Chelsea	3 0
Leicester City v Luton Town	5 5 5 3
Brentford v Burnley	4 2
Portsmouth v Newport County	3 2
Derby County v Cardiff City	2-1

SIXTH ROUND

Hull City v Manchester United	0-1
Wolverhampton Wanderers v West Bromwich Albion	1 0
Leicester City v Brentford	2-0
Portsmouth v Derby County	2 1

SEMI-FINAL

Manchester United v Wolverhampton Wanderers	1-1, 0-1
Leicester City v Portsmouth	3-1

FINAL

Wolverhampton Wanderers v Leicester City	3-1

SCOTTISH FA CUP 1948-49

SECOND ROUND

Motherwell v Rangers	0-3
Partick Thistle v Queen of the South	3-0
Cowdenbeath v East Fife	1-2
Hibernian v Raith Rovers	1-1, 4-3
Clyde v Alloa Athletic	3-1
Ayr United v Morton	0-2
Stenhousemuir v Albion Rovers	5-1
Dundee v St Mirren	0-0, 2-1
Heart of Midlothian v Third Lanark	3-1
Dumbarton v Dundee United	1-1, 3-1

THIRD ROUND

Clyde v Morton	2-0
Heart of Midlothian v Dumbarton	3-0
Rangers	bye
Partick Thistle	bye
East Fife	bye
Hibernian	bye
Stenhousemuir	bye
Dundee	bye

FOURTH ROUND

Rangers v Partick Thistle	4-0
Hibernian v East Fife	0-2
Stenhousemuir v Clyde	0-1
Heart of Midlothian v Dundee	2-4

SEMI-FINAL

Rangers v East Fife	3-0
Clyde v Dundee	2-2, 2-1

FINAL

Rangers v Clyde	4-1

On Saturday 18 September 1948, there were 9 drawn games in Division One of the Football League, a record for any division of the League in a single day.

In both Divisions One and Two, the tally of goals scored during the season was 1303.

Portsmouth, 1948-49 League champions, and Swansea, who finished top of Division Three South, both completed the season without a home defeat. At Fratton Park, Portsmouth won 18 games and drew 3, while Swansea won 20 and drew one at Vetch Field.

Three honours for Bromley

Bromley won the FA Amateur Cup by beating Romford 1-0 at Wembley; they also won the Kent Amateur Cup with the highest score recorded in the final: 9-1. Bromley completed a magnificent season by capturing the Athenian League championship. George Brown, their centre-forward, scored 100 goals during the season. These included a 7, a 6, two 5's, three 4's and five hat-tricks.

In Scotland, Rangers became the first side to achieve the treble, winning the League, the Scottish Cup and the League Cup.

League Tables 1949-50

FIRST DIVISION

		P	W	D	L	F	A	Pts
1	Portsmouth	42	22	9	11	74	38	53
2	Wolves	42	20	13	9	76	49	53
3	Sunderland	42	21	10	11	83	62	52
4	Man United	42	18	14	10	69	44	50
5	Newcastle	42	19	12	11	77	55	50
6	Arsenal	42	19	11	12	79	55	49
7	Blackpool	42	17	15	10	46	35	49
8	Liverpool	42	17	14	11	64	54	48
9	Middlesbrough	42	20	7	15	59	48	47
10	Burnley	42	16	13	13	40	40	45
11	Derby	42	17	10	15	69	61	44
12	Aston Villa	42	15	12	15	61	61	42
13	Chelsea	42	12	16	14	58	65	40
14	WBA	42	14	12	16	47	53	40
15	Huddersfield	42	14	9	19	52	73	37
16	Bolton	42	10	14	18	45	59	34
17	Fulham	42	10	14	18	41	54	34
18	Everton	42	10	14	18	42	66	34
19	Stoke	42	11	12	19	45	75	34
20	Charlton	42	13	6	23	53	65	32
21	Man City	42	8	13	21	36	68	29
22	Birmingham	42	7	14	21	31	67	28

SECOND DIVISION

		P	W	D	L	F	A	Pts
1	Tottenham	42	27	7	8	81	35	61
2	Sheff Wed	42	18	16	8	67	48	52
3	Sheff United	42	19	14	9	68	49	52
4	Southampton	42	19	14	9	64	48	52
5	Leeds	42	17	13	12	54	45	47
6	Preston	42	18	9	15	60	49	45
7	Hull	42	17	11	14	64	72	45
8	Swansea	42	17	9	16	53	49	43
9	Brentford	42	15	13	14	44	49	43
10	Cardiff	42	16	10	16	41	44	42
11	Grimsby	42	16	8	18	74	73	40
12	Coventry	42	13	13	16	55	55	39
13	Barnsley	42	13	13	16	64	67	39
14	Chesterfield	42	15	9	18	43	47	39
15	Leicester	42	12	15	15	55	65	39
16	Blackburn	42	14	10	18	55	60	38
17	Luton	42	10	18	14	41	51	38
18	Bury	42	14	9	19	60	65	37
19	West Ham	42	12	12	18	53	61	36
20	QPR	42	11	12	19	40	57	34
21	Plymouth	42	8	16	18	44	65	32
22	Bradford PA	42	10	11	21	51	77	31

THIRD DIVISION (SOUTH)

		P	W	D	L	F	A	Pts
1	Notts County	42	25	8	9	95	50	58
2	Northampton	42	20	11	11	72	50	51
3	Southend	42	19	13	10	66	48	51
4	Nottm Forest	42	20	9	13	67	39	49
5	Torquay	42	19	10	13	66	63	48
6	Watford	42	16	13	13	45	35	45
7	Crystal Palace	42	15	14	13	55	54	44
8	Brighton	42	16	12	14	57	69	44
9	Bristol Rovers	42	19	5	18	51	51	43
10	Reading	42	17	8	17	70	64	42
11	Norwich	42	16	10	16	65	63	42
12	Bournemouth	42	16	10	16	57	56	42
13	Port Vale	42	15	11	16	47	42	41
14	Swindon	42	15	11	16	59	62	41
15	Bristol City	42	15	10	17	60	61	40
16	Exeter	42	14	11	17	63	75	39
17	Ipswich	42	12	11	19	57	86	35
18	Leyton Orient	42	12	11	19	53	85	35
19	Walsall	42	9	16	17	61	62	34
20	Aldershot	42	13	8	21	48	60	34
21	Newport	42	13	8	21	67	98	34
22	Millwall	42	14	4	24	55	63	32

THIRD DIVISION (NORTH)

		P	W	D	L	F	A	Pts
1	Doncaster	42	19	17	6	66	38	55
2	Gateshead	42	23	7	12	87	54	53
3	Rochdale	42	21	9	12	68	41	51
4	Lincoln	42	21	9	12	60	39	51
5	Tranmere	42	19	11	12	51	48	49
6	Rotherham	42	19	10	13	80	59	48
7	Crewe	42	17	14	11	68	55	48
8	Mansfield	42	18	12	12	66	54	48
9	Carlisle	42	16	15	11	68	51	47
10	Stockport	42	19	7	16	55	52	45
11	Oldham	42	16	11	15	58	63	43
12	Chester	42	17	6	19	70	79	40
13	Accrington	42	16	7	19	57	62	39
14	New Brighton	42	14	10	18	45	63	38
15	Barrow	42	14	9	19	47	53	37
16	Southport	42	12	13	17	51	71	37
17	Darlington	42	11	13	18	56	69	35
18	Hartlepools	42	14	5	23	52	79	33
19	Bradford City	42	12	8	22	61	76	32
20	Wrexham	42	10	12	20	39	54	32
21	Halifax	42	12	8	22	58	85	32
22	York	42	9	13	20	52	70	31

SCOTTISH DIVISION 'A'

		P	W	D	L	F	A	Pts
1	Rangers	30	22	6	2	58	26	50
2	Hibernian	30	22	5	3	86	34	49
3	Hearts	30	20	3	7	86	40	43
4	East Fife	30	15	7	8	58	43	37
5	Celtic	30	14	7	9	51	50	35
6	Dundee	30	12	7	11	49	46	31
7	Partick Thistle	30	13	3	14	55	45	29
8	Aberdeen	30	11	4	15	48	56	26
9	Raith	30	9	8	13	45	54	26
10	Motherwell	30	10	5	15	53	58	25
11	St Mirren	30	8	9	13	42	49	25
12	Third Lanark	30	11	3	16	44	62	25
13	Clyde	30	10	4	16	56	73	24
14	Falkirk	30	7	10	13	48	72	24
15	Queen of the S	30	5	6	19	31	63	16
16	Stirling	30	6	3	21	38	77	15

SCOTTISH DIVISION 'B'

		P	W	D	L	F	A	Pts
1	Morton	30	20	7	3	77	33	47
2	Airdrieonians	30	19	6	5	79	40	44
3	Dunfermline	30	16	4	10	71	57	36
4	St Johnstone	30	15	6	9	64	56	36
5	Cowdenbeath	30	16	3	11	63	56	35
6	Hamilton	30	14	6	10	57	44	34
7	Kilmarnock	30	14	5	11	50	43	33
8	Dundee United	30	14	5	11	74	56	33
9	Queen's Park	30	12	7	11	63	59	31
10	Forfar	30	11	8	11	53	56	30
11	Albion	30	10	7	13	49	61	27
12	Stenhousemuir	30	8	8	14	54	72	24
13	Ayr	30	8	6	16	53	80	22
14	Arbroath	30	5	9	16	47	69	19
15	Dumbarton	30	6	4	20	39	62	16
16	Alloa	30	5	3	22	47	96	13

FA CUP 1949-50

FOURTH ROUND

Arsenal v Swansea Town	2-1
Burnley v Port Vale	2-1
Leeds United v Bolton Wanderers	1-1, 3-2
Charlton Athletic v Cardiff City	1-1, 0-2
Chelsea v Newcastle United	3-0
Chesterfield v Middlesbrough	3-2
Watford v Manchester United	0-1
Portsmouth v Grimsby Town	5-0
Liverpool v Exeter City	3-1
Stockport County v Hull City	0-0, 2-0
Blackpool v Doncaster Rovers	2-1
Wolverhampton Wanderers v Sheffield United	0-0, 4-3
West Ham United v Everton	1-2
Tottenham Hotspur v Sunderland	5-1
Bury v Derby County	2-2, 2-5
Bournemouth v Northampton Town	1-1, 1-2

FIFTH ROUND

Arsenal v Burnley	2-0
Leeds United v Cardiff City	3-1
Chesterfield v Chelsea	1-1, 0-3
Manchester United v Portsmouth	3-3, 3-1
Stockport County v Liverpool	1-2
Wolverhampton Wanderers v Blackpool	0-0, 0-1
Everton v Tottenham Hotspur	1-0
Derby County v Northampton Town	4-2

SIXTH ROUND

Arsenal v Leeds United	1-0
Chelsea v Manchester United	2-0
Liverpool v Blackpool	2-1
Derby County v Everton	1-2

SEMI-FINAL

Arsenal v Chelsea	2-2, 1-0
Liverpool v Everton	2-0

FINAL

Arsenal v Liverpool	2-0

SCOTTISH FA CUP 1949-50

SECOND ROUND

Rangers v Cowdenbeath	8-0
Raith Rovers v Clyde	3-2
Queen of the South v Morton	1-1, 3-0
Aberdeen v Heart of Midlothian	3-1
Celtic v Third Lanark	1-1, 4-1
Partick Thistle v Dundee United	5-0
Stirling Albion v Dumbarton	2-2, 1-1, 6-2
Stenhousemuir v St Johnstone	2-2, 4-2
Dunfermline Athletic v Albion Rovers	2-1
Falkirk v East Fife	2-3

THIRD ROUND

Celtic v Aberdeen	0-1
Dunfermline Athletic v Stenhousemuir	1-4
Rangers	bye
Raith Rovers	bye
Queen of the South	bye
Partick Thistle	bye
Stirling Albion	bye
East Fife	bye

FOURTH ROUND

Rangers v Raith Rovers	1-1, 1-1, 2-0
Queen of the South v Aberdeen	3-3, 2-1
Partick Thistle v Stirling Albion	5-1
Stenhousemuir v East Fife	0-3

SEMI-FINAL

Rangers v Queen of the South	1-1, 3-0
Partick Thistle v East Fife	1-2

FINAL

Rangers v East Fife	3-0

Charlie Mortimore scored 15 goals for Aldershot in Division Three South during 1949-50. These made Mortimore the club's top scorer for the season, and meant that he became the second amateur to head a League club's scoring list since the First World War.

England lose to America
On 28 June 1950, an amazing scoreline came out of Brazil. For at Belo Horizonte, the United States had beaten England 1-0.

On 16 July 1950, 199,854 people watched the World Cup Final in Rio de Janeiro, the official record crowd for any football match.

The Third Division was extended from 44 to 48 clubs as a result of the clamour by minor professional clubs for first-class status. The League management committee proposed the enlargement of each section of the Third Division by two clubs, and this proposal was adopted at the 1950 AGM.

John Charles, Leeds United's centre-half, became Wales' youngest ever international when, on 8 March 1950, at the age of 18 years and 71 days, he played against Northern Ireland.

League Tables 1950-51

FIRST DIVISION

		P	W	D	L	F	A	Pts
1	Tottenham	42	25	10	7	82	44	60
2	Man United	42	24	8	10	74	40	56
3	Blackpool	42	20	10	12	79	53	50
4	Newcastle	42	18	13	11	62	53	49
5	Arsenal	42	19	9	14	73	56	47
6	Middlesbrough	42	18	11	13	76	65	47
7	Portsmouth	42	16	15	11	71	68	47
8	Bolton	42	19	7	16	64	61	45
9	Liverpool	42	16	11	15	53	59	43
10	Burnley	42	14	14	14	48	43	42
11	Derby	42	16	8	18	81	75	40
12	Sunderland	42	12	16	14	63	73	40
13	Stoke	42	13	14	15	50	59	40
14	Wolves	42	15	8	19	74	61	38
15	Aston Villa	42	12	13	17	66	68	37
16	WBA	42	13	11	18	53	61	37
17	Charlton	42	14	9	19	63	80	37
18	Fulham	42	13	11	18	52	68	37
19	Huddersfield	42	15	6	21	64	92	36
20	Chelsea	42	12	8	22	53	65	32
21	Sheff Wed	42	12	8	22	64	83	32
22	Everton	42	12	8	22	48	86	32

SECOND DIVISION

		P	W	D	L	F	A	Pts
1	Preston	42	26	5	11	91	49	57
2	Man City	42	19	14	9	89	61	52
3	Cardiff	42	17	16	9	53	45	50
4	Birmingham	42	20	9	13	64	53	49
5	Leeds	42	20	8	14	63	55	48
6	Blackburn	42	19	8	15	65	66	46
7	Coventry	42	19	7	16	75	59	45
8	Sheff United	42	16	12	14	72	62	44
9	Brentford	42	18	8	16	75	74	44
10	Hull	42	16	11	15	74	70	43
11	Doncaster	42	15	13	14	64	68	43
12	Southampton	42	15	13	14	66	73	43
13	West Ham	42	16	10	16	68	69	42
14	Leicester	42	15	11	16	68	58	41
15	Barnsley	42	15	10	17	74	68	40
16	QPR	42	15	10	17	71	82	40
17	Notts County	42	13	13	16	61	60	39
18	Swansea	42	16	4	22	54	77	36
19	Luton	42	9	14	19	57	70	32
20	Bury	42	12	8	22	60	86	32
21	Chesterfield	42	9	12	21	44	69	30
22	Grimsby	42	8	12	22	61	95	28

THIRD DIVISION (NORTH)

		P	W	D	L	F	A	Pts
1	Rotherham	46	31	9	6	103	41	71
2	Mansfield	46	26	12	8	78	48	64
3	Carlisle	46	25	12	9	79	50	62
4	Tranmere	46	24	11	11	83	62	59
5	Lincoln	46	25	8	13	89	58	58
6	Bradford PA	46	23	8	15	90	72	54
7	Bradford City	46	21	10	15	90	63	52
8	Gateshead	46	21	8	17	84	62	50
9	Crewe	46	19	10	17	61	60	48
10	Stockport	46	20	8	18	63	63	48
11	Rochdale	46	17	11	18	69	62	45
12	Scunthorpe	46	13	18	15	58	57	44
13	Chester	46	17	9	20	62	64	43
14	Wrexham	46	15	12	19	55	71	42
15	Oldham	46	16	8	22	73	73	40
16	Hartlepools	46	16	7	23	64	66	39
17	York	46	12	15	19	66	77	39
18	Darlington	46	13	13	20	59	77	39
19	Barrow	46	16	6	24	51	76	38
20	Shrewsbury	46	15	7	24	43	74	37
21	Southport	46	13	10	23	56	72	36
22	Halifax	46	11	12	23	50	69	34
23	Accrington	46	11	10	25	42	101	32
24	New Brighton	46	11	8	27	40	90	30

THIRD DIVISION (SOUTH)

		P	W	D	L	F	A	Pts
1	Nottm Forest	46	30	10	6	110	40	70
2	Norwich	46	25	14	7	82	45	64
3	Reading	46	21	15	10	88	53	57
4	Plymouth	46	24	9	13	85	55	57
5	Millwall	46	23	10	13	80	57	56
6	Bristol Rovers	46	20	15	11	64	42	55
7	Southend	46	21	10	15	92	69	52
8	Ipswich	46	23	6	17	69	58	52
9	Bournemouth	46	22	7	17	65	57	51
10	Bristol City	46	20	11	15	64	59	51
11	Newport	46	19	9	18	77	70	47
12	Port Vale	46	16	13	17	60	65	45
13	Brighton	46	13	17	16	71	79	43
14	Exeter	46	18	6	22	62	85	42
15	Walsall	46	15	10	21	52	62	40
16	Colchester	46	14	12	20	63	76	40
17	Swindon	46	18	4	24	55	67	40
18	Aldershot	46	15	10	21	56	88	40
19	Leyton Orient	46	15	8	23	53	75	38
20	Torquay	46	14	9	23	64	81	37
21	Northampton	46	10	16	20	55	67	36
22	Gillingham	46	13	9	24	69	101	35
23	Watford	46	9	11	26	54	88	29
24	Crystal Palace	46	8	11	27	33	84	27

SCOTTISH DIVISION 'A'

		P	W	D	L	F	A	Pts
1	Hibernian	30	22	4	4	78	26	48
2	Rangers	30	17	4	9	64	37	38
3	Dundee	30	15	8	7	47	30	38
4	Hearts	30	16	5	9	72	45	37
5	Aberdeen	30	15	5	10	61	50	35
6	Partick Thistle	30	13	7	10	57	48	33
7	Celtic	30	12	5	13	48	46	29
8	Raith	30	13	2	15	52	52	28
9	Motherwell	30	11	6	13	58	65	28
10	East Fife	30	10	8	12	48	66	28
11	St Mirren	30	9	7	14	35	51	25
12	Morton	30	10	4	16	47	59	24
13	Third Lanark	30	11	2	17	40	51	24
14	Airdrieonians	30	10	4	16	52	67	24
15	Clyde	30	8	7	15	37	57	23
16	Falkirk	30	7	4	19	35	81	18

SCOTTISH DIVISION 'B'

		P	W	D	L	F	A	Pts
1	Queen of the S	30	21	3	6	69	35	45
2	Stirling	30	21	3	6	78	44	45
3	Ayr	30	15	6	9	64	40	36
4	Dundee United	30	16	4	10	78	58	36
5	St Johnstone	30	14	5	11	68	53	33
6	Queen's Park	30	13	7	10	56	53	33
7	Hamilton	30	12	8	10	65	49	32
8	Albion	30	14	4	12	56	51	32
9	Dumbarton	30	12	5	13	52	53	29
10	Dunfermline	30	12	4	14	58	73	28
11	Cowdenbeath	30	12	3	15	61	57	27
12	Kilmarnock	30	8	8	14	44	49	24
13	Arbroath	30	8	5	17	46	78	21
14	Forfar	30	9	3	18	43	76	21
15	Stenhousemuir	30	9	2	19	51	80	20
16	Alloa	30	7	4	19	58	98	18

FA CUP 1950-51

FOURTH ROUND

Newcastle United v Bolton Wanderers	3-2
Stoke City v West Ham United	1-0
Luton Town v Bristol Rovers	1-2
Hull City v Rotherham United	2-0
Wolverhampton Wanderers v Aston Villa	3-1
Preston North End v Huddersfield Town	0-2
Sunderland v Southampton	2-0
Newport County v Norwich City	0-2
Blackpool v Stockport County	2-1
Sheffield United v Mansfield Town	0-0, 1-2
Exeter City v Chelsea	1-1, 0-2
Millwall v Fulham	0-1
Derby County v Birmingham City	1-3
Bristol City v Brighton	1-0
Manchester United v Leeds United	4-0
Arsenal v Northampton Town	3-2

FIFTH ROUND

Stoke City v Newcastle United	2-4
Bristol Rovers v Hull City	3-0
Wolverhampton Wanderers v Huddersfield Town	2-0
Sunderland v Norwich City	3-1
Blackpool v Mansfield Town	2-0
Chelsea v Fulham	1-1, 0-3
Birmingham City v Bristol City	2-0
Manchester United v Arsenal	1-0

SIXTH ROUND

Newcastle United v Bristol Rovers	0-0, 3-1
Sunderland v Wolverhampton Wanderers	1-1, 1-3
Blackpool v Fulham	1-0
Birmingham City v Manchester United	1-0

SEMI-FINAL

Newcastle United v Wolverhampton Wanderers	0-0, 2-1
Blackpool v Birmingham City	0-0, 2-1

FINAL

Blackpool v Newcastle United	0-2

SCOTTISH FA CUP 1950-51

SECOND ROUND

Celtic v Duns	4-0
East Stirlingshire v Heart of Midlothian	1-5
Aberdeen v Third Lanark	4-0
St Johnstone v Dundee	1-3
Raith Rovers v Brechin City	5-2
Morton v Airdrieonians	3-3, 1-2
Albion Rovers v Clyde	0-2
Rangers v Hibernian	2-3
Queen's Park v Ayr United	1-3
Motherwell v Hamilton Academicals	4-1

THIRD ROUND

Heart of Midlothian v Celtic	1-2
Airdrieonians v Clyde	4-0
Aberdeen	bye
Dundee	bye
Raith Rovers	bye
Hibernian	bye
Ayr United	bye
Motherwell	bye

FOURTH ROUND

Celtic v Aberdeen	3-0
Dundee v Raith Rovers	1-2
Airdrieonians v Hibernian	0-3
Ayr United v Motherwell	2-2, 1-2

SEMI-FINAL

Celtic v Raith Rovers	3-2
Hibernian v Motherwell	2-3

FINAL

Celtic v Motherwell	1-0

In their first season in the Football League, Scunthorpe United conceded only nine goals in their 23 home matches in Division Three North. In their 23 away games in the same division, Hartlepools United scored only nine times, failing to break a duck in their last 11 fixtures.

Nottingham Forest won the Third Division South championship with a record points total for that division—70.

Billingham Synthonia did not concede a single goal at home in their Northern League programme, though they scored 44.

On 15 November 1950, Leslie Compton, the Arsenal centre-half, played in that position for England against Wales. It was Compton's first international appearance, and at 38 years and 2 months, he is credited with making the oldest international debut in the Home Championship.

FIRST DIVISION

		P	W	D	L	F	A	Pts
1	Man United	42	23	11	8	95	52	57
2	Tottenham	42	22	9	11	76	51	53
3	Arsenal	42	21	11	10	80	61	53
4	Portsmouth	42	20	8	14	68	58	48
5	Bolton	42	19	10	13	65	61	48
6	Aston Villa	42	19	9	14	79	70	47
7	Preston	42	17	12	13	74	54	46
8	Newcastle	42	18	9	15	98	73	45
9	Blackpool	42	18	9	15	64	64	45
10	Charlton	42	17	10	15	68	63	44
11	Liverpool	42	12	19	11	57	61	43
12	Sunderland	42	15	12	15	70	61	42
13	WBA	42	14	13	15	74	77	41
14	Burnley	42	15	10	17	56	63	40
15	Man City	42	13	13	16	58	61	39
16	Wolves	42	12	14	16	73	73	38
17	Derby	42	15	7	20	63	80	37
18	Middlesbrough	42	15	6	21	64	88	36
19	Chelsea	42	14	8	20	52	72	36
20	Stoke	42	12	7	23	49	88	31
21	Huddersfield	42	10	8	24	49	82	28
22	Fulham	42	8	11	23	58	77	27

SECOND DIVISION

		P	W	D	L	F	A	Pts
1	Sheff Wed	42	21	11	10	100	66	53
2	Cardiff	42	20	11	11	72	54	51
3	Birmingham	42	21	9	12	67	56	51
4	Nottm Forest	42	18	13	11	77	62	49
5	Leicester	42	19	9	14	78	64	47
6	Leeds	42	18	11	13	59	57	47
7	Everton	42	17	10	15	64	58	44
8	Luton	42	16	12	14	77	78	44
9	Rotherham	42	17	8	17	73	71	42
10	Brentford	42	15	12	15	54	55	42
11	Sheff United	42	18	5	19	90	76	41
12	West Ham	42	15	11	16	67	77	41
13	Southampton	42	15	11	16	61	73	41
14	Blackburn	42	17	6	19	54	63	40
15	Notts County	42	16	7	19	71	68	39
16	Doncaster	42	13	12	17	55	60	38
17	Bury	42	15	7	20	67	69	37
18	Hull	42	13	11	18	60	70	37
19	Swansea	42	12	12	18	72	76	36
20	Barnsley	42	11	14	17	59	72	36
21	Coventry	42	14	6	22	59	82	34
22	QPR	42	11	12	19	52	81	34

THIRD DIVISION (SOUTH)

		P	W	D	L	F	A	Pts
1	Plymouth	46	29	8	9	107	53	66
2	Reading	46	29	3	14	112	60	61
3	Norwich	46	26	9	11	89	50	61
4	Millwall	46	23	12	11	74	53	58
5	Brighton	46	24	10	12	87	63	58
6	Newport	46	21	12	13	77	76	54
7	Bristol Rovers	46	20	12	14	89	53	52
8	Northampton	46	22	5	19	93	74	49
9	Southend	46	19	10	17	75	66	48
10	Colchester	46	17	12	17	56	77	46
11	Torquay	46	17	10	19	86	98	44
12	Aldershot	46	18	8	20	78	89	44
13	Port Vale	46	14	15	17	50	66	43
14	Bournemouth	46	16	10	20	69	75	42
15	Bristol City	46	15	12	19	58	69	42
16	Swindon	46	14	14	18	51	68	42
17	Ipswich	46	16	9	21	63	74	41
18	Leyton Orient	46	16	9	21	55	68	41
19	Crystal Palace	46	15	9	22	61	80	39
20	Shrewsbury	46	13	10	23	62	86	36
21	Watford	46	13	10	23	57	81	36
22	Gillingham	46	11	13	22	71	81	35
23	Exeter	46	13	9	24	65	86	35
24	Walsall	46	13	5	28	55	94	31

THIRD DIVISION (NORTH)

		P	W	D	L	F	A	Pts
1	Lincoln	46	30	9	7	121	52	69
2	Grimsby	46	29	8	9	96	45	66
3	Stockport	46	23	13	10	74	40	59
4	Oldham	46	24	9	13	90	61	57
5	Gateshead	46	21	11	14	66	49	53
6	Mansfield	46	22	8	16	73	60	52
7	Carlisle	46	19	13	14	62	57	51
8	Bradford PA	46	19	12	15	74	64	50
9	Hartlepools	46	21	8	17	71	65	50
10	York	46	18	13	15	73	52	49
11	Tranmere	46	21	6	19	76	71	48
12	Barrow	46	17	12	17	57	61	46
13	Chesterfield	46	17	11	18	65	66	45
14	Scunthorpe	46	14	16	16	65	74	44
15	Bradford City	46	16	10	20	61	68	42
16	Crewe	46	17	8	21	63	82	42
17	Southport	46	15	11	20	53	71	41
18	Wrexham	46	15	9	22	63	73	39
19	Chester	46	15	9	22	72	85	39
20	Halifax	46	14	7	25	61	97	35
21	Rochdale	46	11	13	22	47	79	35
22	Accrington	46	10	12	24	61	92	32
23	Darlington	46	11	9	26	64	103	31
24	Workington	46	11	7	28	50	91	29

SCOTTISH DIVISION 'A'

		P	W	D	L	F	A	Pts
1	Hibernian	30	20	5	5	92	36	45
2	Rangers	30	16	9	5	61	31	41
3	East Fife	30	17	3	10	71	49	37
4	Hearts	30	14	7	9	69	53	35
5	Raith	30	14	5	11	43	42	33
6	Partick	30	12	7	11	48	51	31
7	Motherwell	30	12	7	11	51	57	31
8	Dundee	30	11	6	13	53	52	28
9	Celtic	30	10	8	12	52	55	28
10	Queen of the S	30	10	8	12	50	60	28
11	Aberdeen	30	10	7	13	65	58	27
12	Third Lanark	30	9	8	13	51	62	26
13	Airdrieonians	30	11	4	15	54	69	26
14	St Mirren	30	10	5	15	43	58	25
15	Morton	30	9	6	15	49	56	24
16	Stirling	30	5	5	20	36	99	15

SCOTTISH DIVISION 'B'

		P	W	D	L	F	A	Pts
1	Clyde	30	19	6	5	100	45	44
2	Falkirk	30	18	7	5	80	34	43
3	Ayr	30	17	5	8	55	45	39
4	Dundee United	30	16	5	9	75	60	37
5	Kilmarnock	30	16	2	12	62	48	34
6	Dunfermline	30	15	2	13	74	65	32
7	Alloa	30	13	6	11	55	49	32
8	Cowdenbeath	30	12	8	10	66	67	32
9	Hamilton	30	12	6	12	47	51	30
10	Dumbarton	30	10	8	12	51	57	28
11	St Johnstone	30	9	7	14	62	68	25
12	Forfar	30	10	4	16	59	97	24
13	Stenhousemuir	30	8	6	16	57	74	22
14	Albion	30	6	10	14	39	57	22
15	Queen's Park	30	8	4	18	40	62	20
16	Arbroath	30	6	4	20	40	83	16

FA CUP 1951-52

FOURTH ROUND

Tottenham Hotspur v Newcastle United	0-3
Swansea Town v Rotherham United	3-0
Notts County v Portsmouth	1-3
Middlesbrough v Doncaster Rovers	1-4
Blackburn Rovers v Hull City	2-0
Gateshead v West Bromwich Albion	0-2
Burnley v Coventry City	2-0
Liverpool v Wolverhampton Wanderers	2-1
Arsenal v Barnsley	4-0
Birmingham City v Leyton Orient	0-1
Luton Town v Brentford	2-2, 0-0, 3-2
Swindon Town v Stoke City	1-1, 1-0
Chelsea v Tranmere Rovers	4-0
Leeds United v Bradford Park Avenue	2-0
West Ham United v Sheffield United	0-0, 2-4
Southend United v Bristol Rovers	2-1

FIFTH ROUND

Swansea Town v Newcastle United	0-1
Portsmouth v Doncaster Rovers	4-0
Blackburn Rovers v West Bromwich Albion	1-0
Burnley v Liverpool	2-0
Leyton Orient v Arsenal	0-3
Luton Town v Swindon Town	3-1
Leeds United v Chelsea	1-1, 1-1, 1-5
Southend United v Sheffield United	1-2

SIXTH ROUND

Portsmouth v Newcastle United	2-4
Blackburn Rovers v Burnley	3-1
Luton Town v Arsenal	2-3
Sheffield United v Chelsea	0-1

SEMI-FINAL

Newcastle United v Blackburn Rovers	0-0, 2-1
Arsenal v Chelsea	1-1, 3-0

FINAL

Newcastle United v Arsenal	1-0

SCOTTISH FA CUP 1951-52

SECOND ROUND

St Mirren v Motherwell	2-3
Clyde v Dunfermline Athletic	3-4
Rangers v Elgin City	6-1
Cowdenbeath v Arbroath	1-4
Heart of Midlothian v Raith Rovers	1-0
St Johnstone v Queen of the South	2-2, 1-3
Airdrieonians v East Fife	2-1
Clachnacuddin v Morton	1-2
Wigtown & Bladnoch v Dundee	1-7
Alloa Athletic v Berwick Rangers	0-0, 1-4
Aberdeen v Kilmarnock	2-1
Leith Athletic v Dundee United	1-4
Hamilton Academicals v Third Lanark	1-1, 0-4
Albion Rovers v Stranraer	1-1, 4-3
Falkirk v Stirling Albion	3-3, 2-1
Dumbarton v Queen's Park	1-0

THIRD ROUND

Dunfermline Athletic v Motherwell	1-1, 0-4
Arbroath v Rangers	0-2
Queen of the South v Heart of Midlothian	1-3
Airdrieonians v Morton	4-0
Dundee v Berwick Rangers	1-0
Dundee United v Aberdeen	2-2, 2-3
Albion Rovers v Third Lanark	1-3
Dumbarton v Falkirk	1-3

FOURTH ROUND

Rangers v Motherwell	1-1, 1-2
Airdrieonians v Heart of Midlothian	2-2, 4-6
Dundee v Aberdeen	4-0
Third Lanark v Falkirk	1-0

SEMI-FINAL

Motherwell v Heart of Midlothian	1-1, 1-1, 3-1
Dundee v Third Lanark	2-0

FINAL

Motherwell v Dundee	4-0

An Englishman from Wales
The first player to appear in an England representative side while not attached to an English club was Charlie Rutter, Cardiff City's right-back. Rutter played for the England 'B' side against the Netherlands 'B' side in Amsterdam, March 1952. England won the match—a kind of forerunner to the Under-23 international games—1-0.

Freddie Steele's move from Mansfield to Port Vale on 28 December 1951 was the first case of a player-manager being transferred from one Football League club to another.

Billy Foulkes of Newcastle United scored with his first kick in his first international appearance for Wales, against England at Cardiff in October 1951.

FIRST DIVISION

		P	W	D	L	F	A	Pts
1	Arsenal	42	21	12	9	97	64	54
2	Preston	42	21	12	9	85	60	54
3	Wolves	42	19	13	10	86	63	51
4	WBA	42	21	8	13	66	60	50
5	Charlton	42	19	11	12	77	63	49
6	Burnley	42	18	12	12	67	52	48
7	Blackpool	42	19	9	14	71	70	47
8	Man United	42	18	10	14	69	72	46
9	Sunderland	42	15	13	14	68	82	43
10	Tottenham	42	15	11	16	78	69	41
11	Aston Villa	42	14	13	15	63	61	41
12	Cardiff	42	14	12	16	54	46	40
13	Middlesbrough	42	14	11	17	70	77	39
14	Bolton	42	15	9	18	61	69	39
15	Portsmouth	42	14	10	18	74	83	38
16	Newcastle	42	14	9	19	59	70	37
17	Liverpool	42	14	8	20	61	82	36
18	Sheff Wed	42	12	11	19	62	72	35
19	Chelsea	42	12	11	19	56	66	35
20	Man City	42	14	7	21	72	87	35
21	Stoke	42	12	10	20	53	66	34
22	Derby	42	11	10	21	59	74	32

SECOND DIVISION

		P	W	D	L	F	A	Pts
1	Sheff United	42	25	10	7	97	55	60
2	Huddersfield	42	24	10	8	84	33	58
3	Luton	42	22	8	12	84	49	52
4	Plymouth	42	20	9	13	65	60	49
5	Leicester	42	18	12	12	89	74	48
6	Birmingham	42	19	10	13	71	66	48
7	Nottm Forest	42	18	8	16	77	67	44
8	Fulham	42	17	10	15	81	71	44
9	Blackburn	42	18	8	16	68	65	44
10	Leeds	42	14	15	13	71	63	43
11	Swansea	42	15	12	15	78	81	42
12	Rotherham	42	16	9	17	75	74	41
13	Doncaster	42	12	16	14	58	64	40
14	West Ham	42	13	13	16	58	60	39
15	Lincoln	42	11	17	14	64	71	39
16	Everton	42	12	14	16	71	75	38
17	Brentford	42	13	11	18	59	76	37
18	Hull	42	14	8	20	57	69	36
19	Notts County	42	14	8	20	60	88	36
20	Bury	42	13	9	20	53	81	35
21	Southampton	42	10	13	19	68	85	33
22	Barnsley	42	5	8	29	47	108	18

FA CUP 1952-53

FOURTH ROUND

Blackpool v Huddersfield Town	1-0
Shrewsbury Town v Southampton	1-4
Arsenal v Bury	6-2
Burnley v Sunderland	2-0
Preston North End v Tottenham Hotspur	2-2, 0-1
Halifax Town v Stoke City	1-0
Sheffield United v Birmingham City	1-1, 1-3
Chelsea v West Bromwich Albion	1-1, 0-0, 1-1, 4-0
Bolton Wanderers v Notts County	1-1, 2-2, 1-0
Manchester City v Luton Town	1-1, 1-5
Hull City v Gateshead	1-2
Plymouth Argyle v Barnsley	1-0
Everton v Nottingham Forest	4-1
Manchester United v Walthamstow Avenue	1-1, 5-2
Aston Villa v Brentford	0-0, 2-1
Newcastle United v Rotherham United	1-3

FIFTH ROUND

Blackpool v Southampton	1-1, 2-1
Burnley v Arsenal	0-2
Halifax Town v Tottenham Hotspur	0-3
Chelsea v Birmingham City	0-4
Luton Town v Bolton Wanderers	0-1
Plymouth Argyle v Gateshead	0-1
Everton v Manchester United	2-1
Rotherham United v Aston Villa	1-3

SIXTH ROUND

Arsenal v Blackpool	1-2
Birmingham City v Tottenham Hotspur	1-1, 2-2, 0-1
Gateshead v Bolton Wanderers	0-1
Aston Villa v Everton	0-1

SEMI-FINAL

Blackpool v Tottenham Hotspur	2-1
Bolton Wanderers v Everton	4-3

FINAL

Blackpool v Bolton Wanderers	4-3

THIRD DIVISION (NORTH)

		P	W	D	L	F	A	Pts
1	Oldham	46	22	15	9	77	45	59
2	Port Vale	46	20	18	8	67	35	58
3	Wrexham	46	24	8	14	86	66	56
4	York	46	20	13	13	60	45	53
5	Grimsby	46	21	10	15	75	59	52
6	Southport	46	20	11	15	63	60	51
7	Bradford PA	46	19	12	15	75	61	50
8	Gateshead	46	17	15	14	76	60	49
9	Carlisle	46	18	13	15	82	68	49
10	Crewe	46	20	8	18	70	68	48
11	Stockport	46	17	13	16	82	69	47
12	Chesterfield*	46	18	11	17	65	63	47
13	Tranmere*	46	21	5	20	65	63	47
14	Halifax	46	16	15	15	68	68	47
15	Scunthorpe	46	16	14	16	62	56	46
16	Bradford City	46	14	18	14	75	80	46
17	Hartlepools	46	16	14	16	57	61	46
18	Mansfield	46	16	14	16	55	62	46
19	Barrow	46	16	12	18	66	71	44
20	Chester	46	11	15	20	64	85	37
21	Darlington	46	14	6	26	58	96	34
22	Rochdale	46	14	5	27	62	83	33
23	Workington	46	11	10	25	55	91	32
24	Accrington	46	8	11	27	39	89	27

*Equal

THIRD DIVISION (SOUTH)

		P	W	D	L	F	A	Pts
1	Bristol Rovers	46	26	12	8	92	46	64
2	Millwall	46	24	14	8	82	44	62
3	Northampton	46	26	10	10	109	70	62
4	Norwich	26	25	10	11	99	55	60
5	Bristol City	46	22	15	9	95	61	59
6	Coventry	46	19	12	15	77	62	50
7	Brighton	46	19	12	15	81	75	50
8	Southend	46	18	13	15	69	74	49
9	Bournemouth	46	19	9	18	74	69	47
10	Watford	46	15	17	14	62	63	47
11	Reading	46	19	8	19	69	64	46
12	Torquay	46	18	9	19	87	88	45
13	Crystal Palace	46	15	13	18	66	82	43
14	Leyton Orient	46	16	10	20	68	73	42
15	Newport	46	16	10	20	70	82	42
16	Ipswich	46	13	15	18	60	69	41
17	Exeter	46	13	14	19	61	71	40
18	Swindon	46	14	12	20	64	79	40
19	Aldershot	46	12	15	19	61	77	39
20	Gillingham	46	12	15	19	55	74	39
21	QPR	46	12	15	19	61	82	39
22	Colchester	46	12	14	20	59	76	38
23	Shrewsbury	46	12	12	22	68	91	36
24	Walsall	46	7	10	29	56	118	24

SCOTTISH FA CUP 1952-53

SECOND ROUND

Dundee v Rangers	0-2
Cowdenbeath v Morton	0-1
Forfar Athletic v Falkirk	2-4
Stirling Albion v Celtic	1-1, 0-3
Raith Rovers v Heart of Midlothian	0-1
St Johnstone v Montrose	1-2
Berwick Rangers v Queen of the South	2-3
Albion Rovers v East Stirlingshire	2-0
Partick Thistle v Clyde	0-2
Buckie Thistle v Ayr United	1-5
Wigtown & Bladnoch v Third Lanark	1-3
Hamilton Academicals v Kilmarnock	2-2, 2-0
Airdrieonians v East Fife	3-0
Hibernian v Queen's Park	4-2
Alloa Athletic v Motherwell	0-2
Aberdeen v St Mirren	2-0

THIRD ROUND

Morton v Rangers	1-4
Falkirk v Celtic	2-3
Heart of Midlothian v Montrose	3-1
Queen of the South v Albion Rovers	2-0
Clyde v Ayr United	8-3
Third Lanark v Hamilton Academicals	1-0
Airdrieonians v Hibernian	0-4
Aberdeen v Motherwell	5-5, 6-1

FOURTH ROUND

Rangers v Celtic	2-0
Heart of Midlothian v Queen of the South	2-1
Clyde v Third Lanark	1-2
Hibernian v Aberdeen	1-1, 0-2

SEMI-FINAL

Rangers v Heart of Midlothian	2-1
Third Lanark v Aberdeen	1-1, 1-2

FINAL

Aberdeen v Rangers	1-1, 0-1

SCOTTISH DIVISION 'A'

		P	W	D	L	F	A	Pts
1	Rangers	30	18	7	5	80	39	43
2	Hibernian	30	19	5	6	93	51	43
3	East Fife	30	16	7	7	72	48	39
4	Hearts	30	12	6	12	59	50	30
5	Clyde	30	13	4	13	78	78	30
6	St Mirren	30	11	8	11	52	58	30
7	Dundee	30	9	11	8	44	37	29
8	Celtic	30	11	7	12	51	54	29
9	Partick	30	10	9	11	55	63	29
10	Queen of the S	30	10	8	12	43	61	28
11	Aberdeen	30	11	5	14	64	68	27
12	Raith Rovers	30	9	8	13	47	53	26
13	Falkirk	30	11	4	15	53	63	26
14	Airdrieonians	30	10	6	14	53	75	26
15	Motherwell	30	10	5	15	57	80	25
16	Third Lanark	30	8	4	18	52	75	20

SCOTTISH DIVISION 'B'

		P	W	D	L	F	A	Pts
1	Stirling	30	20	4	6	64	43	44
2	Hamilton	30	20	3	7	72	40	43
3	Queen's Park	30	15	7	8	70	46	37
4	Kilmarnock	30	17	2	11	74	48	36
5	Ayr	30	17	2	11	76	56	36
6	Morton	30	15	3	12	79	57	33
7	Arbroath	30	13	7	10	52	57	33
8	Dundee United	30	12	5	13	52	56	29
9	Alloa	30	12	5	13	63	68	29
10	Dumbarton	30	11	6	13	58	67	28
11	Dunfermline	30	9	9	12	51	58	27
12	Stenhousemuir	30	10	6	14	56	65	26
13	Cowdenbeath	30	8	7	15	37	54	23
14	St Johnstone	30	8	6	16	41	63	22
15	Forfar	30	8	4	18	54	88	20
16	Albion	30	5	4	21	44	77	14

A Division One match between Aston Villa and Sunderland in September 1952 produced a remarkable goal. It was scored by Peter Aldis, the Aston Villa full-back, who headed the ball into Sunderland's net from 35 yards. This goal, Aldis's first in the League, is reckoned to give Aldis the distance record for a headed goal in League football.

The footballing parson
The only post-War Football League professional who was also a parson was the Reverend Norman Hallam. A Methodist minister, Hallam was right-half for Port Vale in 1952-53. He later played for Barnsley and then Halifax before joining the Midland League club, Goole Town.

FIRST DIVISION

		P	W	D	L	F	A	Pts
1	Wolves	42	25	7	10	96	56	57
2	WBA	42	22	9	11	86	63	53
3	Huddersfield	42	20	11	11	78	61	51
4	Man United	42	18	12	12	73	58	48
5	Bolton	42	18	12	12	75	60	48
6	Blackpool	42	19	10	13	80	69	48
7	Burnley	42	21	4	17	78	67	46
8	Chelsea	42	16	12	14	74	68	44
9	Charlton	42	19	6	17	75	77	44
10	Cardiff	42	18	8	16	51	71	44
11	Preston	42	19	5	18	87	58	43
12	Arsenal	42	15	13	14	75	73	43
13	Aston Villa	42	16	9	17	70	68	41
14	Portsmouth	42	14	11	17	81	89	39
15	Newcastle	42	14	10	18	72	77	38
16	Tottenham	42	16	5	21	65	76	37
17	Man City	42	14	9	19	62	77	37
18	Sunderland	42	14	8	20	81	89	36
19	Sheff Wed	42	15	6	21	70	91	36
20	Sheff United	42	11	11	20	69	90	33
21	Middlesbrough	42	10	10	22	60	91	30
22	Liverpool	42	9	10	23	68	97	28

SECOND DIVISION

		P	W	D	L	F	A	Pts
1	Leicester	42	23	10	9	97	60	56
2	Everton	42	20	16	6	92	58	56
3	Blackburn	42	23	9	10	86	50	55
4	Nottm Forest	42	20	12	10	86	59	52
5	Rotherham	42	21	7	14	80	67	49
6	Luton	42	18	12	12	64	59	48
7	Birmingham	42	18	11	13	78	58	47
8	Fulham	42	17	10	15	98	85	44
9	Bristol Rovers	42	14	16	12	64	58	44
10	Leeds	42	15	13	14	89	81	43
11	Stoke	42	12	17	13	71	60	41
12	Doncaster	42	16	9	17	59	63	41
13	West Ham	42	15	9	18	67	69	39
14	Notts County	42	13	13	16	54	74	39
15	Hull	42	16	6	20	64	66	38
16	Lincoln	42	14	9	19	65	83	37
17	Bury	42	11	14	17	54	72	36
18	Derby	42	12	11	19	64	82	35
19	Plymouth	42	9	16	17	65	82	34
20	Swansea	42	13	8	21	58	82	34
21	Brentford	42	10	11	21	40	78	31
22	Oldham	42	8	9	25	40	89	25

THIRD DIVISION (SOUTH)

		P	W	D	L	F	A	Pts
1	Ipswich	46	27	10	9	82	51	64
2	Brighton	46	26	9	11	86	61	61
3	Bristol City	46	25	6	15	88	66	56
4	Watford	46	21	10	15	85	69	52
5	Northampton	46	20	11	15	82	55	51
6	Southampton	46	22	7	17	76	63	51
7	Norwich	46	20	11	15	73	66	51
8	Reading	46	20	9	17	86	73	49
9	Exeter	46	20	8	18	68	58	48
10	Gillingham	46	19	10	17	61	66	48
11	Leyton Orient	46	18	11	17	79	73	47
12	Millwall	46	19	9	18	74	77	47
13	Torquay	46	17	12	17	81	88	46
14	Coventry	46	18	9	19	61	56	45
15	Newport	46	19	6	21	61	81	44
16	Southend	46	18	7	21	69	71	43
17	Aldershot	46	17	9	20	74	86	43
18	QPR	46	16	10	20	60	68	42
19	Bournemouth	46	16	8	22	67	70	40
20	Swindon	46	15	10	21	67	70	40
21	Shrewsbury	46	14	12	20	65	76	40
22	Crystal Palace	46	14	12	20	60	86	40
23	Colchester	46	10	10	26	50	78	30
24	Walsall	46	9	8	29	40	87	26

THIRD DIVISION (NORTH)

		P	W	D	L	F	A	Pts
1	Port Vale	46	26	17	3	74	21	69
2	Barnsley	46	24	10	12	77	57	58
3	Scunthorpe	46	21	15	10	77	56	57
4	Gateshead	46	21	13	12	74	55	55
5	Bradford City	46	22	9	15	60	55	53
6	Chesterfield	46	19	14	13	76	64	52
7	Mansfield	46	20	11	15	88	67	51
8	Wrexham	46	21	9	16	81	68	51
9	Bradford PA	46	18	14	14	77	68	50
10	Stockport	46	18	11	17	77	67	47
11	Southport	46	17	12	17	63	60	46
12	Barrow	46	16	12	18	72	71	44
13	Carlisle	46	14	15	17	83	71	43
14	Tranmere	46	18	7	21	59	70	43
15	Accrington	46	16	10	20	66	74	42
16	Crewe	46	14	13	19	49	67	41
17	Grimsby	46	16	9	21	51	77	41
18	Hartlepools	46	13	14	19	59	65	40
19	Rochdale	46	15	10	21	59	77	40
20	Workington	46	13	14	19	59	80	40
21	Darlington	46	12	14	20	50	71	38
22	York	46	12	13	21	64	86	37
23	Halifax	46	12	10	24	44	73	34
24	Chester	46	11	10	25	48	67	32

SCOTTISH DIVISION 'A'

		P	W	D	L	F	A	Pts
1	Celtic	30	20	3	7	72	29	43
2	Hearts	30	16	6	8	70	45	38
3	Partick	30	17	1	12	76	54	35
4	Rangers	30	13	8	9	56	35	34
5	Hibernian	30	15	4	11	72	51	34
6	East Fife	30	13	8	9	55	45	34
7	Dundee	30	14	6	10	46	47	34
8	Clyde	30	15	4	11	64	67	34
9	Aberdeen	30	15	3	12	66	51	33
10	Queen of the S	30	14	4	12	72	53	32
11	St Mirren	30	12	4	14	44	54	28
12	Raith	30	10	6	14	56	60	26
13	Falkirk	30	9	7	14	47	61	25
14	Stirling	30	10	4	16	39	62	24
15	Airdrieonians	30	5	5	20	41	92	15
16	Hamilton	30	4	3	23	29	94	11

SCOTTISH DIVISION 'B'

		P	W	D	L	F	A	Pts
1	Motherwell	30	21	3	6	109	43	45
2	Kilmarnock	30	19	4	7	71	39	42
3	Third Lanark	30	13	10	7	78	48	36
4	Stenhousemuir	30	14	8	8	66	58	36
5	Morton	30	15	3	12	85	65	33
6	St Johnstone	30	14	3	13	80	71	31
7	Albion	30	12	7	11	55	63	31
8	Dunfermline	30	11	9	10	48	57	31
9	Ayr	30	11	8	11	50	56	30
10	Queen's Park	30	9	9	12	56	51	27
11	Alloa	30	7	10	13	50	72	24
12	Forfar	30	10	4	16	38	69	24
13	Cowdenbeath	30	9	5	16	67	81	23
14	Arbroath	30	8	7	15	53	67	23
15	Dundee United	30	8	6	16	54	79	22
16	Dumbarton	30	7	8	15	51	92	22

FA CUP 1953-54

FOURTH ROUND

West Bromwich Albion v Rotherham United	4-0
Burnley v Newcastle United	1-1, 0-1
Blackburn Rovers v Hull City	2-2, 1-2
Manchester City v Tottenham Hotspur	0-1
Leyton Orient v Fulham	2-1
Plymouth Argyle v Doncaster Rovers	0-2
Cardiff City v Port Vale	0-2
West Ham United v Blackpool	1-1, 1-3
Sheffield Wednesday v Chesterfield	0-0, 4-2
Everton v Swansea Town	3-0
Headington United v Bolton Wanderers	2-4
Scunthorpe United v Portsmouth	1-1, 2-2, 0-4
Arsenal v Norwich City	1-2
Stoke City v Leicester City	0-0, 1-3
Lincoln City v Preston North End	0-2
Ipswich Town v Birmingham City	1-0

FIFTH ROUND

West Bromwich Albion v Newcastle United	3-2
Hull City v Tottenham Hotspur	1-1, 0-2
Leyton Orient v Doncaster Rovers	3-1
Port Vale v Blackpool	2-0
Sheffield Wednesday v Everton	3-1
Bolton Wanderers v Portsmouth	0-0, 2-1
Norwich City v Leicester City	1-2
Preston North End v Ipswich Town	6-1

SIXTH ROUND

West Bromwich Albion v Tottenham Hotspur	3-0
Leyton Orient v Port Vale	0-1
Sheffield Wednesday v Bolton Wanderers	1-1, 2-0
Leicester City v Preston North End	1-1, 2-2, 1-3

SEMI-FINAL

West Bromwich Albion v Port Vale	2-1
Sheffield Wednesday v Preston North End	0-2

FINAL

West Bromwich Albion v Preston North End	3-2

SCOTTISH FA CUP 1953-54

SECOND ROUND

Falkirk v Celtic	1-2
Stirling Albion v Arbroath	0-0, 3-1
Brechin City v Hamilton Academicals	2-3
Morton v Cowdenbeath	4-0
Tarff Rovers v Partick Thistle	1-9
Peebles Rovers v Buckie Thistle	1-1, 2-7
Motherwell v Dunfermline Athletic	5-2
Coldstream v Raith Rovers	1-10
Third Lanark v Deveronvale	7-2
Rangers v Kilmarnock	2-2, 3-1
Berwick Rangers v Ayr United	5-1
Albion Rovers v Dundee	1-1, 0-4
Queen of the South v Forfar Athletic	3-0
Fraserburgh v Heart of Midlothian	0-3
Hibernian v Clyde	7-0
Duns v Aberdeen	0-8

THIRD ROUND

Stirling Albion v Celtic	3-4
Hamilton Academicals v Morton	2-0
Partick Thistle v Buckie Thistle	5-3
Motherwell v Raith Rovers	4-1
Third Lanark v Rangers	0-0, 4-4, 2-3
Berwick Rangers v Dundee	3-0
Queen of the South v Heart of Midlothian	1-2
Hibernian v Aberdeen	1-3

FOURTH ROUND

Hamilton Academicals v Celtic	1-2
Partick Thistle v Motherwell	1-1, 1-2
Rangers v Berwick Rangers	4-0
Aberdeen v Heart of Midlothian	3-0

SEMI-FINAL

Celtic v Motherwell	2-2, 3-1
Rangers v Aberdeen	0-6

FINAL

Aberdeen v Celtic	1-2

Since the offside rule was changed in 1925, the record number of League games which a club has played in any one season without conceding a goal is 30. Port Vale, with their unpopular yet effective brand of defensive football, set this record in Division Three North, 1953-54. That season, Vale lost but three games, also a record for that division, conceding just 21 goals, a League record.

Stalemate

On 9 January 1954, 15 of the 32 Third Round FA Cup ties played that day ended as draws, a record for the FA Cup competition.

The record Scottish FA Cup win away from home was set on 13 February 1954. Then, in the Second Round, Raith Rovers crumpled Coldstream 10-1 on their own ground.

FIRST DIVISION

		P	W	D	L	F	A	Pts
1	Chelsea	42	20	12	10	81	57	52
2	Wolves	42	19	10	13	89	70	48
3	Portsmouth	42	18	12	12	74	62	48
4	Sunderland	42	15	18	9	64	54	48
5	Man United	42	20	7	15	84	74	47
6	Aston Villa	42	20	7	15	72	73	47
7	Man City	42	18	10	14	76	69	46
8	Newcastle	42	17	9	16	89	77	43
9	Arsenal	42	17	9	16	69	63	43
10	Burnley	42	17	9	16	51	48	43
11	Everton	42	16	10	16	62	68	42
12	Huddersfield	42	14	13	15	63	68	41
13	Sheff United	42	17	7	18	70	86	41
14	Preston	42	16	8	18	83	64	40
15	Charlton	42	15	10	17	76	75	40
16	Tottenham	42	16	8	18	72	73	40
17	WBA	42	16	8	18	76	96	40
18	Bolton	42	13	13	16	62	69	39
19	Blackpool	42	14	10	18	60	64	38
20	Cardiff	42	13	11	18	62	76	37
21	Leicester	42	12	11	19	74	86	35
22	Sheff Wed	42	8	10	24	63	100	26

SECOND DIVISION

		P	W	D	L	F	A	Pts
1	Birmingham	42	22	10	10	92	47	54
2	Luton	42	23	8	11	88	53	54
3	Rotherham	42	25	4	13	94	64	54
4	Leeds	42	23	7	12	70	53	53
5	Stoke	42	21	10	11	69	46	52
6	Blackburn	42	22	6	14	114	79	50
7	Notts County	42	21	6	15	74	71	48
8	West Ham	42	18	10	14	74	70	46
9	Bristol Rovers	42	19	7	16	75	70	45
10	Swansea	42	17	9	16	86	83	43
11	Liverpool	42	16	10	16	92	96	42
12	Middlesbrough	42	18	6	18	73	82	42
13	Bury	42	15	11	16	77	72	41
14	Fulham	42	14	11	17	76	79	39
15	Nottm Forest	42	16	7	19	58	62	39
16	Lincoln	42	13	10	19	68	79	36
17	Port Vale	42	12	11	19	48	71	35
18	Doncaster	42	14	7	21	58	95	35
19	Hull	42	12	10	20	44	69	34
20	Plymouth	42	12	7	23	57	82	31
21	Ipswich	42	11	6	25	57	92	28
22	Derby	42	7	9	26	53	82	23

THIRD DIVISION (SOUTH)

		P	W	D	L	F	A	Pts
1	Bristol City	46	30	10	6	101	47	70
2	Leyton Orient	46	26	9	11	89	47	61
3	Southampton	46	24	11	11	75	51	59
4	Gillingham	46	20	15	11	77	66	55
5	Millwall	46	20	11	15	72	68	51
6	Brighton	46	20	10	16	76	63	50
7	Watford	46	18	14	14	71	62	50
8	Torquay	46	18	12	16	82	82	48
9	Coventry	46	18	11	17	67	59	47
10	Southend	46	17	12	17	83	80	46
11	Brentford	46	16	14	16	82	82	46
12	Norwich	46	18	10	18	60	60	46
13	Northampton	46	19	8	19	73	81	46
14	Aldershot	46	16	13	17	75	71	45
15	QPR	46	15	14	17	69	75	44
16	Shrewsbury	46	16	10	20	70	78	42
17	Bournemouth	46	12	18	16	57	65	42
18	Reading	46	13	15	18	65	73	41
19	Newport	46	11	16	19	60	73	38
20	Crystal Palace	46	11	16	19	52	80	38
21	Swindon	46	11	15	20	46	64	37
22	Exeter	46	11	15	20	47	73	37
23	Walsall	46	10	14	22	75	86	34
24	Colchester	46	9	13	24	53	91	31

THIRD DIVISION (NORTH)

		P	W	D	L	F	A	Pts
1	Barnsley	46	30	5	11	86	46	65
2	Accrington	46	25	11	10	96	67	61
3	Scunthorpe	46	23	12	11	81	53	58
4	York	46	24	10	12	92	63	58
5	Hartlepools	46	25	5	16	64	49	55
6	Chesterfield	46	24	6	16	81	70	54
7	Gateshead	46	20	12	14	65	69	52
8	Workington	46	18	14	14	68	55	50
9	Stockport	46	18	12	16	84	70	48
10	Oldham	46	19	10	17	74	68	48
11	Southport	46	16	16	14	47	44	48
12	Rochdale	46	17	14	15	69	66	48
13	Mansfield	46	18	9	19	65	71	45
14	Halifax	46	15	13	18	63	67	43
15	Darlington	46	14	14	18	62	73	42
16	Bradford PA	46	15	11	20	56	70	41
17	Barrow	46	17	6	23	70	89	40
18	Wrexham	46	13	12	21	65	77	38
19	Tranmere	46	13	11	22	55	70	37
20	Carlisle	46	15	6	25	78	89	36
21	Bradford City	46	13	10	23	47	55	36
22	Crewe	46	10	14	22	68	91	34
23	Grimsby	46	13	8	25	47	78	34
24	Chester	46	12	9	25	44	77	33

SCOTTISH DIVISION 'A'

		P	W	D	L	F	A	Pts
1	Aberdeen	30	24	1	5	73	26	49
2	Celtic	30	19	8	3	76	37	46
3	Rangers	30	19	3	8	67	33	41
4	Hearts	30	16	7	7	74	45	39
5	Hibernian	30	15	4	11	64	54	34
6	St Mirren	30	12	8	10	55	54	32
7	Clyde	30	11	9	10	59	50	31
8	Dundee	30	13	4	13	48	48	30
9	Partick Thistle	30	11	7	12	49	61	29
10	Kilmarnock	30	10	6	14	46	58	26
11	East Fife	30	9	6	15	51	62	24
12	Falkirk	30	8	8	14	42	54	24
13	Queen of the S	30	9	6	15	38	56	24
14	Raith	30	10	3	17	49	57	23
15	Motherwell	30	9	4	17	42	62	22
16	Stirling	30	2	2	26	29	105	6

SCOTTISH DIVISION 'B'

		P	W	D	L	F	A	Pts
1	Airdrieonians	30	18	10	2	103	61	46
2	Dunfermline	30	19	4	7	72	40	42
3	Hamilton	30	17	5	8	74	51	39
4	Queen's Park	30	15	5	10	65	36	35
5	Third Lanark	30	13	7	10	63	49	33
6	Stenhousemuir	30	12	8	10	70	51	32
7	St Johnstone	30	15	2	13	60	51	32
8	Ayr	30	14	4	12	61	73	32
9	Morton	30	12	5	13	58	69	29
10	Forfar	30	11	6	13	63	80	28
11	Albion	30	8	10	12	50	69	26
12	Arbroath	30	8	8	14	55	72	24
13	Dundee United	30	8	6	16	55	70	22
14	Cowdenbeath	30	8	5	17	55	72	21
15	Alloa	30	7	6	17	51	75	20
16	Brechin	30	8	3	19	53	89	19

FA CUP 1954-55

FOURTH ROUND

Everton v Liverpool	0-4
Torquay United v Huddersfield Town	0-1
Hartlepools United v Nottingham Forest	1-1, 1-2
Newcastle United v Brentford	3-2
Sheffield Wednesday v Notts County	1-1, 0-1
Bristol Rovers v Chelsea	1-3
Bishop Auckland v York City	1-3
Tottenham Hotspur v Port Vale	4-2
Swansea Town v Stoke City	3-1
Preston North End v Sunderland	3-3, 0-2
Wolverhampton Wanderers v Arsenal	1-0
West Bromwich Albion v Charlton Athletic	2-4
Birmingham City v Bolton Wanderers	2-1
Doncaster Rovers v Aston Villa	0-0, 2-2, 1-1, 0-0, 3-1
Rotherham United v Luton Town	1-5
Manchester City v Manchester United	2-0

FIFTH ROUND

Liverpool v Huddersfield Town	0-2
Nottingham Forest v Newcastle United	1-1, 2-2, 1-2
Notts County v Chelsea	1-0
York City v Tottenham Hotspur	3-1
Swansea Town v Sunderland	2-2, 0-1
Wolverhampton Wanderers v Charlton Athletic	4-1
Birmingham City v Doncaster Rovers	2-1
Luton Town v Manchester City	0-2

SIXTH ROUND

Huddersfield Town v Newcastle United	1-1, 0-2
Notts County v York City	0-1
Sunderland v Wolverhampton Wanderers	2-0
Birmingham City v Manchester City	0-1

SEMI-FINAL

Newcastle United v York City	1-1, 2-0
Sunderland v Manchester City	0-1

FINAL

Newcastle United v Manchester City	3-1

SCOTTISH FA CUP 1954-55

FIFTH ROUND

Clyde v Albion Rovers	3-0
Morton v Raith Rovers	1-3
Ayr United v Inverness Caledonian	1-1, 2-4
Heart of Midlothian v Hibernian	5-0
Stirling Albion v Aberdeen	0-6
Dundee v Rangers	0-0, 0-1
Airdrieonians v Forfar Athletic	4-3
Dunfermline Athletic v Partick Thistle	4-2
Third Lanark v Queen of the South	2-1
Forres Mechanics v Motherwell	3-4
East Fife v Kilmarnock	1-2
Alloa Athletic v Celtic	2-4
Arbroath v St Johnstone	0-4
Hamilton Academicals v St Mirren	2-1
Falkirk v Stenhousemuir	4-0
Buckie Thistle v Inverness Thistle	2-0

SIXTH ROUND

Clyde v Raith Rovers	3-1
Inverness Caledonian v Falkirk	0-7
Buckie Thistle v Heart of Midlothian	0-6
Aberdeen v Rangers	2-1
Airdrieonians v Dunfermline Athletic	7-0
Third Lanark v Motherwell	1-3
Celtic v Kilmarnock	1-1, 1-0
St Johnstone v Hamilton Academicals	0-1

SEVENTH ROUND

Clyde v Falkirk	5-0
Aberdeen v Heart of Midlothian	1-1, 2-0
Airdrieonians v Motherwell	4-1
Celtic v Hamilton Academicals	2-1

SEMI-FINAL

Aberdeen v Clyde	2-2, 0-1
Airdrieonians v Celtic	2-2, 0-2

FINAL

Celtic v Clyde	1-1, 0-1

A combined effort

Stan Milburn and Jack Froggatt, both Leicester City defenders, are officially recorded as 'sharing one own goal' on 18 December 1954. In the Division One game with Chelsea at Stamford Bridge, Froggatt and Milburn were involved in a misunderstanding in front of goal, and simultaneously booted the ball into the Leicester net, thus sharing the blame. Chelsea won the game by three goals to one.

Stoke City and Bury created an endurance record for an FA Cup match when they met five times in the Third Round in January 1955. Altogether they played for 9 hours and 22 minutes before Stoke won 3-2 at Old Trafford.

On 2 April 1955, Duncan Edwards of Manchester United became the youngest ever England international when, aged 18 years six months, he played against Scotland.

FIRST DIVISION

		P	W	D	L	F	A	Pts
1	Man United	42	25	10	7	83	51	60
2	Blackpool	42	20	9	13	86	62	49
3	Wolves	42	20	9	13	89	65	49
4	Man City	42	18	10	14	82	69	46
5	Arsenal	42	18	10	14	60	61	46
6	Birmingham	42	18	9	15	75	57	45
7	Burnley	42	18	8	16	64	54	44
8	Bolton	42	18	7	17	71	58	43
9	Sunderland	42	17	9	16	80	95	43
10	Luton	42	17	8	17	66	64	42
11	Newcastle	42	17	7	18	85	70	41
12	Portsmouth	42	16	9	17	78	85	41
13	WBA	42	18	5	19	58	70	41
14	Charlton	42	17	6	19	75	81	40
15	Everton	42	15	10	17	55	69	40
16	Chelsea	42	14	11	17	64	77	39
17	Cardiff	42	15	9	18	55	69	39
18	Tottenham	42	15	7	20	61	71	37
19	Preston	42	14	8	20	73	72	36
20	Aston Villa	42	11	13	18	52	69	35
21	Huddersfield	42	14	7	21	54	83	35
22	Sheff United	42	12	9	21	63	77	33

SECOND DIVISION

		P	W	D	L	F	A	Pts
1	Sheff Wed	42	21	13	8	101	62	55
2	Leeds	42	23	6	13	80	60	52
3	Liverpool	42	21	6	15	85	63	48
4	Blackburn	42	21	6	15	84	65	48
5	Leicester	42	21	6	15	94	78	48
6	Bristol Rovers	42	21	6	15	84	70	48
7	Nottm Forest	42	19	9	14	68	63	47
8	Lincoln	42	18	10	14	79	65	46
9	Fulham	42	20	6	16	89	79	46
10	Swansea	42	20	6	16	83	81	46
11	Bristol City	42	19	7	16	80	64	45
12	Port Vale	42	16	13	13	60	58	45
13	Stoke	42	20	4	18	71	62	44
14	Middlesbrough	42	16	8	18	76	78	40
15	Bury	42	16	8	18	86	90	40
16	West Ham	42	14	11	17	74	69	39
17	Doncaster	42	12	11	19	69	96	35
18	Barnsley	42	11	12	19	47	84	34
19	Rotherham	42	12	9	21	56	75	33
20	Notts County	42	11	9	22	55	82	31
21	Plymouth	42	10	8	24	54	87	28
22	Hull	42	10	6	26	53	97	26

THIRD DIVISION (NORTH)

		P	W	D	L	F	A	Pts
1	Grimsby	46	31	6	9	76	29	68
2	Derby	46	28	7	11	110	55	63
3	Accrington	46	25	9	12	92	57	59
4	Hartlepools	46	26	5	15	81	60	57
5	Southport	46	23	11	12	66	53	57
6	Chesterfield	46	25	4	17	94	66	54
7	Stockport	46	21	9	16	90	61	51
8	Bradford City	46	18	13	15	78	64	49
9	Scunthorpe	46	20	8	18	75	63	48
10	Workington	46	19	9	18	75	63	47
11	York	46	19	9	18	85	72	47
12	Rochdale	46	17	13	16	66	84	47
13	Gateshead	46	17	11	18	77	84	45
14	Wrexham	46	16	10	20	66	73	42
15	Darlington	46	16	9	21	60	73	41
16	Tranmere	46	16	9	21	59	84	41
17	Chester	46	13	14	19	52	82	40
18	Mansfield	46	14	11	21	84	81	39
19	Halifax	46	14	11	21	66	76	39
20	Oldham	46	10	18	18	76	86	38
21	Carlisle	46	15	8	23	71	95	38
22	Barrow	46	12	9	25	61	83	33
23	Bradford PA	46	13	7	26	61	122	33
24	Crewe	46	9	10	27	50	105	28

THIRD DIVISION (SOUTH)

		P	W	D	L	F	A	Pts
1	Leyton Orient	46	29	8	9	106	49	66
2	Brighton	46	29	7	10	112	50	65
3	Ipswich	46	25	14	7	106	60	64
4	Southend	46	21	11	14	88	80	53
5	Torquay	46	20	12	14	86	63	52
6	Brentford	46	19	14	13	69	66	52
7	Norwich	46	19	13	14	86	82	51
8	Coventry	46	20	9	17	73	60	49
9	Bournemouth	46	19	10	17	63	51	48
10	Gillingham	46	19	10	17	69	71	48
11	Northampton	46	20	7	19	67	71	47
12	Colchester	46	18	11	17	76	81	47
13	Shrewsbury	46	17	12	17	69	66	46
14	Southampton	46	18	8	20	91	81	44
15	Aldershot	46	12	16	18	70	90	40
16	Exeter	46	15	10	21	58	77	40
17	Reading	46	15	9	22	70	79	39
18	QPR	46	14	11	21	64	86	39
19	Newport	46	15	9	22	58	79	39
20	Walsall	46	15	8	23	68	84	38
21	Watford	46	13	11	22	52	85	37
22	Millwall	46	15	6	25	83	100	36
23	Crystal Palace	46	12	10	24	54	83	34
24	Swindon	46	8	14	24	34	78	30

SCOTTISH LEAGUE 'A'

		P	W	D	L	F	A	Pts
1	Rangers	34	22	8	4	85	27	52
2	Aberdeen	34	18	10	6	87	50	46
3	Hearts	34	19	7	8	99	47	45
4	Hibernian	34	19	7	8	86	50	45
5	Celtic	34	16	9	9	55	39	41
6	Queen of the S	34	16	5	13	69	73	37
7	Airdrieonians	34	14	8	12	85	96	36
8	Kilmarnock	34	12	10	12	52	45	34
9	Partick Thistle	34	13	7	14	62	60	33
10	Motherwell	34	11	11	12	53	59	33
11	Raith	34	12	9	13	58	75	33
12	East Fife	34	13	5	16	61	69	31
13	Dundee	34	12	6	16	56	65	30
14	Falkirk	34	11	6	17	58	75	28
15	St Mirren	34	10	7	17	57	70	27
16	Dunfermline	34	10	6	18	42	82	26
17	Clyde	34	8	6	20	50	74	22
18	Stirling	34	4	5	25	23	82	13

SCOTTISH LEAGUE 'B'

		P	W	D	L	F	A	Pts
1	Queen's Park	36	23	8	5	78	28	54
2	Ayr	36	24	3	9	103	55	51
3	St Johnstone	36	21	7	8	86	45	49
4	Dumbarton	36	21	5	10	83	62	47
5	Stenhousemuir	36	20	4	12	82	54	44
6	Brechin	36	18	6	12	60	56	42
7	Cowdenbeath	36	16	7	13	80	85	39
8	Dundee United	36	12	14	10	78	65	38
9	Morton	36	15	6	15	71	69	36
10	Third Lanark	36	16	3	17	80	64	35
11	Hamilton	36	13	7	16	86	84	33
12	Stranraer	36	14	5	17	77	92	33
13	Alloa	36	12	7	17	67	73	31
14	Berwick	36	11	9	16	52	77	31
15	Forfar	36	10	9	17	62	75	29
16	E Stirlingshire	36	9	10	17	66	94	28
17	Albion	36	8	11	17	58	82	27
18	Arbroath	36	10	6	20	47	67	26
19	Montrose	36	4	3	29	44	133	11

Accrington Stanley set a League record early in the 1955-56 season by fielding a side composed entirely of Scottish-born players. During the season, this team appeared several times. Indeed, all but four of the first-team squad of 19 players the club used that season in the Third Division North were born in Scotland.

On 3 September 1955, Wolves beat Cardiff 9-1 away from home to equal the Division One record away win. Curiously, later in the season, Cardiff won 2-0 at Wolves.

All four countries in the Home Championship finished level with three points, the first time this had ever happened.

FIRST DIVISION

		P	W	D	L	F	A	Pts
1	Man United	42	28	8	6	103	54	64
2	Tottenham	42	22	12	8	104	56	56
3	Preston	42	23	10	9	84	56	56
4	Blackpool	42	22	9	11	93	65	53
5	Arsenal	42	21	8	13	85	69	50
6	Wolves	42	20	8	14	94	70	48
7	Burnley	42	18	10	14	56	50	46
8	Leeds	42	15	14	13	72	63	44
9	Bolton	42	16	12	14	65	65	44
10	Aston Villa	42	14	15	13	65	55	43
11	WBA	42	14	14	14	59	61	42
12	Birmingham*	42	15	9	18	69	69	39
13	Chelsea*	42	13	13	16	73	73	39
14	Sheff Wed	42	16	6	20	82	88	38
15	Everton	42	14	10	18	61	79	38
16	Luton	42	14	9	19	58	76	37
17	Newcastle	42	14	8	20	67	87	36
18	Man City	42	13	9	20	78	88	35
19	Portsmouth	42	10	13	19	62	92	33
20	Sunderland	42	12	8	22	67	88	32
21	Cardiff	42	10	9	23	53	88	29
22	Charlton	42	9	4	29	62	120	22

*Equal

SECOND DIVISION

		P	W	D	L	F	A	Pts
1	Leicester	42	25	11	6	109	67	61
2	Nottm Forest	42	22	10	10	94	55	54
3	Liverpool	42	21	11	10	82	54	53
4	Blackburn	42	21	10	11	83	75	52
5	Stoke	42	20	8	14	83	58	48
6	Middlesbrough	42	19	10	13	84	60	48
7	Sheff United	42	19	8	15	87	76	46
8	West Ham	42	19	8	15	59	63	46
9	Bristol Rovers	42	18	9	15	81	67	45
10	Swansea	42	19	7	16	90	90	45
11	Fulham	42	19	4	19	84	76	42
12	Huddersfield	42	18	6	18	68	74	42
13	Bristol City	42	16	9	17	74	79	41
14	Doncaster	42	15	10	17	77	77	40
15	Leyton Orient	42	15	10	17	66	84	40
16	Grimsby	42	17	5	20	61	62	39
17	Rotherham	42	13	11	18	74	75	37
18	Lincoln	42	14	6	22	54	80	34
19	Barnsley	42	12	10	20	59	89	34
20	Notts County	42	9	12	21	58	86	30
21	Bury	42	8	9	25	60	96	25
22	Port Vale	42	8	6	28	57	101	22

FA CUP 1956-57

FOURTH ROUND

Middlesbrough v Aston Villa	2-3
Bristol City v Rhyl	3-0
Burnley v New Brighton	9-0
Huddersfield Town v Peterborough United	3-1
Newport County v Arsenal	0-2
Bristol Rovers v Preston North End	1-4
Blackpool v Fulham	6-2
West Bromwich Albion v Sunderland	4-2
Wrexham v Manchester United	0-5
Everton v West Ham United	2-1
Wolverhampton Wanderers v Bournemouth	0-1
Tottenham Hotspur v Chelsea	4-0
Southend United v Birmingham City	1-6
Millwall v Newcastle United	2-1
Cardiff City v Barnsley	0-1
Portsmouth v Nottingham Forest	1-3

FIFTH ROUND

Aston Villa v Bristol City	2-1
Huddersfield Town v Burnley	1-2
Preston North End v Arsenal	3-3, 1-2
Blackpool v West Bromwich Albion	0-0, 1-2
Manchester United v Everton	1-0
Bournemouth v Tottenham Hotspur	3-1
Millwall v Birmingham City	1-4
Barnsley v Nottingham Forest	1-2

SIXTH ROUND

Burnley v Aston Villa	1-1, 0-2
West Bromwich Albion v Arsenal	2-2, 2-1
Bournemouth v Manchester United	1-2
Birmingham City v Nottingham Forest	0-0, 1-0

SEMI-FINAL

Aston Villa v West Bromwich Albion	2-2, 1-0
Manchester United v Birmingham City	2-0

FINAL

Aston Villa v Manchester United	2-1

THIRD DIVISION (SOUTH)

		P	W	D	L	F	A	Pts
1	Ipswich	46	25	9	12	101	54	59
2	Torquay	46	24	11	11	89	64	59
3	Colchester	46	22	14	10	84	56	58
4	Southampton	46	22	10	14	76	52	54
5	Bournemouth	46	19	14	13	88	62	52
6	Brighton	46	19	14	13	86	65	52
7	Southend	46	18	12	16	73	65	48
8	Brentford	46	16	16	14	78	76	48
9	Shrewsbury	46	15	18	13	72	79	48
10	QPR	46	18	11	17	61	60	47
11	Watford	46	18	10	18	72	75	46
12	Newport	46	16	13	17	65	62	45
13	Reading	46	18	9	19	80	81	45
14	Northampton	46	18	9	19	66	73	45
15	Walsall	46	16	12	18	80	74	44
16	Coventry	46	16	12	18	74	84	44
17	Millwall	46	16	12	18	64	84	44
18	Plymouth	46	16	11	19	68	73	43
19	Aldershot	46	15	12	19	79	92	42
20	Crystal Palace	46	11	18	17	62	75	40
21	Exeter	46	12	13	21	61	79	37
22	Gillingham	46	12	13	21	54	85	37
23	Swindon	46	15	6	25	66	96	36
24	Norwich	46	8	15	23	61	94	31

THIRD DIVISION (NORTH)

		P	W	D	L	F	A	Pts
1	Derby	46	26	11	9	111	53	63
2	Hartlepools	46	25	9	12	90	63	59
3	Accrington	46	25	8	13	95	64	58
4	Workington	46	24	10	12	93	63	58
5	Stockport	46	23	8	15	91	75	54
6	Chesterfield	46	22	9	15	96	79	53
7	York	46	21	10	15	75	61	52
8	Hull	46	21	10	15	84	69	52
9	Bradford City	46	22	8	16	78	68	52
10	Barrow	46	21	9	16	76	62	51
11	Halifax	46	21	7	18	65	70	49
12	Wrexham	46	19	10	17	97	74	48
13	Rochdale	46	18	12	16	65	65	48
14	Scunthorpe	46	15	15	16	71	69	45
15	Carlisle	46	16	13	17	76	85	45
16	Mansfield	46	17	10	19	91	90	44
17	Gateshead	46	17	10	19	72	90	44
18	Darlington	46	17	8	21	82	95	42
19	Oldham	46	12	15	19	66	74	39
20	Bradford PA	46	16	3	27	66	93	35
21	Chester	46	10	13	23	55	84	33
22	Southport	46	10	12	24	52	94	32
23	Tranmere	46	7	13	26	51	91	27
24	Crewe	46	6	9	31	43	110	21

SCOTTISH FA CUP 1956-57

FIFTH ROUND

Berwick Rangers v Falkirk	1-2
Hibernian v Aberdeen	3-4
Dundee v Clyde	0-0, 1-2
Queen's Park v Brechin City	3-0
Inverness Caledonian v Raith Rovers	2-3
Stenhousemuir v Dundee United	1-1, 0-4
Queen of the South v Dumbarton	2-2, 2-4
Stirling Albion v Motherwell	1-2
Dunfermline Athletic v Morton	3-0
St Mirren v Partick Thistle	1-1, 2-2, 5-1
Heart of Midlothian v Rangers	0-4
Forres Mechanics v Celtic	0-5
Hamilton Academicals v Alloa Athletic	2-2, 5-3
Stranraer v Airdrieonians	1-2
East Fife v St Johnstone	4-0
Kilmarnock v Ayr United	1-0

SIXTH ROUND

Falkirk v Aberdeen	3-1
Queen's Park v Clyde	1-1, 0-2
Raith Rovers v Dundee United	7-0
Motherwell v Dumbarton	1-3
St Mirren v Dunfermline Athletic	1-0
Celtic v Rangers	4-4, 2-0
Hamilton Academicals v Airdrieonians	1-2
East Fife v Kilmarnock	0-0, 0-2

SEVENTH ROUND

Falkirk v Clyde	2-1
Dumbarton v Raith Rovers	0-4
Celtic v St Mirren	2-1
Kilmarnock v Airdrieonians	3-1

SEMI-FINAL

Falkirk v Raith Rovers	2-2, 2-0
Celtic v Kilmarnock	1-1, 1-3

FINAL

Falkirk v Kilmarnock	1-1, 2-1

SCOTTISH FIRST DIVISION

		P	W	D	L	F	A	Pts
1	Rangers	34	26	3	5	96	48	55
2	Hearts	34	24	5	5	81	48	53
3	Kilmarnock	34	16	10	8	57	39	42
4	Raith	34	16	7	11	84	58	39
5	Celtic	34	15	8	11	58	43	38
6	Aberdeen	34	18	2	14	79	59	38
7	Motherwell	34	16	5	13	72	66	37
8	Partick Thistle	34	13	8	13	53	51	34
9	Hibernian	34	12	9	13	69	56	33
10	Dundee	34	13	6	15	55	61	32
11	Airdrieonians	34	13	4	17	77	89	30
12	St Mirren	34	12	6	16	58	72	30
13	Queen's Park	34	11	7	16	55	59	29
14	Falkirk	34	10	8	16	51	70	28
15	East Fife	34	10	6	18	59	82	26
16	Queen of the S	34	10	5	19	54	96	25
17	Dunfermline	34	9	6	19	54	74	24
18	Ayr	34	7	5	22	48	89	19

SCOTTISH SECOND DIVISION

		P	W	D	L	F	A	Pts
1	Clyde	36	29	6	1	122	39	64
2	Third Lanark	36	24	3	9	105	51	51
3	Cowdenbeath	36	20	5	11	87	65	45
4	Morton	36	18	7	11	81	70	43
5	Albion	36	18	6	12	98	80	42
6	Brechin	36	15	10	11	72	68	40
7	Stranraer	36	15	10	11	79	77	40
8	Stirling	36	17	5	14	81	64	39
9	Dumbarton	36	17	4	15	101	70	38
10	Arbroath	36	17	4	15	79	57	38
11	Hamilton	36	14	8	14	69	68	36
12	St Johnstone	36	14	6	16	79	80	34
13	Dundee United	36	14	6	16	75	80	34
14	Stenhousemuir	36	13	6	17	71	81	32
15	Alloa	36	11	5	20	66	99	27
16	Forfar	36	9	5	22	75	100	23
17	Montrose	36	7	7	22	54	124	21
18	Berwick	36	7	6	23	58	114	20
19	E Stirlingshire	36	5	7	24	56	121	17

New man in charge
On 1 January 1957, Alan Hardaker became secretary to the Football League. Hardaker, once an amateur footballer with Hull City, had been assistant secretary since 1951.

After beating Scunthorpe United 2-1, on 19 September 1956, Crewe Alexandra of the Third Division North did not win again until they beat Bradford City 1-0 on 13 April 1957, a League record of 30 games without a win.

FIRST DIVISION

		P	W	D	L	F	A	Pts
1	Wolves	42	28	8	6	103	47	64
2	Preston	42	26	7	9	100	51	59
3	Tottenham	42	21	9	12	93	77	51
4	WBA	42	18	14	10	92	70	50
5	Man City	42	22	5	15	104	100	49
6	Burnley	42	21	5	16	80	74	47
7	Blackpool	42	19	6	17	80	67	44
8	Luton	42	19	6	17	69	63	44
9	Man United	42	16	11	15	85	75	43
10	Nottm Forest	42	16	10	16	69	63	42
11	Chelsea	42	15	12	15	83	79	42
12	Arsenal	42	16	7	19	73	85	39
13	Birmingham	42	14	11	17	76	89	39
14	Aston Villa	42	16	7	19	73	86	39
15	Bolton	42	14	10	18	65	87	38
16	Everton	42	13	11	18	65	75	37
17	Leeds	42	14	9	19	51	63	37
18	Leicester	42	14	5	23	91	112	33
19	Newcastle	42	12	8	22	73	81	32
20	Portsmouth	42	12	8	22	73	88	32
21	Sunderland	42	10	12	20	54	97	32
22	Sheff Wed	42	12	7	23	69	92	31

SECOND DIVISION

		P	W	D	L	F	A	Pts
1	West Ham	42	23	11	8	101	54	57
2	Blackburn	42	22	12	8	93	57	56
3	Charlton	42	24	7	11	107	69	55
4	Liverpool	42	22	10	10	79	54	54
5	Fulham	42	20	12	10	97	59	52
6	Sheff United	42	21	10	11	75	50	52
7	Middlesbrough	42	19	7	16	83	74	45
8	Ipswich	42	16	12	14	68	69	44
9	Huddersfield	42	14	16	12	63	66	44
10	Bristol Rovers	42	17	8	17	85	80	42
11	Stoke	42	18	6	18	75	73	42
12	Leyton Orient	42	18	5	19	77	79	41
13	Grimsby	42	17	6	19	86	83	40
14	Barnsley	42	14	12	16	70	74	40
15	Cardiff	42	14	9	19	63	77	37
16	Derby	42	14	8	20	60	81	36
17	Bristol City	42	13	9	20	63	88	35
18	Rotherham	42	14	5	23	65	101	33
19	Swansea	42	11	9	22	72	99	31
20	Lincoln	42	11	9	22	55	82	31
21	Notts County	42	12	6	24	44	80	30
22	Doncaster	42	8	11	23	56	88	27

THIRD DIVISION (NORTH)

		P	W	D	L	F	A	Pts
1	Scunthorpe	46	29	8	9	88	50	66
2	Accrington	46	25	9	12	83	61	59
3	Bradford City	46	21	15	10	73	49	57
4	Bury	46	23	10	13	94	62	56
5	Hull	46	19	15	12	78	67	53
6	Mansfield	46	22	8	16	100	92	52
7	Halifax	46	20	11	15	83	69	51
8	Chesterfield	46	18	15	13	71	69	51
9	Stockport	46	18	11	17	74	67	47
10	Rochdale	46	19	8	19	79	67	46
11	Tranmere	46	18	10	18	82	76	46
12	Wrexham	46	17	12	17	61	63	46
13	York	46	17	12	17	68	76	46
14	Gateshead	46	15	15	16	68	76	45
15	Oldham	46	14	17	15	72	84	45
16	Carlisle	46	19	6	21	80	78	44
17	Hartlepools	46	16	12	18	73	76	44
18	Barrow	46	13	15	18	66	74	41
19	Workington	46	14	13	19	72	81	41
20	Darlington	46	17	7	22	78	89	41
21	Chester	46	13	13	20	73	81	39
22	Bradford PA	46	13	11	22	68	95	37
23	Southport	46	11	6	29	52	88	28
24	Crewe	46	8	7	31	47	93	23

THIRD DIVISION (SOUTH)

		P	W	D	L	F	A	Pts
1	Brighton	46	24	12	10	88	64	60
2	Brentford	46	24	10	12	82	56	58
3	Plymouth	46	25	8	13	67	48	58
4	Swindon	46	21	15	10	79	50	57
5	Reading	46	21	13	12	79	51	55
6	Southampton	46	22	10	14	112	72	54
7	Southend	46	21	12	13	90	58	54
8	Norwich	46	19	15	12	75	70	53
9	Bournemouth	46	21	9	16	81	74	51
10	QPR	46	18	14	14	64	65	50
11	Newport	46	17	14	15	73	67	48
12	Colchester	46	17	13	16	77	79	47
13	Northampton	46	19	6	21	87	79	44
14	Crystal Palace	46	15	13	18	70	72	43
15	Port Vale	46	16	10	20	67	58	42
16	Watford	46	13	16	17	59	77	42
17	Shrewsbury	46	15	10	21	49	71	40
18	Aldershot	46	12	16	18	59	89	40
19	Coventry	46	13	13	20	61	81	39
20	Walsall	46	14	9	23	61	75	37
21	Torquay	46	11	13	22	49	74	35
22	Gillingham	46	13	9	24	52	81	35
23	Millwall	46	11	9	26	63	91	31
24	Exeter	46	11	9	26	57	99	31

SCOTTISH FIRST DIVISION

		P	W	D	L	F	A	Pts
1	Hearts	34	29	4	1	132	29	62
2	Rangers	34	22	5	7	89	49	49
3	Celtic	34	19	8	7	84	47	46
4	Clyde	34	18	6	10	84	61	42
5	Kilmarnock	34	14	9	11	60	55	37
6	Partick Thistle	34	17	3	14	69	71	37
7	Raith Rovers	34	14	7	13	66	56	35
8	Motherwell	34	12	8	14	68	67	32
9	Hibernian	34	13	5	16	59	60	31
10	Falkirk	34	11	9	14	64	82	31
11	Dundee	34	13	5	16	49	65	31
12	Aberdeen	34	14	2	18	68	76	30
13	St Mirren	34	11	8	15	59	66	30
14	Third Lanark	34	13	4	17	69	88	30
15	Queen of the S	34	12	5	17	61	72	29
16	Airdrieonians	34	13	2	19	71	92	28
17	East Fife	34	10	3	21	45	88	23
18	Queen's Park	34	4	1	29	41	114	9

SCOTTISH SECOND DIVISION

		P	W	D	L	F	A	Pts
1	Stirling Albion	36	25	5	6	105	48	55
2	Dunfermline	36	24	5	7	120	42	53
3	Arbroath	36	21	5	10	89	72	47
4	Dumbarton	36	20	4	12	92	57	44
5	Ayr	36	18	6	12	98	81	42
6	Cowdenbeath	36	17	8	11	100	85	42
7	Brechin	36	16	8	12	80	81	40
8	Alloa	36	15	9	12	88	78	39
9	Dundee United	36	12	9	15	81	77	33
10	Hamilton	36	12	9	15	70	79	33
11	St Johnstone	36	12	9	15	67	85	33
12	Forfar	36	13	6	17	70	71	32
13	Morton	36	12	8	16	77	83	32
14	Montrose	36	13	6	17	55	72	32
15	E Stirlingshire	36	12	5	19	55	79	29
16	Stenhousemuir	36	12	5	19	68	98	29
17	Albion	36	12	5	19	53	79	29
18	Stranraer	36	9	7	20	54	83	25
19	Berwick	36	5	5	26	37	109	15

FA CUP 1957-58

FOURTH ROUND

Everton v Blackburn Rovers	1-2
Cardiff City v Leyton Orient	4-1
Liverpool v Northampton Town	3-1
Newcastle United v Scunthorpe United	1-3
Wolverhampton Wanderers v Portsmouth	5-1
Chelsea v Darlington	3-3, 1-4
Stoke City v Middlesbrough	3-1
York City v Bolton Wanderers	0-0, 0-3
Manchester United v Ipswich Town	2-0
Sheffield Wednesday v Hull City	4-3
West Bromwich Albion v Nottingham Forest	3-3, 5-1
Tottenham Hotspur v Sheffield United	0-3
Bristol Rovers v Burnley	2-2, 3-2
Notts County v Bristol City	1-2
West Ham United v Stockport County	3-2
Fulham v Charlton Athletic	1-1, 2-0

FIFTH ROUND

Cardiff City v Blackburn Rovers	0-0, 1-2
Scunthorpe United v Liverpool	0-1
Wolverhampton Wanderers v Darlington	6-1
Bolton Wanderers v Stoke City	3-1
Manchester United v Sheffield Wednesday	3-0
Sheffield United v West Bromwich Albion	1-1, 1-4
Bristol City v Bristol Rovers	3-4
West Ham United v Fulham	2-3

SIXTH ROUND

Blackburn Rovers v Liverpool	2-1
Bolton Wanderers v Wolverhampton Wanderers	2-1
West Bromwich Albion v Manchester United	2-2, 0-1
Fulham v Bristol Rovers	3-1

SEMI-FINAL

Blackburn Rovers v Bolton Wanderers	1-2
Manchester United v Fulham	2-2, 5-3

FINAL

Bolton Wanderers v Manchester United	2-0

SCOTTISH FA CUP 1957-58

SECOND ROUND

Celtic v Stirling Albion	7-2
Clyde v Arbroath	4-0
Falkirk v St Johnstone	6-3
Montrose v Buckie Thistle	2-2, 1-4
Motherwell v Partick Thistle	2-2, 4-0
Inverness Caledonian v Stenhousemuir	5-2
Morton v Aberdeen	0-1
Raith Rovers v Dundee	0-1
Forfar Athletic v Rangers	1-9
St Mirren v Dunfermline Athletic	1-4
Queen of the South v Stranraer	7-0
Kilmarnock v Vale of Leithen	7-0
Dundee United v Hibernian	0-0, 0-2
Heart of Midlothian v Albion Rovers	4-1
Third Lanark v Lossiemouth	6-1
Queen's Park v Fraserburgh	7-2

THIRD ROUND

Clyde v Celtic	2-0
Buckie Thistle v Falkirk	1-2
Inverness Caledonian v Motherwell	0-7
Dundee v Aberdeen	1-3
Dunfermline Athletic v Rangers	1-2
Kilmarnock v Queen of the South	2-2, 0-3
Heart of Midlothian v Hibernian	3-4
Third Lanark v Queen's Park	5-3

FOURTH ROUND

Clyde v Falkirk	2-1
Motherwell v Aberdeen	2-1
Queen of the South v Rangers	3-4
Hibernian v Third Lanark	3-2

SEMI-FINAL

Clyde v Motherwell	3-2
Rangers v Hibernian	2-2, 1-2

FINAL

Clyde v Hibernian	1-0

In Moscow on 18 May 1958, England played the USSR for the first time ever.

Before the start of the 1957-58 season, it was decided that four Divisions would be introduced in 1958-59. So at the end of the season, the top halves of both Third Divisions formed the new Division Three, and the rest of the teams made up Division Four.

Have boots, will travel
Tony McNamara, a right-winger, played in all four divisions of the Football League inside twelve months. On 12 October 1957, he played his last game for Everton in Division One, and on 27 September 1958 he made his debut for Bury in Division Three. In between, he played in Division Two for Liverpool, and in the Fourth Division for Crewe.

FIRST DIVISION

		P	W	D	L	F	A	Pts
1	Wolves	42	28	5	9	110	49	61
2	Man United	42	24	7	11	103	66	55
3	Arsenal	42	21	8	13	88	68	50
4	Bolton	42	20	10	12	79	66	50
5	WBA	42	18	13	11	88	68	49
6	West Ham	42	21	6	15	85	70	48
7	Burnley	42	19	10	13	81	70	48
8	Blackpool	42	18	11	13	66	49	47
9	Birmingham	42	20	6	16	84	68	46
10	Blackburn	42	17	10	15	76	70	44
11	Newcastle	42	17	7	18	80	80	41
12	Preston	42	17	7	18	70	77	41
13	Nottm Forest	42	17	6	19	71	74	40
14	Chelsea	42	18	4	20	77	98	40
15	Leeds	42	15	9	18	57	74	39
16	Everton	42	17	4	21	71	87	38
17	Luton	42	12	13	17	68	71	37
18	Tottenham	42	13	10	19	85	95	36
19	Leicester	42	11	10	21	67	98	32
20	Man City	42	11	9	22	64	95	31
21	Aston Villa	42	11	8	23	58	87	30
22	Portsmouth	42	6	9	27	64	112	21

SECOND DIVISION

		P	W	D	L	F	A	Pts
1	Sheff Wed	42	28	6	8	106	48	62
2	Fulham	42	27	6	9	96	61	60
3	Sheff United	42	23	7	12	82	48	53
4	Liverpool	42	24	5	13	87	62	53
5	Stoke	42	21	7	14	72	58	49
6	Bristol Rovers	42	18	12	12	80	64	48
7	Derby	42	20	8	14	74	71	48
8	Charlton	42	18	7	17	92	90	43
9	Cardiff	42	18	7	17	65	65	43
10	Bristol City	42	17	7	18	74	70	41
11	Swansea	42	16	9	17	79	81	41
12	Brighton	42	15	11	16	74	90	41
13	Middlesbrough	42	15	10	17	87	71	40
14	Huddersfield	42	16	8	18	62	55	40
15	Sunderland	42	16	8	18	64	75	40
16	Ipswich	42	17	6	19	62	77	40
17	Leyton Orient	42	14	8	20	71	78	36
18	Scunthorpe	42	12	9	21	55	84	33
19	Lincoln	42	11	7	24	63	93	29
20	Rotherham	42	10	9	23	42	82	29
21	Grimsby	42	9	10	23	62	90	28
22	Barnsley	42	10	7	25	55	91	27

FA CUP 1958-59

FOURTH ROUND

Nottingham Forest v Grimsby Town	4-1
Birmingham City v Fulham	1-1, 3-2
Wolverhampton W v Bolton W	1-2
Preston North End v Bradford City	3-2
Charlton Athletic v Everton	2-2, 1-4
Chelsea v Aston Villa	1-2
Blackburn Rovers v Burnley	1-2
Accrington Stanley v Portsmouth	0-0, 1-4
Colchester United v Arsenal	2-2, 0-4
Worcester City v Sheffield United	0-2
Tottenham Hotspur v Newport County	4-1
Norwich City v Cardiff City	3-2
Bristol City v Blackpool	1-1, 0-1
West Bromwich Albion v Brentford	2-0
Stoke City v Ipswich Town	0-1
Leicester City v Luton Town	1-1, 1-4

FIFTH ROUND

Birmingham City v Nottm Forest	1-1, 1-1, 0-5
Bolton W v Preston North End	2-2, 1-1, 1-0
Everton v Aston Villa	1-4
Burnley v Portsmouth	1-0
Arsenal v Sheffield United	2-2, 0-3
Tottenham Hotspur v Norwich City	1-1, 0-1
Blackpool v West Bromwich Albion	3-1
Ipswich Town v Luton Town	2-5

SIXTH ROUND

Nottingham Forest v Bolton Wanderers	2-1
Aston Villa v Burnley	0-0, 2-0
Sheffield United v Norwich City	1-1, 2-3
Blackpool v Luton Town	1-1, 0-1

SEMI-FINAL

Nottingham Forest v Aston Villa	1-0
Norwich City v Luton Town	1-1, 0-1

FINAL

Nottingham Forest v Luton Town	2-1

THIRD DIVISION

		P	W	D	L	F	A	Pts
1	Plymouth	46	23	16	7	89	59	62
2	Hull	46	26	9	11	90	55	61
3	Brentford	46	21	15	10	76	49	57
4	Norwich	46	22	13	11	89	62	57
5	Colchester	46	21	10	15	71	67	52
6	Reading	46	21	8	17	78	63	50
7	Tranmere	46	21	8	17	82	67	50
8	Southend	46	21	8	17	85	80	50
9	Halifax	46	21	8	17	80	77	50
10	Bury	46	17	14	15	69	58	48
11	Bradford City	46	18	11	17	84	76	47
12	Bournemouth	46	17	12	17	69	69	46
13	QPR	46	19	8	19	74	77	46
14	Southampton	46	17	11	18	88	80	45
15	Swindon	46	16	13	17	59	57	45
16	Chesterfield	46	17	10	19	67	64	44
17	Newport	46	17	9	20	69	68	43
18	Wrexham	46	14	14	18	63	77	42
19	Accrington	46	15	12	19	71	87	42
20	Mansfield	46	14	13	19	73	98	41
21	Stockport	46	13	10	23	65	78	36
22	Doncaster	46	14	5	27	50	90	33
23	Notts County	46	8	13	25	55	96	29
24	Rochdale	46	8	12	26	37	79	28

FOURTH DIVISION

		P	W	D	L	F	A	Pts
1	Port Vale	46	26	12	8	110	58	64
2	Coventry	46	24	12	10	84	47	60
3	York	46	21	18	7	73	52	60
4	Shrewsbury	46	24	10	12	101	63	58
5	Exeter	46	23	11	12	87	61	57
6	Walsall	46	21	10	15	95	64	52
7	Crystal Palace	46	20	12	14	90	71	52
8	Northampton	46	21	9	16	85	78	51
9	Millwall	46	20	10	16	76	69	50
10	Carlisle	46	19	12	15	62	65	50
11	Gillingham	46	20	9	17	82	77	49
12	Torquay	46	16	12	18	78	77	44
13	Chester	46	16	12	18	72	84	44
14	Bradford PA	46	18	7	21	75	77	43
15	Watford	46	16	10	20	81	79	42
16	Darlington	46	13	16	17	66	68	42
17	Workington	46	12	17	17	63	78	41
18	Crewe	46	15	10	21	70	82	40
19	Hartlepools	46	15	10	21	74	88	40
20	Gateshead	46	16	8	22	56	85	40
21	Oldham	46	16	4	26	59	84	36
22	Aldershot	46	14	7	25	63	97	35
23	Barrow	46	9	10	27	51	104	28
24	Southport	46	7	12	27	41	86	26

SCOTTISH FA CUP 1958-59

SECOND ROUND

St Mirren v Peebles Rovers	10-0
Airdrieonians v Motherwell	2-7
Montrose v Dunfermline Athletic	0-1
Ayr United v Stranraer	3-0
Fraserburgh v Stirling Albion	3-4
Babcock & Wilcox v Morton	0-5
Celtic v Clyde	1-1, 4-3
Rangers v Heart of Midlothian	3-2
Dundee United v Third Lanark	0-4
Brechin City v Alloa Athletic	3-3, 1-3
Hibernian v Falkirk	3-1
Stenhousemuir v Partick Thistle	1-3
St Johnstone v Queen's Park	3-1
Aberdeen v Arbroath	3-0
Coldstream v Hamilton Academicals	0-4
Dumbarton v Kilmarnock	2-8

THIRD ROUND

St Mirren v Motherwell	3-2
Dunfermline Athletic v Ayr United	2-1
Stirling Albion v Morton	3-1
Celtic v Rangers	2-1
Third Lanark v Alloa Athletic	3-2
Hibernian v Partick Thistle	4-1
St Johnstone v Aberdeen	1-2
Hamilton Academicals v Kilmarnock	0-5

FOURTH ROUND

St Mirren v Dunfermline Athletic	2-1
Stirling Albion v Celtic	1-3
Third Lanark v Hibernian	2-1
Aberdeen v Kilmarnock	3-1

SEMI-FINAL

St Mirren v Celtic	4-0
Third Lanark v Aberdeen	1-1, 0-1

FINAL

St Mirren v Aberdeen	3-1

SCOTTISH FIRST DIVISION

		P	W	D	L	F	A	Pts
1	Rangers	34	21	8	5	92	51	50
2	Hearts	34	21	6	7	92	51	48
3	Motherwell	34	18	8	8	83	50	44
4	Dundee	34	16	9	9	61	51	41
5	Airdrie	34	15	7	12	64	62	37
6	Celtic	34	14	8	12	70	53	36
7	St Mirren	34	14	7	13	71	74	35
8	Kilmarnock	34	13	8	13	58	51	34
9	Partick Thistle	34	14	6	14	59	66	34
10	Hibernian	34	13	6	15	68	70	32
11	Third Lanark	34	11	10	13	74	83	32
12	Stirling	34	11	8	15	54	64	30
13	Aberdeen	34	12	5	17	63	66	29
14	Raith	34	10	9	15	60	70	29
15	Clyde	34	12	4	18	62	66	28
16	Dunfermline	34	10	8	16	68	87	28
17	Falkirk	34	10	7	17	58	79	27
18	Queen of the S	34	6	6	22	38	101	18

SCOTTISH SECOND DIVISION

		P	W	D	L	F	A	Pts
1	Ayr United	36	28	4	4	115	48	60
2	Arbroath	36	23	5	8	86	59	51
3	Stenhousemuir	36	20	6	10	87	68	46
4	Dumbarton	36	19	7	10	94	61	45
5	Brechin	36	16	10	10	79	65	42
6	St Johnstone	36	15	10	11	54	44	40
7	Hamilton	36	15	8	13	76	62	38
8	East Fife	36	15	8	13	83	81	38
9	Berwick	36	16	6	14	63	66	38
10	Albion	36	14	7	15	84	79	35
11	Morton	36	13	8	15	68	85	34
12	Forfar	36	12	9	15	73	87	33
13	Alloa	36	12	7	17	76	81	31
14	Cowdenbeath	36	13	5	18	67	79	31
15	E Stirlingshire	36	10	8	18	50	77	28
16	Stranraer	36	8	11	17	63	76	27
17	Dundee United	36	9	7	20	62	86	25
18	Queen's Park	36	9	6	21	53	80	24
19	Montrose	36	6	6	24	49	96	18

Beginning with the game against France on 3 October 1951, Billy Wright made a world record 70 consecutive appearances for England, ending on 8 May 1959 with the match against the USA. In the Home Championship, he had a record run of 25 games between April 1951 and April 1959.

Denis Law became Scotland's youngest international, when on 18 October 1958, he played against Wales aged just 18 years and 236 days.

The most away wins in any division of the League on a single day is eight, in Division 3, 27 September 1958.

League Tables 1959-60

FIRST DIVISION

		P	W	D	L	F	A	Pts
1	Burnley	42	24	7	11	85	61	55
2	Wolves	42	24	6	12	106	67	54
3	Tottenham	42	21	11	10	86	50	53
4	WBA	42	19	11	12	83	57	49
5	Sheff Wed	42	19	11	12	80	59	49
6	Bolton	42	20	8	14	59	51	48
7	Man United	42	19	7	16	102	80	45
8	Newcastle	42	18	8	16	82	78	44
9	Preston	42	16	12	14	79	76	44
10	Fulham	42	17	10	15	73	80	44
11	Blackpool	42	15	10	17	59	71	40
12	Leicester	42	13	13	16	66	75	39
13	Arsenal	42	15	9	18	68	80	39
14	West Ham	42	16	6	20	75	91	38
15	Man City	42	17	3	22	78	84	37
16	Everton	42	13	11	18	73	78	37
17	Blackburn	42	16	5	21	60	70	37
18	Chelsea	42	14	9	19	76	91	37
19	Birmingham	42	13	10	19	63	80	36
20	Nottm Forest	42	13	9	20	50	74	35
21	Leeds	42	12	10	20	65	92	34
22	Luton	42	9	12	21	50	73	30

SECOND DIVISION

		P	W	D	L	F	A	Pts
1	Aston Villa	42	25	9	8	89	43	59
2	Cardiff	42	23	12	7	90	62	58
3	Liverpool	42	20	10	12	90	66	50
4	Sheff United	42	19	12	11	68	51	50
5	Middlesbrough	42	19	10	13	90	64	48
6	Huddersfield	42	19	9	14	73	52	47
7	Charlton	42	17	13	12	90	87	47
8	Rotherham	42	17	13	12	61	60	47
9	Bristol Rovers	42	18	11	13	72	78	47
10	Leyton Orient	42	15	14	13	76	61	44
11	Ipswich	42	19	6	17	78	68	44
12	Swansea	42	15	10	17	82	84	40
13	Lincoln	42	16	7	19	75	78	39
14	Brighton	42	13	12	17	67	76	38
15	Scunthorpe	42	13	10	19	57	71	36
16	Sunderland	42	12	12	18	52	65	36
17	Stoke	42	14	7	21	66	83	35
18	Derby	42	14	7	21	61	77	35
19	Plymouth	42	13	9	20	61	89	35
20	Portsmouth	42	10	12	20	59	77	32
21	Hull	42	10	10	22	48	76	30
22	Bristol City	42	11	5	26	60	97	27

THIRD DIVISION

		P	W	D	L	F	A	Pts
1	Southampton	46	26	9	11	106	75	61
2	Norwich	46	24	11	11	82	54	59
3	Shrewsbury	46	18	16	12	97	75	52
4	Coventry	46	21	10	15	78	63	52
5	Grimsby	46	18	16	12	87	70	52
6	Brentford	46	21	9	16	78	61	51
7	Bury	46	21	9	16	64	51	51
8	QPR	46	18	13	15	73	54	49
9	Colchester	46	18	11	17	83	74	47
10	Bournemouth	46	17	13	16	72	72	47
11	Reading	46	18	10	18	84	77	46
12	Southend	46	19	8	19	76	74	46
13	Newport	46	20	6	20	80	79	46
14	Port Vale	46	19	8	19	80	79	46
15	Halifax	46	18	10	18	70	72	46
16	Swindon	46	19	8	19	69	78	46
17	Barnsley	46	15	14	17	65	66	44
18	Chesterfield	46	18	7	21	71	84	43
19	Bradford City	46	15	12	19	66	74	42
20	Tranmere	46	14	13	19	72	75	41
21	York	46	13	12	21	57	73	38
22	Mansfield	46	15	6	25	81	112	36
23	Wrexham	46	14	8	24	68	101	36
24	Accrington	46	11	5	30	57	123	27

FOURTH DIVISION

		P	W	D	L	F	A	Pts
1	Walsall	46	28	9	9	102	60	65
2	Notts County	46	26	8	12	107	69	60
3	Torquay	46	26	8	12	84	58	60
4	Watford	46	24	9	13	92	67	57
5	Millwall	46	18	17	11	84	61	53
6	Northampton	46	22	9	15	85	63	53
7	•Gillingham	46	21	10	15	74	69	52
8	Crystal Palace	46	19	12	15	84	64	50
9	Exeter	46	19	11	16	80	70	49
10	Stockport	46	19	11	16	58	54	49
11	Bradford PA	46	17	15	14	70	68	49
12	Rochdale	46	18	10	18	65	60	46
13	Aldershot	46	18	9	19	77	74	45
14	Crewe	46	18	9	19	79	88	45
15	Darlington	46	17	9	20	63	73	43
16	Workington	46	14	14	18	68	60	42
17	Doncaster	46	16	10	20	69	76	42
18	Barrow	46	15	11	20	77	87	41
19	Carlisle	46	15	11	20	51	66	41
20	Chester	46	14	12	20	59	77	40
21	Southport	46	10	14	22	48	92	34
22	Gateshead	46	12	9	25	58	86	33
23	Oldham	46	8	12	26	41	83	28
24	Hartlepools	46	10	7	29	59	109	27

SCOTTISH FIRST DIVISION

		P	W	D	L	F	A	Pts
1	Hearts	34	23	8	3	102	51	54
2	Kilmarnock	34	24	2	8	67	45	50
3	Rangers	34	17	8	9	72	38	42
4	Dundee	34	16	10	8	70	49	42
5	Motherwell	34	16	8	10	71	61	40
6	Clyde	34	15	9	10	77	69	39
7	Hibernian	34	14	7	13	106	85	35
8	Ayr	34	14	6	14	65	73	34
9	Celtic	34	12	9	13	73	59	33
10	Partick Thistle	34	14	4	16	54	78	32
11	Raith Rovers	34	14	3	17	64	62	31
12	Third Lanark	34	13	4	17	75	83	30
13	Dunfermline	34	10	9	15	72	80	29
14	St Mirren	34	11	6	17	78	86	28
15	Aberdeen	34	11	6	17	54	72	28
16	Airdrieonians	34	11	6	17	56	80	28
17	Stirling Albion	34	7	8	19	55	72	22
18	Arbroath	34	4	7	23	38	106	15

SCOTTISH SECOND DIVISION

		P	W	D	L	F	A	Pts
1	St Johnstone	36	24	5	7	87	47	53
2	Dundee United	36	22	6	8	90	45	50
3	Queen of the S	36	21	7	8	94	52	49
4	Hamilton	36	21	6	9	91	62	48
5	Stenhousemuir	36	20	4	12	86	67	44
6	Dumbarton	36	18	7	11	67	53	43
7	Montrose	36	19	5	12	60	52	43
8	Falkirk	36	15	9	12	77	43	39
9	Berwick	36	16	5	15	62	55	37
10	Albion	36	14	8	14	71	78	36
11	Queen's Park	36	17	2	17	65	79	36
12	Brechin	36	14	6	16	66	66	34
13	Alloa	36	13	5	18	70	85	31
14	Morton	36	10	8	18	67	79	28
15	E Stirlingshire	36	10	8	18	68	82	28
16	Forfar	36	10	8	18	53	84	28
17	Stranraer	36	10	3	23	53	79	23
18	East Fife	36	7	6	23	50	87	20
19	Cowdenbeath	36	6	2	28	42	124	14

FA CUP 1959-60

FOURTH ROUND

Wolverhampton v Charlton Athletic	2-1
Huddersfield Town v Luton Town	0-1
Leicester City v Fulham	2-1
West Bromwich Albion v Bolton Wanderers	2-0
Bristol Rovers v Preston North End	3-3, 1-5
Rotherham United v Brighton	1-1, 1-1, 0-6
Scunthorpe United v Port Vale	0-1
Chelsea v Aston Villa	1-2
Sheffield United v Nottingham Forest	3-0
Southampton v Watford	2-2, 0-1
Liverpool v Manchester United	1-3
Sheffield Wednesday v Peterborough United	2-0
Bradford City v Bournemouth	3-1
Swansea Town v Burnley	0-0, 1-2
Crewe Alexandra v Tottenham Hotspur	2-2, 2-13
Blackburn Rovers v Blackpool	1-1, 3-0

FIFTH ROUND

Luton Town v Wolverhampton	1-4
Leicester City v West Bromwich Albion	2-1
Preston North End v Brighton	2-1
Port Vale v Aston Villa	1-2
Sheffield United v Watford	3-2
Manchester United v Sheffield Wednesday	0-1
Bradford City v Burnley	2-2, 0-5
Tottenham Hotspur v Blackburn Rovers	1-3

SIXTH ROUND

Leicester City v Wolverhampton Wanderers	1-2
Aston Villa v Preston North End	2-0
Sheffield United v Sheffield Wednesday	0-2
Burnley v Blackburn Rovers	3-3, 0-2

SEMI-FINAL

Wolverhampton Wanderers v Aston Villa	1-0
Sheffield Wednesday v Blackburn Rovers	1-2

FINAL

Wolverhampton Wanderers v Blackburn Rovers	3-0

SCOTTISH FA CUP 1959-60

SECOND ROUND

Rangers v Arbroath	2-0
•Dunfermline Athletic v Stenhousemuir	2-3
E Stirlingshire v Inverness Caledonian	2-2, 4-1
Hibernian v Dundee	3-0
Elgin City v Forfar Athletic	5-1
St Mirren v Celtic	1-1, 4-4, 2-5
Dundee United v Partick Thistle	2-2, 1-4
Stirling Albion v Queen of the South	3-3, 1-5
Peebles Rovers v Ayr United	1-6
Alloa Athletic v Airdrieonians	1-5
Aberdeen v Clyde	0-2
Montrose v Queen's Park	2-2, 1-1, 1-2
Eyemouth United v Albion Rovers	1-0
Cowdenbeath v Falkirk	1-0
Motherwell v Keith	6-0
Heart of Midlothian v Kilmarnock	1-1, 1-2

THIRD ROUND

Stenhousemuir v Rangers	0-3
East Stirlingshire v Hibernian	0-3
Elgin City v Celtic	1-2
Partick Thistle v Queen of the South	3-2
Ayr United v Airdrieonians	4-2
Clyde v Queen's Park	6-0
Eyemouth United v Cowdenbeath	3-0
Kilmarnock v Motherwell	2-0

FOURTH ROUND

Rangers v Hibernian	3-2
Celtic v Partick Thistle	2-0
Ayr United v Clyde	0-2
Eyemouth United v Kilmarnock	1-2

SEMI-FINAL

Rangers v Celtic	1-1, 4-1
Clyde v Kilmarnock	0-2

FINAL

Rangers v Kilmarnock	2-0

An expensive agreement

In July 1959, the Football League established the copyright on their fixture lists. As a result, the Pools Promoters agreed to pay the League a minimum of £245,000 each year for 10 years. In return, the Pools firms were to be allowed to reprint the fixtures on their coupons.

Cliff Holton of Watford, the 1959-60 Football League leading goalscorer, became the only player since the War to notch two hat-tricks in League matches in successive days. On Good Friday, 15 April 1960, Holton scored three times against Chester. A day later, he hit three more against Gateshead.

FIRST DIVISION

		P	W	D	L	F	A	Pts
1	Tottenham	42	31	4	7	115	55	66
2	Sheff Wed	42	23	12	7	78	47	58
3	Wolves	42	25	7	10	103	75	57
4	Burnley	42	22	7	13	102	77	51
5	Everton	42	22	6	14	87	69	50
6	Leicester	42	18	9	15	87	70	45
7	Man United	42	18	9	15	88	76	45
8	Blackburn	42	15	13	14	77	76	43
9	Aston Villa	42	17	9	16	78	77	43
10	WBA	42	18	5	19	67	71	41
11	Arsenal	42	15	11	16	77	85	41
12	Chelsea	42	15	7	20	98	100	37
13	Man City	42	13	11	18	79	90	37
14	Nottm Forest	42	14	9	19	62	78	37
15	Cardiff	42	13	11	18	60	85	37
16	West Ham	42	13	10	19	77	88	36
17	Fulham	42	14	8	20	72	95	36
18	Bolton	42	12	11	19	58	73	35
19	Birmingham	42	14	6	22	62	84	34
20	Blackpool	42	12	9	21	68	73	33
21	Newcastle	42	11	10	21	86	109	32
22	Preston	42	10	10	22	43	71	30

SECOND DIVISION

		P	W	D	L	F	A	Pts
1	Ipswich	42	26	7	9	100	55	59
2	Sheff United	42	26	6	10	81	51	58
3	Liverpool	42	21	10	11	87	58	52
4	Norwich	42	20	9	13	70	53	49
5	Middlesbrough	42	18	12	12	83	74	48
6	Sunderland	42	17	13	12	75	60	47
7	Swansea	42	18	11	13	77	73	47
8	Southampton	42	18	8	16	84	81	44
9	Scunthorpe	42	14	15	13	69	64	43
10	Charlton	42	16	11	15	97	91	43
11	Plymouth	42	17	8	17	81	82	42
12	Derby	42	15	10	17	80	80	40
13	Luton	42	15	9	18	71	70	39
14	Leeds	42	14	10	18	75	83	38
15	Rotherham	42	12	13	17	65	64	37
16	Brighton	42	14	9	19	61	75	37
17	Bristol Rovers	42	15	7	20	73	92	37
18	Stoke	42	12	12	18	51	59	36
19	Leyton Orient	42	14	8	20	55	78	36
20	Huddersfield	42	13	9	20	62	71	35
21	Portsmouth	42	11	11	20	64	91	33
22	Lincoln	42	8	8	26	48	95	24

THIRD DIVISION

		P	W	D	L	F	A	Pts
1	Bury	46	30	8	8	108	45	68
2	Walsall	46	28	6	12	98	60	62
3	QPR	46	25	10	11	93	60	60
4	Watford	46	20	12	14	85	72	52
5	Notts County	46	21	9	16	82	77	51
6	Grimsby	46	20	10	16	77	69	50
7	Port Vale	46	17	15	14	96	79	49
8	Barnsley	46	21	7	18	83	80	49
9	Halifax	46	16	17	13	71	78	49
10	Shrewsbury	46	15	16	15	83	75	46
11	Hull	46	17	12	17	73	73	46
12	Torquay	46	14	17	15	75	83	45
13	Newport	46	17	11	18	81	90	45
14	Bristol City	46	17	10	19	70	68	44
15	Coventry	46	16	12	18	80	83	44
16	Swindon	46	14	15	17	62	55	43
17	Brentford	46	13	17	16	56	70	43
18	Reading	46	14	12	20	72	83	40
19	Bournemouth	46	15	10	21	58	76	40
20	Southend	46	14	11	21	60	76	39
21	Tranmere	46	15	8	23	79	115	38
22	Bradford City	46	11	14	21	65	87	36
23	Colchester	46	11	11	24	68	101	33
24	Chesterfield	46	10	12	24	67	87	32

FOURTH DIVISION

		P	W	D	L	F	A	Pts
1	Peterborough	46	28	10	8	134	65	66
2	Crystal Palace	46	29	6	11	110	69	64
3	Northampton	46	25	10	11	90	62	60
4	Bradford PA	46	26	8	12	84	74	60
5	York	46	21	9	16	80	60	51
6	Millwall	46	21	8	17	97	86	50
7	Darlington	46	18	13	15	78	70	49
8	Workington	46	21	7	18	74	76	49
9	Crewe	46	20	9	17	61	67	49
10	Aldershot	46	18	9	19	79	69	45
11	Doncaster	46	19	7	20	76	78	45
12	Oldham	46	19	7	20	79	88	45
13	Stockport	46	18	9	19	57	66	45
14	Southport	46	19	6	21	69	67	44
15	Gillingham	46	15	13	18	64	66	43
16	Wrexham	46	17	8	21	62	56	42
17	Rochdale	46	17	8	21	60	66	42
18	Accrington	46	16	8	22	74	88	40
19	Carlisle	46	13	13	20	61	79	39
20	Mansfield	46	16	6	24	71	78	38
21	Exeter	46	14	10	22	66	94	38
22	Barrow	46	13	11	22	52	79	37
23	Hartlepools	46	12	8	26	71	103	32
24	Chester	46	11	9	26	61	104	31

SCOTTISH FIRST DIVISION

		P	W	D	L	F	A	Pts
1	Rangers	34	23	5	6	88	46	51
2	Kilmarnock	34	21	8	5	77	45	50
3	Third Lanark	34	20	2	12	100	80	42
4	Celtic	34	15	9	10	64	46	39
5	Motherwell	34	15	8	11	70	57	38
6	Aberdeen	34	14	8	12	72	72	36
7	Hibernian	34	15	4	15	66	69	34
8	Hearts	34	13	8	13	51	53	34
9	Dundee United	34	13	7	14	60	58	33
10	Dundee	34	13	6	15	61	53	32
11	Partick Thistle	34	13	6	15	59	69	32
12	Dunfermline	34	12	7	15	65	81	31
13	Airdrieonians	34	10	10	14	61	71	30
14	St Mirren	34	11	7	16	53	58	29
15	St Johnstone	34	10	9	15	47	63	29
16	Raith Rovers	34	10	7	17	46	67	27
17	Clyde	34	6	11	17	55	77	23
18	Ayr	34	5	12	17	51	81	22

SCOTTISH SECOND DIVISION

		P	W	D	L	F	A	Pts
1	Stirling Albion	36	24	7	5	89	37	55
2	Falkirk	36	24	6	6	100	40	54
3	Stenhousemuir	36	24	2	10	99	69	50
4	Stranraer	36	19	6	11	83	55	44
5	Queen of the S	36	20	3	13	77	52	43
6	Hamilton	36	17	7	12	84	80	41
7	Montrose	36	19	2	15	75	65	40
8	Cowdenbeath	36	17	6	13	71	65	40
9	Berwick	36	14	9	13	62	69	37
10	Dumbarton	36	15	5	16	78	82	35
11	Alloa	36	13	7	16	78	68	33
12	Arbroath	36	13	7	16	56	76	33
13	East Fife	36	14	4	18	70	80	32
14	Brechin	36	9	9	18	60	78	27
15	Queen's Park	36	10	6	20	61	87	26
16	E Stirlingshire	36	9	7	20	59	100	25
17	Albion	36	9	6	21	60	89	24
18	Forfar	36	10	4	22	65	98	24
19	Morton	36	5	11	20	56	93	21

FA CUP 1960-61

FOURTH ROUND

Leicester City v Bristol City	5-1
Birmingham City v Rotherham United	4-0
Huddersfield Town v Barnsley	1-1, 0-1
Luton Town v Manchester City	3-1
Newcastle United v Stockport County	4-0
Stoke City v Aldershot	0-0, 0-0, 3-0
Sheffield United v Lincoln City	3-1
Bolton Wanderers v Blackburn Rovers	3-3, 0-4
Southampton v Leyton Orient	0-1
Sheffield Wednesday v Manchester United	1-1, 7-2
Brighton v Burnley	3-3, 0-2
Swansea Town v Preston North End	2-1
Scunthorpe United v Norwich City	1-4
Liverpool v Sunderland	0-2
Peterborough United v Aston Villa	1-1, 1-2
Tottenham Hotspur v Crewe Alexandra	5-1

FIFTH ROUND

Birmingham City v Leicester City	1-1, 1-2
Barnsley v Luton Town	1-0
Newcastle United v Stoke City	3-1
Sheffield United v Blackburn Rovers	2-1
Leyton Orient v Sheffield Wednesday	0-2
Burnley v Swansea Town	4-0
Norwich City v Sunderland	0-1
Aston Villa v Tottenham Hotspur	0-2

SIXTH ROUND

Leicester City v Barnsley	0-0, 2-1
Newcastle United v Sheffield United	1-3
Sheffield Wednesday v Burnley	0-0, 0-2
Sunderland v Tottenham Hotspur	1-1, 0-5

SEMI-FINAL

Leicester City v Sheffield United	0-0, 0-0, 2-0
Burnley v Tottenham Hotspur	0-3

FINAL

Leicester City v Tottenham Hotspur	0-2

SCOTTISH FA CUP 1960-61

SECOND ROUND

Buckie Thistle v Raith Rovers	0-2
Celtic v Montrose	6-0
Queen of the South v Hamilton Academicals	0-2
Hibernian v Peebles Rovers	15-1
Brechin City v Duns	5-3
Ayr United v Airdrieonians	0-0, 1-3
Cowdenbeath v Motherwell	1-4
Dundee v Rangers	1-5
East Fife v Partick Thistle	1-3
Kilmarnock v Heart of Midlothian	1-2
Dundee United v St Mirren	0-1
Third Lanark v Arbroath	5-2
Aberdeen v Deveronvale	4-2
Stranraer v Dunfermline Athletic	1-3
Alloa Athletic v Dumbarton	2-0
Forfar Athletic v Morton	2-0

THIRD ROUND

Raith Rovers v Celtic	1-4
Hamilton Academicals v Hibernian	0-4
Brechin City v Airdrieonians	0-3
Motherwell v Rangers	2-2, 5-2
Partick Thistle v Heart of Midlothian	1-2
St Mirren v Third Lanark	3-3, 8-0
Aberdeen v Dunfermline Athletic	3-6
Alloa Athletic v Forfar Athletic	2-1

FOURTH ROUND

Celtic v Hibernian	1-1, 1-0
Motherwell v Airdrieonians	0-1
Heart of Midlothian v St Mirren	0-1
Dunfermline Athletic v Alloa Athletic	4-0

SEMI-FINAL

Celtic v Airdrieonians	4-0
Dunfermline Athletic v St Mirren	0-0, 1-0

FINAL

Celtic v Dunfermline Athletic	0-0, 0-2

Tottenham began the season with 11 consecutive wins, a record, and ended it having won 31 of their 42 games, a First Division record. Spurs' 16 away wins—including an unequalled 8 in a row—was another First Division record. Spurs also equalled Arsenal's Division One record points total of 66.

Burnley were fined £1000 by the Football League for fielding ten reserves in a League match against Chelsea.

The maximum wage restrictions were removed and Johnny Haynes of Fulham became the first British footballer to earn £100 a week.

FIRST DIVISION

	P	W	D	L	F	A	Pts
1 Ipswich	42	24	8	10	93	67	56
2 Burnley	42	21	11	10	101	67	53
3 Tottenham	42	21	10	11	88	69	52
4 Everton	42	20	11	11	88	54	51
5 Sheff United	42	19	9	14	61	69	47
6 Sheff Wed	42	20	6	16	72	58	46
7 Aston Villa	42	18	8	16	65	56	44
8 West Ham	42	17	10	15	76	82	44
9 WBA	42	15	13	14	83	67	43
10 Arsenal	42	16	11	15	71	72	43
11 Bolton	42	16	10	16	62	66	42
12 Man City	42	17	7	18	78	81	41
13 Blackpool	42	15	11	16	70	75	41
14 Leicester	42	17	6	19	72	71	40
15 Man United	42	15	9	18	72	75	39
16 Blackburn	42	14	11	17	50	58	39
17 Birmingham	42	14	10	18	65	81	38
18 Wolves	42	13	10	19	73	86	36
19 Nottm Forest	42	13	10	19	63	79	36
20 Fulham	42	13	7	22	66	74	33
21 Cardiff	42	9	14	19	50	81	32
22 Chelsea	42	9	10	23	63	94	28

SECOND DIVISION

	P	W	D	L	F	A	Pts
1 Liverpool	42	27	8	7	99	43	62
2 Leyton Orient	42	22	10	10	69	40	54
3 Sunderland	42	22	9	11	85	50	53
4 Scunthorpe	42	21	7	14	86	71	49
5 Plymouth	42	19	8	15	75	75	46
6 Southampton	42	18	9	15	77	62	45
7 Huddersfield	42	16	12	14	67	59	44
8 Stoke	42	17	8	17	55	57	42
9 Rotherham	42	16	9	17	70	76	41
10 Preston	42	15	10	17	55	57	40
11 Newcastle	42	15	9	18	64	58	39
12 Middlesbrough	42	16	7	19	76	72	39
13 Luton	42	17	5	20	69	71	39
14 Walsall	42	14	11	17	70	75	39
15 Charlton	42	15	9	18	69	75	39
16 Derby	42	14	11	17	68	75	39
17 Norwich	42	14	11	17	61	70	39
18 Bury	42	17	5	20	52	76	39
19 Leeds	42	12	12	18	50	61	36
20 Swansea	42	12	12	18	61	83	36
21 Bristol Rovers	42	13	7	22	53	81	33
22 Brighton	42	10	11	21	42	86	31

THIRD DIVISION

	P	W	D	L	F	A	Pts
1 Portsmouth	46	27	11	8	87	47	65
2 Grimsby	46	28	6	12	80	56	62
3 Bournemouth	46	21	17	8	69	45	59
4 QPR	46	24	11	11	111	73	59
5 Peterborough	46	26	6	14	107	82	58
6 Bristol City	46	23	8	15	94	72	54
7 Reading	46	22	9	15	77	66	53
8 Northampton	46	20	11	15	85	57	51
9 Swindon	46	17	15	14	78	71	49
10 Hull	46	20	8	18	67	54	48
11 Bradford PA	46	20	7	19	80	78	47
12 Port Vale	46	17	11	18	65	58	45
13 Notts County	46	17	9	20	67	74	43
14 Coventry	46	16	11	19	64	71	43
15 Crystal Palace	46	14	14	18	83	80	42
16 Southend	46	13	16	17	57	69	42
17 Watford	46	14	13	19	63	74	41
18 Halifax	46	15	10	21	62	84	40
19 Shrewsbury	46	13	12	21	73	84	38
20 Barnsley	46	13	12	21	71	95	38
21 Torquay	46	15	6	25	76	100	36
22 Lincoln	46	9	17	20	57	87	35
23 Brentford	46	13	8	25	53	93	34
24 Newport	46	7	8	31	46	102	22

FOURTH DIVISION

	P	W	D	L	F	A	Pts
1 Millwall	44	23	10	11	87	62	56
2 Colchester	44	23	9	12	104	71	55
3 Wrexham	44	22	9	13	96	56	53
4 Carlisle	44	22	8	14	64	63	52
5 Bradford City	44	21	9	14	94	86	51
6 York	44	20	10	14	84	53	50
7 Aldershot	44	22	5	17	81	60	49
8 Workington	44	19	11	14	69	70	49
9 Barrow	44	17	14	13	74	58	48
10 Crewe	44	20	6	18	79	70	46
11 Oldham	44	17	12	15	77	70	46
12 Rochdale	44	19	7	18	71	71	45
13 Darlington	44	18	9	17	61	73	45
14 Mansfield	44	19	6	19	77	66	44
15 Tranmere	44	20	4	20	70	81	44
16 Stockport	44	17	9	18	70	69	43
17 Southport	44	17	9	18	61	71	43
18 Exeter	44	13	11	20	62	77	37
19 Chesterfield	44	14	9	21	70	87	37
20 Gillingham	44	13	11	20	73	94	37
21 Doncaster	44	11	7	26	60	85	29
22 Hartlepools	44	8	11	25	52	101	27
23 Chester	44	7	12	25	54	96	26
24 Accrington Stanley resigned from the League							

SCOTTISH FIRST DIVISION

	P	W	D	L	F	A	Pts
1 Dundee	34	25	4	5	80	46	54
2 Rangers	34	22	7	5	84	31	51
3 Celtic	34	19	8	7	81	37	46
4 Dunfermline	34	19	5	10	77	46	43
5 Kilmarnock	34	16	10	8	74	58	42
6 Hearts	34	16	6	12	54	49	38
7 Partick Thistle	34	16	3	15	60	55	35
8 Hibernian	34	14	5	15	58	72	33
9 Motherwell	34	13	6	15	65	62	32
10 Dundee United	34	13	6	15	70	71	32
11 Third Lanark	34	13	5	16	59	60	31
12 Aberdeen	34	10	9	15	60	73	29
13 Raith Rovers	34	10	7	17	51	73	27
14 Falkirk	34	11	4	19	45	68	26
15 Airdrieonians	34	9	7	18	57	78	25
16 St Mirren	34	10	5	19	52	80	25
17 St Johnstone	34	9	7	18	35	61	25
18 Stirling Albion	34	6	6	22	34	76	18

SCOTTISH SECOND DIVISION

	P	W	D	L	F	A	Pts
1 Clyde	36	15	4	7	108	47	54
2 Queen of the S	36	24	5	7	78	33	53
3 Morton	36	19	6	11	78	64	44
4 Alloa	36	17	8	11	92	78	42
5 Montrose	36	15	11	10	63	50	41
6 Arbroath	36	17	7	12	66	59	41
7 Stranraer	36	14	11	11	61	62	39
8 Berwick	36	16	6	14	83	70	38
9 Ayr	36	15	8	13	71	63	38
10 East Fife	36	15	7	14	60	59	37
11 E Stirlingshire	36	15	4	17	70	81	34
12 Queen's Park	36	12	9	15	64	62	33
13 Hamilton	36	14	5	17	78	79	33
14 Cowdenbeath	36	11	9	16	65	77	31
15 Stenhousemuir	36	13	5	18	69	86	31
16 Forfar	36	11	8	17	68	76	30
17 Dumbarton	36	9	10	17	49	66	28
18 Albion	36	10	5	21	42	74	25
19 Brechin	36	5	2	29	44	123	12

FA CUP 1961-62

FOURTH ROUND

Burnley v Leyton Orient	1-1, 1-0
Everton v Manchester City	2-0
Peterborough United v Sheffield United	1-3
Norwich City v Ipswich Town	1-1, 2-1
Fulham v Walsall	2-2, 2-0
Sunderland v Port Vale	0-0, 1-3
Stoke City v Blackburn Rovers	0-1
Shrewsbury Town v Middlesbrough	2-2, 1-5
Oldham Athletic v Liverpool	1-2
Preston North End v Weymouth	2-0
Manchester United v Arsenal	1-0
Nottingham Forest v Sheffield Wednesday	0-2
Aston Villa v Huddersfield Town	2-1
Charlton Athletic v Derby County	2-1
Wolverhampton Wanderers v West Bromwich Albion	1-2
Plymouth Argyle v Tottenham Hotspur	1-5

FIFTH ROUND

Burnley v Everton	3-1
Sheffield United v Norwich City	3-1
Fulham v Port Vale	1-0
Blackburn Rovers v Middlesbrough	2-1
Liverpool v Preston North End	0-0, 0-0, 0-1
Manchester United v Sheffield Wednesday	0-0, 2-0
Aston Villa v Charlton Athletic	2-1
West Bromwich Albion v Tottenham Hotspur	2-4

SIXTH ROUND

Sheffield United v Burnley	0-1
Fulham v Blackburn Rovers	2-2, 1-0
Preston North End v Manchester United	0-0, 1-2
Tottenham Hotspur v Aston Villa	2-0

SEMI-FINAL

Burnley v Fulham	1-1, 2-1
Manchester United v Tottenham Hotspur	1-3

FINAL

Burnley v Tottenham Hotspur	1-3

SCOTTISH FA CUP 1961-62

SECOND ROUND

Rangers v Arbroath	6-0
Clyde v Aberdeen	2-2, 3-10
Brechin City v Kilmarnock	1-6
Dumbarton v Ross County	2-3
Stirling Albion v Partick Thistle	3-1
East Fife v Albion Rovers	1-0
Stranraer v Montrose	0-0, 1-0
Motherwell v St Johnstone	4-0
Vale of Leithen v Heart of Midlothian	0-5
Morton v Celtic	1-3
Hamilton Academicals v Third Lanark	0-2
Inverness Caledonian v East Stirlingshire	3-0
Dunfermline Athletic v Wigtown	9-0
Queen of the South v Stenhousemuir	0-2
Alloa Athletic v Raith Rovers	1-2
Dundee v St Mirren	0-1

THIRD ROUND

Aberdeen v Rangers	2-2, 5-1
Kilmarnock v Ross County	7-0
Stirling Albion v East Fife	4-1
Stranraer v Motherwell	1-3
Heart of Midlothian v Celtic	3-4
Third Lanark v Inverness Caledonian	6-1
Dunfermline Athletic v Stenhousemuir	0-0, 3-0
Raith Rovers v St Mirren	1-1, 0-4

FOURTH ROUND

Kilmarnock v Rangers	2-4
Stirling Albion v Motherwell	0-6
Celtic v Third Lanark	4-4, 4-0
Dunfermline Athletic v St Mirren	0-1

SEMI-FINAL

Rangers v Motherwell	3-1
Celtic v St Mirren	1-3

FINAL

Rangers v St Mirren	2-0

Triple success

Only once since the War have three players hit hat-tricks for one side in the same League match. Ron Barnes, Roy Ambler and Wyn Davies did this in Wrexham's 10-1 thrashing of Hartlepools in a Fourth Division game on 3 March 1962.

The England player from the Third Division

Johnny Byrne, the Crystal Palace inside-right, became only the third footballer from the Third Division, to appear for England (v Ireland, 22 November 1961) in the Home Championship since the War.

League Tables 1962-63

FIRST DIVISION

		P	W	D	L	F	A	Pts
1	Everton	42	25	11	6	84	42	61
2	Tottenham	42	23	9	10	111	62	55
3	Burnley	42	22	10	10	78	57	54
4	Leicester	42	20	12	10	79	53	52
5	Wolves	42	20	10	12	93	65	50
6	Sheff Wed	42	19	10	13	77	63	48
7	Arsenal	42	18	10	14	86	77	46
8	Liverpool	42	17	10	15	71	59	44
9	Nottm Forest	42	17	10	15	67	69	44
10	Sheff United	42	16	12	14	58	60	44
11	Blackburn	42	15	12	15	79	71	42
12	West Ham	42	14	12	16	73	69	40
13	Blackpool	42	13	14	15	58	64	40
14	WBA	42	16	7	19	71	79	39
15	Aston Villa	42	15	8	19	62	68	38
16	Fulham	42	14	10	18	50	71	38
17	Ipswich	42	12	11	19	59	78	35
18	Bolton	42	15	5	22	55	75	35
19	Man United	42	12	10	20	67	81	34
20	Birmingham	42	10	13	19	63	90	33
21	Man City	42	10	11	21	58	102	31
22	Leyton Orient	42	6	9	27	37	81	21

SECOND DIVISION

		P	W	D	L	F	A	Pts
1	Stoke	42	20	13	9	73	50	53
2	Chelsea	42	24	4	14	81	42	52
3	Sunderland	42	20	12	10	84	55	52
4	Middlesbrough	42	20	9	13	86	85	49
5	Leeds	42	19	10	13	79	53	48
6	Huddersfield	42	17	14	11	63	50	48
7	Newcastle	42	18	11	13	79	59	47
8	Bury	42	18	11	13	51	47	47
9	Scunthorpe	42	16	12	14	57	59	44
10	Cardiff	42	18	7	17	83	73	43
11	Southampton	42	17	8	17	72	67	42
12	Plymouth	42	15	12	15	76	73	42
13	Norwich	42	17	8	17	80	79	42
14	Rotherham	42	17	6	19	67	74	40
15	Swansea	42	15	9	18	51	72	39
16	Portsmouth	42	13	11	18	63	79	37
17	Preston	42	13	11	18	59	74	37
18	Derby	42	12	12	18	61	72	36
19	Grimsby	42	11	13	18	55	66	35
20	Charlton	42	13	5	24	62	94	31
21	Walsall	42	11	9	22	53	89	31
22	Luton	42	11	7	24	61	84	29

THIRD DIVISION

		P	W	D	L	F	A	Pts
1	Northampton	46	26	10	10	109	60	62
2	Swindon	46	22	14	10	87	56	58
3	Port Vale	46	23	8	15	72	58	54
4	Coventry	46	18	17	11	83	69	53
5	Bournemouth	46	18	16	12	63	46	52
6	Peterborough	46	20	11	15	93	75	51
7	Notts County	46	19	13	14	73	74	51
8	Southend	46	19	12	15	75	77	50
9	Wrexham	46	20	9	17	84	83	49
10	Hull	46	19	10	17	74	69	48
11	Crystal Palace	46	17	13	16	68	58	47
12	Colchester	46	18	11	17	73	93	47
13	QPR	46	17	11	18	85	76	45
14	Bristol City	46	16	13	17	100	92	45
15	Shrewsbury	46	16	12	18	83	81	44
16	Millwall	46	15	13	18	82	87	43
17	Watford	46	17	8	21	82	85	42
18	Barnsley	46	15	11	20	63	74	41
19	Bristol Rovers	46	15	11	20	70	88	41
20	Reading	46	16	8	22	74	78	40
21	Bradford PA	46	14	12	20	79	97	40
22	Brighton	46	12	12	22	58	84	36
23	Carlisle	46	13	9	24	61	89	35
24	Halifax	46	9	12	25	64	106	30

FOURTH DIVISION

		P	W	D	L	F	A	Pts
1	Brentford	46	27	8	11	98	64	62
2	Oldham	46	24	11	11	95	60	59
3	Crewe	46	24	11	11	86	58	59
4	Mansfield	46	24	9	13	108	69	57
5	Gillingham	46	22	13	11	71	49	57
6	Torquay	46	20	16	10	75	56	56
7	Rochdale	46	20	11	15	67	59	51
8	Tranmere	46	20	10	16	81	67	50
9	Barrow	46	19	12	15	82	80	50
10	Workington	46	17	13	16	76	68	47
11	Aldershot	46	15	17	14	73	69	47
12	Darlington	46	19	6	21	72	87	44
13	Southport	46	15	14	17	72	106	44
14	York	46	16	11	19	67	62	43
15	Chesterfield	46	13	16	17	70	64	42
16	Doncaster	46	14	14	18	64	77	42
17	Exeter	46	16	10	20	57	77	42
18	Oxford	46	13	15	18	70	71	41
19	Stockport	46	15	11	20	56	70	41
20	Newport	46	14	11	21	76	90	39
21	Chester	46	15	9	22	51	66	39
22	Lincoln	46	13	9	24	68	89	35
23	Bradford City	46	11	10	25	64	93	32
24	Hartlepools	46	7	11	28	56	104	25

SCOTTISH FIRST DIVISION

		P	W	D	L	F	A	Pts
1	Rangers	34	25	7	2	94	28	57
2	Kilmarnock	34	20	8	6	92	40	48
3	Partick Thistle	34	20	6	8	66	44	46
4	Celtic	34	19	6	9	76	44	44
5	Hearts	34	17	9	8	85	59	43
6	Aberdeen	34	17	7	10	70	47	41
7	Dundee United	34	15	11	8	67	52	41
8	Dunfermline	34	13	8	13	50	47	34
9	Dundee	34	12	9	13	60	49	33
10	Motherwell	34	10	11	13	60	63	31
11	Airdrieonians	34	14	2	18	52	76	30
12	St Mirren	34	10	8	16	52	72	28
13	Falkirk	34	12	3	19	54	69	27
14	Third Lanark	34	9	8	17	56	68	26
15	Queen of the S	34	10	6	18	36	75	26
16	Hibernian	34	8	9	17	47	67	25
17	Clyde	34	9	5	20	49	83	23
18	Raith	34	2	5	27	35	118	9

SCOTTISH SECOND DIVISION

		P	W	D	L	F	A	Pts
1	St Johnstone	36	25	5	6	83	37	55
2	E Stirlingshire	36	20	9	7	80	50	49
3	Morton	36	23	2	11	100	49	48
4	Hamilton	36	18	8	10	69	56	44
5	Stranraer	36	16	10	10	81	70	42
6	Arbroath	36	18	4	14	74	51	40
7	Albion	36	18	2	16	72	79	38
8	Cowdenbeath	36	15	7	14	72	61	37
9	Alloa	36	15	6	15	57	56	36
10	Stirling	36	16	4	16	74	75	36
11	East Fife	36	15	6	15	60	69	36
12	Dumbarton	36	15	4	17	64	64	34
13	Ayr	36	13	8	15	68	77	34
14	Queen's Park	36	13	6	17	66	72	32
15	Montrose	36	13	5	18	57	70	31
16	Stenhousemuir	36	13	5	18	54	75	31
17	Berwick	36	11	7	18	57	77	29
18	Forfar	36	9	5	22	73	99	23
19	Brechin	36	3	3	30	39	113	9

FA CUP 1962-63

FOURTH ROUND

Leicester City v Ipswich Town	3-1
Leyton Orient v Derby County	3-0
Manchester City v Bury	1-0
Norwich City v Newcastle United	5-0
Arsenal v Sheffield Wednesday	2-0
Burnley v Liverpool	1-1, 1-2
West Ham United v Swansea Town	1-0
Swindon Town v Everton	1-5
West Bromwich Albion v Nottingham Forest	0-0, 1-2
Middlesbrough v Leeds United	0-2
Southampton v Watford	3-1
Port Vale v Sheffield United	1-2
Portsmouth v Coventry City	1-1, 2-2, 1-2
Gravesend v Sunderland	1-1, 2-5
Charlton Athletic v Chelsea	0-3
Manchester United v Aston Villa	1-0

FIFTH ROUND

Leicester City v Leyton Orient	1-0
Manchester City v Norwich City	1-2
Arsenal v Liverpool	1-2
West Ham United v Everton	1-0
Nottingham Forest v Leeds United	3-0
Southampton v Sheffield United	1-0
Coventry City v Sunderland	2-1
Manchester United v Chelsea	2-1

SIXTH ROUND

Norwich City v Leicester City	0-2
Liverpool v West Ham United	1-0
Nottingham Forest v Southampton	1-1, 3-3, 0-5
Coventry City v Manchester United	1-3

SEMI-FINAL

Leicester City v Liverpool	1-0
Southampton v Manchester United	0-1

FINAL

Leicester City v Manchester United	1-3

SCOTTISH FA CUP 1962-63

SECOND ROUND

Airdrieonians v Rangers	0-6
East Stirlingshire v Motherwell	1-0
Dundee v Montrose	8-0
Brechin City v Hibernian	0-2
Queen's Park v Alloa Athletic	5-1
Ayr United v Dundee United	1-2
Kilmarnock v Queen of the South	0-0, 0-1
Hamilton Academicals v Nairn County	1-1, 2-1
East Fife v Third Lanark	1-1, 0-2
Raith Rovers v Clyde	3-2
St Johnstone v Aberdeen	1-2
Cowdenbeath v Dunfermline Athletic	2-3
Berwick Rangers v St Mirren	1-3
Partick Thistle v Arbroath	1-1, 2-2, 3-2
Gala Fairydean v Duns	1-1, 2-1
Celtic v Heart of Midlothian	3-1

THIRD ROUND

Rangers v East Stirlingshire	7-2
Dundee v Hibernian	1-0
Queen's Park v Dundee United	1-1, 1-3
Queen of the South v Hamilton Academicals	3-0
Third Lanark v Raith Rovers	0-1
Aberdeen v Dunfermline Athletic	4-0
St Mirren v Partick Thistle	1-1, 1-0
Celtic v Gala Fairydean	6-0

FOURTH ROUND

Dundee v Rangers	1-1, 2-3
Dundee United v Queen of the South	1-1, 1-1, 4-0
Raith Rovers v Aberdeen	2-1
St Mirren v Celtic	0-1

SEMI-FINAL

Rangers v Dundee United	5-2
Raith Rovers v Celtic	2-5

FINAL

Rangers v Celtic	1-1, 3-0

Terrible winter disrupts the football programme

The winter of 1962-63 broke all previous records for postponements and abandoned matches due to bad weather. For six weeks, the football programme was wrecked by impossible playing conditions and over 400 League and Cup games were postponed or abandoned in England, Wales and Scotland. The worst-hit day—in fact the worst-hit ever, except for the War years—in England and Scotland was 9 February. Then, 57 games were called off through snow and ice, and only seven were completed. As a result of the severe winter, the football season was extended.

FIRST DIVISION

		P	W	D	L	F	A	Pts
1	Liverpool	42	26	5	11	92	45	57
2	Man United	42	23	7	12	90	62	53
3	Everton	42	21	10	11	84	64	52
4	Tottenham	42	22	7	13	97	81	51
5	Chelsea	42	20	10	12	72	56	50
6	Sheff Wed	42	19	11	12	84	67	49
7	Blackburn	42	18	10	14	89	65	46
8	Arsenal	42	17	11	14	90	82	45
9	Burnley	42	17	10	15	71	64	44
10	WBA	42	16	11	15	70	61	43
11	Leicester	42	16	11	15	61	58	43
12	Sheff United	42	16	11	15	61	64	43
13	Nottm Forest	42	16	9	17	64	68	41
14	West Ham	42	14	12	16	69	74	40
15	Fulham	42	13	13	16	58	65	39
16	Wolves	42	12	15	15	70	80	39
17	Stoke	42	14	10	18	77	78	38
18	Blackpool	42	13	9	20	52	73	35
19	Aston Villa	42	11	12	19	62	71	34
20	Birmingham	42	11	7	24	54	92	29
21	Bolton	42	10	8	24	48	80	28
22	Ipswich	42	9	7	26	56	121	25

SECOND DIVISION

		P	W	D	L	F	A	Pts
1	Leeds	42	24	15	3	71	34	63
2	Sunderland	42	25	11	6	81	37	61
3	Preston	42	23	10	9	79	54	56
4	Charlton	42	19	10	13	76	70	48
5	Southampton	42	19	9	14	100	73	47
6	Man City	42	18	10	14	84	66	46
7	Rotherham	42	19	7	16	90	78	45
8	Newcastle	42	20	5	17	74	69	45
9	Portsmouth	42	16	11	15	79	70	43
10	Middlesbrough	42	15	11	16	67	52	41
11	Northampton	42	16	9	17	58	60	41
12	Huddersfield	42	15	10	17	57	64	40
13	Derby	42	14	11	17	56	67	39
14	Swindon	42	14	10	18	57	69	38
15	Cardiff	42	14	10	18	56	81	38
16	Leyton Orient	42	13	10	19	54	72	36
17	Norwich	42	11	13	18	64	80	35
18	Bury	42	13	9	20	57	73	35
19	Swansea	42	12	9	21	63	74	33
20	Plymouth	42	8	16	18	45	67	32
21	Grimsby	42	9	14	19	47	75	32
22	Scunthorpe	42	10	10	22	52	82	30

THIRD DIVISION

		P	W	D	L	F	A	Pts
1	Coventry	46	22	16	8	98	61	60
2	Crystal Palace	46	23	14	9	73	51	60
3	Watford	46	23	12	11	79	59	58
4	Bournemouth	46	24	8	14	79	58	56
5	Bristol City	46	20	15	11	84	64	55
6	Reading	46	21	10	15	79	62	52
7	Mansfield	46	20	11	15	76	62	51
8	Hull	46	16	17	13	73	68	49
9	Oldham	46	20	8	18	73	70	48
10	Peterborough	46	18	11	17	75	70	47
11	Shrewsbury	46	18	11	17	73	80	47
12	Bristol Rovers	46	19	8	19	91	79	46
13	Port Vale	46	16	14	16	53	49	46
14	Southend	46	15	15	16	77	78	45
15	QPR	46	18	9	19	76	78	45
16	Brentford	46	15	14	17	87	80	44
17	Colchester	46	12	19	15	70	68	43
18	Luton	46	16	10	20	64	80	42
19	Walsall	46	13	14	19	59	76	40
20	Barnsley	46	12	15	19	68	94	39
21	Millwall	46	14	10	22	53	67	38
22	Crewe	46	11	12	23	50	77	34
23	Wrexham	46	13	6	27	75	107	32
24	Notts County	46	9	9	28	45	92	27

FOURTH DIVISION

		P	W	D	L	F	A	Pts
1	Gillingham	46	23	14	9	59	30	60
2	Carlisle	46	25	10	11	113	58	60
3	Workington	46	24	11	11	76	52	59
4	Exeter	46	20	18	8	62	37	58
5	Bradford City	46	25	6	15	76	62	56
6	Torquay	46	20	11	15	80	54	51
7	Tranmere	46	20	11	15	85	73	51
8	Brighton	46	19	12	15	71	52	50
9	Aldershot	46	19	10	17	83	78	48
10	Halifax	46	17	14	15	77	77	48
11	Lincoln	46	19	9	18	67	75	47
12	Chester	46	19	8	19	65	60	46
13	Bradford PA	46	18	9	19	75	81	45
14	Doncaster	46	15	12	19	70	75	42
15	Newport	46	17	8	21	64	73	42
16	Chesterfield	46	15	12	19	57	71	42
17	Stockport	46	15	12	19	50	68	42
18	Oxford	46	14	13	19	59	63	41
19	Darlington	46	14	12	20	66	93	40
20	Rochdale	46	12	15	19	56	59	39
21	Southport	46	15	9	22	63	88	39
22	York	46	14	7	25	52	66	35
23	Hartlepools	46	12	9	25	54	93	33
24	Barrow	46	6	18	22	51	93	30

SCOTTISH FIRST DIVISION

		P	W	D	L	F	A	Pts
1	Rangers	34	25	5	4	85	31	55
2	Kilmarnock	34	22	5	7	77	40	49
3	Celtic	34	19	9	6	89	34	47
4	Hearts	34	19	9	6	74	40	47
5	Dunfermline	34	18	9	7	64	33	45
6	Dundee	34	20	5	9	94	50	45
7	Partick Thistle	34	15	5	14	55	54	35
8	Dundee United	34	13	8	13	65	49	34
9	Aberdeen	34	12	8	14	53	53	32
10	Hibernian	34	12	6	16	59	66	30
11	Motherwell	34	9	11	14	51	62	29
12	St Mirren	34	12	5	17	44	74	29
13	St Johnstone	34	11	6	17	54	70	28
14	Falkirk	34	11	6	17	54	84	28
15	Airdrieonians	34	11	4	19	52	97	26
16	Third Lanark	34	9	7	18	47	74	25
17	Queen of the S	34	5	6	23	40	92	16
18	E Stirlingshire	34	5	2	27	37	91	12

SCOTTISH SECOND DIVISION

		P	W	D	L	F	A	Pts
1	Morton	36	32	3	1	135	37	67
2	Clyde	36	22	9	5	81	44	53
3	Arbroath	36	20	6	10	79	46	46
4	East Fife	36	16	13	7	92	57	45
5	Montrose	36	19	6	11	79	57	44
6	Dumbarton	36	16	6	14	67	59	38
7	Queen's Park	36	17	4	15	57	54	38
8	Stranraer	36	16	6	14	71	73	38
9	Albion	36	12	12	12	67	71	36
10	Raith	36	15	5	16	70	61	35
11	Stenhousemuir	36	15	5	16	83	75	35
12	Berwick	36	10	10	16	68	84	30
13	Hamilton	36	12	6	18	65	81	30
14	Ayr	36	12	5	19	58	83	29
15	Brechin	36	10	8	18	61	98	28
16	Alloa	36	11	5	20	64	92	27
17	Cowdenbeath	36	7	11	18	46	72	25
18	Forfar	36	6	8	22	57	104	20
19	Stirling	36	6	8	22	47	99	20

On 12 October 1963, Tottenham Hotspur had seven players on international duty in the Home Championship, a record. Norman, Greaves and Smith were in the England side that met Wales. The Welsh team included Spurs' brilliant winger, Cliff Jones. Scotland paraded Brown, Mackay and White against Ireland.

Quick off the mark

The fastest goal in first-class football was scored by Jim Fryatt of Bradford Park Avenue on 25 April 1964. Just four seconds after the kick-off, Tranmere Rovers found themselves a goal down. Though a fantastic time, referee R. J. Simon's stop-watch confirmed it.

FA CUP 1963-64

FOURTH ROUND

West Ham United v Leyton Orient	1-1, 3-0
Aldershot v Swindon Town	1-2
Burnley v Newport County	2-1
Chelsea v Huddersfield Town	1-2
Sunderland v Bristol City	6-1
Leeds United v Everton	1-1, 0-2
Barnsley v Bury	2-1
Manchester United v Bristol Rovers	4-1
Ipswich Town v Stoke City	1-1, 0-1
Sheffield United v Swansea Town	1-1, 0-4
West Bromwich Albion v Arsenal	3-3, 0-2
Liverpool v Port Vale	0-0, 2-1
Oxford United v Brentford	2-2, 2-1
Blackburn Rovers v Fulham	2-0
Bedford Town v Carlisle United	0-3
Bolton Wanderers v Preston North End	2-2, 1-2

FIFTH ROUND

West Ham United v Swindon Town	3-1
Burnley v Huddersfield Town	3-0
Sunderland v Everton	3-1
Barnsley v Manchester United	0-4
Stoke City v Swansea Town	2-2, 0-2
Arsenal v Liverpool	0-1
Oxford United v Blackburn Rovers	3-1
Carlisle United v Preston North End	0-1

SIXTH ROUND

West Ham United v Burnley	3-2
Manchester United v Sunderland	3-3, 2-2, 5-1
Liverpool v Swansea Town	1-2
Oxford United v Preston North End	1-2

SEMI-FINAL

West Ham United v Manchester United	3-1
Swansea Town v Preston North End	1-2

FINAL

West Ham United v Preston North End	3-2

SCOTTISH FA CUP 1963-64

SECOND ROUND

Rangers v Duns	9-0
Partick Thistle v St Johnstone	2-0
Morton v Celtic	1-3
Alloa Athletic v Airdrieonians	1-3
East Fife v East Stirlingshire	0-1
Dunfermline Athletic v Fraserburgh	7-0
Aberdeen v Queen's Park	1-1, 2-1
Buckie Thistle v Ayr United	1-3
Hamilton Academicals v Kilmarnock	1-3
Albion Rovers v Arbroath	4-3
St Mirren v Stranraer	2-0
Falkirk v Berwick Rangers	2-2, 5-1
Motherwell v Dumbarton	4-1
Queen of the South v Heart of Midlothian	0-3
Clyde v Forfar Athletic	2-2, 2-3
Brechin City v Dundee	2-9

THIRD ROUND

Rangers v Partick Thistle	3-0
Celtic v Airdrieonians	4-1
East Stirlingshire v Dunfermline Athletic	1-6
Aberdeen v Ayr United	1-2
Kilmarnock v Albion Rovers	2-0
St Mirren v Falkirk	0-1
Motherwell v Heart of Midlothian	3-3, 2-1
Dundee v Forfar Athletic	6-1

FOURTH ROUND

Rangers v Celtic	2-0
Dunfermline Athletic v Ayr United	7-0
Kilmarnock v Falkirk	2-1
Dundee v Motherwell	1-1, 4-2

SEMI-FINAL

Rangers v Dunfermline Athletic	1-0
Kilmarnock v Dundee	0-4

FINAL

Rangers v Dundee	3-1

FIRST DIVISION

		P	W	D	L	F	A	Pts
1	Man United	42	26	9	7	89	39	61
2	Leeds	42	26	9	7	83	52	61
3	Chelsea	42	24	8	10	89	54	56
4	Everton	42	17	15	10	69	60	49
5	Nottm Forest	42	17	13	12	71	67	47
6	Tottenham	42	19	7	16	87	71	45
7	Liverpool	42	17	10	15	67	73	44
8	Sheff Wed	42	16	11	15	57	55	43
9	West Ham	42	19	4	19	82	71	42
10	Blackburn	42	16	10	16	83	79	42
11	Stoke	42	16	10	16	67	66	42
12	Burnley	42	16	10	16	70	70	42
13	Arsenal	42	17	7	18	69	75	41
14	WBA	42	13	13	16	70	65	39
15	Sunderland	42	14	9	19	64	74	37
16	Aston Villa	42	16	5	21	57	82	37
17	Blackpool	42	12	11	19	67	78	35
18	Leicester	42	11	13	18	69	85	35
19	Sheff United	42	12	11	19	50	64	35
20	Fulham	42	11	12	19	60	78	34
21	Wolves	42	13	4	25	59	89	30
22	Birmingham	42	8	11	23	64	96	27

SECOND DIVISION

		P	W	D	L	F	A	Pts
1	Newcastle	42	24	9	9	81	45	57
2	Northampton	42	20	16	6	66	50	56
3	Bolton	42	20	10	12	80	58	50
4	Southampton	42	17	14	11	83	63	48
5	Ipswich	42	15	17	10	74	67	47
6	Norwich	42	20	7	15	61	57	47
7	Crystal Palace	42	16	13	13	55	51	45
8	Huddersfield	42	17	10	15	53	51	44
9	Derby	42	16	11	15	84	79	43
10	Coventry	42	17	9	16	72	70	43
11	Man City	42	16	9	17	63	62	41
12	Preston	42	14	13	15	76	81	41
13	Cardiff	42	13	14	15	64	57	40
14	Rotherham	42	14	12	16	70	69	40
15	Plymouth	42	16	8	18	63	79	40
16	Bury	42	14	10	18	60	66	38
17	Middlesbrough	42	13	9	20	70	76	35
18	Charlton	42	13	9	20	64	75	35
19	Leyton Orient	42	12	11	19	50	72	35
20	Portsmouth	42	12	10	20	56	77	34
21	Swindon	42	14	5	23	63	81	33
22	Swansea	42	11	10	21	62	84	32

FA CUP 1964-65

FOURTH ROUND

Liverpool v Stockport County	1-1, 2-0
Preston North End v Bolton Wanderers	1-2
Leicester City v Plymouth Argyle	5-0
Charlton Athletic v Middlesbrough	1-1, 1-2
West Ham United v Chelsea	0-1
Tottenham Hotspur v Ipswich Town	5-0
Peterborough United v Arsenal	2-1
Swansea Town v Huddersfield Town	1-0
Wolverhampton Wanderers v Rotherham United	2-2, 3-0
Sheffield United v Aston Villa	0-2
Stoke City v Manchester United	0-0, 0-1
Reading v Burnley	1-1, 0-1
Southampton v Crystal Palace	1-2
Sunderland v Nottingham Forest	1-3
Millwall v Shrewsbury Town	1-2
Leeds United v Everton	1-1, 2-1

FIFTH ROUND

Bolton Wanderers v Liverpool	0-1
Middlesbrough v Leicester City	0-3
Chelsea v Tottenham Hotspur	1-0
Peterborough United v Swansea Town	0-0, 2-0
Aston Villa v Wolverhampton Wanderers	1-1, 0-0, 1-3
Manchester United v Burnley	2-1
Crystal Palace v Nottingham Forest	3-1
Leeds United v Shrewsbury Town	2-0

SIXTH ROUND

Leicester City v Liverpool	0-0, 0-1
Chelsea v Peterborough United	5-1
Wolverhampton Wanderers v Manchester United	3-5
Crystal Palace v Leeds United	0-3

SEMI-FINAL

Liverpool v Chelsea	2-0
Manchester United v Leeds United	0-0, 0-1

FINAL

Leeds United v Liverpool	1-2

THIRD DIVISION

		P	W	D	L	F	A	Pts
1	Carlisle	46	25	10	11	76	53	60
2	Bristol City	46	24	11	11	92	55	59
3	Mansfield	46	24	11	11	95	61	59
4	Hull	46	23	12	11	91	57	58
5	Brentford	46	24	9	13	83	55	57
6	Bristol Rovers	46	20	15	11	82	58	55
7	Gillingham	46	23	9	14	70	50	55
8	Peterborough	46	22	7	17	85	74	51
9	Watford	46	17	16	13	71	64	50
10	Grimsby	46	16	17	13	68	67	49
11	Bournemouth	46	18	11	17	72	63	47
12	Southend	46	19	8	19	78	71	46
13	Reading	46	16	14	16	70	70	46
14	QPR	46	17	12	17	72	80	46
15	Workington	46	17	12	17	58	69	46
16	Shrewsbury	46	15	12	19	76	84	42
17	Exeter	46	12	17	17	51	52	41
18	Scunthorpe	46	14	12	20	65	72	40
19	Walsall	46	15	7	24	55	80	37
20	Oldham	46	13	10	23	61	83	36
21	Luton	46	11	11	24	51	94	33
22	Port Vale	46	9	14	23	41	76	32
23	Colchester	46	10	10	26	50	89	30
24	Barnsley	46	9	11	26	54	90	29

FOURTH DIVISION

		P	W	D	L	F	A	Pts
1	Brighton	46	26	11	9	102	57	63
2	Millwall	46	23	16	7	78	45	62
3	York	46	28	6	12	91	56	62
4	Oxford	46	23	15	8	87	44	61
5	Tranmere	46	27	6	13	99	56	60
6	Rochdale	46	22	14	10	74	53	58
7	Bradford PA	46	20	17	9	86	62	57
8	Chester	46	25	6	15	119	81	56
9	Doncaster	46	20	11	15	84	72	51
10	Crewe	46	18	13	15	90	81	49
11	Torquay	46	21	7	18	70	70	49
12	Chesterfield	46	20	8	18	58	70	48
13	Notts County	46	15	14	17	61	73	44
14	Wrexham	46	17	9	20	84	92	43
15	Hartlepools	46	15	13	18	61	85	43
16	Newport	46	17	8	21	85	81	42
17	Darlington	46	18	6	22	84	87	42
18	Aldershot	46	15	7	24	64	84	37
19	Bradford City	46	12	8	26	70	88	32
20	Southport	46	8	16	22	58	89	32
21	Barrow	46	12	6	28	59	105	30
22	Lincoln	46	11	6	29	58	99	28
23	Halifax	46	11	6	29	54	103	28
24	Stockport	46	10	7	29	44	87	27

SCOTTISH FA CUP 1964-65

FIRST ROUND

St Mirren v Celtic	0-3
Dumbarton v Queen's Park	0-0, 1-2
Aberdeen v East Fife	0-0, 0-1
Kilmarnock v Cowdenbeath	5-0
Motherwell v Stenhousemuir	3-2
St Johnstone v Dundee	1-0
Clyde v Morton	0-4
Falkirk v Heart of Midlothian	0-3
Hibernian v E S Clydebank	1-1, 2-0
Ayr United v Partick Thistle	1-1, 1-7
Forfar Athletic v Dundee United	0-3
Rangers v Hamilton Academicals	3-0
Stirling Albion v Arbroath	2-1
Airdrieonians v Montrose	7-3
Inverness Caledonian v Third Lanark	1-5
Queen of the South v Dunfermline Athletic	0-2

SECOND ROUND

Queen's Park v Celtic	0-1
East Fife v Kilmarnock	0-0, 0-3
Motherwell v St Johnstone	1-0
Morton v Heart of Midlothian	3-3, 0-2
Hibernian v Partick Thistle	5-1
Dundee United v Rangers	0-2
Stirling Albion v Airdrieonians	1-1, 2-0
Third Lanark v Dunfermline Athletic	1-1, 2-2, 2-4

THIRD ROUND

Celtic v Kilmarnock	3-2
Motherwell v Heart of Midlothian	1-0
Hibernian v Rangers	2-1
Dunfermline Athletic v Stirling Albion	2-0

SEMI-FINAL

Celtic v Motherwell	2-2, 3-0
Hibernian v Dunfermline Athletic	0-2

FINAL

Celtic v Dunfermline Athletic	3-2

SCOTTISH FIRST DIVISION

		P	W	D	L	F	A	Pts
1	Kilmarnock	34	22	6	6	62	33	50
2	Hearts	34	22	6	6	90	49	50
3	Dunfermline	34	22	5	7	83	36	49
4	Hibernian	34	21	4	9	75	47	46
5	Rangers	34	18	8	8	78	35	44
6	Dundee	34	15	10	9	86	63	40
7	Clyde	34	17	6	11	64	58	40
8	Celtic	34	16	5	13	76	57	37
9	Dundee United	34	15	6	13	59	51	36
10	Morton	34	13	7	14	54	54	33
11	Partick Thistle	34	11	10	13	57	58	32
12	Aberdeen	34	12	8	14	59	75	32
13	St Johnstone	34	9	11	14	57	62	29
14	Motherwell	34	10	8	16	45	54	28
15	St Mirren	34	9	6	19	38	70	24
16	Falkirk	34	7	7	20	43	85	21
17	Airdrieonians	34	5	4	25	48	110	14
18	Third Lanark	34	3	1	30	22	99	7

SCOTTISH SECOND DIVISION

		P	W	D	L	F	A	Pts
1	Stirling Albion	36	26	7	3	84	31	59
2	Hamilton	36	21	8	7	86	53	50
3	Queen of the S	36	16	13	7	84	50	45
4	Queen's Park	36	17	9	10	57	41	43
5	ES Clydebank	36	15	10	11	64	50	40
6	Stranraer	36	17	6	13	74	64	40
7	Arbroath	36	13	13	10	56	51	39
8	Berwick	36	15	9	12	73	70	39
9	East Fife	36	15	7	14	78	77	37
10	Alloa	36	14	8	14	71	81	36
11	Albion	36	14	5	17	56	60	33
12	Cowdenbeath	36	11	10	15	55	62	32
13	Raith	36	9	14	13	54	61	32
14	Dumbarton	36	13	6	17	55	67	32
15	Stenhousemuir	36	11	8	17	49	74	30
16	Montrose	36	10	9	17	80	91	29
17	Forfar	36	9	7	20	63	89	25
18	Ayr	36	9	6	21	49	67	24
19	Brechin	36	6	7	23	53	102	19

Gillingham set the record for an undefeated run of home matches including Cup and League Cup games. From 9 April 1963, Gillingham had gone 52 games—48 of them in the League— at their Priestfield Stadium without a defeat, before losing 1-0 to Exeter on 10 April 1965.

Stan Lynn, Birmingham City's full-back, scored 10 goals (8 from penalties) and ended the 1964-65 season as his club's top League goal-scorer. Only one other full-back—Jimmy Evans of Southend United in 1921-2—has achieved this distinction among Football League clubs.

FIRST DIVISION

	P	W	D	L	F	A	Pts
1 Liverpool	42	26	9	7	79	34	61
2 Leeds	42	23	9	10	79	38	55
3 Burnley	42	24	7	11	79	47	55
4 Man United	42	18	15	9	84	59	51
5 Chelsea	42	22	7	13	65	53	51
6 WBA	42	19	12	11	91	69	50
7 Leicester	42	21	7	14	80	65	49
8 Tottenham	42	16	12	14	75	66	44
9 Sheff United	42	16	11	15	56	59	43
10 Stoke	42	15	12	15	65	64	42
11 Everton	42	15	11	16	56	62	41
12 West Ham	42	15	9	18	70	83	39
13 Blackpool	42	14	9	19	55	65	37
14 Arsenal	42	12	13	17	62	75	37
15 Newcastle	42	14	9	19	50	63	37
16 Aston Villa	42	15	6	21	69	80	36
17 Sheff Wed	42	14	8	20	56	66	36
18 Nottm Forest	42	14	8	20	56	72	36
19 Sunderland	42	14	8	20	51	72	36
20 Fulham	42	14	7	21	67	85	35
21 Northampton	42	10	13	19	55	92	33
22 Blackburn	42	8	4	30	57	88	20

SECOND DIVISION

	P	W	D	L	F	A	Pts
1 Man City	42	22	15	5	76	44	59
2 Southampton	42	22	10	10	85	56	54
3 Coventry	42	20	13	9	73	53	53
4 Huddersfield	42	19	13	10	62	36	51
5 Bristol City	42	17	17	8	63	48	51
6 Wolves	42	20	10	12	87	61	50
7 Rotherham	42	16	14	12	75	74	46
8 Derby	42	16	11	15	71	68	43
9 Bolton	42	16	9	17	62	59	41
10 Birmingham	42	16	9	17	70	75	41
11 Crystal Palace	42	14	13	15	47	52	41
12 Portsmouth	42	16	8	18	74	78	40
13 Norwich	42	12	15	15	52	52	39
14 Carlisle	42	17	5	20	60	63	39
15 Ipswich	42	15	9	18	58	66	39
16 Charlton	42	12	14	16	61	70	38
17 Preston	42	11	15	16	62	70	37
18 Plymouth	42	12	13	17	54	63	37
19 Bury	42	14	7	21	62	76	35
20 Cardiff	42	12	10	20	71	91	34
21 Middlesbrough	42	10	13	19	58	86	33
22 Leyton Orient	42	5	13	24	38	80	23

THIRD DIVISION

	P	W	D	L	F	A	Pts
1 Hull	46	31	7	8	109	62	69
2 Millwall	46	27	11	8	76	43	65
3 QPR	46	24	9	13	95	65	57
4 Scunthorpe	46	21	11	14	80	67	53
5 Workington	46	19	14	13	67	57	52
6 Gillingham	46	22	8	16	62	54	52
7 Swindon	46	19	13	14	74	48	51
8 Reading	46	19	13	14	70	63	51
9 Walsall	46	20	10	16	77	64	50
10 Shrewsbury	46	19	11	16	73	64	49
11 Grimsby	46	17	13	16	68	62	47
12 Watford	46	17	13	16	55	51	47
13 Peterborough	46	17	12	17	80	66	46
14 Oxford	46	19	8	19	70	74	46
15 Brighton	46	16	11	19	67	65	43
16 Bristol Rovers	46	14	14	18	64	64	42
17 Swansea	46	15	11	20	81	96	41
18 Bournemouth	46	13	12	21	38	56	38
19 Mansfield	46	15	8	23	59	89	38
20 Oldham	46	12	13	21	55	81	37
21 Southend	46	16	4	26	54	83	36
22 Exeter	46	12	11	23	53	79	35
23 Brentford	46	10	12	24	48	69	32
24 York	46	9	9	28	53	106	27

FOURTH DIVISION

	P	W	D	L	F	A	Pts
1 Doncaster	46	24	11	11	85	54	59
2 Darlington	46	25	9	12	72	53	59
3 Torquay	46	24	10	12	72	49	58
4 Colchester	46	23	10	13	70	47	56
5 Tranmere	46	24	8	14	93	66	56
6 Luton	46	24	8	14	90	70	56
7 Chester	46	20	12	14	79	70	52
8 Notts County	46	19	12	15	61	53	50
9 Newport	46	18	12	16	75	75	48
10 Southport	46	18	12	16	68	69	48
11 Bradford PA	46	21	5	20	102	92	47
12 Barrow	46	16	15	15	72	76	47
13 Stockport	46	18	6	22	71	70	42
14 Crewe	46	16	9	21	61	63	41
15 Halifax	46	15	11	20	67	75	41
16 Barnsley	46	15	10	21	74	78	40
17 Aldershot	46	15	10	21	75	84	40
18 Hartlepools	46	16	8	22	63	75	40
19 Port Vale	46	15	9	22	48	59	39
20 Chesterfield	46	13	13	20	62	78	39
21 Rochdale	46	16	5	25	71	87	37
22 Lincoln	46	13	11	22	57	82	37
23 Bradford City	46	12	13	21	63	94	37
24 Wrexham	46	13	9	24	72	104	35

SCOTTISH FIRST DIVISION

	P	W	D	L	F	A	Pts
1 Celtic	34	27	3	4	106	30	57
2 Rangers	34	25	5	4	91	29	55
3 Kilmarnock	34	20	5	9	73	46	45
4 Dunfermline	34	19	6	9	94	55	44
5 Dundee United	34	19	5	10	79	51	43
6 Hibernian	34	16	6	12	81	55	38
7 Hearts	34	13	12	9	56	48	38
8 Aberdeen	34	15	6	13	61	54	36
9 Dundee	34	14	6	14	61	61	34
10 Falkirk	34	15	1	18	48	72	31
11 Clyde	34	13	4	17	62	64	30
12 Partick Thistle	34	10	10	14	55	64	30
13 Motherwell	34	12	4	18	52	69	28
14 St Johnstone	34	9	8	17	58	81	26
15 Stirling Albion	34	9	8	17	40	68	26
16 St Mirren	34	9	4	21	44	82	22
17 Morton	34	8	5	21	42	84	21
18 Hamilton	34	3	2	29	27	117	8

SCOTTISH SECOND DIVISION

	P	W	D	L	F	A	Pts
1 Ayr	36	22	9	5	78	37	53
2 Airdrieonians	36	22	6	8	107	56	50
3 Queen of the S	36	18	11	7	83	53	47
4 East Fife	36	20	4	12	72	55	44
5 Raith	36	16	11	9	71	43	43
6 Arbroath	36	15	13	8	72	52	43
7 Albion	36	18	7	11	58	54	43
8 Alloa	36	14	10	12	65	65	38
9 Montrose	36	15	7	14	67	63	37
10 Cowdenbeath	36	15	7	14	69	68	37
11 Berwick	36	12	11	13	69	58	35
12 Dumbarton	36	14	7	15	63	61	35
13 Queen's Park	36	13	7	16	62	65	33
14 Third Lanark	36	12	8	16	55	65	32
15 Stranraer	36	9	10	17	64	83	28
16 Brechin	36	10	7	19	52	92	27
17 E Stirlingshire	36	9	5	22	59	91	23
18 Stenhousemuir	36	6	7	23	47	93	19
19 Forfar	36	7	3	26	61	120	17

FA CUP 1965-66

FOURTH ROUND

Bedford Town v Everton	0-3
Crewe Alexandra v Coventry City	1-1, 1-4
Manchester City v Grimsby Town	2-0
Birmingham City v Leicester City	1-2
Manchester United v Rotherham United	0-0, 1-0
Wolverhampton Wanderers v Sheffield United	3-0
Bolton Wanderers v Preston North End	1-1, 2-3
Tottenham Hotspur v Burnley	4-3
Chelsea v Leeds United	1-0
Shrewsbury Town v Carlisle United	0-0, 1-1, 4-3
Hull City v Nottingham Forest	2-0
Southport v Cardiff City	2-0
Norwich City v Walsall	3-2
West Ham United v Blackburn Rovers	3-3, 1-4
Plymouth Argyle v Huddersfield Town	0-2
Newcastle United v Sheffield Wednesday	1-2

FIFTH ROUND

Everton v Coventry City	3-0
Manchester City v Leicester City	2-2, 1-0
Wolverhampton Wanderers v Manchester United	2-4
Preston North End v Tottenham Hotspur	2-1
Chelsea v Shrewsbury Town	3-2
Hull City v Southport	2-0
Norwich City v Blackburn Rovers	2-2, 2-3
Huddersfield Town v Sheffield Wednesday	1-2

SIXTH ROUND

Manchester City v Everton	0-0, 0-0, 0-2
Preston North End v Manchester United	1-1, 1-3
Chelsea v Hull City	2-2, 3-1
Blackburn Rovers v Sheffield Wednesday	1-2

SEMI-FINAL

Everton v Manchester United	1-0
Chelsea v Sheffield Wednesday	0-2

FINAL

Everton v Sheffield Wednesday	3-2

SCOTTISH FA CUP 1965-66

FIRST ROUND

Celtic v Stranraer	4-0
Dundee v East Fife	9-1
Heart of Midlothian v Clyde	2-1
Hibernian v Third Lanark	4-3
Stirling Albion v Queen's Park	3-1
Dunfermline Athletic v Partick Thistle	3-1
Morton v Kilmarnock	1-1, 0-3
East Stirlingshire v Motherwell	0-0, 1-4
Dumbarton v Montrose	2-1
Queen of the South v Albion Rovers	3-0
Hamilton Academicals v Aberdeen	1-3
Dundee United v Falkirk	0-0, 2-1
Cowdenbeath v St Mirren	1-0
Ayr United v St Johnstone	1-1, 0-1
Alloa Athletic v Ross County	3-5
Rangers v Airdrieonians	5-1

SECOND ROUND

Dundee v Celtic	0-2
Heart of Midlothian v Hibernian	2-1
Stirling Albion v Dunfermline Athletic	0-0, 1-4
Kilmarnock v Motherwell	5-0
Dumbarton v Queen of the South	1-0
Aberdeen v Dundee United	5-0
Cowdenbeath v St Johnstone	3-3, 0-3
Ross County v Rangers	0-2

THIRD ROUND

Celtic v Heart of Midlothian	3-3, 3-1
Dunfermline Athletic v Kilmarnock	2-1
Dumbarton v Aberdeen	0-3
Rangers v St Johnstone	2-0

SEMI-FINAL

Celtic v Dunfermline Athletic	2-0
Aberdeen v Rangers	0-0, 1-2

FINAL

Celtic v Rangers	0-0, 0-1

On 1 January 1966, while they were beating Aldershot 3-2 in a Division Four game, Chester lost both their full-backs, Ray Jones and Bryn Jones, with broken legs.

The World Cup final receipts—£204,805— were a world record for a football match.

At the start of the season, Manchester United had 15 internationals on their staff. They were: Pat Dunne, Harry Gregg, Shay Brennan, Noel Cantwell, Pat Crerand, Bill Foulkes, Denis Law, Nobby Stiles, Tony Dunne, George Best, David Herd, John Connelly, Bobby Charlton, Graham Moore, and David Sadler, then an amateur cap.

FIRST DIVISION

		P	W	D	L	F	A	Pts
1	Man United	42	24	12	6	84	45	60
2	Nottm Forest	42	23	10	9	64	41	56
3	Tottenham	42	24	8	10	71	48	56
4	Leeds	42	22	11	9	62	42	55
5	Liverpool	42	19	13	10	64	47	51
6	Everton	42	19	10	13	65	46	48
7	Arsenal	42	16	14	12	58	47	46
8	Leicester	42	18	8	16	78	71	44
9	Chelsea	42	15	14	13	67	62	44
10	Sheff United	42	16	10	16	52	59	42
11	Sheff Wed	42	14	13	15	56	47	41
12	Stoke	42	17	7	18	63	58	41
13	WBA	42	16	7	19	77	73	39
14	Burnley	42	15	9	18	66	76	39
15	Man City	42	12	15	15	43	52	39
16	West Ham	42	14	8	20	80	84	36
17	Sunderland	42	14	8	20	58	72	36
18	Fulham	42	11	12	19	71	83	34
19	Southampton	42	14	6	22	74	92	34
20	Newcastle	42	12	9	21	39	81	33
21	Aston Villa	42	11	7	24	54	85	29
22	Blackpool	42	6	9	27	41	76	21

SECOND DIVISION

		P	W	D	L	F	A	Pts
1	Coventry	42	23	13	6	74	43	59
2	Wolves	42	25	8	9	88	48	58
3	Carlisle	42	23	6	13	71	54	52
4	Blackburn	42	19	13	10	56	46	51
5	Ipswich	42	17	16	9	70	54	50
6	Huddersfield	42	20	9	13	58	46	49
7	Crystal Palace	42	19	10	13	61	55	48
8	Millwall	42	18	9	15	49	58	45
9	Bolton	42	14	14	14	64	58	42
10	Birmingham	42	16	8	18	70	66	40
11	Norwich	42	13	14	15	49	55	40
12	Hull	42	16	7	19	77	72	39
13	Preston	42	16	7	19	65	67	39
14	Portsmouth	42	13	13	16	59	70	39
15	Bristol City	42	12	14	16	56	62	38
16	Plymouth	42	14	9	19	59	58	37
17	Derby	42	12	12	18	68	72	36
18	Rotherham	42	13	10	19	61	70	36
19	Charlton	42	13	9	20	49	53	35
20	Cardiff	42	12	9	21	61	87	33
21	Northampton	42	12	6	24	47	84	30
22	Bury	42	11	6	25	49	83	28

FA CUP 1966-67

FOURTH ROUND

Brighton & Hove Albion v Chelsea	1-1, 0-4
Fulham v Sheffield United	1-1, 1-3
Manchester United v Norwich City	1-2
Sheffield Wednesday v Mansfield Town	4-0
Sunderland v Peterborough United	7-1
Leeds United v West Bromwich Albion	5-0
Cardiff City v Manchester City	1-1, 1-3
Ipswich Town v Carlisle United	2-0
Rotherham United v Birmingham City	0-0, 1-2
Bolton Wanderers v Arsenal	0-0, 0-3
Tottenham Hotspur v Portsmouth	3-1
Bristol City v Southampton	1-0
Nottingham Forest v Newcastle United	3-0
Swindon Town v Bury	2-1
Wolverhampton Wanderers v Everton	1-1, 1-3
Liverpool v Aston Villa	1-0

FIFTH ROUND

Chelsea v Sheffield United	2-0
Norwich City v Sheffield Wednesday	1-3
Sunderland v Leeds United	1-1, 1-1, 1-2
Manchester City v Ipswich Town	1-1, 3-0
Birmingham City v Arsenal	1-0
Tottenham Hotspur v Bristol City	2-0
Nottingham Forest v Swindon Town	0-0, 1-1, 3-0
Everton v Liverpool	1-0

SIXTH ROUND

Chelsea v Sheffield Wednesday	1-0
Leeds United v Manchester City	1-0
Birmingham City v Tottenham Hotspur	0-0, 0-6
Nottingham Forest v Everton	3-2

SEMI-FINAL

Chelsea v Leeds United	1-0
Tottenham Hotspur v Nottingham Forest	2-1

FINAL

Chelsea v Tottenham Hotspur	1-2

THIRD DIVISION

		P	W	D	L	F	A	Pts
1	QPR	46	26	15	5	103	38	67
2	Middlesbrough	46	23	9	14	87	64	55
3	Watford	46	20	14	12	61	46	54
4	Reading	46	22	9	15	76	57	53
5	Bristol Rovers	46	20	13	13	76	67	53
6	Shrewsbury	46	20	12	14	77	62	52
7	Torquay	46	21	9	16	73	54	51
8	Swindon	46	20	10	16	81	59	50
9	Mansfield	46	20	9	17	84	79	49
10	Oldham	46	19	10	17	80	63	48
11	Gillingham	46	15	16	15	58	62	46
12	Walsall	46	18	10	18	65	72	46
13	Colchester	46	17	10	19	76	73	44
14	Leyton Orient	46	13	18	15	58	68	44
15	Peterborough	46	14	15	17	66	71	43
16	Oxford	46	15	13	18	61	66	43
17	Grimsby	46	17	9	20	61	68	43
18	Scunthorpe	46	17	8	21	58	73	42
19	Brighton	46	13	15	18	61	71	41
20	Bournemouth	46	12	17	17	39	57	41
21	Swansea	46	12	15	19	85	89	39
22	Darlington	46	13	11	22	47	81	37
23	Doncaster	46	12	8	26	58	117	32
24	Workington	46	12	7	27	55	89	31

FOURTH DIVISION

		P	W	D	L	F	A	Pts
1	Stockport	46	26	12	8	69	42	64
2	Southport	46	23	13	10	69	42	59
3	Barrow	46	24	11	11	76	54	59
4	Tranmere	46	22	14	10	66	43	58
5	Crewe	46	21	12	13	70	55	54
6	Southend	46	22	9	15	70	49	53
7	Wrexham	46	16	20	10	76	62	52
8	Hartlepools	46	22	7	17	66	64	51
9	Brentford	46	18	13	15	58	56	49
10	Aldershot	46	18	12	16	72	57	48
11	Bradford City	46	19	10	17	74	62	48
12	Halifax	46	15	14	17	59	68	44
13	Port Vale	46	14	15	17	55	58	43
14	Exeter	46	14	15	17	50	60	43
15	Chesterfield	46	17	8	21	60	63	42
16	Barnsley	46	13	15	18	60	64	41
17	Luton	46	16	9	21	59	73	41
18	Newport	46	12	16	18	56	63	40
19	Chester	46	15	10	21	54	78	40
20	Notts County	46	13	11	22	53	72	37
21	Rochdale	46	13	11	22	53	75	37
22	York	46	12	11	23	65	79	35
23	Bradford PA	46	11	13	22	52	79	35
24	Lincoln	46	9	13	24	58	82	31

SCOTTISH FA CUP 1966-67

FIRST ROUND

Celtic v Arbroath	4-0
Elgin City v Ayr United	2-0
Queen's Park v Raith Rovers	3-2
Stirling Albion v Airdrieonians	1-2
Morton v Clyde	0-1
Motherwell v East Fife	0-1
St Mirren v Cowdenbeath	1-1, 2-0
Inverness Caledonian v Hamilton Academicals	1-3
Heart of Midlothian v Dundee United	0-3
Falkirk v Alloa Athletic	3-1
Partick Thistle v Dumbarton	3-0
Kilmarnock v Dunfermline Athletic	2-2, 0-1
Hibernian v Brechin City	2-0
Berwick Rangers v Rangers	1-0
St Johnstone v Queen of the South	4-0
Aberdeen v Dundee	5-0

SECOND ROUND

Celtic v Elgin City	7-0
Queen's Park v Airdrieonians	1-1, 2-1
Clyde v East Fife	4-1
St Mirren v Hamilton Academicals	0-1
Dundee United v Falkirk	1-0
Partick Thistle v Dunfermline Athletic	1-1, 1-5
Hibernian v Berwick Rangers	1-0
St Johnstone v Aberdeen	0-5

THIRD ROUND

Celtic v Queen's Park	5-3
Clyde v Hamilton Academicals	0-0, 5-1
Dundee United v Dunfermline Athletic	1-0
Hibernian v Aberdeen	1-1, 0-3

SEMI-FINAL

Celtic v Clyde	0-0, 2-0
Dundee United v Aberdeen	0-1

FINAL

Celtic v Aberdeen	2-0

SCOTTISH FIRST DIVISION

		P	W	D	L	F	A	Pts
1	Celtic	34	26	6	2	111	33	58
2	Rangers	34	24	7	3	92	31	55
3	Clyde	34	20	6	8	64	48	46
4	Aberdeen	34	17	8	9	72	38	42
5	Hibernian	34	19	4	11	72	49	42
6	Dundee	34	16	9	9	74	51	41
7	Kilmarnock	34	16	8	10	59	46	40
8	Dunfermline	34	14	10	10	72	52	38
9	Dundee United	34	14	9	11	68	62	37
10	Motherwell	34	10	11	13	59	60	31
11	Hearts	34	11	8	15	39	48	30
12	Partick Thistle	34	9	12	13	49	68	30
13	Airdrieonians	34	11	6	17	41	53	28
14	Falkirk	34	11	4	19	33	70	26
15	St Johnstone	34	10	5	19	53	73	25
16	Stirling	34	5	9	20	31	85	19
17	St Mirren	34	4	7	23	25	81	15
18	Ayr	34	1	7	26	20	86	9

SCOTTISH SECOND DIVISION

		P	W	D	L	F	A	Pts
1	Morton	38	33	3	2	113	20	69
2	Raith	38	27	4	7	95	44	58
3	Arbroath	38	25	7	6	75	32	57
4	Hamilton	38	18	8	12	74	60	44
5	East Fife	38	19	4	15	70	63	42
6	Cowdenbeath	38	16	8	14	70	55	40
7	Queen's Park	38	15	10	13	78	68	40
8	Albion	38	17	6	15	66	62	40
9	Queen of the S	38	15	9	14	84	76	39
10	Berwick	38	16	6	16	63	55	38
11	Third Lanark	38	13	8	17	67	78	34
12	Montrose	38	13	8	17	63	77	34
13	Alloa	38	15	4	19	55	74	34
14	Dumbarton	38	12	9	17	56	64	33
15	Stranraer	38	13	7	18	57	73	33
16	Forfar	38	12	3	23	74	106	27
17	Stenhousemuir	38	9	9	20	62	104	27
18	Clydebank	38	8	8	22	59	92	24
19	E Stirlingshire	38	7	10	21	44	87	24
20	Brechin	38	8	7	23	58	93	23

A great year for Celtic
Celtic won the Scottish League, Cup and League Cup, the Glasgow Cup, and became the first British club to win the European Cup, thus completing a remarkable grand slam.

More directors than players
When Workington increased their board of directors by the addition of a 13th member in October 1966, they found themselves with more directors than full-time players.

FIRST DIVISION

		P	W	D	L	F	A	Pts
1	Man City	42	26	6	10	86	43	58
2	Man United	42	24	8	10	89	55	56
3	Liverpool	42	22	11	9	71	40	55
4	Leeds	42	22	9	11	71	41	53
5	Everton	42	23	6	13	67	40	52
6	Chelsea	42	18	12	12	62	68	48
7	Tottenham	42	19	9	14	70	59	47
8	WBA	42	17	12	13	75	62	46
9	Arsenal	42	17	10	15	60	56	44
10	Newcastle	42	13	15	14	54	67	41
11	Nottm Forest	42	14	11	17	52	64	39
12	West Ham	42	14	10	18	73	69	38
13	Leicester	42	13	12	17	64	69	38
14	Burnley	42	14	10	18	64	71	38
15	Sunderland	42	13	11	18	51	61	37
16	Southampton	42	13	11	18	66	83	37
17	Wolves	42	14	8	20	66	75	36
18	Stoke	42	14	7	21	50	73	35
19	Sheff Wed	42	11	12	19	51	63	34
20	Coventry	42	9	15	18	51	71	33
21	Sheff United	42	11	10	21	49	70	32
22	Fulham	42	10	7	25	56	98	27

SECOND DIVISION

		P	W	D	L	F	A	Pts
1	Ipswich	42	22	15	5	79	44	59
2	QPR	42	25	8	9	67	36	58
3	Blackpool	42	24	10	8	71	43	58
4	Birmingham	42	19	14	9	83	51	52
5	Portsmouth	42	18	13	11	68	55	49
6	Middlesbrough	42	17	12	13	60	54	46
7	Millwall	42	14	17	11	62	50	45
8	Blackburn	42	16	11	15	56	49	43
9	Norwich	42	16	11	15	60	65	43
10	Carlisle	42	14	13	15	58	52	41
11	Crystal Palace	42	14	11	17	56	56	39
12	Bolton	42	13	13	16	60	63	39
13	Cardiff	42	13	12	17	60	66	38
14	Huddersfield	42	13	12	17	46	61	38
15	Charlton	42	12	13	17	63	68	37
16	Aston Villa	42	15	7	20	54	64	37
17	Hull	42	12	13	17	58	73	37
18	Derby	42	13	10	19	71	78	36
19	Bristol City	42	13	10	19	48	62	36
20	Preston	42	12	11	19	43	65	35
21	Rotherham	42	10	11	21	42	76	31
22	Plymouth	42	9	9	24	38	72	27

FA CUP 1967-68

FOURTH ROUND

Carlisle United v Everton	0-2
Coventry City v Tranmere Rovers	1-1, 0-2
Aston Villa v Rotherham United	0-1
Manchester City v Leicester City	0-0, 3-4
Leeds United v Nottingham Forest	2-1
Middlesbrough v Bristol City	1-1, 1-2
Stoke City v West Ham United	0-3
Sheffield United v Blackpool	2-1
Swansea Town v Arsenal	0-1
Birmingham City v Leyton Orient	3-0
Sheffield Wednesday v Swindon Town	2-1
Chelsea v Norwich City	1-0
Fulham v Portsmouth	0-0, 0-1
West Bromwich Albion v Southampton	1-1, 3-2
Tottenham Hotspur v Preston North End	3-1
Walsall v Liverpool	0-0, 2-5

FIFTH ROUND

Everton v Tranmere Rovers	2-0
Rotherham United v Leicester City	1-1, 0-2
Leeds United v Bristol City	2-0
West Ham United v Sheffield United	1-2
Arsenal v Birmingham City	1-1, 1-2
Sheffield Wednesday v Chelsea	2-2, 0-2
Portsmouth v West Bromwich Albion	1-2
Tottenham Hotspur v Liverpool	1-1, 1-2

SIXTH ROUND

Everton v Leicester City	3-1
Leeds United v Sheffield United	1-0
Birmingham City v Chelsea	1-0
West Bromwich Albion v Liverpool	0-0, 1-1, 2-1

SEMI-FINAL

Everton v Leeds United	1-0
West Bromwich Albion v Birmingham City	2-0

FINAL

Everton v West Bromwich Albion	0-1

THIRD DIVISION

		P	W	D	L	F	A	Pts
1	Oxford	46	22	13	11	69	47	57
2	Bury	46	24	8	14	91	66	56
3	Shrewsbury	46	20	15	11	61	49	55
4	Torquay	46	21	11	14	60	56	53
5	Reading	46	21	9	16	70	60	51
6	Watford	46	21	8	17	74	50	50
7	Walsall	46	19	12	15	74	61	50
8	Barrow	46	21	8	17	65	54	50
9	Swindon	46	16	17	13	74	51	49
10	Brighton	46	16	16	14	57	55	48
11	Gillingham	46	18	12	16	59	63	48
12	Bournemouth	46	16	15	15	56	51	47
13	Stockport	46	19	9	18	70	75	47
14	Southport	46	17	12	17	65	65	46
15	Bristol Rovers	46	17	9	20	72	78	43
16	Oldham	46	18	7	21	60	65	43
17	Northampton	46	14	13	19	58	72	41
18	Leyton Orient	46	12	17	17	46	62	41
19	Tranmere	46	14	12	20	62	74	40
20	Mansfield	46	12	13	21	51	67	37
21	Grimsby	46	14	9	23	52	69	37
22	Colchester	46	9	15	22	50	87	33
23	Scunthorpe	46	10	12	24	56	87	32
24	Peterborough	46	20	10	16	79	67	31†

†Peterborough had 19 points deducted for offering irregular bonuses to their players. They were automatically demoted to the Fourth Division.

FOURTH DIVISION

		P	W	D	L	F	A	Pts
1	Luton	46	27	12	7	87	44	66
2	Barnsley	46	24	13	9	68	46	61
3	Hartlepools	46	25	10	11	60	46	60
4	Crewe	46	20	18	8	74	49	58
5	Bradford City	46	23	11	12	72	51	57
6	Southend	46	20	14	12	77	58	54
7	Chesterfield	46	21	11	14	71	50	53
8	Wrexham	46	20	13	13	72	53	53
9	Aldershot	46	18	17	11	70	55	53
10	Doncaster	46	18	15	13	66	56	51
11	Halifax	46	15	16	15	52	49	46
12	Newport	46	16	13	17	58	63	45
13	Lincoln	46	17	9	20	71	68	43
14	Brentford	46	18	7	21	61	64	43
15	Swansea	46	16	10	20	63	77	42
16	Darlington	46	12	17	17	47	53	41
17	Notts County	46	15	11	20	53	79	41
18	Port Vale	46	12	15	19	61	72	39†
19	Rochdale	46	12	14	20	51	72	38
20	Exeter	46	11	16	19	45	65	38
21	York	46	11	14	21	65	68	36
22	Chester	46	9	14	23	57	78	32
23	Workington	46	10	11	25	54	87	31
24	Bradford PA	46	4	15	27	30	82	23

†Port Vale were expelled from the League at the end of the season for making unauthorised payments. They were re-elected immediately.

SCOTTISH FA CUP 1967-68

FIRST ROUND

Rangers v Hamilton Academicals	3-1
Cowdenbeath v Dundee	0-1
Dundee United v St. Mirren	3-1
Heart of Midlothian v Brechin City	4-1
East Fife v Alloa Athletic	3-0
Morton v Falkirk	4-0
Elgin City v Forfar Athletic	3-1
Ayr United v Arbroath	0-2
Celtic v Dunfermline Athletic	0-2
Aberdeen v Raith Rovers	1-1, 1-0
Partick Thistle v Kilmarnock	0-0, 2-1
Clyde v Berwick Rangers	2-0
Motherwell v Airdrieonians	1-1, 0-1
East Stirlingshire v Hibernian	3-5
St Johnstone v Hawick Royal Albert	3-0
Queen of the South v Stirling Albion	1-1, 3-1

SECOND ROUND

Dundee v Rangers	1-1, 1-4
Dundee United v Heart of Midlothian	5-6
East Fife v Morton	0-0, 2-5
Elgin City v Arbroath	2-0
Dunfermline Athletic v Aberdeen	2-1
Partick Thistle v Clyde	3-2
Airdrieonians v Hibernian	1-0
St Johnstone v Queen of the South	5-2

THIRD ROUND

Rangers v Heart of Midlothian	1-1, 0-1
Morton v Elgin City	2-1
Dunfermline Athletic v Partick Thistle	1-0
St Johnstone v Airdrieonians	2-1

SEMI-FINAL

Heart of Midlothian v Morton	1-1, 2-1
Dunfermline Athletic v St Johnstone	1-1, 2-1

FINAL

Dunfermline Athletic v Heart of Midlothian	3-1

SCOTTISH FIRST DIVISION

		P	W	D	L	F	A	Pts
1	Celtic	34	30	3	1	106	24	63
2	Rangers	34	28	5	1	93	34	61
3	Hibernian	34	20	5	9	67	49	45
4	Dunfermline	34	17	5	12	64	41	39
5	Aberdeen	34	16	5	13	63	48	37
6	Morton	34	15	6	13	57	53	36
7	Kilmarnock	34	13	8	13	59	57	34
8	Clyde	34	15	4	15	55	55	34
9	Dundee	34	13	7	14	62	59	33
10	Partick Thistle	34	12	7	15	51	67	31
11	Dundee United	34	10	11	13	53	72	31
12	Hearts	34	13	4	17	56	61	30
13	Airdrieonians	34	10	9	15	45	58	29
14	St Johnstone	34	10	7	17	43	52	27
15	Falkirk	34	7	12	15	36	50	26
16	Raith Rovers	34	9	7	18	58	86	25
17	Motherwell	34	6	7	21	40	66	19
18	Stirling Albion	34	4	4	26	29	105	12

SCOTTISH SECOND DIVISION

		P	W	D	L	F	A	Pts
1	St Mirren	36	27	8	1	100	23	62
2	Arbroath	36	24	5	7	87	34	53
3	East Fife	36	21	7	8	71	47	49
4	Queen's Park	36	20	8	8	76	47	48
5	Ayr	36	18	6	12	69	48	42
6	Queen of the S	36	16	6	14	73	57	38
7	Forfar	36	14	10	12	57	63	38
8	Albion	36	14	9	13	62	55	37
9	Clydebank	36	13	8	15	62	73	34
10	Dumbarton	36	11	11	14	63	74	33
11	Hamilton	36	13	7	16	49	58	33
12	Cowdenbeath	36	12	8	16	57	62	32
13	Montrose	36	10	11	15	54	64	31
14	Berwick	36	13	4	19	34	54	30
15	E Stirlingshire	36	9	10	17	61	74	28
16	Brechin	36	8	12	16	45	62	28
17	Alloa	36	11	6	19	42	69	28
18	Stenhousemuir	36	7	6	23	34	93	20
19	Stranraer	36	8	4	24	41	80	20

FIRST DIVISION

		P	W	D	L	F	A	Pts
1	Leeds	42	27	13	2	66	26	67
2	Liverpool	42	25	11	6	63	24	61
3	Everton	42	21	15	6	77	36	57
4	Arsenal	42	22	12	8	56	27	56
5	Chelsea	42	20	10	12	73	53	50
6	Tottenham	42	14	17	11	61	51	45
7	Southampton	42	16	13	13	57	48	45
8	West Ham	42	13	18	11	66	50	44
9	Newcastle	42	15	14	13	61	55	44
10	WBA	42	16	11	15	64	67	43
11	Man United	42	15	12	15	57	53	42
12	Ipswich	42	15	11	16	59	60	41
13	Man City	42	15	10	17	64	55	40
14	Burnley	42	15	9	18	55	82	39
15	Sheff Wed	42	10	16	16	41	54	36
16	Wolves	42	10	15	17	41	58	35
17	Sunderland	42	11	12	19	43	67	34
18	Nottm Forest	42	10	13	19	45	57	33
19	Stoke	42	9	15	18	40	63	33
20	Coventry	42	10	11	21	46	64	31
21	Leicester	42	9	12	21	39	68	30
22	QPR	42	4	10	28	39	95	18

SECOND DIVISION

		P	W	D	L	F	A	Pts
1	Derby	42	26	11	5	65	32	63
2	Crystal Palace	42	22	12	8	70	47	56
3	Charlton	42	18	14	10	61	52	50
4	Middlesbrough	42	19	11	12	58	49	49
5	Cardiff	42	20	7	15	67	54	47
6	Huddersfield	42	17	12	13	53	46	46
7	Birmingham	42	18	8	16	73	59	44
8	Blackpool	42	14	15	13	51	41	43
9	Sheff United	42	16	11	15	61	50	43
10	Millwall	42	17	9	16	57	49	43
11	Hull	42	13	16	13	59	52	42
12	Carlisle	42	16	10	16	46	49	42
13	Norwich	42	15	10	17	53	56	40
14	Preston	42	12	15	15	38	44	39
15	Portsmouth	42	12	14	16	58	58	38
16	Bristol City	42	11	16	15	46	53	38
17	Bolton	42	12	14	16	55	67	38
18	Aston Villa	42	12	14	16	37	48	38
19	Blackburn	42	13	11	18	52	63	37
20	Oxford	42	12	9	21	34	55	33
21	Bury	42	11	8	23	51	80	30
22	Fulham	42	7	11	24	40	81	25

THIRD DIVISION

		P	W	D	L	F	A	Pts
1	Watford	46	27	10	9	74	34	64
2	Swindon	46	27	10	9	71	35	64
3	Luton	46	25	11	10	74	38	61
4	Bournemouth	46	21	9	16	60	45	51
5	Plymouth	46	17	15	14	53	49	49
6	Torquay	46	18	12	16	54	46	48
7	Tranmere	46	19	10	17	70	68	48
8	Southport	46	17	13	16	71	64	47
9	Stockport	46	16	14	16	67	68	46
10	Barnsley	46	16	14	16	58	63	46
11	Rotherham	46	16	13	17	56	50	45
12	Brighton	46	16	13	17	72	65	45
13	Walsall	46	14	16	16	50	49	44
14	Reading	46	15	13	18	67	66	43
15	Mansfield	46	16	11	19	58	62	43
16	Bristol Rovers	46	16	11	19	63	71	43
17	Shrewsbury	46	16	11	19	51	67	43
18	Orient	46	14	14	18	51	58	42
19	Barrow	46	17	8	21	56	75	42
20	Gillingham	46	13	15	18	54	63	41
21	Northampton	46	14	12	20	54	61	40
22	Hartlepool	46	10	19	17	40	70	39
23	Crewe	46	13	9	24	52	76	35
24	Oldham	46	13	9	24	50	83	35

FOURTH DIVISION

		P	W	D	L	F	A	Pts
1	Doncaster	46	21	17	8	65	38	59
2	Halifax	46	20	17	9	53	37	57
3	Rochdale	46	18	20	8	68	35	56
4	Bradford City	46	18	20	8	65	46	56
5	Darlington	46	17	18	11	62	45	52
6	Colchester	46	20	12	14	57	53	52
7	Southend	46	19	13	14	78	61	51
8	Lincoln	46	17	17	12	54	52	51
9	Wrexham	46	18	14	14	61	52	50
10	Swansea	46	19	11	16	58	54	49
11	Brentford	46	18	12	16	64	65	48
12	Workington	46	15	17	14	40	43	47
13	Port Vale	46	16	14	16	46	46	46
14	Chester	46	16	13	17	76	66	45
15	Aldershot	46	19	7	20	66	66	45
16	Scunthorpe	46	18	8	20	61	60	44
17	Exeter	46	16	11	19	66	65	43
18	Peterborough	46	13	16	17	60	57	42
19	Notts County	46	12	18	16	48	57	42
20	Chesterfield	46	13	15	18	43	50	41
21	York	46	14	11	21	53	75	39
22	Newport	46	11	14	21	49	74	36
23	Grimsby	46	9	15	22	47	69	33
24	Bradford PA	46	5	10	31	32	106	20

SCOTTISH FIRST DIVISION

		P	W	D	L	F	A	Pts
1	Celtic	34	23	8	3	89	32	54
2	Rangers	34	21	7	6	81	32	49
3	Dunfermline	34	19	7	8	63	45	45
4	Kilmarnock	34	15	14	5	50	32	44
5	Dundee United	34	17	9	8	61	49	43
6	St Johnstone	34	16	5	13	66	59	37
7	Airdrieonians	34	13	11	10	46	44	37
8	Hearts	34	14	8	12	52	54	36
9	Dundee	34	10	12	12	47	48	32
10	Morton	34	12	8	14	58	68	32
11	St Mirren	34	11	10	13	40	54	32
12	Hibernian	34	12	7	15	60	59	31
13	Clyde	34	9	13	12	35	50	31
14	Partick Thistle	34	9	10	15	39	53	28
15	Aberdeen	34	9	8	17	50	59	26
16	Raith	34	8	5	21	45	67	21
17	Falkirk	34	5	8	21	33	69	18
18	Arbroath	34	5	6	23	41	82	16

SCOTTISH SECOND DIVISION

		P	W	D	L	F	A	Pts
1	Motherwell	36	30	4	2	112	23	64
2	Ayr	36	23	7	6	82	31	53
3	East Fife	36	21	6	9	82	45	48
4	Stirling	36	21	6	9	67	40	48
5	Queen of the S	36	20	7	9	75	41	47
6	Forfar	36	18	7	11	71	56	47
7	Albion	36	19	5	12	60	56	43
8	Stranraer	36	17	7	12	57	45	41
9	E Stirlingshire	36	17	5	14	70	62	39
10	Montrose	36	15	4	17	59	71	34
11	Queen's Park	36	13	7	16	50	59	33
12	Cowdenbeath	36	12	5	19	54	67	29
13	Clydebank	36	6	15	15	52	67	27
14	Dumbarton	36	11	5	20	46	69	27
15	Hamilton	36	8	8	20	37	72	24
16	Berwick	36	7	9	20	42	70	23
17	Brechin	36	8	6	22	40	78	22
18	Alloa	36	7	7	22	45	79	21
19	Stenhousemuir	36	6	6	24	55	125	18

On 6 May 1969 only 7,843 people were at Hampden Park to see Northern Ireland play Scotland, then the smallest ever crowd at a full home international. There were on average more people at each of Fourth Division Lincoln City's games during the same season.

On 24 August 1968 the main stand at Nottingham Forest's ground caught fire during the game with Leeds and was completely destroyed. Police evacuated the 34,000 crowd and Forest played out the year on neighbouring Notts County's pitch, three hundred yards away.

FA CUP 1968–69

FOURTH ROUND

Newcastle United v Manchester City	0-0, 0-2
Blackburn Rovers v Portsmouth	4-0
Tottenham Hotspur v Wolverhampton Wanderers	2-1
Southampton v Aston Villa	2-2, 1-2
Sheffield Wednesday v Birmingham City	2-2, 1-2
Manchester United v Watford	1-1, 2-0
Bolton Wanderers v Bristol Rovers	1-2
Coventry City v Everton	0-2
West Bromwich Albion v Fulham	2-1
Arsenal v Charlton Athletic	2-0
Preston North End v Chelsea	0-0, 1-2
Stoke City v Halifax Town	1-1, 3-0
Mansfield Town v Southend United	2-1
Huddersfield v West Ham United	0-2
Liverpool v Burnley	2-1
Millwall v Leicester City	0-1

FIFTH ROUND

Manchester City v Blackburn Rovers	4-1
Tottenham Hotspur v Aston Villa	3-2
Birmingham City v Manchester United	2-2, 2-6
Bristol Rovers v Everton	0-1
West Bromwich Albion v Arsenal	1-0
Chelsea v Stoke City	3-2
Mansfield Town v West Ham United	3-0
Liverpool v Leicester City	0-0, 0-1

SIXTH ROUND

Manchester City v Tottenham Hotspur	1-0
Manchester United v Everton	0-1
Chelsea v West Bromwich Albion	1-2
Mansfield Town v Leicester City	0-1

SEMI-FINAL

Manchester City v Everton	1-0
West Bromwich Albion v Leicester City	0-1

FINAL

Leicester City v Manchester City	0-1

SCOTTISH FA CUP 1968–69

FIRST ROUND

Rangers v Hibernian	1-0
Dundee v Hearts	1-2
Dumbarton v St Mirren	0-1
Stenhousemuir v Airdrieonians	0-3
Aberdeen v Berwick Rangers	3-0
Raith Rovers v Dunfermline Athletic	0-2
Montrose v Cowdenbeath	1-0
Kilmarnock v Glasgow University	6-0
Dundee United v Queen's Park	2-1
Ayr United v Queen of the South	1-0
Stranraer v East Fife	3-1
Falkirk v Morton	1-2
East Stirlingshire v Stirling Albion	2-0
St Johnstone v Arbroath	3-2
Motherwell v Clyde	1-1, 1-2
Partick Thistle v Celtic	3-3, 1-8

SECOND ROUND

Rangers v Hearts	2-0
St Mirren v Airdrieonians	1-1, 1-3
Aberdeen v Dunfermline Athletic	2-2, 2-0
Montrose v Kilmarnock	1-1, 1-4
Dundee United v Ayr United	6-2
Stranraer v Morton	1-3
East Stirlingshire v St Johnstone	1-1, 0-3
Clyde v Celtic	0-0, 0-3

THIRD ROUND

Rangers v Airdrieonians	1-0
Aberdeen v Kilmarnock	0-0, 3-0
Dundee United v Morton	2-3
Celtic v St Johnstone	3-2

SEMI-FINAL

Rangers v Aberdeen	6-1
Morton v Celtic	1-4

FINAL

Celtic v Rangers	4-0

FIRST DIVISION

		P	W	D	L	F	A	Pts
1	Everton	42	29	8	5	72	34	66
2	Leeds	42	21	15	6	84	49	57
3	Chelsea	42	21	13	8	70	50	55
4	Derby	42	22	9	11	64	37	53
5	Liverpool	42	20	11	11	65	42	51
6	Coventry	42	19	11	12	58	48	49
7	Newcastle	42	17	13	12	57	35	47
8	Man United	42	14	17	11	66	61	45
9	Stoke	42	15	15	12	56	52	45
10	Man City	42	16	11	15	55	48	43
11	Tottenham	42	17	9	16	54	55	43
12	Arsenal	42	12	18	12	51	49	42
13	Wolves	42	12	16	14	55	57	40
14	Burnley	42	12	15	15	56	61	39
15	Nottm Forest	42	10	18	14	50	71	38
16	WBA	42	14	9	19	58	66	37
17	West Ham	42	12	12	18	51	60	36
18	Ipswich	42	10	11	21	40	63	31
19	Southampton	42	6	17	19	46	67	29
20	Crystal Palace	42	6	15	21	34	68	27
21	Sunderland	42	6	14	22	30	68	26
22	Sheff Wed	42	8	9	25	40	71	25

SECOND DIVISION

		P	W	D	L	F	A	Pts
1	Huddersfield	42	24	12	6	68	37	60
2	Blackpool	42	20	13	9	56	45	53
3	Leicester	42	19	13	10	64	50	51
4	Middlesbrough	42	20	10	12	55	45	50
5	Swindon	42	17	16	9	57	47	50
6	Sheff United	42	22	5	15	73	38	49
7	Cardiff	42	18	13	11	61	41	49
8	Blackburn	42	20	7	15	54	50	47
9	QPR	42	17	11	14	66	57	45
10	Millwall	42	15	14	13	56	56	44
11	Norwich	42	16	11	15	49	46	43
12	Carlisle	42	14	13	15	58	56	41
13	Hull	42	15	11	16	72	70	41
14	Bristol City	42	13	13	16	54	50	39
15	Oxford	42	12	15	15	35	42	39
16	Bolton	42	12	12	18	54	61	36
17	Portsmouth	42	13	9	20	66	80	35
18	Birmingham	42	11	11	20	51	78	33
19	Watford	42	9	13	20	44	57	31
20	Charlton	42	7	17	18	35	76	31
21	Aston Villa	42	8	13	21	36	62	29
22	Preston	42	8	12	22	43	63	28

THIRD DIVISION

		P	W	D	L	F	A	Pts
1	Orient	46	25	12	9	67	36	62
2	Luton	46	23	14	9	77	43	60
3	Bristol Rovers	46	20	16	10	80	59	56
4	Fulham	46	20	15	11	81	55	55
5	Brighton	46	23	9	14	57	43	55
6	Mansfield	46	21	11	14	70	49	53
7	Barnsley	46	19	15	12	68	59	53
8	Reading	46	21	11	14	87	77	53
9	Rochdale	46	18	10	18	69	60	46
10	Bradford City	46	17	12	17	57	50	46
11	Doncaster	46	17	12	17	52	54	46
12	Walsall	46	17	12	17	54	67	46
13	Torquay	46	14	17	15	62	59	45
14	Rotherham	46	15	14	17	62	54	44
15	Shrewsbury	46	13	18	15	62	63	44
16	Tranmere	46	14	16	16	56	72	44
17	Plymouth	46	16	11	19	56	64	43
18	Halifax	46	14	15	17	47	63	43
19	Bury	46	15	11	20	75	80	41
20	Gillingham	46	13	13	20	52	64	39
21	Bournemouth	46	12	15	19	48	71	39
22	Southport	46	14	10	22	48	66	38
23	Barrow	46	8	14	24	46	81	30
24	Stockport	46	6	11	29	27	71	23

FOURTH DIVISION

		P	W	D	L	F	A	Pts
1	Chesterfield	46	27	10	9	77	32	64
2	Wrexham	46	26	9	11	84	49	61
3	Swansea	46	21	18	7	66	45	60
4	Port Vale	46	20	19	7	61	33	59
5	Brentford	46	20	16	10	58	39	56
6	Aldershot	46	20	13	13	78	65	53
7	Notts County	46	22	8	16	73	62	52
8	Lincoln	46	17	16	13	66	52	50
9	Peterborough	46	17	14	15	77	69	48
10	Colchester	46	17	14	15	64	63	48
11	Chester	46	21	6	19	58	66	48
12	Scunthorpe	46	18	10	18	67	65	46
13	York	46	16	14	16	55	62	46
14	Northampton	46	16	12	18	64	55	44
15	Crewe	46	16	12	18	51	51	44
16	Grimsby	46	14	15	17	54	58	43
17	Southend	46	15	10	21	59	85	40
18	Exeter	46	14	11	21	57	59	39
19	Oldham	46	13	13	20	60	65	39
20	Workington	46	12	14	20	46	64	38
21	Newport	46	13	11	22	53	74	37
22	Darlington	46	13	10	23	53	73	36
23	Hartlepool	46	10	10	26	42	82	30
24	Bradford P A	46	6	11	29	41	96	23

SCOTTISH FIRST DIVISION

		P	W	D	L	F	A	Pts
1	Celtic	34	27	3	4	96	33	57
2	Rangers	34	19	7	8	67	40	45
3	Hibernian	34	19	6	9	65	40	44
4	Hearts	34	13	12	9	50	36	38
5	Dundee United	34	16	6	12	62	64	38
6	Dundee	34	15	6	13	49	44	36
7	Kilmarnock	34	13	10	11	62	57	36
8	Aberdeen	34	14	7	13	55	45	35
9	Dunfermline	34	15	5	14	45	45	35
10	Morton	34	13	9	12	52	52	35
11	Motherwell	34	11	10	13	49	51	32
12	Airdrieonians	34	12	8	14	59	64	32
13	St Johnstone	34	11	9	14	50	62	31
14	Ayr	34	12	6	16	37	52	30
15	St Mirren	34	8	9	17	39	54	25
16	Clyde	34	9	7	18	34	56	25
17	Raith	34	5	11	18	32	67	21
18	Partick Thistle	34	5	7	22	41	82	17

SCOTTISH SECOND DIVISION

		P	W	D	L	F	A	Pts
1	Falkirk	36	25	6	5	94	34	56
2	Cowdenbeath	36	24	7	5	81	35	55
3	Queen of the S	36	22	6	8	72	49	50
4	Stirling	36	18	10	8	70	40	46
5	Arbroath	36	20	4	12	76	39	44
6	Alloa	36	19	5	12	62	41	43
7	Dumbarton	36	17	6	13	55	46	40
8	Montrose	36	15	7	14	57	55	37
9	Berwick	36	15	5	16	67	55	35
10	East Fife	36	15	4	17	59	63	34
11	Albion	36	14	5	17	53	64	33
12	E Stirlingshire	36	14	5	17	58	75	33
13	Clydebank	36	10	10	16	47	65	30
14	Brechin	36	11	6	19	47	74	28
15	Queen's Park	36	10	6	20	38	62	26
16	Stenhousemuir	36	10	6	20	47	89	26
17	Stranraer	36	9	7	20	56	75	25
18	Forfar	36	11	1	24	55	83	23
19	Hamilton	36	8	4	24	42	92	20

FA CUP 1969-70

FOURTH ROUND

Chelsea v Burnley	2-2, 3-1
Tottenham Hotspur v Crystal Palace	0-0, 0-1
Charlton Athletic v Queen's Park Rangers	2-3
Derby County v Sheffield United	3-0
Watford v Stoke City	1-0
Gillingham v Peterborough United	5-1
Liverpool v Wrexham	3-1
Southampton v Leicester City	1-1, 2-4
Tranmere Rovers v Northampton Town	0-0, 1-2
Manchester United v Manchester City	3-0
Carlisle United v Aldershot	2-2, 4-1
Middlesbrough v York City	4-1
Swindon Town v Chester	4-2
Sheffield Wednesday v Scunthorpe United	1-2
Blackpool v Mansfield Town	0-2
Sutton United v Leeds United	0-6

FIFTH ROUND

Chelsea v Crystal Palace	4-1
Queen's Park Rangers v Derby County	1-0
Watford v Gillingham	2-1
Liverpool v Leicester City	0-0, 2-0
Northampton Town v Manchester United	2-8
Carlisle United v Middlesbrough	1-2
Swindon Town v Scunthorpe United	3-1
Mansfield Town v Leeds United	0-2

SIXTH ROUND

Queen's Park Rangers v Chelsea	2-4
Watford v Liverpool	1-0
Manchester United v Middlesbrough	1-1, 2-1
Swindon Town v Leeds United	0-2

SEMI-FINAL

Chelsea v Watford	5-1
Manchester United v Leeds United	0-0, 0-0, 0-1

THIRD PLACE PLAY-OFF

Manchester United v Watford	2-0

FINAL

Chelsea v Leeds United	2-2, 2-1

SCOTTISH FA CUP 1969-70

FIRST ROUND

Celtic v Dunfermline Athletic	2-1
Dundee United v Ayr United	1-0
Dumbarton v Forfar Athletic	1-2
Rangers v Hibernian	3-1
East Fife v Raith Rovers	3-0
Morton v Queen of the South	2-0
Albion Rovers v Dundee	1-2
Airdrieonians v Hamilton Academicals	5-0
Motherwell v St Johnstone	2-1
Stranraer v Inverness Caledonian	2-5
Kilmarnock v Partick Thistle	3-0
Montrose v Heart of Midlothian	1-1, 0-1
Falkirk v Tarff Rovers	3-0
St Mirren v Stirling Albion	2-0
Arbroath v Clydebank	1-2
Clyde v Aberdeen	0-4

SECOND ROUND

Celtic v Dundee United	4-0
Forfar Athletic v Rangers	0-7
East Fife v Morton	1-0
Dundee v Airdrieonians	3-0
Motherwell v Inverness Caledonian	3-1
Kilmarnock v Heart of Midlothian	2-0
Falkirk v St Mirren	2-1
Aberdeen v Clydebank	2-1

THIRD ROUND

Celtic v Rangers	3-1
East Fife v Dundee	0-1
Motherwell v Kilmarnock	0-1
Falkirk v Aberdeen	0-1

SEMI-FINAL

Celtic v Dundee	2-1
Kilmarnock v Aberdeen	0-1

FINAL

Celtic v Aberdeen	1-3

Leeds go marching on

Leeds United established a new First Division record for the number of consecutive League games played without a defeat. They completed a run of 34 home and away matches without losing a single game. Their unbeaten run finally ended on 30 August 1969 when they lost 3-2 to Everton, the club that was to take the League title from them.

Six of the Best

George Best scored a record number of goals in a Cup tie, notching six for Manchester United in their 8-2 win over Fourth Division Northampton Town in the fifth round of the FA Cup. Best's team-mate Denis Law, when with Manchester City, once scored six goals in a fourth round tie at Luton, but the match was abandoned and Luton won the replay.

FIRST DIVISION

		P	W	D	L	F	A	Pts
1	Arsenal	42	29	7	6	71	29	65
2	Leeds	42	27	10	5	72	30	64
3	Tottenham	42	19	14	9	54	33	52
4	Wolves	42	22	8	12	64	54	52
5	Liverpool	42	17	17	8	42	24	51
6	Chelsea	42	18	15	9	52	42	51
7	Southampton	42	17	12	13	56	44	46
8	Man United	42	16	11	15	65	66	43
9	Derby	42	16	10	16	56	54	42
10	Coventry	42	16	10	16	37	38	42
11	Man City	42	12	17	13	47	42	41
12	Newcastle	42	14	13	15	44	46	41
13	Stoke	42	12	13	17	44	48	37
14	Everton	42	12	13	17	54	60	37
15	Huddersfield	42	11	14	17	40	49	36
16	Nottm Forest	42	14	8	20	42	61	36
17	WBA	42	10	15	17	58	75	35
18	Crystal Palace	42	12	11	19	39	57	35
19	Ipswich	42	12	10	20	42	48	34
20	West Ham	42	10	14	18	47	60	34
21	Burnley	42	7	13	22	29	63	27
22	Blackpool	42	4	15	23	34	66	23

SECOND DIVISION

		P	W	D	L	F	A	Pts
1	Leicester	42	23	13	6	57	30	59
2	Sheff United	42	21	14	7	73	39	56
3	Cardiff	42	20	13	9	64	41	53
4	Carlisle	42	20	13	9	65	43	53
5	Hull	42	19	13	10	54	41	51
6	Luton	42	18	13	11	62	43	49
7	Middlesbrough	42	17	14	11	60	43	48
8	Millwall	42	19	9	14	59	42	47
9	Birmingham	42	17	12	13	58	48	46
10	Norwich	42	15	14	13	54	52	44
11	QPR	42	16	11	15	58	53	43
12	Swindon	42	15	12	15	61	51	42
13	Sunderland	42	15	12	15	52	54	42
14	Oxford	42	14	14	14	41	48	42
15	Sheff Wed	42	12	12	18	51	69	36
16	Portsmouth	42	10	14	18	46	61	34
17	Orient	42	9	16	17	29	51	34
18	Watford	42	10	13	19	38	60	33
19	Bristol City	42	10	11	21	46	64	31
20	Charlton	42	8	14	20	41	65	30
21	Blackburn	42	6	15	21	37	69	27
22	Bolton	42	7	10	25	35	74	24

THIRD DIVISION

		P	W	D	L	F	A	Pts
1	Preston	46	22	17	7	63	39	61
2	Fulham	46	24	12	10	68	41	60
3	Halifax	46	22	12	12	74	55	56
4	Aston Villa	46	19	15	12	54	46	53
5	Chesterfield	46	17	17	12	66	38	51
6	Bristol Rovers	46	19	13	14	69	50	51
7	Mansfield	46	18	15	13	64	62	51
8	Rotherham	46	17	16	13	64	60	50
9	Wrexham	46	18	13	15	72	65	49
10	Torquay	46	19	11	16	54	57	49
11	Swansea	46	15	16	15	59	56	46
12	Barnsley	46	17	11	18	49	52	45
13	Shrewsbury	46	16	13	17	58	62	45
14	Brighton	46	14	16	16	50	47	44
15	Plymouth	46	12	19	15	63	63	43
16	Rochdale	46	14	15	17	61	68	43
17	Port Vale	46	15	12	19	52	59	42
18	Tranmere	46	10	22	14	45	55	42
19	Bradford City	46	13	14	19	49	62	40
20	Walsall	46	14	11	21	51	57	39
21	Reading	46	14	11	21	48	85	39
22	Bury	46	12	13	21	52	60	37
23	Doncaster	46	13	9	24	45	66	35
24	Gillingham	46	10	13	23	42	67	33

FOURTH DIVISION

		P	W	D	L	F	A	Pts
1	Notts County	46	30	9	7	89	36	69
2	Bournemouth	46	24	12	10	81	46	60
3	Oldham	46	24	11	11	88	63	59
4	York	46	23	10	13	78	54	56
5	Chester	46	24	7	15	69	55	55
6	Colchester	46	21	12	13	70	54	54
7	Northampton	46	19	13	14	63	59	51
8	Southport	46	21	6	19	63	57	48
9	Exeter	46	17	14	15	67	68	48
10	Workington	46	18	12	16	48	49	48
11	Stockport	46	16	14	16	49	65	46
12	Darlington	46	17	11	18	58	57	45
13	Aldershot	46	14	17	15	66	71	45
14	Brentford	46	18	8	20	66	62	44
15	Crewe	46	18	8	20	75	76	44
16	Peterborough	46	18	7	21	70	71	43
17	Scunthorpe	46	15	13	18	56	61	43
18	Southend	46	14	15	17	53	66	43
19	Grimsby	46	18	7	21	57	71	43
20	Cambridge	46	15	13	18	51	66	43
21	Lincoln	46	13	13	20	70	71	39
22	Newport	46	10	8	28	55	85	28
23	Hartlepool	46	8	12	26	34	74	28
24	Barrow	46	7	8	31	51	90	22

SCOTTISH FIRST DIVISION

		P	W	D	L	F	A	Pts
1	Celtic	34	25	6	3	89	23	56
2	Aberdeen	34	24	6	4	68	18	54
3	St Johnstone	34	19	6	9	59	44	44
4	Rangers	34	16	9	9	58	34	41
5	Dundee	34	14	10	10	53	45	38
6	Dundee United	34	14	8	12	53	54	36
7	Falkirk	34	13	9	12	46	53	35
8	Morton	34	13	8	13	44	44	34
9	Motherwell	34	13	8	13	43	47	34
10	Airdrieonians	34	13	8	13	60	65	34
11	Hearts	34	13	7	14	41	40	33
12	Hibernian	34	10	10	14	47	53	30
13	Kilmarnock	34	10	8	16	43	67	28
14	Ayr	34	9	8	17	37	54	26
15	Clyde	34	8	10	16	33	59	26
16	Dunfermline	34	6	11	17	44	56	23
17	St Mirren	34	7	9	18	38	56	23
18	Cowdenbeath	34	7	3	24	33	77	17

SCOTTISH SECOND DIVISION

		P	W	D	L	F	A	Pts
1	Partick Thistle	36	23	10	3	78	26	56
2	East Fife	36	22	7	7	86	44	51
3	Arbroath	36	19	8	9	80	52	46
4	Dumbarton	36	19	6	11	87	46	44
5	Clydebank	36	17	8	11	57	43	42
6	Montrose	36	17	7	12	78	64	41
7	Albion	36	15	9	12	53	52	39
8	Raith	36	15	9	12	62	62	39
9	Stranraer	36	14	8	14	54	52	36
10	Stenhousemuir	36	14	8	14	64	70	36
11	Queen of the S	36	13	9	14	50	56	35
12	Stirling	36	12	8	16	61	61	32
13	Berwick	36	10	10	16	42	60	30
14	Queen's Park	36	13	4	19	51	72	30
15	Forfar	36	9	11	16	63	75	29
16	Alloa	36	9	11	16	56	86	29
17	E Stirlingshire	36	9	9	18	57	86	27
18	Hamilton	36	8	7	21	50	79	23
19	Brechin	36	6	7	23	30	73	19

The unnecessary goalkeeper

One of the strangest events in all football annals happened on 12 May 1971. In the course of the England–Malta game the ball did not cross the England goal-line once and the England goalkeeper, Gordon Banks, did not receive the ball direct from a Maltese player at any time during the game.

A pools punter's best friend

In the 1970-71 season, Tranmere Rovers of the Third Division broke Plymouth Argyle's 50-year-old record by drawing 22 of their 46 League matches, the most ever tied in a single season. In actual fact, Plymouth's drawn percentage was higher as they played 42 and tied 21 games in the 1920-21 season.

FA CUP 1970–71

FOURTH ROUND

Liverpool v Swansea City	3-0
York City v Southampton	3-3, 2-3
Carlisle United v Tottenham Hotspur	2-3
Nottingham Forest v Orient	1-1, 1-0
Everton v Middlesbrough	3-0
Derby County v Wolverhampton Wanderers	2-1
Rochdale v Colchester United	3-3, 0-5
Leeds United v Swindon Town	4-0
Hull City v Blackpool	2-0
Cardiff City v Brentford	0-2
Stoke City v Huddersfield Town	3-3, 0-0, 1-0
West Bromwich Albion v Ipswich Town	1-1, 0-3
Leicester City v Torquay United	3-0
Oxford United v Watford	1-1, 2-1
Chelsea v Manchester City	0-3
Portsmouth v Arsenal	1-1, 2-3

FIFTH ROUND

Liverpool v Southampton	1-0
Tottenham Hotspur v Nottingham Forest	2-1
Everton v Derby County	1-0
Colchester United v Leeds United	3-2
Hull City v Brentford	2-1
Stoke City v Ipswich Town	0-0, 1-0
Leicester City v Oxford United	1-1, 3-1
Manchester City v Arsenal	1-2

SIXTH ROUND

Liverpool v Tottenham Hotspur	0-0, 1-0
Everton v Colchester United	5-0
Hull City v Stoke City	2-3
Leicester City v Arsenal	0-0, 0-1

SEMI-FINAL

Liverpool v Everton	2-1
Stoke City v Arsenal	2-2, 0-2

THIRD PLACE PLAY-OFF

Stoke City v Everton	3-2

FINAL

Liverpool v Arsenal	1-2

SCOTTISH FA CUP 1970–71

THIRD ROUND

Celtic v Queen of the South	5-1
Hibernian v Forfar Athletic	8-1
East Fife v St Mirren	1-1, 1-1, 1-3
St Johnstone v Raith Rovers	2-2, 3-4
Clyde v Brechin City	2-0
Airdrieonians v Alloa Athletic	1-1, 2-0
Rangers v Falkirk	3-0
Aberdeen v Elgin City	5-0
Dundee v Partick Thistle	1-0
Clachnacuddin v Cowdenbeath	0-3
Clydebank v Dundee United	0-0, 1-5
Stirling Albion v Motherwell	3-1
Dunfermline v Arbroath	3-1
Morton v Ayr United	2-0
Queen's Park v Kilmarnock	0-1
Heart of Midlothian v Stranraer	3-0

FOURTH ROUND

Dundee United v Aberdeen	1-1, 0-2
Raith Rovers v Clyde	1-1, 2-0
Morton v Kilmarnock	1-2
Cowdenbeath v Airdrieonians	0-4
St Mirren v Rangers	1-3
Dundee v Stirling Albion	2-0
Celtic v Dunfermline	1-1, 1-0
Heart of Midlothian v Hibernian	1-2

FIFTH ROUND

Rangers v Aberdeen	1-0
Hibernian v Dundee	1-0
Celtic v Raith Rovers	7-1
Kilmarnock v Airdrieonians	2-3

SEMI-FINAL

Hibernian v Rangers	0-0, 1-2
Celtic v Airdrieonians	3-3, 2-0

FINAL

Rangers v Celtic	1-1, 1-2

FIRST DIVISION

		P	W	D	L	F	A	Pts
1	Derby	42	24	10	8	69	33	58
2	Leeds	42	24	9	9	73	31	57
3	Liverpool	42	24	9	9	64	30	57
4	Man City	42	23	11	8	77	45	57
5	Arsenal	42	22	8	12	58	40	52
6	Tottenham	42	19	13	10	63	42	51
7	Chelsea	42	18	12	12	58	49	48
8	Man United	42	19	10	13	69	61	48
9	Wolves	42	18	11	13	65	57	47
10	Sheff United	42	17	12	13	61	60	46
11	Newcastle	42	15	11	16	49	52	41
12	Leicester	42	13	13	16	41	46	39
13	Ipswich	42	11	16	15	39	53	38
14	West Ham	42	12	12	18	47	51	36
15	Everton	42	9	18	15	37	48	36
16	WBA	42	12	11	19	42	54	35
17	Stoke	42	10	15	17	39	56	35
18	Coventry	42	9	15	18	44	67	33
19	Southampton	42	12	7	23	52	80	31
20	Crystal Palace	42	8	13	21	39	65	29
21	Nottm Forest	42	8	9	25	47	81	25
22	Huddersfield	42	6	13	23	27	59	25

SECOND DIVISION

		P	W	D	L	F	A	Pts
1	Norwich	42	21	15	6	60	36	57
2	Birmingham	42	19	18	5	60	31	56
3	Millwall	42	19	17	6	64	46	55
4	QPR	42	20	14	8	57	28	54
5	Sunderland	42	17	16	9	67	57	50
6	Blackpool	42	20	7	15	70	50	47
7	Burnley	42	20	6	16	70	55	46
8	Bristol City	42	18	10	14	61	49	46
9	Middlesbrough	42	19	8	15	50	48	46
10	Carlisle	42	17	9	16	61	57	43
11	Swindon	42	15	12	15	47	47	42
12	Hull	42	14	10	18	49	53	38
13	Luton	42	10	18	14	43	48	38
14	Sheff Wed	42	13	12	17	51	58	38
15	Oxford	42	12	14	16	43	55	38
16	Portsmouth	42	12	13	17	59	68	37
17	Orient	42	14	9	19	50	61	37
18	Preston	42	12	12	18	52	58	36
19	Cardiff	42	10	14	18	56	69	34
20	Fulham	42	12	10	20	45	68	34
21	Charlton	42	12	9	21	55	77	33
22	Watford	42	5	9	28	24	75	19

THIRD DIVISION

		P	W	D	L	F	A	Pts
1	Aston Villa	46	32	6	8	85	32	70
2	Brighton	46	27	11	8	82	47	65
3	Bournemouth	46	23	16	7	73	37	62
4	Notts County	46	25	12	9	74	44	62
5	Rotherham	46	20	15	11	69	52	55
6	Bristol Rovers	46	21	12	13	75	56	54
7	Bolton	46	17	16	13	51	41	50
8	Plymouth	46	20	10	16	74	64	50
9	Walsall	46	15	18	13	62	57	48
10	Blackburn	46	19	9	18	54	57	47
11	Oldham	46	17	11	18	59	63	45
12	Shrewsbury	46	17	10	19	73	65	44
13	Chesterfield	46	18	8	20	57	57	44
14	Swansea	46	17	10	19	46	59	44
15	Port Vale	46	13	15	18	43	59	41
16	Wrexham	46	16	8	22	59	63	40
17	Halifax	46	13	12	21	48	61	38
18	Rochdale	46	12	13	21	57	83	37
19	York	46	12	12	22	57	66	36
20	Tranmere	46	10	16	20	50	71	36
21	Mansfield	46	8	20	18	41	63	36
22	Barnsley	46	9	18	19	32	64	36
23	Torquay	46	10	12	24	41	69	32
24	Bradford City	46	11	10	25	45	77	32

FOURTH DIVISION

		P	W	D	L	F	A	Pts
1	Grimsby	46	28	7	11	88	56	63
2	Southend	46	24	12	10	81	55	60
3	Brentford	46	24	11	11	76	44	59
4	Scunthorpe	46	22	13	11	56	37	57
5	Lincoln	46	21	14	11	77	59	56
6	Workington	46	16	19	11	50	34	51
7	Southport	46	18	14	14	66	46	50
8	Peterborough	46	17	16	13	82	64	50
9	Bury	46	19	12	15	73	59	50
10	Cambridge	46	17	14	15	62	60	48
11	Colchester	46	19	10	17	70	69	48
12	Doncaster	46	16	14	16	56	63	46
13	Gillingham	46	16	13	17	61	67	45
14	Newport	46	18	8	20	60	72	44
15	Exeter	46	16	11	19	61	68	43
16	Reading	46	17	8	21	56	76	42
17	Aldershot	46	9	22	15	48	54	40
18	Hartlepool	46	17	6	23	58	69	40
19	Darlington	46	14	11	21	64	82	39
20	Chester	46	10	18	18	47	56	38
21	Northampton	46	12	13	21	66	79	37
22	Barrow	46	13	11	22	40	71	37
23	Stockport	46	9	14	23	55	87	32
24	Crewe	46	10	9	27	43	69	29

SCOTTISH FIRST DIVISION

		P	W	D	L	F	A	Pts
1	Celtic	34	28	4	2	96	28	60
2	Aberdeen	34	21	8	5	80	26	50
3	Rangers	34	21	2	11	71	38	44
4	Hibernian	34	19	6	9	62	34	44
5	Dundee	34	14	13	7	59	38	41
6	Hearts	34	13	13	8	53	49	39
7	Partick	34	12	10	12	53	54	34
8	St Johnstone	34	12	8	14	52	58	32
9	Dundee United	34	12	7	15	55	70	31
10	Motherwell	34	11	7	16	49	69	29
11	Kilmarnock	34	11	6	17	49	64	28
12	Ayr	34	9	10	15	40	58	28
13	Morton	34	10	7	17	46	52	27
14	Falkirk	34	10	7	17	44	60	27
15	Airdrieonians	34	7	12	15	44	76	26
16	East Fife*	34	5	15	14	34	61	25
17	Clyde	34	7	10	17	33	66	24
18	Dunfermline	34	7	9	18	31	50	23

SCOTTISH SECOND DIVISION

		P	W	D	L	F	A	Pts
1	Dumbarton	36	24	4	8	89	51	52
2	Arbroath	36	22	8	6	71	41	52
3	Stirling	36	21	8	7	75	37	50
4	St Mirren	36	24	2	10	84	47	50
5	Cowdenbeath	36	19	10	7	69	28	48
6	Stranraer	36	18	8	10	70	62	44
7	Queen of the S	36	17	9	10	56	38	43
8	E Stirlingshire	36	17	7	12	60	58	41
9	Clydebank	36	14	11	11	60	52	39
10	Montrose	36	15	6	15	73	54	36
11	Raith	36	13	8	15	56	56	34
12	Queen's Park	36	12	9	15	47	61	33
13	Berwick	36	14	4	18	53	50	32
14	Stenhousemuir	36	10	8	18	41	58	28
15	Brechin	36	8	7	21	41	79	23
16	Alloa	36	9	4	23	41	75	22
17	Forfar	36	6	9	21	32	84	21
18	Albion	36	7	6	23	36	61	20
19	Hamilton	36	4	8	24	31	93	16

Mansfield Town did not score a League goal at home until the 23rd minute of their game against Plymouth Argyle on 18 December 1971. This unrewarded period of 833 minutes of Third Division football at Field Mill is thought to constitute a record-breaking start to any Football League club's season. Mansfield still lost the game 3-2.

Aldershot drew 22 of their Fourth Division fixtures to equal Tranmere Rovers' record of the 1970-71 season. Both Tranmere and Aldershot, however, played 46 games that season and their achievement does not, therefore, compare in percentage terms with Plymouth's feat of 1920-21. That year Argyle drew 21 of their 42 League games.

FA CUP 1971-72

FOURTH ROUND
Liverpool v Leeds United	0-0, 0-2
Cardiff City v Sunderland	1-1, 1-1, 3-1
Everton v Walsall	2-1
Tottenham Hotspur v Rotherham United	2-0
Birmingham City v Ipswich Town	1-0
Portsmouth v Swansea City	2-0
Huddersfield Town v Fulham	3-0
Hereford United v West Ham United	0-0, 1-3
Preston North End v Manchester United	0-2
Millwall v Middlesbrough	2-2, 1-2
Tranmere Rovers v Stoke City	2-2, 0-2
Coventry City v Hull City	0-1
Leicester City v Orient	0-2
Chelsea v Bolton Wanderers	3-0
Derby County v Notts County	6-0
Reading v Arsenal	1-2

FIFTH ROUND
Cardiff City v Leeds United	0-2
Everton v Tottenham Hotspur	0-2
Birmingham City v Portsmouth	3-1
Huddersfield Town v West Ham United	4-2
Manchester United v Middlesbrough	0-0, 3-0
Stoke City v Hull City	4-1
Orient v Chelsea	3-2
Derby County v Arsenal	2-2, 0-0, 0-1

SIXTH ROUND
Leeds United v Tottenham Hotspur	2-1
Birmingham City v Huddersfield Town	3-1
Manchester United v Stoke City	1-1, 1-2
Orient v Arsenal	0-1

SEMI-FINAL
Leeds United v Birmingham City	3-0
Arsenal v Stoke City	1-1, 2-1

FINAL
Leeds United v Arsenal	1-0

SCOTTISH FA CUP 1971-72

THIRD ROUND
Celtic v Albion Rovers	5-0
Dundee v Queen of the South	3-0
Heart of Midlothian v St Johnstone	2-0
Clydebank v East Fife	1-1, 1-0
Dumbarton v Hamilton Academicals	3-1
Raith Rovers v Dunfermline Athletic	2-0
Elgin City v Inverness Caledonian	3-1
Kilmarnock v Alloa Athletic	5-1
Clyde v Ayr United	0-1
Motherwell v Montrose	2-0
Forfar Athletic v St Mirren	0-1
Falkirk v Rangers	2-2, 0-2
Dundee United v Aberdeen	0-4
Morton v Cowdenbeath	1-0
Arbroath v Airdrieonians	1-3
Partick Thistle v Hibernian	0-2

FOURTH ROUND
Celtic v Dundee	4-0
Heart of Midlothian v Clydebank	4-0
Dumbarton v Raith Rovers	0-3
Elgin City v Kilmarnock	1-4
Ayr United v Motherwell	0-0, 1-2
St Mirren v Rangers	1-4
Aberdeen v Morton	1-0
Hibernian v Airdrieonians	2-0

FIFTH ROUND
Celtic v Heart of Midlothian	1-1, 1-0
Raith Rovers v Kilmarnock	1-3
Motherwell v Rangers	2-2, 2-4
Hibernian v Aberdeen	2-0

SEMI-FINAL
Celtic v Kilmarnock	3-1
Rangers v Hibernian	1-1, 0-2

FINAL
Celtic v Hibernian	6-1

FIRST DIVISION

	P	W	D	L	F	A	Pts
1 Liverpool	42	25	10	6	72	42	60
2 Arsenal	42	23	11	8	57	43	57
3 Leeds	42	21	11	10	77	45	53
4 Ipswich	42	17	14	11	55	45	48
5 Wolves	42	18	11	13	66	54	47
6 West Ham	42	17	12	13	67	53	46
7 Derby	42	19	8	15	56	54	46
8 Tottenham	42	16	13	13	58	48	45
9 Newcastle	42	16	13	13	60	51	45
10 Birmingham	42	15	12	15	53	54	42
11 Man City	42	15	11	16	57	60	41
12 Chelsea	42	13	14	15	49	51	40
13 Southampton	42	11	18	13	47	52	40
14 Sheff United	42	15	10	17	51	59	40
15 Stoke	42	14	10	18	61	56	38
16 Leicester	42	10	17	15	40	46	37
17 Everton	42	13	11	18	41	49	37
18 Man United	42	12	13	17	44	60	37
19 Coventry	42	13	9	20	40	55	35
20 Norwich	42	11	10	21	36	63	32
21 Crystal Palace	42	9	12	21	41	58	30
22 WBA	42	9	10	23	38	62	28

SECOND DIVISION

	P	W	D	L	F	A	Pts
1 Burnley	42	24	14	4	72	35	62
2 QPR	42	24	13	5	81	37	61
3 Aston Villa	42	18	14	10	51	47	50
4 Middlesbrough	42	17	13	12	46	43	47
5 Bristol City	42	17	12	13	63	51	46
6 Sunderland	42	17	12	13	59	49	46
7 Blackpool	42	18	10	14	56	51	46
8 Oxford	42	19	7	16	52	43	45
9 Fulham	42	16	12	14	58	49	44
10 Sheff Wed	42	17	10	15	59	55	44
11 Millwall	42	16	10	16	55	47	42
12 Luton	42	15	11	16	44	53	41
13 Hull	42	14	12	16	64	59	40
14 Nottm Forest	42	14	12	16	47	52	40
15 Orient	42	12	12	18	49	53	36
16 Swindon	42	10	16	16	46	60	36
17 Portsmouth	42	12	11	19	42	59	35
18 Carlisle	42	11	12	19	50	52	34
19 Preston	42	11	12	19	37	64	34
20 Cardiff	42	11	11	20	43	58	33
21 Huddersfield	42	8	17	17	36	56	33
22 Brighton	42	8	13	21	46	83	29

FA CUP 1972-73

FOURTH ROUND

Arsenal v Bradford City	2-0
Bolton Wanderers v Cardiff City	2-2, 1-1, 1-0
Carlisle United v Sheffield United	2-1
Chelsea v Ipswich Town	2-0
Coventry City v Grimsby Town	1-0
Derby County v Tottenham Hotspur	1-1, 5-3
Everton v Millwall	0-2
Hull City v West Ham United	1-0
Leeds United v Plymouth Argyle	2-1
Liverpool v Manchester City	0-0, 0-2
Newcastle United v Luton Town	0-2
Oxford United v Queen's Park Rangers	0-2
Sheffield Wednesday v Crystal Palace	1-1, 1-1, 3-2
Sunderland v Reading	1-1, 3-1
West Bromwich Albion v Swindon Town	2-0
Wolverhampton Wanderers v Bristol City	1-0

FIFTH ROUND

Bolton Wanderers v Luton Town	0-1
Carlisle United v Arsenal	1-2
Coventry City v Hull City	3-0
Derby County v Queen's Park Rangers	4-2
Leeds United v West Bromwich Albion	2-0
Manchester City v Sunderland	2-2, 1-3
Sheffield Wednesday v Chelsea	1-2
Wolverhampton Wanderers v Millwall	1-0

SIXTH ROUND

Chelsea v Arsenal	2-2, 1-2
Derby County v Leeds United	0-1
Sunderland v Luton Town	2-0
Wolverhampton Wanderers v Coventry City	2-0

SEMI-FINAL

Arsenal v Sunderland	1-2
Leeds United v Wolverhampton Wanderers	1-0

FINAL

Leeds United v Sunderland	0-1

THIRD DIVISION

	P	W	D	L	F	A	Pts
1 Bolton	46	25	11	10	73	39	61
2 Notts County	46	23	11	12	67	47	57
3 Blackburn	46	20	15	11	57	47	55
4 Oldham	46	19	16	11	72	54	54
5 Bristol Rovers	46	20	13	13	77	56	53
6 Port Vale	46	21	11	14	56	69	53
7 Bournemouth	46	17	16	13	66	44	50
8 Plymouth	46	20	10	16	74	66	50
9 Grimsby	46	20	8	18	67	61	48
10 Tranmere	46	15	16	15	56	52	46
11 Charlton	46	17	11	18	69	67	45
12 Wrexham	46	14	17	15	55	54	45
13 Rochdale	46	14	17	15	48	54	45
14 Southend	46	17	10	19	61	54	44
15 Shrewsbury	46	15	14	17	46	54	44
16 Chesterfield	46	17	9	20	57	61	43
17 Walsall	46	18	7	21	56	66	43
18 York	46	13	15	18	42	46	41
19 Watford	46	12	17	17	43	48	41
20 Halifax	46	13	15	18	43	53	41
21 Rotherham	46	17	7	22	51	65	41
22 Brentford	46	15	7	24	51	69	37
23 Swansea	46	14	9	23	51	73	37
24 Scunthorpe	46	10	10	26	33	72	30

FOURTH DIVISION

	P	W	D	L	F	A	Pts
1 Southport	46	36	10	10	71	48	62
2 Hereford	46	23	12	11	56	38	58
3 Cambridge	46	20	17	9	67	57	57
4 Aldershot	46	22	12	12	60	38	56
5 Newport	46	22	12	12	64	44	56
6 Mansfield	46	20	14	12	78	51	54
7 Reading	46	17	18	11	51	38	52
8 Exeter	46	18	14	14	57	51	50
9 Gillingham	46	19	11	16	63	58	49
10 Lincoln	46	16	16	14	64	57	48
11 Stockport	46	18	12	16	53	53	48
12 Bury	46	14	18	14	58	51	46
13 Workington	46	17	12	17	59	61	46
14 Barnsley	46	14	16	16	58	60	44
15 Chester	46	14	15	17	61	52	43
16 Bradford	46	16	11	19	61	65	43
17 Doncaster	46	15	12	19	49	58	42
18 Torquay	46	12	17	17	44	47	41
19 Peterborough	46	14	13	19	71	76	41
20 Hartlepool	46	12	17	17	34	49	41
21 Crewe	46	9	18	19	38	61	36
22 Colchester	46	10	11	25	48	76	31
23 Northampton	46	10	11	25	40	73	31
24 Darlington	46	7	15	24	42	85	29

SCOTTISH FA CUP 1972-73

THIRD ROUND

Ayr United v Inverness Thistle	3-0
Berwick Rovers v Falkirk	1-3
Brechin City v Aberdeen	2-4
Celtic v East Fife	4-1
Clyde v Montrose	1-1, 2-4
Dumbarton v Cowdenbeath	4-1
Dunfermline Athletic v Dundee	0-3
Elgin City v Hamilton Academicals	0-1
Heart of Midlothian v Airdrieonians	0-0, 1-3
Hibernian v Morton	2-0
Kilmarnock v Queen of the South	2-1
Motherwell v Raith Rovers	2-1
Rangers v Dundee United	1-0
St Mirren v Partick Thistle	0-1
Stirling Albion v Arbroath	3-3, 1-0
Stranraer v St Johnstone	1-1, 2-1

FOURTH ROUND

Ayr United v Stirling Albion	2-1
Dumbarton v Partick Thistle	2-2, 1-3
Kilmarnock v Airdrieonians	0-1
Montrose v Hamilton Academicals	2-2, 1-0
Motherwell v Celtic	0-4
Rangers v Hibernian	1-1, 2-1
Stranraer v Dundee	2-9
Aberdeen v Falkirk	3-1

FIFTH ROUND

Celtic v Aberdeen	0-0, 1-0
Montrose v Dundee	1-4
Partick Thistle v Ayr United	1-5
Rangers v Airdrieonians	2-0

SEMI-FINAL

Ayr United v Rangers	0-2
Celtic v Dundee	0-0, 3-0

FINAL

Celtic v Rangers	2-3

SCOTTISH FIRST DIVISION

	P	W	D	L	F	A	Pts
1 Celtic	34	26	5	3	93	28	57
2 Rangers	34	26	4	4	74	30	56
3 Hibernian	34	19	7	8	74	33	45
4 Aberdeen	34	16	11	7	61	34	43
5 Dundee	34	17	9	8	68	43	43
6 Ayr	34	16	8	10	50	51	40
7 Dundee United	34	17	5	12	56	51	39
8 Motherwell	34	11	9	14	38	48	31
9 East Fife	34	11	8	15	46	54	30
10 Hearts	34	12	6	16	39	50	30
11 St Johnstone	34	10	9	15	52	67	29
12 Morton	34	10	8	16	47	53	28
13 Partick	34	10	8	16	40	53	28
14 Falkirk	34	7	12	15	38	56	26
15 Arbroath	34	9	8	17	39	63	26
16 Dumbarton	34	6	11	17	43	72	23
17 Kilmarnock	34	7	8	19	40	71	22
18 Airdrieonians	34	4	8	22	34	75	16

SCOTTISH SECOND DIVISION

	P	W	D	L	F	A	Pts
1 Clyde	36	23	10	3	68	28	56
2 Dunfermline	36	23	6	7	95	32	52
3 Raith	36	19	9	8	73	42	47
4 Stirling	36	19	9	8	70	39	47
5 St Mirren	36	19	7	10	79	50	45
6 Montrose	36	18	8	10	82	58	44
7 Cowdenbeath	36	14	10	12	57	53	38
8 Hamilton	36	16	6	14	67	63	38
9 Berwick	36	16	5	15	45	54	37
10 Stenhousemuir	36	14	8	14	44	41	36
11 Queen of the S	36	13	8	15	45	52	34
12 Alloa	36	11	11	14	45	49	33
13 E Stirlingshire	36	12	8	16	52	69	32
14 Queen's Park	36	9	12	15	44	61	30
15 Stranraer	36	13	4	19	56	78	30
16 Forfar	36	10	9	17	38	66	29
17 Clydebank	36	9	6	21	48	72	21
18 Albion	36	5	8	23	35	83	18
19 Brechin	36	5	4	27	46	99	14

Arsenal's defeat in the semi-final at Hillsborough prevented them from becoming the first club this century to appear in three consecutive Cup Finals. It also prevented the first 'repeat' Cup Final of the twentieth century as Leeds were their 1972 opponents.

Sunderland, by defeating Leeds 1-0 in the 1973 Cup Final became only the fifth Second Division side to win the FA Cup. On the way they defeated three of the previous holders — Manchester City, Arsenal and Leeds for a remarkably memorable win.

League Tables 1973-74

FIRST DIVISION

		P	W	D	L	F	A	Pts
1	Leeds	42	24	14	4	66	31	62
2	Liverpool	42	22	13	7	52	31	57
3	Derby	42	17	14	11	52	42	48
4	Ipswich	42	18	11	13	67	58	47
5	Stoke	42	15	16	11	54	42	46
6	Burnley	42	16	14	12	56	53	46
7	Everton	42	16	12	14	50	48	44
8	QPR	42	13	17	12	56	52	43
9	Leicester	42	13	16	13	51	41	42
10	Arsenal	42	14	14	14	49	51	42
11	Tottenham	42	14	14	14	45	50	42
12	Wolves	42	13	15	14	49	49	41
13	Sheff United	42	14	12	16	44	49	40
14	Man City†	42	14	12	16	39	46	40
15	Newcastle	42	13	12	17	49	48	38
16	Coventry	42	14	10	18	43	54	38
17	Chelsea	42	12	13	17	56	60	37
18	West Ham	42	11	15	16	55	60	37
19	Birmingham	42	12	13	17	52	64	37
20	Southampton*	42	11	14	17	47	68	36
21	Man United*†	42	10	12	20	38	48	32
22	Norwich*	42	7	15	20	37	62	29

* Three clubs relegated.

† Game at Old Trafford abandoned after 86 minutes. Manchester City, who were leading 1-0, awarded both points.

SECOND DIVISION

		P	W	D	L	F	A	Pts
1	Middlesbrough*	42	27	11	4	77	30	65
2	Luton*	42	19	12	11	64	51	50
3	Carlisle*	42	20	9	13	61	48	49
4	Orient	42	15	18	9	55	42	48
5	Blackpool	42	17	13	12	57	40	47
6	Sunderland	42	19	9	14	58	44	47
7	Nottm Forest	42	15	15	12	57	43	45
8	WBA	42	14	16	12	48	45	44
9	Hull	42	13	17	12	46	47	43
10	Notts County	42	15	13	14	55	60	43
11	Bolton	42	15	12	15	44	40	42
12	Millwall	42	14	14	14	51	51	42
13	Fulham	42	16	10	16	39	43	42
14	Aston Villa	42	13	15	14	48	45	41
15	Portsmouth	42	14	12	16	45	62	40
16	Bristol City	42	14	10	18	47	54	38
17	Cardiff	42	10	16	16	49	62	36
18	Oxford	42	10	16	16	35	46	36
19	Sheff Wed	42	12	11	19	51	63	35
20	Crystal Palace‡	42	11	12	19	43	56	34
21	Preston‡§	42	9	14	19	40	62	31
22	Swindon‡	42	7	11	24	36	72	25

* Three clubs promoted.

‡ Three clubs relegated.

§ Preston had one point deducted for fielding an ineligible player.

THIRD DIVISION

		P	W	D	L	F	A	Pts
1	Oldham‡	46	25	12	9	83	47	62
2	Bristol Rovers‡	46	22	17	7	65	33	61
3	York‡	46	21	19	6	67	38	61
4	Wrexham	46	22	12	12	63	43	56
5	Chesterfield	46	21	14	11	55	42	56
6	Grimsby	46	18	15	13	67	50	51
7	Watford	46	19	12	15	64	56	50
8	Aldershot	46	19	11	16	65	52	49
9	Halifax	46	14	21	11	48	51	49
10	Huddersfield	46	17	13	16	56	55	47
11	Bournemouth	46	16	15	15	54	58	47
12	Southend	46	16	14	16	62	62	46
13	Blackburn	46	18	10	18	62	64	46
14	Charlton	46	19	8	19	66	73	46
15	Walsall	46	16	13	17	57	48	45
16	Tranmere	46	15	15	16	50	44	45
17	Plymouth	46	17	10	19	59	54	44
18	Hereford	46	14	15	17	53	57	43
19	Brighton	46	16	11	19	52	58	43
20	Port Vale	46	14	14	18	52	58	42
21	Cambridge*	46	13	9	24	48	81	35
22	Shrewsbury*	46	10	11	25	41	62	31
23	Southport*	46	6	16	24	35	82	28
24	Rochdale*	46	2	17	27	38	94	21

‡ Three clubs promoted.

* Four clubs relegated.

FOURTH DIVISION

		P	W	D	L	F	A	Pts
1	Peterborough*	46	27	11	8	75	38	65
2	Gillingham*	46	25	12	9	90	49	62
3	Colchester*	46	24	12	10	73	36	60
4	Bury*	46	24	11	11	81	49	59
5	Northampton	46	20	13	13	63	48	53
6	Reading	46	16	19	11	58	37	51
7	Chester	46	17	15	14	54	55	49
8	Bradford	46	17	14	15	58	52	48
9	Newport‡	46	16	14	16	56	65	45
10	Exeter†	45	18	8	19	58	55	44
11	Hartlepool	46	16	12	18	48	47	44
12	Lincoln	46	16	12	18	63	67	44
13	Barnsley	46	17	10	19	58	64	44
14	Swansea	46	16	11	19	45	46	43
15	Rotherham	46	15	13	18	56	58	43
16	Torquay	46	13	17	16	52	57	43
17	Mansfield	46	13	17	16	62	69	43
18	Scunthorpe†	45	14	12	19	47	64	42
19	Brentford	46	12	16	18	48	50	40
20	Darlington	46	13	13	20	40	62	39
21	Crewe	46	14	10	22	43	71	38
22	Doncaster	46	12	11	23	47	80	35
23	Workington	46	11	13	22	43	74	35
24	Stockport	46	7	20	19	44	69	34

† Exeter failed to turn up for their fixture at Scunthorpe and the latter were awarded both points.

‡ Newport had one point deducted for fielding an ineligible player.

* Four clubs promoted.

SCOTTISH FIRST DIVISION

		P	W	D	L	F	A	Pts
1	Celtic	34	23	7	4	82	27	53
2	Hibernian	34	20	9	5	75	42	49
3	Rangers	34	21	6	7	67	34	48
4	Aberdeen	34	13	16	5	46	26	42
5	Dundee	34	16	7	11	67	48	39
6	Hearts	34	14	10	10	54	43	38
7	Ayr	34	15	8	11	44	40	38
8	Dundee United	34	15	7	12	55	51	37
9	Motherwell	34	14	7	13	45	40	35
10	Dumbarton	34	11	7	16	43	58	29
11	Partick	34	9	10	15	33	46	28
12	St Johnstone	34	9	10	15	41	60	28
13	Arbroath	34	10	7	17	52	69	27
14	Morton	34	8	10	16	37	49	26
15	Clyde	34	8	9	17	29	65	25
16	Dunfermline	34	8	8	18	43	65	24
17	East Fife	34	9	6	19	26	51	24
18	Falkirk	34	4	14	16	33	58	22

SCOTTISH SECOND DIVISION

		P	W	D	L	F	A	Pts
1	Airdrieonians	36	28	4	4	102	25	60
2	Kilmarnock	36	26	6	4	96	44	58
3	Hamilton	36	24	7	5	68	38	55
4	Queen of the S	36	20	7	9	73	41	47
5	Raith	36	18	9	9	69	48	45
6	Berwick	36	16	13	7	53	35	45
7	Stirling	36	17	6	13	76	50	40
8	Montrose	36	15	7	14	71	64	37
9	Stranraer	36	14	8	14	64	70	36
10	Clydebank	36	13	8	15	47	48	34
11	St Mirren	36	12	10	14	62	66	34
12	Alloa	36	15	4	17	47	58	34
13	Cowdenbeath	36	11	9	16	59	85	31
14	Queen's Park	36	12	4	20	42	64	28
15	Stenhousemuir	36	11	5	20	44	59	27
16	E Stirlingshire	36	9	5	22	47	73	23
17	Albion	36	7	6	23	38	72	20
18	Forfar	36	5	6	25	42	94	16
19	Brechin	36	5	4	27	33	99	14

FA CUP 1973-74

FOURTH ROUND

Arsenal v Aston Villa	1-1, 0-2
Coventry City v Derby County	0-0, 1-0
Everton v West Bromwich Albion	0-0, 0-1
Fulham v Leicester City	1-1, 1-2
Hereford United v Bristol City	0-1
Liverpool v Carlisle United	0-0, 2-0
Luton Town v Bradford City	3-0
Manchester United v Ipswich Town	0-1
Newcastle United v Scunthorpe United	1-1, 3-0
Nottingham Forest v Manchester City	4-1
Oldham Athletic v Burnley	1-4
Peterborough United v Leeds United	1-4
Portsmouth v Orient	0-0, 1-1, 2-0
Queen's Park Rangers v Birmingham City	2-0
Southampton v Bolton Wanderers	3-3, 2-0
Wrexham v Middlesbrough	1-0

FIFTH ROUND

Bristol City v Leeds United	1-1, 1-0
Burnley v Aston Villa	1-0
Coventry City v Queen's Park Rangers	0-0, 2-3
Liverpool v Ipswich Town	2-0
Luton Town v Leicester City	0-4
Nottingham Forest v Portsmouth	1-0
Southampton v Wrexham	0-1
West Bromwich Albion v Newcastle United	0-3

SIXTH ROUND

Bristol City v Liverpool	0-1
Burnley v Wrexham	1-0
Newcastle United v Nottingham Forest	4-3*, 0-0, 1-0
Queen's Park Rangers v Leicester City	0-2

*FA ordered replay because of crowd invasion. Second and third games both played at Goodison Park.

SEMI-FINAL

Burnley v Newcastle United	0-2
Leicester City v Liverpool	0-0, 1-3

FINAL

Liverpool v Newcastle United	3-0

SCOTTISH FA CUP 1973-74

THIRD ROUND

Aberdeen v Dundee	0-2
Arbroath v Dumbarton	1-0
Celtic v Clydebank	6-1
Cowdenbeath v Ayr United	0-5
Dundee United v Airdrieonians	4-1
Falkirk v Dunfermline Athletic	2-2, 0-1
Forfar Athletic v St Johnstone	1-6
Heart of Midlothian v Clyde	3-1
Hibernian v Kilmarnock	5-2
Montrose v Stirling Albion	1-1, 1-3
Motherwell v Brechin City	2-0
Partick Thistle v Ferranti Thistle	6-1
Queen of the South v East Fife	1-0
Raith Rovers v Morton	2-2, 0-0, 0-1
Rangers v Queen's Park	8-0
Stranraer v St Mirren	1-1, 1-1, 3-2

FOURTH ROUND

Arbroath v Motherwell	1-3
Celtic v Stirling Albion	6-1
Dundee United v Morton	1-0
Dunfermline Athletic v Queen of the South	1-0
Heart of Midlothian v Partick Thistle	1-1, 4-1
Rangers v Dundee	0-3
St Johnstone v Hibernian	1-3
Stranraer v Ayr United	1-7

FIFTH ROUND

Celtic v Motherwell	2-2, 1-0
Dunfermline Athletic v Dundee United	1-1, 0-4
Heart of Midlothian v Ayr United	1-1, 2-1
Hibernian v Dundee	3-3, 0-3

SEMI-FINAL

Celtic v Dundee	1-0
Heart of Midlothian v Dundee United	1-1, 2-4

FINAL

Celtic v Dundee United	3-0

League Tables 1974-75

FIRST DIVISION

		P	W	D	L	F	A	Pts
1	Derby	42	21	11	10	67	49	53
2	Liverpool	42	20	11	11	60	39	51
3	Ipswich	42	23	5	14	66	44	51
4	Everton	42	16	18	8	56	42	50
5	Stoke	42	17	15	10	64	48	49
6	Sheff United	42	18	13	11	58	51	49
7	Middlesbrough	42	18	12	12	54	40	48
8	Man City	42	18	10	14	54	54	46
9	Leeds	42	16	13	13	57	49	45
10	Burnley	42	17	11	14	68	67	45
11	QPR	42	16	10	16	54	54	42
12	Wolverhampton	42	14	11	17	57	54	39
13	West Ham	42	13	13	16	58	59	39
14	Coventry	42	12	15	15	51	62	39
15	Newcastle	42	15	9	18	59	72	39
16	Arsenal	42	13	11	18	47	49	37
17	Birmingham	42	14	9	19	53	61	37
18	Leicester	42	12	12	18	46	60	36
19	Tottenham	42	13	8	21	52	63	34
20	Luton	42	11	11	20	47	65	33
21	Chelsea	42	9	15	18	42	72	33
22	Carlisle	42	12	5	25	43	59	29

SECOND DIVISION

		P	W	D	L	F	A	Pts
1	Man United	42	26	9	7	66	30	61
2	Aston Villa	42	25	8	9	69	32	58
3	Norwich	42	20	13	9	58	37	53
4	Sunderland	42	19	13	10	65	35	51
5	Bristol City	42	21	8	13	47	33	50
6	WBA	42	18	9	15	54	42	45
7	Blackpool	42	14	17	11	38	33	45
8	Hull	42	15	14	13	40	53	44
9	Fulham	42	13	16	13	44	39	42
10	Bolton	42	15	12	15	45	41	42
11	Oxford	42	15	12	15	41	51	42
12	Orient	42	11	20	11	28	39	42
13	Southampton	42	15	11	16	53	54	41
14	Notts County	42	12	16	14	49	59	40
15	York	42	14	10	18	51	55	38
16	Nottm Forest	42	12	14	16	43	55	38
17	Portsmouth	42	12	13	17	44	54	37
18	Oldham	42	10	15	17	40	48	35
19	Bristol Rovers	42	12	11	19	42	64	35
20	Millwall	42	10	12	20	44	56	32
21	Cardiff	42	9	14	19	36	62	32
22	Sheff Wed	42	5	11	26	29	64	21

THIRD DIVISION

		P	W	D	L	F	A	Pts
1	Blackburn	46	22	16	8	68	45	60
2	Plymouth	46	24	11	11	79	58	59
3	Charlton Ath	46	22	11	13	76	61	55
4	Swindon	46	21	11	14	64	58	53
5	Crystal Palace	46	18	15	13	66	57	51
6	Port Vale	46	18	15	13	61	54	51
7	Peterborough	46	19	12	15	47	53	50
8	Walsall	46	18	13	15	67	52	49
9	Preston NE	46	19	11	16	63	56	49
10	Gillingham	46	17	14	15	65	60	48
11	Colchester	46	17	13	16	70	63	47
12	Hereford	46	16	14	16	64	66	46
13	Wrexham	46	15	15	16	65	55	45
14	Bury	46	16	12	18	53	50	44
15	Chesterfield	46	16	12	18	62	66	44
16	Grimsby	46	15	13	18	55	64	43
17	Halifax	46	13	17	16	49	65	43
18	Southend	46	13	16	17	46	51	42
19	Brighton	46	16	10	20	56	64	42
20	Aldershot	46	14	11	21	53	63	38*
21	Bournemouth	46	13	12	21	44	58	38
22	Tranmere	46	14	9	23	55	57	37
23	Watford	46	10	17	19	52	75	37
24	Huddersfield	46	11	10	25	47	76	32

*One point deducted for playing unregistered player.

FOURTH DIVISION

		P	W	D	L	F	A	Pts
1	Mansfield	46	28	12	6	90	40	68
2	Shrewsbury	46	26	10	10	80	43	62
3	Rotherham	46	22	15	9	71	41	59
4	Chester	46	23	11	12	64	38	57
5	Lincoln	46	21	15	10	79	48	57
6	Cambridge	46	20	14	12	62	44	54
7	Reading	46	21	10	15	63	47	52
8	Brentford	46	18	13	15	53	45	49
9	Exeter	46	19	11	16	60	63	49
10	Bradford	46	17	13	16	56	51	47
11	Southport	46	15	17	14	56	56	47
12	Newport	46	19	9	18	68	75	47
13	Hartlepool	46	16	11	19	52	62	43
14	Torquay	46	14	14	18	46	61	42
15	Barnsley	46	15	11	20	62	65	41
16	Northampton	46	15	11	20	67	73	41
17	Doncaster	46	14	12	20	65	79	40
18	Crewe	46	11	18	17	34	47	40
19	Rochdale	46	13	13	20	59	75	39
20	Stockport	46	12	14	20	43	70	38
21	Darlington	46	13	10	23	54	67	36
22	Swansea	46	15	6	25	46	73	36
23	Workington	46	10	11	25	46	66	31
24	Scunthorpe	46	7	15	24	41	78	29

SCOTTISH FIRST DIVISION

		P	W	D	L	F	A	Pts
1	Rangers	34	25	6	3	86	33	56
2	Hibernian	34	20	9	5	69	37	49
3	Celtic	34	20	5	9	81	41	45
4	Dundee United	34	19	7	8	72	43	41
5	Aberdeen	34	16	9	9	66	43	41
6	Dundee	34	16	6	12	48	42	38
7	Ayr	34	14	8	12	50	61	36
8	Hearts	34	11	13	10	47	52	35
9	St Johnstone	34	11	12	11	41	44	34
10	Motherwell	34	14	5	15	52	57	33
11	Airdrie	34	11	9	14	43	55	31
12	Kilmarnock	34	8	15	11	52	68	31
13	Partick	34	10	10	14	48	62	30
14	Dumbarton	34	7	10	17	44	55	24
15	Dumfermline	34	7	9	18	46	66	23
16	Clyde	34	6	10	18	40	63	22
17	Morton	34	6	10	18	31	62	22
18	Arbroath	34	5	7	22	34	66	17

SCOTTISH SECOND DIVISION

		P	W	D	L	F	A	Pts
1	Falkirk	38	26	2	10	76	29	54
2	Queen of the S	38	23	7	8	77	33	53
3	Montrose	38	23	7	8	70	37	53
4	Hamilton	38	21	7	10	69	30	49
5	East Fife	38	20	9	11	57	42	47
6	St Mirren	38	19	8	11	74	52	46
7	Clydebank	38	18	8	12	50	40	44
8	Stirling	38	17	9	12	67	55	43
9	Berwick	38	17	6	15	53	49	40
10	E. Stirlingshire	38	16	8	14	56	52	40
11	Stenhousemuir	38	14	11	13	52	42	39
12	Albion	38	16	7	15	72	64	39
13	Raith	38	14	9	15	48	44	37
14	Stranraer	38	12	11	15	47	69	35
15	Alloa	38	11	11	16	49	56	33
16	Queen's Park	38	10	10	18	41	54	30
17	Brechin	38	9	7	22	44	85	25
18	Meadowbank	38	9	5	24	26	87	23
19	Cowdenbeath	38	5	12	22	39	78	21
20	Forfar	38	1	7	30	27	102	9

FA CUP 1974-75

FOURTH ROUND

Queens Park Rangers v Notts County	3-0
Aston Villa v Sheffield United	4-1
Bury v Mansfield Town	1-2
Carlisle United v West Bromwich Albion	3-2
Chelsea v Birmingham City	0-1
Coventry City v Arsenal	1-1, 3-0
Ipswich Town v Liverpool	1-0
Leatherhead v Leicester City	2-3
Leeds United v Wimbledon	0-0, 1-0
Middlesbrough v Sunderland	3-1
Plymouth Argyle v Everton	1-3
Stafford Rangers v Peterborough United	1-2
Walsall v Newcastle United	1-0
West Ham United v Swindon Town	1-1, 2-1
Derby County v Bristol Rovers	2-0
Fulham v Nottingham Forest	0-0, 1-1, 1-1, 2-1

FIFTH ROUND

Arsenal v Leicester City	0-0, 1-0
Birmingham City v Walsall	2-1
Everton v Fulham	1-2
Ipswich Town v Aston Villa	3-2
Mansfield Town v Carlisle United	0-1
Peterborough United v Middlesbrough	1-1, 2-0
West Ham United v Queen's Park Rangers	2-1
Derby County v Leeds United	0-1

SIXTH ROUND

Arsenal v West Ham United	0-2
Birmingham City v Middlesbrough	1-0
Carlisle United v Fulham	0-1
Ipswich Town v Leeds United	0-0, 1-1, 0-0, 3-2

SEMI-FINAL

Fulham v Birmingham City	1-1, 1-0
West Ham United v Ipswich Town	0-0, 2-1

FINAL

Fulham v West Ham United	0-2

SCOTTISH FA CUP 1974-75

THIRD ROUND

Aberdeen v Rangers	1-1, 2-1
Arbroath v East Stirling	1-0
Ayr United v Queen's Park	1-2
Clyde v Dundee	0-1
Hibernian v Celtic	0-2
Inverness Caledonian v Albion Rovers	0-1
Motherwell v Partick Thistle	0-0, 1-0
Queen of the South v Raith Rovers	2-0
Montrose v Hamilton Academicals	0-0, 0-3
Airdrieonians v Morton	0-0, 3-0
Clydebank v Dunfermline Athletic	2-1
Dumbarton v Inverness Clachnacuddin	2-1
Heart of Midlothian v Kilmarnock	2-0
St. Johnstone v East Fife	1-0
Ross County v Falkirk	1-5
Dundee United v Berwick Rangers	1-1, 1-0

FOURTH ROUND

Airdrieonians v Falkirk	2-0
Arbroath v Albion Rovers	2-0
Celtic v Clydebank	4-1
Hamilton Academicals v Dumbarton	0-1
Motherwell v Queen's Park	4-0
Queen of the South v Heart of Midlothian	0-2
St. Johnstone v Dundee	0-1
Dundee United v Aberdeen	0-1

FIFTH ROUND

Aberdeen v Motherwell	0-1
Arbroath v Airdrieonians	2-2, 0-3
Dumbarton v Celtic	1-2
Heart of Midlothian v Dundee	1-1, 2-3

SEMI-FINAL

Celtic v Dundee	1-0
Airdrieonians v Motherwell	1-1, 1-0

FINAL

Airdrieonians v Celtic	1-3

League Tables 1975-76

FIRST DIVISION

		P	W	D	L	F	A	Pts
1	Liverpool	42	23	14	5	66	31	60
2	QPR	42	24	11	7	67	33	59
3	Man United	42	23	10	10	68	42	56
4	Derby	42	21	11	10	75	58	53
5	Leeds	42	21	9	12	65	46	51
6	Ipswich	42	16	14	12	54	48	46
7	Leicester	42	13	19	10	48	51	45
8	Man City	42	16	12	15	64	46	43
9	Tottenham	42	14	15	13	63	63	43
10	Norwich	42	16	10	16	58	58	42
11	Everton	42	15	12	15	60	66	42
12	Stoke	42	15	11	16	48	50	41
13	Middlesbrough	42	15	10	17	46	45	40
14	Coventry	42	13	14	15	47	57	40
15	Newcastle	42	15	9	18	71	62	39
16	Aston Villa	42	11	17	14	51	59	39
17	Arsenal	42	13	10	19	47	53	36
18	West Ham	42	13	10	19	48	71	36
19	Birmingham	42	13	7	22	57	75	33
20	Wolverhampton	42	10	10	22	51	68	30
21	Burnley	42	9	10	23	43	66	28
22	Sheff United	42	6	10	26	33	82	22

SECOND DIVISION

		P	W	D	L	F	A	Pts
1	Sunderland	42	24	8	10	67	36	56
2	Bristol City	42	19	15	8	59	35	53
3	WBA	42	20	13	9	50	33	53
4	Bolton	42	20	12	10	64	38	52
5	Notts County	42	19	11	12	60	41	49
6	Southampton	42	21	7	14	66	50	49
7	Luton	42	19	10	13	61	51	48
8	Nottm Forest	42	17	12	13	55	40	46
9	Charlton	42	15	12	15	61	72	42
10	Blackpool	42	14	14	14	40	49	42
11	Chelsea	42	12	16	14	53	54	40
12	Fulham	42	13	14	15	45	47	40
13	Orient	42	13	14	15	37	39	40
14	Hull	42	14	11	17	45	49	39
15	Blackburn	42	12	14	16	45	50	38
16	Plymouth	42	13	12	17	48	54	38
17	Oldham	42	13	12	17	57	68	38
18	Bristol Rovers	42	11	16	15	38	50	38
19	Carlisle	42	12	13	17	45	59	37
20	Oxford	42	11	11	20	39	59	33
21	York	42	10	8	24	39	71	28
22	Portsmouth	42	9	7	26	32	61	25

THIRD DIVISION

		P	W	D	L	F	A	Pts
1	Hereford	46	26	11	9	86	55	63
2	Cardiff	46	22	13	11	69	48	57
3	Millwall	46	20	16	10	54	43	56
4	Brighton	46	22	9	15	78	53	53
5	Crystal Palace	46	18	17	11	61	46	53
6	Wrexham	46	20	12	14	66	55	52
7	Walsall	46	18	14	14	74	61	50
8	Preston	46	19	10	17	62	57	48
9	Shrewsbury	46	19	10	17	61	59	48
10	Peterborough	46	15	18	13	63	63	48
11	Mansfield	46	16	15	15	58	52	47
12	Port Vale	46	15	16	15	55	54	46
13	Bury	46	14	16	16	51	46	44
14	Chesterfield	46	17	9	20	69	69	43
15	Gillingham	46	12	19	15	58	68	43
16	Rotherham	46	15	12	19	54	65	42
17	Chester	46	15	12	19	53	62	42
18	Grimsby	46	15	10	21	62	74	40
19	Swindon	46	16	8	22	62	75	40
20	Sheff Wed	46	12	16	18	48	59	40
21	Aldershot	46	13	13	20	59	75	39
22	Colchester	46	12	14	20	41	65	38
23	Southend	46	12	13	21	65	75	37
24	Halifax	46	11	13	22	41	61	35

SCOTTISH PREMIER DIVISION

		P	W	D	L	F	A	Pts
1	Rangers	36	23	8	5	59	24	54
2	Celtic	36	21	6	9	71	42	48
3	Hibernian	36	20	7	9	58	40	43
4	Motherwell	36	16	8	12	57	49	40
5	Hearts	36	13	9	14	39	44	35
6	Ayr	36	14	5	17	46	59	33
7	Aberdeen	36	11	10	15	49	50	32
8	Dundee United	36	12	8	16	46	48	32
9	Dundee	36	11	10	15	49	62	32
10	St Johnstone	36	3	5	28	29	79	11

SCOTTISH FIRST DIVISION

		P	W	D	L	F	A	Pts
1	Partick Thistle	26	17	7	2	47	19	40
2	Kilmarnock	26	16	3	7	44	29	40
3	Montrose	26	12	6	8	53	43	35
4	Dumbarton	26	12	4	10	53	46	29
5	Arbroath	26	11	4	11	41	39	29
6	St Mirren	26	9	8	9	37	37	25
7	Airdrieonians	26	7	11	8	44	41	25
8	Falkirk	26	10	5	11	38	35	24
9	Hamilton	26	7	10	9	37	37	24
10	Queen of the S	26	9	6	11	41	47	23
11	Morton	26	7	9	10	31	40	19
12	East Fife	26	8	7	11	39	53	18
13	Dunfermline	26	5	10	11	30	51	17
14	Clyde	26	5	4	17	34	52	16

SCOTTISH SECOND DIVISION

		P	W	D	L	F	A	Pts
1	Clydebank	26	17	6	3	44	13	40
2	Raith	26	15	10	1	45	22	40
3	Alloa	26	14	7	5	44	28	35
4	Queen's Park	26	10	9	7	41	33	29
5	Cowdenbeath	26	11	7	8	44	43	29
6	Stirling Albion	26	9	7	10	39	32	25
7	Stranraer	26	11	3	12	49	43	25
8	East Stirling	26	8	8	10	33	33	24
9	Albion	26	7	10	9	35	38	24
10	Stenhousemuir	26	9	5	12	39	44	23
11	Berwick	26	7	5	14	32	44	19
12	Forfar	26	4	10	12	28	48	18
13	Brechin	26	6	5	15	28	51	17
14	Meadowbank T	26	5	6	15	24	53	16

FOURTH DIVISION

		P	W	D	L	F	A	Pts
1	Lincoln	46	32	10	4	111	39	74
2	Northampton	46	29	10	7	87	40	68
3	Reading	46	24	12	10	70	51	60
4	Tranmere	46	24	10	12	89	55	58
5	Huddersfield	46	21	14	11	55	41	56
6	Bournemouth	46	20	12	14	57	48	52
7	Exeter	46	18	14	14	56	47	50
8	Watford	46	22	6	18	62	62	50
9	Torquay	46	18	14	14	55	63	50
10	Doncaster	46	19	11	16	75	69	49
11	Swansea	46	16	15	15	66	57	47
12	Barnsley	46	14	16	16	52	48	44
13	Cambridge	46	14	15	17	58	62	43
14	Hartlepool	46	16	10	20	62	78	42
15	Rochdale	46	12	18	16	40	54	42
16	Crewe	46	13	15	18	58	57	41
17	Bradford	46	12	17	17	63	65	41
18	Brentford	46	14	13	19	56	60	41
19	Scunthorpe	46	14	10	22	50	59	38
20	Darlington	46	14	10	22	48	57	38
21	Stockport	46	13	12	21	43	76	38
22	Newport	46	13	9	24	57	90	35
23	Southport	46	8	10	28	41	57	26
24	Workington	46	7	7	32	30	87	27

FA CUP 1975-76

FOURTH ROUND

Bradford City v Tooting & Mitcham United	3-1
Charlton Athletic v Portsmouth	1-1, 3-0
Coventry City v Newcastle United	1-1, 0-5
Derby County v Liverpool	1-0
Huddersfield Town v Bolton Wanderers	0-1
Ipswich Town v Wolverhampton Wanderers	0-0, 0-1
Leeds United v Crystal Palace	0-1
Leicester City v Bury	1-0
Manchester United v Peterborough United	3-1
Norwich City v Luton Town	2-0
Southampton v Blackpool	3-1
Southend United v Cardiff City	2-1
Stoke City v Manchester City	1-0
Sunderland v Hull City	1-0
West Bromwich Albion v Lincoln City	3-2
York City v Chelsea	0-2

FIFTH ROUND

Bolton Wanderers v Newcastle United	3-3, 0-0, 1-2
Chelsea v Crystal Palace	2-3
Derby County v Southend United	1-0
Leicester City v Manchester United	1-2
Norwich City v Bradford City	1-2
Stoke City v Sunderland	0-0, 1-2
West Bromwich Albion v Southampton	1-1, 0-4
Wolverhampton Wanderers v Charlton Athletic	3-0

SIXTH ROUND

Bradford City v Southampton	0-1
Derby County v Newcastle United	4-2
Manchester Utd v Wolverhampton Wanderers	1-1, 3-2
Sunderland v Crystal Palace	0-1

SEMI-FINAL

Manchester United v Derby County	2-0
Southampton v Crystal Palace	2-0

FINAL

Southampton v Manchester United	1-0

SCOTTISH FA CUP 1975-76

THIRD ROUND

Albion Rovers v Partick Thistle	1-2
Alloa Athletic v Aberdeen	0-4
Ayr United v Airdrieonians	4-2
Cowdenbeath v St Mirren	3-0
Dumbarton v Keith	2-0
Dundee v Falkirk	1-2
Dundee United v Hamilton Academicals	4-0
Heart of Midlothian v Clyde	2-2, 1-0
Hibernian v Dunfermline Athletic	3-2
Motherwell v Celtic	3-2
Morton v Montrose	1-3
Queen of the South v St Johnstone	3-2
Raith Rovers v Arbroath	1-0
Rangers v East Fife	3-0
Stenhousemuir v Kilmarnock	1-1, 0-1
Stirling Albion v Forfar Athletic	2-1

FOURTH ROUND

Ayr United v Queen of the South	2-2, 4-5
Cowdenbeath v Motherwell	0-2
Heart of Midlothian v Stirling Albion	3-0
Hibernian v Dundee United	1-1, 2-0
Kilmarnock v Falkirk	3-1
Montrose v Raith Rovers	2-1
Partick Thistle v Dumbarton	0-0, 0-1
Rangers v Aberdeen	4-1

FIFTH ROUND

Dumbarton v Kilmarnock	2-1
Montrose v Heart of Midlothian	2-2, 2-2, 1-2
Motherwell v Hibernian	2-2, 1-1, 2-1
Queen of the South v Rangers	0-3

SEMI-FINAL

Motherwell v Rangers	2-3
Dumbarton v Heart of Midlothian	0-0, 0-3

FINAL

Heart of Midlothian v Rangers	1-3

FIRST DIVISION

		P	W	D	L	F	A	Pts
1	Liverpool	42	23	11	8	62	33	57
2	Man City	42	21	14	7	60	34	56
3	Ipswich	42	22	8	12	66	39	56
4	Aston Villa	42	22	7	13	76	50	51
5	Newcastle	42	18	13	11	64	49	49
6	Man United	42	18	11	13	71	62	47
7	WBA	42	16	13	13	62	56	45
8	Arsenal	42	16	11	15	64	59	43
9	Everton	42	14	14	14	62	64	42
10	Leeds	42	15	12	15	48	51	42
11	Leicester	42	12	18	12	47	60	42
12	Middlesbrough	42	14	13	15	40	45	41
13	Birmingham	42	13	12	17	63	61	38
14	QPR	42	13	12	17	47	52	38
15	Derby	42	9	19	14	50	55	37
16	Norwich	42	14	9	19	47	64	37
17	West Ham	42	11	14	17	46	65	36
18	Bristol City	42	11	13	18	38	48	35
19	Coventry	42	10	15	17	48	59	35
20	Sunderland	42	11	12	19	46	54	34
21	Stoke	42	10	14	18	28	51	34
22	Tottenham	42	12	9	21	48	72	33

SECOND DIVISION

		P	W	D	L	F	A	Pts
1	Wolves	42	22	13	7	84	45	57
2	Chelsea	42	21	13	8	73	53	55
3	Nottm Forest	42	21	10	11	77	43	52
4	Bolton	42	10	11	11	74	54	51
5	Blackpool	42	17	17	8	58	42	51
6	Luton	42	23	6	15	67	48	48
7	Charlton	42	16	16	10	71	58	48
8	Notts County	42	19	10	13	65	60	48
9	Southampton	42	17	10	15	72	67	44
10	Millwall	42	17	13	14	57	53	43
11	Sheff United	42	14	12	16	54	63	40
12	Blackburn	42	15	9	18	42	54	39
13	Oldham	42	14	10	18	52	64	38
14	Hull	42	10	17	15	45	53	37
15	Bristol Rovers	42	12	13	17	53	68	37
16	Burnley	42	11	14	17	46	64	36
17	Fulham	42	11	13	18	44	61	35
18	Cardiff	42	12	10	20	56	67	34
19	Orient	42	9	16	17	37	55	34
20	Carlisle	42	11	12	19	49	75	34
21	Plymouth	42	8	16	18	46	65	32
22	Hereford	42	8	15	19	57	78	31

THIRD DIVISION

		P	W	D	L	F	A	Pts
1	Mansfield	46	28	8	10	78	33	64
2	Brighton	46	25	11	10	83	39	61
3	Crystal Palace	46	23	13	10	68	40	59
4	Rotherham	46	22	15	9	69	44	59
5	Wrexham	46	24	10	12	80	54	58
6	Preston	46	21	12	13	64	43	54
7	Bury	46	23	8	15	64	59	54
8	Sheff Wed	46	22	9	15	65	55	53
9	Lincoln	46	25	14	13	77	70	52
10	Shrewsbury	46	18	11	17	65	59	47
11	Swindon	46	15	15	16	68	75	45
12	Gillingham	46	14	12	18	55	64	44
13	Chester	46	18	8	20	48	58	44
14	Tranmere	46	13	17	16	51	53	43
15	Walsall	46	13	15	18	57	65	41
16	Peterborough	46	13	15	18	55	65	41
17	Oxford	46	12	15	19	55	65	39
18	Chesterfield	46	14	10	22	56	64	38
19	Port Vale	46	11	16	19	47	71	38
20	Portsmouth	46	11	14	21	43	70	35
21	Reading	46	13	9	24	49	73	35
22	Northampton	46	13	8	25	60	75	34
23	Grimsby	46	12	9	25	45	69	33
24	York	46	10	12	24	50	89	32

FOURTH DIVISION

		P	W	D	L	F	A	Pts
1	Cambridge	46	26	13	7	87	40	65
2	Exeter	46	25	12	9	70	46	62
3	Colchester	46	25	9	12	77	43	59
4	Bradford	46	23	13	10	71	51	59
5	Swansea	46	25	8	13	82	68	58
6	Barnsley	46	23	9	14	62	39	55
7	Watford	46	18	15	13	67	55	51
8	Doncaster	46	21	9	16	61	65	51
9	Huddersfield	46	19	12	15	60	49	50
10	Southend	46	15	19	12	52	45	49
11	Darlington	46	18	13	15	59	64	49
12	Crewe	46	19	11	16	47	60	49
13	Bournemouth	46	15	18	13	55	44	48
14	Stockport	46	13	19	14	53	57	45
15	Brentford	46	18	7	21	77	76	43
16	Torquay	46	17	9	20	59	67	43
17	Aldershot	46	16	11	19	45	59	43
18	Rochdale	46	13	12	21	50	59	38
19	Newport	46	14	10	22	42	58	38
20	Scunthorpe	46	13	11	22	49	73	37
21	Halifax	46	11	14	21	47	58	36
22	Hartlepool	46	10	12	24	47	73	32
23	Southport	46	3	19	24	53	77	25
24	Workington	46	4	11	31	41	102	19

SCOTTISH PREMIER DIVISION

		P	W	D	L	F	A	Pts
1	Celtic	36	23	9	4	79	39	55
2	Rangers	36	18	10	8	62	37	46
3	Aberdeen	36	16	11	9	56	42	43
4	Dundee United	36	16	9	11	54	45	41
5	Partick Thistle	36	11	13	12	40	44	35
6	Hibernian	36	8	18	10	34	35	34
7	Motherwell	36	10	11	14	57	50	32
8	Ayr	36	11	8	17	44	68	30
9	Hearts	36	7	13	16	49	66	27
10	Kilmarnock	36	4	9	23	32	71	17

SCOTTISH FIRST DIVISION

		P	W	D	L	F	A	Pts
1	St Mirren	39	25	12	2	91	38	62
2	Clydebank	39	24	10	5	89	38	58
3	Dundee	39	21	9	9	90	55	51
4	Morton	39	20	10	9	77	52	50
5	Montrose	39	16	9	14	61	62	41
6	Airdrieonians	39	13	12	14	63	58	38
7	Dumbarton	39	14	9	16	63	68	37
8	Arbroath	39	17	3	19	46	62	37
9	Queen of the S	39	11	13	15	58	65	35
10	Hamilton	39	11	14	18	44	55	32
11	St Johnstone	39	8	13	18	44	64	29
12	East Fife	39	8	13	18	40	71	29
13	Raith	39	8	11	20	45	68	27
14	Falkirk	39	6	8	25	36	85	20

SCOTTISH SECOND DIVISION

		P	W	D	L	F	A	Pts
1	Stirling	39	22	11	6	59	29	55
2	Alloa	39	19	13	7	73	45	51
3	Dunfermline	39	20	10	11	52	36	50
4	Stranraer	39	20	6	13	74	53	46
5	Queens Park	39	17	11	11	65	51	45
6	Albion	39	15	12	12	74	60	42
7	Clyde	39	15	11	13	68	65	41
8	Berwick	39	13	10	16	37	51	36
9	Stenhousemuir	39	15	5	19	38	49	35
10	E Stirlingshire	39	12	8	19	47	63	32
11	Meadowbank	39	8	16	15	41	57	32
12	Cowdenbeath	39	13	5	21	45	64	31
13	Brechin	39	7	12	20	51	77	26
14	Forfar	39	7	10	22	43	68	24

FA CUP 1976-77

FOURTH ROUND

Arsenal v Coventry	3-1
Aston Villa v West Ham	3-0
Birmingham v Leeds	1-2
Blackburn v Orient	3-0
Cardiff v Wrexham	3-2
Chester v Luton	1-0
Colchester v Derby	1-1, 0-1
Ipswich v Wolverhampton Wanderers	2-2, 0-1
Liverpool v Carlisle	3-0
Manchester United v Queen's Park Rangers	1-0
Middlesbrough v Hereford	4-0
Northwich Victoria v Oldham	1-3*
Port Vale v Burnley	2-1
Swindon v Everton	2-2, 1-2
Nottingham Forest v Southampton	3-3, 1-2
Newcastle v Manchester City	1-3

FIFTH ROUND

Aston Villa v Port Vale	3-0
Cardiff v Everton	1-2
Derby v Blackburn	3-1
Leeds v Manchester City	1-0
Liverpool v Oldham	3-1
Middlesbrough v Arsenal	4-1
Southampton v Manchester United	2-2, 1-2
Wolverhampton Wanderers v Chester	1-0

SIXTH ROUND

Everton v Derby	2-0
Liverpool v Middlesbrough	2-0
Manchester United v Aston Villa	2-1
Wolverhampton Wanderers v Leeds	0-1

SEMI-FINALS

Everton v Liverpool	2-2, 0-3
(both games at Maine Rd)	
Leeds v Manchester United	1-2
(at Hillsborough)	

FINAL

Liverpool v Manchester United	1-2

*played at Maine Rd.

SCOTTISH FA CUP 1976-77

THIRD ROUND

Airdrie v Celtic	1-1, 0-5
Arbroath v Brechin	1-0
Dunfermline v Aberdeen	0-1
East Fife v Clyde	2-1
East Stirling v Albion	0-3
Heart of Midlothian v Dumbarton	1-1, 1-0
Morton v Ayr United	0-1
Motherwell v Kilmarnock	3-0
Queen's Park v Alloa	0-0, 0-1
Queen of the South v Montrose	3-2
Rangers v Falkirk	3-1
St Mirren v Dundee	4-1
Stirling Albion v Elgin City	1-1, 2-3
St Johnstone v Dundee	1-1, 2-4
Hamilton v Clydebank	0-0, 0-3
Hibernian v Partick Thistle	3-0

FOURTH ROUND

Arbroath v Hibernian	1-1, 2-1
Dundee v Aberdeen	0-0, 2-1
East Fife v Albion	2-1
Heart of Midlothian v Clydebank	1-0
Motherwell v St Mirren	2-1
Queen of the South v Alloa	2-1
Rangers v Elgin City	3-0
Celtic v Ayr United	1-1, 3-1

FIFTH ROUND

Celtic v Queen of the South	5-1
Heart of Midlothian v East Fife	0-0, 3-1
Rangers v Motherwell	2-0
Arbroath v Dundee	1-3

SEMI-FINALS

Celtic v Dundee	2-0
Rangers v Heart of Midlothian	2-0

FINAL

Celtic v Rangers	1-0

FIRST DIVISION

		P	W	D	L	F	A	Pts
1	Nottm Forest	42	25	14	3	69	24	64
2	Liverpool	42	24	9	9	65	34	57
3	Everton	42	22	11	9	76	45	55
4	Man City	42	20	12	10	74	51	52
5	Arsenal	42	21	10	11	60	37	52
6	WBA	42	18	14	10	62	53	50
7	Coventry	42	18	12	12	75	62	48
8	Aston Villa	42	18	10	14	57	42	46
9	Leeds	42	18	10	14	63	53	46
10	Man United	42	16	10	16	67	63	42
11	Birmingham	42	16	9	17	55	60	41
12	Derby	42	14	13	15	54	59	41
13	Norwich	42	11	18	13	52	66	40
14	Middlesbrough	42	12	15	15	42	54	39
15	Wolves	42	12	12	18	51	64	36
16	Chelsea	42	11	14	17	46	69	36
17	Bristol City	42	11	13	18	49	53	35
18	Ipswich	42	11	13	18	47	61	35
19	QPR	42	9	15	18	47	64	33
20	West Ham	42	12	8	22	52	69	32
21	Newcastle	42	6	10	26	42	78	22
22	Leicester	42	5	12	25	26	70	22

SECOND DIVISION

		P	W	D	L	F	A	Pts
1	Bolton	42	24	10	8	63	33	58
2	Southampton	42	22	13	7	70	39	57
3	Tottenham	42	20	16	6	83	49	56
4	Brighton	42	22	12	8	63	38	56
5	Blackburn	42	16	13	13	56	60	45
6	Sunderland	42	14	16	12	67	59	44
7	Stoke	42	16	10	16	53	49	42
8	Oldham	42	13	16	13	54	58	42
9	Crystal Palace	42	13	15	14	50	47	41
10	Fulham	42	14	13	15	49	49	41
11	Burnley	42	15	10	17	56	64	40
12	Sheff United	42	16	8	18	62	73	40
13	Luton	42	14	10	18	54	52	38
14	Orient	42	10	18	14	43	49	38
15	Notts County	42	11	16	15	54	62	38
16	Millwall	42	12	14	16	49	57	38
17	Charlton	42	13	12	17	55	68	38
18	Bristol Rovers	42	13	12	17	61	77	38
19	Cardiff	42	13	12	17	51	71	38
20	Blackpool	42	12	13	17	59	60	37
21	Mansfield	42	10	11	21	49	69	31
22	Hull	42	8	12	22	34	52	28

THIRD DIVISION

		P	W	D	L	F	A	Pts
1	Wrexham	46	23	15	8	78	45	61
2	Cambridge	46	23	12	11	72	51	58
3	Preston	46	20	16	10	63	38	56
4	Peterborough	46	20	16	10	47	33	56
5	Chester	46	16	22	8	59	56	54
6	Walsall	46	18	17	11	61	50	53
7	Gillingham	46	15	20	11	67	60	50
8	Colchester	46	15	18	13	55	44	48
9	Chesterfield	46	17	14	15	58	49	48
10	Swindon	46	16	16	14	67	60	48
11	Shrewsbury	46	16	15	15	63	57	47
12	Tranmere	46	16	15	15	57	52	47
13	Carlisle	46	14	19	13	59	59	47
14	Sheff Wed	46	15	16	15	50	52	46
15	Bury	46	13	19	14	62	56	45
16	Lincoln	46	15	15	16	53	61	45
17	Exeter	46	15	14	17	49	59	44
18	Oxford	46	13	14	19	64	67	40
19	Plymouth	46	11	17	18	61	68	39
20	Rotherham	46	13	13	20	51	68	39
21	Port Vale	46	8	20	18	46	67	36
22	Bradford	46	12	10	24	56	86	34
23	Hereford	46	9	14	23	34	60	32
24	Portsmouth	46	7	17	22	31	75	31

FOURTH DIVISION

		P	W	D	L	F	A	Pts
1	Watford	46	30	11	5	85	38	71
2	Southend	46	25	10	11	66	39	60
3	Swansea	46	23	10	13	87	47	56
4	Brentford	46	21	14	11	86	54	56
5	Aldershot	46	19	16	11	67	47	54
6	Grimsby	46	21	11	14	57	51	53
7	Barnsley	46	18	14	14	61	49	50
8	Reading	46	18	14	14	55	52	50
9	Torquay	46	16	15	15	57	56	47
10	Northampton	46	17	13	16	63	68	47
11	Huddersfield	46	15	15	16	63	55	45
12	Doncaster	46	14	17	15	52	65	45
13	Wimbledon	46	14	16	16	66	67	44
14	Scunthorpe	46	14	16	16	50	55	44
15	Crewe	46	15	14	17	50	69	44
16	Newport	46	16	11	19	65	73	43
17	Bournemouth	46	14	15	17	41	51	43
18	Stockport	46	16	10	20	56	56	42
19	Darlington	46	14	13	19	52	59	41
20	Halifax	46	10	21	15	52	62	41
21	Hartlepool	46	15	7	24	51	84	37
22	York	46	12	12	22	50	69	36
23	Southport	46	6	19	21	52	76	31
24	Rochdale	46	8	8	30	43	85	24

SCOTTISH PREMIER DIVISION

		P	W	D	L	F	A	Pts
1	Rangers	36	24	7	5	76	39	55
2	Aberdeen	36	22	9	5	68	29	53
3	Dundee United	36	16	8	12	42	32	40
4	Hibernian	36	15	7	14	51	43	37
5	Celtic	36	15	6	15	63	54	36
6	Motherwell	36	13	7	16	45	52	33
7	Partick	36	14	5	17	52	64	33
8	St Mirren	36	11	8	17	52	63	30
9	Ayr	36	9	6	21	36	68	24
10	Clydebank	36	6	7	23	23	64	19

SCOTTISH FIRST DIVISION

		P	W	D	L	F	A	Pts
1	Morton	39	25	8	6	85	42	58
2	Hearts	39	24	10	5	77	42	58
3	Dundee	39	25	7	7	91	44	57
4	Dumbarton	39	16	17	6	65	48	49
5	Stirling	39	15	12	12	60	52	42
6	Kilmarnock	39	14	12	13	52	46	40
7	Hamilton	39	12	12	15	54	56	36
8	St Johnstone	39	15	6	18	52	64	36
9	Arbroath	39	11	13	15	42	55	35
10	Airdrieonians	39	12	10	17	50	64	34
11	Montrose	39	10	9	20	55	71	29
12	Queen of the S	39	8	13	18	44	68	29
13	Alloa	39	8	8	23	44	84	24
14	East Fife	39	4	11	24	39	74	19

SCOTTISH SECOND DIVISION

		P	W	D	L	F	A	Pts
1	Clyde	39	21	11	7	71	32	53
2	Raith	39	19	15	5	63	38	53
3	Dunfermline	39	18	12	9	64	41	48
4	Berwick	39	16	16	7	68	51	48
5	Falkirk	39	15	14	10	51	46	44
6	Forfar	39	17	8	14	61	55	42
7	Queen's Park	39	13	15	11	52	51	41
8	Albion	39	16	8	15	68	68	40
9	East Stirling	39	15	8	16	55	65	38
10	Cowdenbeath	39	13	8	18	75	78	34
11	Stranraer	39	13	7	19	54	59	33
12	Stenhousemuir	39	10	10	19	43	67	30
13	Meadowbank	39	6	10	23	43	89	22
14	Brechin	39	7	6	26	45	73	20

FA CUP 1977-78

FOURTH ROUND

Arsenal v Wolverhampton Wanderers	2-1
Bolton Wanderers v Mansfield Town	1-0
Brighton & Hove Albion v Notts County	1-2
Bristol Rovers v Southampton	2-0
Chelsea v Burnley	6-2
Derby County v Birmingham City	2-1
Ipswich v Hartlepool	4-1
Manchester United v West Bromwich Albion	1-1, 2-3
Middlesbrough v Everton	3-2
Millwall v Luton Town	4-0
Newcastle United v Wrexham	2-2, 1-4
Nottingham Forest v Manchester City	2-1
Orient v Blackburn Rovers	3-1
Stoke City v Blyth Spartans	2-3
Walsall v Leicester City	1-0
West Ham United v Queen's Park Rangers	1-1, 1-6

FIFTH ROUND

Arsenal v Walsall	4-1
Bristol Rovers v Ipswich	2-2, 0-3
Derby County v West Bromwich Albion	2-3
Orient v Chelsea	0-0, 2-1
Middlesbrough v Bolton Wanderers	2-0
Millwall v Notts County	2-1
Queen's Park Rangers v Nottingham Forest	1-1, 1-3
Wrexham v Blyth Spartans	1-1, 2-1

SIXTH ROUND

Middlesbrough v Orient	0-0, 1-2
Millwall v Ipswich	1-6
West Bromwich Albion v Nottingham Forest	2-0
Wrexham v Arsenal	2-3

SEMI-FINALS

Arsenal v Orient	3-0
Ipswich v West Bromwich Albion	3-1

FINAL

Arsenal v Ipswich	0-1

SCOTTISH FA CUP 1977-78

THIRD ROUND

Aberdeen v Ayr United	2-0
Albion Rovers v Morton	0-1
Airdrieonians v Heart of Midlothian	2-3
Arbroath v Motherwell	0-4
Berwick Rangers v Rangers	2-4
Celtic v Dundee	2-1
Dumbarton v Alloa Athletic	2-1
Hamilton Academicals v Dundee United	1-4
Hibernian v East Fife	4-0
Meadowbank v Inverness Caledonia	2-1
Partick Thistle v Cowdenbeath	1-1, 1-0
Queen of the South v Montrose	2-2, 3-1
St Johnstone v Brechin City	2-1
St Mirren v Kilmarnock	1-2
Stirling Albion v Clydebank	0-0 (abandoned), 3-0
Vale of Leithen v Queen's Park	0-1

FOURTH ROUND

Aberdeen v St Johnstone	3-0
Celtic v Kilmarnock	1-1, 0-1
Dumbarton v Heart of Midlothian	1-0
Dundee United v Queen of the South	3-0
Morton v Meadowbank	3-0
Motherwell v Queen's Park	1-3
Rangers v Stirling Albion	1-0
Hibernian v Partick Thistle	0-0, 1-2

FIFTH ROUND

Aberdeen v Morton	2-2, 2-1
Dundee United v Queen's Park	2-0
Partick Thistle v Dumbarton	2-1
Rangers v Kilmarnock	4-1

SEMI-FINALS

Aberdeen v Partick Thistle	4-2
Rangers v Dundee United	2-0

FINAL

Rangers v Aberdeen	2-1

EUROPEAN CHAMPION CLUBS' CUP

1955-56 **REAL MADRID**
Paris 12 June 1956 Attendance 38,329
Real Madrid (2) **4** **Reims** (2) **3**
di Stefano, Rial 2, Leblond, Templin,
Marquitos Hidalgo
Real: Alonso, Atienza, Lesmes, Munoz, Marquitos, Zaggara, Joseito, Marchal, di Stefano, Rial, Gento
Reims: Jacquet, Zimny, Giraudo, Leblond, Jonquet, Siatka, Hidalgo, Glovacki, Kopa, Bliard, Templin

1956-57 **REAL MADRID**
Madrid 30 May 1957 Attendance 125,000
Real Madrid (0) **2** **Fiorentina** (0) **0**
di Stefano, Gento
Real: Alonso, Torres, Lesmes, Munoz, Marquitos, Zaggara, Kopa, Mateos, di Stefano, Rial, Gento
Fiorentina: Sarti, Magnini, Cervato, Scaramucci, Orzan, Segato, Julinho, Gratton, Virgili, Montuori, Bizzarri

1957-58 **REAL MADRID**
Brussels 29 May 1958 Attendance 67,000
Real Madrid (0) (2) **3** **AC Milan** (0) (2) **2**
di Stefano, Rial, Gento Schiaffino, Grillo
Real: Alonso, Atienza, Lesmes, Santisteban, Santamaria, Zaggara, Kopa, Joseito, di Stefano, Rial, Gento
AC Milan: Soldan, Fontana, Beraldo, Bergamaschi, Maldini, Radice, Danova, Liedholm, Schiaffino, Grillo, Cucchiaroni

1958-59 **REAL MADRID**
Stuttgart 3 June 1959 Attendance 80,000
Real Madrid (1) **2** **Reims** (0) **0**
Mateos, di Stefano
Real: Dominguez, Marquitos, Zaggara, Santisteban, Santamaria, Ruiz, Kopa, Mateos, di Stefano, Rial, Gento
Reims: Colonna, Rodzik, Giraudo, Penverne, Jonquet, Leblond, Lamartine, Bliard, Fontaine, Piantoni, Vincent

1959-60 **REAL MADRID**
Glasgow 18 May 1960 Attendance 127,621
Real Madrid (3) **7** **Eintracht Frankfurt** (1) **3**
di Stefano 3, Puskas 4 Kress, Stein 2
Real: Dominguez, Marquitos, Pachin, Vidal, Santamaria, Zaggara, Canario, Del Sol, di Stefano, Puskas, Gento
Eintracht: Loy, Lutz, Hoefer, Weilbacher, Eigenbrodt, Stinka, Kress, Lindner, Stein, Pfaff, Meier

1960-61 **BENFICA**
Berne 31 May 1961 Attendance 33,000
Benfica (2) **3** **Barcelona** (1) **2**
Aguas, Ramallets (og), Coluna Kocsis, Czibor
Benfica: Costa Pereira, Joao, Angelo, Neto, Germano, Cruz, Augusto, Santana, Aguas, Coluna, Cavem
Barcelona: Ramallets, Foncho, Gracia, Verges, Gensana, Garay, Kubala, Kocsis, Evaristo, Suarez, Czibor

1961-62 **BENFICA**
Amsterdam 2 May 1962 Attendance 68,000
Benfica (2) **5** **Real Madrid** (3) **3**
Aguas, Cavem, Coluna Puskas 3
Eusebio 2 (1 pen)
Benfica: Costa Pereira, Joao, Angelo, Cavem, Germano, Cruz, Augusto, Eusebio, Aguas, Coluna, Simoes
Real: Araquistain, Casado, Miera, Felo, Santamaria, Pachin, Tejada, Del Sol, di Stefano, Puskas, Gento

1962-63 **AC MILAN**
Wembley 22 May 1963 Attendance 45,000
AC Milan (0) **2** **Benfica** (1) **1**
Altafini 2 Eusebio
Milan: Ghezzi, David, Trebbi, Benitez, Maldini, Trapattoni, Pivatelli, Dino Sani, Altafini, Rivera, Mora
Benfica: Costa Pereira, Cavem, Cruz, Humberto, Raul, Coluna, Augusto, Santana, Torres, Eusebio, Simoes

1963-64 **INTER MILAN**
Vienna 27 May 1964 Attendance 72,000
Inter Milan (1) **3** **Real Madrid** (0) **1**
Mazzola 2, Milani Felo
Inter: Sarti, Burgnich, Facchetti, Tagnin, Guarneri, Picchi, Jair, Mazzola, Milani, Suarez, Corso
Real: Vicente, Isidro, Pachin, Zoco, Santamaria, Muller, Amancio, Felo, di Stefano, Puskas, Gento

1964-65 **INTER MILAN**
Milan 27 May 1965 Attendance 80,000
Inter Milan (1) **1** **Benfica** (0) **0**
Jair
Inter: Sarti, Burgnich, Facchetti, Bedin, Guarneri, Picchi, Jair, Mazzola, Peiro, Suarez, Corso
Benfica: Costa Pereira, Cavem, Cruz, Neto, Germano, Raul, Augusto, Eusebio, Torres, Coluna, Simoes

1965-66 **REAL MADRID**
Brussels 11 May 1966 Attendance 38,714
Real Madrid (0) **2** **Partizan Belgrade** (0) **1**
Amancio, Serena Vasovic
Real: Araquistain, Pachin, Sanchis, Pirri, De Felipe, Zoco, Serena, Amancio, Grosso, Velasquez, Gento
Partizan: Soskic, Jusufi, Migailovic, Becejac, Rasovic, Vasovic, Bajic, Kovacevic, Hasanagic, Galic, Pirmajer

1966-67 **CELTIC**
Lisbon 25 May 1967 Attendance 45,000
Celtic (0) **2** **Inter Milan** (1) **1**
Gemmell, Chalmers Mazzola (pen)
Celtic: Simpson, Craig, Gemmell, Murdoch, McNeill, Clark, Johnstone, Wallace, Chalmers, Auld, Lennox
Inter: Sarti, Burgnich, Facchetti, Bedin, Guarneri, Picchi, Domenghini, Mazzola, Cappellini, Biccli, Corso

1967-68 **MANCHESTER UNITED**
Wembley 29 May 1968 Attendance 100,000
Manchester United (0) (1) **4** **Benfica** (0) (1) **1**
Charlton 2, Best, Kidd Graca

United: Stepney, Brennan, Dunne, Crerand, Foulkes, Stiles, Best, Kidd, Charlton, Sadler, Aston
Benfica: Henrique, Adolfo, Cruz, Graca, Humberto, Jacinto, Augusto, Eusebio, Torres, Coluna, Simoes

1968-69 **AC MILAN**
Madrid 28 May 1969 Attendance 50,000
AC Milan (2) **4** **Ajax Amsterdam** (0) **1**
Prati 3, Sormani Vasovic
Milan: Cudicini, Anquiletti, Schnellinger, Maldera, Rosato, Trapattoni, Hamrin, Lodetti, Sormani, Rivera, Prati
Ajax: Bals, Suurbier (sub Muller), Van Duivenbode, Pronk, Hulsoff, Vasovic, Swart, Cruyff, Danielson, Groot (sub Nuninga), Keizer

1969-70 **FEYENOORD**
Milan 6 May 1970 Attendance 50,000
Feyenoord (1) (1) **2** **Celtic** (1) (1) **1**
Israel, Kindvall Gemmell
Feyenoord: Graafland, Romeyns, Laseroms, Israel, Van Duivenbode, Hasil, Jansen, Van Hanegem, Wery, Kindvall, Mouljin (sub Haak)
Celtic: Williams, Hay, Gemmell, Murdoch, McNeill, Brogan, Johnstone, Lennox, Wallace, Auld (sub Connolly), Hughes

1970-71 **AJAX AMSTERDAM**
Wembley 2 June 1971 Attendance 90,000
Ajax Amsterdam (1) **2** **Panathinaikos** (0) **0**
Van Dijk, Haan
Ajax: Stuy, Vasovic, Suurbier, Hulsoff, Rijinders (sub Haan), Neeskens, Swart (sub Blankenburg), Muhren, Keizer, Van Dijk, Cruyff
Panathinaikos: Economopoulos, Tomaras, Vlahos, Elefetrakis, Kamaras, Sourpis, Grammos, Filokouris, Antoniadis, Domazos, Kapsis

1971-72 **AJAX AMSTERDAM**
Rotterdam 31 May 1972 Attendance 67,000
Ajax Amsterdam (0) **2** **Inter Milan** (0) **0**
Cruyff 2
Ajax: Stuy, Suurbier, Blankenburg, Hulshoff, Krol, Neeskens, Haan, Muhren, Swart, Cruyff, Keizer
Inter: Bordon, Burgnich, Bellugi, Oriali, Facchetti, Bedin, Mazzola, Giubertoni (sub Bertini), Jair, Pellicarro, Boninsegna, Frustalupi

1972-73 **AJAX AMSTERDAM**
Belgrade 30 May 1973 Attendance 93,500
Ajax Amsterdam (0) **1** **Juventus** (0) **0**
Rep
Ajax: Stuy, Suurbier, Blankenburg, Hulshoff, Krol, Neeskens, Haan, G. Muhren, Rep, Cruyff, Keizer
Juventus: Zoff, Longobucco, Marchetti, Furino, Morini, Salvadore, Altafini, Causio (sub Cuccureddu), Anastasi, Capello, Bettega (sub Haller)

1973-74 **BAYERN MUNICH**
Brussels 15 May 1974 Attendance 65,000
Bayern Munich (0) (0) **1** **Atletico Madrid** (0) (0) **1**
Schwarzenbeck Luis
Brussels 17 May 1974 Attendance 65,000
Bayern Munich (1) **4** **Atletico Madrid** (0) **0**
Muller 2, Hoeness 2
Bayern Munich: Maier, Hansen, Breitner, Schwarzenbeck, Beckenbauer, Roth, Torstensson (sub Durnberger first match), Zobel, Muller, Hoeness, Kappelmann
Atletico Madrid: Reina, Melo, Capon, Adelardo (sub Benegas second match), Heredia, Eusebio, Luis, Garate, Salcedo (sub Alberto in first match), Ufarte (sub Becerra in both matches), Alberto (Irureta played in first match)

1974-75 **BAYERN MUNICH**
Paris 28 May 1975 Attendance 50,000
Bayern Munich (0) **2** **Leeds United** (0) **0**
Roth, Muller
Bayern Munich: Maier, Durnberger, Andersson (sub Weiss), Schwarzenbeck, Beckenbauer, Roth, Torstensson, Zobel, Muller, Hoeness (sub Wunder), Kappelmann
Leeds United: Stewart, Reaney, F. Gray, Bremner, Madeley, Hunter, Lorimer, Clarke, Jordan, Giles, Yorath (sub E. Gray)

1975-76 **BAYERN MUNICH**
Glasgow 12 May 1976 Attendance 54,864
Bayern Munich (0) **1** **St. Etienne** (0) **0**
Roth
Bayern Munich: Maier, Hansen, Schwarzenbeck, Beckenbauer, Horsmann, Roth, Durnberger, Kappelmann, Rummenigge, Muller, Hoeness
St. Etienne: Curkovic, Repellini, Piazza, Lopez, Janvion, Bathenay, Santini, Larque, P. Revelli, H. Revelli, Sarramanga (sub Rocheteau)

1976-77 **LIVERPOOL**
Final: Rome 25.5.77 Attendance 57,000
Liverpool (1) **3** **Borussia Monchengladbach** (0) **1**
McDermott, Smith, Neal (pen) Simonsen
Liverpool: Clemence, Neal, Jones, Smith, Kennedy, Hughes, Keegan, Case, Heighway, Callaghan, McDermott.
Borussia Monchengladbach: Kneib, Vogts, Klinkhammer, Wittkamp, Schaffer, Wohlers (sub Hannes), Bonhoff, Wimmer (sub Kulik), Stielike, Simonsen, Heynckes.

1977-78 **LIVERPOOL**
Wembley 10.5.78 Attendance 92,000
Liverpool (0) **1** **FC Bruges** (0) **0**
Dalglish
Liverpool: Clemence, Neal, Thompson, Hansen, Hughes, McDermott, Kennedy, Souness, Case (sub Heighway), Fairclough, Dalglish
FC Bruges: Jensen, Bastijns, Krieger, Leekens, Maes (sub Volders), Cools, De Cubber, Vandereycken, Ku (sub Sanders), Simoen, Sorensen

Right A clash between Liverpool's Emlyn Hughes and Cools of Bruges during the first leg of the 1975/76 EUFA Cup final. Liverpool won the Cup for the second time in four years. The following season they graduated to winning the European Cup and then confirmed their status as the best side in Europe by retaining it in 1978.

FAIRS CUP WINNERS AND FINALS

1955-58 BARCELONA
First Leg: Stamford Bridge 5.3.58 Attendance 45,466
London (1) 2 **Barcelona** (2) 2
Greaves, Langley (pen) Tajada, Martinez
Second Leg: Barcelona 1.5.58 Attendance 62,000
Barcelona (3) 6 **London** (0) 0
Suarez 2, Evaristo 2,
Martinez, Verges

London: **First Leg:** Kelsey (Arsenal) ; Sillett P. (Chelsea), Langley (Fulham) ;
Blanchflower (Spurs), Norman (Spurs), Coote (Brentford) ;
Groves (Arsenal), Greaves (Chelsea), Smith (Spurs), Haynes
(Fulham), Robb (Spurs).
Second Leg: Kelsey (Arsenal) ; Wright (West Ham), Cantwell (West Ham) ;
Blanchflower (Spurs), Brown (West Ham), Bowen (Arsenal) ;
Medwin (Spurs), Groves (Arsenal), Smith (Spurs), Bloomfield
(Arsenal), Lewis (Chelsea).

1958-60 BARCELONA
First Leg: Birmingham 29.3.60 Attendance 40,500
Birmingham City (0) 0 **Barcelona** (0) 0
Second Leg: Barcelona 4.5.60 Attendance 70,000
Barcelona (2) 4 **Birmingham City** (0) 1
Martinez, Czibor 2, Coll Hooper

1960-61 AS ROMA
First Leg: Birmingham 27.9.61 Attendance 21,005
Birmingham City (0) 2 **AS Roma** (1) 2
Hellawell, Orritt Manfredini 2
Second Leg: Rome 11.10.61 Attendance 60,000
AS Roma (0) 2 **Birmingham City** (0) 0
Farmer (og), Pestrin

1961-62 VALENCIA
First Leg: Valencia 8.9.62 Attendance 65,000
Valencia 6 **Barcelona** 2
Second Leg: Barcelona 12.9.62 Attendance 60,000
Barcelona 1 **Valencia** 1

1962-63 VALENCIA
First Leg: Zagreb 12.6.63 Attendance 40,000
Dynamo Zagreb (1) 1 **Valencia** (0) 2
Zambata Waldo, Urtiaga
Second Leg: Valencia 26.6.63 Attendance 55,000
Valencia 2 **Dynamo Zagreb** 0
Mano, Nunez

1963-64 REAL ZARAGOZA
Final: Barcelona 24.6.64 Attendance 50,000
Real Zaragoza (1) 2 **Valencia** (1) 1
Villa, Marcelino Urtiaga

1964-65 FERENCVAROS
Final: Turin 23.6.65 Attendance 25,000
Ferencvaros (1) 1 **Juventus** (0) 0
Fenyvesi

1965-66 BARCELONA
First Leg: Barcelona 14.9.66 Attendance 70,000
Barcelona (0) 0 **Real Zaragoza** (1) 1
Canario
Second Leg: Zaragoza 21.9.66 Attendance 70,000
Real Zaragoza (1) 2 **Barcelona** (1) 4
Marcelino 2 Pujol 3, Zaballa

1966-67 DYNAMO ZAGREB
First Leg: Zagreb 30.8.67 Attendance 40,000
Dynamo Zagreb (1) 2 **Leeds United** (0) 0
Cercer 2
Second Leg: Leeds 6.9.67 Attendance 35,604
Leeds United (0) 0 **Dynamo Zagreb** (0) 0

1967-68 LEEDS UNITED
First Leg: Leeds 7.8.68 Attendance 25,368
Leeds United (1) 1 **Ferencvaros** (0) 0
Jones
Second Leg: Budapest 11.9.68 Attendance 70,000
Ferencvaros (0) 0 **Leeds United** (0) 0
Leeds Sprake ; Reaney, Cooper, Bremner, Charlton, Hunter, Lorimer,
United : Madeley, Jones, Giles (sub Hibbitt), Gray (sub O'Grady).

1968-69 NEWCASTLE UNITED
First Leg: Newcastle 29.5.69 Attendance 60,000
Newcastle United (0) 3 **Ujpest Dozsa** (0) 0
Moncur 2, Scott
Second Leg: Budapest 11.6.69 Attendance 37,000
Ujpest Dozsa (2) 2 **Newcastle United** (0) 3
Bene, Gorocs Moncur, Arentoft, Foggon
Newcastle McFaul ; Craig, Clark, Gibb, Burton, Moncur, Scott, Robson,
United : Davies, Arentoft, Sinclair. (Foggon substituted for Scott in first leg
and for Sinclair in second leg).

1969-70 ARSENAL
First Leg: Brussels 22.4.70 Attendance 37,000
Anderlecht (2) 3 **Arsenal** (0) 1
Devrindt, Mulder 2 Kennedy
Second Leg: London 28.4.70 Attendance 51,612
Arsenal (1) 3 **Anderlecht** (0) 0
Kelly, Radford, Sammels
Arsenal : Wilson ; Storey, McNab, Kelly, McLintock, Simpson, Armstrong,
Sammels, Radford, George (sub Kennedy in first leg), Graham.

1970-71 LEEDS UNITED
First Leg: Turin 26.5.71 Attendance 65,000
Juventus (0) 0 **Leeds United** (0) 0
(game abandoned after 51 minutes)
Turin 28.5.71 Attendance 65,000
Juventus (1) 2 **Leeds United** (0) 2
Bettega, Capello Madeley, Bates
Second Leg: Leeds 3.6.71 Attendance 42,483
Leeds United (1) 1 **Juventus** (1) 1
Clarke Anastasi
Leeds Sprake ; Reaney, Cooper, Bremner, Charlton, Hunter, Lorimer,
United : Clarke, Jones (sub Bates in first leg), Giles,
Madeley (sub Bates in second leg).
(Leeds won on the 'away goals count double' rule).

UEFA CUP WINNERS AND FINALS

1971-72 TOTTENHAM HOTSPUR
First Leg: Wolverhampton 3.5.72 Attendance 45,000
Wolverhampton Wanderers (0) 1 **Tottenham Hotspur** (0) 2
McCalliog Chivers 2
Second Leg: Tottenham 17.5.72 Attendance 48,000
Tottenham Hotspur (1) 1 **Wolverhampton Wanderers** (0) 1
Mullery Wagstaffe
Tottenham Jennings, Kinnear, Knowles, Mullery, England, Beal, Coates (sub Pratt
Hotspur : in first leg), Perryman, Chivers, Peters, Gilzean.

1972-73 LIVERPOOL
First Leg: Liverpool 10.5.73 Attendance 41,169
Liverpool (3) 3 **Borussia Monchengladbach** (0) 0
Keegan 2, Lloyd
Second Leg: Monchengladbach 23.5.73 Attendance 35,000
Borussia Monchengladbach (2) 2 **Liverpool** (0) 0
Liverpool : Clemence, Lawler, Lindsay, Smith, Lloyd, Hughes, Keegan, Cormack,
Toshack, Heighway (sub Hall in first leg, Boersma in second leg),
Callaghan

1973-74 FEYENOORD
First Leg: Tottenham 21.5.74 Attendance 46,281
Tottenham Hotspur (1) 2 **Feyenoord** (1) 2
England, Van Daele og Van Hanegem, De Jong
Second Leg: Rotterdam 29.5.74 Attendance 68,000
Feyenoord (1) 2 **Tottenham Hotspur** (0) 0
Rijsbergen, Ressel
Feyenoord : Treytel, Rijsbergen, Van Daele, Israel, Vos, Ramljak (Van Hanegem
in first leg), Jansen, De Jong, Ressel, Schoemaker, Kristensen
(subs Boskamp, Wery)

1974-75 BORUSSIA MONCHENGLADBACH
First Leg: Dusseldorf 7.5.75 Attendance 45,000
Borussia Monchengladbach (0) 0 **Twente Enschede** (0) 0
Second Leg: Enschede 21.5.75 Attendance 24,500
Twente Enschede (0) 1 **Borussia Monchengladbach** (2) 5
Drost Heynckes 3, Simonsen 2 (1 pen.)

Borussia Kleff, Wittkamp, Vogts, Klinkhammer (Stielike played in
Monchen- first leg), Surau (sub Schafer in second leg), Bonhof, Wimmer
gladbach : (sub Koppel second leg), Danner (sub Del Haye first leg),
Simonsen, Jensen, Heynckes (Kulik played in first leg)

1975-76 LIVERPOOL
First Leg: Liverpool 28.4.76 Attendance 56,000
Liverpool (0) 3 **Bruges** (2) 2
Kennedy, Case, Keegan (pen) Lambert, Cools
Second Leg: Bruges 19.5.76 Attendance 32,000
Bruges (1) 1 **Liverpool** (1) 1
Keegan Lambert (pen)
Liverpool : Clemence, Smith, Neal, Thompson, Kennedy, Hughes, Keegan, Case
(Fairclough played in first leg), Heighway, Toshack (sub Case first leg,
sub Fairclough second leg), Callaghan

1976-77 JUVENTUS
First Leg: Turin 4.5.77 Attendance 75,000
Juventus (1) 1 **Athletico Bilbao** (0) 0
Tardelli
Second Leg: Bilbao 18.5.77 Attendance 43,000
Athletico Bilbao (1) 2 **Juventus** (1) 1
Irureta, Carlos Bettega
Juventus : Zoff, Cuccureddu, Morini, Scirea, Gentile, Causio,
Tardelli, Furino, Benetti, Boninsegna (sub Spinosi),
Bettega

1977-78 PSV EINDHOVEN
First Leg: Corsica 26.4.78 Attendance 15,000
Bastia (0) 0 **PSV Eindhoven** (0) 0
Second Leg: Eindhoven 9.5.78 Attendance 27,000
PSV Eindhoven (1) 3 **Bastia** (0) 0
W. Van der Kerkhof, Deijkers,
Van der Kuylen
PSV Van Beveren, Krijgh, Stevens, Van Kraay (sub Deacy),
Eindhoven Brandts, W. Van der Kerkhof, Poortvliet, Van der Kuylen,
Lubse, Deijkers, R. Van der Kerkhof

EUROPEAN CUP WINNERS CUP FINALS

1960-61   **FIORENTINA**
First Leg: Glasgow   17.5.61   Attendance 80,000
     Rangers   (0) **0**   **Fiorentina**   (1) **2**
                          Milan 2
Second Leg: Florence   27.5.61   Attendance 50,000
     Fiorentina   (1) **2**   **Rangers**   (1) **1**
     Milan, Hamrin   Scott
Rangers: Ritchie, Shearer, Caldow, Davis, Paterson, Baxter, Wilson, McMillan, Scott, Brand, Hume (Millar in second leg)

1961-62   **ATLETICO MADRID**
Final: Glasgow   10.5.62   Attendance 27,389
     Atletico Madrid   (1) **1**   **Fiorentina**   (1) **1**
     Peiro   Hamrin
Replay: Stuttgart   5.9.62   Attendance 45,000
     Atletico Madrid   (2) **3**   **Fiorentina**   (0) **0**
     Jones, Mendoca, Peiro

1962-63   **TOTTENHAM HOTSPUR**
Final: Rotterdam   15.5.63   Attendance 25,000
     Tottenham Hotspur   (2) **5**   **Atletico Madrid**   (0) **1**
     Greaves 2, White, Dyson 2   Collar (pen)
Tottenham Hotspur: Brown, Baker, Henry, Blanchflower, Norman, Marchi, Jones, White, Smith, Greaves, Dyson

1963-64   **SPORTING LISBON**
Final: Brussels   13.5.64   Attendance 9,000
     Sporting Lisbon   (1) (3) **3**   **MTK Budapest**   (1) (3) **3**
     Figueiredo 2, Dansky (og)   Sandor 2, Kuti
Replay: Antwerp   15.5.64   Attendance 18,000
     Sporting Lisbon   (1) **1**   **MTK Budapest**   (0) **0**
     Morais

1964-65   **WEST HAM UNITED**
Final: Wembley   19.5.65   Attendance 100,000
     West Ham United   (0) **2**   **TSV Munich 1860**   (0) **0**
     Sealey 2
West Ham United: Standen, Kirkup, Burkett, Peters, Brown, Moore, Sealey, Boyce, Hurst, Dear, Sissons

1965-66   **BORUSSIA DORTMUND**
Final: Glasgow   5.5.66   Attendance 41,657
     Borussia Dortmund   (0) (1) **2**   **Liverpool**   (0) (1) **1**
     Held, Yeats (og)   Hunt
Liverpool: Lawrence, Lawler, Byrne, Milne, Yeats, Stevenson, Callaghan, Hunt, St John, Smith, Thompson

1966-67   **BAYERN MUNICH**
Final: Nuremberg   31.5.67   Attendance 69,480
     Bayern Munich   (0) (0) **1**   **Rangers**   (0) (0) **0**
     Roth
Rangers: Martin, Johansen, Provan, Jardine, McKinnon, Greig, Henderson, Smith (A), Hynd, Smith (D), Johnston

1967-68   **AC MILAN**
Final: Rotterdam   23.5.68
     AC Milan   (2) **2**   **SV Hamburg**   (0) **0**
     Hamrin 2

1968-69   **SLOVAN BRATISLAVA**
Final: Basle   21.5.69
     Slovan Bratislava   (3) **3**   **Barcelona**   (1) **2**
     Cvetler, Hrivnak, Jan Capkovic   Zaldua, Rexach

1969-70   **MANCHESTER CITY**
Final: Vienna   29.4.70   Attendance 10,000
     Manchester City   (2) **2**   **Gornik Zabrze**   (0) **1**
     Young, Lee penalty   Oslizlo
Manchester City: Corrigan, Book, Pardoe, Doyle (Bowyer), Booth, Oakes, Heslop, Bell, Lee, Young, Towers

1970-71   **CHELSEA**
Final: Athens   19.5.71   Attendance 42,000
     Chelsea   (0) (1) **1**   **Real Madrid**   (0) (1) **1**
     Osgood   Zoco
Replay: Athens   21.5.71   Attendance 24,000
     Chelsea   (2) **2**   **Real Madrid**   (0) **1**
     Dempsey, Osgood   Fleitas
Chelsea: *Final:* Bonetti, Boyle, Harris, Hollins (Mulligan), Dempsey, Webb, Weller, Cooke, Osgood (Baldwin), Hudson, Houseman
     Replay: Bonetti, Boyle, Harris, Cooke, Dempsey, Webb, Weller, Baldwin, Osgood (Smethurst), Hudson, Houseman

1971-72   **RANGERS**
Final: Barcelona   24.5.72   Attendance 45,000
     Rangers   (2) **3**   **Moscow Dynamo**   (0) **2**
     Stein, Johnston 2   Eschtrekov, Makiovic
Rangers: McCloy, Jardine, Mathieson, Greig, Johnstone, Smith, McLean, Conn, Stein, Macdonald, Johnston

1972-73   **AC MILAN**
Final: Salonika   16.5.73   Attendance 45,000
     AC Milan   (1) **1**   **Leeds United**   (0) **0**
     Chiaguri
AC Milan: Vecchi, Sabadini, Zignoli, Anquilletti, Turone, Rosato (sub Dolci), Sogliano, Benetti, Bigon, Rivera, Chiaguri
Leeds United: Harvey, Reaney, Cherry, Bates, Madeley, Hunter, Lorimer, Jordan, Jones, Gray (F). Yorath (sub McQueen)

1973-74   **FC MAGDEBURG**
Final: Rotterdam   8.5.74   Attendance 5,000
     FC Magdeburg   (1) **2**   **AC Milan**   (0) **0**
     Lanzi og, Seguin
FC Magdeburg: Schultz, Enge, Zapf, Gaube, Abraham, Tyll, Pommerenke, Seguin, Raugust, Sparwasser, Hoffman
AC Milan: Pizzaballa, Anquilletti, Sabadini, Lanzi, Schnellinger, Maldera, Tresoldi, Benetti, Bigon, Rivera, Bergamaschi

1974-75   **DYNAMO KIEV**
Final: Basle   14.5.75   Attendance 13,000
     Dynamo Kiev   (2) **3**   **Ferencvaros**   (0) **0**
     Onischenko (2), Blochin
Dynamo Kiev: Rudakov, Fomenko, Troshkin, Reshko, Matvienko, Muntian, Konkov, Burjak, Kolotov, Onischenko, Blochin
Ferencvaros: Geczi, Pataki, Martos, Rab, Megyesi, Nyilasi (sub Onhaus), Juhasz, Mucha, Szabo, Mate, Magyar

1975-76   **ANDERLECHT**
Final: Brussels   5.5.76   Attendance 58,000
     Anderlecht   (1) **4**   **West Ham United**   (1) **2**
     Rensenbrink 2 (1 pen)   Holland, Robson
     Van der Elst 2
Anderlecht: Ruiter, Lomme, Broos, Van Binst, Thissen, Dockx, Coeck (sub Vercauteren), Van der Elst, Ressel, Haan, Rensenbrink
West Ham United: Day, Coleman, Bonds, T. Taylor, Lampard (sub A. Taylor), McDowell, Brooking, Paddon, Holland, Jennings, Robson

1976-77   **HAMBURG**
Final: Amsterdam   11.5.77   Attendance 65,000
     Hamburg   (0) **2**   **Anderlecht**   (0) **0**
     Volkert (pen)
     Magath
Hamburg: Kargus, Kaltz, Ripp, Nogly, Hidien, Steffenhagen, Keller, Reimann, Memering, Magath, Volkert
Anderlecht: Ruiter, Van Binst, Vanden Daele, Broos, Thissen, Van der Elst, Coeck, Haan, Dockx (sub Vanpoucke), Ressel, Rensenbrink

1977-78   **ANDERLECHT**
Final: Paris   3.5.78   Attendance 48,679
     Anderlecht   (3) **4**   **Wien**   (0) **0**
     Rensenbrink (2)
     Van Binst (2)
Anderlecht: De Bree, Van Binst, Broos, Dusbaba, Thissen, Van der Elst, Haan, Nielsen, Coeck, Vercauteren (sub Dockx), Rensenbrink
Wien: Baumgartner, R. Sara, J. Sara, Obermayer, Baumeister, Prohaska, Daxbacher (sub Martinez), Gasselich, Morales (sub Drazen), Pirkner, Parits

Additional pictures supplied by
Associated Press 73
Colorsport 2, 4/5, 6/7, 22, 23B, 39B, 40T, 41,
43, 54, 55, 62, 63, 71, 145, 147, 154L, 156, 229, endpapers
Ray Green 38
London Express News & Features Service 39T
Radio Times Hulton Picture Library 157, 172, 173, 174
Sportapics 23T, 70
Sporting Pictures 8, 57
Syndication International 24, 40, 42, 77